Innovative Document Summarization Techniques:

Revolutionizing Knowledge Understanding

Alessandro Fiori
IRCC, Institute for Cancer Research and Treatment, Italy

A volume in the Advances in Data Mining and Database Management (ADMDM) Book Series

Managing Director:	Lindsay Johnston
Production Manager:	Jennifer Yoder
Development Editor:	Allyson Gard
Acquisitions Editor:	Kayla Wolfe
Typesetter:	Michael Brehm
Cover Design:	Jason Mull

Published in the United States of America by
Information Science Reference (an imprint of IGI Global)
701 E. Chocolate Avenue
Hershey PA 17033
Tel: 717-533-8845
Fax: 717-533-8661
E-mail: cust@igi-global.com
Web site: http://www.igi-global.com

Library of Congress Cataloging-in-Publication Data

Innovative document summarization techniques : revolutionizing knowledge understanding / Alessandro Fiori, editor.
     pages cm
  Includes bibliographical references and index.
  Summary: "This book evaluates some of the existing approaches to information retrieval and summarization of digital documents, as well as highlighting current research and future developments"-- Provided by publisher.
  ISBN 978-1-4666-5019-0 (hardcover) -- ISBN 978-1-4666-5020-6 (ebook) -- ISBN 978-1-4666-5021-3 (print & perpetual access) 1. Automatic abstracting. 2. Electronic information resources--Abstracting and indexing. 3. Information storage and retrieval systems. 4. Text processing (Computer science) 5. Information science--Statistical methods. I. Fiori, Alessandro, 1982- editor of compilation.
  Z695.92.I55 2014
  025.04--dc23
                              2013037489

This book is published in the IGI Global book series Advances in Data Mining and Database Management (ADMDM) (ISSN: 2327-1981; eISSN: 2327-199X)

British Cataloguing in Publication Data
A Cataloguing in Publication record for this book is available from the British Library.

All work contributed to this book is new, previously-unpublished material. The views expressed in this book are those of the authors, but not necessarily of the publisher.

For electronic access to this publication, please contact: eresources@igi-global.com.

Advances in Data Mining and Database Management (ADMDM) Book Series

ISSN: 2327-1981
EISSN: 2327-199X

MISSION

With the large amounts of information available to businesses in today's digital world, there is a need for methods and research on managing and analyzing the information that is collected and stored. IT professionals, software engineers, and business administrators, along with many other researchers and academics, have made the fields of data mining and database management into ones of increasing importance as the digital world expands. The **Advances in Data Mining & Database Management (ADMDM) Book Series** aims to bring together research in both fields in order to become a resource for those involved in either field.

COVERAGE

- Cluster Analysis
- Customer Analytics
- Data Mining
- Data Quality
- Data Warehousing
- Database Security
- Database Testing
- Decision Support Systems
- Enterprise Systems
- Text Mining

IGI Global is currently accepting manuscripts for publication within this series. To submit a proposal for a volume in this series, please contact our Acquisition Editors at Acquisitions@igi-global.com or visit: http://www.igi-global.com/publish/.

Titles in this Series

For a list of additional titles in this series, please visit: www.igi-global.com

Innovative Document Summarization Techniques Revolutionizing Knowledge Understanding
Alessandro Fiori (IRCC, Institute for Cancer Research and Treatment, Italy)
Information Science Reference • copyright 2014 • 272pp • H/C (ISBN: 9781466650190) • US $175.00 (our price)

Emerging Methods in Predictive Analytics Risk Management and Decision-Making
William H. Hsu (Kansas State University, USA)
Information Science Reference • copyright 2014 • 367pp • H/C (ISBN: 9781466650633) • US $175.00 (our price)

Data Science and Simulation in Transportation Research
Davy Janssens (Hasselt University, Belgium) Ansar-Ul-Haque Yasar (Hasselt University, Belgium) and Luk Knapen
(Hasselt University, Belgium)
Information Science Reference • copyright 2014 • 350pp • H/C (ISBN: 9781466649200) • US $175.00 (our price)

Big Data Management, Technologies, and Applications
Wen-Chen Hu (University of North Dakota, USA) and Naima Kaabouch (University of North Dakota, USA)
Information Science Reference • copyright 2014 • 342pp • H/C (ISBN: 9781466646995) • US $175.00 (our price)

Innovative Approaches of Data Visualization and Visual Analytics
Mao Lin Huang (University of Technology, Sydney, Australia) and Weidong Huang (CSIRO, Australia)
Information Science Reference • copyright 2014 • 464pp • H/C (ISBN: 9781466643093) • US $200.00 (our price)

Data Mining in Dynamic Social Networks and Fuzzy Systems
Vishal Bhatnagar (Ambedkar Institute of Advanced Communication Technologies and Research, India)
Information Science Reference • copyright 2013 • 412pp • H/C (ISBN: 9781466642133) • US $195.00 (our price)

Ethical Data Mining Applications for Socio-Economic Development
Hakikur Rahman (University of Minho, Portugal) and Isabel Ramos (University of Minho, Portugal)
Information Science Reference • copyright 2013 • 359pp • H/C (ISBN: 9781466640788) • US $195.00 (our price)

Design, Performance, and Analysis of Innovative Information Retrieval
Zhongyu (Joan) Lu (University of Huddersfield, UK)
Information Science Reference • copyright 2013 • 508pp • H/C (ISBN: 9781466619753) • US $195.00 (our price)

XML Data Mining Models, Methods, and Applications
Andrea Tagarelli (University of Calabria, Italy)
Information Science Reference • copyright 2012 • 538pp • H/C (ISBN: 9781613503560) • US $195.00 (our price)

www.igi-global.com

701 E. Chocolate Ave., Hershey, PA 17033
Order online at www.igi-global.com or call 717-533-8845 x100
To place a standing order for titles released in this series, contact: cust@igi-global.com
Mon-Fri 8:00 am - 5:00 pm (est) or fax 24 hours a day 717-533-8661

Ilija Subašić, *KU Leuven, Belgium*

Josef Steinberger. *University of West Bohemia, Czech Republic*

Ralf Steinberger, *Joint Research Centre, Italy*

Hristo Tanev, *Joint Research Centre, Italy*

Marco Turchi, *Fondazione Bruno Kessler, Italy*

Natalia Vanetik, *Shamoon College of Engineering, Israel*

Mathias Verbeke, *KU Leuven, Belgium*

Vanni Zavarella, *Joint Research Centre, Italy*

Table of Contents

Section 1
General-Purpose and Domain-Specific Methods

Section 2
Social Networks and Web News Summarization

Section 3
Multilingual Summarization

Detailed Table of Contents

Section 1
General-Purpose and Domain-Specific Methods

Chapter 1

Sean Sovine, Marshall University, USA
Hyoil Han, Marshall University, USA

A number of multi-document summarization approaches aim at extracting a subset of sentences that contain the most relevant information in a document collection. Thus, a fundamental task is sentence ranking, according to a relevance score that defines the importance of each sentence for inclusion in a summary. This chapter overviews state-of-the-art and most successful works focused on sentence ranking methods. A categorization of these approaches is provided to analyze in-depth all of their aspects.

Chapter 2

Uri Mirchev, Ben Gurion University of the Negev, Israel
Mark Last, Ben Gurion University of the Negev, Israel

Graph models are usually exploited to represent relationships among terms, concepts, and sentences. However, these representations also allow capturing different aspects of a document collection. In this chapter, the authors propose the SentRel (Sentence Relations) method based on recursive importance inference from a three-tiered graph representation of a document collection and its refinement in the process of summary construction. Moreover, the approach is language-independent and domain-independent. Results on the TAC 2011 dataset show good results with respect to state-of-the-art summarization systems which require a different set of textual entities.

Chapter 3

Marina Litvak, Shamoon College of Engineering, Israel
Natalia Vanetik, Shamoon College of Engineering, Israel

A summary should preserve the content and meaning of the original document collection. In the extractive summarization task, this issue can be modeled as a maximum coverage problem. The authors define a system of linear inequalities to describe the content of the given document set. Each sentence is modeled by a hyperplane, and the intersections between these hyperplanes represent all possible summaries. The summary extraction task is re-formulated as finding the point on a convex polytope closest to the given hyperplane, which can be solved efficiently with linear programming. Experimental results on the DUC 2002 and MultiLing 2013 collections show good performance with respect to the other competitors.

Chapter 4

Angela Locoro, University of Genova, Italy
Massimo Ancona, University of Genova, Italy

Document summarization can help scientists of diverse fields, such as historians and archaeologists. Indeed, understanding and describing past or present societies is a complex task that involves the analysis of written sources (e.g., books, scientific papers). The Herodotus tool aims to support domain experts in the reasoning tasks over complex interactions characterizing a society in order to explain the causes of events and predict future events according to changes in some factors. The chapter presents the Interactive Summary Extractor Tool (ISET), whose aim is to extract and organize text summaries for archaeological and historical documental sources. The approach is designed to simplify the user interaction and improve the results according to the user interests.

Chapter 5

Paulo Cesar Fernandes de Oliveira, Anhanguera University, Brazil

A challenging issue in document summarization is the evaluation of results. This task is usually subjective, costly, time consuming, and, if it is human-assisted, it can generate some bias. Thus, several works have been addressing the definition of metrics and instruments to automatically evaluate the quality of summaries. This chapter provides a comprehensive survey of several evaluation metrics and proposes an automatic summary evaluation method. Experimental results show high-level correlation of the proposed evaluation approach with human judgments.

Section 2
Social Networks and Web News Summarization

Chapter 6

Atefeh Farzindar, NLP Technologies Inc., Canada & Université de Montréal, Canada

Online social networking sites (e.g., Facebook, YouTube) have revolutionized the ways of communication among individuals, groups, and communities, and altered everyday practices. Social media have become a primary source of intelligence, because they are often the first response to key events and allow for highly dynamic content. Thus, summarization approaches can improve social media retrieval and event detection. The chapter overviews the approaches to social media summarization and methods for update summarization, network activity summarization, event-based summarization, and opinion summarization. Moreover, a review of the existing evaluation metrics oriented to capturing the intrinsic quality of the summaries and their usefulness to the human user is provided.

Chapter 7

Summarization research is expanding to real-world areas where the payoffs are high, the datasets are often huge, and the tasks are very complex. The principal example is opinion summarization from large datasets that generally include a high degree of noise and little editorial structure. To deal with this kind of real-world problem, the chapter discusses three major aspects that must be considered and adhered to when designing opinion summarization systems: (1) simple and modular techniques, (2) domain knowledge, and (3) evaluation metrics.

Chapter 8

With the advent of the Internet and its broad diffusion, digital information is becoming more and more readily available, and users need suitable tools to select, filter, and extract only the relevant material. In the contextual advertising field, automatically suggesting ads within the content of a generic Webpage is a challenging task. The authors present several novel summarization approaches to extracting summaries from Web pages. A comparison with state-of-the-art techniques and the assessment of whether the proposed techniques can be successfully applied to contextual advertising are performed. The proposed methods achieve good performance with respect to well-known text summarization techniques.

Chapter 9

Applications based on summarization systems should allow humans to get a maximum coverage picture of everyday news story in a limited time, avoiding redundancy. NewSum is a real, multi-document, multilingual news summarization application that deals with the issues caused by the nature of real-world news. The method exploits the representation of n-gram graphs to perform sentence selection and redundancy removal for the summaries. Clustering approaches are used to detect events and topics. An open architecture for responsive summarization in a mobile setting is also presented. To understand the market applicability of the system, a pool of non-experts evaluated the quality of the summaries and the usefulness of the application in reading news.

Chapter 10

Bettina Berendt, KU Leuven, Belgium

Mark Last, Ben-Gurion University of the Negev, Israel

Ilija Subašić, KU Leuven, Belgium

Mathias Verbeke, KU Leuven, Belgium

News is delivered at an increasingly fast pace and provided over a variety of software and hardware platforms, in particular mobile devices. Thus, several new methods for automated news summarization have been developed, with a particular interest in temporal text mining, graph-based methods, and graphical interfaces. An overview of these methods and a discussion of the challenges associated with evaluation frameworks are provided. Based on the results of case studies, the authors examine the fundamental aspects to build summarization and document search interfaces.

Section 3
Multilingual Summarization

Chapter 11

Kamal Sarkar, Jadavpur University, India

In the age of electronic media, online information is available in several different languages other than English, such as Chinese, Spanish, French, Hindi, etc. With the rapid growth of Web documents, automatic summarization can be an indispensable solution to reduce the information overload and the redundancy. The chapter overviews various state-of-the-art methods with special emphasis on multilingual summarizers. The different approaches are grouped based on their characteristics and the document representation exploited.

Chapter 12

Josef Steinberger, University of West Bohemia, Czech Republic

Ralf Steinberger, Joint Research Centre, Italy

Hristo Tanev, Joint Research Centre, Italy

Vanni Zavarella, Joint Research Centre, Italy

Marco Turchi, Fondazione Bruno Kessler, Italy

News gathering and analysis systems produce a huge amount of articles per day. Automatic summarization systems can provide the main contents of the news to the final users, but they must deal with the highly redundant information and multilingual resources. The chapter discusses recent frameworks based on Latent Semantic Analysis (LSA) that show good performance across many different languages. Starting from these methods, the authors show how domain-specific aspects can be used and a compression and paraphrasing method can be plugged in. A discussion of summarization evaluation in different languages is also presented, and two new approaches are introduced.

Chapter 13

When summarization approaches deal with multilingual document collections, many issues arise, correlated to the dependence on language and linguistic knowledge. In this chapter, the language-dependent challenges and the most relevant works focused on language-independent algorithms are presented. The advantages and disadvantages of the discussed methods are analyzed in order to provide an overview of methods dealing with multilingual collections. Finally, new perspectives are presented to design language-independent systems.

Foreword

Internet-age readers are overwhelmed by a huge mass of textual documents available in a variety of different digital formats. Hence, the capability of summarizing this wealth of information to focus the reader's attention on the most significant portions of a text, or of a document collection, is becoming a pressing need. This book provides a valuable, in-depth coverage of automated document summarization techniques (i.e., techniques that automatically produce a succinct overview of the most important concepts covered by one or more documents).

Automatic summarization may be performed by means of different techniques, based on NLP, machine learning, and data mining. The resulting summary typically contains either the most relevant sentences or the most prominent keywords in the document or in the collection. The book chapters introduce a variety of approaches to document summarization, together with methods to assess the quality of the generated summaries. They provide a thorough review of the state-of-the-art in this new and interesting text analysis domain.

Summarization techniques find application in rather diverse domains. The book covers a selection of the most relevant application domains, ranging from Web document summarization to user opinion inference in social network data. A challenging issue, covered in the book but still to be explored, is addressing the different languages in which documents are available. Several book chapters cover multilingual summarization (i.e. the capability of dealing with multiple languages by means of the same summarization technique).

Elena Baralis
Politecnico di Torino, Italy

Elena Baralis *has been a full professor at the Dipartimento di Automatica e Informatica of the Politecnico di Torino since January 2005. She holds a Master degree in Electrical Engineering and a Ph.D. in Computer Engineering, both from Politecnico di Torino. Her current research interests are in the field of database systems and data mining, more specifically on mining algorithms for very large databases and sensor/stream data analysis. She has published over 80 papers in international journals and conference proceedings. She has served on the program committees or as area chair of several international conferences and workshops, among which are VLDB, IEEE ICDM, ACM SAC, DaWak, ACM CIKM, and PKDD.*

Preface

In the information era, while the amount of electronic documents keeps growing exponentially, the time available to the final users to process the information tends to decrease. Moreover, text documents represent a powerful resource to infer new knowledge by means of data mining techniques. For instance, by analyzing the document content, it is possible to extract user interests, community opinions, and expand the knowledge about a specific domain. To help users quickly gain knowledge and ease the discovery of new information from text documents, a significant research effort has been devoted to the study and the development of automated summarization tools, which produce a concise overview of the most relevant document content (i.e., a summary). Extracting a succinct and informative description of document collections is fundamental to allowing users to quickly familiarize themselves with the information of interest. For example, the summary of a collection of news documents regarding the same topic may provide a synthetic overview of the most relevant news facets. Differently, the summarization of social network data can support the identification of relevant information about a specific event, and the inference of user and community interests and opinions.

During recent years, a considerable number of automated summarization tools have been proposed. For instance, summarizers have been developed oriented to producing concise representations of a single document and/or a collection of documents discussing the same topics. Both general-purpose and domain-oriented approaches may be identified. In addition, summarization systems may be classified as: (1) sentence-based, if they partition documents into sentences and select the most informative ones for inclusion in the summary, or (2) keyword-based, if they detect salient keywords that summarize the document content. All these approaches usually exploit statistical metrics, text mining algorithms and/ or Natural Language Processing (NLP) methods. For instance, clustering-based approaches, probabilistic or co-occurrence-based strategies, graph-based algorithms, and itemset-based methods have already been proposed. Some systems also allow the management and the analysis of text documents in different languages. However, the evaluation of summaries represents a significant hurdle and can be very expensive in terms of time and resources. Thus, it is always difficult to identify which system can achieve the best results in the context of interest. The definition of automatic evaluation systems for text summaries is still an open research task.

This book provides a comprehensive discussion of the state of the art in document summarization. The reader will find in-depth discussion of the approaches focused on multilingual, domain-oriented and Web-oriented summarization tasks. Furthermore, some current real-world applications in several fields, such as contextual advertising, social networks, and archeology, are also provided.

The audience for the book includes—but is not limited to—students, lecturers, researchers, and practitioners of information technology, computer science, and bioinformatics. Developers and consumers will be interested in discovering how document summarization can improve their productivity in real applications, while researchers and students can learn more about the main concepts of the state-of-the-art document summarization approaches. This book can also make an academic reference work by providing comprehensive coverage of the document summarization field. Through predictions of future trends, analysis of techniques and technologies, and focuses on real application scenarios, this book will be a useful instrument for developing new document summarization tools suited to different application fields.

The book comprises 13 chapters and is organized as follows.

Section 1, "General-Purpose and Domain-Specific Methods," consists of 5 chapters and provides a good overview of the data representation and evaluation metrics adopted by general-purpose and domain-specific summarizers.

Chapter 1, "Classification of Sentence Ranking Methods for Multi-Document Summarization," overviews state-of-the-art and most successful works focused on sentence-ranking methods. Since multi-document summarization approaches extract a subset of sentences that contain the most relevant information, the sentence-ranking task is fundamental to defining their importance for inclusion in a summary according to a relevance score. A categorization of ranking methods is also provided to highlight the different properties of each group.

Chapter 2, "Multi-Document Summarization by Extended Graph Text Representation and Importance Refinement," proposes the SentRel (Sentence Relations) method based on recursive importance inference from a three-tiered graph representation of a document collection and its refinement in the process of summary construction. Differently from other methods, the graph representation is not used to encode the relationships among terms, concepts, and/or sentences, but to capture different correlations among the documents in the collection. The approach is both language-independent and domain-independent and achieves good results with respect to state-of-the-art summarization systems on the TAC 2011 dataset.

Chapter 3, "Efficient Summarization with Polytopes," defines a system of linear inequalities to describe the content of the given document set. Each sentence is modeled by a hyperplane, and the intersections between these hyperplanes represent all possible summaries. Since a summary should preserve the content and meaning of the original document collection, the summary extraction task is re-formulated as finding the point on a convex polytope closest to the given hyperplane, which can be solved efficiently with linear programming. Experimental results on the DUC 2002 and MultiLing 2013 collections show good performance with respect to the other competitors.

Chapter 4, "Interactive Summaries by Multi-Pole Information Extraction for the Archaeological Domain," presents the application of a document summarization approach in a specific domain, the archeological one. The chapter proposes the Interactive Summary Extractor Tool (ISET), whose aim is to extract and organize text summaries for archeological and historical documental sources. This system is integrated in the Herodotus tool that supports domain experts in the reasoning tasks over complex interactions characterizing a society, in order to explain causes of events and predict future events according to some factor changes. The goal of the ISET tool is to improve summarization results according to user interests, thus simplifying the interaction with the system.

Chapter 5, "Evaluation Metrics for the Summarization Task," provides a comprehensive survey about several summary evaluation metrics. Indeed, the evaluation of summary quality is a challenging task, since, in many cases, it is subjective, costly, time consuming, and, if human-assisted, it can generate some bias. For these reasons, several works have targeted the definition of metrics and instruments to automatically evaluate the quality of summaries. The chapter, besides analyzing the most recent and used evaluation metrics, proposes an automatic summary evaluation method that shows high-level correlation with human judgments.

Section 2, "Social Networks and Web News Summarization," consists of 5 chapters and illustrates how summarization approaches can provide a succinct representation of relevant information related to social media data, events, and user/community interests.

Chapter 6, "Social Network Integration in Document Summarization," introduces the summarization approaches applied to social media data. Indeed, the advent of online social networking sites (e.g., Facebook, YouTube) has revolutionized the way people communicate and declared the social media as a primary source of knowledge about key events. This chapter overviews the most recent approaches to social media summarization and methods for update summarization, network activity summarization, event-based summarization, and opinion summarization. Moreover, a review of the existing evaluation metrics oriented to capturing the intrinsic quality of summaries and their usefulness to the human user is also provided.

Chapter 7, "Approaches to Large-Scale User Opinion Summarization for the Web," deals with the new frontiers of summarization research, where the payoffs are high, the datasets often huge, and the tasks very complex. The main example is the opinion summarization of large datasets that generally include high degrees of noise and little editorial structure. This chapter aims at defining the best practices to design an opinion summarization system by identifying three major aspects: (1) simple and modular techniques, (2) domain knowledge, and (3) evaluation metrics.

Chapter 8, "Novel Text Summarization Techniques for Contextual Advertising," introduces several novel summarization approaches to extracting summaries from Web pages in order to improve the quality of suggested ads. A comparison with state-of-the-art techniques and an assessment of whether the proposed techniques can be successfully applied to contextual advertising are presented. The proposed methods achieve good performance with respect to well-known text summarization techniques.

Chapter 9, "NewSum: 'N-Gram Graph'-Based Summarization in the Real World," describes the application of a summarization approach in a real use case scenario: multilingual news summarization. The proposed system, named NewSum, deals with the issues caused by the nature of real-world news by exploiting the n-gram graph representation to perform sentence selection and redundancy removal for the summaries. Clustering approaches are also used to detect events and topics. An open architecture for responsive summarization in a mobile setting is also presented. To understand the market applicability of the system, a pool of non-experts evaluated the quality of the summaries and the usefulness of the application in reading news.

Chapter 10, "New Formats and Interfaces for Multi-Document News Summarization and its Evaluation," presents news summarizers. In particular, it overviews automatic methods based on temporal text mining and graph-based methods and discusses the challenges associated with evaluation frameworks. Moreover, the graphical interfaces developed for the analysis and the search of summaries are analyzed in-depth, and, according to the results of case studies, the fundamental aspects in designing effective summarization and document search interfaces are identified.

Section 3, "Multilingual Summarization," consists of 3 chapters and covers the multilingual aspect of the summarization task. The state-of-the-art works addressing this issue are analyzed with a specific focus on the data representation and the text mining methods exploited during the summarization process.

Chapter 11, "Multilingual Summarization Approaches," overviews various state-of-the-art methods with special emphasis on multilingual summarizers. Indeed, in the age of electronic media, online information is available in several different languages other than English, and automatic summarization systems can be an indispensable solution to reduce the information overload and redundancy. The approaches presented are grouped based on their characteristics and the exploited document representation to highlight their main differences and the performance achieved in different scenarios.

Chapter 12, "Aspects of Multilingual News Summarization," discusses recent frameworks based on Latent Semantic Analysis (LSA) that showed good performance across many different languages. Starting from these methods, the authors show how domain-specific aspects can be used and a compression and paraphrasing method can be plugged in. A discussion of summarization evaluation in different languages is also presented, and two new approaches are introduced.

Chapter 13, "Language Independent Summarization Approaches," analyzes the language-dependent challenges and the most relevant works focused on language-independent algorithms. The advantages and disadvantages of the discussed methods dealing with multilingual collections are analyzed. Finally, new perspectives are presented to design language-independent systems.

Document summarization is an appealing research field that can provide useful tools for improving the accessibility to large volumes of data contained in document collections. Good summarization systems may also help in acquiring knowledge about a specific domain (e.g., biology) quickly and without redundancy and in understanding event causes (e.g., historical events) and many other aspects of human knowledge published over heterogeneous text resources. The objective of this work is to provide a clear and consolidated view of current summarization methods and their application to real scenarios. We seek to explore new methods to model text data, extract the relevant information according to the user interests and evaluate the quality and usefulness of the extracted summaries. We believe that a considerable research effort will be required in the future to improve the quality of these systems, for instance, in terms of computational load and readability of the summary. Different application domains might also benefit from summarization techniques and allow scientists to enhance their works. We also believe that multilingual approaches will be the next generation of summarization systems.

We are confident that professionals, researchers, and students in the fields of text mining, natural language processing, text summarization, and social network analysis will be able to use this book to learn more about the ways in which summarization techniques can prove useful in different environments.

Alessandro Fiori
Institute for Cancer Research and Treatment (IRCC), Italy

Acknowledgment

This book would not have been possible without the cooperation of many people: the authors, the reviewers, my colleagues, the staff at IGI Global, and my family.

To the authors who have each spent a lot of time and energy writing, editing, and rewriting their chapters over the last year, without you there would be no book. To the reviewers, many of whom were also authors and therefore did double duty, your constructive feedback has made each and every chapter the best it can be. We appreciate the time you spent reading and discerning the chapters.

To all my colleagues not directly involved with the writing or reviewing of chapters, without your ideas, discussions, and support, this book would have remained just an idea. A special thank to my colleague, Alberto, who helped me many times during the last year.

To all of the staff at IGI Global, in particular Allyson Gard and Alyssa Sweigart, I thank you for your continued support, advice, and assistance with all aspects of the project from its initial proposal up through the final publication approvals.

To my parents, my grandmother, my wife Maria and my dog Sophie, without your love and support, there would be no book. This book is devoted to you!

Alessandro Fiori
IRCC, Institute for Cancer Research and Treatment, Italy

Section 1
General-Purpose and Domain-Specific Methods

Chapter 1
Classification of Sentence Ranking Methods for Multi-Document Summarization

Sean Sovine
Marshall University, USA

Hyoil Han
Marshall University, USA

ABSTRACT

Modern information technology allows text information to be produced and disseminated at a very rapid pace. This situation leads to the problem of information overload, in which users are faced with a very large body of text that is relevant to an information need and no efficient and effective way to locate within the body of text the specific information that is needed. In one example of such a scenario, a user might be given a collection of digital news articles relevant to a particular current event and may need to rapidly generate a summary of the essential information relevant to the event contained in those articles. In extractive MDS, the most fundamental task is to select a subset of the sentences in the input document set in order to form a summary of the document set. An essential component of this task is sentence ranking, in which sentences from the original document set are ranked in order of importance for inclusion in a summary. The purpose of this chapter is to give an analysis of the most successful methods for sentence ranking that have been employed in recent MDS work. To this end, the authors classify sentence ranking methods into six classes and present/discuss specific approaches within each class.

DOI: 10.4018/978-1-4666-5019-0.ch001

INTRODUCTION

Automatic text summarization is one attempt to solve the problem of information overload, and consists of the study of automated techniques for extracting key information from a body of text and using that information to form a concise summary of the documents in the set. The ideal of automatic summarization work is to develop techniques by which a machine can generate summaries that successfully imitate summaries generated by human beings. The category of automatic summarization actually contains a wide range of variations of the basic summarization task. This variety arises because of the many different purposes that exist for generating a summary, the different possible definitions of what a text summary is, and the great variety that exists in possible input data sources for a summarization algorithm.

The types of automatic summarization task can be divided on several axes. First, the input data that is to be summarized may be known to belong to a specific domain, or the task may be considered *generic* or predominately domain-independent. The input data may be from a single source document, or from multiple source documents. In the case that the input data consists of a set of documents from different sources with a common topic, the task is referred to as multi-document summarization (MDS). The summarization task may be *informative*, so that the summarization algorithm attempts to determine the key information in the input data using features of the input data set. On the other hand, the task may be *focused* summarization, in which the consumer of the summary has a particular question or specific topic that will be used to guide and motivate the summarization process. Many summarization systems are currently designed to incorporate aspects of informative and focused summarization. Finally, summarization may be *abstractive* or *extractive* (Nenkova & McKeown, 2011; Radev, Hovy, & McKeown, 2002; Sparck Jones, 1999).

Abstractive summaries are like those typically created by human summarizers, where the summary is composed of language that is generated specifically for the purpose of the summary. Extractive summaries, by contrast, are composed of sentences or parts of sentences that are extracted from the text of the input documents—and possibly rearranged or compressed—to form the final summary, with few other modifications (Nenkova & McKeown, 2011; Radev, Hovy, & McKeown, 2002). This chapter addresses extractive MDS systems. Currently, most summarization systems developed and tested for research purposes are extractive in nature.

Most current summarization research is focused on a generic multi-document summarization task that also features a query-focused component. This is largely due to conventions developed during the course of the Document Understanding Conferences (DUC) and Text Analysis Conferences (TAC) (NIST 2011; NIST 2013). The evaluation tasks developed during the DUC/TAC conferences are by far the most widely used methodologies for evaluating automatic summarization systems. We discuss the DUC/TAC conferences and their evaluation methodologies further in the section *Evaluation Methodologies*.

Systems developed for the DUC/TAC evaluation task are largely domain-independent, but are designed to be tested using corpora of newswire documents containing multiple topic-focused document sets. These systems are often intended to generate summaries that are both informative and focused, but some of these systems are either exclusively informative or exclusively focused in approach. Some experimental evidence suggests that, while current MDS systems are achieving continually higher levels of quality in the summaries they generate, the performance of these current systems has not yet reached the theoretical maximum of the extractive approach, which is the extractive summary containing the optimal set of document sentences (Bysani, Reddy, & Varma, 2009).

BACKGROUND

All extractive summarization systems contain three essential components: sentence ranking, summary generation, and pre- and post-processing. Figure 1 shows the overall process of multi-document summarization. In extractive MDS, summaries are formed by extracting sentences from the input document set. This fact implies that the fundamental question of extractive MDS is which sentences are most important for inclusion in the summary. In general, most systems approach this decision in two stages. The first stage, sentence ranking, involves determining the importance of each sentence based on various features of the individual sentence. The second stage, summary generation, then considers sentences in combination.

In summary generation, it matters not only which sentences have the best individual qualities as candidates for a summary, but also what the qualities of these sentences are in combination as a candidate summary. Aside from selecting the most relevant and informative sentences for a summary, summary generation must also address the issue of redundancy, which occurs when two sentences are selected for inclusion in a summary that both contain highly similar content.

Pre- and post-processing includes all other steps that occur before sentence ranking and after summary generation, respectively. Significant issues in pre-processing include segmenting source text into individual sentences, removing text that is not desirable for inclusion in a summary, such as headlines or author contact information, and converting sentences into an internal representation. The most common internal representation for a sentence is a bag-of-words vector format, in which each sentence is represented by a vector of counts of tokens appearing in the sentence, where this vector contains a within-sentence count for each token in the vocabulary of the entire document set. The most significant issue in post-processing is summary ordering. The sentences in a summary should be ordered in a fashion that yields a coherent and readable summary, with a logical progression from one sentence to the next.

In this chapter, we focus on the various methods that have been successfully utilized for sentence ranking in recent MDS research. In most systems, sentence ranking and summary generation are clearly defined, separate phases. However, there are some MDS methods, which we describe, that violate this separation. Taking this into consideration, as we describe each implementation of a sentence ranking method, if necessary we also briefly describe the summary generation method that is utilized by an implementation. As pre- and post-processing tasks are generally highly similar across most MDS systems, we only describe pre-and-post processing considerations for particular MDS systems when they are both highly unique and relevant to the sentence ranking process of the system.

EVALUATION METHODOLOGIES

The Document Understanding Conference (DUC) was envisioned and organized in 2000, based on a research initiative of the United States government and sponsored by the National Institute of Standards and Technology (NIST), as an annual conference that would facilitate and provide a common forum for research in text summarization

Figure 1. Overview of multi-document summarization process

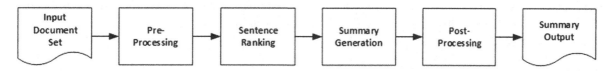

and question answering. Part of the vision of the DUC conference was to establish a standardized procedure for evaluating the quality of output produced by summarization systems. The DUC conference later became part of the Text Analysis Conference (TAC), which was established in 2008 and includes summarization as well as related areas of research in natural language processing (NLP). Since 2001, the DUC/TAC conferences have been singularly instrumental to progress in summarization research, and the evaluation methodologies developed at these conferences are almost universally employed for evaluation in summarization research efforts.

The DUC/TAC conferences have featured a variety of summarization tasks, but the most consistent task presented at these conferences has been a query-focused multi-document summarization task. This is the task that is most often used as a benchmark in summarization research. The format of the DUC/TAC multi-document summarization task is as follows: Participants are given a collection of document sets, in which each document set contains a number of documents focused on a single topic. For example, in the TAC task, participants are given 44 sets of 10 documents. Along with each set there is a query or information need description that is intended to be used by the summarization system to focus the summary. The participant is instructed to generate a summary of each document set in the collection using the participant's MDS system with the document set and query as input, with no human intervention. The system-generated summary for each document set is then evaluated against the accompanying human-generated summaries, which NIST provides, using one of the DUC/TAC methodologies described below (NIST 2011; NIST 2013).

The empirical evaluations for the systems described in this chapter are all based on the standardized DUC/TAC methodologies – ROUGE and Pyramid. ROUGE, is a fast, automated method based on *n*-gram matching between machine (or system-generated) summaries and human-generated reference summaries. Pyramid is a content-based human evaluation method that involves locating units of content that overlap between machine and human-generated summaries. Each Pyramid content unit is weighted by how many human-generated summaries contain that content unit. The efficiency of ROUGE and the fact that it is an automated evaluation allow summarization researchers to obtain evaluations of their work in a reasonable amount of time while requiring little human effort (Lin, 2004). Pyramid offers a more rigorous evaluation based on human understanding of the conceptual content of the human and machine summaries, but is not feasible for most individual research efforts, due to the significant amount of time and human effort that is required to complete a Pyramid evaluation (Nenkova, Passonneau, McKeown, 2007).

In this chapter, we present evaluation results for each of the methods discussed as a validation of the utility of the method and as evidence of the potential of similar methods in future research. This chapter contains a survey and classification of recent approaches to sentence ranking. To rigorously evaluate each of the sentence ranking methods presented in this chapter against each other would require a special study. This special study would have to isolate the sentence ranking aspect of the summarization process, in such a way that the pre- and post-processing and summary generation phases would be held fixed while the method of sentence ranking is interchanged, allowing the performance of each method to be tested using the same data set with only the parameter of the sentence ranking method being varied. This special study would be of great benefit to the MDS research community, and it is hoped that future researchers will undertake such a study, though it is admitted that such study would be a significant undertaking.

SENTENCE RANKING METHODS

Classification of Sentence Ranking Method

The goal of sentence ranking in an MDS system is to compare sentences in the input document set and rank them according to importance for inclusion in a summary of the input document set. Sentence ranking is normally accomplished by formulating a score for each sentence that gives a numerical estimate of the relative importance of each sentence. Sentence scores are typically based on features of the individual sentences and features of the document set as a whole. In some cases, sentence scores are formulated using an external source of information—such as a query or topic statement in the case of focused summarization—or a collection of background documents.

In the current literature there is a wide variety of approaches to the problem of sentence ranking in MDS. One factor that varies widely among these approaches is the level of structure that each sentence ranking method extracts from the text in the input document set. We present a classification of sentence ranking methods that proceeds from those utilizing the simplest, most superficial structure to those utilizing the richest, most complex structure.

Methods for sentence ranking can be classified based on the type of information obtained from the document set to be utilized in the ranking process. The classes of sentence ranking methods that we discuss are: *simple word frequency-based methods*, *word clustering and co-occurrence methods*, *singular value decomposition (SVD) methods*, *probabilistic topic-modeling methods*, *graph-based methods,* and *linguistics/natural language processing (NLP) methods*. We discuss each of these classes in detail in the proceeding subsections. Because of the great amount of effort and creativity that has gone into MDS research in recent years, it would be very difficult to exhaustively represent and classify the many approaches to sentence ranking found in MDS research. Therefore, this chapter attempts to present those approaches that are among the most important and that show a great amount of promise for motivating future investigations.

The vast majority of MDS systems utilize a bag-of-words vector representation of sentences that maintains only word-count information for each sentence, disregarding word order information. An example of such a vector for a sentence s_1 is as follows:

$$\vec{s}_1 = \left\langle w_1, w_2, w_3, \ldots, w_n \right\rangle$$

where n is the number of unique tokens in the input document set vocabulary, which is considered to be an ordered list of all tokens occurring at least once in the input document set. In this example, sentence s_1 would contain w_1 instances of the first token in the document set vocabulary, and similarly s_1 would contain w_j instances of the jth word in the document set vocabulary. In the following descriptions of sentence ranking methods and system implementations, it can be assumed that unless stated otherwise, all systems described utilize the bag-of-words vector representation for sentences.

Most summarization systems also feature a stop-word removal component during the pre-processing phase, during which all document tokens are converted into words, usually by converting all characters to lowercase, discarding non-word tokens, and stemming the remaining word tokens. Stop-word removal involves removing extremely common words that have little informative value from the document vocabulary, and is usually accomplished by comparing input document tokens to a pre-defined list of stop-words. In this chapter, 'words' and 'terms' are used interchangeably.

Many sentence ranking methods have a number of parameters that must be optimized based on a set of training data in order to maximize performance or to suit user preference. At times these parameters are adjusted by hand, but in many cases, some machine learning method is used with supervised learning to find the optimal set of parameters. This chapter is more focused on the aspects of the sentence ranking problem that are unique to the MDS problem, and thus we do not provide an in depth discussion of machine learning algorithms. Further, we do not discuss specific optimization algorithms in conjunction with any sentence ranking method unless that algorithm is integral to the method.

Simple Word Frequency-Based Method

In simple word frequency-based methods, each sentence is ranked based on the occurrence frequency, in some context, of words occurring in the sentence. For example, a basic system might maintain a count of the frequency of each word in the entire document set vocabulary and, for each sentence, calculate the score of that sentence as the average frequency of a word occurring in that sentence. Sentence ranking methods of this class are by far the simplest, both conceptually and computationally, but the specific approaches we discuss below show that MDS systems with simple word frequency-based sentence ranking can exhibit very strong performance based on current evaluation methods.

The motivating hypothesis for word-frequency methods is as follows: once frequent words that convey little meaningful information—that is, stop words—are removed, the relative frequency with which each remaining word occurs in the document set reflects the importance of that word to the content of the document set. This hypothesis is fairly easy to accept, as it seems to be sensible to assume that a word that is important to the main topic of the document set will occur in many sentences of the document set. There is also another

assumption underlying the use of simple word-frequency. This assumption is that, though there may be several synonymous words corresponding to the topic of a document set, at least one of these words is repeated significantly in the document set, where significance is measured by the relative frequency of the word. Experimental results, which demonstrate that systems using simple word-frequency perform very well, confirm the validity of these motivating hypotheses.

The system CLASSY developed by Conroy, Schlesinger, Rankel, and O'Leary (2010) for the Text Analysis Conference (TAC) 2010, utilizes basic word frequency information to provide a score for each document set sentence. These scores are then used to select a set of top-scoring sentences whose total word count exceeds the desired number of words for the target summary length. Finally, a set of procedures is applied to this set of selected sentences in order to find a subset of these sentences that maximizes the total score of selected sentences while minimizing the redundancy among the selected sentences. This subset is then ordered using a Traveling Salesperson algorithm to form the final summary (Cormen, Leiserson, & Rivest, 2011).

The sentence score generated by the CLASSY system for a sentence x is calculated using the formula

$$s(x) = \frac{1}{|x|} \sum_{w \in x} P(w),$$

where $P(w)$ is an estimated probability score called the *approximate oracle score* and $|x|$ is the number of words in x. The approximate oracle score is intended to estimate the probability that a word w will occur in a human-generated summary of the document set, and is calculated using the following formula

$$P\left(w\right) = \frac{1}{4}q\left(w\right) + \frac{1}{4}s\left(w\right) + \frac{1}{2}p\left(w\right)$$

where $q(w)$ is equal to 1 if w is a term appearing in the query for the document set, and equal to 0 otherwise, $s(w)$ is equal to 1 if w is a signature term for the document set, and equal to 0 otherwise, and $p(w)$ is the relative frequency of occurrence of the term w in the document set (Conroy, Schlesinger, & O'Leary, 2007). A signature term is a term that is determined to occur with significantly greater frequency in the input document set than would be expected in a background collection of documents not focused on a particular topic (Conroy, Schlesinger, O'Leary, & Goldstein, 2006).

CLASSY originated with the system submitted by Conroy, Schlesinger, O'Leary, and Goldstein (2006) to Document Understanding Conference (DUC) 2006, which was itself a continuation of prior work. This system underwent some minor revisions from year-to-year until 2010, but each year performed among the top systems submitted to the DUC and TAC conferences.

The system PYTHY, which was developed by Toutanova, Brockett, Gamon, Jagarlamudi, Suzuki, and Vanderwende (2007) and submitted to DUC 2007, also uses a sentence ranking method that is based primarily on simple word frequency-based features. The PYTHY system calculates the score of a given sentence as a linear combination of a large number of numerical features, which are calculated individually for each sentence. Thus, the formula for the score of a sentence x is

$$S\left(x\right) = \sum_{k=1}^{K} w_k f_k\left(x\right)$$

where $f_k(x)$ is the kth feature, w_k gives the weight of the kth feature, and there are K features calculated for each sentence. A supervised machine learning method is utilized to find the optimal values for the coefficients w_k. The objective function for this machine learning optimization is a measure

of how well the pairwise sentence comparisons of the system match those generated based on an evaluation of the importance of sentences in the training data.

The features for PYTHY include the following: *SumClusterFrequency* is the average relative frequency of words in a sentence, where the relative frequency of a word is considered based on the occurrence of that word in the context of the entire document set. *SumTopicFrequency* is the average frequency of words in a sentence, where the relative frequency of a word is based on the occurrence of that word in the context of the query or topic description. Similarly, there are features *SumClusterHeadlineFrequency* and *SumDocumentFrequency* which utilize the frequency of a word within the collection of headlines from the input documents, and within the document in which the sentence occurs, respectively. Also, the system utilizes features *SumDocumentStartFrequency* and *SumClusterStartFrequency*, which consider the frequencies of words in the first 100 words of the document the sentence occurs in and the first 100 words of all documents in the document collection, respectively.

The PYTHY system also uses features based on variations of the cluster and topic frequency features, in which the frequency of bigrams, multi-word expressions, and skip bigrams are considered. Bigrams are pairs of consecutive words that occur in the document set, multi-word expressions are named entities and other significant word collocations, and skip bigrams are pairs of document words that occur with at most two words in between their respective occurrences. Also utilized are variations of the cluster- and topic-based frequency features that consider all tokens, rather than only words that have been determined to be vocabulary words during the pre-processing phase.

PYTHY utilizes a sentence simplification system which generates at most four progressively simplified versions of each sentence and adds these simplified sentences back to the list of document sentences for summary formation. This sentence simplification is based upon information obtained from a linguistic parse of the sentences. To incorporate simplified sentences into the sentence selection process, the PYTHY sentence ranking system considers features that indicate whether a sentence is simplified and the length of the simplified sentence as a proportion of the length of the original sentence.

PYTHY also utilizes the following features: a pair of binary indicator features that equal to 1 only if the length of a sentence is less than a given number of words (five or ten), the relative position of the sentence in the source document, a pair of binary indicator features that are equal to 1 only if the position of a sentence is less than a given value (five or ten), and a binary indicator feature that is equal to 1 only if the sentence contains a verb. Finally, PYTHY uses an *inverse document frequency* (IDF) based feature that is equal to -1 times the sum of the logarithm of the sentence frequency of each word in the sentence, where the sentence frequency of a word is the number of sentences in the document set that contain the word.

PYTHY exhibits a high level of summary quality, and scored among the top systems in the DUC 2007. As we have seen, the PYTHY system utilizes a nearly exhaustive collection of frequency-based features, in addition to length, position, and heuristic full-sentence features. Summary generation in PYTHY is performed using an iterative, greedy approach in which sentences are selected one-by-one in decreasing order by score, where scores are updated after each selection so that the scores of sentences containing words also contained in already selected sentences are penalized incrementally.

As with the CLASSY system above, the performance of PYTHY shows that simple word frequency-based systems can be very effective. Further, these systems are both conceptually quite simple and are based on the simple hypotheses described above.

Word Clustering and Co-Occurrence Method

Some issues arise immediately when considering words as features of documents and sentences for the purpose of summarization. One such issue is that of synonymy, where two distinct words have equivalent meanings. A related issue is co-reference, where a single entity or concept may be denoted by multiple distinct names. These issues can have particular significance whenever a query or topic description is being used to focus the summarization task. Often a query or topic statement is a series of words or a set of brief sentences. As such, the query or topic statement is likely to contain a few significant keywords to motivate the sentence ranking process, but is not likely to contain a variety of distinct words that refer to any single concept.

As an example, consider a sentence in a set of articles about a political candidate for the office of prime minister who is also the current prime minister. It may be the case that the term 'candidate' occurs with a high level of frequency in the collection of articles and refers to the current prime minister, but the term 'incumbent', also referring to the current prime minister who is running for re-election, occurs somewhat rarely in the set. Thus, a sentence containing highly relevant information, but utilizing the term incumbent and not the term candidate, may not be selected for use in a summary by a frequency-based sentence ranking method. It is possible that the sentence would contain other high-frequency terms, but this example demonstrates how synonymy and co-reference can be a problem for word frequency-based summarization algorithms.

One method that has been utilized by MDS systems for addressing the issues of synonymy and co-reference is *word clustering*. In this method, words that have related meanings or refer to related concepts in the context of the input documents are clustered together. In this way, the presence of one such word in a sentence has essentially the same effect as if the whole cluster of contextually related words appeared in the sentence.

Another method that is closely related to word clustering involves the utilization of *co-occurrence* information. Co-occurrence information models the frequency with which two words in a document set occur in the same context, or 'near-by' one another. That is, the strength of co-occurrence between two words measures how often those two words occur together in the document set, where "together" can be defined in various ways. The motivating idea of co-occurrence methods is that words that occur in similar contexts tend to have related meanings.

The MDS method submitted to DUC 2007 by Pingali, Rahul, and Vasudeva (2007) utilizes both word clustering and co-occurrence methods. This system ranks sentences based on a simple weighted average of two feature scores: a query independent score and a query dependent score. The query independent score is intended to capture the relevance of the sentence to the topic that is featured in the input document set, and the query dependent score is intended to capture the relevance of the sentence to the user-supplied query, based on co-occurrence information contained in the document set. Thus, the query independent portion of the score addresses informative summarization and the query dependent portion addresses focused summarization.

To calculate the query independent score for each sentence, the system first generates

1. A probabilistic model of the probability of particular word occurring in the collection of all words in the input document set, and
2. A similar model of the probability of a particular word occurring in a randomly selected set of background documents.

Once these models are constructed the method of distributional clustering is used to combine sets of words into clusters. In this method, first the classification probability distribution $P(D|w)$

for an unknown document containing word w is calculated for each word in the input document set using a naïve Bayes model. Next, word clusters are formed by identifying sets of words that have similar classification distributions $P(D|w)$. A new naïve Bayes model is then generated by setting $P(D|w)$ for each word within each cluster C equal to a weighted average that is calculated over the values of $P(D|w)$ for each word w in C (Baker & McCallum, 1998). The new naïve Bayes model formed by the word clustering process is then used to generate the query independent score for a sentence x using the formula

$$S_{Ind}(x) = \frac{P(D)\prod_{t=1}^{|x|}P(w_t \mid D)}{P(D)\prod_{t=1}^{|x|}P(w_t|D) + P(\hat{D})\prod_{t=1}^{|x|}P(w_t \mid \hat{D})}$$

where D represents the input document set and $\hat{D}$ represents the randomly selected set of background documents.

In calculating the query dependent score, the system first estimates a co-occurrence model based on a sliding window of length k. The question that motivates this model is, "if a particular word w occurs in a document in the input document set, what is the probability that a particular word y will occur within a distance of at most k words of w?" Once this model has been constructed, it is utilized in the following manner: First, for each word w within a sentence x, the model is used to locate all words that co-occur with word w with a probability greater than a threshold value T and add those words to a new version of sentence x that will be used for calculating the query dependent score. We denote this new version of x by x'. Given this expanded sentence, the formula for calculating the query dependent score for sentence x goes as follows:

$$S_{Dep}(x) = \prod_{w \in x'}P(w \mid x')\sum_{y \in Query}P(y|w, D)P(y|D),$$

where $P(w \mid x')$ reflects the occurrence frequency of w within the modified query x', $P(y|w,D)$ is the co-occurrence probability of word y occurring within a window of k words of word w in the input document set, and $P(y|D)$ is the probability of word y based on occurrence frequency in the input document set.

The MDS system presented by Pingali, Rahul, and Vasudeva (2007) at DUC 2007 performed extremely well in the DUC evaluation, outscoring all other systems submitted to that conference in the ROUGE evaluation. It is interesting to note that this system utilizes both word clustering and co-occurrence. It is also worth noting that this system utilizes a set of methods that are motivated by a probabilistic theoretical background.

The system presented by Amini and Usunier (2007) at DUC 2007 also utilizes word clustering for sentence ranking. This system first generates a bag-of-documents vector representation for each word, in which a word w is represented by the vector $\vec{w}$. This vector $\vec{w}$ is defined by

$$\vec{w} = \left\langle tf\left(w, d_1\right), tf\left(w, d_2\right), \ldots, tf\left(w, d_n\right) \right\rangle$$

where $tf(w, d_i)$ represents the number of times the word w occurs in the document i. This vector representation is then utilized in conjunction with the CEM algorithm, a classification variant of the well-known EM algorithm, to produce clusters of related terms which form a partition of the total vocabulary of the input document set (Celeux & Govaert, 1992).

Sentence ranking in the system by Amini and Usunier is performed based on a score given to each sentence, which is a linear combination of four features. The first feature, F_1, is simply the number of common terms between the sentence x and the document set query q. The second feature, F_2, is the weighted cosine similarity of the sentence x and the query q, which is calculated using the following formula:

$$Cos\left(x, q\right) = \frac{\sum_{w \in x \cap q} c_q\left(w\right) c_x\left(w\right)}{\sum_{w \in q}\left[c_q\left(w\right)\right]^2 \sum_{w \in x}\left[c_x\left(w\right)\right]^2}$$

In this formula, $c_n(w)$ is equal to the product of the frequency of term w in n (which could be the sentence x or the query q) and the number of documents in the input document set in which w appears. The third feature, F_3, is equal to the sum of the logarithms of the document frequencies of all words appearing in both the sentence and the set of words contained in clusters that contain query words. Similarly, the fourth feature, F_4, is equal to the sum of the logarithms of the document frequencies of all words appearing in both the sentence and the set of words contained in clusters containing words from the topic title of the document set (DUC document sets are given topic titles).

The weights for the four features are as assigned using the following formula

$$S(x) = 0.2*F_1(x) + 0.04*F_2(x) + 0.4*F_3(x) + 0.36*F_4(x)$$

From this formula, we can see that the features F_3 and F_4, which are the two features using word clusters, are given the highest weight. Amini and Usunier point out that there is a low level of correlation between the rankings induced by each individual feature when compared with each other feature. This implies that the features are capturing complementary information. Complementarity among features is a desirable quality, because it indicates that the system is not obtaining redundant information from the set of features.

This system was ranked among the top performing systems in the DUC 2007 evaluation. An outstanding feature of this system is that it utilizes only features based on the topic title and query words for the summary document set. That is, each feature is a query-dependent feature. Thus, the system developed by Amini and Usunier is designed to exclusively perform focused summarization.

Singular Value Decomposition Method

As mentioned above, the bag-of-words vector format is a very widely-used format for representing document sentences in text summarization algorithms. Whenever a data set exists that consists of a set of data vectors of uniform format—like the set of bag-of-words vectors—a matrix can be formed from those vectors, and the potential exists to perform an analysis of that data set using matrix methods. For example, suppose the vocabulary of the input document set contains m unique words and n sentences. Then, an m x n term-sentence matrix can be formed whose columns are sentence bag-of-words vectors and whose rows are term bag-of-sentence vectors.

One of the most frequently utilized matrix methods in data analysis is the singular value decomposition (SVD). The singular value decomposition of a data matrix A (m x n) is as follows:

$$A = USV^T$$

where U is an m x m matrix with columns that are orthogonal unit vectors that are eigenvectors of AA^T, S is a diagonal matrix containing on its main diagonal the singular values of A in descending order from top to bottom, and V is an n x n matrix with columns that are orthogonal unit vectors that are eigenvectors of A^TA (Kalman, 2006). SVD was first introduced for use in text summarization by Gong and Liu (2001).

Conceptually, singular value decomposition is a process by which a matrix is decomposed into a product of orthogonal matrices. Given this product representation, the column vectors of the original matrix can be represented as linear combinations of a new set of orthogonal vectors. In effect, this method allows a set of data vectors to be represented in terms of linear combinations of the vectors of a new orthogonal basis, where this new basis is comprised of vectors represent-

ing fundamental patterns of the data set. Further, the process gives this new basis in an ordered fashion, with a number called a singular value that corresponds to each vector in the new basis, such that the magnitude of each singular value corresponds to the relative importance of the corresponding vector in this new basis (Kalman, 2006). In summary, SVD allows one to identify fundamental patterns that exist in the data which are ranked by importance and to understand how vectors in the original data set can be represented as combinations of these fundamental patterns.

Steinberger and Ježek (2004), describe a method for utilizing SVD in text summarization. In this method, first a weighted term-by-sentence matrix A is formed. Next, the SVD, USV^T of matrix A is obtained. Sentence scores are then calculated based on the matrix V. In the SVD of A, column r of the matrix V represents the coefficients of the linear combination of basis vectors from matrix U (which are weighted by the singular values in matrix S) that can be used to reconstruct the bag-of-words-vector for sentence r. The sentence score based on matrix V is a weighted vector-length score, where each component is weighted by its corresponding singular value. The formula for this score for sentence r is

$$s_r = \sqrt{\sum_{i=1}^{n} v_{ir} \sigma_i^2}$$

where v_{ir} is the rth component of the column of V corresponding to sentence r, σ_i is the ith singular value, and n is the number of dimensions utilized in the SVD process.

SVD methods for sentence ranking in MDS are able to capture patterns in the underlying structure of the data set formed by the bag-of-words vector representations of sentences and to locate sentences that have the strongest correspondence to the most significant patterns. In the following section, we discuss another method that uses SVD in conjunction with probabilistic topic modeling methods, whichfurther illustrate how SVD can be used in MDS.

Probabilistic Topic Modeling Method

Probabilistic topic models are used to discover underlying themes that exist within a body of text. In describing these models, the term textual entity is used to denote either documents or sentences, depending on the details of the model. In a probabilistic topic model, it is assumed that a body of text is generated by a random process. In this process, for each word w in each document, first a topic t is drawn at random, and then the word w is drawn at random from a distribution over words, $P(w|T=t)$, corresponding to the topic t. Thus, in a topic model, each topic is modeled using a multinomial distribution over words.

In a topic model, each textual entity (document or sentence) has a set of parameters that defines the distribution of topics within that entity, so that within a particular entity e (document or sentence), topics for words within e are drawn at random from the distribution $P(t|E=e)$ of topics within e. Thus, in a topic model of a collection of text, topics are defined by distributions over words, of the form $P(w|T=t)$, and textual entities (documents or sentences) are defined by distributions over topics, of the form $P(t|E=e)$. For example, consider latent Dirichlet allocation (LDA). In the LDA model, each document d within a collection of documents has a distribution over topics, $P(t|D=d)$, which defines that particular document, and each topic t is modeled using a distribution over words, $P(w|T=t)$ (Blei, 2012).

In MDS, a set of documents with a common topic is summarized in such a way that the summary represents the essential content of the document set in a concise form. Some topic modeling approaches to MDS start with the assumption that the common topic of the documents in the collection of input documents is actually comprised of a set of related subtopics. Some of these approaches propose that the summary of the document collection should contain a representation of the subtopics that make up the topic of the collection. Other approaches to MDS that utilize probabilistic topic models posit the existence of a primary topic and a set of secondary topics and use the topic model to emphasize the primary topic in forming the summary.

Arora and Ravindran (2008) introduce an MDS approach that utilizes singular value decomposition (SVD) and LDA for the process of sentence ranking and summary generation. In their approach to MDS, Arora and Ravindran first utilize LDA to produce a topic model for the input document set. In this model, for each document D_k in the document set there is a distribution over topics, denoted $P(T_j|D_k)$, and for each topic T_j in the model there is a distribution over words, denoted $P(w_i|T_j)$. Using this model, a matrix A_j is formed for each topic T_j, in which each column is a weighted bag-of-words vector corresponding to a sentence in the input document set. The weight for the entry in the ith row, corresponding to word w_i, in the nth column of matrix A_j corresponding to sentence S_{kr}, the rth sentence in document D_k, is equal to

$$[A_j]_{in} = P(w_i|T_j)\, P(T_j|D_k)$$

if sentence S_{kr} contains word w_i, and 0 otherwise.

Next, each of the matrices A_j is submitted to the process of SVD, in order to yield an orthonormal basis for each topic, with basis vectors ordered by importance. Recall that the SVD process also yields the set of coefficients for representing the original sentence vectors in topic representation matrix A_j as a linear combination of these new ordered basis vectors for the corresponding topic T_j. Further, due to the SVD process, the vector of coefficients for each sentence is normalized to unit length. Thus, by examining the sentence coefficient vectors with respect to a particular topic it is possible to locate the sentence

$\dot{S}$ that depends most strongly on a particular basis vector v for topic T_j. This sentence $\dot{S}$ will be the sentence whose vector representation in the new basis has the largest coefficient among all sentence vectors in the component corresponding to the basis vector v.

Finally, in the method of Arora and Ravindran (2008), topics are ranked by probability using the formula

$$P\left(T_j\right) = \sum_{k=1}^{M} P\left(T_j | D_k\right) P\left(D_k\right),$$

where M is the number of documents in the input document set. Though Arora and Ravindran do not specify, it is likely that $P(D_k)$ is a uniform distribution. Another option would be to define $P(D_k)$ based on the relative length of each document. For summary generation, an iterative process is used to select one sentence pertaining to each topic until the desired summary length is achieved. This selection is performed in such a way that the kth sentence to be selected for topic j is the sentence that corresponds most strongly to the kth basis vector for topic j. Thus, in this method, sentences are ranked based on the importance of topics and based on the representation of sentences in terms of SVD basis vectors for each topic.

The motivation for this method is that the basis vectors generated by the SVD process represent fundamental patterns in the topic-weighted bag-of-words data matrices, and that the orthogonality of these vectors implies that there should be little or no redundancy in the information captured by any two distinct basis vectors. Thus, by selecting sentences corresponding to the most important basis vectors for each topic, the system is selecting the most fundamental sentences for each topic, while at the same time avoiding redundancy. In the evaluation of Arora and Ravindran (2008), this system outperformed top systems from DUC 2002 significantly and slightly outperformed a baseline MDS system using LDA without SVD, based on a ROUGE evaluation.

In work by Haghighi and Vanderwende (2009), a probabilistic topic model is introduced that is designed to perform MDS. This model is similar to the LDA model, but with a richer structure that captures information relevant to the MDS task. This model is geared toward separating content that is related to the primary topic of the document set from content that is related specifically to subtopics of the document set and content that is unrelated to the common topic of the document set.

There are several distributions over words (referred to as topics) that make up this model: a background distribution $P_B(w)$ that models non-content and stop-words, a set of content distributions $P_{C_i}\left(w\right)$ that model subtopics of the essential document set content, and for each document, a document-specific distribution $P_D(w)$ that models content that is specific to a single document. In this approach, a document set is modeled as being generated by the following probabilistic process.

In this model, first the parameters of the set of content distributions $P_{C_i}\left(w\right)$ and the background distribution $P_B(w)$ are randomly drawn. Among these content distributions, one distribution, $P_{C_0}\left(w\right)$, is designated the general content distribution, which pertains to the primary theme of the document set, while the other content distributions are designated as specific content distributions, which pertain to subtopics. Then, a document specific distribution $P_{D_j}\left(w\right)$ is drawn corresponding to each document D_j. For each sentence s, a distribution $P(t|S=s)$ over topics is drawn for that sentence that determines the probability that a word in that sentence will be either a content word, a document specific word, or a background word.

Within each sentence s, for each word w, a drawing is made from that sentence's topic distribution $P(t|S=s)$ to determine which topic the word w will belong to, and then the word w is drawn from the distribution $P(w|T=t)$ for that topic. If the word w is a content word, then a drawing is first made from a binomial distribution $P(g|S=s)$, to determine if word w is a general content word or if word w is a specific content word. In this model, content words in sentences that occur earlier in a document are more heavily weighted toward general content, while content words in sentences that occur later in the document are weighted slightly more toward specific content. It is assumed in the model that a single specific distribution c_i will be drawn for each sentence, which will be used for all specific topic words that occur in that sentence. To reflect the observation that adjacent sentences are more likely to address the same specific topics, the set of specific content distributions for all sentences is modeled using a sticky HMM model that ensures adjacent sentences are more likely to draw the same specific content word distribution (Barzilay & Lee, 2004).

The parameters for this rich, multilayered topic model are estimated using Gibbs sampling (Blei, Griffiths, Jordan, and Tenenbaum, 2004). Utilizing the estimated model parameters, sentences are selected for the final summary one-at-a-time. At each iteration, the sentence is selected for addition to the candidate summary Z that minimizes the Kullback-Leibler (KL) divergence of the general content word distribution of the document set from the word distribution of the summary Z. KL divergence is calculated using the following formula:

$$D(P_{c_0} || P_Z) = \sum_{w \in Vocab} \ln\left(\frac{P_{c_0}(w)}{P_Z(w)}\right) P_{c_0}(w)$$

where $P_{c_0}(w)$ represents the general content word distribution with parameters estimated as described above, $P_Z(w)$ represents the distribution of words in the candidate summary, and the sum-

mation is over the set of all words occurring in the input document set.

In evaluations conducted by Haghighi and Vanderwende, this system performed comparably to the PYTHY system described above. However, the results of a quality-based user evaluation conducted by Haghighi and Vanderwende demonstrated that users preferred summaries by this system over those generated by the system PYTHY, in the categories "overall," "non-redundancy," "coherence," and "focus," with significance in each category. An advantage of this method is that it allows a separate summary to be generated to address each specific content distribution in the document set, by replacing the general content distribution in the KL divergence formula above with one of the specific content distributions.

The primary advantage of topic modeling-based sentence ranking is that it allows a summarization system to provide more structure in the summary. By identifying the subtopics that make up the unifying topic of the input document set, a summary can be structured in a way that reflects the structure of the topic. Similar to SVD, topic models reveal underlying structure in the data of the input document set and allow sentences to be related to important patterns in this structure. Further, topic modeling methods allow the central theme of the topic to be separated from the secondary themes of the topic, so that the central theme can be emphasized in the summary.

Graph-Based Method

Another way to think about the importance of a sentence in a topic-focused document set is in terms of how strongly that sentence relates to the other sentences in the document set. It is the information that describes the common topic of the document set that one is interested in extracting in MDS. Intuitively, since the important sentences for a summary are related to the unifying topic of the document set, these sentences should contain information that is found throughout the set, and so important sentences should be in general highly related to other sentences. Thus, the problem of sentence ranking for MDS can be viewed as a search to identify the sentences that contain information that is most central to the document set, where the centrality of a sentence means that, on average, that sentence is significantly related to other sentences in the document set.

If we define a notion of similarity between sentences, then we can view a document set as a graph in which each sentence is represented by a corresponding vertex, and between each pair of related sentences there is an edge whose weight corresponds to the similarity between the two sentences. That is, we consider similarity to be the measure of relatedness between sentences. Observe that since similarity between sentences is typically defined in a way that is symmetric, this graph will be undirected. Given this graph representation of the document set, it is possible to utilize graph-theoretic methods for calculating the importance of a node in the graph representation, which corresponds to a sentence in the document set.

In work by Erkan and Radev (2004), a graph-based method is utilized for sentence ranking that is based on the PageRank algorithm that powers the Google search engine (Brin and Page, 1998). In this work, similarity between sentences is defined using a modified version of cosine centrality in which terms are weighted by their respective inverse document frequencies (IDF). IDF was first introduced by Karen Sparck Jones (1999), and for word w, is equal to

$$IDF\left(w\right) = \log\left(\frac{N}{n_w}\right),$$

where N is the number of documents in the collection and n_w is equal to the number of documents containing word w. The IDF-weighted cosine similarity defined is as follows:

$$Cos_{IDF}(x,y)=$$

$$\frac{\sum_{w \in x \cap y} c_y\left(w\right) c_x\left(w\right)\left[IDF\left(w\right)\right]^2}{\sum_{w \in y}[c_y\left(w\right)IDF\left(w\right)]^2 \sum_{w \in x}[c_x\left(w\right)IDF\left(w\right)]^2}$$

where $c_x(w)$ is the number of occurrences of term w in sentence x and $c_y(w)$ is the number of occurrences of term w in sentence y. Using this similarity metric, a graph is constructed to represent the input document set, in the manner described above. Recall that a graph can be represented by an adjacency matrix, which is a matrix containing the edge weight between any two nodes in the matrix (or 0 if there is no edge between two nodes).

The fundamental concept of node importance in a graph is that an important node is one which is linked to by many other nodes. Thus, the importance of a node is measured by the number of nodes it is connected to. Given that edges between sentences in the document set graph representation set are weighted by similarity, this importance measure can be improved by considering the impact of edge weights in this calculation. However, it also makes a great deal of sense to consider the not only the number of other nodes a particular node is connected to, but also the importance of those other nodes as well. For example, consider the case in which a particular node in the document graph is linked to by many other nodes, none of which are themselves important. This would give an artificially high importance to the node in consideration. In contrast, a truly important node might be connected to fewer other nodes, where each of these other nodes is itself important. This line of reasoning motivates the following formula for calculating node importance:

$$p\left(u\right) = \sum_{v \in adj(u)} \frac{Cos_{IDF}\left(x,v\right)}{\sum_{z \in adj(v)} Cos_{IDF}\left(z,v\right)} p\left(v\right)$$

where *adj(u)* is the set of all nodes adjacent to *u* in the document set graph. Observe that this formula is recursive in that the importance of each node (sentence) is calculated based on the importance of each other node it is connected to.

Erkan and Radev discuss how the above formula can be represented using a matrix equation,

p=B$^\mathrm{T}$p

where **p** is a vector containing the importance values for each node and **B** is the adjacency matrix for the graph. By slightly modifying **B**, this matrix can be made into a stochastic matrix, which then allows the authors to ground the calculation of the final node importance score in the theory of Markov chains. Specifically, by adding a small constant value to each entry of the matrix and normalizing row-wise so that each row sums to one, Markov chain theory tells us that there is a stationary distribution for **p**. This distribution can be interpreted in terms of random walks: if a walker were to start at any node in the graph and randomly walk from one node to the next through the graph, as the number of steps taken tends to infinity, the distribution of probabilities of arriving at each node would converge to a specific distribution. This distribution is what is referred to as the stationary distribution. This stationary distribution is the final *LexRank* score for sentences in the graph representation, as defined by Erkan and Radev.

The theory of Markov chains also supplies an iterative algorithm for calculating the *LexRank* score. The version of this algorithm given by Erkan and Radev proceeds as follows: first, the vector $\mathbf{p}_0$ is initialized to a small constant value in each component. Given vector $\mathbf{p}_k$, the vector $\mathbf{p}_{k+1}$ is obtained by multiplying $\mathbf{p}_k$ by the modified version of matrix **B**. After obtaining $\mathbf{p}_{k+1}$, the distance between $\mathbf{p}_k$ and $\mathbf{p}_{k+1}$ is calculated using the Frobenius norm. If this distance is less than some predetermined threshold value, then the score vector is found to have satisfactorily

converged, otherwise the process continues. In an empirical evaluation, Erkan and Radev demonstrated that an MDS system using the *LexRank* sentence ranking algorithm was able to outscore the top systems submitted to DUC 2004 using the ROUGE evaluation method.

Mihalcea and Tarau (2004) independently proposed a graph-based algorithm for sentence ranking based on *PageRank* called *TextRank*. This algorithm is nearly identical to *LexRank*, with the most significant difference being the choice of similarity metric. *TextRank* utilizes a similarity metric based on content overlap that is defined as follows:

$$Sim\left(u,v\right) = \frac{\left|\left\{w \mid w \in u \ \& w \in v\right\}\right|}{\log\left(\left|u\right|\right) + \log\left(\left|v\right|\right)}$$

where *u* and *v* are sentences and *w* represents a word contained in both *u* and *v*.

Mihalcea and Tarau tested a summarization system using *TextRank* on the DUC 2002 single-document summarization task and found this system performed comparably to top-performing systems submitted to that conference.

Graph-based methods for sentence ranking take into consideration relationships between sentences throughout an entire document collection, and thus are able to identify sentences that are most strongly connected to other sentences. These methods depend on a definition of similarity or relatedness between sentences. As we have seen, similarity between sentences may be defined in a number of ways, and therefore it is possible that graph methods could be adapted for use in conjunction with other methods we discuss in this chapter. Further, by incorporating multiple types of edges between sentences, it would be possible to incorporate multiple senses of similarity into a single graph representation. As demonstrated by the algorithm given by Erkan and Radev, graph methods can be implemented using relatively simple and efficient algorithms. All of these advantages suggest that graph-based methods hold much potential for continued exploration in MDS research.

Linguistics/Natural Language Processing Method

All of the methods we have looked at so far have utilized features that are based on distributions of words as they occur within different spans of text. Typically, these distributions have originated with word counts and been treated probabilistically, in some cases after being submitted to data analysis techniques such as SVD, LDA, or distributional clustering. However, in working with text data, researchers in the fields of natural language processing (NLP) and computational linguistics have moved beyond the surface features described by word counts to linguistic structures that exist at deeper levels in the structure of the text. Two examples of such structures are predicate-argument structures (or semantic frames) and discourse structure. We describe two approaches to sentence ranking in MDS that utilize these structures and other linguistic concepts and NLP techniques, such as paraphrase recognition and text segmentation.

Wang, Li, Zhu, and Ding (2008) introduce an MDS method that involves defining a semantic similarity metric for document set sentences based on semantic roles contained within those sentences and utilizing symmetric non-negative matrix factorization (SNMF) on the symmetric sentence similarity matrix to produce clusters of sentences. In this method, it is proposed that each sentence cluster corresponds to a subtopic of the document set.

Semantic roles are constituents within a clause that have a semantic relation to the predicate of the clause (Marquez, Carreras, Litkowski, & Stevenson, 2008). For example, in the sentence '*a man went to the store*', the word *went* is the sole predicate, and *a man* and *to the store* comprise arguments to the predicate. In the context of se-

mantic roles, an argument is a set of words that all serve as part of the same semantic role with respect to the predicate.

Given a non-negative, symmetric $n \times n$ data matrix A, symmetric non-negative matrix factorization is the process of finding a non-negative $n \times r$ matrix H such that

$$A \approx HH^T$$

where $\approx$ dictates approximate equality. The number r is a positive integer between 1 and n that is a parameter of the SNMF procedure. The matrix H can be used to cluster the row-elements of A by assigning row element i of H (corresponding to the element represented by row i of A) to the cluster corresponding to the column j for which it has the highest value. In this way, r clusters are obtained that form a partition of the set of row elements of A.

In the method of Wang, Li, Zhu, and Ding, first a semantic role parse of the document set is obtained that contains a set of frames for each sentence in the document set. A frame consists of a predicate and the set of arguments of that predicate which occur within a single sentence. Next, a measure of similarity is computed between each pair of sentences in the input document set, as follows.

Consider a sentence s_1 and a sentence s_2 in the input document set. The similarity between sentences s_1 and s_2 based on frames is computed using the following method: Let f_1 and f_2 be two frames. Similarity between frames f_1 and f_2 is defined as the sum of the similarities of common roles between the two frames divided by the number of roles in the frame that contains more roles, as in the following equation:

$$fSim\left(f_1, f_2\right) = \frac{\sum_{r_1 \in f_1} \sum_{r_2 \in f_2} rSim\left(r_1, r_2\right)}{\max\left\{\left|f_1\right|, \left|f_2\right|\right\}},$$

where $rSim(r_1,r_2)$ is the role similarity between roles r_1 and r_2 and $|f_n|$ is the number of roles in f_n. Observe that *fSim* is a symmetric function with respect to its two inputs.

Similarity between two roles is defined to be the number of terms in the role containing fewer terms that are related to a term contained in the role containing more terms, divided by the number of terms in the role containing more terms. To define role similarity $rSim(r_1,r_2)$ between roles r_1 and r_2, a function g that takes as input two roles r_1 and r_2, is first defined as follows:

$$g\left(r_1,r_2\right) = \frac{tSim\left(r_1,r_2\right)}{|r_1|}$$

where $tSim(r_1,r_2)$ is the number of terms in r_2 that are related to at least one term in r_1, and $|r_1|$ is the number of terms in r_1. In the calculation of $tSim(r_1,r_2)$, two terms are considered to be related if they are either identical, or if one of the following WordNet relations exists between them: synonym, hypernym, hyponym, meronym, or holynym. WordNet is a lexical database that contains a network of semantic relations between terms (Miller, 1995).

Given the function g, $rSim(r_1,r_2)$ is calculated using the following equation:

$$rSim(r_1,r_2) = \begin{cases} 0 & \text{if } r_1, r_2 \text{ are of different types,} \\ g(r_1,r_2) & \text{if } |r_2| \leq |r_1| \\ g(r_2,r_1) & \text{if } |r_2| > |r_1| \end{cases}$$

Role type designates the relation that an argument has to its predicate. For example, the role *agent* designates the entity that carries out the action of the predicate. In the sentence '*John thanked Bill*', John is the agent, who performed the action of thanking. Finally, similarity between

sentences s_1 and s_2 is calculated using the following (symmetric) formula:

$$sim(s_1,s_2) = \max\{fSim(f_1,f_2) \mid f_1 \in s_1, f_2 \in s_2\}$$

After sentence similarity scores are calculated, a sentence-sentence similarity matrix A is formed from the pairwise similarity scores between each pair of sentences in the input document set, and sentence clusters are obtained by factoring this symmetric similarity matrix using SNMF. Sentences are then ranked based on a linear combination of two features.

For a sentence S, the first feature is defined as

$$F_1 = \frac{1}{|C(i)| - 1} \sum_{j \in C(i), i \neq j} sim\left(S_i, S_j\right),$$

where the summation is over all sentences in the cluster $C(i)$ containing sentence i, except for sentence i itself, $|C(i)|$ is the number of sentences in the cluster $C(i)$, and $sim(S_i,S_j)$ is the semantic sentence similarity measure defined above. The second feature is defined as the similarity between the sentence and the query.

Evaluation performed by Wang, Li, Zhu, and Ding showed that this system outperformed the average score of systems submitted to DUC 2006 and DUC 2005, respectively. Though these evaluation results are not as remarkable as the results presented in other work discussed in this chapter, we believe the application of sentence clustering and the unique semantic sentence similarity metric presented in this work exhibit potential for further exploration, possibly in conjunction with other methods discussed in this chapter.

Harabagiu and Lacatusu (2010) introduce a method for performing MDS that utilizes topic themes. Harabagiu and Lacatusu define a *topic theme* as "a type of knowledge representation that encodes a facet of the knowledge pertaining to a topic." The method introduced by Harabagiu and Lacatusu relies primarily on predicate-argument structures, which are obtained from input document set sentences using a semantic parser. A predicate-argument structure is comprised of a predicate and all of the arguments – or sets of words that fill a semantic role – of that predicate. A predicate-argument structure contains the same information that comprises a semantic frame, as discussed above in describing the work of Wang, Li, Zhu, and Ding.

Harabagiu and Lacatusu define a *topic theme* as consisting of a predicate, which is located in one or more sentences in the input document set and a set of semantically consistent arguments that appear with occurrences of that predicate in the input document set. Harabagiu and Lacatusu (2010) consider that a predicate may be found in multiple sentences in different forms and with different wordings, and so an algorithm for paraphrase recognition is utilized to identify when two predicates with different wordings are actually the same. Semantic consistency between two arguments is verified by checking for words within the two arguments that fall into the same WordNet class. Thus, a topic theme consists of a predicate that occurs at least once in the input document set and a set of consistent arguments that occur in conjunction with that predicate within the input document set. This work makes extensive use of NLP tools, such as WordNet and paraphrase recognition algorithms.

After generating the set of topic themes from the input document set, a representation of these themes is created and specific predicate representatives are chosen for each theme using a classifier with input features that include word frequency information, relations between words obtained from predicate-argument structures, and information related to semantic frames. Next, relations are obtained between themes using linguistic *cohesion* and *coherence* relationships. Cohesion relationships are related to co-occurrence in that they infer relatedness through proximity. In this work, Harabagiu and Lacatusu consider coherence relationships between themes occurring in the same sentence, in successive sentences, or in the same text segment, using segments of related text obtained from an NLP tool for text segmentation. Coherence relations are based on the theory of discourse structure. Discourse relations describe semantic relations between segments of text occurring within a document, which are typically phrases or sentences (Louis, Joshi, & Nenkova, 2010). The relations utilized in this work are contrast, cause-explanation-evidence, condition, and elaboration, and each class of relation is recognized using an independent classifier.

Themes are organized into a ranked structure in which each theme is given a score based on the following features: average position of occurrence of the theme within source documents, density of the theme in the document set, a cohesion-based connectivity measure, and a coherence-based connectivity measure. The connectivity measures capture the connectedness of a theme to other themes. Finally, sentences are selected based on the themes that they contain. Each sentence is given a score based on

1. The position of the themes contained within the sentence in the ranked list of themes and
2. A score that is calculated based on the arguments contained within the sentence.

This second measure assigns a weight to each argument of each theme within a sentence. For each argument, this weight is inversely proportional to the number of appearances of the argument in the theme it belongs to. Sentences are ranked based on the assigned sentence scores.

Harabagiu and Lacatusu evaluated their method against high-performing MDS methods developed by other authors as well as against a variation of the topic themes method utilizing a graph-based structure for scoring themes in place of the linked list of themes. The linked list theme structure exhibited the strongest performance in this evaluation. It also outperformed the highest performing system from DUC 2004. This method exemplifies an approach to MDS that makes use of sophisticated methods from computational linguistics and natural language processing (NLP) to obtain linguistic information about sentences for use in the sentence ranking process.

By extracting more linguistic structure—both syntactic and semantic—from the input document set, linguistics/NLP-based methods for sentence ranking are able to identify relations in the text that other methods based on more superficial features such as word-frequency are not aware of. This deeper structure allows such methods to capture significant relationships that are indicators of the topic of the input document set, as in the theme structures described in Harabagiu and Lacatusu. The semantic sentence similarity measure introduced by Wang, Li, Zhu, and Ding presents a refinement of the typical frequency-based similarity measure that seems to hold much potential for further investigation. The quality of summaries generated using these linguistics/NLP methods depends on the strength of the linguistics/NLP tools that are utilized. As these tools continue to improve in accuracy and sophistication as the result of current research, the MDS methods based on these tools should continue to improve as well.

Analysis of Sentence Ranking Method Classification

Consideration of the sentence ranking methods discussed above demonstrates that there exists a wide variety of approaches to the problem of sentence ranking in MDS. One factor that varies widely among the different classes discussed above is the level of structure that each sentence ranking method extracts from the text in the input document set. Roughly, the methods presented in this chapter proceed from those utilizing the simplest, most superficial structure to those utilizing the richest, most complex structure.

Word frequency is a surface feature, and word-frequency ranking methods tend to use this feature in simple and straightforward ways. Frequent terms are seen as an indicator of importance in these method. Word clustering methods build on the concept of word frequency by clustering similar terms, and thus extract a structure from the text that indicates how words in the text can be grouped based on their contexts. Co-occurrence is similar to word clustering, and models the level of cohesion between individual words in the text. Word clustering and co-occurrence provide some compensation for the problems of synonymy and co-reference that arise when using only superficial word-based features.

SVD methods introduce a more detailed analysis of the text data by utilizing the term-sentence matrix formed from the bag-of-words representation of document set sentences and revealing fundamental underlying patterns in the text data that exist at the sentence level. Topic modeling methods also identify patterns of word usage, which are modeled as probability distributions, as these patterns occur at the level of sentence, document, and entire document set, and within a background of general content. Using these distributional patterns, a ranking method is able to identify the sentences in the document set that most strongly relate to the primary topic of the document set.

Graph-based methods utilize the concept of connectivity among graph nodes, taking into account the relationship of each sentence to each other sentence in order to locate the sentences that are most central to the document set as a whole. Finally, linguistics/NLP methods utilize syntactic and semantic linguistic structures occurring within and between sentences of the input document set in order to find relationships between sentences and important syntactic or semantic structures. It is worth noting that for all classes other than the class of linguistics/NLP methods, the features of the text that are utilized are essentially language agnostic, and so with little modification, these methods could be utilized for summarizing corpora of text in languages other than English.

Along with the level of structure that is extracted from the text, the level of complexity also varies from one class of method to the next. In general, as the extracted structure becomes more complex, the conceptual complexity of methods increases. The computational complexity of methods varies widely between methods of different classes as well, though it does not seem to correlate with structure in a straightforward way. For example, the simple word frequency-based methods for sentence ranking entail the least computational complexity, because they are based on simple counting operations. On the other hand, the graph-based methods are considerably more complex in a conceptual sense, but they can be computed using efficient algorithms that involve only counting, vector multiplication, and vector-matrix multiplication.

It is also of interest that systems in each class appear to be capable of producing a high level of performance, despite the varying levels of structure and complexity that each class entails. There are a number of factors that we hypothesize to contribute to this. One factor is that the sentence ranking method is not the entirety of the summarization process. It could be that the other stages—pre- and post-processing and summary generation—also have a powerful influence on the outcome of the summarization process. The specific methods described in this chapter in conjunction with each method class utilize differing implementations of the overall summarization process. Thus, it is possible that one system could have a stronger sentence ranking component and a relatively weaker summary generation component, for example, while another system could have a relatively weaker sentence ranking component but a very strong summary generation component, and both systems would perform strongly in evaluation.

In order to truly ascertain the relative strength of each method, it would be necessary to perform an evaluation in which a system was implemented with fixed pre- and post-processing and summary generation components while allowing the sentence ranking method to be an interchangeable component. In this evaluation, the sentence ranking method would be the only independent variable.

Another factor that could explain the similarity of performance of different methods is the nature of current methodologies for evaluating summaries. It is possible that current evaluation metrics, while being very useful, do not pick up some subtleties among machine summaries that would be noticed by a human reader. The DUC/TAC conferences have attempted to account for subtle differences in summary quality with the more subjective responsiveness and readability/fluency scores included in their summary evaluations. A survey of user preferences based on the subjective judgment of summary quality was conducted by Haghighi and Vanderwende (2009), revealing that users preferred the summaries generated by a topic model-based system over the summaries generated by the word frequency-based system *PYTHY*, though the ROUGE scores of the two systems were statistically indistinguishable.

As discussed in the *Evaluation Methodology* section, the ROUGE and Pyramid evaluation metrics differ in approach as well as cost. Since the word frequency-based methods attempt to generate a summary that has word-frequency characteristics resembling those of the entire document, it makes intuitive sense to hypothesize that these methods would maximize the ROUGE score. This is because ROUGE scores are based on n-gram overlap between a system-generated summary and human-generated reference summaries, which essentially a measurement of the overlap of surface word frequency features between the two.

By contrast, it seems reasonable that the more structured methods—particularly the linguistic/NLP methods—would capture information of a more conceptual nature. If this is the case, then these methods should exhibit higher performance in the Pyramid evaluation. In the optimal situation, every system would be evaluated using the Pyramid method, which seems to be the most accurate reflection of the quality of a machine-generated summary relative to a human-generated summary. Unfortunately, the cost in time and effort of the Pyramid method makes it infeasible for the iterative research process, and most research efforts do not have the resources to conduct a Pyramid evaluation. Having a Pyramid evaluation of all of the methods presented in this chapter on a common data set and task would provide a valuable insight into the relative strengths of the methods presented here.

It is possible that new evaluation methodologies will reveal more subtle, yet important, differences in the summaries produced by systems utilizing sentence ranking methods of different classes. Hopefully, research will be continued to improve methods for summary evaluation. The optimal evaluation method would be highly informative, in the manner of Pyramid, but also reasonably efficient, like ROUGE. To this end, the TAC conference has featured the AESOP task in which researchers develop new evaluation metrics for MDS and submit them for evaluation (NIST, 2013).

Finally, if one considers a set of sentences within a document set that comprises an optimal set of sentences for forming a summary, it is likely that there are signatures present at each level of structure that distinguish sentences in this set from other document set sentences. That is, a single optimal summary sentence could contain frequent terms, could contain words from significant word clusters, could have strong relations to singular vectors and topics within a topic model, could be central in the document graph, and could contain significant linguistic structures. Or, that sentence could have some subset of this set of features. If this is the case, a ranking method that uses all of these features in combination could prove to be more effective than a method based on only one feature.

FUTURE RESEARCH DIRECTION

It would be beneficial to have a comprehensive scientific evaluation of each sentence ranking method against the other. Such an evaluation would involve fixing all aspects of the MDS process while varying the sentence ranking method, as the only independent variable. This evaluation would allow the relative strength of each ranking method to be objectively determined. It would also be useful to obtain information about the complementarity of each of these methods, which would involve investigating similarities and differences between the rankings generated by each pair of methods.

One way to quantify the complementarity among methods would be to utilize each possible pairing of two methods in order to determine whether a system using a pair combination would outperform a system using only one of the constituents the pair. Another way to quantify complementarity would be to perform a correlational study of the rankings produced by each method with each other method or with a set of rankings that is human generated. If there were complementarity among different methods, it would be possible to construct a system that utilizes all methods in combination. As mentioned above, such a method could prove to be more powerful than a method using a single type of feature. Since the ranking for each method can be calculated independently, by utilizing parallel processing, such a system could run in the nearly same amount of time that is required to run the least efficient of the individual techniques.

Evaluation procedure is very important to summarization research. Evaluation results are the only guide researchers have at their disposal when developing new techniques, and so the summarization methods developed by researchers are very much dependent on the evaluation techniques available. While the Pyramid method gives the most accurate assessment of the relationship a machine summary to human-generated summaries, the time and effort this method requires makes it infeasible in the research process. The ROUGE method is reasonably effective and extremely efficient, but it has the significant drawback of not directly addressing the conceptual content of a summary. As this discussion illustrates, we believe that further research into methods for evaluating summary quality is a very important factor in the progress of summarization research. We hope that evaluation procedures can keep pace with progress in the stock of techniques that are available for application to the MDS process.

CONCLUSION

We have discussed methods for ranking sentences in extractive MDS. Extractive MDS systems usually consist of the three phases: pre- and post-processing, sentence ranking, and summary generation. Sentence ranking is fundamental to the processing of extractive MDS and is closely related to summary generation. In some methods for extractive MDS, sentence ranking and summary generation are interlocking aspects of a single process.

We have discussed six classes of sentence ranking methods. The first class, word frequency-based methods, is the simplest conceptually. Methods in this class utilize basic word frequency statistics based on the occurrence of terms within the input document set. The second class, word clustering and co-occurrence methods, involves clustering related words and measuring cohesion between pairs of words. Methods in the third class, singular value decomposition methods, utilize an SVD of the matrix formed from the sentence bag-of-words vectors to locate fundamental sentence-level patterns in the data of these vectors. The relation of sentences to these patterns provides a measure of sentence importance.

In methods of the fourth class, probabilistic topic modeling methods, documents are modeled as having been generated by a random process involving mixtures of word distributions. These methods allow content that is related to the primary topic of the input document set to be separated from other, less relevant content. The fifth class, graph-based methods, contains methods that rank each sentence based on the importance of the node corresponding to that sentence in a graph representation of the document set, using methods for graph-based node importance. The sixth class, linguistic/NLP methods, involves utilizing NLP tools to identify significant syntactic and semantic structures within the text of the input document set, so that sentences can be ranked based on their respective relationships to these structures.

The level of structure that is extracted from the information in the input document set for the purpose of sentence ranking varies significantly from one class to another, with the simple word-frequency methods extracting the least structured information and the linguistic/NLP methods extracting the most structured information. The complexity of sentence ranking methods also varies from one class to another, both in a conceptual sense and in a computational sense. However, computational efficiency is not directly correlated with the level of structure or conceptual complexity of a method. Performance evaluation, using the methodology of the DUC and TAC conferences, gives evidence that systems with sentence extraction methods from each of aforementioned classes can be highly effective in the task of MDS.

It is possible that other phases of the extractive MDS process—summary generation and pre- and post-processing—could also have a significant impact on the performance of an MDS system. Thus, it would be beneficial to perform an evaluation in which all other aspects of the MDS process are held fixed while the sentence ranking method is varied, in order to accurately determine the relative strengths of different methods. It is also possible that a different evaluation methodology could reveal subtle differences between methods that are ignored current evaluation techniques.

The nature of methods developed in MDS research is strongly related to the evaluation methods used in the research process. Thus, we believe efforts should continue to improve evaluation methodologies for MDS. One such effort is the TAC AESOP task (NIST, 2013). Finally, it is possible that complementary exists between sentence ranking methods of different classes, so that it would be possible to obtain a more powerful sentence ranking method by utilizing methods from different classes in combination.

REFERENCES

Amini, M. R., & Usunier, N. (2007). *A contextual query expansion approach by term clustering for robust text summarization*. Paper presented at Document Understanding Conference 2007. Rochester, NY.

Arora, R., & Ravindran, B. (2008). Latent dirichlet allocation and singular value decomposition-based multi-document summarization. In *Proceedings of the Eighth IEEE International Conference on Data Mining (ICDM 2008)*. IEEE Press.

Baker, L. D., & McCallum, A. K. (1998). Distributional clustering of words for text classification. In *Proceedings of the 21st Annual International ACM SIGIR Conference on Research and Development in Information Retrieval* (pp. 96-103). New York: ACM Press.

Barzilay, R., & Elhadad, M. (1997). Using lexical chains for text summarization. In *Proceedings of the ACL/EACL'97 Workshop on Intelligent Scalable Text Summarization* (pp. 10–17). ACL.

Blei, D. M. (2012). Probabilistic topic models. *Communications of the ACM, 55*(4), 77–84. doi:10.1145/2133806.2133826

Blei, D. M., Griffiths, T. L., Jordan, M. I., & Tenenbaum, J. B. (2004). Hierarchical topic models and the nested Chinese restaurant process. In *Neural Information Processing Systems*. Cambridge, MA: The MIT Press.

Boguraev, B., & Kennedy, C. (1997). Salience-based content characterization of text documents. In *Proceedings of the ACL/EACL'97 Workshop on Intelligent Scalable Text Summarization* (pp. 2–9). ACL.

Brin, S., & Page, L. (1998). The anatomy of a large-scale hypertextual web search engine. *Computer Networks and ISDN Systems, 30*(1–7), 107–117.

Celeux, G., & Govaert, G. (1992). A classification EM algorithm for clustering two stochastic versions. *Journal of CSDA, 14*(3), 315–332.

Conroy, J. M., Schlesinger, J. D., & O'Leary, D. P. (2007). *CLASSY 2007 at DUC 2007*. Paper presented at Document Understanding Conference 2007. Rochester, NY.

Conroy, J. M., Schlesinger, J. D., O'Leary, D. P., & Goldstein, J. (2006). *Back to basics: CLASSY 2006*. Paper presented at Document Understanding Conference 2006. Rochester, NY.

Conroy, J. M., Schlesinger, J. D., Rankel, P. A., & O'Leary, D. P. (2010). *Guiding CLASSY toward more responsive summaries*. Paper presented at Text Analysis Conference 2010. Gaithersburg, MD.

Cormen, T. H., Leiserson, C. E., & Rivest, R. L. (2011). *Introduction to algorithms*. Cambridge, MA: The MIT Press.

Erkan, G., & Radev, D. (2004). Lexrank: Graph-based centrality as salience in text summarization. *Journal of Artificial Intelligence Research, 22*(1), 457–479.

Gong, Y., & Liu, X. (2001). Generic text summarization using relevance measure and latent semantic analysis. In *Proceedings of the 24th Annual International ACM SIGIR Conference on Research and Development in Information Retrieval* (pp. 19-25). ACM.

Harabagiu, S., & Lacatusu, F. (2010). Using topic themes for multi-document summarization. *ACM Transactions on Information Systems, 28*(3), 13:1-13:47.

Harman, D., & Over, P. (2004). The effects of human variation in duc summary evaluation. In *Proceedings of Text Summarization Branches out Workshop at ACL 2004*. ACL.

Kalman, D. (2006). A singularly valuable decomposition: The SVD of a matrix. *The College Mathematics Journal, 27*(1), 2–23. doi:10.2307/2687269

Lin, C. (2004). ROUGE: A package for automatic evaluation of summaries. In *Proceedings of the 42nd Annual Meeting of the Association for Computational Linguistics*. ACL.

Marcu, D. (2000). *DUC summarization roadmap*. Paper presented at NIST Ad-Hoc Review Committee for Planning Long-Term Research and Evaluation in Question Answering and Summarization. Retrieved from http://www-nlpir.nist.gov/projects/duc/roadmap.html

Marquez, L., Carreras, X., Litkowski, K. C., & Stevenson, S. (2008). Semantic role labeling: An introduction to the special issue. *Computational Linguistics, 34*(2), 145–159.

Mihalcea, R., & Tarau, P. (2004). Textrank: Bringing order into texts. [EMNLP.]. *Proceedings of EMNLP, 2004*, 404–411.

Miller, G. (1995). WordNet: A lexical database for English. *Communications of the ACM, 38*(11), 39–41. doi:10.1145/219717.219748

National Institute of Standards and Technology (NIST). (2011). *Document understanding conferences*. Retrieved July 21, 2013 from http://duc.nist.gov

National Institute of Standards and Technology (NIST). (2013). *Text analysis conference (TAC)*. Retrieved July 21, 2013 from http://www.nist.gov/tac

Nenkova, A. (2005). Automatic text summarization of newswire: Lessons learned from the document understanding conference. In *Proceedings of the 20th National Conference on Artificial Intelligence* (pp. 1436-1441). AAAI.

Nenkova, A., & McKeown, K. (2011). Automatic summarization. *Foundations and Trends in Information Retrieval, 5*(2-3), 103–233. doi:10.1561/1500000015

Nenkova, A., Passonneau, R., & McKeown, K. (2007). *The pyramid method: Incorporating human content selection variation in summarization evaluation*. ACM Transactions on Speech and Language Processing. doi:10.1145/1233912.1233913

Pingali, P., Rahul, K., & Vasudeva, V. (2007). *IIIT Hyderabad at DUC 2007*. Paper presented at Document Understanding Conference 2007. Rochester, NY.

Radev, D. R., Hovy, E., & McKeown, K. (2002). Introduction to the special issue on summarization. *Computational Linguistics, 28*(4), 399–408.

Sparck Jones, K. (1999). Automatic summarising: Factors and directions. In I. Mani, & M. Maybury (Eds.), *Advances in automatic text summarisation* (pp. 1–12). Cambridge, MA: MIT Press.

Toutanova, K., Brockett, C., Gamon, M., Jagarlamudi, J., Suzuki, H., & Vanderwende, L. (2007). *The PYTHY summarization system: Microsoft research at DUC 2007*. Paper presented at Document Understanding Conference 2007. Rochester, NY.

Wang, D., Li, T., Zhu, S., & Ding, C. (2008). Multi-document summarization via sentence-level semantic analysis and symmetric matrix factorization. In *Proceedings of the International ACM SIGIR Conference (SIGIR 2008)* (pp. 307-314). New York: ACM Press.

ADDITIONAL READING

Baker, C. F., Fillmore, C. J., & Lowe, J. B. (1998). The Berkely FrameNet project. In *COLING-ACL '98: Proceedings of the Conference* (pp. 86-90). San Francisco, CA: Morgan Kaufmann.

Blei, D., Ng, A., & Jordan, M. (2003). Latent Dirichlet Allocation. *Journal of Machine Learning Research*, *3*, 993–1022.

Bysani, P., Reddy, V. B., & Varma, V. (2009). Modeling novelty and feature combination using support vector regression for update summarization. In *The 7th International Conference on Natural Language Processing* (ICON 2008).

Clark, A., Fox, C., & Shalom, L. (2012). *The handbook of computational linguistics and natural language processing*. Malden, MA: Wiley-Blackwell.

Darwiche, A. (2009). *Modeling and Reasoning with Bayesian Networks*. New York, NY: Cambridge University Press.

Gildea, D., & Jurafsky, D. (2002). Automatic labeling of semantic roles. *Journal of Computational Linguistics*, *28*(3), 245–288.

Gilks, W. R., Richardson, S., & Spiegelhalter, D. (1995). *Markov Chain Monte Carlo in Practice*. Boca Raton, FL: Champan & Hall / CRC.

Koller, D., & Friedman, N. (2009). Probabilistic graphical models: Principles and Techniques. Cambridge, MA: MIT Press.

Lee, D. D., & Seung, H. S. (1999). Learning the parts of objects with nonnegative matrix factorization. *Nature*, *401*, 788–791.

Lee, D. D., & Seung, H. S. (2000). Algorithms for non-negative matrix factorization. In *Advances in Neural Information Processing* (Proceedings of NIPS 2000) (pp. 556-562). Cambridge, MA: MIT Press.

Lin, C. (2004). ROUGE: A package for automatic evaluation of summaries. In *Text Summarization Branches Out: Proceedings of the ACL-04 Workshop* (pp. 74-81). Cambridge, MA: MIT Press.

Louis, A., Joshi, A., & Nenkova, A. (2010). Discourse indicators for content selection in summarization. In *Proceedings of SIGDIAL 2010: the 11th Annual Meeting of the Special Interest Group on Discourse and Dialogue* (pp. 147–156). Association for Computational Linguistics.

Manning, C. D., & Schuetze, H. (1999). *Foundations of staticstical natural language processing*. Cambridge, MA: MIT Press.

Marcu, D. (1999). The automatic construction of large-scale corpora for summarization. In *Proceedings of the 22nd ACM SIGIR Conference* (pp. 137-144). New York, NY: ACM Press.

McKeown, K., Passonneau, R. J., Elson, D. K., Nenkova, A., & Hirschberg, J. (2005). Do summaries help?: A task-based evaluation of multi-document summarization. In *Proceedings of the ACM SIGIR Conference on Research and Development in Information Retrieval* (pp. 210-217). New York, NY: ACM Press.

Palmer, M., Gildea, D., & Kingsbury, P. (2005). The Proposition Bank: A corpus annotated with semantic roles. *Computational Linguistics Journal*, *31*(1), 2–33.

Skillicorn, D. (2007). *Understanding Complex Datasets: Data Mining with Matrix Decompositions*. Boca Raton, FL: Chapman & Hall / CRC.

Sovine, S., & Han, H. (2013). A computationally efficient system for high-performance multi-document summarization. In *Proceedings of the 26th International Florida Artificial Intelligence Research Society* (FLAIRS) Conference.

Steinberger, J., Poesio, M., Kabadjov, M., & Ježek, K. (2007). Two uses of anaphora resolution in summarization. *Information Processing & Management*, *43*(6), 1663–1680. doi:10.1016/j.ipm.2007.01.010

Steyvers, M., & Griffiths, T. (2006). Probabilistic Topic Models. In T. Landauer, D. Mcnamara, S. Dennis, & W. Kintsch (Eds.), *Handbook of Latent Semantic Analysis*. Hillsdale, NJ: Erlbaum.

Vanderwende, L., Suzuki, H., Brockett, C., & Nenkova, A. (2007). Beyond SumBasic: Task-focused summarization with sentence simplification and lexical expansion. *Information Processing & Management*, *43*(6), 1606–1618. doi:10.1016/j.ipm.2007.01.023

Yi, W., Goodman, J., Vanderwende, L., & Suzuki, H. (2007). Multi-document summarization by maximizing informative content-words. In *Proceedings of the 20th International Joint Conference on Artificial Intelligence* (IJCAI '07) (pp. 1776-1782). San Francisco, CA: Morgan Kaufmann.

KEY TERMS AND DEFINITIONS

Extractive Multi-Document Summarization: A set of techniques for performing MDS in which key sentences from the source document set are extracted to form the summary.

Graph-Based Methods: Sentence ranking methods that form a graph representation of document set sentences and utilize graph-based centrality measures to define sentence importance.

Linguistics/Natural Language Processing Methods: Sentence ranking methods that utilize deeper syntactic and semantic structures obtained from the text using linguistics or natural language processing techniques and rank sentences based on their respective relations to these structures.

Multi-Document Summarization (MDS): The study of automated techniques for extracting key information from a set of documents with a common topic and using that information to form a concise summary of the documents in the set.

Pre- and Post-Processing: All the steps in extractive MDS that occur before sentence ranking and after summary generation, including the extraction of usable sentences from input documents and converting them into an internal representation.

Probabilistic Topic Modeling Methods: Sentence ranking methods based on topics, which are word distributions that are discovered within a body of text, where which documents or sentences are represented as mixtures of topic word distributions.

Sentence Ranking: The stage of extractive MDS that involves determining the importance of each sentence for inclusion in the summary based on various features of the individual sentence.

Simple Word-Frequency Based Methods: Sentence ranking methods in which each sentence is ranked based on the frequency occurrence frequency, in some context, of words appearing in that sentence.

Singular Value Decomposition Methods: Sentence ranking methods that utilize a matrix representation of document set sentences along with the singular value decomposition of this word-sentence matrix to obtain a representation of each sentence as a combination of fundamental patterns in the underlying structure the word-sentence matrix data. Sentences are ranked in these methods based on their respective relationships to these fundamental patterns.

Summary Generation: The stage of extractive MDS that considers sentences in combination in order to find the combination of sentences that form the best summary of the document set content while containing minimal internal redundancy.

Word-Clustering Methods: Sentence ranking methods that addressing the issues of synonymy and co-reference by clustering together words that have related meanings or refer to related concepts in the context of the input documents or by measuring the cohesion between terms in the input document set.

Chapter 2

Multi–Document Summarization by Extended Graph Text Representation and Importance Refinement

Uri Mirchev
Ben Gurion University of the Negev, Israel

Mark Last
Ben Gurion University of the Negev, Israel

ABSTRACT

Automatic multi-document summarization is aimed at recognizing important text content in a collection of topic-related documents and representing it in the form of a short abstract or extract. This chapter presents a novel approach to the multi-document summarization problem, focusing on the generic summarization task. The proposed SentRel (Sentence Relations) multi-document summarization algorithm assigns importance scores to documents and sentences in a collection based on two aspects: static and dynamic. In the static aspect, the significance score is recursively inferred from a novel, tripartite graph representation of the text corpus. In the dynamic aspect, the significance score is continuously refined with respect to the current summary content. The resulting summary is generated in the form of complete sentences exactly as they appear in the summarized documents, ensuring the summary's grammatical correctness. The proposed algorithm is evaluated on the TAC 2011 dataset using DUC 2001 for training and DUC 2004 for parameter tuning. The SentRel ROUGE-1 and ROUGE-2 scores are comparable to state-of-the-art summarization systems, which require a different set of textual entities.

DOI: 10.4018/978-1-4666-5019-0.ch002

1. INTRODUCTION

The amount of information on the web is huge and it continues to increase dramatically, causing the effect of data overload. The purpose of *multi-document summarization* is extracting important information from an input collection of topic-related documents and representing it in a concise and usable form. Since one of the reasons for data overload is the fact that many documents share the same or similar topics, automatic multi-document summarization has drawn much attention in recent years. Text summarization is challenging because of its cognitive nature and interesting because of its practical applications. For example, every day many news websites publish articles discussing the same hot topic of the day. One can read all these articles to achieve the complete understanding of the news topic. Alternatively, multi-document summarization can be used, giving the reader one exhaustive story covering the topic. Summarization can also be applied to information retrieval. We can run a summarizer on a search engine output, generating a unified summary of the information contained in result pages, hence letting the user save the time spent on viewing these pages.

Manual summarization of large document collections is a time-consuming and difficult task, which requires a significant intellectual effort. Therefore, automation of the summarization process is required. McKeown, et al. (2005) conducted experiments to determine whether multi-document summaries measurably improve the user performance and experience. Four groups of users were asked to perform the same fact-gathering tasks by reading online news under different conditions: no summaries at all, single-sentence summaries drawn from one of the articles, automated summaries, and human summaries. The results showed that the quality of submitted reports was significantly better and the user satisfaction was higher using both automated and human multi-document summaries rather than relying on the source documents only.

The automated text summarization area has been extensively explored during the last decade, mostly due to DUC and TAC annual competitions. Thousands of research works have been conducted and published on the subject of multi-document generic summarization. However, despite the significant efforts dedicated to design of novel summarization approaches, the automated summary quality is still far from being perfect. Thus, in the TAC 2011 competition (Text Analysis Conference www.nist.gov/tac) on English dataset, the best summarization system (*ID2*) achieved performance of 0.46 in terms of ROUGE-1 recall score vs. the upper bound of 0.52 obtained by the *topline* system based on human summaries.

In this chapter, we offer a fresh look at the summarization process by enhancing the graph representation of a document collection. We also propose that decision about including a sentence in a summary should be influenced by the previously selected sentences. This feature is expressed in the continuous refinement of the sentence importance score. We introduce an algorithm called SentRel (Sentence Relations) for automated summarization of a topic-related document collection. The algorithm copes with the generic summarization task, where the goal is to reflect the most important information described by the input collection. To achieve this goal, the proposed extractive summarization algorithm distills the most relevant sentences from the collection into a short extract, which can be quickly digested by the end-user.

Our summarization approach is based on the mutual reinforcement principle used to compute global importance of the sentences, representing the text corpus as a tripartite graph. In addition, the importance scores of textual entities (i.e. documents and sentences) are iteratively updated by the current summary content. The ordinal and chronological dependencies of sentences in a multi-document summary are calculated beforehand from a training dataset(s) accompanied by gold standard summaries. The SentRel algorithm is greedy, since it iteratively chooses the most important sentences for the summary. The choice of each summary sentence is based on the global information recursively inferred from the tripartite graph, taking into account the partial summary built during the previous iterations.

The goal of the current research is to explore the contribution of the following features:

1. Incorporating a layer of virtual nodes in a graph representation of the text corpus based on the mutual reinforcement principle.
2. Refining the importance scores of candidate documents based on the chronological index of each document in the collection and the current summary content.
3. Refining the importance scores of candidate sentences with respect to the sentences previously selected for the summary based on the ordinal index of each sentence in its source document.

These are the main characteristics of the proposed multi-document summarization algorithm:

1. *Extractive* as it uses original sentences in the output summary.
2. *Language-independent* as it exploits no syntactic features of the input language.
3. *Monolingual* as it assumes that all input documents are written in the same language.
4. *Domain-independent* as it makes no assumptions about the nature of the corpus to be summarized.
5. *Autonomous* as it involves no external tools or knowledge bases.

This chapter is organized as follows. In Section 2, we provide some background on automated multi-document summarization with an emphasis on graph-based representations of summarized collections. Section 3 presents the SentRel summarization algorithm. The algorithm performance

is compared empirically to the state-of-the-art multi-document summarization methods in Section 4. The contributions of the proposed approach and the directions for future research are discussed in Section 5.

2. BACKGROUND

2.1 Multi-Document Summarization Approaches

Multi-document summarization deals with a cluster of topic-related documents. It is more complex than single-document summarization, since articles can be written by different authors, having different writing styles and using a different document structure. Moreover, articles will inevitably overlap in their content being related to the same topic or will have contradictory views regarding the target topic, leading to conflicting information. In addition, single-document summaries usually keep the original order of the sentences in an input article, which is not necessarily the case for multi-document summaries, where summary sentences may be drawn from different input sources in different order. Each summarization method can be categorized with respect to its summary generation approach, summarization task, language dependency, and the learning process. These categories are briefly described below.

We distinguish between two different approaches to summary generation. *Extractive summarization* makes use of complete sentences from the corpus whereas *abstractive summarization* involves the process of reformulation and even may use novel terms to form a summary. An advantage of extractive summarization over abstractive one is that it assures grammatical correctness at least at the local level (of sentences) while abstractive does not. Automatic abstractive summaries often give worse results compared to extractive summaries, due to the challenges faced by the abstractive techniques, the biggest of which being the representation problem.

We also distinguish between two different categories of summarization tasks. *Domain-specific summarization* is adapted for particular information sphere (e.g. dissertation abstracts, people's autobiographies) whereas *domain-independent summarization* makes no assumptions about the nature of the summarized corpus. Domain-specific summarization relies on characteristics of a given domain. For example, Zhou, et al. (2005) suggests that all biographies share certain standard biographical elements. This improves summarization quality but, on the other hand, limits the summarizer effectiveness to very specific cases, whereas generic systems are applicable to a wide range of scenarios, although with moderate performance.

A *language-dependent* method solves the summarization problem by exploiting syntactic features of an input language while a *language-independent* method relies mostly on statistical features computed from the corpus. A language-dependent method is generally more sophisticated than a language-independent one since it requires a deep syntactic analysis of the corpus. The lion's share of research was done in the language-independent domain and a significant number of innovations in this area have their origins in information retrieval techniques.

Supervised summarization has a learning phase, training on summaries written by human annotators whereas *unsupervised summarization* relies on input documents only. Supervised summarization requires high quality training data prepared by professionals and the training process may take hours and even days of computer run time. Opposite to the supervised approach, an unsupervised technique has no training phase dealing only with information that can be found in the source documents. For instance, Erkan & Radev

(2004) represent text input by a graph and defines a sentence salience as a graph centrality score.

The SentRel method presented in this chapter is aimed at multi-document generic extractive summarization. It is language-independent, as it uses only statistical features of the input text, and it is supervised as it is trained on a corpus of human-generated multi-document summaries.

2.2 Generic Summarization Methods

Erkan and Radev (2004) proposed the LexRank approach, for multi-document extractive summarization. A sentence importance is based on the concept of eigenvector centrality in a graph of sentences. LexRank is based on the concept of authority in the web network, where the more important pages point to the target page, the more important it must be. The web network is considered as a graph, where the nodes represent entities (pages) and the edges express relations between them. The corpus sentences can also be viewed as a graph, where nodes represent sentences and edges represent inter-sentence relationships in terms of cosine similarity. The basic assumption of the approach is that sentences that are similar to many other sentences in the cluster are more important and therefore will better represent the topic of the cluster. The transition matrix is constructed indicating sufficient similarity as transition between the sentences and the PageRank algorithm (Page, Brin, Motwani, & Winograd, 1999) is applied. Finally, a summary is constructed from *N* top-scored sentences.

Wan and Yang (2008) used cluster-based analysis for multi-document summarization, by incorporating the cluster-level information into the process of sentence ranking. Documents usually cover few topic themes, and here, which can be represented by clusters of topic-related sentences. The basic assumption of this approach is that sentences in an important theme cluster should be ranked higher than sentences in other theme clusters, and an important sentence in a theme cluster should be ranked higher than other sentences in that cluster. Two models are proposed to exploit cluster-level information for sentences ranking. The models are:

- **Cluster-Based Conditional Markov Random Walk Model:** This model is based on a bipartite graph with sentence and cluster levels. Sentence-to-sentence relationships are expressed by the sentence similarity, sentence-to-cluster relationships are expressed by their correlation. Then, the PageRank algorithm (Page, Brin, Motwani, & Winograd, 1999) is applied to the bipartite graph for obtaining salient sentences.

- **Cluster-Based HITS Model:** This model is also based on a two-layer graph of sentences and clusters. Here, a distinction is made between hubs and authorities, which have mutual reinforcement relationship. Good hubs are connected to many good authorities and a good authority is connected to many good hubs. Objects in the cluster layer are considered as hubs and objects in the sentence layer are considered as authorities. This model uses only sentence-to-cluster relationships. Then, the HITS algorithm (Kleinberg, 1998) is applied to the graph and the sentence saliency is computed as its authority score.

Mihalcea and Tarau (2005) describe multilingual and multi/single document summarization methods based on graph node ranking algorithms. The basic idea is that of "voting" or "recommendation". When one vertex is connected to another vertex, it is casting a vote for that vertex. The higher is the number of votes that are cast for a given vertex, the higher is the importance of the vertex.

In single-document summarization, the goal is to score sentences and to choose N highest scored sentences to summary. Vertices represent sentences and weighted edges represent inter-sentence relations in terms of content overlap. The idea of recommendation is implemented by the content overlap relations: a sentence containing some term recommends another sentence, which contains that term. Vertices are ranked by the PageRank (Page, Brin, Motwani, & Winograd, 1999) or the HITS (Kleinberg, 1998) algorithms. The resulting sentence graph can be interpreted in the following ways:

- **Undirected Graph**
- **Directed Forward Graph:** Edge orientation according to sentence appearance in the text
- **Directed Backward Graph:** Edge orientation according to inverse sentence appearance in the text

Multi-document summarization is done via the "meta" summarization phase. First, for each input document, a single document summary is created, as described above. Next, all single-document summaries are treated as one document and summarized by a single-document summarization technique, so that a summary of summaries is created.

Shen and Li (2010) formulated the multi-document summarization task as a minimum dominating set problem. The graph is generated from a corpus of text documents, where sentences are represented by nodes connected by edges only if the similarity of the corresponding sentences exceeds a threshold. Shen and Li suppose that a summary should represent the whole corpus of sentences in terms of information coverage. Consequently, every sentence of the corpus should either be a part of the summary or be similar to at least one sentence of the summary. Additionally, a summary should be as short as possible. In order to produce a generic summary, a greedy approximation algorithm is used and the minimum dominating set of the graph is constructed, choosing at each stage a sentence having a maximal contribution to information coverage.

Lin and Bilmes (2010) formulated the multi-document summarization task as maximizing a submodular function (a discrete analog of convex function) under a budget constraint problem. A budget constraint is natural in summarization tasks since the summary length is often limited. For example, in the generic summarization task of DUC'04 (Document Understanding Conference 2004) competition, the summary length was restricted to 665 bytes, whereas in TAC'11 (Text Analysis Conference 2011) competition, the evaluation ROUGE score was punished if the summary length was less than 240 or greater than 250 words. The authors sought to achieve an informative and compact summary by combining information coverage maximization with redundancy minimization. For this purpose, they defined a submodular objective function, which measures the summary quality. Their objective function expresses the summary's informativeness in terms of information coverage while penalizing for redundancy. At each stage, the greedy algorithm adds a new sentence to the summary as long as the sentence maximizes and increases the objective function value, penalizing for its length, and as long as the total summary length is not exceeded. This approach is similar to (Shen & Li, 2010), where the summary is also composed by increasing its information coverage, but without considering the summary redundancy and the candidate sentence length.

Schlesinger & Conroy (2011) proposed a supervised and language-independent summarization algorithm named "CLASSY". It was trained on DUC 2005 and 2007 datasets, ignoring a document set topic. The term scoring was calculated by Bayes term weighting. It has calculated as the expected maximum likelihood estimate of the probability that a term would be included in a human-generated summary.

The following features were used to calculate a sentence score:

1. Log of the Dunning signature term statistic.
2. Text rank computed by term co-occurrence in sentences. The terms with a signature term p-value less than 0.001 were excluded.
3. Log of probability that a term occurs in a sentence in the cluster of documents to be summarized.
4. Log of probability that a term occurs in a sentence with one or more signature terms in the cluster of documents to be summarized.

The CLASSY algorithm participated in the TAC 2011 competition and was referenced there as "ID2" system. It obtained ROUGE-1 recall score of 0.46481, which is the second best after the topline system.

Steinberger & Kabadjov (2011) proposed an unsupervised and language-independent summarization algorithm based on Single Value Decomposition (SVD). First, a term-by-sentence matrix is built from the corpus. A column represents the weighted term-frequency vector of the sentence j in a given set of documents. The weighting scheme includes a binary local weight and an entropy-based global weight. Then SVD is applied to identify and extract semantically important sentences. The result is the matrix $A = USV^T$ reducing the matrix $F = SV^T$ to r dimensions, where r can be fine-tuned. Sentence selection starts with measuring the length of sentence vectors in the matrix F. The vector length serves as a measure for importance of a sentence within the top cluster topics. The sentence whose corresponding vector has the largest length is selected to the summary. After placing it in the summary, the topic/sentence distribution in the matrix F is updated by subtracting the information contained in that sentence. As a result, the vector length of similar sentences is decreased, preventing within-summary redundancy. The process is continued with a sentence, which has the largest vector length. This algorithm participated in the TAC 2011 competition and was referenced there as "ID3" system. It obtained ROUGE-2 recall score of 0.17330, which is the second best after the topline system.

The MUSE (MUltilingual Sentence Extractor) approach to single-document summarization (Litvak & Last, 2013) uses a linear combination of 31 language-independent features from various categories for ranking each sentence in a document. These features do not require any morphological or syntactic analysis of the summarized text and they may include the sentence position in a document, the number of characters and words in a sentence, the sentence similarity to the document title, and other statistical metrics. The value of each MUSE feature expresses a particular aspect of sentence significance in the text corpus. In (Litvak & Last, 2013), a weighted linear combination of the MUSE features is used for calculating the importance score of document sentences.

The MUSE features are listed in Table 1 (Litvak & Last, 2013). The vector-based features listed in Table 1 use *tf* or *tf-idf* term weights to evaluate sentence importance. In contrast, the representation used by the graph-based methods (all except TextRank) is based on the word-based graph representation models described by (Schenker, Bunke, Last, & Kandel, 2005), who showed that such graph representations can outperform the vector space model on several text mining tasks. In the word-based graph representation used by MUSE, nodes represent unique terms (distinct words) and edges represent order-relationships between two terms. There is a directed edge from term *A* to term *B* if a term *A* occurrence immediately precedes the term *B* occurrence in any sentence of the document. For the TextRank score calculation (based on (Mihalcea & Tarau, 2005) and denoted by ML_TR in Table 1), MUSE builds a sentence-based graph representation where nodes stand for sentences and edges for similarity relationships.

According to the experimental results presented in (Litvak & Last, 2013), MUSE significantly outperforms TextRank (Mihalcea & Tarau, 2005) on three different languages: English, Hebrew, and Arabic.

In this chapter, we propose the following enhancements of the state-of-the-art methods for generic multi-document summarization:

1. We make use of MUSE scores for estimating the importance of each sentence in the summarized collection.
2. We utilize the chronological indices of documents included in the summary for refining the importance score of each candidate document.
3. We utilize the ordinal indices of sentences included in the summary for refining the importance score of each candidate sentence.

2.3 Performance Evaluation in Summarization

The purpose of a summary evaluation is assessing of its overall quality. Evaluation of a summary can be performed in an intrinsic or extrinsic manner, depending on whether the goal is to assess the summary itself (i.e. according to its information content) or its effectiveness for reaching the goals of a third party application (e.g., IR). In the intrinsic evaluation, the summary informativeness is determined by comparing its content to the gold standard summary. In the case of extrinsic evaluation, the third party system performance is estimated. For example, in the text categorization domain, a document summarizer can serve as a noise filter, providing the summary sentences, rather than the entire document content, as an input to the categorization algorithm. Then the summarizer will be evaluated by the categorization performance of the resulting system.

Table 1. The MUSE features (Litvak & Last, 2013)

Score name	Description
POS_F	Closeness to the beginning of the document.
POS_L	Closeness to the end of the document.
POS_B	Closeness to the borders of the document.
LEN_W	Number of *words* in the sentence.
LEN_CH	Number of *characters* in the sentence.
LUHN	Based on keywords closure.
KEY	Sum of the keywords frequencies.
COV	Ratio of keywords number (Coverage).
TF	Average term frequency for all sentence words.
TFISF	Term frequency inversed sentence frequency.
SVD	Singular value decomposition application on text corpus.
TITLE_O	Overlap similarity to the title.
TITLE_J	Jaccard similarity to the title.
TITLE_C	Cosine similarity to the title.
D_COV_O	Overlap similarity to the document complement.
D_COV_J	Jaccard similarity to the document complement.
D_COV_C	Cosine similarity to the document complement.
LUHN_DEG	Graph-based extensions of LUHN, KEY and COV measures respectively.
KEY_DEG	KEY_DEG Node degree is used instead of a word frequency: words are considered COV_DEG significant if they
COV_EG	are represented by nodes having a degree higher than a predefined threshold.
DEG	Average degree for all sentence nodes.
GRASE	Frequent sentences from *bushy* paths are selected. Each sentence in the *bushy* path gets a domination score that is the number of edges with its label in the path normalized by the sentence length. The relevance score for a sentence is calculated as a sum of its domination scores over all paths.
LUHN_PR	Graph-based extensions of LUHN, KEY and COV measures respectively.
KEY_PR	KEY_PR Node PageRank score is used instead of a word frequency: words are considered COV_PR significant if
COV_PR	they are represented by nodes having a PageRank score higher than a predefined threshold.
PR	Average PageRank for all sentence nodes.
TITLE_E_O	Overlap-based edge matching between title and sentence graphs.
TITLE_E_J	Jaccard-based edge matching between title and sentence graphs.
D_COV E_O	Overlap-based edge matching between sentence and a document complement graphs.
D_COV_E_J	Jaccard-based edge matching between sentence and a document complement graphs.
ML_TR	Multilingual version of TextRank without morphological analysis, sentence score equals to PageRank.

Another aspect of the summary evaluation approaches is the automation issue. Evaluation can be human-assisted or automatic. In human-assisted evaluation approaches, human participation is an integral part of the evaluation process. For example, in the Pyramid evaluation (Nenkova, Passonneau, & McKeown, 2007), conceptually equal pieces of information (Summary Content Units) across model summaries are manually identified. In the DUC'04 conference, the summaries are evaluated with respect to linguistic quality aspects (Grammaticality, Non-redundancy, Referential clarity, Focus, and Structure and Coherence). Each quality aspect has the related question that is to be answered by human assessors according to a five-point scale. In automatic evaluation approaches, a summary quality is determined by a computer program, which compares human-generated ("model") summaries to system-generated ("peer") summaries. For example, ROUGE (Lin, 2004) automatically compares model versus peer summary in terms of overlapping units such as n-gram, word sequences and word pairs. The ParaEval approach (Zhou, Lin, Munteanu, & Hovy, 2006) extends the strict lexical matching of ROUGE by considering paraphrase and synonym semantic closeness.

We will use the ROUGE package (Lin, 2004) to automatically evaluate our multi-document summarization system. ROUGE is an abbreviation of Recall-Oriented Understudy for Gisting Evaluation. It is a family of evaluation measures for automatically assessing the summary quality from different perspectives. ROUGE compares peer summary (computer generated) to several model summaries (gold standard created by professional human abstractors) by counting the number of overlapping units such as n-gram, word sequences and word pairs. These are ROUGE measures: ROUGE-N, ROUGE-L, ROUGE-W, ROUGE-S and ROUGE-SU. ROUGE-N stands for N-gram Co-Occurrence Statistics, which measures n-gram recall between a candidate summary and a set of model ones. ROUGE-L views a summary sentence as a sequence of words. It looks for the longest common sub-sequence between a reference summary sentence and every candidate summary sentence. ROUGE-W means Weighted Longest Common Subsequence (LCS). It extends the ROUGE-L measure by storing the length of consecutive matches encountered so far in a regular two-dimensional dynamic programming table and computing LCS. ROUGE-S is Skip-Bigram Co-Occurrence Statistics. It measures the overlap of skip bigrams between a peer summary and a set of model summaries, counting pairs of words in their sentence order. ROUGE-SU serves as an extension of the ROUGE-S measure, giving credit to a candidate sentence even if it does not have any word pair co-occurring with its references but does have a single word co-occurrence.

The ROUGE script output is influenced by the options provided by an evaluator. For example, it can be decided whether both model and system summaries should be stemmed using the Porter stemmer or whether the stop words should be removed before computing various statistics. Also, the script may be configured to control the summary length limit by considering only the first n bytes or words in the model/system summary. Currently, ROUGE is the most popular summary evaluation method due to its high correlation with human assigned summary scores. ROUGE is a fully automatic, simple and intuitive evaluation method. It can be easily applied to multiple languages, since it does not require either syntactic or grammatical analysis of the input text.

3. THE SENTREL MULTI-DOCUMENT SUMMARIZATION ALGORITHM

3.1 The Architectural View

Figure 1 presents the architectural view of the proposed approach. In the training phase, we calculate the chronological dependencies of documents and the ordinal dependencies of sentences from a benchmark corpus of document sets and their abstractive or extractive gold standard summaries. In the summarization phase, we build a tripartite graph representation of the document set to be summarized. Then we repeatedly calculate the chronological importance off each document in the corpus, select the most important document, calculate the ordinal importance of each sentence in the selected document, and select the most important sentence to be added to the summary.

Figure 1. The SentRel architecture

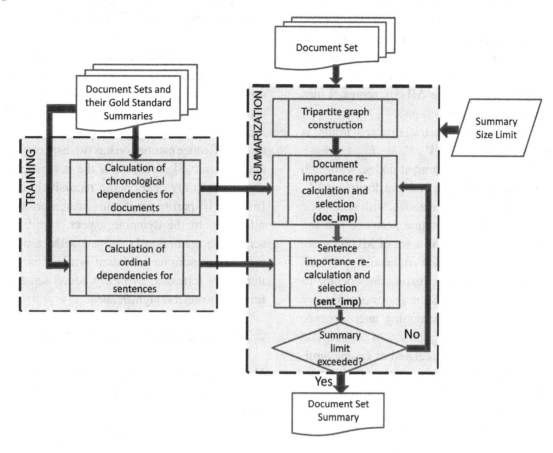

Once the summary size limit is exceeded, the algorithm terminates and outputs the document set summary.

3.2 Extended Graph Representation of the Text Corpus

We propose a tripartite symmetric directed graph representation of the text corpus. The graph includes three layers of disjoint entities: documents, sentences, and MUSE (Litvak & Last, 2013) scores. Document nodes represent corpus documents; sentence nodes represent document sentences, and MUSE score nodes represent MUSE scores calculated for the corpus sentences. This is a virtual layer since MUSE score nodes do not represent any textual entities (such as documents or sentences). A document node and a sentence node

are connected by an edge if their cosine similarity exceeds a predefined threshold and the similarity is assigned as a weight to the corresponding edge. Sentence nodes are also connected by an edge if their cosine similarity is greater than a threshold, and the cosine similarity value serves as a weight for the connecting edge. We do not define edges connecting document nodes, since most documents in the summarized text corpus are expected to be similar to each other, being all related to the same topic. Each sentence node is connected to 31 MUSE (Litvak & Last, 2013) score nodes calculated for that sentence with the score values assigned to edges weights. We let the information flow through these nodes towards the related sentence, implementing the concept of voting-based recommendation. Unlike the single-document summarization algorithm presented in

(Litvak & Last, 2013), SentRel does not calculate a weighted linear combination of MUSE scores.

Figure 2 schematically illustrates document set representation by a tripartite graph. Rectangles denote documents, empty circles denote sentences, and solid circles denote MUSE scores. Lines denote inter-node connections.

The tripartite symmetric directed graph is defined formally as $G = (V_D, V_S, V_M, E_{DS}, E_{SS}, E_{SM})$. $V_D = \{d_i\}$ is a set of document nodes, with each node d_i corresponding to a unique document i, $V_S = \{s_j\}$ is a set of sentence nodes, with each node s_j corresponding to a unique sentence j in the corpus, and $V_M = \{m_k\}$ is a set of MUSE score nodes associated with each sentence. $E_{DS} = \{e_{ij}:d_i \in V_D, s_j \in V_S\}$ is a set of edges expressing document-sentence relations and $E_{SS} = \{e_{j'j''}:s_{j'}, s_{j''} \in V_S, s_{j'} \neq s_{j''}\}$ is a set of edges expressing inter-sentence relations. The weights w_{ij} and $w_{j'j''}$ of edges e_{ij} and $e_{j'j''}$, respectively, are calculated as cosine similarities between the corresponding textual entities and an edge e_{ij} or $e_{j'j''}$ is generated if the cosine similarity exceeds a threshold β. $E_{SM} = \{e_{jk}:s_j \in V_S, m_k \in V_m\}$ is a set of edges expressing MUSE scores of each sentence, where the weight w_{jk} denotes the value of the MUSE score k calculated for the sentence s_j.

3.3 Sentence Importance Calculation and Refinement

In order to decide which sentences will represent the text corpus in the summary, the significance scores of documents and sentences should be estimated. Higher score value denotes higher importance. According to the SentRel approach, the significance estimation has two aspects: static and dynamic. Significance of the static aspect is determined only once, being recursively drawn from the tri-partite graph: this is an a priori significance. In the dynamic aspect, significance scores are continuously refined with respect to the current summary content while it is being iteratively refreshed by newly added sentences; this is a posteriori significance.

3.3.1 Static Significance Calculation

Nodes significance is calculated by applying the HITS (Kleinberg, 1998) algorithm on the tripartite graph G. HITS implements the mutual reinforcement principle computing recursively the graph node scores. The application of the HITS algorithm in the multi-document summarization context can be justified by a strong analogy to conditions

Figure 2. Document set representation by tripartite graph

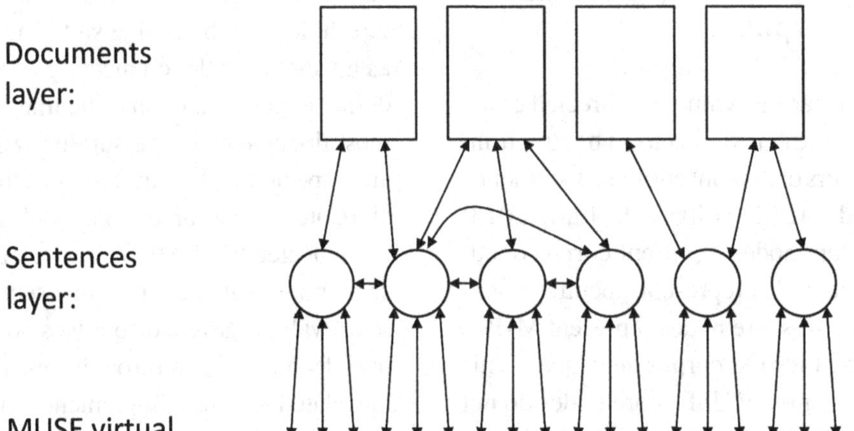

Documents layer:

Sentences layer:

MUSE virtual layer:

for using the algorithm in the IR domain. In the IR domain, the algorithm focuses on a relatively small collection of pages (i.e. 200) relevant to the query. In our case, the graph size is of the same order of magnitude and all textual units are related to the same topic. Also, we see the iterative mutual reinforcement as a recommendation process, where textual entities (sentences) addressing the same concept cast vote for each another, while virtual entities (MUSE scores of each sentence) serve as an extra support for the textual entities. Implementing the mutual reinforcement principle on the three-layer graph, which represents the text corpus, captures the following intuition:

1. A document is important if it is related to important sentences
2. A sentence is important if:
    a. It is related to important documents
    b. It shares a common concept with other important sentences
    c. It is supported by high MUSE scores

The HITS approach distinguishes between two kinds of scores calculated per node: hub and authority, which mutually reinforce each other. Hubs and authorities of all nodes are uniformly initialized to one prior to running HITS.

The hub score update is defined in Equation 1 as the sum of outgoing nodes authority scores.

$$G(n_i).H^{(t+1)} = \sum_{n_j \in Out(n_i)} w_{ij} \times G(n_j).A^{(t)} \qquad (1)$$

The authority score update is defined in Equation 2 as the sum of incoming nodes hub scores.

$$G(n_i).A^{(t+1)} = \sum_{n_j \in In(n_i)} w_{ij} \times G(n_j).H^{(t)} \qquad (2)$$

where

$G(n_i).H^{(t+1)}$- denotes hub score of node n_i from graph G at iteration $t+1$.

$G(n_i).A^{(t+1)}$- denotes authority score of node n_i from graph G at iteration $t+1$.

$Out(n_i)$- denotes the set of nodes which are pointed to by the node n_i.

$In(n_i)$- denotes the set of nodes which point to the node n_i.

w_{ij} - weight associated with an edge which connects the nodes n_i, n_j.

To ensure convergence, hub and authority scores are normalized. The scores are being updated until their convergence is achieved. After normalization, the squared authority and hub scores of all graph nodes are summed-up to one.

Figure 3 demonstrates the first 20 iterations of hub and authority scores computation for the first sentence from the "M0000.english" document taken from the TAC 2011 English dataset. A score value was sampled after each iteration. Since this is a symmetric directed graph, the hub and the authority scores of each node finally converge to the same value.

3.3.2 Importance Refinement

After document and sentence significance scores were calculated by the HITS algorithm, they are refined in the process of summary construction. We assume that the textual unit's significance is influenced by the current content of the summary, and therefore the static significance score should be updated as long as the summary content is being changed too. The significance score is updated based on the previously selected key sentences. Statically determined importance is modified by the probabilities calculated beforehand on particular dataset(s) accompanied by abstractive or extractive gold standard summaries.

Figure 3. Sentence scores computation with HITS

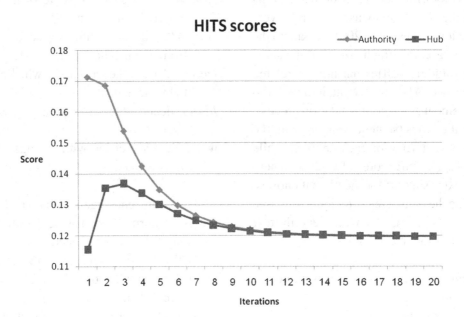

3.3.2.1 Chronological Document Dependencies

To obtain documents chronological dependencies, the conditional probability of a document to become active given another active document is calculated. A document becomes "active" when at least one of its sentences is included in the summary. The corresponding sentence becomes "active" as well. We utilize the publication date information available for each document in a dataset. Documents are sorted in chronological order, which usually represents the development of event(s) discussed in the document set. We denote by *CIP (m/n)* the conditional probability for a document with a chronological index *m* to become active given that the previous sentence was extracted from a document with chronological index *n*. This probability is calculated from a benchmark corpus of gold standard summaries (such as DUC 2001) using Equation 3.

$$CIP(m \ / \ n) = \frac{\sum_{i=1}^{N} \delta_{mn}^{i}}{\sum_{i=1}^{N} \sigma_{n}^{i}} \qquad (3)$$

where *m* and *n* are document chronological indices in a document set summarized by a gold standard summary *i*. *N* is the total number of gold standard summaries in a benchmark collection. δ_{mn}^{i} is the matching function between two chronological indices in a gold standard summary *i* (calculated by Equation 4).

$$\delta_{mn}^{i} =$$
$$\begin{cases} 1, & \begin{cases} \exists j : \arg\max_{l}\max_{h} c\_o(v_j^i, s_h^l(i)) = n \text{ and} \\ \exists k \neq j \arg\max_{l}\max_{h} c\_o(v_k^i, s_h^l(i)) = m \end{cases} \\ 0, & \text{otherwise} \end{cases}$$
$$(4)$$

where

v_j^i and v_k^i – sentences j and k in a gold standard summary i

$s_h^l(i)$ – original sentence with ordinal index h from a document with a chronological index l in a document set summarized by the gold standard summary i

$c\_o\,(a, b)$ – content overlap between sentences a and b (number of common words shared by both sentences)

We search the document set, which is summarized by the gold standard summary i, for an original sentence $s_h^l(i)$ having the maximum content overlap, in terms of the number of common words, with each summary sentence. Then we retrieve the chronological index l of a document containing the sentence $s_h^l(i)$. The $\delta_{mn}^{\ i}$ matching function takes the value of one for gold standard summary i if the chronological index of at least one document corresponding to a summary sentence is n and the chronological index of at least one document corresponding to a different summary sentence is m. Otherwise, it is equal to zero.

The nominator of Equation 3 counts the number of gold standard summaries that include sentences based on documents with chronological indices m and n. In the denominator, we count the number of gold standard summaries that include at least one sentence based on a document with the chronological index n. The corresponding matching function is calculated by Equation 5.

$$\sigma_n^i = \begin{cases} 1, \exists j : \arg\max_l \max_h c\_o(v_j^i, s_h^l(i)) = n \\ 0, \ \text{otherwise} \end{cases}$$

(5)

In addition, we denote by *CIP (m)* the global probability for a document with a chronological index m to become "active" disregarding other active documents. This probability is calculated by Equation 6.

$$CIP(m) = \frac{\sum_{i=1}^{N} \sigma_m^i}{N}$$

(6)

where

$$\sigma_m^i = \begin{cases} 1, \exists j : \arg\max_l \max_h c\_o(v_j^i, s_h^l(i)) = m \\ 0, \ \text{otherwise} \end{cases}$$

(7)

The difference between *CIP (m/n)* and *CIP (m)* is tested for statistical significance using the Binomial distribution and only the *CIP (m/n)* values at the significance level of 0.05 and higher are preferred.

3.3.2.2 Ordinal Sentences Dependencies

We exploit the fact that the summary may contain sentences belonging to the same document. To obtain ordinal sentence dependencies, conditional probability of a sentence from a particular document to become active is calculated, given other active sentence(s) from the same document. As indicated above, a sentence becomes "active" if it is included in the summary. Here, the most basic sentence feature is exploited – its physical position in the document. We denote by *OIP (m/n)* the conditional probability of a sentence with ordinal index m to become active given that a sentence with index n is currently active, where the indexes n, m represent the physical order of sentences in the same document. This probability is calculated from a benchmark corpus of gold standard summaries (such as DUC 2001) using Equation 8.

$$OIP(m \,/\, n) = \frac{\sum_{i=1}^{N} \sum_{j=1}^{S_i} \alpha_{mn}^{ij}}{\sum_{i=1}^{N} \sum_{j=1}^{S_i} \beta_n^{ij}}$$

(8)

where m and n are ordinal indices of sentences in a document. N is the total number of gold standard summaries in a benchmark collection. S_i is the number of documents summarized by a gold standard summary i. α_{mn}^{ij} is the matching function between two ordinal indices of sentences in a document j summarized by the gold standard summary i (calculated by Equation 9 in Box 1) where

v_a^i and v_b^i – sentences with ordinal indices a and b from the gold standard summary i

$s_h^l(i)$ – original sentence with an ordinal index h from a document l summarized by a gold standard summary i.

We search the document set, which is summarized by the gold standard summary i, for an original sentence $s_h^l(i)$ having the maximum content overlap, in terms of the number of common words, with each summary sentence. Then we retrieve the ordinal index h of the sentence $s_h^l(i)$ and the index of its document l. The α_{mn}^{ij} matching function takes the value of one for a document j in a document set i if the document j contains an active sentence with an ordinal index n and an active sentence with an ordinal index m. Otherwise, it is equal to zero.

The nominator of Equation 9 counts the number of documents that include active sentences with ordinal indices m and n. In the denominator, we count the number of documents that include an

active sentence with the ordinal index n. The corresponding matching function is calculated by Equation 10.

$$\beta_n^{ij} = \begin{cases} 1, \exists a : \arg\max_h \max_l c\_o(v_a^i, s_h^l(i)) = n \\ \quad \text{and} \arg\max_l \max_h c\_o(v_a^i, s_h^l(i)) = j \\ 0, \text{ otherwise} \end{cases}$$

(10)

In addition, we denote by *OIP (m)* the global probability of a sentence with ordinal index m to become active disregarding other active sentences in the same document. This probability is calculated by Equation 11.

$$OIP(m) = \frac{\sum_{i=1}^{N} \sum_{a=1}^{L_i} \gamma_m^{ia}}{\sum_{i=1}^{N} L_i}$$

(11)

where L_i is the number of sentences in the collection summarized by the gold standard summary i

The nominator of Equation 11 counts the number of sentences with ordinal index m, which are active w.r.t. the gold standard summary i. In the denominator, we count the total number of sentences in the collections summarized by all gold standard summaries. The corresponding matching function is calculated by Equation 12.

Box 1. Equation 9

$$\alpha_{mn}^{ij} = \begin{cases} 1, & \begin{cases} \exists a : \arg\max_h \max_l c\_o(v_a^i, s_h^l(i)) = n \text{ and } \arg\max_l \max_h c\_o(v_a^i, s_h^l(i)) = j \text{ and} \\ \exists b \neq a : \arg\max_h \max_l c\_o(v_b^i, s_h^l(i)) = m \text{ and } \arg\max_l \max_h c\_o(v_b^i, s_h^l(i)) = j \end{cases} \\ 0, & \text{otherwise} \end{cases}$$

$$\gamma_m^{ia} = \begin{cases} 1, & \arg\max_h \max_l c\_o(v_a^i, s_h^l(i)) = m \\ 0, & \text{otherwise} \end{cases}$$

(12)

The difference between *OIP (m/n)* and *OIP (m)* is tested for statistical significance using the Binomial distribution and only the *OIP (m/n)* values at the significance level of 0.05 and higher are preferred.

3.4 Main Flow of the Algorithm

In the beginning, a multi-layer graph representation of the text corpus is built and global importance of documents and sentences is calculated. After that, sentences are repeatedly chosen until the target summary reaches the desired length. A representative sentence selection involves two stages. In the first stage, the documents global importance is refined and the most important document is determined, changing its state to "active". In the second stage, the importance score of each sentence in the active document sentences is refined and the most significant sentence is identified. Finally, this sentence is appended to the summary.

The summarization algorithm depends on input parameters listed in Table 2. The parameter values remain constant during the whole summarization process.

The function **main_flow** in Box 2 describes the summarization process in a formal way.

3.5 Document Importance Calculation

Document final importance value is calculated as its authority score inferred recursively from the text graph and refined with respect to the sentences previously selected to form the summary content. According to the SentRel approach, it is believed that a high authority score of the document indicates its global significance. The refinement concept complements the document global significance. The function **doc_imp** in Box 3 formally defines document importance calculation.

3.6 Sentence Importance Calculation

Sentence importance value is calculated as a combination of two factors: its authority score and length (number of words). The importance is rewarded by the authority score and penalized by the sentence length. We assume that a high authority score of the sentence indicates its global significance and therefore it should be positively considered. On the other hand, since the summary is constrained by the amount of content it may hold, the sentence length has a negative effect.

Table 2. SentRel input parameters

Parameter name	Description	Range
α	Sentence authority weight	[0,1]
β	Minimal textual units relationship strength	[0,1]
γ	Sentence length weight	[0,1]
ζ	Sentence diversity threshold	[0,1]
η	Document top candidate sentences	N
k	Percentage of the most important documents (when documents are sorted in descending order of importance)	[0,1]

Box 2. Function: **main_flow**

```
Input:
    D - collection of topic related documents D={d_i:0 ≤ i < |D|}
    d_i is a single document in D consisting of sentences.
    d_i ={s_j^i: 0≤ j< | d_i |}, s_j^i is a sentence j which belongs to the document i.


    MAX_LENGTH- summary maximal length (the length can be expressed in words or letters).


    k -percentage of the most important documents in a collection.

Output: S - peer summary


1.  Construct a tripartite graph representation of the document set
2.  Calculate the static importance of the graph nodes
3.  WHILE S.length < MAX_LENGTH DO
        3.1.    Recalculate the importance of each document d_i (using the function doc_imp)
        3.2.    Set the status of the most important document d_i* to "active"
        3.3.    Recalculate the importance of each sentence s_j^i* in document d_i*, j < η
                (using the function sent_imp)
        3.4.    Add the most important sentence s_j*^i* in document d_i* to the summary S
        3.5.    Set the status of s_j*^i* to "active"
4.  RETURN S
```

After the static sentence importance was calculated, it is refined in each iteration with respect to the document sentences previously selected to be included in the summary. The function **sent_imp** (Box 4) formally defines the sentence importance calculation.

4. EVALUATION

4.1 Training

Our algorithm was trained on the DUC 2001 and DUC 2004 datasets. The chronological and ordinal dependencies were pre-calculated on the DUC 2001 training and testing datasets accompanied by 400 word limited human summaries, allowing maximal coverage for ordinal probabilities. The most successful configuration of the algorithm settings was found using the DUC 2004 dataset.

In order to find the appropriate values for the input parameters, 1800 different candidate combinations were enumerated, see Table 3. Each combination was evaluated by the ROUGE script with the input from DUC 2004 competition: "-a -c 95 -b 665 -m -n 4 -w 1.2 -d", see Table 4 for more details.

Finally, the configuration, which maximized the ROUGE-2 recall score was selected as an optimal, see Table 5.

According to the best found configuration, all collection documents ($k = 1$) and all document sentences ($\eta = 15$) should participate in summarization process. Sentence static importance is almost fully considered ($\alpha = 0.8$) punished by small amount of its length ($\gamma = 0.05$). Only sentences whose content overlap with summary was less than half were allowed ($\zeta = 0.5$). Textual units (documents and sentences) are considered to be related if their similarity exceeds minimum value of 0.01 ($\beta = 0.01$).

Box 3. Function: **doc_imp**

```
Input:
    S - Summary
    G' - Text collection graph
    d_i - Document i
    m_i - the chronological index of the document i
    D - Topic-related documents collection

Output:
    w_i - Refined document importance

1. If the number of active sentences in d_i is 2 return zero
2. Else, continue
3. Set the initial document importance w_i to its authority score
4. If the summary is empty, multiply the document importance w_i by its global
   chronological probability CIP(m_i)
5. Else
6. Get the chronological index c of the document containing the sentence added
   to the summary in the previous iteration
    6.1.  If the conditional probability CIP (m_i/c) is statistically
          significant, multiply the document importance w_i by it
    6.2.  Else
    6.3.  Multiply the document importance w_i by the average chronological
          conditional probabilities across all documents in D given c
7. Return w_i
```

We focused on the maximization of ROUGE-2 recall because in the most cases it correlates better to human summaries than the rest of ROUGE measures (Lin, ROUGE: A Package for Automatic Evaluation of Summaries).

4.2 Testing

Our algorithm was evaluated on the dataset of the TAC 2011 summarization track (Giannakopoulos, et al., 2011) focusing on ROUGE-1 and ROUGE-2 recall scores. The scores were calculated by the ROUGE script with the following input parameters: "-a -x -2 4 -u -c 95 -r 1000 -n 2 -f A -p 0.5 -t 0 -d", which was a part of TAC 2011 competition

requirements. See Table 4 for detailed description of these parameters. Our algorithm was trained and tested only on the English version of the dataset because the computation of MUSE metrics had been adapted to the English language.

The proposed approach performance was compared with the systems that participated in the TAC 2011 competition (Giannakopoulos, et al., 2011) including the global baseline and topline systems. The baseline summarization system (*ID9*) represents the document set by a bag-of-words, calculates a centroid of the document set, and chooses the sentences, which are most similar to the centroid. The topline system (*ID10*) uses human summaries as given in the

Box 4. Function: **sent_imp**

```
Input:
    s_j^i - Sentence j in document i
    S - Summary
    G' - Text collection graph
    d_i - Document i
    α - Sentence authority weight
    γ - Sentence length weight
    ζ - Sentence redundancy threshold
    η - Document top candidate sentences
    m_j^i - ordinal index of sentence j in the document i
    n_i - the ordinal index of the previous active sentence in the document i

Output:
    w'_j^i - Refined importance of sentence j in document i
```

1. If the sentence redundancy (maximum content overlap between the sentence s_j^i and a summary sentence) exceeds the diversity threshold ζ, return zero
2. Else, continue
3. Calculate the static importance value of the sentence as a difference between its weighted authority score and its weighted length normalized by the maximum length of a sentence in the document i: $w'_j^i = \alpha \times A_j^i - \gamma \times SL_j^i / max_j\{ SL_j^i \}$
4. Get the document active sentence
5. If no document sentence have participated in the summary yet, multiply the importance value w'_j^i of the sentence j by the global ordinal probability $OIP\ (m_j^i)$ based on its ordinal index m_j^i in the document i
6. Else
   6.1. If the conditional probability $OIP\ (m_j^i\ /n_i)$ is statistically significant, multiply the sentence importance by it
   6.2. Else
   6.3. Multiply the sentence importance by the average conditional ordinal probabilities across all document sentences in d_i given n_i.
7. Return w'_j^i

process of summarization. Human summaries are represented by a graph and merged into the unified representative graph. Random summaries are generated by combining sentences from the original texts. These summaries are matched to the representative graph and the most similar summary is selected as the topline summary.

Our summarization algorithm was compared with the systems participated in TAC 2011 competition. The evaluation results were tested for statistical significance by the paired *t*-test assuming two-tailed distribution. The difference was considered significant in case of *p*-value < 0.05.

Table 3. SentRel algorithm settings

Parameter name	Description	Purpose	Range	Candidate values
α	Sentence authority	Weight	[0, 1]	0.05, 0.15, 0.3, 0.5, 0.8, 1
β	Strength of textual units relationship	Threshold	[0, 1]	0.01
γ	Sentence length	Weight	[0, 1]	0.05, 0.2, 0.5, 0.8, 1
ζ	Sentence diversity	Threshold	[0, 1]	0, 0.1, 0.3, 0.5, 0.8
η	Document top candidate sentences	Threshold	$\mathbb{N}$	5, 10, 15
k	Percentage of the most important documents	Threshold	[0, 1]	0.3, 0.5, 0.8, 1

Table 4. ROUGE script input parameters

Parameter	Description
-a	Evaluate all systems specified in the ROUGE-eval-config-file
-x	Do not calculate ROUGE-L
-2 4	Compute skip bigram (ROGUE-S) co-occurrence, when maximum gap length between two words (skip-bigram) is 4
-u	Compute skip bigram including unigram
-c 95	Specify confidence interval of 95%
-r 1000	Specify 1000 sampling points in bootstrap resampling
-n N	Compute ROUGE-N up to N - max n-gram length
-f A	Select model average as scoring formula
-p 0.5	Relative importance of recall and precision ROUGE scores is 0.5
-t 0	Compute average ROUGE by averaging over the whole test corpus instead of sentences, using sentence as a counting unit
-d	Print per evaluation average score for each system
-b 665	Only use the first 665 bytes in the system summary for the evaluation
-m	Stem both model and system summaries using Porter stemmer before computing various statistics
-w 1.2	Weighting factor of 1.2 for longest common subsequence

Table 5. Optimal configuration of the SentRel algorithm

Parameter name	α	β	γ	ζ	η	k
Value	0.8	0.01	0.05	0.5	15	1

4.3 Evaluation Results

Table 6 shows the TAC 2011 evaluation results in terms of ROUGE-1 recall. It can be seen from the table that our algorithm was significantly outperformed only by the topline system. The *ID2* system (Schlesinger & Conroy, 2011) performed better than *SentRel* but its result was not significantly different from ours. In the other cases, our algorithm has reached higher score than the other systems, whereas the difference vs. two of them (ID4, ID3) is not statistically significant.

Table 6. Evaluation results on TAC11 dataset, recall of ROUGE-1

System	Score	P-Value	Is significant
ID10 (topline)	0.52488	0.00061	Yes
ID2	0.46481	0.81767	No
Sentrel	0.45224	-	-
ID4	0.44423	0.36316	No
ID3	0.43169	0.23058	No
ID5	0.41092	0.01861	Yes
ID1	0.40524	0.04613	Yes
ID7	0.39586	0.00960	Yes
ID8	0.38714	0.00432	Yes
ID9 (baseline)	0.38105	0.00230	Yes
ID6	0.35470	0.00227	Yes

Table 7. Evaluation results on TAC11 dataset, recall of ROUGE-2

System	Score	P-Value	Is significant
ID10 (topline)	0.25177	0.00205	Yes
ID3	0.17330	0.85953	No
ID2	0.17052	0.70107	No
Sentrel	0.16765	-	-
ID4	0.15170	0.13324	No
ID5	0.13605	0.02332	Yes
ID8	0.12144	0.00705	Yes
ID1	0.12125	0.04117	Yes
ID9 (baseline)	0.10962	0.00283	Yes
ID6	0.10655	0.01371	Yes
ID7	0.09662	0.00162	Yes

Table 7 describes TAC 2011 evaluation results in terms of ROUGE-2 recall. It can be seen from the table that our algorithm was significantly outperformed only by the topline system. *ID3* (Steinberger & Kabadjov, 2011) and *ID2* (Schlesinger & Conroy, 2011), which were overviewed in sub-section 2.2, performed better than *SentRel* but their result was not significantly different from it. In the other cases, our algorithm has reached higher score than the other systems whereas the difference vs. the *ID4* system is not statistically significant.

Table 8 and Table 9 show TAC 2011 descriptive statistics of the algorithms performance in terms of ROUGE-1 and ROUGE-2 recall scores, respectively.

4.4 Discussion

Our evaluation results, in terms of ROUGE-1 and ROUGE-2 recall, show that the proposed algorithm (SentRel) performs at nearly the same level as the best systems participating in the TAC 2011 multi-document summarization challenge.

Table 8. TAC11 ROUGE-1 recall descriptive statistics

System	Mean[1]	Standard deviation	Min	Max
Sentrel	0.45580	0.02518	0.42065	0.51467
ID1	0.40560	0.05997	0.33463	0.50459
ID2	0.46495	0.04703	0.40208	0.55832
ID3	0.43193	0.05209	0.36576	0.53997
ID4	0.44417	0.05294	0.31621	0.50399
ID5	0.41105	0.04379	0.35798	0.48624
ID6	0.35498	0.06424	0.24967	0.47467
ID7	0.39596	0.04581	0.31258	0.45067
ID8	0.38713	0.04919	0.31836	0.44706
ID9 (baseline)	0.38117	0.04362	0.30323	0.44444
ID10 (topline)	0.52501	0.03024	0.48508	0.56356

[1]Mean values are slightly different from those presented in Table 6. It happened because this mean value is calculated according to the output of rouge script which tends to print rounded values. The same phenomenon is observed in Table 7 and Table 9 respectively.

Table 9. TAC11 ROUGE-2 recall descriptive statistics

System	Mean	Standard deviation	Min	Max
Sentrel	0.17347	0.03768	0.11528	0.26238
ID1	0.12155	0.05594	0.05890	0.22356
ID2	0.17065	0.05024	0.08854	0.25395
ID3	0.17356	0.06046	0.09067	0.27105
ID4	0.15169	0.04645	0.05423	0.22163
ID5	0.13616	0.03340	0.07552	0.18553
ID6	0.10676	0.05317	0.02865	0.20482
ID7	0.09666	0.03513	0.04167	0.15119
ID8	0.12141	0.03758	0.06380	0.16779
ID9 (baseline)	0.10972	0.02739	0.06347	0.14173
ID10 (topline)	0.25193	0.04475	0.18359	0.31459

However, our method builds upon different elements of the summarized collection. Whereas the two leading systems (denoted as ID2 and ID3) refer mainly to terms, sentences, and term-sentence relationships, the graph structure used by SentRel includes the following three entity types: sentences, documents, and MUSE scores. Unlike the state-of-the-art systems, SentRel also considers the chronological index of each document and the ordinal index of each sentence. On the other hand, individual terms comprising each sentence are excluded from the SentRel graph representation, which makes it less dependent on language-specific resources like stop word lists and stemming algorithms. As indicated in the next section, this result may lead to multi-document summarization algorithms that rely on more compact graph structures than the state-of-the-art methods.

5 CONCLUSION AND FUTURE RESEARCH

We proposed a new multi-document summarization algorithm, called SentRel, which is based on recursive importance inference from a three-tiered graph representation of a textual corpus and its refinement in the process of the summary construction. The algorithm evaluation on TAC 2011 showed that its performance is not significantly different from the state-of-the-art summarization systems, which have shown the best results in that competition. In contrast to those systems, SentRel does not rely on term-sentence relationships. In addition, our algorithm is language-independent and domain-independent, and consequently it does not exploit any language-specific syntactic features or external resources. In the view of the promising evaluation results, we believe that the ideas presented in this chapter deserve further exploration and elaboration. Possible directions for future enhancements of the proposed algorithm are outlined below.

The proposed summarization algorithm can be enhanced by external text processing tools (e.g. OpenNLP) and knowledge bases (e.g. WordNet, Thesaurus, Wikipedia) if they are available for a particular language. In the current version of the summarization algorithm, the parameter η (used in function **sent_imp**) controls the maximal number of summary sentences per document. This parameter is global for all collection documents. The algorithm can be extended so that each document will have a sentence limit of its own based on the importance of a specific document. According to the current approach, the ordinal probabilities for importance refinement are applied without the consideration of the summary content. This feature can be extended by applying different sets of probabilities in each summary construction iteration. In the current graph representation, a particular sentence is supported by all MUSE scores. Consequently, each sentence node is connected to all MUSE nodes in the text graph.

This graph structure can be reduced by pruning the connections with low MUSE scores. Another possible modification of the graph structure is defining one node for each MUSE score and then connecting all sentence nodes to the same MUSE node. Since the number of MUSE scores is much lower than the number of distinct terms in a document collection, the resulting graph will be much more compact than the structures based on the sentence-term relationships that are used by the state-of-the-art methods. At present, the mutual reinforcement principle is implemented by the HITS algorithm (Kleinberg, 1998); it can be easily replaced by the PageRank algorithm (Page, Brin, Motwani, & Winograd, 1999).

REFERENCES

Erkan, G., & Radev, D. (2004). LexRank: Graph-based lexical centrality as salience in text summarization. *Journal of Artificial Intelligence Research*, 457–479.

Giannakopoulos, G., El-Haj, M., Favre, B., Litvak, M., Steinberger, J., & Varma, V. (2011). TAC 2011 multiling pilot overview. In *Proceedings of Text Analysis Conference (TAC-2011)*. National Institute of Standards and Technology.

Kleinberg, J. (1998). Authoritative sources in a hyperlinked environment. In *Proceedings of the Ninth Annual ACM-SIAM Symposium on Discrete Algorithms* (SODA '98). ACM.

Lin, C. (2004). ROUGE: A package for automatic evaluation of summaries. In *Proceedings of the ACL-04 Workshop* (pp. 74-81). Association for Computational Linguistics.

Lin, H., & Bilmes, J. (2010). Multi-document summarization via budgeted maximization of submodular functions. In *Proceedings of the 2010 Annual Conference of the North American Chapter of the Association for Computational Linguistics (HLT '10)* (pp. 912-920). Stroudsburg, PA: Association for Computational Linguistics.

Litvak, M., & Last, M. (2013, September). Cross-lingual training of summarization systems using annotated corpora in a foreign language. *Information Retrieval, 5*(16), 629-656.

McKeown, K., Passonneau, R. J., Elson, D. K., Nenkova, A., & Hirschberg, J. (2005). Do summaries help? In *Proceedings of the 28th Annual International ACM SIGIR Conference on Research and Development in Information Retrieval (SIGIR '05)* (pp. 210-217). New York, NY: ACM.

Mihalcea, R., & Tarau, P. (2005). A language independent algorithm for single and multiple document summarization. In *Proceedings of International Joint Conference on Natural Language Processing (IJCNLP'2005)*. IEEE.

Nenkova, A., Passonneau, R., & McKeown, K. (2007). *The pyramid method: Incorporating human content selection variation in summarization evaluation.* ACM Transactions on Speech and Language Processing. doi:10.1145/1233912.1233913

Page, L., Brin, S., Motwani, R., & Winograd, T. (1999). *The pagerank citation ranking: Bringing order to the web.* Stanford Digital Libraries.

Schenker, A., Bunke, H., Last, M., & Kandel, A. (2005). *Graph-theoretic techniques for web content mining.* Singapore: World Scientific.

Schlesinger, J. M., & Conroy, J. D. (2011). CLASSY 2011 at TAC: Guided and multi-lingual summaries and evaluation metrics. In *Proceedings of the Fourth Text Analysis Conference (TAC 2011)*. Gaithersburg, MD: National Institute of Standards and Technology.

Shen, C., & Li, T. (2010). Multi-document summarization via the minimum dominating set. In *Proceedings of the 23rd International Conference on Computational Linguistics (COLING '10)* (pp. 984-992). Association for Computational Linguistics.

Steinberger, J., & Kabadjov, M. (2011). JRC's participation at TAC 2011: Guided and multilingual summarization tasks. In *Proceedings of the Fourth Text Analysis Conference (TAC 2011)*. Gaithersburg, MD: National Institute of Standards and Technology.

Wan, X., & Yang, J. (2008). Multi-document summarization using cluster-based link analysis. In *Proceedings of the 31st Annual International ACM SIGIR Conference on Research and Development in Information Retrieval (SIGIR '08)*. ACM.

Zhou, L., Lin, C.-Y., Munteanu, D. S., & Hovy, E. (2006). ParaEval: Using paraphrases to evaluate summaries automatically. In *Proceedings of the Main Conference on Human Language Technology Conference of the North American Chapter of the Association of Computational Linguistics (HLT-NAACL '06)* (pp. 447-454). Stroudsburg, PA: Association for Computational Linguistics.

Zhou, L., Ticrea, M., & Hovy, E. (2005). Multi-document biography summarization. In *Proceedings of Conference on Empirical Methods in Natural Language Processing (EMNLP)*. EMNLP.

ADDITIONAL READING

Barzilay, R., Elhadad, N., & McKeown, K. (2002). Inferring strategies for sentence ordering in multidocument news summarization. *Journal of Artificial Intelligence Research*, 35–55.

Bollegala, D., Okazaki, N., & Ishizuka, M. (2006). A bottom-up approach to sentence ordering for multi-document summarization. In Proceedings of the 21st International Conference on Computational Linguistics and the 44th annual meeting of the Association for Computational Linguistics (ACL-44). Association for Computational Linguistics (pp. 385-392). Stroudsburg, PA, USA.

Boros, E., Kantor, P., & Neu, D. (2001). A Clustering Based Approach to Creating Multi-Document Summaries. Proceedings of the 24th annual international ACM SIGIR conference on research and development in information retrieval.

Bysani, P. (2010). Detecting novelty in the context of progressive summarization. In Proceedings of the NAACL HLT 2010 Student Research Workshop (HLT-SRWS '10). Association for Computational Linguistics (pp. 13-18). Stroudsburg, PA, USA.

Filippova, K. (2010). Multi-sentence compression: finding shortest paths in word graphs. In Proceedings of the 23rd International Conference on Computational Linguistics (COLING '10). Association for Computational Linguistics (pp. 322-330). Stroudsburg, PA, USA.

Honarpisheh, M. A., Ghassem-Sani, G., & Mirroshandel, S. A. (2008). A Multi-Document Multi-Lingual Automatic Summarization System. In IJCNLP (pp. 733-738).

Ma, T., & Wan, X. (2010). Multi-document Summarization Using Minimum Distortion. In Proceedings of the 2010 IEEE International Conference on Data Mining (ICDM '10) (pp. 354-363). Washington, DC, USA: IEEE Computer Society.

Radev, D. R., Hovy, E., & McKeown, K. (2002). Introduction to the special issue on summarization. *Computational Linguistics*, 28(4), 399–408. doi:10.1162/089120102762671927

Saggion, H. (2006). Multilingual Multidocument Summarization Tools and Evaluation. International Conference on Language Resources and Evaluation (LREC).

Varadarajan, R., & Hristidis, V. (2005, October). Structure-based query-specific document summarization. In Proceedings of the 14th ACM international conference on Information and knowledge management (pp. 231-232). ACM.

Wan, X. (2010). Towards a unified approach to simultaneous single-document and multi-document summarizations. In Proceedings of the 23rd International Conference on Computational Linguistics (COLING '10) (pp. 1137-1145). Stroudsburg, PA, USA: Association for Computational Linguistics.

Wan, X., Li, H., & Xiao, J. (2010). Cross-language document summarization based on machine translation quality prediction. In Proceedings of the 48th Annual Meeting of the Association for Computational Linguistics (ACL '10). (pp. 917-926). Stroudsburg, PA, USA.

Wang, D., & Li, T. (2010). Many are better than one: improving multi-document summarization via weighted consensus. In Proceeding of the 33rd international ACM SIGIR conference on Research and development in information retrieval (SIGIR '10) (pp. 809-810). New York, NY, USA.

Wang, D., Zhu, S., Li, T., & Gong, Y. (2009). Multi-document summarization using sentence-based topic models. In Proceedings of the ACL-IJCNLP 2009 Conference Short Papers (ACL Short '09) (pp. 297-300). Association for Computational Linguistics, Stroudsburg, PA, USA.

Wei, F., Li, W., Lu, Q., & He, Y. (2010). A document-sensitive graph model for multi-document summarization. *Knowledge and Information Systems*, 245–259. doi:10.1007/s10115-009-0194-2

Xiaodan, X. (2010). Study on Sub Topic Clustering of Multi-documents Based on Semi-supervised Learning. 2nd International Workshop on Database Technology and Applications. Wuhan, China: IEEE Computer Society.

Xiong, Y., Liu, H., & Li, L. (2010). Multi-Document summarization based on improved features and clustering. International Conference on Natural Language Processing and Knowledge Engineering (NLP-KE) (pp. 1 - 5).

Zhang, J., Cheng, X., Xu, H., Wang, X., & Zeng, Y. (2008). Summarizing Dynamic Information with Signature Terms Based Content Filtering. Retrieved 09 06, 2011, from TAC 2008 Proceedings Papers [Cited: 11 21, 2012]: http://www.nist.gov/tac/publications/2008/papers.html.

Zhao, L., Wu, L., & Huang, X. (2009). Using query expansion in graph-based approach for query-focused multi-document summarization. *Information Processing & Management*, *45*(1), 35–41. doi:10.1016/j.ipm.2008.07.001

KEY TERMS AND DEFINITIONS

Abstractive Summarization: Involves the process of reformulation of the original text and even may use novel terms to form a summary.

Domain-Specific Summarization: Adapted for particular information sphere (e.g. dissertation abstracts, people's autobiographies).

Extractive Summarization: Selection of a subset of the most relevant fragments from a source text into the summary. The fragments can be paragraphs, sentences, key phrases or keywords.

Generic Summarization: Makes no assumptions about the nature of the summarized corpus.

Language-Independent Summarization: Exploits no syntactic features of the input language.

Monolingual Summarization: Assumes that all input documents are written in the same language.

MUltilingual Sentence Extractor (MUSE): An extractive generic single-document summarization approach, which uses a linear combination of language-independent features for ranking each sentence in a text document.

Query-Based Summarization: Processes a document (or a set of documents) to be summarized as well as a query expressing the user's interest.

Recall-Oriented Understudy for Gisting Evaluation (ROUGE): An automated method for comparing a computer-generated summary to gold standard summaries (generated by human annotators) in terms of overlapping units such as n-grams, word sequences, and word pairs.

Symmetric Directed Graph: A directed graph D is called symmetric, where for every arc in D, the corresponding inverted arc also belongs to D.

Supervised Summarization Algorithm: Trained on summaries written by human annotators.

Unsupervised Summarization Algorithm: Relies on input documents only.

Chapter 3
Efficient Summarization with Polytopes

Marina Litvak
Shamoon College of Engineering, Israel

Natalia Vanetik
Shamoon College of Engineering, Israel

ABSTRACT

The problem of extractive summarization for a collection of documents is defined as the problem of selecting a small subset of sentences so that the contents and meaning of the original document set are preserved in the extract in best possible way. In this chapter, the authors present a linear model for the problem of extractive text summarization, where they strive to obtain a summary that preserves the information coverage as much as possible in comparison to the original document set. The authors measure the information coverage in terms and reduce the summarization task to the maximum coverage problem. They construct a system of linear inequalities that describes the given document set and its possible summaries and translate the problem of finding the best summary to the problem of finding the point on a convex polytope closest to the given hyperplane. This re-formulated problem can be solved efficiently with the help of linear programming. The experimental results show the partial superiority of our introduced approach over other systems participated in the generic multi-document summarization tasks of the DUC 2002 and the MultiLing 2013 competitions.

INTRODUCTION

Automated text summarization is an active field of research attracting much attention from both academic and industrial communities. Summarization is important for IR systems since it helps to access large repositories of textual data efficiently by identifying the essence of a document and indexing a repository. Also, summarization provides end users shorter versions of the original documents that retain their most important points and, as result, saves time user needs for getting conclusions and decisions. Taxonomically, we distinguish between *single-document*, where a

DOI: 10.4018/978-1-4666-5019-0.ch003

summary per single document is generated, and *multi-document*, where a summary per cluster of related documents is generated, summarization. Also, we distinguish between automatically generated *extract*— the most salient fragments of the input document/s (e.g., sentences, paragraphs, etc.) and *abstract*— re-formulated synopsis expressing the main idea of the input document/s. Since generating abstracts requires a deep linguistic analysis of the input documents, most existing summarizers work in extractive manner (Mani and Maybury, 1999). Moreover, extractive summarization can be applied to cross-lingual/multilingual domains (Litvak et al., 2010).

In this paper we deal with the problem of extractive summarization. Our method can be generalized for both single-document and multi-document summarization. Since the method includes only very basic linguistic analysis, it can be applied to multiple languages.

Formally speaking, in this paper we introduce:

- A novel text representation model expanding a classic Vector Space Model (Salton et al., 1975) to Hyperplane and Half-spaces;
- A distance measure between text and information coverage we wish to preserve;
- A re-formulated extractive summarization problem as an optimization task and its solution using fractional linear programming.
- Multiple possible objective functions for extractive summarization.

The main challenge of this paper is a new text representation model making possible to represent an exponential number of extracts without computing them explicitly, and finding the optimal one by simple optimizing an objective function in polynomial time.

This chapter is organized as follows: next section depicts related work, the following sections describe problem setting and definitions, introduce a new text representation model and a possible

distance measure between text and information coverage, refer summarization task as a distance optimization in a new text representation model and introduce multiple objective functions. Experiments section describes experiment setup and results. The consequent conclusions and the summary of the proposed future work follow in the last section.

BACKGROUND

Extractive summarization can be considered as an optimization problem in a very natural way—we need to extract *maximum* information in *minimal* number of words. Unfortunately, this problem is known as NP-hard, and there is no known polynomial algorithm which can tell, given a solution, whether it is optimal. Many researchers worked in this direction last decade, formulating the summarization as optimization problem and solving it using such *approximation* techniques like a standard hill-climbing algorithm (Hassel and Sjobergh, 2006), A* search algorithm (Aker et al., 2010), regression models (Ouyang et al., 2011), and evolutionary algorithms (Alfonseca and Rodriguez, 2003; Kallel et al., 2004; Liu et al., 2006).

Some authors measure information by text units like terms, N-grams, etc. and reduce summarization to the maximum coverage problem (Takamura and Okumura, 2009). The maximum coverage model extracts sentences to a summary to cover as many terms/N-grams as possible. Despite a great performance (Takamura and Okumura, 2009; Gillick and Favre, 2009) in summarization field, maximum coverage problem, as a private case of a general optimization task, is known as NP-hard (Khuller et al., 1999). Some works attempt to find a near-optimum solution by greedy approach (Filatova, 2004; Wan, 2008; Takamura and Okumura, 2009). Linear programming helps to find a more accurate approximated solution to the maximum coverage problem and became very popular in summarization field in the last years (McDonald, 2007; Gillick and Favre, 2009; Woodsend and Lapata, 2010; Nishikawa, Hasegawa, and Kikui, 2010; Makino et al., 2011). However, most mentioned works use Integer Linear Programming and exponential number of constrains. The difference from our approach lies in time complexity (ILP is NP-hard), and the form and number of constraints. For example, in (McDonald, 2007) constraints are hard-coded and express only the relevance and redundancy between text units, while sentence structure and other term properties are not taken into account.

Trying to solve a trade-off between summary quality and time complexity, we propose a novel summarization model solving the approximated maximum coverage problem by fractional (not integer) *linear programming* in polynomial time. We measure information coverage by terms and strive to obtain a summary that preserves the optimal (minimal or maximal) value of the chosen objective function (for example, total term frequency) as much as possible in comparison to the original document.

Various objective functions combining different parameters like term's position and its frequency are introduced and evaluated.

DEFINITIONS

Problem Setting

We are given a set of sentences[1] $S_1, ..., S_n$ derived from a document or a cluster of related documents speaking on some subject. Meaningful words in these sentences are entirely described by terms[2] $T_1, ..., T_m$.

Our goal is to find a subset $S_{i1}, ..., S_{ik}$ consisting of sentences such that

1. There are at most N terms in these sentences.
2. Term frequency is preserved as much as possible w.r.t. the original sentence set.
3. Redundant information among k selected sentences is minimized.

Text Preprocessing

In order to build the matrix and then the polytope model, one needs to perform the basic text preprocessing including sentence splitting and tokenization. Also, additional steps like stopwords removal, stemming, synonym resolution, etc. may be performed for resource-rich languages. Since the main purpose of these methods is to reduce the matrix dimensionality, the resulted model will be more efficient.

The Matrix Model

In this section we present the matrix model that we use to represent text data – the term count matrix. A *term count matrix* is a real matrix $A_{TC} = (a_{ij})$ of size m×n where $a_{ij} = k$ if term T_i appears in the sentence S_j precisely k times.

Here, columns of A_{TC} describe sentences and rows describe terms. Since we are not interested in redundant sentences, in the case of multi-document summarization, we can initially select meaningful sentences by clustering all the columns as vectors in $\mathbb{R}^n$ and choose a single representative from each cluster. In this case columns of A_{TC} describe representatives of sentence clusters.

The total number of words (term appearances) in the document, denoted by S, can be computed from the matrix A_{TC} as

$$S = \sum_i \sum_j a_{ij} \tag{1}$$

Here and further, we refer to A_{TC} as the *sentence-term* matrix corresponding to the given document/s.

Example 1: Given the following text of $n = 3$ sentences and $m = 5$ (normalized) terms:

S_1 = A fat cat is a cat that eats fat meat.

S_2 = My cat eats fish but he is a fat cat.

S_3 = All fat cats eat fish and meat.

Matrix A_{TC} corresponding to the text above has the following *shape:*

$$
\begin{array}{c}
\\
T_1 = fat \\
T_2 = cat \\
T_3 = eat \\
T_4 = fish \\
T_5 = meat
\end{array}
\begin{bmatrix}
S_1 & S_2 & S_3 \\
a_{11} = 2 & a_{12} = 1 & a_{13} = 1 \\
a_{21} = 2 & a_{22} = 2 & a_{23} = 1 \\
a_{31} = 1 & a_{32} = 1 & a_{33} = 1 \\
a_{41} = 0 & a_{42} = 1 & a_{43} = 1 \\
a_{51} = 1 & a_{52} = 0 & a_{53} = 1
\end{bmatrix}
$$

where a_{ij} are term counts. The total count of terms in this matrix is

$$
S = \sum_{i=1}^{5} \sum_{j=1}^{3} a_{ij} = 16
$$

The Goal

In this setting, our goal can be reformulated as the problem of finding subset $i_1, ..., i_k$ of matrix columns from A_{TC}, so that the chosen submatrix represents the best possible summary under some constraints.

Constraints may be defined as upper and/or lower bounds on the total number of terms or words in the summary. Since it is hard to determine what is the best summary mathematically (this task is usually left to human experts), we wish to express summary quality as a linear function of the underlying matrix. We strive to find a summary that gives an optimal value once the function in question has been determined.

FROM MATRIX MODEL TO POLYTOPE

Hyperplanes and Half-Spaces

Extractive summarization aims at extracting a subset of sentences that covers as much non-redundant information as possible w.r.t. the source document/documents. Here we introduce a new efficient text representation model with purpose of representing all possible extracts without computing them explicitly.

Since the number of potential extracts is exponential in the number of sentences, we would be saving a great portion of computation time. Finding an optimal extract of text units is a general problem for various Information Retrieval tasks like: Question Answering, Literature Search, etc., and our model can be efficiently applied on all these tasks.

In our representation model, each sentence is represented by hyperplane, and all sentences derived from a document form hyperplane intersections (a polytope). Then, all possible extracts can be represented by subplanes of our hyperplane intersections and as such are not located far from the boundary of the polytope. Therefore, intuitively, the boundary of the resulting polytope is a good approximation for extracts that can be generated from the given document.

The Approach

Let $A := A_{TC}$ be the sentence-term matrix of given document(s). We view every column of matrix A as a *linear constraint* representing a hyperplane in $\mathbb{R}^{mn}$.

An occurrence of term t_i in sentence S_j is represented by variable x_{ij}. Note that the maximality constraint on the number of terms in the summary can be easily expressed as a constraint on the sum of these variables.

Example 2: This example demonstrates variables corresponding to the 5×3 matrix A_{TC} of Example 1.

$$
\begin{array}{c}
\quad S_1 \quad S_2 \quad S_3 \\
\begin{array}{c} T_1 \\ T_2 \\ T_3 \\ T_4 \\ T_5 \end{array}
\begin{bmatrix}
x_{11} & x_{12} & x_{13} \\
x_{21} & x_{22} & x_{23} \\
x_{31} & x_{32} & x_{33} \\
x_{41} & x_{42} & x_{43} \\
x_{51} & x_{52} & x_{53}
\end{bmatrix}
\end{array}
$$

Together all the columns of A define a system of linear inequalities, and we also express constrains on the number of terms or words (words is an appearance of a term in a sentence; the same word can appear in a sentence more than once) in the extract we seek.

Every sentence in our document is a hyperlane in $\mathbb{R}^{mn}$ expressed with the help of columns

$$A[\,][\,j] = [a_{1j}, \ldots, a_{mj}]$$

of A and variables

$$x_j = [x_{1j}, \ldots, x_{mj}] \text{ for all } 1 \leq j \leq n$$

representing appearances of terms in sentences.

We define a system of linear inequalities

$$A[\,][j] \cdot x_j^T = \sum_{i=1}^{m} a_{ij} x_{ij} \leq A[\,][j] \cdot 1^T = \sum_{i=1}^{m} a_{ij} \tag{2}$$

for all $1 \leq j \leq n$.

Every inequality of this form defines a hyperplane H_i and it lower half-space specified by Equation (2):

$$A[\,][j] \cdot x_j^T = A[\,][j] \cdot 1^T$$

and with normal vector $\mathbf{n} = (\mathbf{n}_{xy})$

$$
n_{xy} = \begin{cases} a_{xy} & 1 \leq x \leq m \wedge y = j \\ 0 & \text{otherwise} \end{cases} \tag{3}
$$

To express the fact that every term is either present or absent from the chosen extract, we add constraints

$$0 \leq x_{ij} \leq 1 \tag{4}$$

Intuitively, entire hyperplane H_i and therefore every point $p \in H_i$ represents sentence S_i. Since each extractive summary is a subset of sentences of the original document(s), we observe intersections of hyperplanes as objects that represent these summaries.

Define the intersection of two hyperplanes, say H_i and H_j, as a representation of two-sentence summary containing sentences S_i and S_j. Then a subset of r sentences is represented by intersection of r hyperplanes.

Example 3: Sentence-term matrix A_{TC} of Example 1 defines the following hyperplane equations.
$$H_1: 2x_{11}+2x_{21}+x_{31}+x_{51} = 2+2+1+1 = 6$$
$$H_2: x_{12}+2x_{22}+x_{32}+x_{42} = 5$$
$$H_3: x_{13}+x_{23}+x_{33}+x_{43}+x_{53} = 5$$

Here, a summary consisting of the first and the second sentence is expressed by the intersection of hyperplanes H_1 and H_2. Figure 1 shows how a two-dimensional projection of hyperplanes H_1, H_2, H_3 and their intersections look like.

Summary Constraints

We express summarization constraints in the form of linear inequalities in $\mathbb{R}^{mn}$, using the columns of the sentence-term matrix A as linear constraints. Maximality constraint on the number of terms in the summary can be easily expressed as a constraint on the sum of term variables x_{ij}. Since we are

Figure 1. Two-dimensional projection of hyperplane intersection

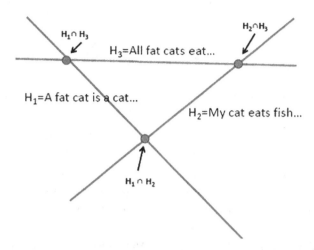

looking for summaries that consist of at least T_{min} and at most T_{max} terms, we introduce the following linear constraint.

$$T_{min} \le \sum_{i=1}^{m} \sum_{j=1}^{n} x_{ij} \le T_{max} \qquad (5)$$

Indeed, every variable x_{ij} stands for an appearance of term i in sentence j, and we intend for their sum to express the number of terms in selected sentences.

Example 4: Equation (5) for Example 1, $T_{min} = 6$ and $T_{max} = 11$ has the form

$$0 \le x_{ij} \le 1, \forall i, j$$
$$6 \le \sum_{i=1}^{5} \sum_{j=1}^{3} x_{ij} \le 11$$

Additionally, we may have constraints on the minimal W_{min} and maximal W_{max} number of words in the summary. We take into account only words that remain in the text after stop-word removal and stemming. The difference between the number terms and the number of words in a summary is that a single term can appear more than once in a sentence. Therefore, the total number of words in the text is expressed by summing up the elements

of its term-count matrix. Therefore, minimality and maximality constraints for words are expressed by the following linear inequality.

$$W_{min} \le \sum_{i=1}^{m} \sum_{j=1}^{n} a_{ij} x_{ij} \le W_{max} \qquad (6)$$

Example 5: Equation (6) for the sentence-term matrix of Example 1 for $W_{min} = 6$ $W_{max} = 11$ has the form

$$6 \le 2x_{11} + 2x_{21} + x_{31} + x_{51} + x_{12} + x_{22} + 2x_{32} + x_{42} + x_{52} + x_{13} + x_{23} + x_{33} + x_{43} + vx_{53} \le 11$$

If we set $T_{min} = 6$ and $T_{max} = 10$, the corresponding constraint of (5) has the form

$$6 \le x_{11} + x_{21} + x_{31} + x_{51} + x_{12} + x_{22} + 2x_{32} + x_{42} + x_{52} + x_{13} + x_{23} + x_{33} + x_{43} + x_{53} \le 10$$

The Polytope Model

Having defined linear inequalities that describe each sentence in a document separately and the total number of terms in sentence subset, we can now look at them together as a system:

$$\begin{cases} \sum_{i=1}^{m} a_{i1} x_{i1} \leq \sum_{i=1}^{m} a_{i1} \\ \quad \dots \qquad \qquad . \\ \sum_{i=1}^{m} a_{in} x_{in} \leq \sum_{i=1}^{m} a_{in} \\ T_{\min} \leq \sum_{i=1}^{m} \sum_{j=1}^{n} x_{ij} \leq T_{\max} \\ W_{\min} \leq \sum_{i=1}^{m} \sum_{j=1}^{n} a_{ij} x_{ij} \leq W_{\max} \\ \qquad 0 \leq x_{ij} \leq 1 \end{cases} \quad (7)$$

First n inequalities describe sentences $S_1, \dots, S_n$, the next two inequalities describes constraints on the total number of terms and words in a summary, and the final constraint determines upper and lower boundaries for all sentence-term variables.

Since every inequality in the system (7) is linear, the entire system describes a convex polyhedron in $\mathbb{R}^{mn}$, which we denote by **P**. Faces of **P** are determined by intersections of hyperplanes

$$H_j, 1 \leq j \leq n$$

$$T_{min} = \sum_{i=1}^{m} \sum_{j=1}^{n} x_{ij}$$

$$T_{\max} = \sum_{i=1}^{m} \sum_{j=1}^{n} x_{ij}$$

$$W_{min} = \sum_{i=1}^{m} \sum_{j=1}^{n} a_{ij} x_{ij}$$

$$W_{\max} = \sum_{i=1}^{m} \sum_{j=1}^{n} a_{ij} x_{ij}$$

$$x_{ij} = 0, 1 \leq i \leq m, 1 \leq j \leq n$$

$$x_{ij} = 1, 1 \leq i \leq m, 1 \leq j \leq n$$

Intersections of H_i's represent subsets of sentences (see Figure 2 for illustration), as the following property shows.

Property 1: Equation of the intersection $H_{1, \dots, k}$ $= H_1 \cap \dots \cap H_k$ (which is a hyperplane by itself) satisfies

$$\sum_{i=1}^{m} \sum_{j=1}^{k} a_{ij} x_{ij} = \sum_{i=1}^{m} \sum_{j=1}^{k} a_{ij} .$$

Proof: The intersection $H_{1, \dots, k}$ has to satisfy all the equations of $H_1, \dots, H_k$. Therefore, summing up equalities (2) for $H_1, \dots, H_k$ we have $\sum_{i=1}^{m} \sum_{j=1}^{k} a_{ij} x_{ij} = \sum_{i=1}^{m} \sum_{j=1}^{k} a_{ij}$. Note that the choice of indexes $1, \dots, k$ was arbitrary and the property holds for any subset of indexes.

Figure 2. Intersection of hyperplanes

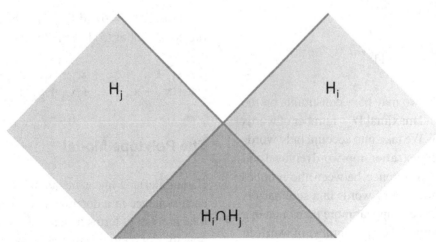

Therefore, the hypersurfaces representing sentence sets we seek are in fact hyperplane intersections that form the boundaries of the polytope **P**.

OBJECTIVE FUNCTIONS FOR SUMMARIZATION

We assume here that the surface of the polyhedron **P** is a suitable representation of all the possible sentence subsets (its size, of course, is not polynomial in m and n since the number of vertices of **P** can reach $O(2^n)$). Fortunately, we do not need to scan the whole set of **P**'s surfaces but rather to find the point on **P** that optimizes (minimizes or maximizes) the chosen objective function. In this section we describe objective functions that we used for summarization and the changes in the model that were required for each of these functions.

Maximal Weighted Term Sum

This objective function requires polytope **P** constructed with the sentence-term matrix A_{TC}.

Every term T_i, $i = 1..m$, may participate in sentences $S_1, ..., S_n$ and is therefore expressed by variables $x_{1i}, ..., x_{ni}$ in inequalities of **P** defining those sentences. We therefore define term variables $t_1, ..., t_m$ as sums of their appearances in all the sentences.

$$t_i = \sum_{j=1}^{n} x_{ij}, 1 \leq i \leq m \qquad (8)$$

The weighted sum of terms then becomes the weighted sum of term variables that we wish to maximize. We define the corresponding objective function as

$$\max \sum_{i=1}^{m} w_i t_i \qquad (9)$$

where w_i denotes term weight in the objective function. We explore several options for term weights:

POS_EQ: Unweighted sum where all terms are equally important

$w_i = 1$ for all i;

POS_F: Closeness to the beginning of the document – the term is more important if it first appears in the beginning of a document:

$$w_i = \frac{1}{app(i)},$$

where $app(i)$ is the index of a sentence in the document where the term T_i first appeared;

POS_L: Closeness to the end of the document – the term is more important if it first appears closer to the end of a document:

$w_i = app(i)$;

POS_B: Closeness to borders of the document – the term is more important if it first appears close to the beginning or the end of a document:

$$w_i = \max\left\{app(i), \frac{1}{app(i)}\right\};$$

TF: Normalized term frequency

$w_i = tf(i)$,

where $tf(i)$ is the normalized term frequency of T_i computed as the number of times the term appears in the document divided by the total number of term appearances of all the terms;

TF-ISF: Term frequency multiplied by inverse sentence frequency

$w_i = tf(i) \times isf(i),$

where *tf(i)* is the normalized term frequency of T_i and *isf(i)* is inverse sentence frequency of T_i defined as

$$1 - \frac{\log \left| \left\{ S_j \mid T_i \in S_j \right\} \right|}{\log n}$$

Example 6: In Example 1 we have term variables t_i

$t_1 = x_{11} + x_{12} + x_{13}$
$t_2 = x_{21} + x_{22} + x_{23}$
$t_3 = x_{31} + x_{32} + x_{33}$
$t_4 = x_{41} + x_{42} + x_{43}$
$t_5 = x_{51} + x_{52} + x_{53}$

Weighted term objective function then has the form

$\max w_1 t_1 + w_2 t_2 + w_3 t_3 + w_4 t_4 + w_5 t_5$

For the metric *POS_EQ*, $1 \leq i \leq 5$ we have objective function

$\max t_1 + t_2 + t_3 + t_4 + t_5$

Distance Functions

This section describes objective functions for summary optimization that have the form of distance function, i.e. they optimize the distance from the generated summary to some point that represents the "ideal" summary. We describe here two such functions. For these functions we aim to find a point on the polytope **P** which is the closest to the chosen vector $p = (p_1, ..., p_m)$. The vector expresses document properties we wish to preserve per term for all the terms $T_1, ..., T_m$. We use term variables $t_1, ..., t_m$ defined in Equation (8) and seek to minimize the distance between $t = (t_1, ..., t_m)$ and the "ideal" vector $p = (p_1, ..., p_m)$.

Maximal Term Coverage with Minimal Repetition

Here, our best point contains all the terms precisely once, thus minimizing repetition but increasing coverage:

$p = (1,...,1)$ (10)

The distance between a point on **P** and the target point *p* is expressed via variables $t_1, ..., t_m$ as

$$\sqrt{\sum_{i=1}^{m} \left(t_i - 1 \right)^2}$$

In order to find the minimum of this function, it is sufficient to minimize the expression under the root sign. Therefore we define the objective function as

$$\min \sum_{i=1}^{m} \left(t_i - 1 \right)^2 \qquad (11)$$

This is a quadratic programming problem. Quadratic programming problems can be solved efficiently both theoretically and practically (Karmarkar, 1984; Khachiyan, 1996; Berkelaar, 1999). If quadratic programming is not supported by a particular LP solving software, then we seek to minimize Manhattan distance between the polytope and the target point:

$$\sum_{i=1}^{m} \left| t_i - 1 \right| \qquad (12)$$

In order to express absolute values in a system of linear inequalities, we use the well-known trick of defining auxiliary variables t_i^+, t_i^- and adding to the system equalities

$$t_i - 1 = t_i^+ - t_i^-, \quad 1 \le i \le m$$

Then objective function has the form

$$\min \sum_{i=1}^m \left(t_i^+ + t_i^- \right) \tag{13}$$

Example 7: For Example 1 Euclidean distance minimization function has the form

$$\min \sum_{i=1}^5 \left(t_i - 1 \right)^2$$

In order to minimize Manhattan distance, we define auxiliary variables

$$t_1 - 1 = t_1^+ - t_1^-, t_2 - 1 = t_2^+ - t_2^-,$$
$$t_3 - 1 = t_3^+ - t_3^-, t_4 - 1 = t_4^+ - t_4^-, t_5 - 1 = t_5^+ - t_5^-,$$

and get an objective function of form

$$\min \sum_{i=1}^5 \left(t_i^+ + t_i^- \right)$$

Minimal Distance to Term Frequency

We use here document frequencies as the target (best) point

$$p = (tf_1, ..., tf_m) \tag{14}$$

where tf_i is the normalized term frequency of term T_i computed as

$$tf_i = \frac{\sum_{j=1}^n a_{ij}}{\sum_{i=1}^m \sum_{j=1}^n a_{ij}}$$

Generated summary is described by the point

$$t = \left(\frac{t_1}{\sum_{i=1}^m t_i}, ..., \frac{t_m}{\sum_{i=1}^m t_i} \right)$$

where

$$\frac{t_j}{\sum_{i=1}^m t_i} = \frac{\sum_i^m x_{ij}}{\sum_i^m \sum_{j=1}^n x_{ij}}$$

is the term frequency of term T_j in generated summary. In order to find the point on **P** which is the closest to p, we need to compute term frequencies in the chosen summary. Thus we need to address rational function optimization in a system of linear inequalities.

To do so, we introduce additional variable

$$r = \frac{1}{\sum_{i=1}^m t_i} \tag{15}$$

and replace all variables x_{ij} with variables r_{ij} representing $r \cdot x_{ij}$, and variables r_i representing $r \cdot t_i$.

Introducing new variables gives us the system

$$\begin{cases} \sum_{i=1}^m a_{ij} r_{ij} \le \sum_{i=1}^m a_{ij}, 1 \le j \le n \\ r T_{\min} \le \sum_{i=1}^m \sum_{j=1}^n r_{ij} \le r T_{\max} \\ r W_{\min} \le \sum_{i=1}^m \sum_{j=1}^n a_{ij} r_{ij} \le r W_{\max} \\ 0 \le r_{ij} \le r \\ r_i = \sum_{j=1}^n r_{ij}, 1 \le i \le m \\ \sum_{i=1}^m \sum_{j=1}^n r_{ij} = 1 \end{cases} \tag{16}$$

of linear inequalities that expresses the fact that we are looking for new rational variables. Then minimal distance objective function is

$$\min \sqrt{\sum_{i=1}^{m} \left(r_i - tf_i \right)^2} \qquad (17)$$

which is equivalent to the quadratic objective function

$$\min \sum_{i=1}^{m} \left(r_i - tf_i \right)^2 \qquad (18)$$

In case of Manhattan distance the following linear function needs to be used.

$$\min \sum_{i=1}^{m} \left| r_i - tf_i \right| \qquad (19)$$

Example 8: For Example 1 and constraint $W_{max} = 12$ we represent the "ideal" summary by the term frequency vector of the document:

$$p = (0.25, 0.3125, 0.1875, 0.125, 0.125)$$

Introduction of rational variables gives us the following system of inequalities:

$$2r_{11} + 2r_{21} + r_{31} + r_{51} \le 6r$$
$$r_{12} + 2r_{22} + r_{32} + r_{42} \le 5r$$
$$r_{13} + r_{23} + r_{33} + r_{43} + r_{53} \le 5r$$

where r is defined according to (15). The system is completed with equations

$$0 \le r_{ij} \le r, \text{ for all } 1 \le i \le 5, 1 \le j \le 3$$

$$\sum_{i=1}^{5} \sum_{j=1}^{3} a_{ij} r_{ij} \le 12r$$

$$r_i = \sum_{j=1}^{3} r_{ij}, \quad 1 \le i \le 5$$

$$\sum_{i=1}^{5} \sum_{j=1}^{3} r_{ij} = 1$$

Objective function for Euclidean distance has the form

$$\min \sum_{i=1}^{5} \left(r_i - p_i \right)^2$$

and for Manhattan distance the function is

$$\min \sum_{i=1}^{5} \left(r_i^+ + r_i^- \right)$$

where $r_1 - 0.25 = r_1^+ - r_1^-$, $r_2 - 0.3125 = r_2^+ - r_2^-$, $r_3 - 0.1875 = r_3^+ - r_3^-$, $r_4 - 0.125 = r_4^+ - r_4^-$, and $r_5 - 0.125 = r_5^+ - r_5^-$.

Sentence Overlap

For this type of objective functions we use sentence-term matrix A_{TC} as a basis for polytope construction.

Recall that sentences S_j and S_k in the text are represented by hyperplanes

$$\sum_{i=1}^{m} a_{ij} x_{ij} = \sum_{i=1}^{n} a_{ij}$$

and

$$\sum_{i=1}^{m} a_{ik} x_{ik} = \sum_{i=1}^{n} a_{ik}$$

respectively in polytope **P**. For each pair of sentences $S_j, S_k, j < k$, we define auxiliary variables ovl_{jk} that express the similarity between S_j and S_k. For every term T_i that appears in both sentences the weight $w(a_{ij}, a_{ik})$ of sentence overlap for the term T_i is defined as

$$w\left(a_{ij}, a_{ik} \right) = \begin{cases} 1 & \text{if } T_i \text{ is present in both } S_j \text{ and } S_k \\ 0, & \text{otherwise} \end{cases}.$$

Overlap variable ovl_{jk} for the pair of sentences S_j, S_k is defined as sentence intersection divided by sentence union, according to *Jaccard similarity coefficient* formula:

$$ovl_{jk} = \frac{\left| S_j \cap S_k \right|}{\left| S_j \cup S_k \right|} = \frac{\sum_{i=1}^{m} w\left(a_{ij}, a_{ik}\right)\left(x_{ij} + x_{ik}\right)}{\sum_{i=1}^{m}\left(a_{ij} + a_{ik}\right)} \tag{20}$$

As a result, the overlap of two sentences S_j and S_k is represented by a variable ovl_{jk} which is a weighted sum of variables x_{ij}:

$$ovl_{jk} = \sum_{i=1}^{m} \omega_i \left(x_{ij} + x_{ik}\right) \tag{21}$$

where

$$\omega_i = \frac{\sum_{i=1}^{m} w\left(a_{ij}, a_{ik}\right)}{\sum_{i=1}^{m}\left(a_{ij} + a_{ik}\right)}$$

according to (21). To minimize all pairwise sentence overlaps in the final summary, we define the objective function

$$\min \sum_{j=1}^{n} \sum_{k=j+1}^{n} ovl_{jk} \tag{22}$$

Example 9: In Example 1 for overlap weights $\min(a_{ij}, a_{ik})$ sentence overlaps are defined as

$$ovl_{12} = \frac{1}{11}\left(\left(x_{11} + x_{12}\right) + 2\left(x_{21} + x_{22}\right) + \left(x_{31} + x_{32}\right)\right)$$

$$ovl_{23} = \frac{1}{10}$$
$$\left(\left(x_{12} + x_{13}\right) + \left(x_{22} + x_{23}\right) + \left(x_{32} + x_{33}\right) + \left(x_{42} + x_{43}\right)\right)$$
$$ovl_{13} = \frac{1}{11}$$
$$\left(\left(x_{11} + x_{13}\right) + \left(x_{21} + x_{23}\right) + \left(x_{31} + x_{33}\right) + \left(x_{51} + x_{53}\right)\right)$$

Maximal Bigram Sum

In the fields of computational linguistics and probability, an n-gram is a contiguous sequence of n items from a given sequence of text or speech. An n-gram could be any combination of text units, letters or terms/words. An n-gram of size 1 is referred to as a "unigram"; size 2 is called a "bigram." Note that we consider any continuous pair of words or words separated by stopwords only to be a bigram.

The purpose of this objective function is to maximize bigram coverage in the chosen summary. This task requires additional information about which bigrams (T_i, T_j) where T_i, T_j are terms, are present in every sentence. The information can be easily extracted from the initial text during the computation of sentence-term matrix. To implement this objective function, we define variables for every bigram in the text:

$$bi_{ij} \text{ for all bigrams } (T_i, T_j) \tag{23}$$

Each sentence is then also a weighted sum of its bigrams

$$S_i = \sum_{(T_j, T_k) \in S_i} w_{jk} bi_{jk} \tag{24}$$

where w_{jk} denotes the number of times a bigram appears in the sentence. The objective function has the form

$$\max \sum_{i,j} bi_{ij}$$
$$\text{where } \forall i, j \; 0 \le bi_{ij} \le 1 \tag{25}$$

Example 10: In Example 1 we have 2-grams *fat,cat, cat,eat, eat,fat, fat,meat, eat,fish, fish,meat,* each appearing at most once in a sentence. Bigram variables are

$$bi_{12}, bi_{23}, bi_{31}, bi_{15}, bi_{34}, bi_{45},$$

and new sentence equalities then have the form

$$S_1 = bi_{12} + bi_{23} + bi_{31} + bi_{15}$$

$S_2 = bi_{23} + bi_{34} + bi_{12}$

$S_3 = bi_{12} + bi_{23} + bi_{34} + bi_{45}$

The objective function is defined as

$$\max\ bi_{12} + bi_{23} + bi_{31} + bi_{15} + bi_{34} + bi_{45}$$

EXTRACTING THE SUMMARY

Since the LP method not only finds the minimal distance but also presents an evidence to that minimality in the form of a point $x = (x_{ij})$, we use the point's data to find what sentences belong to the chosen summary.

Viewing x as a matrix, which equations of H_i the point x satisfies as equalities. If equality holds, x lies on H_i and therefore the sentence S_i is contained in the summary. Otherwise, S_i does not belong to the chosen summary. This test is straightforward and takes $O(mn)$ time. In a case of insufficient summary length, the sentences nearest to the point x are extracted to a summary in a greedy manner.

More formally, let $x = (x_{ij})$ be the point that optimizes a chosen objective function. To determine which sentence subset it describes, we perform the following.

1. Determine *normalized distance* from x to every sentence hyperplane:

$$dist_j = \frac{\sum_{i=1}^{m} \left(a_{ij} - x_{ij} \right)}{\sum_{i=1}^{m} a_{ij}}$$

Note that x lies in lower half-spaces of sentence hyperplanes and thus $\sum_{i=1}^{m} x_{ij} \leq \sum_{i=1}^{m} a_{ij}$. The above expression is in fact L_1 distance from x to H_j, and other types of distances can be used.

2. Sort distances d_j in increasing order and obtain sorted list $d_{j_1}, ..., d_{j_m}$.
3. Add sentences $S_{j_1}, ..., S_{j_k}$ for maximal k that satisfies the word count constraint.

The intuition behind our approach is as follows. Since we use fractional linear programming, the point x is an approximation of the best summary and as such it does not describe the sentences exactly. Therefore, we need to compute the distance data in order to find the sentences that are closest (L_1-wise, in our example) to the point x.

EXPERIMENTS

Experiment Setup

In order to evaluate the quality of our approach, we measured its efficiency in terms of time complexity and accuracy, and compared our approach to multiple summarizers participated in the generic multi-document summarization tasks of the DUC 2002 (DUC, 2002) and MultiLing 2013 (MultiLing, 2013) competitions, and human performance as well. Our software was implemented in Java using lpsolve (Berkelaar, 1999). We used following objective functions in our experiments.

1. Maximal weighted term sum function, defined in Equation (9) and denoted by $OBJ_1^{weight\_type}$ where *weight_type* is one of POS_EQ, POS_L, POS_F, POS_B, TF, TF-ISF described in Section "Maximal Weighted Term Sum."
2. Maximal term coverage with minimal repetition function denoted by OBJ_2 and defined in Equation (13).
3. Minimal distance to term frequency function denoted by OBJ_3 and defined in Equation (19).
4. Minimal sentence overlap function, denoted by OBJ_4 and defined in Equation (22).

5. Maximal bigram sum function, denoted by OBJ_5 and defined in Equation (25).

We conduct the experiments on the datasets from the Document Understanding Conference (DUC) run by NIST in 2002 and the MultiLing 2013 dataset. The dataset of DUC 2002 contains 59 document collections, each having about 10 documents and two manually created abstracts for lengths 50, 100, and 200 words. We generated summaries of size 200 words and compared their quality to the Gold Standard summaries of the same size. The MultiLing dataset is composed of 15 document sets, each of 10 related documents, and three manually created abstracts of 250 words length. The same length constraint was applied to the generated summaries. The dataset contains parallel corpora in several languages.

One of the evaluation criteria used in DUC, the well-known automatic summarization evaluation package ROUGE (Lin, 2004), is used to evaluate the effectiveness of our approach vs. summarizers participated in the generic multi-document summarization task of the DUC 2002 and the MultiLing 2013 competitions. The recall scores of ROUGE-N for $N \in \{1, 2\}$, ROUGE-L, ROUGE-W-1.2, and ROUGE-SU4 which are based on N-gram, Longest Common Subsequence (LCS), Weighted Longest Common Subsequence (WLCS), and Skip-bigram plus unigram, with maximum skip-distance of 4, matching between system summaries and reference summaries, respectively, are reported in Tables 1 through 4.

Table 1. Evaluation results: DUC 2002

system	rouge-1	system	rouge-2	system	rouge-L	system	rouge-W-1.2	system	rouge-SU4
I	0.844	A	0.761	A	0.834	I	0.285	A	0.762
A	0.843	I	0.760	I	0.834	A	0.284	I	0.759
B	0.843	B	0.754	B	0.831	B	0.282	B	0.753
G	0.827	G	0.744	G	0.816	E	0.280	G	0.745
H	0.826	E	0.744	E	0.812	G	0.280	E	0.745
E	0.821	J	0.726	H	0.810	J	0.274	J	0.728
J	0.818	H	0.724	J	0.807	H	0.271	H	0.727
F	0.801	F	0.713	F	0.789	F	0.270	F	0.716
C	0.799	C	0.700	C	0.786	C	0.267	C	0.704
19	0.642	19	0.460	19	0.620	19	0.192	19	0.463
24	0.621	24	0.436	24	0.596	24	0.185	24	0.439
29	0.619	21	0.430	20	0.596	21	0.183	21	0.434
20	0.618	20	0.426	29	0.595	20	0.180	20	0.429
21	0.612	28	0.425	21	0.589	29	0.180	29	0.426
28	0.578	29	0.423	28	0.559	28	0.175	28	0.422
OBJ_1^{TF}	0.572	$OBJ_1^{POS\_F}$	0.373	OBJ_1^{TF}	0.548	$OBJ_1^{POS\_F}$	0.163	25	0.374
OBJ_3	0.570	OBJ_3	0.367	OBJ_3	0.546	OBJ_1^{TF}	0.162	$OBJ_1^{POS\_F}$	0.368
OBJ_5	0.569	OBJ_1^{TF}	0.367	OBJ_5	0.543	OBJ_5	0.162	OBJ_3	0.365
$OBJ_1^{POS\_F}$	0.566	25	0.365	$OBJ_1^{POS\_F}$	0.542	OBJ_3	0.162	OBJ_1^{TF}	0.365
25	0.566	$OBJ_1^{POS\_EQ}$	0.363	$OBJ_1^{POS\_EQ}$	0.539	25	0.161	OBJ_5	0.361
$OBJ_1^{POS\_EQ}$	0.565	$OBJ_1^{POS\_B}$	0.362	25	0.539	$OBJ_1^{POS\_EQ}$	0.160	$OBJ_1^{POS\_EQ}$	0.359
OBJ_4	0.562	OBJ_5	0.362	OBJ_4	0.538	OBJ_1^{TF-ISF}	0.159	$OBJ_1^{POS\_B}$	0.358
OBJ_1^{TF-ISF}	0.561	OBJ_4	0.358	OBJ_1^{TF-ISF}	0.536	OBJ_4	0.159	OBJ_1^{TF-ISF}	0.357
OBJ_2	0.559	OBJ_1^{TF-ISF}	0.358	OBJ_2	0.533	$OBJ_1^{POS\_B}$	0.158	OBJ_4	0.356
$OBJ_1^{POS\_B}$	0.552	OBJ_2	0.354	$OBJ_1^{POS\_B}$	0.529	OBJ_2	0.157	OBJ_2	0.353
$OBJ_1^{POS\_L}$	0.549	$OBJ_1^{POS\_L}$	0.353	$OBJ_1^{POS\_L}$	0.526	$OBJ_1^{POS\_L}$	0.156	$OBJ_1^{POS\_L}$	0.351
31	0.549	31	0.339	31	0.519	31	0.153	31	0.349
16	0.517	16	0.313	16	0.488	16	0.145	16	0.328
22	0.449	22	0.271	22	0.427	22	0.128	22	0.282
GI	0.412	GI	0.100	-	-	-	-	-	-

Table 2. Evaluation results: MultiLing 2013-English

system	rouge-1	system	rouge-2	system	rouge-L	system	rouge-W-1.2	system	rouge-SU4
C	0.767	C	0.630	C	0.755	A	0.236	C	0.628
A	0.765	A	0.626	A	0.752	C	0.236	A	0.624
B	0.755	B	0.610	B	0.742	B	0.233	B	0.610
D	0.732	D	0.592	D	0.721	D	0.226	D	0.586
ID1	0.633	ID1	0.432	ID21	0.615	ID1	0.176	ID1	0.423
ID21	0.632	ID21	0.428	ID1	0.615	ID21	0.176	ID21	0.421
ID11	0.624	ID11	0.421	ID11	0.605	ID11	0.174	ID11	0.413
ID4	0.620	ID4	0.416	ID4	0.601	ID4	0.173	ID4	0.410
ID2	0.617	ID2	0.413	ID2	0.599	ID2	0.172	ID2	0.409
ID61	0.578	OBJ_5	0.369	OBJ_5	0.557	OBJ_5	0.159	ID61	0.371
OBJ_5	0.576	ID61	0.368	ID61	0.554	OBJ_4	0.158	OBJ_5	0.366
OBJ_4	0.570	OBJ_4	0.367	OBJ_4	0.553	ID61	0.157	ID6	0.364
$OBJ_1^{POS\_L}$	0.558	ID6	0.364	$OBJ_1^{POS\_B}$	0.542	$OBJ_1^{POS\_B}$	0.154	OBJ_4	0.362
$OBJ_1^{POS\_B}$	0.558	OBJ_1^{TF}	0.358	$OBJ_1^{POS\_L}$	0.541	ID6	0.154	$OBJ_1^{POS\_L}$	0.354
OBJ_1^{TF}	0.557	$OBJ_1^{POS\_L}$	0.357	ID6	0.540	OBJ_1^{TF}	0.154	OBJ_1^{TF}	0.354
ID6	0.557	$OBJ_1^{POS\_B}$	0.356	OBJ_1^{TF}	0.538	$OBJ_1^{POS\_L}$	0.153	OBJ_2	0.352
OBJ_2	0.556	OBJ_2	0.354	OBJ_2	0.538	OBJ_2	0.153	$OBJ_1^{POS\_B}$	0.352
$OBJ_1^{POS\_F}$	0.553	$OBJ_1^{POS\_EQ}$	0.351	$OBJ_1^{POS\_F}$	0.532	$OBJ_1^{POS\_F}$	0.152	$OBJ_1^{POS\_F}$	0.347
$OBJ_1^{POS\_EQ}$	0.545	OBJ_1^{TF-ISF}	0.350	$OBJ_1^{POS\_EQ}$	0.531	$OBJ_1^{POS\_EQ}$	0.152	$OBJ_1^{POS\_EQ}$	0.346
OBJ_1^{TF-ISF}	0.545	$OBJ_1^{POS\_F}$	0.349	OBJ_1^{TF-ISF}	0.529	OBJ_1^{TF-ISF}	0.151	OBJ_1^{TF-ISF}	0.345
OBJ_3	0.525	OBJ_3	0.322	OBJ_3	0.504	OBJ_3	0.144	OBJ_3	0.322
ID3	0.503	ID3	0.310	ID3	0.481	ID3	0.138	ID3	0.313

Table 3. Evaluation results: MultiLing 2013-Hebrew

system	rouge-1	system	rouge-2	system	rouge-L	system	rouge-W-1.2	system	rouge-SU4
A	0.689	A	0.598	A	0.682	A	0.218	A	0.579
C	0.672	C	0.585	C	0.666	C	0.216	C	0.565
B	0.647	B	0.562	B	0.642	B	0.210	B	0.544
ID61	0.520	ID61	0.393	ID2	0.511	ID61	0.151	ID61	0.361
ID2	0.519	ID2	0.388	ID61	0.511	ID2	0.150	ID2	0.357
ID4	0.505	OBJ_5	0.380	ID4	0.495	ID4	0.147	ID4	0.343
OBJ_5	0.493	ID4	0.376	OBJ_5	0.488	OBJ_5	0.145	OBJ_5	0.342
OBJ_1^{TF-ISF}	0.481	OBJ_1^{TF-ISF}	0.372	OBJ_1^{TF-ISF}	0.475	OBJ_1^{TF-ISF}	0.142	OBJ_1^{TF-ISF}	0.334
$OBJ_1^{POS\_EQ}$	0.479	$OBJ_1^{POS\_EQ}$	0.369	$OBJ_1^{POS\_EQ}$	0.474	$OBJ_1^{POS\_EQ}$	0.142	$OBJ_1^{POS\_EQ}$	0.332
OBJ_1^{TF}	0.479	ID6	0.358	OBJ_1^{TF}	0.471	OBJ_1^{TF}	0.140	ID6	0.327
OBJ_4	0.476	OBJ_1^{TF}	0.357	OBJ_4	0.470	OBJ_4	0.139	OBJ_1^{TF}	0.323
ID6	0.475	OBJ_4	0.352	ID6	0.468	OBJ_4	0.139	OBJ_4	0.318
$OBJ_1^{POS\_L}$	0.470	$OBJ_1^{POS\_L}$	0.350	$OBJ_1^{POS\_L}$	0.462	$OBJ_1^{POS\_L}$	0.138	$OBJ_1^{POS\_L}$	0.315
$OBJ_1^{POS\_B}$	0.461	$OBJ_1^{POS\_B}$	0.338	$OBJ_1^{POS\_B}$	0.454	$OBJ_1^{POS\_B}$	0.134	$OBJ_1^{POS\_B}$	0.306
$OBJ_1^{POS\_F}$	0.457	$OBJ_1^{POS\_F}$	0.338	$OBJ_1^{POS\_F}$	0.450	$OBJ_1^{POS\_F}$	0.133	$OBJ_1^{POS\_F}$	0.304
OBJ_3	0.447	OBJ_2	0.329	OBJ_3	0.439	OBJ_2	0.131	OBJ_2	0.296
OBJ_2	0.442	OBJ_3	0.324	OBJ_2	0.436	OBJ_3	0.130	OBJ_3	0.294
ID11	0.396	ID11	0.269	ID11	0.381	ID11	0.112	ID11	0.246
ID1	0.370	ID21	0.244	ID21	0.354	ID1	0.103	ID21	0.225
ID21	0.369	ID1	0.243	ID1	0.351	ID21	0.103	ID1	0.224

Table 4. Evaluation results: MultiLing 2013-Arabic

system	rouge-1	system	rouge-2	system	rouge-L	system	rouge-W-1.2	system	rouge-SU4
A	0.830	A	0.689	A	0.800	A	0.202	A	0.716
B	0.820	B	0.665	B	0.786	B	0.198	B	0.698
ID61	0.774	ID61	0.558	ID61	0.729	ID61	0.161	ID61	0.601
ID4	0.772	ID4	0.550	ID4	0.726	ID4	0.161	ID4	0.596
$OBJ_1^{POS\_F}$	0.743	ID2	0.512	$OBJ_1^{POS\_F}$	0.696	ID2	0.150	ID2	0.557
OBJ_4	0.740	$OBJ_1^{POS\_F}$	0.499	ID2	0.694	$OBJ_1^{POS\_F}$	0.149	$OBJ_1^{POS\_F}$	0.551
OBJ_1^{TF-ISF}	0.736	ID6	0.496	OBJ_4	0.694	ID6	0.148	OBJ_4	0.549
$OBJ_1^{POS\_EQ}$	0.736	OBJ_4	0.494	$OBJ_1^{POS\_EQ}$	0.692	OBJ_4	0.146	ID6	0.549
ID6	0.732	ID11	0.486	OBJ_1^{TF-ISF}	0.691	$OBJ_1^{POS\_EQ}$	0.145	$OBJ_1^{POS\_EQ}$	0.541
$OBJ_1^{POS\_L}$	0.730	$OBJ_1^{POS\_L}$	0.485	ID6	0.690	OBJ_1^{TF-ISF}	0.145	OBJ_1^{TF-ISF}	0.540
OBJ_2	0.730	$OBJ_1^{POS\_EQ}$	0.484	$OBJ_1^{POS\_L}$	0.684	$OBJ_1^{POS\_L}$	0.144	$OBJ_1^{POS\_L}$	0.539
ID2	0.729	OBJ_1^{TF-ISF}	0.483	OBJ_2	0.683	$OBJ_1^{POS\_B}$	0.144	ID11	0.536
$OBJ_1^{POS\_B}$	0.727	ID1	0.483	$OBJ_1^{POS\_B}$	0.682	OBJ_2	0.142	OBJ_2	0.535
ID11	0.714	OBJ_2	0.480	OBJ_1^{TF}	0.659	OBJ_5	0.140	$OBJ_1^{POS\_B}$	0.534
ID1	0.710	$OBJ_1^{POS\_B}$	0.479	ID11	0.658	OBJ_1^{TF}	0.136	ID1	0.533
OBJ_1^{TF}	0.704	ID21	0.467	OBJ_5	0.655	ID11	0.134	ID21	0.520
OBJ_3	0.704	OBJ_5	0.464	ID1	0.654	ID1	0.133	OBJ_3	0.517
ID21	0.700	OBJ_3	0.460	OBJ_3	0.649	OBJ_3	0.133	OBJ_1^{TF}	0.511
ID3	0.691	OBJ_1^{TF}	0.454	ID21	0.643	ID3	0.130	OBJ_5	0.508
OBJ_5	0.689	ID3	0.449	ID3	0.638	ID21	0.127	ID3	0.504

Experimental Results

As it can be seen from Table 1, our approach given best objective functions outperforms 4 systems participated in DUC 2002 competition in terms of ROUGE-1, ROUGE-2, ROUGE-L, and ROUGE-W-1.2, and 3 systems in terms of ROUGE-SU4. Moreover, GI (Global Inference, Knapsack) algorithm from (McDonald, 2007), also using linear programming, performs worse than our approach. Position-based weights behave as expected on this corpus: closeness to the beginning of a document is the best indication of relevance, while closeness to the end of a document, conversely, the worst one.

The evaluation results on the MultiLing'13 English, Hebrew and Arabic data can be seen in Tables 2, 3 and 4, respectively. As it can be seen from the results, only 2 to 3 out of 8 systems are outperformed by our system in English, 4 to 5 out of 7 systems in Hebrew, and 5 to 6 out of 8 systems in Arabic. It is worth to note that ID6 and ID61 are baseline systems, where ID61 is a baseline generating summaries from Gold Standard sentences while improving coverage of Gold Standard summaries.

In order to figure out the reasons of such inaccurate performance, we performed an additional experiment measuring the coverage of gold standard terms by the terms selected by our model.[3] Results confirm that all selected terms appear in gold standard summaries, and both precision and recall are high. However, since we are performing sentence extraction without preceding compression, our summaries contain "garbage" terms not selected by our algorithm as well, thus decreasing precision and recall. Better performance of our approach for longer summaries can be considered as an additional proof of this inference. An interesting outcome has been observed—our generated summaries cover document terms (in terms of recall) better than gold standard summaries do. The most simple and intuitive explanation for that is the difference between abstracts (gold standard) and extracts (generated).

CONCLUSION AND FUTURE WORK

In this chapter we present a linear programming model for the problem of extractive summarization. We represent the document as a sentence-term matrix whose entries contain term count values and view this matrix as a set of intersecting hyperplanes. Every possible summary of a document is represented as an intersection of two or more hyperlanes, and one additional constraint is used to limit the number of terms in a summary. We consider the summary to be the best if the optimal (maximal or minimal) value of objective function is achived during summarization, and in this case the summarization problem translates into the problem of finding a point on a convex polytope (defined by linear inequalities) which is the closest to the hyperplane describing overall term frequencies in the document. We introduce multiple objective functions optimizing summary (as a point on a convex polytope) properties.

Linear programming problem can be solved in polynomial time (Karmarkar, 1984; Khachiyan, 1996; Khachiyan and Todd, 1993). Numerous packages and applications are available, such as (Berkelaar, 1999), (Makhorin, 2000) etc. So, the theoretical time complexity of our approach is polynomial (quadratic, being more precise). Practically, running time of single document summarization takes a few seconds with lpsolve package, even though it employs the simplex approach.

The experiments conducted on multiple datasets and languages show partial superiority of our approach over other systems. The following conclusions are made based on the obtained results.

1. Our approach performs better on Hebrew and Arabic than on English data. The possible reasons for that are as follows. Hebrew and Arabic, unlike English, have simple sentence splitting rules, where particular punctuation marks indicate sentence boundaries. Also, normalization of terms (stopwords removal and stemming) was not performed for Hebrew and Arabic. Apparently, the filtered during this stage information cause accuracy loss in distance measurement.

2. The lack of deep morphological analysis and NLP techniques also may affect the quality of the generated summaries, while permitting multilingual text processing.

3. Striving to preserve terms collection of the summarized documents as much as possible does not perform well when the results compared to Gold Standard *abstracts*. Despite better coverage of document terms, resulted extracts may contain different vocabulary, affecting the ROUGE scores. Two approaches can handle this problem—using different information measures for maximal coverage and/or using different evaluation metrics.

4. Adding entire sentences to summaries decrease precision and recall metrics due to "garbage" information they carry. Therefore, sentence compression is required in order to see the "actual" results of the optimization procedure.

5. The general problem of automated summarization is that there is no single objective function (so far) that describes the best summary. Many authors tried to express the optimum by combining multiple objectives into single *weighted function* (Edmundson, 1969; Radev et al., 2001; Saggion et al., 2003; Litvak et al., 2010).

In future, we intend to work on the following directions.

1. To come up with different objective functions that take into consideration redundant information, like "garbage" terms. The classic example is a *profit* function that is usually calculated as a subtraction of redundant information from the utility value.

2. Perform sentence compression in order to reduce the amount of redundant information in selected sentences.

3. To adapt our approach to *query-based* summarization by adapting objective functions.

4. To find the optimal linear combination of the proposed objective functions in order to consider multiple parameters describing summary quality.

Our approach, in its current state, has the following benefits vs. other summarizers.

1. It is *unsupervised* method that does not require any annotated data and training sources.

2. It is based on the 'maximal coverage' principle, considering all possible extracts and solving it in *polynomial time*.

3. It uses a *novel* text representation model *independently* from the objective functions describing the summary quality. As such, one can easily to add more functions without changing the model. In contrast, in most of works using linear programming for extracting sentences, objective functions are embedded into the model (McDonald, 2007).

4. Since our approach does not require any morphological analysis, it is totally *language-independent*, as our experimental results confirm.

ACKNOWLEDGMENT

Authors thank Igor Vinokur for implementing the introduced approach and performing experiments. This research was partially funded by U.S. Department of Navy, Office of Naval Research.

REFERENCES

Aker, A., Cohn, T., & Gaizauskas, R. (2010). Multidocument summarization using A* search and discriminative training. In *Proceedings of the 2010 Conference on Empirical Methods in Natural Language Processing, EMNLP '10*. (pp. 482–491). EMNLP.

Alfonseca, E., & Rodriguez, P. (2003). Generating extracts with genetic algorithms. In *Proceedings of the 2003 European Conference on Information Retrieval (ECIR'2003)*. (pp. 511–519). ECIR.

Berkelaar, M. (1999). *lp-solve free software*. Retrieved from http://lpsolve.sourceforge.net/5.5/

DUC. (2002). *Document understanding conference*. Retrieved from http://duc.nist.gov/pubs. html#2002.

Edmundson, H. P. (1969). New methods in automatic extracting. *Transaction of the ACM, 16*(2), 264–285.

Filatova, E. (2004). Event-based extractive summarization. In *Proceedings of ACL Workshop on Summarization* (pp. 104–111). ACL.

Gillick, D., & Favre, B. (2009). A scalable global model for summarization. In *Proceedings of the NAACL HLT Workshop on Integer Linear Programming for Natural Language Processing* (pp. 10–18). NAACL.

Hassel, M., & Sjobergh, J. (2006). Towards holistic summarization: Selecting summaries, not sentences. In *Proceedings of LREC - International Conference on Language Resources and Evaluation*. LREC.

Kallel, F. J., Jaoua, M., Hadrich, L. B., & Hamadou, A. B. (2004). Summarization at LARIS laboratory. In *Proceedings of the Document Understanding Conference*. Academic Press.

Karmarkar, N. (1984). New polynomial-time algorithm for linear programming. *Combinatorica*, *4*, 373–395. doi:10.1007/BF02579150

Khachiyan, L. G. (1996). Rounding of polytopes in the real number model of computation. *Mathematics of Operations Research*, *21*, 307–320. doi:10.1287/moor.21.2.307

Khachiyan, L. G., & Todd, M. J. (1993). On the complexity of approximating the maximal inscribed ellipsoid for a polytope. *Mathematical Programming*, *61*, 137–159. doi:10.1007/BF01582144

Khuller, S., Moss, A., & Naor, J. S. (1999). The budgeted maximum coverage problem. *Information Processing Letters*, *70*(1), 39–45. doi:10.1016/S0020-0190(99)00031-9

Lin, C.-Y. (2004). Rouge: A package for automatic evaluation of summaries. In *Proceedings of the Workshop on Text Summarization Branches Out (WAS 2004)* (pp. 25–26). WAS.

Litvak, M., Last, M., & Friedman, M. (2010). A new approach to improving multilingual summarization using a genetic algorithm. In *Proceedings of the 48th Annual Meeting of the Association for Computational Linguistics* (pp. 927–936). ACL.

Litvak, M., & Vanetik, N. (2012). Polytope model for extractive summarization. In *Proceedings of International Conference on Knowledge Discovery and Information Retrieval* (pp. 281-286). Academic Press.

Liu, D., Wang, Y., Liu, C., & Wang, Z. (2006). Multiple documents summarization based on genetic algorithm. *Fuzzy Systems and Knowledge Discovery*, *4223*, 355–364. doi:10.1007/11881599_40

Makhorin, A. O. (2000). *GNU linear programming kit*. Retrieved from http://www.gnu.org/software/glpk/

Makino, T., Takamura, H., & Okumura, M. (2011). Balanced coverage of aspects for text summarization. *In Proceedings of Text Analysis Conference*. TAC.

Mani, I., & Maybury, M. (1999). *Advances in automatic text summarization*. Cambridge, MA: MIT Press.

McDonald, R. (2007). A study of global inference algorithms in multi-document summarization. *Advances in Information Retrieval*, 557-564.

MultiLing. (2013). Retrieved from http://multiling.iit.demokritos.gr/pages/view/662/multiling-2013

Nishikawa, H., Hasegawa, T., & Kikui, G. (2010). Opinion summarization with integer linear programming formulation for sentence extraction and ordering. In Proceedings of Coling 2010: Poster Volume (pp. 910–918). Coling.

Ouyang, Y., Li, W., Li, S., & Lu, Q. (2011). Applying regression models to query-focused multi-document summarization. *Information Processing & Management*, *47*, 227–237. doi:10.1016/j.ipm.2010.03.005

Radev, D., Blair-Goldensohn, S., & Zhang, Z. (2001). Experiments in single and multidocument summarization using MEAD. In *Proceedings of First Document Understanding Conference*. Academic Press.

Saggion, H., Bontcheva, K., & Cunningham, H. (2003). Robust generic and query-based summarisation. *In Proceedings of the Tenth Conference on European Chapter of the Association for Computational Linguistics* (pp. 235–238). EACL.

Salton, G., Yang, C., & Wong, A. (1975). A vector-space model for information retrieval. *Communications of the ACM*, 18.

Takamura, H., & Okumura, M. (2009). Text summarization model based on maximum coverage problem and its variant. In *Proceedings of the 12th Conference of the European Chapter of the Association for Computational Linguistics* (pp. 781–789). EACL.

Wan, X. (2008). Using only cross-document relationships for both generic and topic-focused multi-document summarizations. *Information Retrieval*, *11*(1), 25–49. doi:10.1007/s10791-007-9037-5

Woodsend, K., & Lapata, M. (2010). Automatic generation of story highlights. *In Proceedings of the 48th Annual Meeting of the Association for Computational Linguistics* (pp. 565–574). ACL.

ADDITIONAL READING

Barzilay, R., Elhadad, N., & McKeown, K. R. (2002). Inferring strategies for sentence ordering in multidocument news summarization. *Journal of Artificial Intelligence Research*, *17*, 35–55.

Chowdary, C. R., & Kumar, P. S. (2009) Esum: An efficient system for query-specific multi-document summarization. In ECIR (Advances in Information Retrieval), pp. 724–728.

Dan, G., & Benoit, F. (2009). A scalable global model for summarization. Proceedings of the Workshop on Integer Linear Programming for Natural Language Processing, pp. 10–18.

Erkan, G., & Radev, Dragomir R. (2004). Lexrank: Graph-based centrality as salience in text summarization. [JAIR]. *Journal of Artificial Intelligence Research*.

Giannakopoulos, G., El-Haj, M., Favre, B., Litvak, M., Steinberger, J., & Varma, V. (2011). TAC 2011 MultiLing Pilot Overview. Proceedings of the Text Analysis Conference 2011.

Lin, C.-Y., & Hovy, E. (2002). From single to multi-document summarization: A prototype system and its evaluation. In Proceedings of the ACL, pp. 457–464.

Litvak, M., & Last, M. (2010). Language-independent techniques for automated text summarization. M. Last and A. Kandel (Editors), Web intelligence and security, IOS Press, NATO Science for Peace and Security Series, 2010, pp. 209–240.

Lovins, J. B. (1968). Development of a stemming algorithm. *Mechanical Translation and Computational Linguistics*, *11*, 22–31.

Luhn, H. P. (1958). The automatic creation of literature abstracts. IBM Journal: 159–165.

Manning, C. D., Raghavan, P., & Schütze, H. (2008). *Introduction to information retrieval.* Cambridge University Press. doi:10.1017/CBO9780511809071

Manning, C. D., & Schütze, H. (1999). *Foundations of statistical natural language processing.* The MIT Press.

Martins, A., & Smith, N. A. (2009). Summarization with a joint model for sentence extraction and compression. *Proceedings of the Workshop on Integer Linear Programming for Natural Language Processing*, 2009, pp. 1–9.

McKeown, K., Passonneau, R. J., Elson, D. K., Nenkova, A., Hirschberg, J. (2005). Do summaries help? A task-based evaluation of multi-document summarization. SIGIR'05, Salvador, Brazil, August 15–19.

McKeown, K. R., & Radev, D. R. (1995). Generating summaries of multiple news articles. In *Proceedings, ACM Conference on Research and Development in Information Retrieval SIGIR'95*, pages 74–82.

Pitler. E. (2010). Methods for sentence compression. Technical Report.

Radev, D., Jing, H., Stys, M., & Tam, D. (2004). Centroid-based summarization of multiple documents. *Information Processing & Management*, *40*, 919–938. doi:10.1016/j.ipm.2003.10.006

Salton, G., Wong, A., & Yang, C. S. (1975). A vector space model for automatic indexing. *Communications of the ACM*, *18*(11), 613–620. doi:10.1145/361219.361220

Soubbotin, M., & Soubbotin, S. (2005). Trade-off between factors influencing quality of the summary. document understanding workshop (DUC), Vancouver, B.C., Canada, October 9–10, 2005.

Youngjoong, K. (2012). *A study of term weighting schemes using class information for text classification. SIGIR'12*. ACM.

Zellig, H. (1954). Distributional structure. *Word*, *10*(2/3), 146–162.

KEY TERMS AND DEFINITIONS

Automatic Summarization: A process of reducing a text document with a computer program in order to create a summary that retains the most important points of the original document.

Convex Polytope: A special case of a polytope, having the additional property that it is also a convex set of points in the n-dimensional space R^n.

Extractive Summarization: A process of selecting a subset of existing words, phrases, or sentences in the original text to form the summary.

Linear Programming (LP) or Linear Optimization: A mathematical method for determining a way to achieve the best outcome (such as maximum profit or lowest cost) in a given mathematical model for some list of requirements represented as linear relationships. Linear programming is a specific case of mathematical programming (mathematical optimization).

Natural Language Processing (NLP): Computerized processes intended to result in natural language understanding and natural language generation and to enable computers to understand and communicate in human language, whether spoken, written, or published. It is also the name of the field devoted to the study and development of these processes.

Polyhedron: A geometric object bounded by planes, which exists in any general number of dimensions.

Polytope: A closed polyhedron (polyhedron of finite volume).

Stemming: The process for reducing inflected (or sometimes derived) words to their stem, base or root form—generally a written word form.

Stop Words: Are words which are filtered out prior to, or after, processing of natural language data (text). There is not one definite list of stop words which all tools use, if even used.

ENDNOTES

[1]   Since an extractive summarization usually deals with sentence extraction, this paper also focuses on sentences. Generally, our method can be used for extracting any other text units like phrases, paragraphs, etc.

[2]   normalized meaningful words

[3]   It's important to note that our model selects *terms* in sentences *gradually*. Therefore, in order to rank and extract sentences, we measure the distance between vectors of selected terms and sentences.

Chapter 4

Interactive Summaries by Multi-Pole Information Extraction for the Archaeological Domain

Angela Locoro
University of Genova, Italy

Massimo Ancona
University of Genova, Italy

ABSTRACT

Understanding and describing past or present societies is a complex task, as it involves a multi-faceted analysis of the norms, interactions, and evolutions that characterize them. This serves as the motivation for developing a tool, named Herodotus, aiming at supporting domain experts, such as historians or archaeologists, in the reasoning tasks over complex interactions characterizing a society in order to explain why some event took place and, possibly, to predict what could happen when some factors change. An important part of Herodotus is the text mining module that is responsible for the extraction of knowledge from written sources, such as books and scientific papers. Machines cannot always help users in dealing with natural language, because of the variety, ambiguity and non-rigidity that language shows in its use; they can only try to process information in a meaningful way for users. Information Extraction (IE) is the technology that pulls specific information from large volumes of unstructured texts and stores this information in structured forms. Users can then consult, compose, and analyze them. Domain-based IE should focus on an analysis of a specific state of affairs and, in this way, it can obtain more precise and detailed results. This helps domain experts to deal with the complexity of their everyday objects and environments. This chapter is centered on the Interactive Summary Extractor tool, whose scope is to organize, in a partially automated but substantially interactive way, text summaries for archaeological and historical documental sources. The texts so analyzed will help domain experts to collect data, viewing a synthesized version of it, compose such summaries in units of sense for the particular archaeological study or research that is in place, and so on. Summaries can then be modified, stored, retrieved and managed for later elaboration.

DOI: 10.4018/978-1-4666-5019-0.ch004

INTRODUCTION AND MOTIVATIONS

Searching and structuring information for archaeologists is a complex task: information has to be collected from disparate sources in different languages and environments, often apparently unrelated, and structured into an organic (multimedia) form. For example, documentation on the mechanism of "Antikythera" ("Antikythera Mechanism," 2013) has an unexpected, but fundamental relation with Cicero, mentioning that two of such devices have been constructed by Archimedes. This fact, paired with the sophistication of the device technology, suggested to the authors of the research in (Edmunds & Freeth, 2011), the assertion: "even if only one device of this kind is so far known to have survived, it was based on the tradition of a long line of precursors."

Another example is represented by the description of the embalming process performed by Ancient Egyptians and described in detailed form by Herodotus in volume II of his book "Histories," from which the archaeologists could formulate ideas on how this ancient practice was performed. These examples point out how wide is the environment and how disparate are the sources to be explored by archaeologists for collecting information about specific historic facts, techniques, objects and instruments.

Our system, named *Herodotus*, is going to be an evolution of a previous system (Ancona et al., 2005), which will serve as a support for making plans for the preservation of the natural and cultural heritage represented in such scenarios. In addition, the same tool used by the domain experts might be exploited for presenting the cultural and natural heritage and for training people in knowing, appreciating, respecting and, possibly, helping to safeguard it.

More specifically, the aim of Herodotus is to semi-automatically extract knowledge from collections of ancient books, scientific publications, paintings, images and documents reporting findings of archaeological excavations, to create a formalized *electronic institution*, or *e-institution*, (Bogdanovych, 2007) modeling an open multi-agent system (MAS) that mimics norms and relations of the real life relative to a specific archaeological area and historical time.

In this Chapter, we will describe the *Interactive Summary Extractor Tool* (ISET from now on), which will be part of the Herodotus text mining module and whose prototype is under implementation and evaluation. Text Mining may span from simple keyword matching (KM), which only superficially determines meaning, to a complete parsing, structuring and reasoning task, which attempts to understand the whole semantics of texts. The term information extraction (IE) usually defines activities similar to the last example. Nonetheless, KM may provide and support more granularities when trying to combine atomic methods to locate sentences of importance to the user's subject area and application. There are several structures significant for archaeologists that can be searched and extracted from plain texts, ranging from simple keywords and key-phrases to text summaries, object properties and relations, as well as rules and even ontologies or taxonomies.

ISET is an interactive tool for the summarization of single documents. The tool functionalities range from keywords and phrases extraction to text summaries. In this version, all the intelligent actions are intended to be committed to the care of a human user: the system computes keywords frequencies and key-phrases related to them, but the task of organizing or structuring all the concepts discovered is demanded to the user. In particular, for ad-hoc texts, summarization will have the purpose of highlighting all portions of text that could be relevant to a specific theme. The originality of our tool lays in two main factors:

- The interactivity and lightness of the approach, resulting in more flexibility, user-oriented capacities, and easy access where a low speed connectivity may be the only available.

- The exploitation of a multi-pole approach, with three keywords and key-phrases extraction algorithms that can be run in parallel in order to obtain better results with respect to a single approach technique.

In particular, the work presented in the Chapter aims at assessing the strengths and weaknesses of each algorithm in order to define the basis for their further combination.

In general, parametric and semi-automatic instruments are preferable and considered more convenient than full automated approaches. An approach of this kind is more easily adaptable to an interactive use. This basic design choice does not preclude future experiences for extending ISET to more complex tasks such as the redundancy control over the different summary methods, the conversion of plain text (e.g., PDF files or WEB pages) into structured (and formalized) knowledge with the support of more sophisticate algorithms and instruments, and so on. These extensions will depend on the experimentation of the present version and on the interest of domain experts into more automated approaches to the problem.

ISET, AN INTERACTIVE TEXT SUMMARIZER

The present version of the ISET tool is based on an interactive keyword/key-phrase and summary highlighter (i.e., highlighting all sentences considered relevant), and an interactive summarizer. The keyword/key-phrase highlighter points out and underlines all relevant words of a text. The words are displayed in color, each color driven by a codified grammar that identifies the main parts of a discourse. The keyword highlighter assigns to each word a statistical estimation rate to be a possible keyword, rate that is displayed in different tones of the color used for displaying each keyword. At this point the user can re-exam phrases, include/exclude some keywords, discard or modify selected key-phrase or sentences of a summary, and so on. A summary has only a temporary use: the main output produced does not need to be lexically perfect – its scope is to reduce the cost for the user of reading the full document in order to select the relevant parts. As depicted in the introduction, in a domain like the archaeological one, experts need to collect and put together disparate sources of historic knowledge by manually exploring and filtering relevant information. In such scenario, a tool for information extraction can only play the first-aid role of selecting the relevant information inside a text, by automatically analyzing the text itself and extracting keywords based on the statistical importance that they have at text level.

Interactively means that users are allowed to move flexibly between summaries and the whole document. In addition, an interactive tool should supply a uniform and stable behavior, e.g., when the user varies an input parameter in a given interval the measured output should reveal an almost linear response. Nothing is more frustrating than a tool producing large variations of the output, against small variations of the input conditions, which may lead to an all-or-nothing answer in some cases.

To these aims, ISET will be composed of a user interface similar to a text editor (where input texts should not be modified but only annotated in several ways). The program includes several functions for data extraction, all implemented in separate modules, in order to make them easily replaceable. Most functions perform the same task with different methods and the user has the capability of activating them in alternative or in parallel, in order to select the best results in an interactive execution fashion. Most algorithms require a dictionary built from a corpus. In ISET we provide, for each function, at least one algorithm not requiring a corpus-based implementation. Moreover, we include a basic dictionary (easily changeable) implicitly adopted by all algorithms requiring a corpus-based information.

ISET implements three basic automated selection processes: a *keyword extractor (KE)*, a *key-phrase extractor (PE)*, and a *text summarizer (TS)*. The user has the capability of applying each function to the whole text or to a selected part, she/he can also modify the function *execution mode* (e.g., to modify the parameter on which the function depends, like the maximum number of selected keywords/ key-phrases, or even to include or exclude in/from the set of keywords a specific word). In what follows, a brief description of the main functionalities of the ISET tool is depicted.

Keyword extraction: The keyword extractor selects a set of relevant keywords that identify the main topics described in the document. Keywords play a fundamental role in an interactive tool: ISET provides them to users by the application of three different computations: TF-IDF ("Tf-idf," 2013); standard deviation of inter-word spacing (Ortuño et al., 2002; Berryman et al., 2002), named "sigma-rank" from now on; zipf law statistics (Li, 1992), named "zipf" from now on.

To the best of our knowledge, the application of some of these approaches to the summarization of texts was never experimented. Thus, this Chapter is characterized by a novel approach in the use of well known measures for natural language text statistics, as well as measures that are native of other domains, such as signal processing and DNA sequencing (Ortuño M. et al 2002). Empirical studies show that the "attraction between words is a phenomenon that plays an important role in both language processing, and DNA sequence analysis, and it has been modeled for information retrieval and speech recognition purposes" (Herrera & Pury, 2008).

The choice to use and provide users with three methods for keywords extraction is motivated by their different features, some of which have been

anticipated above, that can be combined in order to obtain a better result. In particular:

- Tf-idf exploits information based on both the single document (tf), and the corpus to which it belongs to (idf).
- "sigma-rank" is computed on each single text and, at least in our formulation and employment, it does not exploit corpus-based information. Nevertheless, other authors claim that documents with comparable "sigma-ranks" could be a symptom of similar style, hence such measure may indicate that documents belong to the same author / corpus or, vice versa, that an author's / corpus style may be measured by "sigma-rank" computation.
- "zipf" has been discovered and conceived as a general law, whose validity is independent from the object of its application, being a single text or a corpus. Hence, it should prove its stability whatever is the source of its application.

Key-phrase extraction: The *key-phrases extractor* selects multi-words key-terms possessing the distinguishing property of being linguistic descriptors of the document (single keywords are the proper sub-case of this study). Also key-phrase extraction is based on statistical methods.

Text summarization: This function is a direct product of ISET above functionalities: a summary is displayed in form of outlined sentences of the original text, after the keywords and key-phrase extraction phases. In an interactive tool such functionality can be easily performed by the user and does not represent a goal of the system: the aim of ISET text summarizer is to highlight the portion of text which results to be more relevant after an interactive session performed between the user and ISET. For this reason, the text summarizer is parametric and task oriented: it selects and outlines sentences on the base of a set of keywords / key-phrases selected and ordered by importance by the user (in general extracted by the above algorithms) and creates a shortened version of (a part of) the input text by outlining its pertinent parts.

In what follows, a description of the keywords and key-phrase extraction algorithms implemented in ISET is depicted in detail, along with experiments conducted on a corpus of Greek mythology texts, and the evaluation and discussion of the results obtained by the summarization approaches of the tool. The experiments presented in this study exploit bounded parameters instead of flexible ones. This is due to the necessity of testing our algorithms in a systematic way, in order to measure the performances of our approaches to summarization, and provide an analysis of the strengths and weaknesses for each of the three approaches examined.

Keywords and Key-Phrases Extraction: Algorithms Description

The ISET module for keywords and key-phrases extraction is based on text processing techniques for the normalization of data and on three keyword extraction techniques as a preparation for the summarization of texts.

Given a document or set of documents written in plain text, each of them undergoes the following steps:

- **Stopwords Removal:** According to the stopword list found in (Savoy, 2013) for the English language, a pre-processing of each text is carried out in order to cut the stopwords in it.
- **POS Tagging:** By exploiting the Stanford POS Tagger (Toutanova & Manning, 2000) on each document, a list of words is tagged and filtered by noun and verb-related POS. This list was necessary in the phase of lemmatization of words, which we applied only to nouns and verbs (being the only

two kinds of words to have morphological inflections in our texts).

- **Lemmatization:** The lemmatization of words is done for each document, only on inflected word forms (nouns and verbs) by using WordNet (Didion, 2012). This operation is necessary in order to compute frequencies on word lemmas as a sum of frequencies of word inflections, while applying the same values to each of the different word forms in the original text. This gives an equal score to each word represented by the same lemma during the keywords computation.
- **Word Statistics Computation and Word Ranking:** In this phase, the three keyword extraction methods used by ISET are applied to the words in a text. In particular, for each approach, the frequency of each word and word lemma is computed according to the relative formulas. Stopwords are excluded; adjectives and adverbs become words, whereas nouns and verbs become word lemmas in the next.

The keyword extraction algorithm is based on the following three approaches:

- **Tf-idf Word Ranking:** Let w be a word or word lemma inside a text, d the text document under analysis, and D the document corpus. The tf-idf formula is composed of the following:

$$Tf = \frac{f(w,d)}{\max(f(t,d) : t \in d)}$$

being t each term (word or word lemma) in the document

$$Idf = \log \frac{|D|}{\Sigma(d \in D : w \in d)}$$

$Tf-idf=tf*idf$

- **Sigma-Rank:** For each inter-word spacing between each word and word lemma inside a text, a set of word spacing of the form $s = \{x_1,...,x_n\}$ is obtained. Let M be the statistic mean of the set s, n be the cardinality of s. For each set, a scaled standard deviation σ_d is computed, according to the following formula:

$$\sigma_d = \frac{1}{M}\sqrt{\frac{\sum_{i=1,...,n}(x_i - M)^2}{n-1}}$$

- **Zipf Ranking:** The zipf law is computed for each word and word lemma, as follows

$$P(r) = \frac{C}{r^a}$$

with r as the rank (position) of a word based on its absolute frequency (number of occurrences inside the text taken into exam), C as constant that has been fixed to 0.1, and *alpha* as an exponent that has been approximated to 1. In this way, the law expresses a distribution law of the words that depends on the inverse of the word rank.

Once the list of candidate keywords is created and ranked for a document, by exploiting one or more of the above ranking scores, the user is requested, for example, to examine it and to establish a threshold below which no word will be considered in the keyword selection, or to select manually the first n words that she/he feels are interesting to be considered for candidate text keywords, while discarding the others, or to delegate to the threshold automatically set by the system the selection of keywords among those in the list.

This selection will then be exploited by the algorithm to provide the text summarization.

Summarization Task

Once a list of candidate keywords is obtained for each text, the second phase of the algorithm works as follows:

- It computes the number of keywords inside each sentence in the text being analyzed, ranks all sentences based on the number of keywords inside it, and computes the number of sentences for each keyword frequency.
- It extracts the key-phrases based on a the number of keywords per sentence, chosen between a range.
- It reports the subset of key-phrases to the user, as a selection among the whole set of sentences of the document, in the same order in which they appear in the original text.

The user may choose to adjust the range of values among which the number of keywords is parameterized for sentence extraction, and run the key-phrase extraction phase once again, or she / he may choose to simply discard manually the sentences that she / he thinks are redundant, or she / he may decide to change the order of the sentences from the original document. Prior to this, the procedure can be set to manual, and a panel to drive the summarization procedure is presented to the user.

For example, if a user chooses to run IMET on a document by "sigma-rank" extractor, the output will be the one in Table 1 (taken by a real example from one of our experiments on the document "Eridanus"). The output will display the number of candidate key-phrases grouped by number of keywords, and shows the results ranked by number of candidate key-phrases:

Table 1. An example of output taken by a real experiment on the document with title "Eridanus," after running the "sigma-rank" algorithm. On the first column a list of keyword frequencies is reported; on the second column the number of keyphrases in the document with such number of keywords is displayed.

Document "Eridanus"	
Keyword_frequency	Number_of_candidate_key-phrases
4	4
1	3
2	3
3	2
5	1
6	1
7	1

The user may choose to compose her / his summary according to simple statistic rules. For example:

- Take the 50% of candidate key-phrases (i.e. only the first two lines of the above example are considered for key-phrase extraction).
- Take only key-phrases for which the number of keywords ranges from 1 to 3 (i.e. only takes 8 key-phrases, the ones that correspond to the keyword frequencies 1,2 and 3 in the above example).
- Take only key-phrases whose frequency corresponds to the statistical mode of the data (i.e. only key-phrases with 5, 6 and 7 keywords values are selected in the above example).
- Take only key-phrases with the same number of keywords and above a certain frequency (i.e. by looking at the right column, the user choose a threshold below which data are cut).

EXPERIMENTS

The Wikipedia Corpus

The Wikipedia corpus has been chosen for preliminary experiments on the ISET module. In particular, the dataset selected is composed of 147 documents, among the 150 texts that are classified under the Wikipedia category of Greek gods ("Greek gods," 2013). The choice of this specific dataset was dictated by several factors:

- The need to test our tool on documents of the history and archaeology domains.
- The need to simulate a real scenario where archaeologists access online resources (such as Wikipedia) in order to obtain on-the-fly notions and ready-at-hand information, and are able to synthesize / combine them for further elaboration and reuse.
- The free and widespread availability of a corpus, without copyright issues, which allow a presentation of full results of experiments.
- The style of Wikipedia corpus, which is characterized by plain English sentences and words, and that, as it is claimed by its maintainers, was conceived to "minimize the use of ambiguous words, of jargon, and of vague or unnecessarily complex wording." In addition, sentences are structured in a similar way throughout the text, and even the document structure, which privileges a model of informativeness placed at the beginning of the documents and at the beginning of each subsection, was relevant for measuring an automatic or semi-automatic summarization task.
- The size of the documents in the corpus (which was quite uniform, see Table 2 for a pointwise analysis of the 72 documents selected among the corpus to be summarized).

- The uniform style of the corpus, either structural (in the disposition of information) and linguistic (in the choice of expression and of expressiveness).
- The easiness, due to the size of the documents and to the plain style of the content, for a domain expert to manually summarize part of the corpus in a straightforward way, for providing reference summaries that were necessary for the evaluation of our summarization algorithms.

For the experiments conducted in this study the corpus has been classified into smaller categories, and results and discussion are based on this further classification. In particular, based on the size of the text in the corpus, each document belongs to one of the following categories:

- Large size text: above 14 KB
- Medium size text: from 6 to 14 KB
- Small size text: from 2 to 6 KB

Table 2 shows the average size, average number of tokens and average number of lemmas of the 72 documents that have been summarized. The Table is split in three rows, representing the above classification of files.

Texts below ~2 KB have only been considered in the computation of statistics, i.e., as part of the corpus, but were not considered for summarization, as most of them is composed of less than 10 sentences in total.

Wikipedia texts have been extracted from the "Edit" Tab text of the Wikipedia page, by discarding the following Wikipedia sections from each document extracted: "See Also," "Notes," "References," "Bibliography," and "External Links," whenever present.

In order to extract plain texts from Wikipedia wiki syntax ("Mediawiki, Help Formatting," 2013) we used a tool for preprocessing wiki texts ("Bliki engine," 2013), and we further refine the extraction task with cleaning operations, both automatic and manual, such as for example the deletion of resilient wiki syntax (e.g., after running the Bliki, double brackets, i.e., "{{text}}" were still there).

The Experimental Settings

For each document in the corpus, the three statistics have been computed as depicted in the previous Section of the Chapter. Summaries have been created for 72 out of 147 documents (see Table 2), which corresponds to the set of file with a size above 2 KB, as clarified above.

In particular, for this set of experiments, fixed thresholds have been set for each of the measures computed for ranking keywords, and a fixed value range of keyword frequency per sentence has been established. Table 3 depicts the values in detail. In particular, for each method, the range of values found is reported, as well as the fixed thresholds, and the selected range of keyword frequency values.

For each file in the experiments that has been summarized (72 in total) and evaluated (30 in total), the results are reported in the next Section according to different perspectives. As shown in Table 2, for each file classification

Table 2. The documents of the corpus with average tokens and word lemmas. The Table is split in three rows, one for each of the file size categories.

	Avg Size KB	Avg #tokens	Avg #lemmas	Total Documents
Large size files	32	5,134	1,798	13
Medium size files	9	1,371	627	18
Small size files	3	489	258	41

Table 3. Values range of the three indexes computed over the corpus, fixed thresholds, and selected keyword frequency values range, for extracting key-phrases during the experiments.

Keyword extraction method	Value range	Fixed threshold	Value range of keywords in key-phrases for summary extraction
tfidf	5.66 – 0.07	0.25	\<between 4 and 7 keywords\>
Sigma-rank	2.83 - 0	0	\<between 4 and 7 keywords\>
zipf	0.1 - 0	0.005	\<between 4 and 7 keywords\>

set (large, medium and small size file) a subset of summaries has been selected for manual evaluation. In particular, on a total of 30 files chosen for evaluation, 6 large size, 16 medium size and 8 small size files were the ones chosen by domain experts for creating reference summaries by hand.

Results and Evaluation

Table 4 reports the number of key-phrases extracted for each of the evaluated summaries (30 in total) obtained with "tfidf," "sigma-rank" and "zipf" (columns 2, 3, and 4, named "tfidf," "s-rank," and "zipf, respectively, for each document table). The key-phrases are split for number of keywords contained (column 1 named "kw fr," for each document table).

The Table shows that, for large size files (the first 6 document tables), the distribution of key-phrases along the dimension of keyword frequency is more uniform for "sigma-rank" summaries, whereas "zipf" summaries show a tendency for extracting less keywords, and "tfidf" shows even a less uniform behaviour. With fewer exception "tfidf" always extracts less keyphrases with respect to "sigma-rank."

For medium size files (the central 16 document tables), the situation is specular: "tfidf" shows most of the time to overcome "sigma-rank" in number of key-phrases extracted, whereas "zipf"

has a similar behaviour to the one observed for large size files.

Finally, in the third set (the last 8 that belong to small size files) similar behaviours are observable only between single word frequencies dimension (e.g. for keyword frequency 4 the similarities are higher than with other keyword frequencies). The last document table (Hesperus) shows how disparate the summaries may be for one file: "tfidf" has extracted the most part of its key-phrase among those with keyword frequency 7, whereas "zipf" has extracted quite the same number of key-phrases among those with word frequency 4.

This outline an interesting trend: the "zipf" approach tends to provide shorter summaries if compared to the other two methods. "tfidf" is conditioned by the weight of keywords of the whole corpus, hence it extracts keyphrases with high frequency keywords, whereas "sigma-rank" should privileges the extraction of more keyphrases with fewer keyword frequencies (as it relies only on a single text to compute the relevancy of words), by looking at the results.

Table 5 reports the Jaccard similarity coefficient (ranging in the interval [0,1]) measured between each pair of summaries obtained for each file (72 in total), i.e. the "tfidf" against the "sigma-rank," the "tfidf" against the "zipf," and the "sigma-rank" against the "zipf," respectively. Let S_1 and S_2 be two summaries (i.e., set of key-phrases) of the same file obtained with two methods. According to the following formula:

Table 4. Each table shows, for each document, the 3 evaluated summaries, 30 for each method (tfidf, s-rank, and zipf) applied to the 30 original texts, for a total of 90 summaries. Each column shows, for each document summarized and each summary method, the number of key-phrases obtained. Column 1 shows the keyword frequencies groups (namely, 4, 5, 6 and 7, which are the keyword ranges extracted for our experiments).

Pluto				Dioniso				Homer			
kw fr	tfidf	s-rank	zipf	kw fr	tfidf	s-rank	zipf	kw fr	tfidf	s-rank	zipf
4	39	53	5	4	32	16	4	4	16	15	
5	33	51	1	5	17	20	2	5	21	11	
6	17	48		6	12	20	1	6	14	26	1
7	11	50		7	12	15		7	14	13	

Hades				Hephaestos				Cronus			
kw fr	tfidf	s-rank	zipf	kw fr	tfidf	s-rank	zipf	kw fr	tfidf	s-rank	zipf
4	13	11	6	4	4	11	1	4	4	11	
5	12	4	1	5	5	11	2	5	5	12	5
6	9	15	1	6	5	5		6	8	4	
7	3	5	1	7	5	8		7	3	4	

Helios				Uranus				Apis			
kw fr	tfidf	s-rank	zipf	kw fr	tfidf	s-rank	zipf	kw fr	tfidf	s-rank	zipf
4	3	10		4	2	10	2	4	1	5	5
5	6	6	1	5	2	7	2	5	4	4	1
6	3	7		6		2	2	6	3	6	
7	8	5		7	2	3		7	4	3	1

Anemoi				Adonis				Asopus			
kw fr	tfidf	s-rank	zipf	kw fr	tfidf	s-rank	zipf	kw fr	tfidf	s-rank	zipf
4	4	16	6	4	4	5	1	4	7	2	3
5	7	12	2	5	2	4		5	5	8	2
6	3	4		6	5	3		6	3	2	3
7	8			7	4	4		7		5	1

Asclepius				Atlas				Aeulus			
kw fr	tfidf	s-rank	zipf	kw fr	tfidf	s-rank	zipf	kw fr	tfidf	s-rank	zipf
4	3	6	2	4	3	3	3	4	4	12	
5	5	3		5		4	1	5	3	4	5
6	3	1		6	2	3		6	3	2	1
7	7	3		7	4	4		7	3	4	

Caerus				Glaucus				Achelous			
kw fr	tfidf	s-rank	zipf	kw fr	tfidf	s-rank	zipf	kw fr	tfidf	s-rank	zipf
4	4	6	2	4	3	6	2	4	6	5	4
5	10	4	2	5	6	5	4	5	4	2	1
6	4	4		6	1	3		6	1	4	2
7	2	2		7	6	3	1	7	2	1	1

continued on following page

Table 4. Continued

Panean				Phorphorus				Triton			
kw fr	tfidf	s-rank	zipf	kw fr	tfidf	s-rank	zipf	kw fr	tfidf	s-rank	zipf
4	1	6	6	4		2	3	4	3	4	
5	3	2	1	5			2	5	1	4	1
6	6	1	1	6		3	1	6	4	1	1
7	5	2	2	7	1	2		7	5	2	2

Aristaeus			
kw fr	tfidf	s-rank	zipf
4	1	4	
5	1	2	2
6	3	2	
7	1	2	1

Oceanus				Eros				Morpheus			
kw fr	tfidf	s-rank	zipf	kw fr	tfidf	s-rank	zipf	kw fr	tfidf	s-rank	zipf
4	2	2	2	4	4	3		4	2	10	1
5	1	2	1	5		7	3	5	5	2	
6			1	6	4	4	1	6	5	1	1
7	2	1		7	5	1		7	2	2	

Melicerts				Erotes				Eridanos			
kw fr	tfidf	s-rank	zipf	kw fr	tfidf	s-rank	zipf	kw fr	tfidf	s-rank	zipf
4		5	2	4	8	5	5	4		4	3
5		2	1	5	6	6	2	5		1	2
6		2	1	6	4	4	1	6	2	1	1
7	2	1	1	7		2		7	2	1	1

Phobos				Hesperus			
kw fr	tfidf	s-rank	zipf	kw fr	tfidf	s-rank	zipf
4		4	3	4		1	3
5	2	1	1	5	2		
6	1			6		2	1
7	1			7	1	1	3

$$JC(S_1, S_2) = \left| \frac{S_1 \cap S_2}{S_1 \cup S_2} \right|$$

This analysis shows whether there is a similarity for summaries obtained with different approaches, and quantifies it for the obtained results (in this specific scenario, we measure the similarity between key-phrases extracted by pair-wise different methods). The measure is symmetric, so we only report one-way computation when comparing two methods.

The Table reports the average (arithmetic mean) of the Jaccard coefficient similarity and the standard deviation, both computed on each of the categories of files according to the file size.

Table 5. The documents of the corpus with average jaccard coefficient similarity computed over each category of file size, for each of the three methods exploited. Bold values represent the highest average similarity and standard deviation.

| | Jaccard similarity coefficient, average and standard deviation | | | | | |
| | tfidf vs σ-rank | | tfidf vs zipf | | σ-rank vs zipf | |
	Avg	σ	Avg	σ	Avg	σ
Large file size	0.15	0.042	0.01	0.005	0.01	0.004
Medium file size	0.11	**0.043**	0.05	0.024	0.12	0.031
Small file size	0.06	0.020	0.04	0.015	**0.35**	0.037

"Tfidf" summaries are more similar to "sigma-rank" ones for large size files, whereas the other two pairs show a low similarity (which is also confirmed by the low variance). More similarities are shown between "sigma-rank" and "zipf" summaries for small size files, even if there is a higher variance in the results. Medium size texts summaries show the highest average jaccard coefficient between "sigma-rank" and "zipf," followed by "tfidf" and "sigma-rank" that have also the highest variance among the results.

Table 6 shows the results of the evaluation in terms of Precision, Recall and F-Measure. Let S be the set of sentences of a summary and S_r be the set of sentences of the relative reference summary, precision has been computed as

$$Pr(S, S_r) = \frac{|S \cap S_r|}{|S|}$$

Recall has been computed as

$$Rec(S, S_r) = \frac{|S \cap S_r|}{|S_r|}$$

An F-Measure has been computed as

$$f - Meas(S, S_r) = \frac{2 * Pr(S, S_r) * Rec(S, S_r)}{Pr(S, S_r) + Rec(S, S_r)}$$

All the above measures return as a result a number between [0,1]. For the sake of readability, all the results in the next table are multiplied by 100 and discussed as if they were percentages.

The well known pattern of a higher precision leading to a lower recall is also observable in the present evaluation results. The best precision (100%) is obtained by running "zipf" as a method; the highest recall is again obtained by "zipf" (100%), but only in one case (Anemoi summary). In all the other cases it results that, on average, the recall for "zipf" (18%) is lower than those obtained by "tfidf" (22%) and "sigma-rank" (31%), respectively. The best F-Measure (67%) is obtained by the "sigma-rank" approach.

In particular, for large size texts, the best precision is obtained by "zipf" (67%), the best recall and F-measures are obtained by "sigma-rank" (42% and 46%, respectively). With fewer exceptions, "sigma-rank" is the best performing method in terms of recall and F-measure if compared with the other two.

For medium size texts, the best precision is obtained by "zipf" (100%), and also the best recall (100%). It is worth noticing that, despite the 100% single result, every other recall for the "zipf" experiments is lower than the recall for "sigma-rank." The best recalls are obtained, on average, by "sigma-rank" (29% against 19% and 18% of "tfidf" and "zipf," respectively) that gives also the highest performance in terms of F-Measure (55%).

Table 6. Precision, recall, and F-Measure computed against the reference summaries, for each text and for each method applied to it. Bold values highlight the higher precision, recall and F-Measure for each of the different methods in the three parts of the Table, whereas the bold and italic style highlights the highest precision, recall and F-measure among the set of results considered as a whole (in each of the three parts).

Name (Wikipedia page title)	Prec, Rec and F-Meas of summary against reference summary								
	Tfidf summaries			S-Rank summaries			Zipf summaries		
	Prec	Rec	F-M	Prec	Rec	F-M	Prec	Rec	F-M
Pluto	6	31	9	2	25	4	0	0	0
Dionysus	19	25	22	24	29	27	43	6	1
Homer	**28**	**35**	**31**	28	35	31	38	7	11
Hades	15	26	19	23	37	28	38	**16**	**22**
Hephaestus	17	10	12	37	37	37	50	3	6
Cronus	17	9	12	**50**	*42*	*46*	*67*	6	11
Helios	9	6	7	26	28	27	*100*	6	11
Uranus	50	13	21	44	35	39	50	13	21
Apis	33	12	17	53	24	33	*100*	21	34
Anemoi	41	23	30	40	33	36	43	*100*	16
Adonis	71	**33**	45	54	23	33	*100*	3	6
Asopus	**73**	**33**	**46**	54	29	38	6	12	21
Asclepius	24	17	20	36	17	23	5	4	8
Atlas	17	6	9	67	**47**	*55*	5	12	19
Aeolus	31	14	20	60	43	50	*100*	18	3
Caerus	40	**33**	36	40	25	31	33	4	7
Glaucus	50	29	36	43	29	34	40	10	15
Achelous	50	32	39	56	26	36	57	21	31
Paean	29	31	30	27	23	25	50	31	**38**
Phosphorus	0	0	0	60	30	40	40	20	27
Triton	27	19	22	57	25	35	0	0	0
Aristaeus	0	0	0	*100*	32	48	*100*	5	9
Oceanus	0	0	0	20	14	17	67	29	40
Eros	38	28	32	38	28	32	*100*	11	20
Morpheus	31	40	35	25	30	27	50	1	17
Melicertes	0	0	0	38	33	35	60	33	43
Erotes	67	**50**	**57**	58	35	42	71	25	37
Eridanos	**75**	30	43	*100*	**50**	*67*	75	30	43
Phobos	67	17	27	40	17	24	67	17	27
Hesperus	4	43	7	25	14	18	67	*57*	**62**

For small size texts, the best precision performance is given by "zipf" (100%), the best recall is assigned to "zipf" (57%), but, on average, the recall is better for "sigma-rank" (28% against 26% by "tfidf" and 25% by "zipf"), while "tfidf" shows the highest recall for 3 summaries out of 8. The best F-Measure on average is assignable to "zipf," as it results of around 36% against 25% of "tfidf" and 33% of "sigma-rank." As a single experiment it is assigned to "sigma-rank" (67%).

A trend that is observable from the data is the inverse performance relation between "tfidf" and "zipf" on medium size texts and small size texts. Whenever "zipf" shows a very poor recall (e.g. Adonis, Asclepius, Caerus, Triton, and Morpheus summaries), "tfidf" shows a recall and an F-Measure that are better or equal to "sigma-rank" ones (in at least 3 summaries out of 5 they are better).

A further evaluation was conducted by using the ROUGE tool (Lin, 2004a). In particular, as summaries extracted with our algorithms and manual summaries provided by domain experts are all in form of a selection of whole sentences from the original texts, a meaningful measure for our evaluation purposes is the ROUGE-W one. We recall here that this measure aims at considering the order of sentences between a reference summary and its candidate summaries, and at giving a higher score to consecutive matches between sentences belonging to compared summaries.

Table 7 shows the results of the ROUGE-W evaluation run for each of the 3 candidate summaries against the reference summary, for the 30 texts examined. As there is only one reference summary for each file, the average precision, average recall and average F-Measure returned by the tool are the same as the single precision, recall and F-Measure, so we only show the last one.

These results outline that "sigma-rank" outperforms "tfidf" and "zipf" in terms of recall and F-Measure, with fewer exceptions (like in the evaluation of Table 6). In addition, "tfidf" has a

worst performance if compared with the evaluation of Table 6, whereas "zipf" provides the best precision for the most part of experiments (as in Table 6 evaluation).

This further elaboration outlines some strengths and weaknesses of the approaches experimented, in form of general rules that may be derived from the data at hand. For large size texts, as well as for medium size texts, the "sigma-rank" seems to outperform the other two methods; for small size texts the "zipf" approach operates better than the others. Precision plays an important role in a tool like ours, where the user should be able to extract relevant knowledge first and than refine the search for complete knowledge. The corpus knowledge that "tfidf" includes in its computation does not seem to bring any improvement in tasks such as text summarization of a single text, even if the texts that we choose for our experiments can be considered a corpus for their uniformity of style and topic. Moreover, the correlation between "tfidf" and "zipf" on medium size texts and small size texts that was observed in Table 6 is no more applicable to the evaluation results of Table 7. This result further lowers the performance evaluation of "tfidf" for our summarization task.

RELATED WORK

Text summarization is a well-established research field, for which numerous approaches have been proposed to date (Nenkova & McKeown, 2012).

The main conferences in the field (DUC and TAC, which includes DUC from 2008 on) aim at collecting Natural Language Processing communities around well defined and large scale evaluation methodologies for text analysis. An important task in the community is the Summarization Track. Reeve and Hyoil (2007) exploit an approach based on a term frequency distribution. Basically, the approach consists in

Table 7. ROUGE-W evaluation results. In bold the highest precision, recall and F-Measure for each document

Name (Wikipedia page title)	ROUGE-W Prec, Rec and F-Meas								
	Tfidf summaries			S-Rank summaries			Zipf summaries		
	Prec	Rec	F-M	Prec	Rec	F-M	Prec	Rec	F-M
Pluto	6	**26**	9	5	21	8	**25**	8	**12**
Dionysus	17	13	15	23	**15**	**18**	**31**	5	9
Homer	26	**15**	**19**	26	14	18	**31**	5	9
Hades	21	11	15	23	**14**	**17**	**39**	10	16
Hephaestus	27	3	6	30	**16**	**21**	**40**	5	9
Cronus	27	3	6	35	**11**	**17**	**36**	5	9
Helios	17	3	6	22	**13**	**17**	**68**	3	5
Uranus	39	2	3	29	**14**	**19**	**46**	10	16
Apis	33	2	5	**38**	**8**	**13**	36	6	11
Anemoi	35	7	12	35	**20**	**25**	**47**	9	15
Adonis	46	6	11	34	**13**	**18**	**76**	2	4
Asopus	43	**13**	**19**	**45**	12	**19**	39	7	12
Asclepius	24	5	8	**35**	**12**	**18**	20	1	2
Atlas	37	3	6	**47**	**18**	**26**	38	5	10
Aeolus	31	4	7	37	**14**	**20**	**55**	7	13
Caerus	**31**	10	15	**31**	17	**22**	28	5	8
Glaucus	38	15	22	37	**16**	**23**	**44**	12	19
Achelous	40	12	18	39	13	19	**51**	**15**	**23**
Paean	32	8	12	34	15	21	**50**	**26**	**34**
Phosphorus	**55**	1	1	33	**8**	**13**	39	7	12
Triton	27	5	9	**31**	**11**	**17**	20	6	9
Aristaeus	28	1	3	**53**	**15**	**24**	50	6	11
Oceanus	20	1	2	35	6	10	**64**	**17**	**27**
Eros	33	6	10	40	**16**	**23**	49	10	17
Morpheus	26	13	17	25	**24**	**24**	**39**	6	10
Melicertes	24	1	3	32	**15**	21	**47**	15	**23**
Erotes	45	**25**	**32**	43	22	29	**54**	15	23
Eridanos	**59**	6	10	55	**30**	**39**	44	23	30
Phobos	40	5	8	34	7	11	**47**	**17**	**24**
Hesperus	**48**	7	12	37	18	24	42	**30**	**35**

first creating a frequency distribution model of the text, and then generating the summary by selecting those sentences that best match the frequency distribution model. Verma et al. (2007) use an approach to text summarization based on ontologies. A user formulates a query in terms of keywords and the ontologies are used to interpret it. A rank is given for selection of sentences that have a minimal distance to the query. Gong et al. (2010), put Wikipedia texts in the summarization loop, by extracting conceptual features from it. The methods is based on a link probability measure that determines the "keyphrasesness" of wiki links. A concept disambiguation procedure follows, as well as the position in Wikipedia text, the sentence length and weight features calculations, based on which a sentence-based extractive summary is finally generated and evaluated.

Most of the existing techniques propose a scoring function to measure the importance of sentences in a text and create a summary including the top-ranked sentences.

He et al. (2012) generate a summary by selecting the sentences that best reconstruct the original document. Each sentence s is assigned a set of related sentences that are representative of the meaning of s based on a reconstruction function. The sentences included in the summary are those that best approximate the entire document, or minimize the reconstruction error.

Gong and Liu (2001) and Steinberger and Jezek (2004) use *latent semantic analysis* (LSA) to identify semantically important sentence. Indeed, LSA is able to capture the relationships between terms and can therefore cluster terms and sentences. More specifically, a document is represented as a terms by sentences matrix, where each column vector represents the weighted term-frequency vector of a sentence in the document. By performing a singular value decomposition of the matrix, the singular vectors are identified which represent the salient topics of the document; the

sentences that are included in the summary are those that best represent each topic.

The method proposed by Goldstein et al. (1999) generates a summary containing sentences that receive a high score based on statistical and linguistic features. The strong point of this approach is that the weights assigned to each feature can be tuned to generate different summaries, based on the type of a document. For instance, a summary of a news article would typically include the first sentence, and therefore the position of a sentence in the text should be assigned a large weight.

Conroy and O'Leary (2001) describe a hidden Markov model that computes a probability that each sentence is a summary sentence given a set of features. The considered features are: the position of the sentence in the document, the position of the sentence within its paragraph, the number of terms in the sentence, how likely the terms are, given a baseline of terms, and how likely sentence terms are, given the document terms.

Shen et al. (2007) propose an approach based on conditional random fields. Their framework views a document as a sequence of sentences and the summarization procedure labels the sentences by 1 and 0, where 1 evidently means that the sentence should be included in the summary. The label of a sentence depends on the label of the others.

Other approaches (Erkan & Radev, 2004; Mihalcea & Tarau, 2005) model the document as a graph and apply one of the existing iterative algorithms to score the nodes, such as HITS or PageRank. The nodes of the graph correspond to sentences, while the edges express the relatedness between two sentences; for instance, two sentences are considered related if they have a significant overlap of tokens. Optionally, the edges can have a weight to signify the strength of the association between two sentences. The sentences that are included in the summary are those corresponding to top-scored nodes.

The generation of a summary of multiple documents is a generalization of the text summarization problem. Here the challenge is that information across multiple documents can overlap and yet they can be also very different; as a result, a summary should cover the differences without replicating overlapping information.

Wang et al. (2008) describe an algorithm that decomposes the documents into sentences and creates a sentence by sentence matrix containing the pairwise sentence semantic similarity; by performing a symmetric matrix factorization, the sentences are grouped into clusters, each cluster containing similar sentences; finally, the most representative sentences of each cluster are selected to form the summary.

The method described by Wan and Yang (2008) uses an adapted markov random walk model.

As opposed to most of the research we came across, which focuses on generating static summaries that cannot be customized based on specific needs, we propose an interactive tool that leverages users' feedback.

Interactive tools, which are closely related to what we propose in this chapter are those of (Jones et al., 2002; House, 1997). In particular, Jones et al. (2002) propose to score sentences to be included in the summary based on their keyphrases, which are identified by using a Naïve Bayes classifier. Each sentence is then scored based on the scores of the key-phrases it contains. The scored sentences are then fed into the user interface, which includes different customization tools for the user to modify the summary.

CONCLUSION AND FUTURE DIRECTIONS

In this Chapter an approach for interactive text summarization in the domain of history and archaeology has been depicted. The procedure to treat each document and to extract a list of keywords and key-phrases has been detailed, and experiments and results have been provided on an ad-hoc corpus taken from Wikipedia, in the domain of Greek mythology.

The three algorithms for the keywords extraction phase have been explained and the results obtained for each of them have been evaluated and discussed.

Future directions aims at exploring new combination of words and frequency counts based on the "sigma-rank" approach applied to bigrams extraction, instead of single terms, in order to exploit them as keywords and / or combine them with unique words.

The user interface will be improved with panels for all the above options; the panel to select, adjust and tune the parameters for the summarization task will be developed in a user friendly fashion.

Although the present version of ISET limits the level of information extraction to simple algorithms, it has result to be effective when used in an interactive environment. We plan to experiment this version with archaeologists before going into more sophisticated algorithms and in the adoption of more sophisticated tools that could help the users to produce an output to be directly fed into a *rule* and an *ontology extractor (OE)*. In this context, we will design an interactive tool for helping archaeologists in searching and organizing textual information in rich infrastructures in a bottom-up approach starting from keywords and keyphrases, continuing with relations and, through successive abstractions, eventually ending with an ontology. In the latter case, the role of the user is fundamental: finding relations and concept leading to the definition of an ontology is a task that cannot be performed by an algorithm alone; it is mainly a task of the user: our tool will provide simple primitives and hints for supporting him in this job.

These extensions will depend on the success of the experimentation of the present version and on the interest of our users in the use of less intuitive and more formal approaches to the problem.

REFERENCES

Ancona, M., Scagliola, N., & Traverso, A. (2005). *Application of 3G cellular phones to cultural heritage: The agamemnon project.* Paper presented at the International Workshop on Recording, Modeling and Visualization of Cultural Heritage. New York, NY.

Antikytera Mechanism. (n.d.). *Wikipedia.* Retrieved from http://en.wikipedia.org/wiki/Antikythera_mechanism

Baker, C. F., & Fellbaum, C. (2009). WordNet and FrameNet as complementary resources for annotation. In *Proceedings of the Third Linguistic Annotation Workshop*, ACL-IJCNLP, (pp. 125–129). ACL.

Berryman, M. J., Allison, A., & Abbott, D. (2002). Signal processing and statistical methods in analysis of text and DNA. In *Proceedings of SPIE: Biomedical Applications of Micro and Nanoengineering.* SPIE.

Bliki Engine. (n.d.). Retrieved from http://code.google.com/p/gwtwiki/

Bogdanovych, A. (2007). *Virtual institutions.* (PhD Thesis). University of Technology of Sydney, Sydney, Australia.

Conroy, J. M., & O'Leary, D. P. (2001). Text summarization via hidden markov models. In *Proceedings of the 24th Annual International ACM SIGIR Conference on Research and Development in Information Retrieval* (pp. 406-407). ACM.

Das, D., & Martins, A. (2007). *A survey on automatic text summarization. Literature Survey for the Language and Statistics II Course at CMU.* Pittsburgh, PA: CMU.

De Silva, L., & Jayaratne, L. (2009). *Semi-automatic extraction and modeling of ontologies using wikipedia XML corpus,* Applications of Digital Information and Web Technologies.

Didion, J. (2012). *The java wordnet library (JWNL).* Retrieved from http://sourceforge.net/projects/jwordnet/

DUC. (n.d.). *Document understanding conference.* Retrieved from http://www-nlpir.nist.gov/projects/duc/index.html

Edmunds, M.G., & Freeth, T. (2011). Using computation to decode the first known computer. *IEEE Computer*, 32-39.

Erkan, G., & Radev, D. R. (2004). Lexpagerank: Prestige in multi-document text summarization. In *Proceedings of EMNLP* (Vol. 4). EMNLP.

Goldstein, J., Kantrowitz, M., Mittal, V., & Carbonell, J. (1999). Summarizing text documents: Sentence selection and evaluation metrics. In *Proceedings of the 22nd Annual International ACM SIGIR Conference on Research and Development in Information Retrieval*, (pp. 121-128). ACM.

Gong, S., Qu, Y., & Tian, S. (2010). Summarization using wikipedia. In *Proceedings of the Text Analysis Conference.* TAC.

Gong, Y., & Liu, X. (2001). Generic text summarization using relevance measure and latent semantic analysis. In *Proceedings of the 24th Annual International ACM SIGIR Conference on Research and Development in Information Retrieval*, (pp. 19-25). ACM.

Greek Gods. (n.d.). *Wikipedia.* Retrieved from http://en.wikipedia.org/wiki/Category:Greek_gods

Hassanpour, S., O'Connor, M. J., & Das, A. K. (2011). A framework for the automatic extraction of rules from online text. *LNCS, 6826*, 266–280.

He, Z., Chen, C., Bu, J., Wang, C., Zhang, L., Cai, D., & He, X. (2012). *Document summarization based on data reconstruction.* Paper presented at the Twenty-Sixth AAAI Conference on Artificial Intelligence. New York, NY.

Help Formatting. (n.d.). *MediaWiki*. Retrieved April 10, 2013, from http://www.mediawiki.org/wiki/Help:Formatting

Herrera, J. P., & Pury, P. A. (2008). Statistical keyword detection in literary corpora. *The European Physical Journal C, 63*(1), 135–146.

House, D. (1997). *Interactive text summarization for fast answers*. Retrieved from http://www.mitre.org/pubs/edge/july_97/tirst.htm

Jones, S., Lundy, S., & Paynter, G. W. (2002). Interactive document summarization using automatically extracted keyphrases. In *Proceedings of the 35th Hawaii Int. Conf. on System Science*. IEEE.

Klein, D., & Manning, C. D. (2003). Accurate unlexicalized parsing. In *Proceedings of the 41st Meeting of the Association for Computational Linguistics*, (pp. 423-430). ACL.

Li, W. (1992). Random texts exhibit Zipf's-law-like word frequency distribution. *IEEE Transactions on Information Theory*, 1842–1845. doi:10.1109/18.165464

Lin, C. Y. (2004a). ROUGE: A package for automatic evaluation of summaries. In *Proceedings of the Workshop on Text Summarization Branches Out* (WAS 2004). WAS.

Manning, C. D., & Schutze, H. (1999). *Foundations of statistical natural language processing*. Cambridge, MA: MIT Press.

McDonald, D. M., & Chen, H. (2006). Summary in context: Searching versus browsing. *ACM Transactions on Information Systems, 24*(1), 111–141. doi:10.1145/1125857.1125861

Mihalcea, R., & Tarau, P. (2005). A language independent algorithm for single and multiple document summarization. In *Proceedings of IJCNLP*, (vol. 5). IJCNLP.

Miller, G. A. (1995). *WordNet: A lexical database for English*. WordNet.

Nenkova, A., & McKeown, K. (2012). A survey of text summarization techniques. In *Mining Text Data* (pp. 43–76). Berlin: Springer. doi:10.1007/978-1-4614-3223-4_3

Ortuño, M., Carpena, P., Bernaola-Galván, P., Muñoz, E., & Somoza, A. M. (2002). Keyword detection in natural languages and DNA. *Europhysics Letters, 57*, 759–764. doi:10.1209/epl/i2002-00528-3

Patel, C., Supekar, K., & Lee, Y. (2003). OntoGenie: Extracting ontology instances from WWW. In *Proceedings of Human Language Technology for the Semantic Web and Web Services*. ISWC.

Reeve, L. H., & Hyoil, H. (2007). A term frequency distribution approach for the duc-2007 update task. In *Proceedings of the Document Understanding Conference*. DUC.

Sarah, M., & Taylor, S. M. (2004). Information extraction tools: Deciphering human language. *IT Professional, 6*(6), 28–34. doi:10.1109/MITP.2004.82

Savoy, J. (2013). *IR multilingual resources at UniNE*. Retrieved from http://members.unine.ch/jacques.savoy/clef/

Schutz, A., & Buitelaar, P. (2005). *RelExt: A tool for relation extraction from text in ontology extension*. Academic Press. doi:10.1007/11574620_43

Shen, D., Sun, J. T., Li, H., Yang, Q., & Chen, Z. (2007). Document summarization using conditional random fields. In *Proceedings of the 20th International Joint Conference on Artificial Intelligence*, (vol. 7, pp. 2862-2867). IEEE.

Shi, L., & Mihalcea, R. (2004). *Open text semantic parsing using FrameNet and WordNet*. Paper presented at HLT-NAACL 2004. New York, NY.

Steinberger, J., & Jezek, K. (2004). Using latent semantic analysis in text summarization and summary evaluation. [ISIM.]. *Proceedings of ISIM, 04*, 93–100.

TAC. (n.d.). *Text analysis conference*. Retrieved from http://www.nist.gov/tac/about/index.html

Tf-idf. (n.d.). *Wikipedia*. Retrieved April 10, 2013, from http://en.wikipedia.org/wiki/Tf-idf

Toutanova, K., & Manning, C. D. (2000). Enriching the knowledge sources used in a maximum entropy part-of-speech tagger. In *Proceedings of the Joint SIGDAT Conference on Empirical Methods in Natural Language Processing and Very Large Corpora* (EMNLP/VLC-2000), (pp. 63-70). ACM.

Verma, R., Ping, C., & Wei, L. (2007). A semantic free-text summarization system using ontology knowledge. In *Proceedings of Document Understanding Conference*. DUC.

Wan, X., & Yang, J. (2008). Multi-document summarization using cluster-based link analysis. In *Proceedings of the 31st Annual International ACM SIGIR Conference on Research and Development in Information Retrieval*, (pp. 299-306). ACM.

Wang, D., Li, T., Zhu, S., & Ding, C. (2008). Multi-document summarization via sentence-level semantic analysis and symmetric matrix factorization. In *Proceedings of the 31st Annual International ACM SIGIR Conference on Research and Development in Information Retrieval*, (pp. 307-314). ACM.

Wang, G., Yu, Y., & Haiping, Z. (2007). *PORE: Positive-only relation extraction from wikipedia text*. In *Proceedings of the 6th International Semantic Web and 2nd Asian Conference on Asian Semantic Web Conference*, (pp. 580-594). Springer.

Zipf, G. K. (1949). *Human behavior and the principle of least effort*. Reading, MA: Addison-Wesley.

ADDITIONAL READING

Ancona, M., Mascardi, V., Quercini, G., Bogdanovych, H., de Lumley, H., Papaleo, L., et al. (2010). Virtual institutions for preserving and simulating the culture of Mount Bego's ancient people. In Proc. of the 11th, p. 5-8, doi: doi:10.2312/PE/VAST/VAST10S/001-004.

Ardito, C., Buono, P., Costabile, M. F., Lanzilotti, R., & Fioriello, S. (2012). *New Channels, Creativity, EUD for creating Engaging Experiences of Cultural Heritage*, In Proceedings of CDCH, part of VL/HCC 2012.

Arnold, D. (2008). *Editorial for inaugural issue of JOCCH: Pasteur's Quadrant: Cultural heritage as inspiration for basic research in computer science*. ACM J. Comput. Cultur. Heritage 1, 1. *Article, 1*, 1–13. doi: doi:10.1145/1367080.1367081

Barber, M., van Regteren Altena, J. F., & Brandt, R.Council of Europe. (1999). *European Bronze Age Monuments: A Multilingual Glossary of Archaeological Terminology. Cultural Heritage Series*. Council of Europe.

Bimber, O., Chang, C.K. (2011). *Computational Archaeology: Reviving the Past with Present-Day Tools*, Computer, vol.44, no.7, pp.30,31, doi: 10.1109/MC.2011.201.

Bogdanovich, A., Papaleo, L., Ancona, M., Mascardi, V., Quercini, G., Simoff, S., et al. (2009). *Integrating Agents and Virtual Institutions for Sharing Cultural Heritage on the Web*. In Proceedings of the Workshop On Intelligent Cultural Heritage (Satellite workshop of the AI*IA 2009: International Conference of the Italian Association for Artificial Intelligence).

Ch'ng, E., Chapman, H., Gaffney, V., Murgatroyd, P., Gaffney, C., Neubauer, W. (2011). *From Sites to Landscapes: How Computing Technology Is Shaping Archaeological Practice*, Computer, vol.44, no.7, pp.40,46, doi: 10.1109/MC.2011.162.

Collao, A., Jr., Diaz-Kommonen, L., Kaipainen, M., & Pietarila, J. (2003). *Soft ontologies and similarity cluster tools to facilitate exploration and discovery of cultural heritage resources,* In 14th International Workshop on Database and Expert Systems Applications (DEXA'03), vol., no., pp.75,79 doi: 10.1109/DEXA.2003.1232001.

Diamond, J. M. (2005). *Collapse: How Societies Choose to Fail or Succeed.* Viking Press.

Kilfeather, E., McAuley, J., Corns, A., & McHugh, O. (2003). *An ontological application for archaeological narratives.* In 14th International Workshop on Database and Expert Systems Applications (DEXA'03), vol., no., pp.110,114, doi: 10.1109/DEXA.2003.1232007.

Lampe K.H., Riede K., Doerr M. (2008). *Research between natural and cultural history information: Benefits and IT-requirements for transdisciplinarity.* J. Comput. Cult. Herit. 1, 1, Article 4, 22 pages. DOI=10.1145/1367080.1367084.

Laycock R. G., Drinkwater D., Day A. M. (2008). *Exploring cultural heritage sites through space and time.* J. Comput. Cult. Herit. 1, 2, Article 11, 15 pages. DOI=10.1145/1434763.1434768.

Locoro, A., Grignani, D., & Mascardi, V. (2011). MANENT: An Infrastructure for Integrating, Structuring and Searching Digital Libraries. In *Learning Structure and Schemas from Documents, Studies in Computational Intelligence* (pp. 315–341). Springer. doi:10.1007/978-3-642-22913-8_15

Locoro, A., Mascardi, V., & Briola, D. Martelli M. Ancona M., Deufemia V., Paolino L.,Tortora G., Polese G., Francese R. (2012). *The Indiana MAS Project: Goals and Preliminary Results,* Proceedings of the Workshop from Objects to Agents (dagli Oggetti agli Agenti), WOA 2012, ceur-ws.org, vol. 892.

Mabroukeh N.R., Ezeife, C. I. (2010). *A taxonomy of sequential pattern mining algorithms.* ACM Comput. Surv. 43, 1, Article, 41 pages. DOI=10.1145/1824795.1824798.

Mascardi V., Briola D., Locoro A., Grignani D., Deufemia V., Paolino L., Bianchi N., de Lumley H., Malafronte D., Ricciarelli A. (2014). A Holonic Multi-Agent System for Sketch, Image and Text Interpretation in the Rock Art Domain. To appear in International Journal of Innovative Computing, Information and Control, issn: 1349-4198.

Mulholland, P., & Zdrahal, Z. (2003). *Knowledge support for story construction, exploration and personalization in Cultural Heritage Forums.* In 14th International Workshop on Database and Expert Systems Applications (DEXA'03).

North, D. C. (1989). Institutions and economic growth: An historical introduction. *World Development, Elsevier, 17*(9), 1319–1332. doi:10.1016/0305-750X(89)90075-2

North, D. C. (1991). Institutions. *The Journal of Economic Perspectives, 5*(1), 97–112. doi:10.1257/jep.5.1.97

Oberländer-Târnoveanu, I. (2005). Multilingual Access to Cultural Heritage Resources. *Internet Archaeology, 18.* doi: doi:10.11141/ia.18.7

Papaleo, L., Quercini, G., Mascardi, V., Ancona, M., Traverso, A., & de Lumley, H. (2011). *Agents and Ontologies for Understanding and Preserving the Rock Art of Mount Bego.* In Proceedings of ICAART 2011, 3rd International Conference on Agents and Artificial Intelligence.

Petrovic, V., Gidding, A., Wypych, T., Kuester, F., Defanti, T.A., Levy, T.E. (2011). *Dealing with Archaeology's Data Avalanche,* Computer, vol.44, no.7, pp.56,60, doi: 10.1109/MC.2011.161.

Smith, G., Maher, M. L., & Gu, N. (2007). *Designing Virtual Worlds for 3D Electronic Institutions, Computer-Aided Architectural Design Futures (CAADFutures)* (pp. 397–400). Springer. doi:10.1007/978-1-4020-6528-6_29

Young, O. R. (1989). *International Cooperation: Building Regimes for Natural Resources and the Environment.* Cornell University Press.

Young, O. R. (1997). *Global Governance: Drawing Insights from the Environmental Experience.* MIT Press.

Zara, J., & Slavik, P. (2003). *Cultural heritage presentation in virtual environment: Czech experience.* In 14th International Workshop on Database and Expert Systems Applications (DEXA'03), vol., no., pp.92,96, doi: 10.1109/DEXA.2003.1232004.

KEY TERMS AND DEFINITIONS

Digital Preservation: The series of managed activities necessary to ensure continued access to digital materials for as long as necessary, involving the planning, resource allocation, and application of preservation methods and technologies to ensure that digital information of continuing value remains accessible and usable.

Information Extraction: The task of automatically extracting structured information from unstructured and/or semi-structured machine-readable documents.

Interactive Summarization: Is the process of text summarization conducted with the involvement of a user in the Information Extraction loop.

Keyword Extraction: Is a subtask of information extraction. The goal of keyword extraction is to automatically extract relevant terms from a given text or corpus.

Natural Language Processing: Is a field of computer science, artificial intelligence, and linguistics concerned with the interactions between computers and human (natural) languages. Many challenges in NLP involve natural language understanding -- that is, enabling computers to derive meaning from human or natural language input.

Sentence Extraction: Is a technique used for automatic summarization of a text. Sentence extraction is a low-cost approach compared to more knowledge-intensive deeper approaches which require additional knowledge bases such as ontologies or linguistic knowledge.

Text Summarization: Is the process of reducing a text document in order to create a summary that retains the most important points of the original document.

Chapter 5
Evaluation Metrics for the Summarization Task

Paulo Cesar Fernandes de Oliveira
Anhanguera University, Brazil

ABSTRACT

Summary evaluation is a challenging issue. It is subjective, costly, time consuming, and, if it is human-assisted, can generate some bias. Due to this, several attempts have been made in the last decades in order to avoid all these drawbacks. Those attempts focused on automatic summary evaluation. This chapter provides a comprehensive survey about studies that have dealt with this topic and proposes and describes the development of an automatic summary evaluation method. In addition, it presents some experiments that have been carried out in order to assess the method's performance.

INTRODUCTION

The aim of this chapter is twofold. First, it surveys studies which have dealt with summary evaluation, and metrics developed therein. Second, it proposes and describes the development of an automatic summary evaluation method, and the implementation of a computational framework.

It is interesting, for the purpose of this chapter, to start by considering a definition of *evalua-*

tion. According to Rutman (1984), evaluation is a process where certain procedures are applied in order to obtain valid and reliable evidence on the manner and extent to which specific activities produce the measured results. Even though the definition is given in the context of the social science, it is potentially appropriate to automatic text summarization (ATS).

There are two keywords in this definition, namely, procedures and results. Procedures can be thought as an *algorithm*, which is a finite set of procedures or instructions for attaining some task. The measured results produced by the application

DOI: 10.4018/978-1-4666-5019-0.ch005

of certain procedures are in fact, the *outcome* of the evaluation process.

Hence, the evaluation process should describe and implement an algorithm which will be used by an evaluator; this activity will result in an outcome. Putting it into the ATS context, the algorithm provides means for assessing the level of the quality of a summary in relation to its original text, and the outcome is a score that will represent this level of quality of the summary under test. In general terms, the evaluation will produce a metric that will allow one to say "the quality of this summary is good or not."

However, summary evaluation is not a straightforward task. Research on this field has tried to respond to a fundamental but complex and subjective question: what constitutes a good summary? As yet, there is not a clear answer. The debate in the ATS literature regarding suitable evaluation metrics for measuring the quality of summaries has been massive.

Another feature related to this topic is that the majority of evaluation methods developed so far have depended on human intervention, and therefore have the drawbacks of being time consuming and expensive, as we will show in the next section.

On the other hand, if a researcher, for example, needs an evaluation method which is fast and is not influenced by human error or subjectivity, an automatic evaluation method could be the answer. Many approaches have been developed on this topic, using a variety of metrics such as sentence recall, sentence ranking, content-based, and so on (e.g. (Saggion, Radev, Teufel, Lam, & Strassel, 2002); (Radev, Jing, & Budzikowska, 2000); (Donaway, Drummey, & Mather, 2000)).

BACKGROUND

Due to a crescent interest in summary evaluation in the past several years, some studies will be described in this section. In order to do this description in a more systematic fashion, we will

follow an interesting classification proposed by Tucker (1999). He suggested four approaches, namely: direct evaluation; target-based evaluation; task-based evaluation and automatic evaluation.

Direct Evaluation

In this approach, people, following some guidelines, look at the summaries and decide directly whether they are *good* or not.

Earl (1970), developed a program which produced summaries by sentence extraction. The evaluation process did not consider the overall acceptability of the summaries. Instead, each sentence in each extract was considered either to be *worthy of extracting* or *not worthy of extracting*. She created an algorithm to choose the sentences based on a percentage score, i.e. the proportion of sentences that were acceptable. Four chapters from a technical book were used as the text corpus for all the experiments and, according to the author, the criteria of *relevance* and *comprehensibility* was adopted. She pointed out that the results were *very encouraging*.

Brandow, Mitze, & Rau (1995) designed and implemented a summarization system called ANES, which performs domain-independent summarization of news documents. The evaluation of ANES involved generating summaries (extracts) of 60, 150 and 250 words for a text corpus of 250 newspaper stories. These summaries were then compared to those generated by a system called *Searchable Lead* – a commercial product by Mead Data Central. Experienced news analysts using *content* and *readability* criteria as guidelines executed the evaluation process. Each summary was read and judged by the analysts with the corresponding source text. The authors concluded that the "most surprising result of the experiment was the adequacy of producing summaries consisting only of the first sentences in a story."

In order to be able to assess the quality of summaries more precisely, Minel, Nugier and Piat (1997) described two protocols – FAN and

MLUCE. The FAN protocol deals with *legibility* of a summary independently from the source text. Two judges read 27 abstracts and assessed them counting the presence of dangling anaphora, tautological sentences, and the overall legibility (as being *very bad*, *mediocre*, *good* or *very good*). There was very little variation in assessment between the judges, reported the authors. The MLUCE protocol deals with the summary content and the use of it. Two applications were selected using MLUCE: allowing the reader to decide whether to read the source text and, helping the reader to write a synthesis of the source text. This experiment lasted a total of eight months. Comparing the results between the two protocols, very little convergence was shown, argued the authors.

Target-Based Evaluation

For target-based evaluation, a person reads the source text and produces a summary (target) from it. Then summaries to be evaluated are compared with the target, measuring how close they are to the target.

DeJong (1982) described two evaluations of FRUMP, in each of which the system was run in real time on 120 UPI (United Press International) news stories. In one experiment, the system ran for a day, using 48 out of 60 sketchy scripts. For the second experiment, FRUMP ran for six days, but used only 7 out of 60 sketchy scripts. In both experiments, the stories were classified according to whether the system processed them correctly or not. On both evaluations, FRUMP could understand some of the 120 stories. According to the author, the results suggested that FRUMP often produced relevant summaries (extracts) when an appropriate script was selected. However, some confusing summaries were produced due to failures in the script selection.

Paice and Jones (1993) proposed a method that focused on concept identification rather than sentence extraction. They classified these concepts as focal and non-focal. For a corpus, they used 54 research papers in the area of the crop agriculture. Percentages of the focal and non-focal concepts in the source text were calculated to verify whether they were included in the summary. In fact, they measured the summary's coverage (hit rate) of these concepts in terms of Correct, Incorrect, and Missing. The authors found that the success hit rate for the focal concept was higher than the non-focal concept.

Johnson, Paice, Black & Neal (1993) outlined an interesting approach to evaluation. A template was created which reflected the discourse structure of the text. It was divided into sections (e.g. aim, methods and findings) and was used to identify concepts in the text. To each concept a numerical score was assigned indicating their relative importance. The metric used to check the quality of a summary was simply the sum of the scores of concepts included in the summary (abstract). Johnson and his colleagues concluded that, "our objectives have been met ... [However,] much [work] remains to be done" (p.232, 236).

Miike, Itoh, Ono & Sumita (1994) developed a prototype of a Japanese-language summarization system named BREVIDOC. The evaluation carried out used 90 technical papers from the monthly Toshiba Review and editorials from the Asahi newspaper. The researchers chose key sentences which they thought should be included in the summary (the target). Their system produced summaries (abstracts) of these documents in lengths of 24% and 30%, and the percentage each key sentence covered, was calculated. The coverage of the key sentences was 51% for summaries at 24% length and 41% for summaries at 30% length.

From a professionally produced abstract which contained sentences from an original document selected by *inspiration* (c.188 technical papers), Kupiec, Pedersen & Chen (1995) used a combination of automatic and manual techniques to classify sentences in the manual abstracts. Two measures were introduced:

1. The fraction of summary sentences which are faithfully reproduced by the summarizer.
2. The fraction of all matchable sentences that were selected.

Their summarizer was trained and evaluated with these 2 measures. The authors reported that the results were in agreement with Edmundson (1969), but suggested that their combination of cue phrases, location information and sentence-length scores, produced more accurate results.

Salton, Singhal, Mitra & Buckley (1997) selected 50 articles from the Funk and Wagnalls Encyclopedia. For each document, two summaries (extracts) were constructed manually by choosing two individuals who identified the most important paragraphs in the article. The measure used to check the system's performance was the amount of overlap between the automatic and the manual summaries. The degree of overlapping was classified in four different ways: optimistic where the target selected was the manual extract which had the most overlap with the automatic one; pessimistic where the target selected was the manual extract which had the least overlap with the automatic one; intersection where the target was selected by taking the paragraphs contained in both manual extracts; and union where the target was selected by taking all paragraphs contained in either of the manual extracts. Salton et al pointed out that: "in view of the fact that extracts generated by two humans for the same article are surprisingly dissimilar, the performance of the automatic text summarization methods is acceptable." In other words, the overlap between the two manual extracts was, on average, 46%. The evaluation measures for automatic extraction methods were on average: 46% for optimistic, 31% for pessimistic, 47% for intersection and 55% for union.

Lin and Hovy (2002) have discussed manual and automatic evaluations using data from the Document Understanding Conference 2001 (DUC 2004). For each document or document set (c. 600 documents), one human summary (extract) was created as the *ideal* model. Then assessors, who created the *ideal* summary, did pairwise comparisons between their summaries and the system-generated summaries. They used the Summary Evaluation Environment (SEE) 2.0 (Lin, 2001) to support the evaluation process. Lin and Hovy observed that inter-human agreement was low, which means that using a single model as reference summary is not adequate. Another observation was the relative performance of the systems in terms of rankings: the performance changes when the instability of human judgment is considered.

Task-Based Evaluation

The approaches discussed so far, namely direct and target-based evaluations have a significant problem: if one needs the summaries produced by these approaches, will these summaries be helpful in a determined situation? This is the characteristic of task-based evaluation: rather than attempt to evaluate the qualities of the summaries directly, the approach measures the ability of users to perform some task for which the summaries ought to help these users. One particular area where this kind of evaluation is appropriate is information retrieval.

Hand (1997), working for the TIPSTER Phase III (which includes MUC and TREC), proposed a "formal, large-scale, multiple task, multiple system evaluation" – TIPSTER SUMMAC Text Summarization Evaluation. As a text corpus, it used 1000 documents containing newspaper articles and belonging to TREC test collections. Hand pointed out that the evaluation of text summarization would "be task-based, judging the utility of a summary to a particular task." Two tasks were suggested: subject categorization which evaluated generic summaries; and the other, adhoc retrieval which evaluated user-directed summaries. For the first task, participants received the documents and produced indicative and neutral summaries from them. For the second task they received the documents and the queries used; thus they had the opportunity to produce indicative summaries focused on the query topic. For both tasks, *professional information analysts* read the summaries and documents and categorized or judged the summaries' relevance, as appropriate. In TIPSTER SUMMAC's concluding report (Mani, et al., 1998), it was pointed out: "SUMMAC has established definitively in a large-scale evaluation that automatic text summarization is very effective in relevance assessment tasks."

Automatic Evaluation

The automatic evaluation approach tries to automate the process of summary evaluation in order, for example, to reduce the cost of other evaluation approaches. The summaries are processed automatically to assess to what degree the criteria are met (e.g. *accuracy*, *usefulness*, *suitability*, and so on).

Lin and Hovy (2003) applied an automatic summary evaluation using the accumulative *n-gram*[1] matching scores to verify the correlation between automatic evaluation and direct (human) evaluation. Using 600 newswire articles from DUC 2001 collection set in their experiment, they found that the *n-gram* statistics are a good automatic scoring metric because the system consistently correlated highly with human assessments. More discussion about this study will be given later in the chapter.

Pastra and Saggion (2003) used a weighted average of similar length phrase matches (*n-grams*) as a metric to evaluate their summaries. Part of a corpus (Hong Kong Newspaper Corpus), consisting of English and Chinese texts, and containing translations of each other was used for this experiment. From this corpus, the researchers have used only three document clusters, each consisting of ten documents in English. The documents of each cluster were assessed by three judges providing a score on a scale from 0 to 10, and expressing how important the sentence was for the topic of the cluster, which is, in fact, the utility judgement. Summaries for each document were produced

based on the utility judgement given by the judges and represented the *gold standard* or reference for the experiment. Also, the documents were summarized automatically (extracts) by a summarization module within the GATE architecture (Cunningham, Maynard, Bontcheva, & Tablan, 2002), at five different compression rates: 10%, 20%, 30%, 40% and 50% (i.e. candidate summaries). They had run the metric comparing the reference summaries with the candidate summaries. From the preliminary results obtained, the authors concluded that:

1. In order to obtain reliable results, the metric should be performed over system generated summaries using multiple references rather than a single reference.
2. Running this metric .".. over system generated summaries at multiple compression rates and estimating the average rank of each system might yield consistent and reliable results even with a single reference summary and therefore compensate for lack of multiple reference summaries."
3. Their work needs to be scaled considerably.

Ahmad, Vrusias and Oliveira (2003) trained and tested a Kohonen Self Organising Feature Map (SOFM), using 102 Reuters news-wires texts with 1000 cycles. After this phase, the summaries (extracts) of the same 102 texts were assigned over the trained SOFM and checked to see if they were in the same position as their original full text. The central idea is: if the summaries occupy a similar position, there is an indication that they are *good*, that is; the summaries contain the chief points of the texts. In their experiment, the authors reported that just over 81% of the summaries occupied the same coordinates on the map as their full text. This experiment is also described in more detail later in this Chapter.

We provided, in the paragraphs above, an explanation of some summary evaluation approaches which have been investigated by the scientific community, following an interesting classification proposed by Tucker (1999). We could see that an astonishing amount of attention has been devoted to the summary evaluation problem. Looking at the number of systems described, it gives us an idea of the considerable amount of practical effort expended on this matter to date. As a consequence, dozens of measures of effectiveness and performance have been proposed in the literature. What follows is an exploratory description of these measures or metrics, namely, Information Retrieval-based Metrics, Statistical-based Metrics, and Content-based Metrics.

First of all, it is convenient to provide some explanations about similarity. Similarity is an intricate concept which has been widely argued and discussed in many fields, such as information theory (Cover & Thomas, 1991), psychology (Tversky, 1977) and linguistics (Frawley, 1992). In natural language processing it has also been widely used. Clough (Clough, 2003), for example, pointed out that text similarity is measured using a basic assumption: "the greater the similarity (or fewer the differences) between texts; the more likely it is that a relationship of some kind exits between them" (p.17). In fact, the task here is to compute some kind of similarity score which indicates the probable existence of a particular relationship between the texts.

Under this assumption, the following reasoning will be used: we want to detect if there is coincidence between a pair of texts, e.g. the full text and the summary. If the degree of coincidence is high, we will assume that they are similar; as a consequence, the quality of the summary is a measure of the degree in which the summary and the original text are similar. To express this in another way: the similarity score or the evaluation metric quantifies how similar two texts are in providing an estimation of the goodness of this similarity.

Information Retrieval-Based Metrics

Information Retrieval (IR) research studies the retrieval of information from a collection of written documents, usually expressed in natural language. In order to measure the retrieval performance (effectiveness) of computer systems designed to extract these documents from a data-base following a user's query, two metrics have been used, namely precision and recall.

Precision and Recall were defined in the context of IR (Baeza-Yates & Ribeiro-Neto, 1999), (Salton & McGill, 1983), (van Rijsbergen, 1979), but are used in summary evaluation as well. Figure 1 taken from Baeza-Yates and Ribeiro-Neto (1999) represents a set theory approach which defines these metrics.

Looking at Figure 1, they are defined as follows:

- **Precision:** The number of relevant documents returned by the system divided by the total number of documents retrieved by the system.

$$\text{Precision} = P = \frac{|S|}{|R|} \qquad (1)$$

- **Recall:** The number of relevant documents returned by the system divided by the total number of relevant document in the corpus.

$$\text{Recall} = R = \frac{|S|}{|A|} \qquad (2)$$

Some alternative measures were proposed over the years. As an example, a single measure, which combines precision and recall into a single score, was attempted. One such measure is *F-measure* (i.e. F_β), which is the harmonic mean of recall and precision (van Rijsbergen, 1979). It is computed as:

Figure 1. IR metrics Precision and recall (Adapted from Baeza-Yates & Ribeiro-Neto, 1999, page 75)

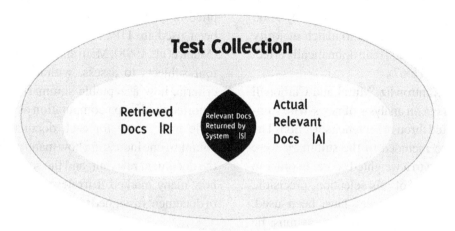

$$F_{\beta} = \frac{\left(\beta^2 + 1\right) \times R \times P}{R + \beta^2 \times P} \qquad (3)$$

where β is a weighting factor which assigns different relative importance to precision and recall. In other words, β is a parameter which quantifies the P/R ratio relating to a user who assigns β times as much importance to recall as precision. If β =1, we will have:

$$F_{\beta} = \frac{2 \times R \times P}{R + P} \qquad (4)$$

One can argue that *precision* measures how many of the answers that you get are right; and recall measures how many right answers you get. Findings in IR experiments show that there is usually a trade-off between them, i.e. as the precision of the system improves the recall gets worse and vice-versa. Hence, systems reports achieving 100% precision and recall are very rare.

As can be seen, precision and recall are very easy to calculate, making them motivating and attractive for many researchers. In text summarization in general, they are used when a summary is compared against a target summary, i.e. a *gold standard*, thus calculating the accuracy of this

comparison (see task-based evaluation section). Donaway, Drummey, & Mather (2000), for example, slightly modified the formulas:

$$\text{Precision} = \frac{J}{K} \qquad (5)$$

$$\text{Recall} = \frac{J}{M} \qquad (6)$$

$$F = \frac{2 \times J}{M + K} \qquad (7)$$

where M is the number of sentences in a document, J is the number of sentences a summary has in common with the document, and K is the number of sentences in a summary to be evaluated.

There are some examples of IR-based metrics applications. These include the work of Jing, McKeown, Barzilay and Elhadad (1998) who carried out an experiment to study the target-based evaluation method. In their results, they observed that the summary length affects the evaluation's consistency. Another observation reported was about the use of these metrics. They claimed: "... precision and recall are not the best measures for computing summary quality. This is due to the fact that a small change in the summary output (e.g. replacing 1 sentence with an equally good equivalent which happens not to match majority opinion [of the assessors]) can dramatically affect a system's score" (p.67).

Goldstein, Kantrowitz, Mittal and Carbonell (1999) carried out an analysis of news-wire summaries generated through sentence selection. The sentences to be included in the summary were ranked according to a weighted score. In order to evaluate the quality of this selection, precision, recall and F-measure curves have been used. They also pointed out that two aspects must be taken into account when dealing with evaluation of summarization systems, namely the compression ratios and the features of the document set.

Statistical-Based Metrics

Kappa is a statistical evaluation metric (Siegel & Castellan, 1988) which is widely accepted in the field of content analysis (Krippendorff, 1980), (Weber, 1990). Furthermore, Carletta (1996) argued for the adoption of this measure in the area of discourse and dialogue analysis as a reliability measure.

Kappa (i.e. K) is a coefficient of agreement and is defined by the formula (Siegel & Castellan, 1988):

$$K = \frac{P(A) - P(E)}{1 - P(E)} \qquad (8)$$

where $P(A)$ is the proportion of times that the judges agree and $P(E)$ is the proportion of times that we would expect them to agree by chance. $K = 0$ when there is no agreement other than that which would be expected by chance. $K = 1$ when there is total agreement.

It appears that with Kappa it is possible to measure the agreement between subjects by counting the proportion of times they agree or disagree on a decision.

However, one can ask: how Kappa can be applied in summary evaluation? Well, Kappa has been used in TIPSTER SUMMAC evaluation (Mani, et al., 1998). Mani and his colleagues asked four subjects to assess, without given explicit criteria, how acceptable summaries were. They reported the Kappa computation as: "construct a table with a row for each document, and two columns, one indicating how many judges marked the document relevant, and the second indicating how many marked it irrelevant. The proportion of documents assigned to the jth category (relevant/irrelevant) is, $p_j = \dfrac{C_j}{\left(N \times k\right)}$ where C_j is the total for column j, N is the number of documents and k is the number of judges. The expected proportion of agreement on category j is p^2_j, assuming subjects assign documents to categories at random. $P(E)$ is thus the sum of the expected proportion of agreement on relevant and the expected agreement on irrelevant" (p.19).

According to Mani and his colleagues, only on 36% of the data, was there unanimous agreement amongst these four subjects, which resulted in a Kappa coefficient of 0.24. They concluded based on the experimental results, that there was a large disagreement amongst these four subjects overall.

Another relevant work in text summarization which employs this metric is shown by Radev et al. (2003). In this paper they presented a large-scale meta-evaluation using a huge corpus consisting of: a) 100 million automatic summaries in English and Chinese; b) 10,000 manual extracts and abstracts; and c) 200 Million automatic document and summary retrievals using 20 queries. Performing extensive experiments, they concluded that Kappa offers significant advantages over precision and recall.

Content-Based Metrics

These metrics measure the similarity of the content of two texts: a reference text and a candidate text at a more fine-grained level than just sentences (Radev, et al., 2003).

The first metric, *Cosine*, belongs to a class of measures of semantic similarity and is best conceptualized as a measure of vector similarity. For example, if we want to calculate the semantic similarity between two words, we need to represent them as vectors in a multi-dimensional space, the so-called *vector space model*.

The *vector space model* is the most widely used information retrieval model (Salton, Wong, & Yang, 1975), (Salton & McGill, 1983). Documents and queries are expressed using a vector whose components are all the possible index terms (*t*). Each index term has an associated weight that indicates the importance of the index term in the document (or query). In other words, the document d_j and the query q are represented as t-dimensional vectors. Figure 2 shows documents and queries in a three dimensional space.

Basically the idea here is to observe the closeness between the documents and the query, i.e. the most relevant documents for a specific query are those which are represented by the vectors closest to the query. The closeness is computed by just choosing the documents which have the smallest angle with the query vector.

As we said earlier, *Cosine* is a measure of vector similarity. This means that in the vector space model, in order to evaluate the degree of similarity of a document d_j with regard to the query q, we compute the correlation between the two vectors. This calculation is performed by the cosine of the angle between these two vectors (i.e. d_j and q) using the following formula:

$$\cos\left(\vec{d_j}, \vec{q}\right) = \frac{\vec{d_j} \cdot \vec{q}}{\left|\vec{d_j}\right| \times \left|\vec{q}\right|} = \frac{\sum_{i=1}^{n} d_{j_i} \cdot q_i}{\sqrt{\sum_{i=1}^{n} d_{j_i}^2} \sqrt{\sum_{i=1}^{n} q_i^2}} \qquad (9)$$

Let us give an example of this calculation. In Figure 3 we show a vector space with two dimen-

sions. The entities represented in the space are the query q represented by the vector (0.4, 0.8), and two documents d_1 and d_2 with the following coordinates: (0.8, 0.3), and (0.2, 0.7) respectively. Applying the formula, we will have:

$$\cos\left(d_1, q\right) = \cos\left(\alpha_1\right)$$
$$= \frac{\left(0.8 \times 0.4\right) + \left(0.3 \times 0.8\right)}{\sqrt{0.8^2 + 0.3^2} \times \sqrt{0.4^2 + 0.8^2}} = \frac{0.56}{0.7641} = 0.73$$
$$(10)$$

$$\cos\left(d_2, q\right) = \cos\left(\alpha_2\right)$$
$$= \frac{\left(0.2 \times 0.4\right) + \left(0.7 \times 0.8\right)}{\sqrt{0.2^2 + 0.7^2} \times \sqrt{0.4^2 + 0.8^2}} = \frac{0.64}{0.6511} = 0.98$$
$$(11)$$

The results show that document d_2 is most similar to query q.

Cosine is applied in summary evaluation by evaluating the quality of a summary considering its similarity with the full document. It is called content-based metric because it considers the similarity of the content of the summary to the content of the full document. The metric gives the cosine of the angle between the two documents, i.e. full text and summary. Documents with high cosine similarity are deemed to be similar.

We will now describe two relevant studies which used the cosine metric.

Firstly, Donaway, Drummey and Mather (2000) employed this metric in order to compare it with traditional ones; that is, precision and recall metrics. They used fifteen documents from the TREC collection. Four expert judges have been asked to create extract summaries (*ground truths*) for each of the documents. Each *ground truth* summary should contain as many sentences as necessary to be an *ideal* summary. The judges selected those sentences. Donaway and his colleagues compared automatically generated summaries against the ideal *ground truths* summaries using the metrics described above and produced a ranking of the

Figure 2. Vector representation of words and queries in a 3D space

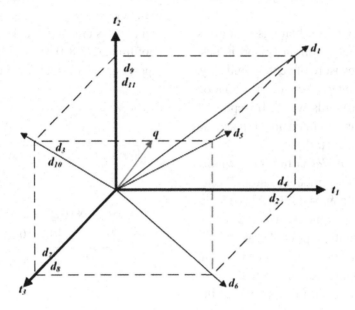

Figure 3. Example of vector space in 2D representation

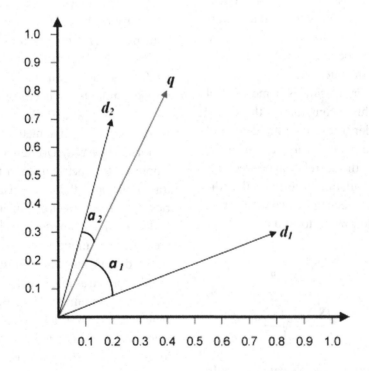

summaries based on the metric's score. They reported that content-based metrics (i.e. *cosine*) resulted in a high correlation between rankings in comparison to precision-recall metrics.

Secondly, interested in a comparative evaluation of evaluation measures for summarization, Saggion, Radev, Teufel and Lam (2002) presented a framework which assesses summaries in English and Chinese using three content-based metrics, namely, *cosine*, word overlap (i.e. *unigram/bigram*), and longest common subsequence (see the following metrics descriptions in this section). They pointed out that these metrics have advantages over precision-recall metrics.

Another content-based metric is *n-gram*[2] matching. *N-gram* is one of the oldest and most useful tools in language processing. It is a model of word prediction which was first proposed by Andrei Andreyevich Markov, a Russian mathematician, in 1913 (Markov, 1913). Markov developed what are now called Markov chains (*bigrams* and *trigrams*[3]) in order to predict if an upcoming letter in a text novel of Pushkin called *Eugene Onyegin* was a consonant (C) or a vowel (V). He classified twenty thousand letters as C or V and calculated whether the probability of a *bigram* or *trigram* for a given letter could be a vowel given the previous one or two letters.

Before continuing with *n-gram*'s definition and description, let us explain why this model or approach is one of the most useful tools. The task of guessing the next word is fundamental in areas like hand-writing recognition, speech recognition, statistical machine translation and spelling error detection (Jurafsky & Martin, 2000).

An *n-gram* model uses the previous *n* - 1 words to predict the next one. The task of predicting the next word can be formulated as a probability function *P*:

$$P\left(w_n \mid w_1 \cdots w_{n-1}\right) = \frac{P\left(w_1 \cdots w_n\right)}{P\left(w_1 \cdots w_{n-1}\right)} \qquad (12)$$

However, a problem appears here. It is not easy to calculate the probability of a word given a long sequence of preceding words. Imagine, for example, if we had to count the number of times every word occurs following every long string. This problem is resolved making a simplification or in other words, an assumption: we consider the probability of a word given only the single previous word (i.e. a bigram model). This assumption is called a Markov assumption, where we assume that we can predict the probability of some future unit without looking too far into the past. By generalizing the process, we have:

- **Bigram:** Looks one word behind: first order Markov model
- **Trigram:** Looks two words behind: second order Markov model
- **N-Gram:** Looks *n* – 1 words behind: *n* – 1st order Markov model

To illustrate this point we will discuss an example taken from Jurafsky and Martin (2000), where a speech-understanding system called Berkeley Restaurant is used. In this system, users ask questions about restaurants in Berkeley, California, and the system displays appropriate information from a database which contains information about local restaurants. Here is an example of a user query:

I want to eat British food.

Following Jurafsky and Martin (2000), Table 1 shows a sample of the bigram probabilities for words that can follow the word eat and other bigram probabilities. Those words were taken from the sentences spoken by the users.

The calculation of the probability for the user query is carried out by multiplying the appropriate bigram probabilities is shown in Box 1 (<s> is a special word which means "start of sentence" or beginning of the text).

Table 1. A sample of bigram probabilities (adapted from Jurafsky and Martin (2000), page 199)

eat on	0.16	eat Thai	0.03
eat some	0.06	eat breakfast	0.03
eat lunch	0.06	eat in	0.02
eat dinner	0.05	eat Chinese	0.02
eat at	0.04	eat Mexican	0.02
eat a	0.04	eat tomorrow	0.01
eat Indian	0.04	eat dessert	0.007
eat today	0.03	eat British	0.001
<s> I	0.25	I want	0.32
want to	0.65	to eat	0.26
British food	0.60		

Box 1. Bigram probabilities

```
P(I want to eat British food) = P(I | <s>) P(want | I) P(to | want) P(eat | to)
                                P(British | eat) P(food | British)
                              = 0.25 * 0.32 * 0.65 * 0.26
                              * 0.001 * 0.60
                              = 0.000008
```

As mentioned earlier, an *n-gram* probability is the conditional probability of a word given the previous *n* – 1 words. Sometimes some *n-grams* are missing, which suggests that there is an occurrence of a number of cases of zero probability, reflecting the data sparseness. Manning and Schutze (1999) justify this problem saying that "while a few words are common, the vast majority of words are very uncommon – and longer n-grams involving them are thus much rarer again" (p.198). The sparseness of the data is mainly the result of the limited size of the corpus.

Several techniques were developed in order to assign non-zero probability to these zero probability *n-grams*. This task, which is called smoothing, provides a better way of estimating some of the zero-probability and low-probability *n-grams* and assigning them non-zero values (Jurafsky & Martin, 2000). Commonly used smoothing algorithms include: Katz's Backing-off (Katz, 1987);

Good-Turing Discounting (Good, 1953); Witten-Bell Discounting (Bell, Cleary, & Witten, 1990), (Witten & Bell, 1991) and Deleted Interpolation (Chen & Goodman, 1998).

According to Lin and Och (2004a), *n-gram* based metrics have been in use for automatic evaluation of Machine Translation (MT), resulting in BLEU (Papineni, Roukos, Ward, & Zhu, 2001) and NIST scores (Doddington, 2002).

BLEU is a precision based metric (Papineni, Roukos, Ward, & Zhu, 2001) and is based on the notion that there may be several "perfect" translations of a given source sentence; following the same idea, there may also be several equally good summaries for a single source document.

Lin and Hovy (2003) used a similar concept to automatic summary evaluation. They have used accumulative *n-gram* matching scores computed automatically between ideal summaries and system generated summaries as a performance metric indicator. In their experiments, the authors have found that the *n-gram* co-occurrence metric correlated highly and positively with human evaluations. Just for comparison purposes, a BLEU score was also applied to the same experiment. However, they concluded that the application of BLEU evaluation procedures did not give good results.

Carrying out an in-depth study, Lin (2004) introduced a package called ROUGE, which stands for Recall-Oriented Understudy for Gisting Evaluation. ROUGE, in contrast to BLEU, is, as the name suggests, a recall based metric. The package contains four different metrics, namely ROUGE-N (N-gram Co-occurrence Statistics), ROUGE-L (Longest Common Subsequence), ROUGE-W (Weighted Longest Common Subsequence) and ROUGE-S (Skip-bigram Co-occurrence Statistics). The first three have been used as official metrics in DUC 2004, a large-scale summarization evaluation conference sponsored by NIST (National Institute of Standards and Technology). Following his intuition that ROUGE scores should correlate highly with human scores, Lin (2004) computed the correlation between those two scores using DUC 2001, DUC 2002 and DUC 2003 evaluation data, which contain human judgments. He concluded that ROUGE metrics could be used in automatic summary evaluation, especially in single document summarization tasks.

Due to the importance and relevance BLEU and ROUGE have in the context of this chapter, it is perhaps important to discuss the two metrics in some detail.

The BLEU Metric

This metric was proposed as an evaluation method of Machine Translation (MT) by Papineni, Roukos, Ward and Zhu (2001). According to the authors, "the closer a machine translation is to a professional human translation; the better it is" (p.1). Basically, two elements are considered in this context, namely, a reference translation and

a candidate translation. The main task is then to compare *n-grams* of the candidate with the *n-grams* of the reference translation and count the number of matches; the more the matches, the better the candidate translation. Also, the matches have two features such as: they are position-independent and for simplicity reasons, as pointed out by the authors, only *unigram* matches are computed.

BLEU, as defined by Papineni et al (2001), is a precision-based metric; or a "modified *n-gram* precision" (p.2), as they call it, and it is computed as follows:

$$p_n = \frac{\sum\limits_{C \in \{Candidates\}} \sum\limits_{n-gram \in C} Count_{clip}(n-gram)}{\sum\limits_{C \in \{Candidates\}} \sum\limits_{n-gram \in C} Count(n-gram)}$$

(13)

where $Count_{clip}(n\text{-}gram)$ is the maximum number of *n-grams* co-occurring in a candidate translation and a reference translation, and $Count(n\text{-}gram)$ is the number of *n-grams* in the candidate translation.

The reason why BLEU is a precision-based metric is explained by the authors as follows: in the formula above, the denominator is always the number of *n-grams* in the candidate translation instead of the reference(s). This causes a problem in computing recall as illustrated by the following example given by Papineni and his colleagues in their paper (p.5):

Candidate 1: I always invariably perpetually do.
Candidate 2: I always do.
Reference 1: I always do.
Reference 2: I invariably do.
Reference 3: I perpetually do.

As we can see, Candidate 1 recalls more words from the references, but it is not a good translation. Thus, recall computed over the set of all reference words is not a good measure.

In order to prevent very short translations that try to maximize their precision scores, BLEU includes a brevity penalty (BP):

$$BP = \begin{cases} 1 & if\ |c| > |r| \\ e^{(1-|r|/|c|)} & if\ |c| \leq |r| \end{cases} \qquad (14)$$

where |c| is the length of the candidate translation and |r| is the length of the reference translation.

BP is an exponential multiplicative factor that only penalizes candidates shorter than their reference translations. In other words, it favors candidate translations with sizes similar to references.

Finally, the BLEU metric is computed as follows:

$$BLEU = BP \cdot \exp\left(\sum_{n=1}^{N} w_n \log p_n\right) \qquad (15)$$

where N is the length of n-grams and w_n is a weighting factor[4].

Looking at the formula, first the geometric average of the modified n-gram precisions – p_n is computed, using n-grams up to length N and positive weights w_n summing to one; and then the result is multiplied by the brevity penalty factor explained above.

The ROUGE Metric

ROUGE is a kind of package used to evaluate summaries, and was proposed by Lin & Hovy (2003), and Lin (2004). It includes several automatic evaluation methods that measure the similarity between summaries, namely, ROUGE-N, ROUGE-L, ROUGE-W and ROUGE-S. We will describe each of them in the following paragraphs.

ROUGE-N (N-gram Co-occurrence Statistics): Is an n-gram recall-based metric between a candidate summary and a set of reference summaries, and is computed as follows:

$$ROUGE - N$$
$$= \frac{\displaystyle\sum_{S\in\{reference\ summaries\}} \sum_{gram_n \in S} Count_{match}\left(gram_n\right)}{\displaystyle\sum_{S\in\{reference\ summaries\}} \sum_{gram_n \in S} Count\left(gram_n\right)} \qquad (16)$$

where n is the length of the *n-gram*; $gram_n$ is the number of *n-grams* co-occurring in a candidate summary and a set of reference summaries; and $Count_{match}(gram_n)$ is the maximum number of *n-grams* co-occurring in a candidate summary and a set of reference summaries.

Looking at the formula above, especially in the denominator, we see that it contains the total sum of the number of *n-grams* occurring in the reference summary. ROUGE scores computed are recall-based, whereas BLEU is a precision-based metric; BLEU's denominator is always the number of *n-grams* in the candidate translation rather than the reference(s).

ROUGE-N can also be calculated when one uses multiple references. If this is the case, a pairwise summary level ROUGE-N between a candidate summary s and every reference, r_i, in the reference set is computed. As result, the maximum of pairwise summary-level ROUGE-N scores as the final multiple reference ROUGE-N score is taken. This can be expressed as:

$$ROUGE\text{-}N_{multi} = \arg\max_i ROUGE\text{-}N(r_i, s) \qquad (17)$$

ROUGE-L (Longest Common Subsequence): Is based on a string matching problem of finding the *longest common subsequence* (LCS) of two strings (Cormen, Leiserson, Rivest, & Stein, 2001). The LCS formal definition is as follows:

- A *sequence* is a list $X = \left(x_1, x_2, \cdots, x_n\right)$, (e.g. $\left(A, G, C, G, T, A, G\right)$); or a list $Y = \left(y_1, y_2, \cdots, y_n\right)$, (e.g. $\left(G, T, C, A, G, A\right)$).

- A *subsequence* of X is an ordered sublist of X (e.g. (G,C,T,A), however, not (T,C,G)).

- A common subsequence of two sequences X and Y is a subsequence of both of them, e.g.

$$(G,C,A) \, or \, (G,C,G,A)$$
$$or \, (G,T,A,G) \, or \, (G,C,A,G)$$

- The LCS, or *longest common subsequence* of X and Y is their longest possible common subsequence. In the example, since no common subsequence of length 5 exists there are 3 LCS's:

$$(G,C,G,A) \, or \, (G,T,A,G) \, or \, (G,C,A,G).$$

LCS has applications in several fields, such as:

- **Molecular Biology**: Where DNA sequences (genes) can be represented as sequences of four letters *ACGT*, for example, corresponding to the four submolecules forming DNA. One way of computing how similar two sequences are is to find the length of their longest common subsequence.

- **File Comparison**: In the Unix operating system there is a program called "diff," which is used to compare two different versions of the same file, and to determine what changes have been made to the file. The program works by finding a longest common subsequence of the lines of the two files; any line in the subsequence has not been changed, so what it displays is the remaining set of lines that have changed. In this case each line of a file is a single complicated character in a string.

- **Lexicon Construction for Translation**: Melamed (1995) used LCS in identifying cognate candidates during construction of N-best translation lexicon from parallel text (i.e. bitext). In order to measure the cognateness between a pair of words, he calculated the ratio between the length of their longest (not necessarily contiguous) common subsequence and the length of the longer word, which he called LCSR (*Longest Common Subsequence Ratio*). Melamed (1995) used as an example words in French and English, e.g. *gouvernement* (French), which is 12 characters long, has 10 characters that appear in the same order in *government* (English). Thus, the LCSR for these two words is 10/12.

- **Automatic Summarization Evaluation:** Saggion, Radev, Teufel and Lam (2002) proposed a framework for evaluating summaries in English and Chinese using a normalized pairwise LCS in order to compare the similarity between the sentences of two texts using the following formula:

$$2 \times lcs(X,Y) = len(x) + len(Y) - edit_{di}(X,Y) \quad (18)$$

where X and Y are the sequences; *lcs(X,Y)* is the longest common subsequence between X and Y; *len(X)* and *len(Y)* are the length of string X and Y, respectively; and $edit_{di}(X,Y)$ is the minimum number of deletions and insertions needed to transform X into Y (Crochemore & Rytter, 2003).

ROUGE-L is applied in two different levels, *sentence-level* and *summary-level*. For details, please refer to Lin (2004).

Sentence-Level: Here a sentence of a summary is viewed as a sequence of words and the argument is that the longer the LCS of two summary sentences is, the more similar the two summaries are. Thus, in order to estimate the similarity between a reference summary X of length *m* and a candidate summary Y of length *n*, a LCS-based F-measure which is ROUGE-L, is defined as follows:

$$F_{lcs} = \frac{\left(1 + \beta^2\right) R_{lcs} P_{lcs}}{R_{lcs} + \beta^2 P_{lcs}} \tag{19}$$

Earlier, we pointed out that F-measure combines precision and recall into a single metric and for the specific case of , it represents their harmonic mean. Consequently, the composite factors (i.e. LCS-based recall and LCS-based precision) are:

$$R_{lcs} = \frac{LCS\left(X, Y\right)}{m} \tag{20}$$

$$P_{lcs} = \frac{LCS\left(X, Y\right)}{n} \tag{21}$$

where $LCS(X,Y)$ is the length of the *longest common subsequence* between X and Y, and β is a weighting factor which assigns different relative importance to precision and recall. In other words, β is a parameter which quantifies the *P/R* ratio relating to a user who assigns β times as much importance to recall than precision. In DUC, $\beta \rightarrow \infty$, i.e. β is set to a very big number. For that reason, only R_{lcs} is considered. Note that when $X = Y$, ROUGE-L=1; and when $LCS(X,Y) = 0$, i.e. there is nothing in common between X and Y, *ROUGE-L=0*.

Summary-Level: Analogously, when LCS-based F-measure metric is applied to summary-level, the union LCS matches between a reference summary sentence (r_i), and every candidate summary sentence (c_j) is taken. Thus, the computation of the summary-level LCS-based F-measure, given a reference summary of u sentences containing a total of m words and a candidate summary of v sentences containing a total of n words, is:

$$R_{lcs} = \frac{\sum_{i=1}^{u} LCS_{\cup}\left(r_i, C\right)}{m} \tag{22}$$

$$P_{lcs} = \frac{\sum_{i=1}^{u} LCS_{\cup}\left(r_i, C\right)}{n} \tag{23}$$

$$F_{lcs} = \frac{\left(1 + \beta^2\right) R_{lcs} P_{lcs}}{R_{lcs} + \beta^2 P_{lcs}} \tag{24}$$

where $LCS \cup (r_i, C)$ is the LCS score of the union *longest common subsequence* between reference sentence r_i and candidate summary C. Once more, β is set to a very big number in DUC, and only R_{lcs} is considered.

For instance, if $r_i = w_1\ w_2\ w_3\ w_4\ w_5$, and C contains two sentences: $c_1 = w_1\ w_2\ w_6\ w_7\ w_8$ and $c_2 = w_1\ w_3\ w_8\ w_9\ w_5$, then *the longest common subsequence* of r_i and c_1 is "$w_1\ w_2$" and the *longest common subsequence* of r_i and c_2 is "$w_1\ w_3\ w_5$." The union *longest common subsequence* of r_i, c_1, and c_2 is "$w_1\ w_2\ w_3\ w_5$" and $LCS \cup (r_i, C) = 4/5$.

ROUGE-W (Weighted Longest Common Subsequence): This metric has the function to improve the LCS when there are consecutive matches like (example extracted from Lin (2004)):

- Let $X = \left\{\underline{A}\ \underline{B}\ \underline{C}\ \underline{D}\ E\ F\ G\right\}$ be a reference sequence.
- Let $Y_1 = \left\{\underline{A}\ \underline{B}\ \underline{C}\ \underline{D}\ H\ I\ K\right\}$ and $Y_2 = \left\{\underline{A}\ H\ \underline{B}\ K\ \underline{C}\ I\ \underline{D}\right\}$ be two candidate sequences.

If we compute ROUGE-L, Y_1 and Y_2 will have the same score. Because Y_1 has consecutive matches, Y_1 will be chosen. A question arises: how to choose Y_1 rather than Y_2? This can be resolved by a technique called dynamic programming (Cormen, Leiserson, Rivest, & Stein, 2001).

The basic idea of this technique is to solve a problem using the following three-step process:

1. Break down the problem into smaller subproblems;

2. Solve these problems optimally using this three-step process recursively;

3. Use these optimal solutions to construct an optimal solution for the original problem.

The subproblems are, themselves, solved by dividing them into sub-subproblems, and so on, until we reach some simple case that is easy to solve. In each breaking down step the solutions to problems we have already solved should be saved (i.e., *stored*). Then, if we need to solve the same problem later, we can retrieve and use our already-computed solution. This approach is called *memoization*. If we are sure we won't need a particular solution anymore, we can throw it away to save space.

Lin (2004) applied dynamic programming using a bi-dimensional array c^5 which ends at word x_i of X and word y_j of Y, in order to store (*memoize*) the length of consecutive matches encountered so far, and called it weighted LCS (WLCS). A variable k has been used to indicate the length of the current consecutive matches ending at words x_i and y_j. Thus, like in ROUGE-L, an F-measure metric based on WLCS can be computed as follows, given a sequence X of length m and a sequence Y of length n:

$$R_{wlcs} = f^{-1}\left(\frac{WLCS(X,Y)}{f(m)}\right) \quad (25)$$

$$P_{wlcs} = f^{-1}\left(\frac{WLCS(X,Y)}{f(n)}\right) \quad (26)$$

$$F_{wlcs} = \frac{\left(1+\beta^2\right)R_{wlcs}P_{wlcs}}{R_{wlcs}+\beta^2 P_{wlcs}} \quad (27)$$

where f^{-1} is the inverse function of $f(k)=k^2$ (Lin preferred to use a close inverse form in order to normalize the final ROUGE-W score: $f^{-1}(k)=k^{1/2}$); β is a weighting factor which assigns different relative importance to precision and recall.

ROUGE-W is then the WLCS-based F-measure, shown above. Using the equation above in the example given in the beginning of this metric explanation, the ROUGE-W scores for the sequences Y_1 and Y_2 are 0.571 and 0.286 respectively. Consequently, Y_1 would be ranked higher than Y_2 using WLCS.

ROUGE-S (Skip-Bigram Co-Occurrence Statistics): Gappy bigrams or *Skip-bigrams* are pairs of words in any sentence order, which allow gaps. *Skip-bigram* co-occurrence statistics measure the overlap of *skip-bigrams* between a candidate summary and a set of reference summaries. The following example, taken from Lin's paper (Lin, 2004), illustrates how the metric works. Supposing that S_1 is the reference summary sentence, and S_2, S_3 and S_4 are the candidate summary sentences:

S_1: Police killed the gunman
S_2: Police kill the gunman
S_3: The gunman kill police
S_4: The gunman police killed

In this case, each sentence has a combination of $C_2^4 = 6$ *skip-bigrams*:

$$C_2^4 = \frac{4!}{2!\times(4-2)!} = \frac{4!}{\left(2!\times 2!\right)} = \frac{24}{4} = 6$$

that is,

S_1 **skip-bigrams**: (*police killed, police the, police gunman, killed the, killed gunman, the gunman*) = 6

S_2 **skip-bigram** **matches with** S_1: (*police the, police gunman, the gunman*) = 3

S_3**skip-bigram matches with**S_1: (*the gunman*) = 1

S_4 **skip-bigram** **matches with** S_1: (*the gunman, police killed*) = 2

Assuming that X is a reference summary and Y is a candidate summary, the *skip-bigram*-based F-measure is computed as follows:

$$R_{skip2} = \frac{SKIP2\left(X,Y\right)}{C\left(m,2\right)} \quad (28)$$

$$P_{skip2} = \frac{SKIP2\left(X,Y\right)}{C\left(n,2\right)} \quad (29)$$

$$F_{skip2} = \frac{\left(1+\beta^2\right)R_{skip2}P_{skip2}}{R_{skip2}+\beta^2 P_{skip2}} \quad (30)$$

where $SKIP2(X,Y)$ is the number of *skip-bigram* matches between X and Y, β controls the relative importance of P_{skip2} and R_{skip2}, and C is the combination function.

Considering the four sentences example taken from Lin (2004), with $\beta = 1$ and S_1 as the reference summary, the ROUGE-S score for S_2 is 0.5; S_3 is 0.167; and S_4 is 0.333. Hence, S_2 is better than S_3 and S_4, and S_4 is better than S_3. Based on this figures, Lin affirmed:

This result is more intuitive than using BLEU-2 and ROUGE-L. One advantage of skip-bigram vs. BLEU is that it does not require consecutive matches but is still sensitive to word order. Comparing skip-bigram with LCS, skip-bigram counts all in-order matching word pairs while LCS only counts one longest common subsequence (p.6).

Sometimes some spurious matches like "the the" or "of in," can appear and might be counted as valid matches. To avoid these matches, the maximum skip distance, d_{skip}, can be limited between two in-order words that are allowed to form a *skip-bigram*. For example, if d_{skip} is set to 0 then ROUGE-S is equal to the *bigram* overlap F-measure. If d_{skip} is set to 4 then only word pairs of at most 4 words distant can form *skip-bigrams*.

The skip distance can be adjusted by counting the *skip-bigram* matches, $SKIP2(X,Y)$, within the maximum skip distance, and replacing the denominator $C(m,2)$ of R_{skip2} equation; and $C(n,2)$ of P_{skip2} equation, with the actual numbers of within distance *skip-bigrams* from the reference and the candidate respectively. ROUGE-S with the maximum skip distance of N is called ROUGE-SN.

ROUGE-SU (An extension of ROUGE-S): ROUGE-S presents a problem. No credit is given to a candidate sentence if it does not have any word pair co-occurring with its reference. Let us consider the following example, taken from Lin[44]:

S_5: Gunman the killed police

In this case, the ROUGE-S score for this sentence is zero. Observing well, S_5 is the exact reverse of S_1 and there is no *skip-bigram* match between them. In order to avoid this, ROUGE-S can be extended with the addition of *unigram* as counting unit. This extended version is then called ROUGE-SU.

Recently, two more content-based metrics have been proposed: Basic Elements (BE) (Hovy, Lin, & Zhou, 2005) (Hovy, Lin, Zhou, & Fukumoto, 2006) and The Pyramid Method (Nenkova & Passonneau, 2004) (Nenkova, Passonneau, & McKeown, 2007). We will describe them in the next paragraphs.

The BE Metric

This metric uses smaller meaningful (semantic) units of information called Basic Elements. These units are defined as a triple (i.e. *head | modifier | relation |*):

- The *head* of a major syntactic constituent (e.g. noun, verb, adjective or adverbial phrase) and
- Two other arguments *(modifier* and *relation)* which are dependents of that head (Hovy, Lin, & Zhou, 2005) (Hovy, Lin, Zhou, & Fukumoto, 2006).

The triple mentioned in the definition is, in fact, a kind of a structure which aims to handle the semantic relationship of terms within a sentence. And doing so, the information matching between two sentences that have the same meaning (e.g. alternative phrasing), although are expressed in different ways, becomes easier.

In order to extract these semantic units automatically, the BE framework is composed by four modules:

- **BE Breakers:** Create individual BE units given a text
- **BE Scorers:** Assign scores to each BE unit individually
- **BE Matcher:** Rates the similarity of two BE units
- **BE Score Integrators:** Produce a score given a list rated BE units

The workflow is simple. The inputs to the system are the reference summaries, and the BE Breakers module produces a chosen list of BEs, which are ranked from the most important to the least important.

In a similar way, the candidate summaries are submitted to this module as well; and the candidates BEs are compared against the reference BEs for scoring.

The authors identified some matching strategies which needed to be studied and implemented. The first two are already implemented. They are:

- **Lexical Identity:** Words should match exactly, exclusive of alteration
- **Lemma Identity:** Words' root forms must match (Wordnet is used for obtaining the root forms)
- **Synonym Identity:** Words and their synonyms (any) match (Wordnet is used for obtaining synonyms)
- **Distributional Similarity:** Words similarity is calculated through the cosine distance using the Clustering By Committee (CBC) package (Lin & Pantel, 2002)
- Phrasal Paraphrase Matching (approximate)
- **Semantic Generalization Match:** BE words are substituted by semantic gener-

alizations (e.g. "Mother Theresa" by "human") and matched afterwards (Named Entity Recognition and WordNet is used for the generalization)

The method's performance was assessed using correlation. In order to do so, the authors compared BE against ROUGE, Pyramid Method (it will be described in the next section) and the responsiveness score used by NIST in DUC 2005 (Dang, 2005). Based on the results, they concluded that BE correlated more highly with the responsiveness score than the Pyramid Method. They used the Spearman and Pearson correlation coefficient for the evaluation procedure. However, BE had a slightly higher Pearson correlation than ROUGE, but ROUGE outperformed slightly better using the Spearman correlation.

The Pyramid Method Metric

Departing from the notion that there is no single best model summary, Nenkova, Passonneau and McKeown (2007) proposed this metric. The central idea of this method is that the information contained in the reference texts is not compared on a sentence level; rather, on a smaller or clausal level which was defined by the authors as Summarization Content Units (SCUs). In order to clarify the SCU definition, we will provide an example, adapted from (Nenkova & Passonneau, 2004). There are four reference summaries taken from the DUC 2003 dataset. According to the authors, after a kind of an annotation procedure, two SCU's could be identified, and they are denoted by the underlining in Box 2. The first SCU indicates that *two Libians were accused/indicted (of the Lockerbie bombing)* and the second SCU indicates that this *indictment occurred in 1991*.

After the SCUs' identification, a kind of a weighted inventory, in the form of a pyramid, is created and is shown in Figure 4. This inventory is based on the SCUs appearance in the reference summaries. In other words, if a SCU appears in

Box 2.

Reference 1 – In 1998 <u>two Libyans indicted in 1991</u> for the Lockerbie bombing were still in Libya.

Reference 2 – <u>Two Libyans were indicted in 1991</u> for blowing up a Pan Am jumbo jet over Lockerbie, Scotland in 1988.

Reference 3 – <u>Two Libyans, accused</u> by the United States and Britain of bombing a New York bound Pan Am jet over Lockerbie, Scotland in 1988, killing 270 people, for 10 years were harbored by Libya who claimed the suspects could not get a fair trial in America or Britain.

Reference 4 – <u>Two Libyan suspects were indicted in 1991</u>.

all reference summaries, it is given the highest weight (i.e. the total number of reference summaries). But, if a SCU appears only in one summary, the lowest weight of 1 is assigned to it. Consequently, the pyramid has tiers (i.e. layers) equal to the number of reference summaries. In our case, the pyramid has 4 tiers, also referred to as "pyramid of order 4," the first SCU (*two Libians were accused/indicted*) has weight of 4 (*w=4*), and the second SCU (*indictment occurred in 1991*) has weight of 3 (*w=3*).

The pyramid formation came from the notion that the tiers "descend" with the highest weight SCUs appearing at the top, and the SCUs with lowest weight appearing in the bottom tiers. And based on that, the degree of informativeness of a

Figure 4. Example of the pyramid with SCUs identified for the top two tiers (Adapted from Nenkova & Passonneau, 2004)

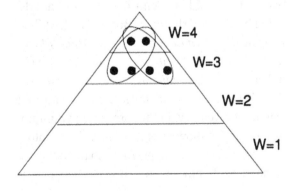

summary, or in other words, the Pyramid score (P), can be computed as the ratio of the sum of the weights of the SCUs (D) to the sum of the weights of an optimal summary with the same number of SCUs (Max). Such scores range from 0 to 1, with higher scores indicating that relatively more of the content is as highly weighted as possible. The authors pointed out that a summary is considered optimal if it contains more (or even all) SCUs from the top tiers and less from the lower tiers, as long as the length allows. Those SCUs from top tiers can be understood of as the most salient information from the text as all (or most) of the reference summaries include this information. The equation is given below:

$$P = \frac{D}{Max} \qquad (31)$$

From this equation, we will illustrate how D and Max are calculated.

$$D = \sum_{i=1}^{n} w_{T_i} \times D_i \qquad (32)$$

where the pyramid has *n* tiers, with tier T_n on the top, and T_1 on the bottom. w_{Ti} is the weight and D_i is the number of SCUs in the candidate summary that appear in T_i.

$$Max = \sum_{i=j+1}^{n} w_{T_i} \times |T_i| + j \times \left(X - \sum_{i=j+1}^{n} |T_i| \right)$$
(33)

where $j = \max_i \left(\sum_{t=i}^{n} |T_i| \geq X \right)$

In the equation above, j is the index of the lowest tier an optimally informative summary will draw from. X is the summary size in SCUs, $|T_i|$ is the number of SCUs in tier T_i.

This method presents an advantage. It relies on semantic matching rather than exact string matching for scoring; that is, the ideas or concepts conveyed in the text are matched rather than exact words. Unfortunately, there is a drawback. It is not completely automatic (i.e. semi-automatic), which involves a lot of human tasks, namely, the reference summaries creation, the SCU annotation procedure, and the comparison of reference SCUs with candidate summaries. As a consequence, the method becomes time consuming, expensive (in case of financial compensation to the people involved) and labor intensive.

Brief Conclusions

The groundwork for this chapter has now been established. We have reviewed approaches regarding summary evaluation, and also certain evaluation metrics which have been used so far. Nevertheless, some comments about this review must be made.

In terms of summary evaluation, following a categorization given by Tucker (1999), we have reviewed four categories, namely, direct evaluation, target-based evaluation, task-based evaluation and automatic evaluation. These categories revealed several challenging problems which provided some insights, and are discussed below.

Firstly, if one wants to carry out a large-scale evaluation where human experts are required to make judgments of a large number of summaries, and if one is expecting to obtain meaningful results,

this will have, as consequence, an increasing of the cost.

Secondly, target-based comparison is based on the assumption that the target ideally should contain some underlying qualities such as *coherence, readability,* and *representativeness.* This is not the possible; and it has pointed out by Tucker (1999):

... not all desirable properties of a summary can be captured in a target. Whereas criteria of importance or representativeness can be approximated as, say, coverage of key sentences or concepts, it is difficult to see how one could do something similar for criteria of cohesiveness or clarity. So typically, target-based comparison evaluation is restricted to issues of summary content, not its expression (p. 55).

Thirdly, for summaries evaluated in a real life situation, a clearly set out task has to be created in order to model this situation. However, it is not easy to create such tasks and put them into an experiment, because the task design can be biased towards genre, length of text or a particular summarization technology; this must be avoided. Also, it is complicated to design a task according to the users' or application's needs. In the Document Understanding Conferences (DUC, 2004), for instance, we can see how carefully the tasks were planned and designed.

Finally, several issues need to be resolved when one wants to evaluate summaries. The review has suggested that if we could completely automate the process of summary evaluation, making it cheaper and faster while retaining some of the advantages of the approaches when we discussed the most relevant summary evaluation metrics, progress will be achieved; this has motivated this chapter.

The evaluation metrics reviewed show a constant preoccupation amongst researchers in evaluating their summarization systems. The great diversity indicates the importance that has been given to this topic. We can classify the metrics in two broad categories: classical metrics and modern metrics.

The classical metrics (Recall, Precision, Kappa and Cosine) have been used extensively over the last four decades. Even though these metrics had their origins in IR and Statistics, they could perfectly be adapted to the summarization field due to the facility of computerized implementation. They can be considered as standard. The very frequent use of these metrics has shown that researchers wanted to judge the performance of their systems, and to do so, focused their efforts on improving the systems.

The modern metrics, *n-gram* based metrics, originated from a concept conceived in 1913 by Markov (1913); and currently they have been used widely in MT and Summary Evaluation, indicating, a central trend.

BLEU, for example, proposed in a seminal paper by Papineni *et al.* (2001), has as main objective to help in automatic evaluation of MT. However, BLEU can be extended to other areas, as the authors argue: ".. we believe that our approach of using the *n-gram* similarity of a candidate to a set of references has wider applicability than MT; for example, it could be extended to the evaluation of natural language generation and summarization systems" (p.9, italics added). We report later in this chapter an experiment comparing our metric's performance with BLEU.

ROUGE 2004, the metric which has been adopted by the summarisation research community. In fact, ROUGE is an adaptation of BLEU's concept – the *best match length*, which is the reference translation length most similar to the candidate translation. In a similar vein, Lin and Hovy (2003), and later Lin (2004) implemented the concept: the more similar a summary made by a computer is to a human expert summary, the better it is.

Finally, the last two metrics reviewed (i.e. Pyramid and BE) presented a concern, which were built upon the attainments and drawbacks of the previous methods – the idea of semantic fragments

of text with variable length and aiming to be as reliable in assessing the quality of summaries as humans normally do.

In the next section, we will thoroughly describe our automatic evaluation metric – VERT, which has some motivations derived from BLEU and ROUGE.

MAIN FOCUS OF THE CHAPTER

The Proposed Method

This section presents a detailed description of our evaluation method. We have developed a method, called VERT-F, which deals with the matching between sentences, based in content bearing words using a graph theory method. This graph theory method, based on bipartite matching, leads to the well-known precision and recall that form the basis of IR-metrics.

VERT-F: N-Gram Matching

N-gram matching procedures are used typically in linguistic pattern recognition models and we have discussed earlier in this chapter two major metrics, (i.e. ROUGE and BLEU), that are based on *n-gram* matching. There is a considerable interest in machine translation in this context when cross-lingual patterns between source and target translation are matched to assess the effectiveness of a translation system.

Turian, Shen and Melamed (2003), for instance, proposed an interesting machine translation evaluation procedure which inspired us in the development of VERT-F. The idea is based on the intersection of two texts[6] (i.e. the reference and the candidate) and what these texts have in common. A comparison is then carried out using a grid which presents the commonality between these two texts. In order to illustrate this comparison, consider two texts:

Figure 5. Bitext grid showing the relationship between a reference text (X axis) and its corresponding candidate text (Y axis)

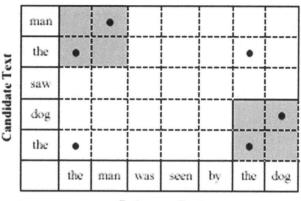

Reference Text: The man was seen by the dog
Candidate Text: The dog saw the man

The common unigrams are: the, man, dog; and the bigrams are: the man, the dog.

This is shown in the bitext grid in Figure 5. If a word appears in the reference text and in the candidate text, there is a hit; represented as a bullet in Figure 5.

The first suggestion then would be to count the number of hits in the grid. However, there is a risk of double-counting, that is, words that appear more than once in both texts. See the word "the" in Figure 5, for instance. In order to avoid double-counting, a subset of the hits is taken such that there are no hits in the same row or column. Double-counting is avoided through the use of the "maximum bipartite matching problem" (MBMP), which is discussed in graph theory (Cormen, Leiserson, Rivest, & Stein, 2001), (The Open University, 2001). In graph theory, a bipartite graph is a special graph where the set of vertices can be divided into two disjoint sets with two vertices of the same set never sharing an edge. The problem is formalized as follows:

Definition: Let G=(V, E) be a bipartite graph in which V can be partitioned into two sets V_1 and V_2 such that $V=V_1 \cup V_2$. A matching M on G is a subset of the edges of G such that each vertex in G is incident with no more than one edge in M. A maximum matching is a perfect matching between vertices of G, that is, a subgraph which pairs every vertex with exactly one other vertex.

In order to illustrate the working of the MBMP, consider the following example adapted from (The Open University, 2001): five people have each won a holiday to one of five resorts – Blackpool, Cannes, Edinburgh, Paris and San Francisco. Of the winners, one will go only to UK, one will not go to France or Scotland, two will not go to UK and the fifth will go only to San Francisco. The bipartite graph representing the winners and their destinations is shown in Figure 6.

Let us suppose that one wants to determine whether it is possible for each winner to go to a different resort by finding a maximum bipartite matching in this graph. By visual inspection and according to the definition given above, one maximum matching for this example is represented in Figure 7 (the thickened edges are a maximum matching).

Figure 6. A bipartite graph example

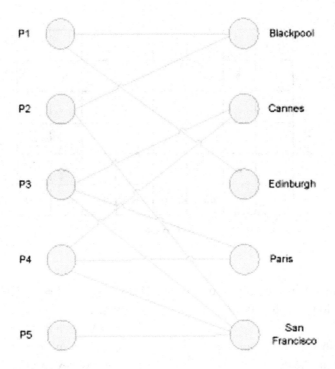

Figure 7. Maximum matching example

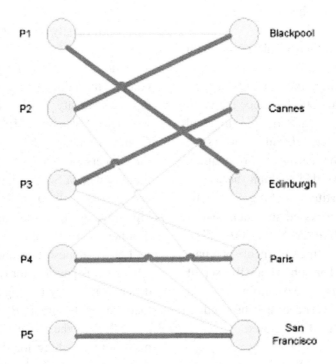

Figure 8. Graph representation of the example shown in Figure 5

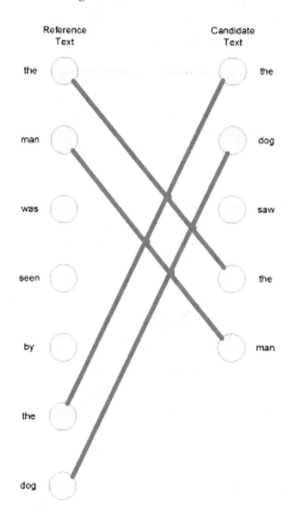

The bitext grid for the candidate and reference text (see Figure 5) now can be represented using MBMP as in Figure 8.

From the definition of the *maximum bipartite matching problem*, the maximum match size (MMS) of a bitext is the size of any maximum matching for that bitext. The MMS in Figure 8 includes two vertices between the four instances for the nodes in the graph, together with one vertex each for man and dog nodes.

One can show that the MMS value divided by the length of the candidate text (C) or divided by the length of the reference text (R) will lead to the recall and precision metrics. Recall and precision are the most common metrics used to evaluate NLP systems ((Salton & McGill, 1983), (van Rijsbergen, 1979)), as we described in a earlier section. According to Salton and McGill, and van Rijsbergen, when one compares a set of candidate items Y to a set of reference items X, we will have:

$$recall\left(Y\middle|X\right) = \frac{\left|X \cap Y\right|}{\left|X\right|}$$

$$precision\left(Y\middle|X\right) = \frac{\left|X \cap Y\right|}{\left|Y\right|} \tag{34}$$

Taking the idea of the intersection of a pair of texts described earlier, and applying the recall and precision definition to it, we will obtain, respectively:

$$recall\left(Candidate\middle|\text{Reference}\right)$$
$$= \frac{MMS\left(Candidate, \text{Reference}\right)}{\left|\text{Reference}\right|} \tag{35}$$

$$precision\left(Candidate\middle|\text{Reference}\right)$$
$$= \frac{MMS\left(Candidate, \text{Reference}\right)}{\left|Candidate\right|} \tag{36}$$

We will use the *f-measure*, as our proposed metric, which is a combination of precision and recall:

$$F_\beta = \frac{\left(1 + \beta^2\right) \times precision \times recall}{\beta^2 \times precision + recall} \tag{37}$$

and for $\beta = 1$ we will have:

$$F_\beta = \frac{2 \times precision \times recall}{\left(precision + recall\right)} \tag{38}$$

In fact, *f-measure* is the harmonic mean of the recall and precision metrics.

The Computational Framework

We have implemented the metric described in the previous sections and incorporated it into a general framework. Our new automatic summary evaluation system is called VERT, Valuation using Enhanced Rationale Technique, comprises VERT-F. The idea for the name is derived from two previous systems, namely BLEU[7] (Papineni, Roukos, Ward, & Zhu, 2001) and ROUGE[8] (Lin, 2004).

VERT consists of two main components: a *Tokenizer* for text pre-processing and selection of candidate terms for evaluation and an *Evaluator* which processes the candidate terms according to the metric chosen by the user. There is also an additional component called *Auxiliary Modules*, which contains a *Stopword Remover* and a *Stemmer*. Figure 9 provides an overview of the VERT system architecture.

The first component, the *Tokenizer*, contains three modules:

- **Sentence Boundary Identifier:** This module identifies sentences delimiters with the following regular expression pattern: [! | . | ." | .' | ?]+
- **Word Boundary Identifier:** Similarly, this module also identifies any word delimited by the previous pattern. Some exceptions to this rule are applied in abbreviations, such as full stops in social titles (e.g. Rev., Prof., Gen.); in qualifications (e.g. Ph.D., M.D.); in place names (e.g. U.K., U.S.A.) and in initials for first and middle names (e.g. J. B. Hall)
- **Word Frequency Counter:** This module collects and extracts the words or terms, updating their frequency counts.

In the second component, the *Evaluator*, the VERT-F algorithm is performed. Finally, the additional component – *Auxiliary Modules*, comprises two modules:

- **Stopword Remover:** This module identifies and eliminates frequently occurring words (the so-called closed class words), such as some verbs (e.g. *be*, *have*, *should*), conjunctions (e.g. *and*, *because*), pronouns (e.g. *nobody*, *anybody*) and determiners (e.g. *the*, *a/an*).
- **Stemmer:** This module reduces the terms to their root form. In order to accomplish this, the module makes use of morphological and derivational transformation rules. For example, plurals of nouns like *cats – cat*; and derivational endings in verbs such as *ing*, *es*, *s*, *ed*, are transformed and/or removed.

VERT Experiment

The major goal of the experiments reported in this section, is to investigate the performance of a new procedure for summary evaluation, VERT, described in earlier sections. In addition, the evaluation procedure must not depend on human intervention; it should be carried out automatically. This is essential because one of the aims of this chapter is to propose a new method to evaluate summaries, which would not be viable if the analysis was manual.

For us, the efficacy of an automatic evaluation metric must be assessed through correlation comparison between the automatic metric scores and human scores. This means that the automatic scores should correlate highly with human scores (Lin, 2004). If they do correlate, we can affirm that the automatic metric can be used to evaluate summaries. We believe that this criterion forms the fundamental *ground-truth* for the evaluation of our metric (i.e. VERT-F). As Mani (2000) argues:

Figure 9. VERT system architecture

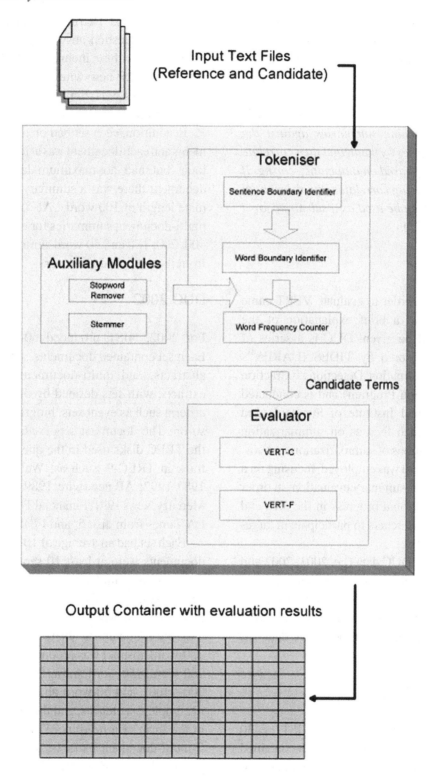

There are a number of considerations that need to be kept in mind when using automatic comparison measures. Even when passages are extracted, there are task-specific considerations that will warrant a human comparison of the machine summary against the reference summary. Luckily, there is a way around this dilemma. Ideally, one would compare the machine summaries against the reference summaries by hand, and then correlate it with a measure based on automatic scoring. If the automatic scoring correlates with the manual method, it can then be used as a substitute for it on this task (p.233).

Data Set

The data used in order to evaluate VERT came from DUC. First, a brief explanation of the DUC's role will be given. DUC is a series of conferences sponsored by TIDES (DARPA[9]'s Translingual Information Detection, Extraction and Summarization Program) and is conducted by NIST (National Institute of Standards and Technology), which focuses on summarization and in the evaluations of summarization systems. In 2000, a road map was employed, focusing on a long-term plan for summary evaluation, in order to stimulate additional progress in the area and also to enable researchers to participate in large-scale experiments.

We have used DUC data (i.e. 2001, 2002 and 2003), because such a corpus contains 3 years of human judgments, and this would make our efficacy assessment possible and feasible. In what follows, general information about DUC data will be provided.

DUC 2001

60 reference sets were produced by NIST, i.e. 30 for training and 30 for testing. Each set contained documents, per-document summaries, and multi-document summaries, with sets defined by different types of criteria such as event sets, opinion sets, and so on. The document sets used data from the TREC (Text Retrieval Conferences) disks used in the question-answering track in TREC-9. Specifically these include: Wall Street Journal 1987-1992; AP newswire 1989-1990; San Jose Mercury News 1991; Financial Times 1991-1994; LA Times from disk 5; and FBIS from disk 5.

In addition, each set had on average 10 documents and each document was at least 10 sentences long, but had no maximum length. For each document there was a summary of the approximate length of 100 words. Also, there were four multi-document summaries for each set, namely, 400, 200, 100 and 50 word summaries produced from the 400 words summary.

DUC 2002

For 2002, NIST produced 60 reference sets. Each set contained documents, single-document abstracts, and multi-document abstracts and extracts, with sets defined by different types of criteria such as event sets, biographical sets, and so on. The document sets contained data from the TREC disks used in the question-answering track in TREC-9, such as: Wall Street Journal 1987-1992; AP newswire 1989-1990; San Jose Mercury News 1991; Financial Times 1991-1994; LA Times from disk 5; and FBIS from disk 5.

Each set had an average of 10 documents. The documents were at least 10 sentences long, but had no maximum length. Each document had a single-document abstract, with an approximate length of 100 words. Additionally, there were four multi-document abstracts for each set. A 200-word abstract was produced first, and then a 100-word, a 50-word, and a 10-word abstract. The 200-, 100-, and 50-word abstracts were written in complete sentences, and the 10-word abstract, in the form of a headline. Finally, each set had 2 multi-document extracts, a 400-word extract produced first, and then a 200-word extract from it. Each extract consisted of some subset of the sentences in the document set.

DUC 2003

DUC 2003 used documents from the TDT (Topic Detection and Tracking) and TREC collections. Specifically, these included:

- **30 TREC Document Clusters:** NIST assessors chose 30 clusters of TREC documents related to subjects of interest to them. Each subset contained on average 10 documents. The documents came from the following collections: AP newswire, 1998-2000; New York Times newswire, 1998-2000; Xinhua News Agency (English version), 1996-2000.
- **30 TDT Document Clusters:** NIST assessors chose 30 TDT topics/events/timespans and a subset of the documents TDT annotators found for each topic/event/timespan. Each subset contained on average 10 documents, and the documents came from the same collections identified above.
- **30 TREC Novelty Track Document Clusters:** NIST staff chose 30 TREC Novelty Track question topics and a subset of the documents TREC assessors found relevant to each topic. Each subset contained on average 22 documents. The documents came from the following collections: Financial Times of London, 1991-1994; Federal Register, 1994; FBIS, 1996; Los Angeles Times 1989-1990.

From DUC data we have used the following corpus for this study:

- Summaries of single documents of about 100 words for DUC 2001 and DUC 2002. In total, 15 systems submitted 3,304 summaries for DUC 2001. For DUC 2002, 17 systems submitted 7,359 summaries.
- Very short summaries of single documents of about 10 words for DUC 2003, where 14 systems submitted in total 8,050 summaries.

Evaluation of Evaluation

We pointed out in the beginning of this section that the assessment of an automatic evaluation metric should be carried out through correlation analysis. In the statistical literature, this type of analysis makes use of measures of correlation, which are, according to Sheskin (2000), "descriptive statistical measures that represent the degree of relationship between two or more variables." These descriptive measures are known as correlation coefficients. Those coefficients, when calculated, produce a value within the range of −1 to +1. If a value of +1 is obtained, there is a perfect positive correlation; if a value of −1 is obtained, there is a perfect negative correlation, and a value of zero indicates no correlation at all. This range (−1 to +1), in fact, denotes the strength of the relationship between the two variables.

A question arises at this point: is it possible to determine if one metric is "better" than another through correlation analysis? In other words, how to proceed in comparative evaluations, like ROUGE versus VERT, for instance? In comparative evaluations we believe that the answer is ranking correlation (Voorhees, 2000), (Voorhees & Tice, 2000). What we mean is the rankings produced by a particular scoring method (an evaluation metric, in our context) are more important than the scores themselves. This insight is given by Kendall's Tau (τ) correlation coefficient (Sheskin, 2000). Kendall's τ calculates the "distance" between two rankings as the minimum number of pairwise adjacent swaps necessary to convert one ranking into the other. The "distance" value, which is normalized by the number of items being ranked, is the correlation coefficient. In other words, Kendall's τ depends on the number of inversions in the rank order of one variable when the other variable is ranked in order. If the correlation is 1.0, we have two identical rankings; if it is -1.0, we have a correlation between a ranking and its perfect inverse; and if it is 0.0, there is no correlation.

We then computed, for each set of DUC data (i.e. 2001, 2002 and 2003), the Kendall's τ correlation coefficient. This correlation coefficient was computed between the system's average VERT-F scores, and its respective mean coverage scores as assigned by NIST assessors. Human judges assigned the mean coverage scores where they examined the percentage of content overlap between a manual summary and the candidate summary using Summary Evaluation Environment (Lin, 2001) developed by the University of Southern California's Information Sciences Institute.

Table 2 shows the Kendall's τ correlation coefficient of VERT-C and VERT-F scores versus human judgments on DUC 2001 and 2002 data, which consist of single summaries of 100 words, and also on DUC 2003 data, which consist of very short summaries of 10 words.

As can be seen in Table 2, VERT-F achieved a good correlation with human scores. The reason is because VERT-F is based on the matching of all words between a reference text and a candidate text; that is, each text is split in clauses (a word is the minimum clause in this case), and the matching is carried out.

One might ask: what about the comparative evaluations? What about ROUGE and BLEU against VERT? Similarly, we computed Kendall's τ between ROUGE, BLEU and human scores. These values are shown in Table 3.

We decided to put all the results into a chart in order to illustrate better the metrics performances. Looking at Figure 10, we observe that the best performance was achieved by ROUGE, which outperforms our metric VERT-F, and BLEU. On the other hand, VERT-F and ROUGE comparatively presented almost the same performance. BLEU showed the poorest performance amongst the other metrics. These results also highlight the achievement of our proposed metric VERT; or more specifically VERT-F.

Brief Conclusions

The previous section (i.e. VERT Experiment) has presented the experiments conducted in order to test VERT's performance.

We have utilized correlation analysis, a kind of statistical investigation which makes use of correlation coefficients. These coefficients quantify

Table 2. Kendall's τ correlation coefficient of VERT scores versus human scores for DUC 2001, 2002 and 2003 data

DUC	VERT-F vs. Humans
2001	0.91
2002	0.89
2003	0.95

Table 3. Kendall's τ correlation coefficient of BLEU and ROUGE scores versus human scores for DUC data

DUC	BLEU vs. Human	ROUGE vs. Human
2001	0.64	0.85
2002	0.54	0.99
2003	0.05	0.97

Figure 10. Comparative chart

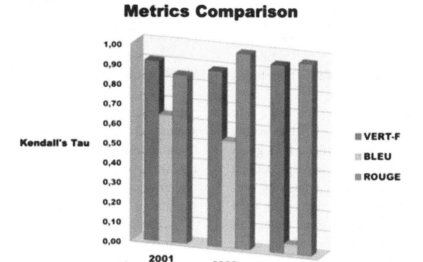

the degree of relationship between two or more variables. Kendall's τ correlation coefficient has been used. The outcomes of the experiment revealed that VERT-F scores correlated highly and positively in relation to human scores, which can be considered a relevant attainment to this investigation.

We also have found that doing a comparative evaluation (ranking correlation) amongst BLEU, ROUGE and VERT against human scores, ROUGE outperformed the other two. However, VERT-F had a similar performance in relation to ROUGE, the official metric used by NIST, and we therefore conclude that VERT-F can be considered as an automatic summary evaluation metric.

In brief, we believe that the notion of ranking correlation, that is, comparative evaluation, is central to summary evaluation research; or more specifically, evaluation of evaluation. Using, as background, a mature discipline like statistics, we can confirm that our evaluation experiments are significant and their results are consistent. Moreover, our work contributed to solid advance in the state of the art.

Another VERT Experiment

VERT had the opportunity to participate in the Text Analysis Conference (TAC) Summarization Track in 2010 and 2011. This event can be considered as another experiment for our system. Firstly, a brief description of TAC will be given.

According to NIST, TAC (2011) is a "series of evaluation workshops organized to encourage research in Natural Language Processing (NLP) and related applications, by providing a large test collection, common evaluation procedures, and a forum for organizations to share their results." TAC encompasses a set of tasks identified as "tracks," where each of which concentrates on a particular subproblem of NLP. The tracks are: Question Answering, Recognizing Textual Entailment, Summarization and Knowledge Base Population. In our case, the Summarization Track.

TAC Summarization Track (TAC ST) started in 2008, and can be considered as the DUC's predecessor. It has two purposes:

1. Aiming to foster research in automatic text summarization; and
2. Providing a common evaluation framework for automatic summarization systems.

In 2011, TAC ST was composed by three tasks:

1. **Guided Summarization**: The aim's task is to write a short summary (~100 words) of a set of 10 newswire articles for a given topic, where the topic falls into a predefined category. Participants (and human summarizers) are given a list of aspects for each category, and a summary must include all aspects found for its category. Moreover, an "update" component of the guided summarization task is to write a 100-word "update" summary of a subsequent 10 newswire articles for the topic, under the assumption that the user has already read the earlier articles. The evaluation criteria for the summaries will be *readability*, *content*, and *overall responsiveness*.

2. **Automatically Evaluating Summaries of Peers (AESOP):** The aim's task is to automatically score a summary for a given metric. The focus was on metrics that reflect summary content, such as *overall responsiveness*, *content* (pyramid) and *readability*. VERT has participated in this task.

3. **Multiling Pilot:** The aim's task is to stimulate the use of multi-lingual algorithms for summarization, including the effort of transforming an algorithm or a set of resources from a mono-lingual to a multi-lingual version.

Data Set

NIST has used all test data and summaries produced within the TAC 2011 Guided Summarization task. In fact, the same collection from the newswire portion of the TAC 2010 KBP Source Data (LDC Catalog no. LDC2010E12). It comprises news articles taken from several sources such as the New York Times, the Associated Press, and the Xinhua News Agency newswires. The news collection spans the time-period 2007-2008.

VERT Submission

The TAC data set consisted of human-authored summaries (i.e. model summaries) and automatic (non-model) summaries. In order to process our run, we have used these model summaries as the reference summaries, and the others as candidate summaries.

According to NIST, 7 participants submitted 22 metrics in the AESOP task, resulting in 25 metrics which were evaluated. These submissions have been labeled by a random number (i.e. 1 up to 25). Submissions 1, 2 and 3 refer to ROUGE-2, ROUGE-SU4, and BE baselines, respectively. Our team submitted only 1 run (ID no. 4).

For each of our automatic metric submitted, NIST computed Pearson's, Spearman's, and Kendall's correlations with Pyramid, Overall Responsiveness and Overall Readability.

Table 4 and Table 5 show the NIST calculations results for VERT participation against the 3 scores above, and for the initial and the update summaries, respectively (All Peers case).

Table 4 shows that in terms of correlation with Pyramid score, VERT-F obtained a very good degree of correlation for the 3 correlation coefficients (i.e. rank 1 for Pearson, and rank 2 for Spearman and rank 3 for Kendall). It is a remarkable performance, if it is compared to the 24 others metrics.

Meanwhile, the correlations with the Responsiveness score, our system achieved rank 1 for the Pearson coefficient, and rank 2 for both Spearman and Kendall coefficients. That was a good performance as well.

And finally, the correlations with the Readability score; VERT-F reached rank 1 for Pearson and Kendall coefficients, and rank 2 for Spearman, which is a good performance too.

Table 4. The 3 correlations of the AESOP metrics with the pyramid, responsiveness and readability scores for the initial summaries

Initial Summaries									
Run no.	**Correlations with Pyramid**			**Correlations with Responsiveness**			**Correlations with Readability**		
	P	S	K	P	S	K	P	S	K
4	r	rho	tau	r	rho	tau	r	rho	tau
	0.974	0.933	0.785	0.972	0.894	0.740	0.926	0.672	0.519
Rank	2	1	3	1	2	2	1	2	1
Baseline 1	0.752	0.864	0.703	0.779	0.948	0.609	0.663	0.498	0.374
Baseline 2	0.763	0.886	0.723	0.810	0.966	0.629	0.682	0.533	0.400
Baseline 3	0.781	0.878	0.720	0.784	0.941	0.590	0.683	0.531	0.387
Min	0.113	0.179	0.078	0.093	0.187	0.090	0.049	0.083	0.036
Mean	0.720	0.750	0.609	0.703	0.708	0.552	0.653	0.505	0.374
Max	0.975	0.933	0.799	0.972	0.899	0.748	0.926	0.674	0.674
Std.Dev.	0.325	0.298	0.279	0.330	0.272	0.243	0.329	0.219	0.177

Obs.: P, S and K stand for Pearson, Spearman and Kendall, respectively

Table 5. The 3 correlations of the AESOP metrics with the pyramid, responsiveness and readability scores for the updated summaries

Updated Summaries									
Run no.	**Correlations with Pyramid**			**Correlations with Responsiveness**			**Correlations with Readability**		
	P	S	K	P	S	K	P	S	K
4	r	rho	tau	r	rho	tau	r	rho	tau
	0.950	0.873	0.695	0.974	0.911	0.762	0.934	0.663	0.507
Rank	3	5	5	2	2	2	1	1	1
Baseline 1	0.775	0.851	0.684	0.717	0.869	0.710	0.712	0.550	0.399
Baseline 2	0.730	0.883	0.720	0.675	0.903	0.743	0.686	0.558	0.405
Baseline 3	0.740	0.848	0.686	0.649	0.808	0.637	0.611	0.415	0.287
Min	0.017	0.159	0.103	-0.058	0.063	0.018	-0.043	-0.101	-0.116
Mean	0.680	0.697	0.552	0.652	0.693	0.554	0.626	0.426	0.307
Max	0.953	0.891	0.731	0.975	0.912	0.764	0.934	0.663	0.663
Std.Dev.	0.358	0.282	0.237	0.392	0.331	0.284	0.366	0.281	0.225

Obs.: P, S and K stand for Pearson, Spearman and Kendall, respectively

As can be seen in Table 5, our system has obtained a satisfactory performance with the Pyramid score, that is, rank 3 for Pearson and rank 5 for both Spearman and Kendall coefficients.

For the Responsiveness score, VERT-F achieved rank 2 for all 3 coefficients, which can be considered a good performance.

For the Readability score, VERT-F achieved rank 1 for all 3 coefficients. That was a very good performance.

Brief Conclusions

TAC 2011 results have shown that our automatic evaluation metric accomplished an excellent and robust performance, especially when compared to the other 24 participants.

Furthermore, our system scores correlated highly and positively in relation to the official NIST scores, which confirms Mani's statement (2000) (please see p. 125).

CONCLUSION

In this section an overview of the main findings obtained so far will be provided. The implications of the results obtained in VERT system evaluation presented in this chapter are discussed in this section. Also, the directions in which this work can be taken forward are addressed.

The present study has some implications for the manner in which summaries can be evaluated automatically. The major finding is the confirmation that an automatic evaluation metric can be used for such a task: VERT-F is promising in that the statistics it produces has a high-level correlation with human judgments. The correlation analysis mentioned above, determines the degree to which two variables co-vary (i.e., vary in relationship to one another). In other words, the analysis assesses the degree of relationship between two variables, in our case, the automatic metric score and human assigned score. If a good correlation

is obtained, the use of automatic scores to predict corresponding human judgment scores may be undertaken. In this sense, the approach pursued in this investigation follows Lin's approach (2004). This is evident by the emphasis placed throughout VERT experiment on assessing its efficacy and reliability in the *VERT Experiment* and *Another VERT Experiment* sections.

Additionally, the investigation presented in this chapter contributes to current research on summary evaluation metrics. We reviewed the main summary evaluation metrics which have been applied to the study of this topic. Three main threads were identified: studies which used IR-based metrics (i.e. precision, recall, f-measure): Jing, McKeown, Barzilay & Elhadad (1998), and Goldstein, Kantrowitz, Mittal & Carbonell (1999); studies which used Statistical-based metrics (i.e. Kappa): Radev et al. (2003), and Mani et al. (1998); and studies which approached content-based metrics (i.e. cosine, n-gram): Donaway, Drummey & Mather (2000), Saggion, Radev, Teufel & Lam (2002), Lin and Hovy (2003) and Lin (2004). With VERT, the summarization research community can apply a valuable resource in order to evaluate their systems.

The results of the present study also suggest a complement to automatic evaluation of MT, like BLEU (Papineni, Roukos, Ward, & Zhu, 2001), and NIST (Doddington, 2002), which is a variant of BLEU and ROUGE (Lin & Och, 2004b). In the latter, Lin described two new evaluation methods for machine translation. Based on empirical results and using eight MT systems' outputs, their human assessment data, and the reference translations from the 2003 NIST Chinese MT Evaluation (NIST, 2003), he concluded that both methods correlate with human judgments very well in terms of adequacy and fluency. Therefore, having access to these high quality large-scale human judgments used by Lin, and which were very hard to obtain, future research can explore application of VERT in MT.

Finally, automatic summary evaluation is still in its infancy. Although it is a science and an art, it is nevertheless still limited. General advances in this field will therefore require increasingly efficient and robust methods of automatic assessment; in general terms, this growth of activity and interest will be welcomed. It will be essential for the progress and health of summarization, in both intellectual and practical terms.

REFERENCES

Ahmad, K., Vrusias, B., & Oliveira, P. C. (2003). Summary evaluation and text categorization. In *Proceedings of the 26th Annual International ACM SIGIR Conference on Research and Development in Informaion Retrieval* (pp. 443-444). ACM.

Baeza-Yates, R., & Ribeiro-Neto, B. (1999). *Modern information retrieval*. New York: ACM Press.

Bell, T. C., Cleary, J. G., & Witten, H. (1990). *Text compression*. Englewood Cliffs, NJ: Prentice Hall.

Brandow, R., Mitze, K., & Rau, L. (1995). Automatic condensation of electronic publications by sentence selection. *Information Processing & Management, 31*(5), 675–685. doi:10.1016/0306-4573(95)00052-I

Carletta, J. (1996). Assessing agreement on classification tasks: The Kappa statistic. *Computational Linguistics, 22*(2), 249–254.

Chen, S. F., & Goodman, J. (1998). *An empirical study of smoothing techniques for language modeling (Technical Report)*. Cambridge, MA: Harvard University.

Clough, P. D. (2003). *Measuring text reuse.* (PhD Thesis). University of Sheffield, Sheffield, UK.

Cormen, T., Leiserson, C., Rivest, R., & Stein, C. (2001). *Introduction to algorithms* (2nd ed.). Cambridge, MA: MIT Press.

Cover, T. M., & Thomas, J. A. (1991). *Elements of information theory*. New York: Wiley-Blackwell. doi:10.1002/0471200611

Crochemore, M., & Rytter, W. (2003). *Jewels of stringology: Text algorithms* (2nd ed.). Singapore: World Scientific Publishing.

Cunningham, H., Maynard, D., Bontcheva, K., & Tablan, V. (2002). GATE: A framework and graphical development environment for robust NLP tools. In *Proceedings of the 40th Anniversary Meeting of the Association for Computational Linguistics* (ACL'02). Philadelphia, PA: ACL.

Dang, H. (2005). Overview of DUC 2005. In *Proceedings of the Document Understanding Conferences (DUC)*. Vancouver, Canada: NIST.

DeJong, G. F. (1982). An overview of the frump system. In W. Lehnert, & M. Ringle (Eds.), *Strategies for natural language processing* (pp. 149–176). Academic Press.

Doddington, G. (2002). Automatic evaluation of machine translation quality using n-gram co-occurrence statistics. In *Proceedings of the Second International Conference on Human Language Technology Research* (pp. 138-145). San Francisco, CA: Morgan Kaufmann.

Donaway, R. L., Drummey, K. W., & Mather, L. A. (2000). A comparison of rankings produced by summarization evaluation measures. In *Proceedings of NAACL-ANLP 2000 Workshop on Text Summarization* (pp. 69-78). Association for Computational Linguistics.

DUC. (2004). *The document understanding conference*. Retrieved from http://duc.nist.gov

Earl, L. (1970). Experiments in automatic extracting and indexing. *Information Storage and Retrieval, 6*(4), 313–330. doi:10.1016/0020-0271(70)90025-2

Edmundson, H. P. (1969). New methods in automatic abstracting. *Journal of the Association for Computing Machinery*, *16*(2), 264–285. doi:10.1145/321510.321519

Firmin, T., & Chrzanowski, M. J. (1999). An evaluation of automatic text summarization systems. In I. Mani, & M. T. Maybury (Eds.), *Advances in automatic text summarization* (pp. 325–336). Cambridge, MA: MIT Press.

Frawley, W. (1992). *Linguistic semantics*. New York: Routledge.

Goldstein, J., Kantrowitz, M., Mittal, V., & Carbonell, J. (1999). Summarizing text documents: Sentence selection and evaluation metrics. In *Proceedings of the 22nd Annual International ACM SIGIR Conference on Research and Development in Information Retrieval* (pp. 121-128). ACM.

Good, I. J. (1953). The population frequencies of species and the estimation of population parameters. *Biometrika*, *40*(3/4), 237–264. doi:10.2307/2333344

Hand, T. F. (1997). A proposal for task-based evaluation of text summarisation systems. In *Proceedings of the ACL/EACL'97 Workshop on Intelligent Scalable Text Summarization* (pp. 31-38). ACL.

Hovy, E., Lin, C.-Y., & Zhou, L. (2005). Evaluating DUC 2005 using basic elements. In *Proceedings of the Document Understanding Conferences (DUC)*. Vancouver, Canada: NIST.

Hovy, E., Lin, C.-Y., Zhou, L., & Fukumoto, J. (2006). Automated summarization evaluation with basic elements. In *Proceedings of the Fifth Conference on Language Resources and Evaluation (LREC)* (pp. 899-902). Genoa, Italy: LREC.

Jing, H., McKeown, K., Barzilay, R., & Elhadad, M. (1998). Summarization evaluation methods: Experiments and analysis. In *Working Notes of the Workshop on Intelligent Text Summarization* (pp. 60-68). Academic Press.

Johnson, F. C., Paice, C. D., Black, W. J., & Neal, A. P. (1993). The application of linguistic processing to automatic abstract generation. *Journal of document and text management*, *1*(3), 215-241.

Jurafsky, D., & Martin, J. H. (2000). *Speech and language processing: an introduction to natural language processing, computational linguistics, and speech recognition*. Upper Saddle River, NJ: Prentice-Hall International.

Katz, S. (1987). Estimation of probabilities from sparse data for the language model component of a speech recognizer. *IEEE Transactions on Acoustics, Speech, and Signal Processing*, *35*(3), 400–401. doi:10.1109/TASSP.1987.1165125

Krippendorff, K. (1980). *Content analysis: An introduction to its methodology*. Beverly Hills, CA: Sage Publications.

Kupiec, J., Pedersen, J., & Chen, F. (1995). A trainable document summariser. In *Proceedings of the 18th Annual International ACM SIGIR Conference on Research and Development in Information Retrieval* (pp. 68-73). ACM.

Lin, C.-Y. (2001). *Summary evaluation environment*. Retrieved from http://www.isi.edu/~cyl/SEE

Lin, C.-Y. (2004). ROUGE: A package for automatic evaluation of summaries. In *Proceedings of the Workshop on Text Summarization Branches Out (WAS 2004)*. WAS.

Lin, C.-Y., & Hovy, E. (2002). Manual and automatic evaluation of summaries. In *Proceedings of the ACL 2002 Workshop on Automatic Summarization*, (vol. 4, pp. 45-51). Association for Computation Linguistics.

Lin, C.-Y., & Hovy, E. (2003). Automatic evaluation of summaries using n-gram co-occurrence statistics. In *Proceedings of the 2003 Conference of the North American Chapter of the Association for Computational Linguistics on Human Language Technology*, (pp. 71-78). ACL.

Lin, C.-Y., & Och, F. J. (2004a). Automatic evaluation of machine translation quality using longest common subsequence and skip-bigram statistics. In *Proceedings of the 42nd Annual Meeting on Association for Computational Linguistics* (pp. 605-612). Association for Computational Linguistics.

Lin, C.-Y., & Och, F. J. (2004b). ORANGE: A method for evaluating automatic evaluation th metrics for machine translation. In *Proceedings of the 20th International Conference on Computational Linguistics* (pp. 501-507). Association for Computational Linguistics.

Lin, D., & Pantel, P. (2002). Concept discovery from text. In *Proceedings of the 19th International Conference on Computational Linguistics (COLING-02)* (pp. 1-7). Taipei, Taiwan: Association for Computational Linguistics.

Mani, I. (2000). *Automatic summarization*. Amsterdam: John Benjamins Publishing Company.

Mani, I., Firmin, T., House, D., Chrzanowski, M., Klein, G., & Hirschman, L. et al. (1998). *The TIPSTER SUMMAC text summarisation evaluation: Final report*. The MITRE Corporation.

Manning, C. D., & Schutze, H. (1999). *Foundations of statistical natural language processing*. Cambridge, MA: MIT Press.

Markov, A. (1913). An example of statistical investigation in the text of 'Eugene Onyegin' illustrating coupling of 'tests' in chains. In *Proceedings of the Academy of Sciences of St. Petersburg* (pp. 153-162). Academy of Sciences of St. Petersburg.

Melamed, I. D. (1995). Automatic evaluation and uniform filter cascades for inducing n-best translation lexicons. In *Proceedings of the 3rd Workshop on Very Large Corpora (WVLC3)* (pp. 184-198). WVLC.

Miike, S., Itoh, E., Ono, K., & Sumita, K. (1994). A full-text retrieval system with a dynamic abstract generation function. In *Proceedings of the 17th Annual International ACM SIGIR Conference on Research and Development in Information Retrieval* (pp. 152-161). ACM.

Minel, J., Nugier, S., & Piat, G. (1997). How to appreciate the quality of automatic text summarisation? Examples of FAN And MLUCE protocols and their results on SERAPHIN. In I. Mani & M. Maybury (Ed.), *Proceedings of ACL/EACL Workshop on Intelligent Scalable Text Summarization* (pp. 25-30). ACL.

Nenkova, A., & Passonneau, R. (2004). Evaluating content selection in summarization: The pyramid method. In *Proceedings of the Joint Annual Meeting of Human Language Technology and the North American Chapter of the Association for Computational Linguistics (HLT-NAACL)* (pp. 145-152). Boston, MA: NAACL.

Nenkova, A., Passonneau, R., & McKeown, K. (2007). The pyramid method: Incorporating human content selection variation in summarization evaluation. *ACM Transactions on Speech and Language Processing, 4*(1), 1–23.

NIST. (2003). *The 2003 NIST machine translation evaluation plan (MT-03)*. Retrieved from http://www.itl.nist.gov/iad/mig/tests/2003/doc/mt03_evalplan.v2.pdf

Open University. (2001). *Networks 3 - Assignment and transportation* (2nd ed.). Open University Worldwide.

Paice, C. D., & Jones, P. A. (1993). The identification of important concepts in highly structured technical papers. In *Proceedings of the 16th Annual International ACM SIGIR Conference of Research and Development in Information Retrieval* (pp. 69-78). ACM.

Papineni, K., Roukos, S., Ward, T., & Zhu, W.-J. (2001). *BLEU: A method for automatic evaluation of machine translation.* Academic Press. doi:10.3115/1073083.1073135

Pastra, K., & Saggion, H. (2003). Colouring summaries BLEU. In *Proceedings of the EACL 2003 Workshop on Evaluation Initiatives in Natural Language Processing: Are Evaluation Methods, Metrics and Resources Reusable?* (pp. 35-42). Association for Computational Linguistics.

Radev, D., Teufel, S., Saggion, H., Lam, W., Blitzer, J., Qi, H., et al. (2003). Evaluation challenges in large-scale document summarization. In *Proceedings of the 41st Annual Meeting of the Association for Computational Linguistics* (pp. 375-382). Association for Computational Linguistics.

Radev, D. R., Jing, H., & Budzikowska, M. (2000). Centroid-based summarization of multiple documents: Sentence extraction, utility based evaluation, and user studies. In *Proceedings of NAACL-ANLP 2000 Workshop on Text Summarisation* (pp. 21-29). NAACL.

Rutman, L. (1984). *Evaluation research methods: A basic guide.* Beverly Hills, CA: Sage Publications.

Saggion, H., Radev, D., Teufel, S., & Lam, W. (2002). Meta-evaluation of summaries in a cross-lingual environment using content-based metrics. In *Proceedings of the 19th International Conference on Computational Linguistics* (pp. 1-7). ACL.

Saggion, H., Radev, D., Teufel, S., Lam, W., & Strassel, S. M. (2002). Developing Infrastructure for the evaluation of single and multi-document summarization systems in a cross-lingual environment. In *Proceedings of the Third International Conference on Language Resources And Evaluation (LREC 2002)* (pp. 747-754). LREC.

Salton, G., & McGill, M. J. (1983). *Introduction to modern information retrieval.* New York: McGraw Hill.

Salton, G., Singhal, A., Mitra, M., & Buckley, C. (1997). Automatic text structuring and summarization. *Information Processing & Management, 33*(2), 193–207. doi:10.1016/S0306-4573(96)00062-3

Salton, G., Wong, A., & Yang, C. S. (1975). Vector space model for automatic indexing. *Communications of the ACM, 18*(11), 613–620. doi:10.1145/361219.361220

Sheskin, D. J. (2000). *Handbook of parametric and nonparametric statistical procedures* (2nd ed.). Academic Press.

Siegel, S., & Castellan, N. J. Jr. (1988). *Nonparametric statistics for the behavioral sciences.* New York: McGraw-Hill.

TAC. (2011). *The text analysis conference.* Retrieved 2011 30-October from http://www.nist.gov/tac/

Tratz, S., & Hovy, E. (2008). Summarization evaluation using transformed basic elements. In *Proceedings of the Text Analysis Conference (TAC-08).* Gaithersburg, MD: NIST.

Tucker, R. (1999). *Automatic summarising and the CLASP system.* (PhD thesis). University of Cambridge Computer Laboratory, Cambridge, UK.

Turian, J. P., Shen, L., & Melamed, I. D. (2003). Evaluation of machine translation and its evaluation. [New Orleans, LA: MT.]. *Proceedings of MT Summit, IX,* 386–393.

Tversky, A. (1977). Features of similarity. *Psychological Review*, *84*(4), 327–352. doi:10.1037/0033-295X.84.4.327

van Rijsbergen, C. (1979). *Information retrieval* (2nd ed.). London: Butterworths.

Voorhees, E. M. (2000). Variations in relevance judgments and the measurement of retrieval effectiveness. *Information Processing & Management*, *36*(5), 697–716. doi:10.1016/S0306-4573(00)00010-8

Voorhees, E. M., & Tice, D. M. (2000). Overview of the TREC-9 question answering track. In *Proceedings of the Ninth Text REtrieval Conference (TREC-9)*. TREC.

Weber, R. P. (1990). *Basic content analysis* (2nd ed.). Thousand Oaks, CA: Sage Publications.

Witten, H., & Bell, T. C. (1991). The zero-frequency problem: Estimating the probabilities of novel events in adaptive text compression. *IEEE Transactions on Information Theory*, *37*(4), 1085–1094. doi:10.1109/18.87000

ADDITIONAL READING

Dalianis, H., Hassel, M., de Smedt, K., Liseth, A., Lech, T. C., & Wedekind, J. (2004). Porting and evaluation of automatic summarization. In H. Holmboe (Ed.), *Nordisk Sprogteknologi 2003: Årbog for Nordisk Språkteknologisk Forskningsprogram 2000-2004*. Museum Tusculanums Forlag.

de Smedt, K., Liseth, A., Hassel, M., & Dalianis, H. (2005). How short is good? An evaluation of automatic summarization. In H. Holmboe (Ed.), *Nordisk Sprogteknologi 2004: Årbog for Nordisk Språkteknologisk Forskningsprogram 2000-2004*. Museum Tusculanums Forlag.

Firmin, T., & Chrzanowski, M. J. (1999). An Evaluation of Automatic Text Summarization Systems. In I. Mani, & M. T. Maybury (Eds.), *Advances in Automatic Text Summarization* (pp. 325–336). MIT Press.

Hassel, M. (2004). *Evaluation of automatic text summarization: a practical implementation*. Licentiate Thesis, Royal Institute of Technology, Department of Numerical Analysis and Computer Science.

Hovy, E., & Lin, C.-Y. (2002). Manual and Automatic Evaluation of Summaries. In U. Hahn, & D. Harman (Ed.), *Proceedings of the Workshop on Text Summarization at the 40th Meeting of the Association for Computational Linguistics*.

Lloret, E., & Palomar, M. (2012). Text summarisation in progress: a literature review. *Artificial Intelligence Review*, *37*(1), 1–41. doi:10.1007/s10462-011-9216-z

Mani, I. (2001). Summarization evaluation: an overview. *Proceedings of the North American Chapter of the Association for Computational Linguistics (NAACL). Workshop on Automatic Summarization*.

Murray, G., Kleinbauer, T., Poller, P., Becker, T., Renals, S., & Kilgour, J. (2009). Extrinsic summarization evaluation: A decision audit task. *ACM Transactions on Speech and Language Processing*, *6*(2), 1–29. doi:10.1145/1596517.1596518

Nanba, H., & Okumura, M. (2006). An automatic method for summary evaluation using multiple evaluation results by a manual method. *Proceedings of the COLING/ACL on Main conference poster sessions (COLING-ACL '06)*. Stroudsburg, PA, USA: Association for Computational Linguistics.

Nenkova, A., & McKeown, K. (2011). Automatic Summarization. *Foundations and Trends in Information Retrieval*, *5*(2-3), 103–233. doi:10.1561/1500000015

Owczarzak, K., & Dang, H. T. (2009). Evaluation of automatic summaries: metrics under varying data conditions. *Proceedings of the 2009 Workshop on Language Generation and Summarisation (ACL-IJCNLP)* (pp. 23–30). Suntec, Singapore.

Pardo, T., Antiqueira, L., Nunes, M., Oliveira, O., Jr., & Costa, L. (2006). Using Complex Networks for Language Processing: The Case of Summary Evaluation. *Proceedings of the 4th International Conference on Communications, Circuits and Systems – ICCCAS.* Guilin, China.

Schilder, F., & Kondadadi, R. (2009). A Metric for Automatically Evaluating Coherent Summaries via Context Chains. *IEEE International Conference on Semantic Computing (ICSC'09)* (pp. 65-70). IEEE.

Sparck Jones, K., & Galliers, J. R. (1996). *Evaluating Natural Language Processing Systems: An Analysis and Review.* Secaucus, NJ, USA: Springer-Verlag New York, Inc.

Torres-Moreno, J.-M., Saggion, H., Cunha, I., SanJuan, E., & Velázquez-Morales, P. (2010). Summary Evaluation with and without References. *Polibits, 42,* 13–20.

Yatsko, V., & Vishnyakov, T. (2007). A method for evaluating modern systems of automatic text summarization. *Automatic Documentation and Mathematical Linguistics, 41*(3), 93–103. doi:10.3103/S0005105507030041

Zhou, L., Lin, C.-Y., Munteanu, D. S., & Hovy, E. (2006). ParaEval: using paraphrases to evaluate summaries automatically. *Proceedings of the main conference on Human Language Technology Conference of the North American Chapter of the Association of Computational Linguistics (HLT-NAACL '06).* Stroudsburg, PA, USA: Association for Computational Linguistics.

KEY TERMS AND DEFINITIONS

Abstract: A summary, at least some of whose material is not present in the original document.

Extract: A summary consisting entirely of material copied from the input.

Generic Summary: A summary aimed at a particular, usually broad, readership community.

Graph: A set of dots called vertices (or nodes) connected by lines called edges (or arcs).

Indicative Summary: A summary used to identify the main topics in the source text.

Informative Summary: A summary that conveys the important information in the source text.

N-Gram: Consecutive sequences of *n* characters; i.e. any substring of length *n*.

Precison: An information retrieval performance measure that quantifies the fraction of retrieved documents which are known to be relevant.

Recall: An information retrieval performance measure that quantifies the fraction of known relevant documents which were effectively retrieved.

Stopwords: Words which occur frequently in a text or document, e.g. articles, prepositions and conjunctions (also called stoplist).

Summary: A concise representation of a source text capturing the main points of the text, and acting as surrogate.

Token: An atomic element within a string.

Tokenize: tokenizing is the operation of splitting up a string of characters into a set of tokens.

User-Focused Summary: A summary tailored to the requirements of a particular user or group of users (also called topic-focused summary).

Vector Model: A classical model of document retrieval based on representing documents and queries as vectors in *n*-dimensional space.

Word: The fundamental building block or unit of language.

ENDNOTES

[1] *n-gram:* consecutive sequences of *n* characters. However it will be used to mean a sequence of *n* words throughout this chapter.

[2] *Gram* is a Greek word which means letter

[3] We intend to use the Latin/Greek number prefix. So, for us Bigram = 2-gram; Trigram = 3-gram and Tetragram or Quadrigram = 4-gram

[4] Papineni et al used $N=4$ and $w_n=1/N$

[5] An algorithm for ROUGE-W is shown in Lin's paper Lin (2004), page 5

[6] *Bitext* is the employed term used by Turian and his colleagues.

[7] BLEU stands for BiLingual Evaluation Understudy

[8] ROUGE stands for Recall-Oriented Understudy for Gisting Evaluation

[9] DARPA stands for Defense Advanced Research Projects Agency

Section 2
Social Networks and Web News Summarization

Chapter 6
Social Network Integration in Document Summarization

Atefeh Farzindar
NLP Technologies Inc., Canada & Université de Montréal, Canada

ABSTRACT

In this chapter, the author presents the new role of summarization in the dynamic network of social media and its importance in semantic analysis of social media and large data. The author introduces how summarization tasks can improve social media retrieval and event detection. The author discusses the challenges in social media data versus traditional documents. The author presents the approaches to social media summarization and methods for update summarization, network activities summarization, event-based summarization, and opinion summarization. The author reviews the existing evaluation metrics for summarization and the efforts on evaluation shared tasks on social data related tracks by ACL, TREC, TAC, and SemEval. In conclusion, the author discusses the importance of this dynamic discipline and great potential of automatic summarization in the coming decade, in the context of changes in mobile technology, cloud computing, and social networking.

1. INTRODUCTION

Automatic summarization of traditional media such as written press and articles has been a popular research domain over the past 25 years. Document summarization is typically performed

DOI: 10.4018/978-1-4666-5019-0.ch006

to save reading time by reducing the amount of information presented to users. Several online news agencies use clustering techniques to categorize news articles and provide pseudo-summaries. In addition, summarizing specific types of documents, such as legal decisions, drew a lot of attention in the research field and the marketing of automatic systems (Farzindar and Lapalme 2004). The purpose of these approaches is to exploit the thematic structure of documents in order to improve coherence and readability of the summary. In recent years, we have been facing new challenges in processing social media data and its integration in document summarization. Texts in social media are extremely noisy, ungrammatical; they do not adhere to conventional rules and they are subject to continuously changing conventions.

Over the past few years, online social networking sites (Facebook, Twitter, Youtube, Flickr, MySpace, LinkedIn, Metacafe, Vimeo, etc.) have revolutionized the way we communicate with individuals, groups and communities, and altered everyday practices (Boyd and Ellison, 2007). Nearly one in four people worldwide will use social networks in 2013, according to an eMarketer report (New Media Trend Watch, 2013), "Worldwide Social Network Users: 2013 Forecast and Comparative Estimates". Social media has become a primary source of intelligence because it has become the first response to key events issued by highly dynamic contents generated by 1.73 billion users in 2013. Social media statistics for 2012 has shown that Facebook has grown to more than 800 million active users, adding more than 200 million in a single year. Twitter now has 100 million active users and LinkedIn has over 64 million users in North America alone (Digital Buzz, 2012). Recently, workshops such as Semantic Analysis in Social Media (Farzindar and Inkpen, 2012) and NAACL/HLT workshop on Language Analysis in Social Media (Farzindar et Al. 2013) have been increasingly focusing on the impact of social media on our daily lives, both on a personal and a professional level.

Social media data is the collection of open source information which can be obtained publicly via Blogs and micro-blogs, Internet forums, user-generated FAQs, chat, podcasts, online games, tags, ratings and comments. Social media data has several properties: the nature of conversation is social which are posted in real-time. Geolocating a group of topically-related conversations is important as it includes emotions, neologisms, credibility/rumors and incentives. The texts are non-structured and are presented in many formats and written by different people in many languages and styles. Also the typography mistakes and chat slang have become increasingly prevalent on social networking sites like Facebook and Twitter. The authors are not professional writers and the pockets of sources in thousands of places on the www.

Monitoring and analyzing this rich and continuous flow of user-generated content can yield unprecedentedly valuable information, which would not have been available from traditional media outlets. Summarization can play a key role in semantic analysis of social media and Social Media Analytics. This has given rise to the emerging discipline of Social Media Analytics, which draws from Social Network Analysis, Machine Learning, Data Mining, Information Retrieval (IR), automatic summarization, and Natural Language Processing (NLP) (Melville et al. 2009).

In the context of analyzing social networks and document summarization, finding powerful methods and algorithms to extract the relevant data in large volumes, various and free formats from multiple sources and languages, is a scientific challenge. Automatic processing and summarization of such data needs to evaluate the appropriate research methods for information extraction, automatic categorization, clustering, indexing data and statistical machine translation.

The sheer volume of social media data and the incredible rate at which new content is created makes manual summarization, or any other meaningful manual analysis, largely infeasible. In many applications the amount of data is too large for effective real-time human evaluation and analysis of the data for a decision maker.

Traditionally, a distinction is made between extractive and abstractive summaries. The former is defined as consisting entirely of content extracted from the input, while the latter contains some content not present in the source (e.g. paraphrased material) (Mani, 2001) and (Mani and Maybury, 1999).

In social media, the real time event search and the need for event detection raise an important issue (Farzindar and Khreich 2013). The purpose of dynamic information retrieval and real time event searches is to effectively execute search strategies on many features, where search queries consider multiple dimensions including their spatial and temporal relationship. In this case, the summarization task of social data in the form of various documents from multiple sources becomes important to support the event search and detection of relevant information. Summarization approaches can also be distinguished based on whether they target the summarization of a single document or a collection of related documents. Unlike traditional news summarization, the opinion and sentiment of authors increase an additional dimension to summarization of social media data. The different sizes of source documents—such as a combination of multi-tweets and blogs—and content variability render the task of summarizing multi-documents from social data difficult.

Summarization of the sense of a day- or week-worth of conversations in social networks for a group of topically-related conversations or about a specific event presents the challenge of Cross-Language Summarization. Also social media summarization methods for the information of interest to the analyst for preferential inclusion drive us to domain-based applications of summarization.

Cross-Language Document Summarization from Social Media Data

The application of existing summarization techniques to social media from different languages and multiple resources is faced with several additional challenges; the tools for text analysis are typically designed for specific languages. The main research issue therefore lies in assessing whether to develop language-independent approaches, or language-specific approaches. Also users do not only publish the contents in English but in a multitude of languages. This means that due to the language barrier, many users cannot access all available content. The use of machine translation technology can help bridge the language gap in these situations. The integration of machine translation and summarization open opportunities for Cross-Language Summarization.

Domain-Based Applications of Summarization

The huge volume of publicly available information on social networks and web open-source intelligence can be used to benefit different areas such as industry, public safety and security, and healthcare. Some innovative integration into social media monitoring, and some model scenarios of government-user applications in coordination and situational awareness will be addressed. It will show how summarization can help governments interpret data in near real-time and provide enhanced command decision at the strategic and operational levels.

- **Industry:** There is great interest for social media data monitoring and summarization in the industry. Social media data can dramatically improve business intelligence and help the industry. Businesses could achieve several goals by integrating social data into their corporate BI systems, such as branding and awareness, customer/prospect engagement and improving customer service. Online marketing, product recommendation and reputation management are some examples of real-world applications for summarization.

- **Defence and Homeland Security** are greatly interested in studying these sources of information and summaries to understand situations, and perform *sentiment analysis* of a group of individuals with common interests, and also to be alerted against potential threats to defence and public safety. In this section, we will discuss the issue of information flow from social networks such as MySpace, Facebook, Skyblog, and Twitter. We will present methods for information extraction in Web 2.0 to find links between data entities, and to analyze the characteristics and dynamism of networks through which organizations and discussions evolve. Social data is often significant in meaning. In this context, aggregate social behaviour can provide valuable information for the sake of national security.

- **Healthcare:** Over time, social media became part of common healthcare. The healthcare industry uses social media tools for building community engagement and fostering better relationships with their clients. The use of Twitter to discuss recommendations for providers and consumers (patients, families, or caregivers), ailments, treatments, and medication, are only a few examples of social media in healthcare. This was initially referred to as social health.

This chapter focuses on presenting how Social network integration in document summarization can help develop innovative tools and integrate appropriate linguistic information in various fields as mentioned above.

The chapter describes four major topics:

- **Challenges in Social Media Data:** This section focuses on the difficulty of social media data versus traditional texts such as news articles and scientific papers.
- **Social Media Summarization Approaches:** This section will compare existing approaches to social media summarization and method adaptation. We will also investigate the new problem of event detection in social media and summariza-

tion of events of interest. In addition, we will present the multi-document summarization and dynamic information retrieval created by microblogs, namely Tweets subjected to a 140-character limit.

- **Evaluation:** We will present the evaluation metrics and objective testing/benchmarking for social media from a natural language processing (NLP) and summarization standpoint.
- **Conclusion and Future Prospects:** The last section will summarize the methods and real-world applications described in this chapter. We will conclude with the high potential for research, given the summarization needs of end-users.

2. CHALLENGES IN SOCIAL MEDIA TEXT

Social media text differs significantly from typical news reports or scientific texts targeted by traditional summarization efforts. Many of the differences that characterize social media texts can be attributed to the same source that makes social media such an interesting and important target of inquiry: that the use of social networks has made everybody a potential author. As a result, the language is now closer to the user than to any prescribed norms (Zhou and Hovy, 2006; Beverungen and Kalita, 2011). Blogs, tweets, and status updates are written in an informal, conversational tone – often more of a "stream of consciousness" than the carefully thought out and meticulously edited works that might be expected in traditional print media. This informal nature of social media texts presents new challenges to all levels of automatic language processing.

At the surface level, several issues pose challenges to basic NLP tools developed for traditional data. Inconsistent (or absent) punctuation and capitalization can make detection of sentence boundaries quite difficult – sometimes even for human readers, as in the following tweet: "#qcpoli enjoyed a hearty laugh today with #plq debate audience for @jflisee #notrehome tune was that the intended reaction?" Emoticons, incorrect or non-standard spelling, and rampant abbreviation complicate tokenization and part-of-speech tagging, among other tasks. Traditional tools must be adapted to consider new variations such as letter repetition (*"heyyyyyy"*), which are different from common spelling errors. Grammaticality, or frequent lack thereof, is another concern for any syntactic analyses of social media texts, where fragments can be as commonplace as actual full sentences and the choice between *there, they're,* and *their* can seem to be made at random.

Social media is also much noisier than traditional print media. Like much else on the Internet, social networks are plagued with spam, ads, and all manner of other unsolicited, irrelevant, or distracting content. Even by ignoring these forms of noise, much of the genuine, legitimate content on social media can be seen as irrelevant with respect to most information needs. André, Bernstein, and Luther (2012) demonstrate this in a study that assesses user-perceived value of tweets. They collected over forty thousand ratings of tweets from followers, in which only 36% of tweets were rated as "worth reading," while 25% were rated as "not worth reading." The least valued tweets were so-called presence maintenance posts (e.g. *"Hullo twitter!"*). Pre-processing to filter out spam and other irrelevant content, or models that are better capable of coping with noise are essential in any language processing efforts targeting social media.

Several characteristics of social media text are of particular concern to summarization efforts. Particularities of a given medium and the way in which that medium is used can have a profound impact on what constitutes a successful summarization approach. For example, the 140-character limit imposed on Twitter posts makes for individual tweets that are rather contextually impoverished compared to a more traditional document. However,

redundancy can become a problem for summarization over multiple tweets due in part to the practise of retweeting posts. Sharifi et al. (2010) note the redundancy of information as a major issue with microblog summarization in their experiments with data mining techniques to automatically create summary posts of Twitter trending topics.

A major challenge facing event detection and summarization of events of interest from multiple Twitter streams are therefore to separate the mundane and polluted information from interesting real-world events. In practice, highly scalable and efficient approaches are required for handling and processing the increasingly large amount of Twitter data (especially for real-time event detection). Other challenges are inherent to Twitter design and usage. These are mainly due to the short length of tweet messages the frequent use of (dynamically evolving) informal, irregular and abbreviated words, the large number of spelling and grammatical errors, and the use of improper sentence structure and mixed languages. Such data sparseness, lack of context, and diversity of vocabulary make the traditional text analysis techniques less suitable for tweets (Metzler et al., 2007). In addition, different events may enjoy different popularity among users, and can differ significantly in content, number of messages and participants, time periods, inherent structure, and causal relationships (Nallapati et al., 2004).

Across all forms of social media, subjectivity is an ever-present trait. While traditional news texts may strive to present an objective, neutral account of factual information, social media texts are much more subjective and opinion-laden. Whether or not the ultimate information need lies directly in opinion summarization or mining, sentiment analysis plays a much greater role in summarization of social texts.

Topic drift is much more prominent in social media, both because of the conversational tone of social texts and the continuously streaming nature of social media. (Zhou and Hovy, 2006)

There are also entirely new dimensions to be explored, where new sources of information and types of features need to be assessed and exploited. While traditional texts can be seen as largely static and self-contained, the information presented in social media, such as online discussion forums, blogs, and Twitter posts, is highly dynamic, and involves interaction among various participants. This can be seen as an additional source of complexity that may hamper traditional summarization approaches, but it is also an opportunity, making available additional context that can aid in summarization or making possible entirely new forms of summarization. For instance, Hu et al. (2007) suggest summarizing a blog post by extracting representative sentences using information from user comments. Chua and Asur (2013) exploit temporal correlation in a stream of tweets to extract relevant tweets for event summarization. Lin et al. (2009) address summarization not of the content of posts or messages, but of the social network itself by extracting temporally representative users, actions, and concepts in Flickr data.

Standard summarization approaches applied to social media data are therefore confronted with difficulties due to non-standard spelling, noise, limited sets of features, and errors in determining the number of clusters.

Some NLP techniques, including normalization, term expansion, improved feature selection, and noise reduction, have been proposed to improve clustering performance in Twitter news (Beverungen and Kalita, 2011). Identifying proper names and language switch in a sentence would require rapid and accurate name entity recognition, and language detection techniques.

Recent research efforts focus on the analysis of language in social media for understanding social behavior and building socially aware systems. The goal is the analysis of language with implications for fields such as computational linguistics, sociolinguistics and psycholinguistics. For example Eisenstein (Eisenstein, 2013) studies

the phonological variation and factors when get transcribed into social media text.

3. SOCIAL MEDIA SUMMARIZATION APPROACHES

Automatic summarization from multiple social media sources is a highly active research topic that aims at reducing and aggregating the amount of information presented to users. This section will formalize a variety of more advanced approaches, and present their advantages and limitations. In addition, summarization can be very useful for other tasks such as classification and clustering of data from social media because the number of features is also reduced. However, the tools for text analysis and summarization are typically designed for specific sources and languages. A major objective of these approaches is to assess whether to develop language-independent approaches, or develop and combine specific approaches for each language.

As mentioned earlier, the social media scale is enormous. Combined with the high-level of noise present in social media, this guarantees that most texts are certain to be irrelevant for any particular information need. Accordingly, any summarization task – and indeed most other NLP tasks – must be framed slightly differently than in traditional domains. In particular, there is an inherent need to narrow in on relevant content, and, as such, some form of information retrieval and/or detection of specific phenomena is generally a prerequisite to summarization. Also, there is less of a focus on what individual "documents" are about, but rather how they can contribute to a summary of some real-world phenomenon. In this section we distinguish between using social media data in automated summarization and using summarization for social media retrieval and event detection. We focus on the following type of summarization.

3.1 Update Summarization

Update summarization is a fairly recent area linking news summarization to online and dynamic settings. Update summarization uses web documents, such as blogs, reviews, news articles, to identify new information on a topic. As defined at Text Retrieval Conference (TREC) 2008, the update summarization task consists in a short (~ 100-word) summary of a set of newswire articles, under the assumption that the user has already read a given set of earlier articles.

Delort and Alfonseca (2011) propose a news multi-document summarization system called DUALSUM, using an unsupervised probabilistic approach based on Topic-Model to identify novelty in a document collection, and applying it to generate summary updates.

Li et al. (2012) present a method for update summarization which used a Multi-level Hierarchical Dirichlet Process (HDP) Model. It proposes clustering as a three-level HDP model, which reveals the diversity and commonality between aspects discovere from two different periods of time as history and update.

In 2013, TREC defines Temporal Summarization. Unexpected news events such as natural disasters represent a unique information access problem where the performance of traditional approaches deteriorates. For example, immediately after an event, the corpus may be sparsely populated with relevant content. Even when, after a few hours, relevant content is available, it is often inaccurate or highly redundant. At the same time, crisis events demonstrate a scenario where users urgently need information, especially if they are directly affected by the event. The goal of this track is to develop systems which allow users to efficiently monitor the information associated with an event over time. Specifically, the approaches which can broadcast useful, new, and timely sentence-length updates about a developing event, and can track the value of important event-related attributes (e.g. number of fatalities, financial impact).

3.2 Network Activity Summarization

Social media text is by definition social in nature. Individual posts are not static, isolated pieces of text, but are inherently linked to other posts and users according to the parameters of the specific social network. Information about the relations between textual (or other media) entries and interactions between users – i.e. information about the structure and activity of the network itself – can be useful for summarization, both as additional sources of information to aid in summarization of the content of the network, and as a target of summarization in and of itself.

Liu et al. (2012) leverage social network features to adapt a graph-based summarization approach to the task of summarizing tweets. They overcome the issue of the brevity of tweets, and the corresponding difficulty of determining salience based solely on terms within a tweet by incorporating "social signals" of salience from the network. Specifically, they make use of the notion of re-tweets and number of followers as indicators of salience: tweets that are re-tweeted more often and/or that are posted by users with a higher number of followers are considered more salient. They also incorporate a tweets-per-user threshold to ensure summaries maintain some degree of user diversity.

3.3 Event Summarization

Event summarization seeks to extract social media text representative of some real-world event. Here, an event can be broadly defined as any occurrence unfolding over some spatial and temporal scope (Farzindar and Khreich 2013). In practice, the aim is not to summarize any and all events, but events of interest. Unlike in news reports, where events mentioned are, by definition, newsworthy, events of interest must first be identified in social media before they can be summarized. Also, summarization tasks can improve social media retrieval.

For this purpose Twitter is a popular social media tool because the user can communicate with short information, which is easier to consume and faster to spread. In addition, the Twitter stream can contain a link with points to a blog or a webpage with detailed information. One interesting approach for social media summarization is to detect the event of interest from Twitter and summarize the blogs related to the event. In this section, we present some event detection approaches from Twitter streams.

Twitter is currently the most popular and fastest-growing microblogging service, with more than 140 million users producing over 400 million tweets per day – mostly from cellphones – as of June 2012. Twitter enables users to post status updates, or tweets, no longer than 140 characters to a network of followers using various communication services (e.g., cell phones, emails, Web interfaces, or other third-party applications). Even though tweets are limited in size, Twitter is updated hundreds of millions of times a day by people all over the world, and its content varies tremendously based on user interests and behaviors (Java et al., 2007; Krishnamurthy et al., 2008; Zhao and Rosson, 2009).

Event detection techniques are classified according to the event type (specified or unspecified), detection task (retrospective or new event detection) and detection method (supervised or unsupervised).

3.3.1 Specified vs. Unspecified Event Detection

Depending on the available information on the event of interest, event detection can be classified into specified and unspecified techniques. Since no prior information is available about the event, the unspecified event detection techniques rely on the temporal signal of social media stream to detect the occurrence of a real-world event. These techniques typically require monitoring for bursts or trends in social media stream, grouping the features with identical trend into events, and ultimately classifying the events into different categories. On the other hand, the specified event detection relies on specific information and features that are known about the event, such as a venue, time, type, and description, which are provided by the user or from the event context. These features can be exploited by adapting traditional information retrieval and extraction techniques (such as filtering, query generation and expansion, clustering, and information aggregation) to the unique characteristics of social media data.

a. Unspecified Event Detection

The nature of Twitter posts reflect events as they unfold, hence these tweets are particularly useful for unknown event detection. Unknown events of interest are typically driven by emerging events, breaking news and general topics that attract the attention of a large number of Twitter users. Since no event information is available, unknown events are typically detected by exploiting the temporal patterns or signal of Twitter stream. New events of general interest exhibit a burst of features in Twitter stream yielding, for instance, a sudden increased use of specific keywords. Bursty features that occur frequently together in tweets can then be grouped into trends (Mathioudakis and Koudas, 2010). In addition to trending events, endogenous or non-event trends are also abundant on Twitter (Naaman et al., 2011). Techniques for unspecified event detection in Twitter must therefore discriminate trending events of general interest from the trivial or non-event trends (exhibiting similar temporal pattern) using salable and efficient algorithms. The techniques described below have tried to address these challenges.

Sankaranarayanan et al. (2009) proposed a news processing system based on Twitter, called TwitterStand, to capture tweets that correspond to late breaking news. They employ Naive Bayes classifier to separate news from irrelevant information, and an online clustering algorithm based on weighted term vector according to tf-idf and cosine similarity to form clusters of news. In addition, hashtags are used to reduce clustering errors. Clusters are also associated with time information for management and for determining the clusters of interest. Other issues addressed include removing the noise and determining the relevant locations associated with the tweets.

Phuvipadawat and Murata (2010) presented a method to collect, group, rank and track breaking news from Twitter. They first sample tweets (through Twitter streaming API) using predefined search queries, e.g., "#breakingnews" and "#breaking news" keyword, and index their content with Apache Lucene. Similar messages are then grouped together to form a news story. Similarity between messages is based on tf-idf with an increased weight for proper noun terms, hashtags, and usernames. Proper nouns are identified using Stanford Named Entity Recognizer (NER) trained on conventional news corpora. They use a weighted combination of number of followers (reliability) and the number of re-tweeted messages (popularity) with a time Adjustment for the freshness of the message to rank each cluster. New messages are included in a cluster if they are similar to the first message and to the top k terms in that cluster. The authors stress the importance of proper nouns identification to enhance the similarity comparison between tweets, and hence improve the overall system accuracy. An application based on the proposed method called Hot-stream has been developed.

Petrovi´c et al. (2010) adapted the online NED approach proposed for news media (Allan et al., 2000), which is based on cosine similarity between documents to detect new events that have never appeared in previous tweets. They focused on improving the efficiency of online NED algorithm, and proposed a constant time and space approach based on an adapted variant of the locality sensitive hashing (LSH) methods (Gionis et al., 1999), which limits the search to a small number of documents. However, they did not consider replies, retweets, and hashtags in their experiments, or the significance of newly detected events (e.g., trivial or not). Results have shown that ranking according to the number of users is better than ranking according to the number of tweets, and considering entropy of the message reduces the amount of spam messages in output.

Becker et al. (2011a) focused on online identification of real-world event content and its associated Twitter messages using an online clustering technique, which continuously clusters similar tweets, and then classifies the clusters content into real-world events or non-events. These non-events involve Twitter-centric topics, which are trending activities in Twitter that do not reflect any real-world occurrences (Naaman et al., 2011). Twittercentric activities are difficult to detect, because they often share similar temporal distribution characteristics with real-world events. Their clustering approach is based on a classical (threshold-based) incremental clustering algorithm that has been proposed for NED in news documents (Allan et al., 1998). Each message is represented as a tf-idf weight vector of its textual content, and cosine similarity is used to compute the distance from a message to cluster centroids. In addition to traditional pre-processing steps such as stop-word elimination and stemming, the weight of hashtag terms are doubled since they are considered a strong indicative of the message content. The authors combined temporal, social, topical, and Twitter-centric features. The temporal features rely on term frequency that appear in the set of messages associated with a cluster over time. The social features include the percentage of messages containing users interaction (i.e., retweets, replies and mentions) out of all messages in a cluster. The topical features are based on the hypothesis that event clusters tend to revolve around a central topic, whereas non-event clusters often revolve around various common terms (e.g., "sleep" or "work") that do not reflect a single theme. Twittercentric features are based on the frequency of multi-word hashtags with special capitalization (e.g., #BadWrestlingNames). Since the clusters constantly evolve over time, the features are periodically updated for old clusters and computed for newly formed ones. Finally, a support vector machine (SVM) classifier is trained on a labeled set of cluster features, and used to decide whether or not the cluster (and its associated messages) contains real-world event information.

Long et al. (2011) adapted a traditional clustering approach by integrating some specific features into the characteristics of microblog data. These features are based on "topical words", which are more popular than others with respect to an event. Topical words are extracted from daily messages based on word frequency, word occurrence in hashtag and word entropy. A (top-down) hierarchical divisive clustering approach is employed on a co-occurrence graph (connecting messages in which topical words co-occur) to divide topical words into event clusters. To track changes among events at different time, a maximum weighted bipartite graph matching is employed to create event chains, with a variation of Jaccard coefficient as similarity measures between clusters. Finally, cosine similarity augmented with a time interval between messages is used to find the top-k most relevant posts that summarize an event. These event summaries are then linked to event chain cluster and plotted on the time line. For event detection, the authors found that top-down divisive clustering outperforms both k-means and traditional hierarchical clustering algorithms.

Weng and Lee (2011) proposed an event detection based on clustering of discrete wavelet signal built from individual words generated by Twitter. In contrast with Fourier transforms, which has been proposed for event detection from traditional media, wavelet transformation are localized in both time and frequency domain, and hence able to identify the time and the duration of a bursty event within the signal. Wavelets convert the signals from the time domain to time-scale domain where the scale can be considered as the inverse of frequency. Signal construction is based on time-dependent variant of DFIDF (Document Frequency-Inverse Document Frequency), where DF counts the number of tweets (document) containing a specific word, while IDF accommodates word frequency up to the current time step. A sliding-window is then applied to capture the change over time using the H-measure (normalized wavelet entropy). Trivial words are filtered out based on (a threshold set on) signals cross-correlation, which measure similarity between two signals as function of a time-lag. The remaining words are then clustered to form events with a modularity-based graph partitioning technique, which splits the graph into subgraphs each corresponding to an event. Finally, significant events are detected based on the number of words and the cross-correlation among the words related to an event.

Similarly, Cordeiro (2012) proposed a continuous wavelet transformation based on hashtag occurrences combined with a topic model inference using Latent Dirichlet Allocation (LDA) (Blei et al., 2003). Instead of individual words, hashtags are used for building wavelet signals. An abrupt increase in the number of a given hashtag is considered a good indicator of an event that is happening at a given time. Therefore, all hashtags were retrieved from tweets and then grouped in intervals of five minutes. Hashtag signals are constructed over time by counting the hashtag mentions in each interval, grouping them into separated time series (one for each hashtag), and concatenating all tweets that mention the hashtag during each time series. Adaptive filters are then used to remove noisy hashtag signals, before applying the continuous wavelet transformation and getting a time-frequency representation of the signal. Next, wavelet peak and local maxima detection techniques are used to detect peaks and changes in the hashtag signal. Finally, when an event is detected within a given time interval, LDA is applied to all tweets related to the hashtag in each corresponding time series in order to extract a set of latent topics, which provide an improved summary of event description.

b. Specified Event Detection

Specified event detection includes known or planned social events. These events could be partially or fully specified with the related content or metadata information such as location, time, venue and performers. The techniques described below attempt to exploit Twitter textual content or metadata information or both, using a wide range of machine learning, data mining, and text analysis techniques.

Popescu and Pennacchiotti (2010) focused on identifying controversial events that provoke public discussions with opposing opinions in Twitter, such as controversies involving celebrities. Their detection framework is based on the notion of a Twitter snapshot, a triplet consisting of a target entity (e.g., Barack Obama), a given time period (e.g., 1 day) and a set of tweets about the entity from the target time period. Given a set of Twitter snapshots, an event detection module first distinguishes between event and non-event snapshots using a supervised Gradient Boosted Decision Trees (GBDT) (Friedman, 2001), trained on manually labeled dataset. To rank these event snapshots, a controversy model assigns higher scores to controversial-event snapshots, based on a regression algorithm applied to a large number of features. The employed features are based on Twitter-specific characteristics including linguistic, structural, buzziness, sentiment, and controversy features, and on external features such as news buzz and web-news controversy. These external features require time alignment of entities in news media and Twitter sources, to capture entities that are trending in both sources as they are more likely to refer to real-world events. The authors have also proposed to merge the two stages (detection and scoring) into a single-stage system by including the event detection score as an additional feature into the controversy model, which yielded an improved performance. Feature analysis of the single-stage system revealed that the events core is the most relevant feature since

it discriminates event from non-event snapshots. Hashtags are found to be important semantic features for tweets, since they help identify the topic of a tweet and estimate the topical cohesiveness of a set of tweets. Nevertheless, external features based on news and the Web are also useful, hence correlation with traditional media helps validate and explain social media reactions. In addition, the linguistic, structural and sentiment features also provide considerable effects. The authors concluded that a rich, varied set of features is crucial for controversy detection.

In a successive work, Popescu et al. (2011) employed the same framework described above, but with additional features to extract events and their descriptions from Twitter. The key idea is based on the importance and the number of the entities to capture commonsense intuitions about event and non-event snapshots. As observed by the authors: "Most event snapshots have a small set of important entities and additional minor entities while nonevent snapshots may have a larger set of equally unimportant entities". These new features are inspired from the document aboutness system (Paranjpe, 2009), and aim at ranking the entities in a snapshot with respect to their relative importance to the snapshot. This includes relative positional information (e.g. offset of term in snapshot), term-level information (term frequency, Twitter corpus IDF), and snapshot-level information (length of snapshot, category, language). Opinion extraction tools such as an Off-the-shelf Part-of-Seepch (POS) tagger and regular expressions have also been applied for improved event and main entity extraction. The number of snapshots containing action verbs, the buzziness of an entity in the news on a given day and the number of reply tweets are among the most useful new features found by the authors.

Benson et al. (2011) present a novel approach to identify Twitter messages for concert events using a factor graph model, which simultaneously analyzes individual messages, clusters them according to event type, and induces a canonical value for each event property. The motivation is to infer a comprehensive list of musical events from Twitter (based on artist/venue pairs) to complete an existing list (e.g., city event calendar table) by discovering new musical events mentioned by Twitter users that are difficult to find in other media sources. At the message level, this approach relies on a Conditional Random Field (CRF) to extract the name of the artist and location of the event. The input features to CRF model include word shape; a set of regular expressions for common emoticons, time references, and venue types; a bag of words for artist names extracted from external source (e.g., Wikipedia) and a bag of words for city venue names. Clustering is guided by term popularity, which is an alignment score among the message term labels (artist, venue, none) and some candidate value (e.g., specific artist or venue name). To capture the large text variation in Twitter messages, this score is based on a weighted combination of term similarity measures, including complete string matching, and adjacency and equality indicators scaled by the opposite document frequency. In addition, a uniqueness factor (favoring single messages) is employed during clustering to uncover rare event messages that are dominated by the popular ones, and to discourage various messages from the same events to cluster into multiple events. On the other hand, a consistent indicator is employed to discourage messages from multiple events to form a single cluster. The factor graph model is then employed to capture the interaction between all components and provide the final decision. The output of the model is a clustering of messages based on a musical event, where each cluster is represented by an artist-venue pair.

Lee and Sumiya (2010) present a geo-social local event detection system based on modeling and monitoring crowd behaviors via Twitter, to identify local festivals. They rely on geographical regularities deduced from the usual behavior patterns of crowds using geotags. First, Twitter geo-tagged data is collected and pre-processed over a long period of time for a specific region (Fujisaka et al., 2010). The region is then divided into several regions of interest (ROI) using the k-means algorithm, applied to the geographical coordinates (longitudes/latitudes) of the collected data. Geographical regularities of crowd within each ROI are then estimated from historical data based on three main features: the number of tweets, users and moving users within a ROI. Statistics for these features are then accumulated over historical data using a six-hour time interval to form the estimated behavior of crowd within each ROI. Finally, unusual events in the monitored geographical area can be detected by comparing statistics from new tweets to those of the estimated behavior. The authors found that an increased user activity (moving inside or coming to a ROI) combined with an increased number of tweets provide strong indicator of local festivals.

Sakaki et al. (2010) exploited tweets to detect specific types of events like earthquakes and typhoons. They formulated event detection as a classification problem, and trained an SVM on a manually labeled Twitter data set comprising positive events (earthquakes and typhoons) and negative events (other events or non-events). Three types of features have been employed, the number of words (statistical), the keywords in a tweet message, and the words surrounding users query (contextual). Analysis of the number of tweets over time for earthquakes and typhoons data revealed an exponential distribution of events. Parameters of the exponential distribution are estimated from historical data and then used for computation of a reliable wait time (during which more information is being gathered from related tweets) before raising an alarm. Experiments have shown that the statistical feature by itself provided the best results, while a small improvement in performance was achieved by the combination of the three features. The authors have also applied Kalman filtering and particle filtering (Fox et al., 2003) for estimation of earthquake center and typhoon trajectory from Twitter temporal and spatial information. They found that particle filters outperformed Kalman filters in both cases, due to the inappropriate Gaussian assumption of the latter for this type of problems.

Becker et al. (2011) presented a system for augmenting information about planned events with Twitter messages, using a combination of simple rules and query building strategies. To identify Twitter messages for an event, they begin with simple and precise query strategies derived from the event description and its associated aspects (e.g., combining time and venue). An annotator is then asked to label the results returned by each strategy for over 50 events which provide high-precision tweets. To improve recall, they employ term-frequency analysis and co-location techniques on the resulting high-precision tweets to identify descriptive event terms and phrases, which are then used recursively to define new queries. In addition, they build queries using URL and hashtag statistics from the high precision tweets for an event. Finally, they build a rule-based classifier to select among this new set of queries, and then use the selected queries to retrieve additional event messages. In a related work, Becker et al. (2011b) proposed centrality-based approaches to extract high-quality, relevant, and useful Twitter messages related to an event. These approaches are based on the observation that the most topically central messages in a cluster are more likely to reflect key aspects of the event than other, less central cluster messages. The techniques from both works have recently been extended and incorporated into a more general approach that aims at identifying social media contents for known events across different social media sites (Becker et al., 2012).

Massoudi et al. (2011) employed a generative language modeling approach based on query expansion and microblog "quality indicators" to retrieve individual microblog messages. However, the authors only considered the existence of a query term within a specific post and discarded its local frequency. The quality indicators include part of the blog "credibility indicators" proposed

by Weerkamp and de Rijke (2008) such as emoticons, post length, shouting, capitalization, and the existence of hyperlinks, extended with specific microblog characteristics such as a recency factor, and the number of reposts and followers. The recency factor is based on difference between the query time and the post time. The values provided with these microblog-specific indicators are averaged into a single value and are weight-combined with the credibility indicators to compute the overall prior probability for a microblog post. The query expansion technique selects top k terms that occur in a userspecified number of posts close to the query date. The final query is therefore a weighted mixture of the original and the expanded query. The combination of the quality indicator terms and the microblog characteristics has been shown to outperform each method alone. In addition, tokens with numeric or non-alphabetic characters have turned out beneficial for query expansion.

Rather than retrieving individual microblog messages in response to an event query, Metzler et al. (2012) proposed retrieving a ranked list (or timeline) of historical event summaries. The search task involves temporal query expansion, timespan retrieval and summarization. In response to a user query, this approach retrieves a ranked set of timespans based on the occurrence of the query keywords. In this work the authors suggest dividing the microblog stream into hourly-based timespans. A burstiness score is then computed for all terms that occur in messages posted during each of the retrieved timespans. This score is based on the frequency of term occurrence within the timespan retrieved from the entire microblog archive. The idea is to capture terms that are heavily discussed and trending during a retrieved timespan because they are more likely to be related to the query. The scores for each term are aggregated (using geometric mean) over all retrieved timespans, and the k-highest weighted terms are considered for query expansion. The expanded query is now used to identify the 1,000 highest scoring timespans, with respect to the term expansion weight and to the cosine similarity between the burstiness of the query terms and the burstiness of the timespan terms. Adjacent timespans (contiguous in time) are then merged into longer time interval to form the final ranked list. To produce a short summary for each retrieved time interval, a small set of query-relevant messages posted during the timespan are then selected. These relevant messages are retrieved as top ranked message according to a weighted variant of the query likelihood scoring function, which is based on the burstiness score for expansion terms and a Dirichlet smoothed language modeling estimate for each term in the message. The authors showed that their approach is more robust and effective than the traditional relevance-based language models (Lavrenko and Croft, 2001) applied to the collected Twitter corpus and to English Gigaword corpus.

Gu et al. (2011) proposed an event modeling approach called ETree for event modeling from Twitter stream. ETree employs n-gram-based content analysis techniques to group a large number of event-related messages into semantically-coherent information blocks, an incremental modeling process to construct hierarchical theme structures, and a life cycle-based temporal analysis technique to identify potential causal relationships between information blocks. The n-gram model is used to detect frequent key phrases among a large number of event-related messages, where each phrase represents an initial information block. Semantically-coherent messages are merged into the corresponding information block. The weighted cosine similarity is computed between each of the remaining messages (does not include any key phrase) and each information block. Messages with high similarities are then merged into the corresponding information block. In addition, replies to tweets are also merged into the corresponding information block. An incremental (top-down) hierarchical algorithm based on weighted cosine similarity is proposed to construct and update the theme structures,

where each theme is considered as a tree structure with information blocks as leaf nodes and subtopics as internal nodes. For instance, when a new tweet becomes available, it may be assigned to an existing theme or node or may become a new theme (in this case the hierarchy must be re-constructed). Finally, casual relationship between information blocks are computed based on content (weighted cosine) similarity and temporal relevance. Temporal information is based on the time boundaries of each information block as well as on the temporal distribution reflecting the number of messages posted within each time period. The authors show that the n-gram-based block identification generates coherent information blocks with high coverage. An event is considered coherent if more than half of its information blocks are relevant, while the coverage of an event is defined as the percentage of messages that are captured into one of the identified information blocks. In addition, ETree is shown more efficient compared to its non-incremental version and to TSCAN – a widely used algorithm that derives major themes of events from the eigenvectors of a temporal block association matrix (Chen and Chen, 2008).

c. New vs. Retrospective Event

Similar to event detection from conventional media, (Allan, 2002) and (Yang et al., 1998, 2002), event detection in Twitter can also be classified into retrospective and new event detection depending on the task and application requirements as well as on the type of event. Since new event detection (NED) techniques involve continuous monitoring of Twitter signal for discovering new events in near real-time, they are naturally suited for detecting unknown real-world events or breaking news. In general, trending events on Twitter could be aligned with real-world breaking news. However, sometimes a comment, person or photo related to real-world breaking news may become more trending on Twitter than the original event. One such example is Bobak Ferdowsi's hair style on social media during NASA's operation in 2012, where media reported: 'Mohawk guy' Bobak Ferdowsi's hair goes viral as Curiosity lands on Mars.

Although NED approaches do not impose any assumption on the event, they are not restricted to unspecified event detection. When the monitoring task involves specific events (natural disasters, celebrities, etc.) or a specific information about the event description (e.g., geographical location), these information could be integrated into the NED system by, for instance, using filtering techniques (Sakaki et al., 2010) or exploiting additional features such as the controversy (Popescu and Pennacchiotti, 2010) or the geo-tagged information (Lee and Sumiya, 2010), to better focus on the event of interest. Most NED approaches could also be applied to historical data in order to detect and analyze past events.

While most research focuses on new event detection to exploit the timely information provided by Twitter stream, recent studies showan interest in retrospective event detection from Twitter's historical data. Existing microblog search services, such as those offered by Twitter and Google, only provide limited search capabilities that allow individual microblog posts to be retrieved in response to a query (Metzler et al., 2012). The challenges in finding Twitter messages relevant to a given user query are mainly due to the sparseness of the tweets and the large number of vocabulary mismatch (which is dynamically evolving). For example, relevant messages may not contain any query term, or new abbreviations or hashtags may emerge with the event. Traditional query expansion techniques rely on terms that co-occur with query terms in relevant documents. In contrast, event retrieval from Twitter data focuses on temporal and dynamic query expansion techniques. Recent research efforts have started to focus on providing more structured and comprehensive summaries of Twitter events.

d. Detection Methods and Features

Event detection from Twitter stream draws on techniques from different fields, which are extensively covered in the literature, including Machine Learning and Data Mining (Murphy, 2012; Hastie et al., 2009), Natural Language Processing (Manning and Schütze, 1999; Jurafsky and Martin, 2009), Information Extraction (Hogenboom et al., 2011), Text Mining (Hogenboom et al., 2011; Aggarwal, 2011), and Information Retrieval (Baeza-Yates and Ribeiro-Neto, 2011).

3.3.2 Summarization of Events from Social Media

The summarization task for a given event of interest is an active domain. Chong and Asur (2013) proposed a search and summarization framework to extract relevant representative tweets from an unfiltered tweet stream in order to generate a coherent and concise summary of an event. It introduced two topic models that take advantage of temporal correlation in the data to extract relevant tweets for summarization.

Xu et al. (2013) study automatic tweet summarization task using event and information extraction (IE). They proposed an event-graph based method using IE techniques that is able to create summaries of variable length for different topics. This approach first extracts event information including named entities and event phrases from tweets then construct event graphs that represent the relationship between them. The method ranks and partitions the events using PageRank-like algorithms, and creates summaries of variable length for different topics.

3.4 Opinion Summarization

Summarization task can help the better understanding of opinion mining and sentiment analysis in social networks. As mentioned previously, social texts tend to be much more subjective and opinion-laden than traditional texts. It can thus be a great resource for businesses and other organizations to keep apprised of the public opinion regarding their products and services. Automated opinion summarization techniques are essential to leverage this immense source of opinion data. Such techniques may target a general assessment of sentiment polarity regarding a particular product or service, which can be invaluable for marketing or reputation management (e.g. "Do customers feel positive or negative regarding a particular brand or product?"). Opinion summarization may also target more specific query-based information, such as "Which particular features do customers like best about a given product?"

However the summarization task is framed, sentiment analysis is necessarily an integral part of any opinion summarization task, and constitutes a challenging area of inquiry in its own right. Sentiment analysis includes both determination of polarity (i.e. positive, negative, neutral) and sentiment degree (e.g. strong, weak). At the word level, these can be determined by consulting an opinion dictionary, containing sentiment information for each word. This may consist in a list of words annotated for sentiment either manually, such as the General Inquirer list, or augmented through corpus analysis or automated processing of lexical resources like WordNet.

Mithun (2012) presents an approach to extractive, query-based opinion summarization of blogs. Extraction and ranking of sentences is performed based on query and topic similarity in a traditional fashion using tf.idf, but also based on a "subjectivity score". The latter is calculated based on the polarity and sentiment degree of words within the sentence, as determined from MPQA subjectivity lexicon. Extracted sentences must match the polarity of the query. The degree of sentiment of the sentence, determined both from the number of subjective words therein and how strongly weighted each word is, also affects the ranking of the sentence for extraction.

4. EVALUATION

The evaluation methods and challenges of summarization from social media data is a critical issue. Spark Jones and Galliers (1995) proposed to divide the evaluation into two types: intrinsic methods and extrinsic methods. An intrinsic evaluation measures the properties of the nature of the subject and to assess its objective, while extrinsic evaluation measure aspects concerning the impacts and effects of its precise function for a human user.

There are different intrinsic and extrinsic evaluation methods and review the quality measures used in Text REtrieval Conference (TREC), DUC (Document Understanding Conference), TAC (Text Analysis Conference) and US National Institute of Standards and Technology (NIST) evaluations. The quality of a summary is assessed mostly on its content and linguistic quality such as coherence and grammaticality.

For intrinsic evaluation purposes, the summaries produced by machine could be compared with the reference summaries written by professional abstractors. This evaluation is recall-based, which measures how many of the reference summary sentences the machine summary contains. For measuring recall, the most common way is using the so-called ROUGE (Recall-Oriented Understudy for Gisting Evaluation) measure (Lin, 2004). The ROUGE software is proposed which determines the quality of a summary by comparing it to ideal summaries created by humans. ROUGE compares the summarization output with the human-generated summary based on n-grams match. The score of ROUGE-N is based on the number of n-grams occurring at the reference summary side. Recall can be computed with respect to unigram, bigram, trigram, or 4-gram matching. For example, ROUGE-2 computes the number of two successive words occurring between the machine summary and ideal summary. For measuring ROUGE-L, we view a summary sentence as a sequence of words. This evaluation computes the longest common subsequence of words to estimate the similarity between two summaries.

An extrinsic evaluation measures the quality of a system in term of its utility to solve a particular task (Giannakopoulos, Karkaletsis, and Vouros, 2006). For example, in a query-based summary the end goal is to answer the user query. In this case, human judges evaluate the summary output in terms of how well it answers the users query and not necessarily how it compares with a gold standard.

The above mentioned evaluation metrics are used to evaluate both opinionated and news article based summarization approaches and could be adapted for social media summarization. Shared evaluation tasks such as DUC and TAC competitions also use these methods to evaluate participants' summary.

TAC 2008 manual evaluations including Pyramid evaluation results that in all criteria, automatic systems are weaker than humans. Interestingly, in the automatic evaluations using ROUGE-2 and ROUGE-SU4, there was no significant performance difference between human and automatic systems; they achieved similar ROUGE scores. Dang and Owczarzak (2008) explains this the following ways: ''automatic metrics, based on string matching, are unable to appreciate a summary that uses different phrases than the reference text, even if such a summary is perfectly fine by human standards''. On the other hand, the TAC 2008 update summarization task showed that a significant gap exists between automatic summarizers and human summarizers based on manual evaluation of summaries. This indicates that ROUGE may not be the most effective tool to evaluate summaries. The same phenomenon is encountered in Mithun (2012)'s summary content evaluation.

According to Das and Martins (2007) a universal strategy to evaluate summarization systems is still absent. Summary evaluation is a difficult task because no ideal summary is available for a set of

documents. It is also difficult to compare different summaries and establish a baseline because of the absence of standard human or automatic summary evaluation metrics. On the other hand, manual evaluation is very expensive. According to Lin (2004), large scale manual evaluations of all participants' summaries as in the DUC 2003 conference would require over 3000 hours of human effort to evaluate summary content and linguistic qualities. A study by Das and Martins (2007) showed that evaluating the content of a summary is more difficult compared to evaluating its linguistic quality.

There is a need for more investigation on development of benchmark corpora and task-oriented evaluation methods for linguistic analysis in social media.

Temporal Summarization defined in TREC 2013 has the goal of developing systems that allow users to efficiently monitor the information associated with an event over time. The objective in this evaluation is to measure the precision, recall, timeliness, and novelty of updates provided by a system.

International workshop on Semantic Evaluation (SemEval-2013) proposed semantic evaluation exercises for sentiment analysis in Twitter. The task has two sub-tasks: an expression-level task and a message-level task. The first task consists of Contextual Polarity Disambiguation; by giving a message containing a marked instance of a word or a phrase, determine whether that instance is positive, negative or neutral in that context. Second task defined as a Message Polarity Classification; by giving a message, decide whether the message is of positive, negative, or neutral sentiment. For messages conveying both a positive and negative sentiment, whichever is the stronger sentiment should be chosen.

As extrinsic evaluation Xu et al. (2013) used human judgment automatic tweet summarization task using event and information extraction (IE). Xu evaluated human judgment for summarization and Event-related information extracted from tweets. In this evaluation human annotators were asked to rate the system for completeness and compactness. Completeness refers to how well the summary covers the important content in the tweets. Compactness refers to how much meaningful and non-redundant information is in the summary.

We emphasize on the need for publicly available corpora and test benchmarks in order to allow a comprehensive evaluation of performance, and on the need for an objective comparison of different approaches.

5. CONCLUSION AND FUTURE PROSPECTS

In this chapter we have considered different aspects for Social network integration in document summarization. Social network information, or open-source intelligence, is a form of intelligence gathering management that involves seeking, selecting, and acquiring information from publicly available sources, and analyzing it to produce actionable intelligence. Automatic summarization is an important theme in semantic analysis of social media and big data.

This chapter presented a distinction between traditional extractive and abstractive summaries and summarization of social media data. We described the approaches using social media in summarization and using automatic summarization for better social media retrieval and event detection. We introduced some innovative applications and use for automatic summarization in conjunction with social media analytics. We mentioned some demine-based applications such as health care, security & defence, and industry business intelligence: consumer operations and daily lives.

We highlighted the new role of summarization in the dynamic network of social media and the need for information extraction and event detection. Several workshops organized by the Association for Computational Linguistics (ACL) and special issues in scientific journals dedicated to semantic analysis in social media show how much this research field is active. The efforts on evaluation shared tasks on social data related tracks, such as update summarization, temporal summarization and event-based summarization, testimony to this fact.

We summed up the argument made by the book chapter, namely that summarization continues to be a dynamic discipline of great importance to the future of natural language processing. This purpose of this chapter is to help clarify the strengths and weaknesses of social media summarization, underlining the areas in need of more research and investigation for the future. In conclusion, we point out the fact that more work needs to be done in order to build a summarization corpora from social media that could help accelerate progress in the field. There are several summarization possibilities in the coming decade, in the context of changes in mobile technology, cloud computing and social networking.

REFERENCES

Afantenos, S., Karkaletsis, V., & Stamatopoulos, P. (2005). Summarization from medical documents: A survey. *Artificial Intelligence in Medicine, 33*(2), 157–177. doi:10.1016/j.artmed.2004.07.017 PMID:15811783

Aggarwal, C. C. (2011). An introduction to social network data analytics. In *Social network data analytics.* New York: Springer. doi:10.1007/978-1-4419-8462-3_1

Allan, J. (2002). *Topic detection and tracking: Event-based information organization.* Norwell, MA: Kluwer Academic Publishers. doi:10.1007/978-1-4615-0933-2

Allan, J., Papka, R., & Lavrenko, V. (1998). Online new event detection and tracking. In *Proceedings of the 21st Annual International ACM SIGIR Conference on Research and Development in Information Retrieval*, SIGIR '98. ACM.

André, P., Bernstein, M. S., & Luther, K. (2012). Who gives a tweet? Evaluating microblog content value. In *Proceedings of the ACM 2012 Conference on Computer Supported Cooperative Work*. IEEE.

Baeza-Yates, R. A., & Ribeiro-Neto, B. (2011). *Modern information retrieval the concepts and technology behind search* (2nd ed.). Harlow, UK: Pearson Education Ltd.

Becker, H., Chen, F., Iter, D., Naaman, M., & Gravano, L. (2011). Automatic identification and presentation of Twitter content for planned events. In *Proceedings of International AAAI Conference on Weblogs and Social Media*. AAAI.

Becker, H., Iter, D., Naaman, M., & Gravano, L. (2012). Identifying content for planned events across social media sites. In *Proceedings of the Fifth ACM International Conference on Web Search and Data Mining*, WSDM '12. ACM.

Becker, H., Naaman, M., & Gravano, L. (2010). Learning similarity metrics for event identification in social media. In *Proceedings of WSDM*, (pp. 291–300). WSDM.

Becker, H., Naaman, M., & Gravano, L. (2011a). Beyond trending topics: Real-world event identification on Twitter. In *Proceedings of ICWSM*. ICWSM.

Becker, H., Naaman, M., & Gravano, L. (2011b). Selecting quality Twitter content for events. In *Proceedings of International AAAI Conference on Weblogs and Social Media*. AAAI.

Benson, E., Haghighi, A., & Barzilay, R. (2011). Event discovery in social media feeds. In *Proceedings of the 49th Annual Meeting of the Association for Computational Linguistics: Human Language Technologies*. ACL.

Beverungen, G., & Kalita, J. (2011). Evaluating methods for summarizing twitter posts. In *Proceedings of WSDM'11*. Hong Kong, China: WSDM.

Blei, D., M., Andrew, Y. N., & Jordan, I. M. (2003). Latent dirichlet allocation. *Journal of Machine Learning Research, 3*, 993–1022.

Boyd, D. M., & Ellison, B. N. (2007). Social network sites: Definition, history, and scholarship. *Journal of Computer-Mediated Communication, 13*(1), 210–230. doi:10.1111/j.1083-6101.2007.00393.x

Chakrabarti, D., & Punera, K. (2011). Event summarization using tweets. In *Proceedings of the Fifth International AAAI Conference on Weblogs and Social Media* (pp. 66-73). AAAI.

Chen, C. C., & Chang Chen, M. (2008). Tscan: A novel method for topic summarization and content anatomy. In *Proceedings of the 31st Annual International ACM SIGIR Conference on Research and Development in Information Retrieval*, SIGIR '08. ACM.

Chong Tat Chua, F., & Asur, S. (2013). Automatic summarization of events from social media. In *Proceedings of the Seventh International AAAI Conference on Weblogs and Social Media* (ICWSM). AAAI.

Chua, F. C. T., & Asur. (2013). Automatic summarization of events from social media. In *Proceedings of the Seventh International AAAI Conference on Weblogs and Social Media* (ICWSM 2013). AAAI.

Cordeiro, M. (2012). Twitter event detection: Combining wavelet analysis and topic inference summarization. In *Proceedings of Doctoral Symposium on Informatics Engineering*. DSIE.

Dang, H. T., & Owczarzak, K. (2008). Overview of the TAC 2008 update summarization task. In *Proceedings of the Text Analysis Conference*. Gaithersburg, MD: TAC.

Das, D., & Martins, A. F. T. (2007). *A survey on automatic text summarization*. Retrieved from http://www.cs.cmu.edu/~nasmith/LS2/das-martins.07.pdf

Delort, J., & Alfonseca, E. (2012). DualSum: A topic-model based approach for update summarization. In *Proceeding of EACL 2012*. Avignon, France: EACL.

Digital Buzz. (2012). *Infographic: Social media statistics for 2012*. Retrieved from http://www.digitalbuzzblog.com/social-media-statistics-stats-2012-infographic/

Eisenstein, J. (2013). Phonological factors in social media writing. In *Proceedings of the NAACL/HLT 2013 Workshop on Language Analysis in Social Media* (LASM 2013). Atlanta, GA: LASM.

Farzindar, A. (2012). Industrial perspectives on social networks. In *Proceedings of EACL 2012 - Workshop on Semantic Analysis in Social Media*. EACL.

Farzindar, A., Danescu-Niiculescu-Mizil, C., Gamon, M., Inkpen, D., & Nagarajan, M. (Eds.). (2013). *Proceedings of the NAACL/HLT workshop on language analysis in social media* (LASM 2013). Atlanta, GA: NAACL.

Farzindar, A., & Inkpen, D. (Eds.). (2012). *Proceedings of the workshop on semantic analysis in social media* (SASM). Avignon, France: Association for Computational Linguistics.

Farzindar, A., & Khreich, W. (2013). A Survey of Techniques for Event Detection in Twitter, accepted in special Issue of the Computational Intelligence, an International Journal, on Semantic analysis in social networks.

Farzindar, A., & Lapalme, G. (2004). LetSum, an automatic legal text summarizing system, legal knowledge and information systems. In *Proceedings of Jurix 2004: the Sevententh Annual Conference*. Berlin: IOS Press.

Fox, D., Hightower, J., Liao, L., Schulz, D., & Borriello, G. (2003). Bayesian filtering for location estimation. *IEEE Pervasive Computing / IEEE Computer Society [and] IEEE Communications Society, 2*, 24–33. doi:10.1109/MPRV.2003.1228524

Friedman, J. H. (2001). Greedy function approximation: A gradient boosting machine. *Annals of Statistics, 29*, 1189–1232. doi:10.1214/aos/1013203451

Fujisaka, T., Lee, R., & Sumiya, K. (2010). Discovery of user behavior patterns from geo-tagged micro-blogs. In *Proceedings of the 4th International Conference on Uniquitous Information Management and Communication*, ICUIMC '10. ACM.

Giannakopoulos, G., Karkaletsis, V., & Vouros, G. (2006). *Automatic multi-document summarization and prior knowledge: Past, present and vision* (Technical Report DEMO-2006-2). Demokritos, Greece: NCSR.

Gionis, A., Indyk, P., & Motwani, R. (1999). Similarity search in high dimensions via hashing. In *Proceedings of the 25th International Conference on Very Large Data Bases*, VLDB '99. Morgan Kaufmann Publishers Inc.

Gu, H., Xie, X., Lv, Q., Ruan, Y., & Shang, L. (2011). ETree: Effective and efficient event modeling for real-time online social media networks. In Proceedings of Web Intelligence and Intelligent Agent Technology (WI-IAT), 2011 IEEE/WIC/ACM, (Vol. 1, pp. 300–307). IEEE.

Hastie, T., Tibshirani, R., & Friedman, J. (2009). *The elements of statistical learning: Data mining, inference, and prediction* (2nd ed.). Berlin: Springer. doi:10.1007/978-0-387-84858-7

Hogenboom, F., Frasincar, F., Kaymak, U., & Jong, F. (2011). An overview of event extraction from text. In *Proceedings of Workshop on Detection, Representation, and Exploitation of Events in the Semantic Web* (DeRiVE 2011). CEUR.

Hu, M., Sun, A., & Lim, E. (2007). Comments-oriented blog summarization by sentence extraction. In *Proceedings of 16th CIKM*, (pp. 901—904). CIKM.

Java, A., Song, X., Finin, T., & Tseng, B. (2007). Why we Twitter: Understanding microblogging usage and communities. In *Proceedings of the 9th WebKDD and 1st SNA-KDD 2007 Workshop on Web Mining and Social Network Analysis*, WebKDD/SNA-KDD '07. ACM.

Jurafsky, D., & Martin, H. J. (2009). *Speech and language processing an introduction to natural language processing, computational linguistics, and speech recognition* (2nd ed.). Upper Saddle River, NJ: Prentice Hall.

Krishnamurthy, B., Gill, P., & Arlitt, M. (2008). A few chirps about Twitter. In *Proceedings of the First Workshop on Online Social Networks*, WOSN '08. ACM.

Lavrenko, V., & Croft, W. B. (2001). Relevance based language models. In *Proceedings of the 24th Annual International ACM SIGIR Conference on Research and Development in Information Retrieval*, SIGIR '01. ACM.

Lee, R., & Sumiya, K. (2010). Measuring geographical regularities of crowd behaviors for Twitter-based geo-social event detection. In *Proceedings of the 2nd ACM SIGSPATIAL International Workshop on Location Based Social Networks*, LBSN '10. ACM.

Li, J., & Li, S. Wang. X., Tian, Y., & Chang, B. (2012). Key laboratory of computational linguistics. Peking University.

Lin, Y. C. (2004). ROUGE: A package for automatic evaluation of summaries. In *Proceedings of the ACL-04 Workshop*. ACL.

Lin, Y., Sundaram, H., & Kelliher, A. (2009). *Summarization of large scale social network activity: Acoustics, speech, and signal processing*. Academic Press.

Liu, K.-L., Li, W.-J., & Guo, M. (2012). Emoticon smoothed language models for Twitter sentiment analysis. In *Proceedings of the Twenty-Sixth AAAI Conference on Artificial Intelligence*. AAAI.

Long, R., Wang, H., Chen, Y., Jin, O., & Yu, Y. (2011). Towards effective event detection, tracking and summarization on microblog data. In *Web-Age Information Management (LNCS)* (Vol. 6897, pp. 652–663). Berlin: Springer. doi:10.1007/978-3-642-23535-1_55

Mani, I. (2001). *Automatic summarization*. Amsterdam, The Netherlands: John Benjamins Publishing Co.

Mani, I., & Maybury, M. (1999). *Advances in automatic text summarization*. Cambridge, MA: MIT Press.

Manning, C. D., & Schütze, H. (1999). *Foundations of statistical natural language processing*. Cambridge, MA: MIT Press.

Massoudi, K., Tsagkias, M., Rijke, M., & Weerkamp, W. (2011). Incorporating query expansion and quality indicators in searching microblog posts. In *Proceedings of the 33rd European Conference on Advances in Information Retrieval*, ECIR'11. Springer-Verlag.

Mathioudakis, M., & Koudas, N. (2010). TwitterMonitor: Trend detection over the Twitter stream. In *Proceedings of SIGMOD Conference*. Indianapolis, IN: ACM.

Melville, P., Sindhwani, V., & Lawrence, R. (2009). Social media analytics: Channeling the power of the blogosphere for marketing insight. In *Proceedings of the Workshop on Information in Networks* (WIN-2009). New York: WIN.

Metzler, D., Cai, C., & Hovy, E. H. (2012). Structured event retrieval over microblog archives. In *Proceedings of HLT-NAACL*, (pp. 646–655). NAACL.

Metzler, D., Dumais, S., & Meek, C. (2007). Similarity measures for short segments of text. In *Proceedings of the 29th European Conference on IR Research*, ECIR'07. Springer-Verlag.

Mithun, S. (2012*). Exploiting rhetorical relations in blog summarization*. (PhD thesis). Department of Computer Science and Software Engineering, Concordia University, Montreal, Canada.

Murphy, K. P. (2012). *Machine learning: A probabilistic perspective*. Cambridge, MA: MIT Press.

Naaman, M., Becker, H., & Gravano, L. (2011). Hip and trendy: Characterizing emerging trends on Twitter. *Journal of the American Society for Information Science and Technology*, 62(5), 902–918. doi:10.1002/asi.21489

Nallapati, R., Feng, A., Peng, F., & Allan, J. (2004). Event threading within news topics. In *Proceedings of the Thirteenth ACM International Conference on Information and Knowledge Management*, CIKM '04. ACM.

New Media Trend Watch. (2013). *Social networking and UGC*. Retrieved from http://www.newmediatrendwatch.com/world-overview/137-social-networking-and-ugc

Paranjpe, D. (2009). Learning document aboutness from implicit user feedback and document structure. In *Proceedings of the 18th ACM Conference on Information and Knowledge Management*, CIKM '09. ACM.

Petrovic, S., Osborne, M., & Lavrenko, V. (2010). Streaming first story detection with application to Twitter. In *Proceedings of Human Language Technologies: The 2010 Annual Conference of the North American Chapter of the Association for Computational Linguistics*, HLT'10. Association for Computational Linguistics.

Phuvipadawat, S., & Murata, T. (2010). Breaking news detection and tracking in Twitter. In *Proceedings of IEEE/WIC/ACM International Conference on Web Intelligence and Intelligent Agent Technology* (WI- IAT). IEEE.

Popescu, A.-M., & Pennacchiotti, M. (2010). Detecting controversial events from Twitter. In *Proceedings of the 19th ACM International Conference on Information and Knowledge Management*, CIKM '10. ACM.

Popescu, A.-M., Pennacchiotti, M., & Paranjpe, D. (2011). Extracting events and event descriptions from Twitter. In *Proceedings of the 20th International Conference Companion on World Wide Web*. ACM.

Sakaki, T., Okazaki, M., & Matsuo, Y. (2010). Earthquake shakes Twitter users: Real-time event detection by social sensors. In *Proceedings of the 19th international conference on World Wide Web*, WWW '10. ACM.

Sankaranarayanan, J., Samet, H., Teitler, B. E., Lieberman, M. D., & Sperling, J. (2009). Twit-terStand: News in tweets. In *Proceedings of the 17th ACM SIGSPATIAL International Conference on Advances in Geographic Information Systems*, GIS '09. ACM.

Sharifi, B., Hutton, M., & Kalita, J. (2010). Experiments in microblog summarization. In *Proceedings of NAACL-HLT 2010*. Los Angeles, CA: NAACL.

Spark-Jones, K., & Galliers, R. J. (1995). Evaluating natural language processing systems: An analysis and review. *Lecture Notes in Artificial Intelligence, 1083.*

Weerkamp, W., & Rijke, M. (2008). Credibility improves topical blog post retrieval. In *Proceedings of ACL*, (pp. 923–931). ACL.

Weng, J., & Lee, B. S. (2011). Event detection in Twitter. In *Proceedings of ICWSM*. ICWSM.

Xu, W., Grishman, R., Meyers, A., & Ritter, A. (2013). A preliminary study of tweet summarization using information extraction. In *Proceedings of the NAACL/HLT 2013 Workshop on Language Analysis in Social Media* (LASM 2013). Atlanta, GA: NAACL.

Yang, Y., Pierce, T., & Carbonell, J. (1998). A study of retrospective and on-line event detection. In *Proceedings of the 21st Annual International ACM SIGIR Conference on Research and Development in Information Retrieval*, SIGIR '98. ACM.

Yang, Y., Zhang, J., Carbonell, J., & Jin, C. (2002). Topic-conditioned novelty detection. In *Proceedings of the Eighth ACM SIGKDD International Conference on Knowledge Discovery and Data Mining*. ACM.

Zhao, D., & Rosson, B. R. (2009). How and why people Twitter: The role that micro-blogging plays in informal communication at work. In *Proceedings of the ACM 2009 International Conference on Supporting Group Work*. ACM.

Zhou, L., & Hovy, E. (2006). On the summarization of dynamically introduced information: Online discussions and blogs. In *Proceedings of AI'06 Spring Symposium on Computational Approaches to Analyzing Weblogs*. AI.

ADDITIONAL READING

Barbier, G., Feng, Z., Gundecha, P., Liu, H., *Provenance Data in Social Media*, Synthesis Lectures on Data Mining and Knowledge Discovery, Morgan & Claypool publishers. Farzindar, A., & Inkpen, D. editors. Special issue of Computational Intelligence, an International Journal on Semantic analysis in social networks

Farzindar, A., Danescu-Niiculescu-Mizil, C., Gamon, M., Inkpen, D., & Nagarajan, M. (Eds.). (2013). Proceedings of the NAACL/HLT workshop on Language Analysis in Social Media (LASM 2013), The 2013 Conference of the North American Chapter of the Association for Computational Linguistics: Human Language Technologies, Atlanta, Georgia, June 13, 2013.

Farzindar, A., & Inkpen, D. (Eds.). (2012). Proceedings of the Workshop on Semantic Analysis in Social Media (SASM). Association for Computational Linguistics, Avignon, France, April 23, 2012.

Liu, B. *Sentiment Analysis and Opinion Mining (Introduction and Survey)*, Synthesis Lectures on Human Language Technologies, Morgan & Claypool Publishers. Russell, M. *Mining the Social Web, Analyzing Data from Facebook, Twitter, LinkedIn, and Other Social Media Sites*, O'Reilly Media Publisher.

KEY TERMS AND DEFINITIONS

Automatic Summarization: Reducing a text in order to summarize the major points of the original document in a manner sensitive to the application or user's need.

Information Extraction: The automatic extraction of structured information such as entities, relations or events from unstructured documents.

Microblogging: A broadcast medium in the form of blogging featuring small content allowing users to exchange small elements such as short sentences, individual images, or video links.

Semantic Analysis in Social Media: Analysing, understanding and enabling social networks using natural language interfaces and human behaviour on the web, e-learning environments, cyber communities and educational or online shared workspaces.

Social Computing: A term for an area of computer science that is concerned with the intersection of social behaviour and computational systems.

Social Event Detection: Discovers social events and identifies related media items.

Social Event Summarization: To extract social media text representative of some real-world event. In practice, the aim is not to summarize any and all events, but only events of interest.

Social Event: A planned public or social event that can be broadly defined as any occurrence unfolding over some spatial and temporal scope. A social event is planned by people, attended by people, and the media providing the event are captured by people.

Social Media Summarization: Automatic summarization from multiple social media sources aiming to reduce and aggregate the amount of information presented to users.

Social Media Text: A written content of a social nature.

Social Media: Web-based medium designed to be disseminated through social interaction among people in which they create, share, and exchange information and ideas through highly accessible and scalable publishing techniques in virtual communities and networks.

Social Networking Service: A web-based platform to build social networks among people who share interests and activities.

Update Summarization: Update summarization uses web documents, such as blogs, reviews, news articles, to identify new information on a topic, under the assumption that the user has already read a given set of earlier articles.

Chapter 7
Approaches to Large-Scale User Opinion Summarization for the Web

William Darling
Xerox Research Centre Europe, France

ABSTRACT

This chapter discusses approaches to applying text summarization research to the real-world problem of opinion summarization of user comments. Following a brief overview of the history of research in text summarization, the authors consider large scale user opinion summarization on the Web, a summarization problem that is distinct from the traditional domain that the research has focused on until very recently. More specifically, they consider opinion summarization of large datasets that generally include large degrees of noise and little editorial structure. To deal with this kind of real-world problem, the chapter addresses three major areas that must be considered and adhered to when designing systems for this type of problem: simple techniques, domain knowledge, and evaluative testing. Each area is covered in detail, and throughout the chapter, the lessons are applied to a case study that aims to apply the recommendations to designing a real-world opinion summarization system for a fictional book publisher.

INTRODUCTION

The research literature in automatic text summarization is extensive and spans nearly seven decades. The focus in this research has traditionally centered most strongly on summarization of news articles (Gong & Liu, 2001; Nenkova, et al., 2006; Haghighi & Vanderwende, 2009; Nenkova &

McKeown, 2011), but in recent years has expanded in diverse directions to, most notably, opinion summarization (Hu & Liu, 2004; Blair-Goldensohn, et al., 2008; Lerman, et al., 2009; Lu, et al., 2009). Opinion summarization is of immense interest to corporations and governments, who can act more effectively when they understand the viewpoints of their customers or citizens that are being laid bare each day in Internet forums and social networks, but are so disparate and numerous that they can-

DOI: 10.4018/978-1-4666-5019-0.ch007

not be efficiently digested without some service in between the raw data and the ultimate consumer.

Part of the impetus of the disparate evolution in text summarization's domain can be attributed to its application to real-world problems. While news summarization is interesting, in practice it is often unnecessary due to the concise and structured nature of newswire writing and the common existence of an already-included high quality succinct summary: the headline. Further, news summarization (as far as the task has commonly been defined in the literature) is arguably not a "real-world problem"; the datasets are small, the payoff is low, and the task is generally accomplished easily by humans.

In contrast, the areas that summarization research is expanding to are primarily those that can be considered real-world problems. Here, the payoffs are high, the datasets are often huge (making the problems interesting by virtue of fitting into the *in vogue* area of "big data'") and the tasks are those that, rather than simplifying or optimizing the efficiency of an existing practice, could not be done without the help of algorithmic – often machine learning based – approaches. The principal example is opinion summarization (Liu & Zhang, 2012). This broad field encompasses disparate research tasks that include, *inter alia*, topic modeling, sentence scoring, clustering, sentiment analysis, subjectivity prediction, and user modeling. Building a powerful and mature system for real-world use in this area necessitates expertise in at least a large subset of all of these areas, plus the experience and knowledge required to make them work together synoptically.

What it does not necessarily require, however, is "advanced" or overly complicated models. Peter Norvig and others have argued convincingly that in general more data with simple models beats less data with complex models (Halevy, et al., 2009). While Norvig's statement was with respect to machine learning in general, and in particular to cases where large amounts of data are available, the sentiment at least appears to be particularly apt

with respect to text summarization. Models that have existed for several years tend to perform on par with more recent complicated methods and the simpler models are often easier to implement and scale much better. When these simple methods are coupled with domain-specific targeted assumptions about the structure of the input and the types of meta information that are available, impressive results can be easily achieved. In this Chapter, we explain powerful yet simple techniques for opinion summarization that build on these ideas.

This Chapter gives a practical overview to large-scale user opinion summarization particularly through the web. It broadly addresses three major areas that must be considered and adhered to when designing modern opinion summarization systems that tackle the real-world problems associated with understanding a collection of individual's viewpoints from opinionated text data. Here, we consider real-world problems to consist of tasks where there are large amounts of unstructured data, there is generally no gold-standard or notion of an objectively correct answer, and that can in some way be considered as *practical* or *commercial* in that there is a conceivable situation where the system would be commercially viable (in either an industrial or governmental context). While each of the three major areas necessarily feed on each other, they will be presented sequentially. They include: (1) relying on simple techniques; (2) domain knowledge and specialization; and (3) testing and evaluation. Following discussions of how best to utilize existing techniques and how to design and undertake competent testing and evaluation of a real-world user opinion summarization system, the Chapter will conclude with a brief look at where summarization research is headed in the near future. Throughout the Chapter, the recommendations will be exemplified by application to an informal case study involving the implementation of a book review summarization system for a publishing company. The case study considers specific existing techniques to implement, the domain knowledge that might be included, a proper evaluation framework, and how to tie all of the parts together into a coherent whole.

BACKGROUND

Research into automatic text summarization dates back to the 1950's at IBM. Luhn's pioneering work on scientific research article summarization concentrated on the word frequency counts of an input text and this view remains largely the basis of most summarization work today (Luhn, 1958). Luhn's summarization system took a shallow view of the summarization task referred to as *extractive* summarization. To generate a summary, a method first segments the input into multiple sentences and then *scores* or *orders* the sentences according to some function $f(S)$ where $f(S)$ is large for sentences that are *representative* of the input and low for sentences that are not as important to the main message of the input text. A summary is then generated by selecting the highest scoring sentences and concatenating them together to form the output. This approach – which remains the most common method for performing any class of automatic text summarization (Nenkova & McKeown, 2011) – is contrasted with *abstractive* summarization where a summary is created by paraphrasing or rewriting the input in a more succinct version. The latter approach, while more difficult and still rarely employed in summarization systems, is more akin to the summarization that is performed by humans.

Luhn's method determines the *representativeness* or *significance* of a sentence by a combination of its contained words' frequency counts and the sentence's relative position in the input. Luhn's rational for this approach was that for an author to emphasize an important point, she will typically need to repeat certain words as the argument is elaborated; these words that are used extensively will then be correlated with the sentences which are of high importance. Nenkova, *et al.* (2006) later provided an empirical justification for relying on

term frequency by observing humans participants creating summaries and comparing the words they chose to the frequency of the words in the input; it was shown that generally, the more often a word appears in an input text, the more likely it is that the word will appear in a model summary generated by a human (Nenkova, et al., 2006).

Luhn's work is also among the earliest to discuss stop-words in the context of natural language processing (NLP). Semantically empty words such as "the", "and", "a", and "of" that serve only a syntactic purpose in connecting content words to form coherent natural language sentences are commonly referred to as stop-words and a standard pre-processing step in most NLP tasks involves filtering them out of the input using a pre-computed list. Luhn instead established a high-frequency word cutoff such that the important words in a document would be those high-frequency words that were below the cutoff where stop-words would tend to begin to appear. To quantitatively determine the importance of each sentence, Luhn's method then scores each sentence by the number of high-frequency words it contains that are below the stop-word cutoff, but that are above another cutoff that determines where the important words begin. A summary is then made up by iteratively extracting the sentences with the highest importance score until the desired summary length is met. Despite this method's simplicity, modern state-of-the-art summarization systems rarely diverge from its basic principle of choosing sentences with a high ratio of content to non-content words where content words are determined based on their frequency in the input. Sentence selection based on word frequency has been shown to closely mimic the approach that humans take when summarizing an input (Nenkova, et al., 2006), and has been empirically shown to provide results that are commensurate with more complex and modern methods (Darling, 2010).

Later summarization techniques began to rely on sentence-based features, which originated with Edmundson (1969). Edmundson's techniques

Figure 1. Frequency-ordered list of word frequency for Jane Austen's Emma (left) and Shakespeare's Macbeth (right). The words in blue are likely stop-words; the words in red are unimportant background words; and the words in green are the important content words following Luhn's intuition.

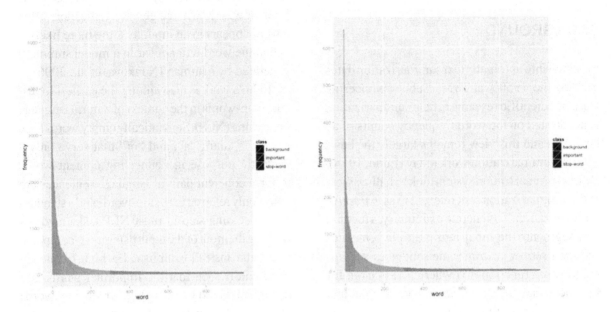

considered three principal features that he called "cue", "title", and "location". The weights of these features were learned in an early supervised learning framework, contrary to the unsupervised approach taken by Luhn. The "cue" feature, for example, gives greater weight to sentences that contain *bonus* words, and gives negative weight to sentences that contain *stigma* words. These words are learned from paired training data where content words that are commonly found in both input texts and their related summaries are chosen as *bonus* words and vice versa. This feature is highly dependent on the given domain, and some example bonus words in the research paper summarization domain might include *significant* and *conclusion* because the important messages from the paper might likely be found in sentences containing these words.

The "title" feature is more straightforward and simply gives stronger weight to a sentence that contains words that also appear in the title of the text. The intuition here is that these words are clearly important because they were used to give a highly succinct overview of the text in the form of its title. This feature tends to work well when a title is available (Darling, 2010), but is of course unusable when the input contains no title. The third feature considered by Edmundson is sentence location. The weights for this feature can again be learned by domain but intuitively one could argue that sentences appearing near the beginning and end of an input should generally be weighted more heavily because writers will tend to convey their most important points in introducing and concluding the subject matter. This can be a particularly powerful feature in certain domains; Lin & Hovy (1997) were able to achieve impressive results using *only* position as a feature in a restricted domain. This feature is also very useful in the news domain because of the structure of most news articles. Taking the first *n* sentences of a newswire article as a summarization method results in a strong baseline and was studied in depth by Nenkova (2005).

Supervised learning of features for a specific domain is very popular for text summarization and many modern systems use this approach including many of the highest performing systems at the Text Analysis Conference (TAC) which caters to the practical construction of text summarization systems (Owczarzak & Dang, 2011). The ultimate methods used to learn and combine features are varied and include SVMs, Naïve Bayes, Decision Tress, and Genetic Algorithms (Kupiec, et al., 1995; Hovy & Lin, 1998; Lin, 1999; Okurowski, et al., 2000). The number and types of features have grown since Edmundson's work and will now commonly include by sentence (in addition to the original cue, title, and location): average term frequency; number of words; degree of sentence node; page rank of sentence node; length of sentence vector in a latent subspace; and *tf-ids* / *tf-idf* scores; etc. (Litvak, et al., 2010). Recent supervised approaches also take advantage of features computed using hierarchical topic model distributions (Celikyilmaz & Dilek Hakkani-Tur, 2010) and other advanced machine learning methods.

Other common classes of methods that have developed in addition to those based on word frequency include topic signatures (Lin & Hovy, 2000), sentence clustering and selection (McKeown, et al., 1999), graph-based approaches based on PageRank-like algorithms (Erkan & Radev, 2004), lexical chains (Barzilay & Elhadad, 1997), and unsupervised topic modeling-based approaches (Daumé & Marcu, 2006; Haghighi & Vanderwende, 2009; Darling & Song, 2011b). We have gone over some of the most primary basics of text summarization simply because the core of these methods still carries over to the most recent work that is being produced in the area and we will build on them in the coming sections. See (Nenkova & McKeown, 2011) for an extensive recent survey of common techniques used in text summarization research. Before we discuss specific techniques for opinion summarization, however, we spend some time discussing the widespread

problem in summarization of redundancy, and how it is generally dealt with.

Dealing with Redundancy

One problem endemic to nearly every text summarization method is redundancy and we therefore make note of it here. With only a small amount of space to convey the important content from an input, there is absolutely no room for taking up valuable space by repeating information. The issue is less extreme for traditional single document summarization but becomes increasingly important with the move to multi-document summarization as though multiple documents may contain diverse and connected important information that can complement each other, when articles discuss the same theme there will almost always exist some kind of redundancy with respect to introducing the topic or touching upon salient common points. This will prove to be an especially important consideration in designing a system that seeks to summarize user comments, as we will move to shortly, because there will nearly always be some kind of overlap in users' views, and generally the aim of a summary is to see a broad yet succinct view of the input so as to maximize the understanding of the disparate themes present in the original documents. This is especially true when performing opinion summarization where the user of the system will likely be interested in the views that users or citizens have on a wide array of issues rather than simply a view of *the* most prevalent issue being discussed (though the latter meta information is clearly also of use).

Creating a summary can be thought of as an optimization problem where we are seeking to maximize important content while minimizing overlap or redundancy. Figure 2 shows a collection of sentences from an input visualized in a 2d space where the closer two points are to each other corresponds to their semantic similarity. There are three clusters of points and each cluster can be thought of as a sub-topic of the main theme

Figure 2. Sentences from an input visualized in a 2d space where the closer two points are to each other corresponds to their semantic similarity. There are three clusters of points denoted by color where each cluster can be thought of as a sub-topic of the input.

expressed in the input documents. Because there are far more sentences in the green cluster (four times as many as the other two), simple statistical techniques that aim to replicate the input word frequency distribution in the summary will likely only choose sentences from the green cluster, ignoring the interesting information contained in the red and blue clusters. Further, if the method simply selects sentences that are very likely under the input word frequency distribution (points near the middle of the green cluster), these sentences may very well be *too* similar to each other and the length-limited summary will be poor in information content due to space being taken up by repeated content.

There are two common classes of approach for dealing with redundancy: one that treats redundancy avoidance as a separate step in the summarization pipeline, and another that makes it part of the scoring method itself. For the former,

any method that scores sentences can be employed, and then when sentence selection occurs, sentences can be skipped if they are too similar to any of the sentences that have already been chosen, or their score could be weighted downwards depending on how similar they are to previously selected sentences. The most common choice for detecting sentence similarity is the cosine similarity measure in the vector space model used traditionally in information retrieval systems (Singhal, 2001). A method that follows this procedure and fits into the above example is that of McKeown, et al. who cluster similar sentences together and then select representative sentences from each of the clusters while avoiding redundancy (McKeown, 1999). The latter method – where redundancy avoidance forms part of the scoring technique – considers the problem of redundancy within the summarization model. The most famous of these techniques is Maximal Marginal Relevance (MMR) which greedily selects sentences by iteratively selecting the sentence which maximizes the score of a combination of similarity to a summarization query and dissimilarity to the already selected sentences (Carbonell & Goldstein, 1998):

$$MMR = \text{argmax}_{s \in S} [\lambda \text{Sim}_1(s, Q) - (1 - \lambda)\text{max}_{t \in C} \text{Sim}_2(s, t)]$$

where S is the set of candidate sentences segmented from the input, C is the set of sentences that have already been selected for summary inclusion, Q is the summarization query which in generic summarization can be considered as the centroid of the input space (Gong & Liu, 2001; Nenkova & McKeown, 2011), and $\lambda \in [0,1]$ is a parameter learned on a development set that controls the contribution from the relevancy measure and the redundancy avoiding measure. MMR is a framework and the similarity functions Sim_1 and Sim_2 can be set to whatever works best for the problem at hand. However, generally they are the same function and the cosine similarity measure is employed (Carbonell & Goldstein, 1998). As mentioned above, it is important to keep this problem in mind in any summarization context, but it can become increasingly significant when summarizing opinions on a large-scale as there will nearly always contain a large degree of redundant overlap.

Why Opinion Summarization?

This chapter does not aim to cover the state of the art in all areas of summarization research. Instead, here we are considering text summarization as it is used by companies and encountered by users specifically in everyday life. We will therefore briefly look at some of the summarization systems that exist in the real world and assess their usefulness. The conclusion is that user opinion summarization on the web may be the most interesting application and also the most useful. While text summarization has been a topic of interest for natural language processing and machine learning researchers for many years, it is just in the past few years that it has started to become important as an application area in the real world. This is almost entirely thanks to the user-driven model of Web 2.0 and the enormous amounts of data that are being made available in forums, social networks, and review sites.

Prior to the advent of the "user-centered" Web, where the most popular websites have shifted from static providers of information disconnected from the user to providers of services that augment the data that users provide themselves (e.g. Facebook, Flickr, Twitter, etc.), there were few examples of text summarization systems in real world use. Mac OS X has included a little-known extractive text summarization service since 2005 which is likely based on term frequency statistics. Microsoft Word has also included an extractive summarization

tool called AutoSummarize since 2003 that is known to be based on term frequency statistics. Nevertheless, it is safe to say that neither of these systems have experienced widespread use and neither are well known by users; these services are seen more as toys that perhaps small groups of users find useful for specific types of tasks. A more professional example of a summarization system deployed in the real world is the software "DecisionExpress" which is a professional legal decision text summarization system developed by NLP Technologies and described in (Chieze, et al., 2010). The system is based on domain-specific linguistic rules and extracts content from the input at either a sentence or paragraph level. As NLP Technologies is a private company it is unknown how widely used the software is, but it is marketed as a serious tool for legal professionals who are interested in having access to the key points in legal decisions in a given area that are released over a certain time period.

There are likely other isolated examples of text summarization being used for professional purposes in this manner as software products provided for a particular industry, but by far the most glaring example of its recent success is through the Internet and enabling more advanced Web 2.0 services. These include news summaries on Google News; product and service review summaries for travel destinations (Tripadvisor, Booking.com, Hotels.com); restaurants (Yelp.com, Zagat.com, Google+); products (Amazon); and even summarized user comments on Facebook. This view of summarization may not align itself perfectly with a common *a priori* understanding of what automatic text summarization entails, but it represents the foremost example of text summarization being used in the real world right now. Throughout the remainder of this Chapter, an overview of this interpretation of real-world text summarization will be provided, and we will outline a framework for a first approach to take in designing a large scale user opinion summarization system of data collected from users in the Web 2.0 environment.

LARGE SCALE USER OPINION SUMMARIZATION

While summarization systems that aim to distill and re-present *facts* more succinctly than in their original incarnation represent ambitious research and development goals, fully useful and accurate systems that fit within this domain are still not entirely within our grasp. Here, we describe approaches to summarizing people's opinions both because with thousands or millions of different inputs it would be impossible to digest all of the relevant data (making summary generation something that would be impossible without automatic techniques), and because the data from users' opinions available to other users on review sites and to corporations and governments in addressing problems with their products or policies represents an opportunity to truly offer a next level of information that would not have been possible before Web 2.0 and the tools that make it possible.

The problems associated with summarizing user opinions are many. First, there are generally two levels of semantic meaning that one is interested in with respect to an opinion: the target of the opinion (what is the user referring to?) and its valence (is it a positive, negative, or neutral opinion?). Both levels subsume numerous sub-levels as well and can be thought of as a hierarchy. In the context of our case study that aims to build an opinion summarization system for a publisher, if the target is a specific book, for example, one opinion may concentrate on the plot line (commonly referred to as an *aspect*) while another may consider the writing style. These distinct aspects should be treated separately. The valence can also become much more complex. A user's opinion with respect to a particular book's writing style may be nuanced in the sense that she ascribes a positive opinion to it but only for a subset of its use. For example, a single sentence may both praise and criticize an author's writing style, and therefore assigning the sentence a single valence or "sentiment" score may be ambiguous. In citizen opinion summarization, it may be impossible to attribute a traditional fixed-point sentimental score to an opinion if, for example, the comment entails a structured criticism and suggestion for a policy; it would be nonsensical to say that this could fit into either a "for" or "against" cluster of opinions with respect to a proposed law. Finally, identifying the opinion holder is itself often nontrivial (Kim & Hovy, 2005). A common example is when a user quotes another to apply some context to her position; determining the overall valence of the stated opinion then becomes an even more complex task.

Another difficulty in summarizing user opinions lies in their textually unstructured nature. In the news article domain, inputs are highly structured, copy-edited, and succinctly written to begin with. As such, even random sentence selection will often result in a readable summary where the reader will likely be able to grasp at least the underlying theme of the input. In fact, informal experiments have shown that, on average, randomly selecting sentences from the Document Understanding Conference (Dang, 2006) and Text Analysis Conference (Owczarzak and Dang, 2011) newswire datasets and applying simple redundancy avoidance techniques results in a system that can generally perform on par with respect to ROUGE scores as other systems that competed in these summarization competitions. ROUGE (Recall-Oriented Understudy for Gisting Evaluation) is the standard metric for automatically evaluating text summarization systems and is based on counting n-gram overlaps between the candidate summary and a set of references (Lin, 2004). Contrast newswire summarizations with opinion summarization which includes texts that are typically unstructured, at times rambling, and nearly always far from succinct.

A random sentence selection procedure run on this latter kind of input will almost surely result in an incomprehensible output that is of no value to a user.

Despite these hurdles, however, opinion summarization research is flourishing, and the obtainable results are impressive (Hu & Liu, 2004; Liu, et al., 2005; Blair-Goldensohn, et al. 2008). Opinion summarization, as a sub-task of the umbrella term text summarization, encompasses a number of research areas that include feature extraction, sentiment analysis, clustering, association mining, and many others. A quality system will generally have to draw on many of these areas and techniques, and it is important that the researcher or developer designing a system is at least familiar with the basic approaches that are commonly employed. But this Chapter does not aim to be a survey of sentiment analysis or opinion mining. For a full overview, see (Liu, 2012; Liu & Zhang, 2012). Instead, we offer a broad view of the approach that one might take when initially faced with a summarization problem that involves real world data and that will be used by real world users. Again, we are focusing on real world problems in the context of opinion summarization most likely provided as a web service or as a system that makes use of user content gathered through the web and that is then used to gain information with respect to a product, service, policy, or general outlook held by some subset of the population. To offer a service like this, we advocate taking a three-pronged framework-like approach that centers on simple statistical techniques, strong domain adaptation, and rigorous testing. Centering upon these three values will ensure a modular, improvable system that works from the beginning and that can become more complex with time, expertise, and resources. We begin with an outline of simple techniques. These are methods that are usually easily understandable, are simple to implement, and tend to scale well. But they are not poorly performing, and that in a sense

is the philosophical purpose of the next section. We aim to show that simple techniques, strung together, result in maintainable systems that provide good performance and excellent quality.

Simple Techniques

Despite the recorded successes in improved ROUGE (Lin, 2004) and Pyramid (Nenkova & Passonneau, 2004) scores found in the literature through successively more elaborate and complex models, text summarization systems in a practical environment have tended to excel when based on simple statistical methods. This is a common theme in practical machine learning evidenced by recent position papers (Wagstaff, 2012), and by business decisions taken by companies with strong investments in machine learning systems. As an example, following the "Netflix challenge" where the online video streaming company Netflix awarded $1M USD to the team that was successful in improving their existing recommendation engine by an improvement in Root Mean Squared Error of 10%, Netflix nevertheless did not implement the winning entry because – though its theoretical accuracy was demonstrated to be higher – its implementation complexity and speed were not adequate for use in a commercial system. In recent Document Understanding Conference (DUC) and Text Analysis Conference (TAC) summarization track competitions, the best performers tended to make use of simple statistical techniques that had demonstrated generally good (but not incredible) performance, and that were then augmented with some common sense additions that were typically guided by some measure of domain knowledge (Nenkova, et al., 2006; Darling, 2010). This section will examine the most powerful simple methods and discuss why these methods tend to perform on par with those that are more complex.

While Luhn made use of term frequency in his original text summarization system and rationalized its use by explaining that an author must elaborate important points which leads to high frequency use of important terms (Luhn, 1958), it was later empirically shown by Nenkova, et al. (2006) that sentences containing common words show up in summaries manually created by human volunteers. More precisely, the higher the frequency of a word in the input, the more likely it was to appear in a manually created summary. This provides the empirical justification for term frequency to be used as an important feature (Nenkova, et al., 2006; Darling, 2010). The principal problem associated with a simple technique that selects sentences based on a high average word probability under the estimated unigram distribution of the input is that the raw unigram distribution may not be the best model for the important content contained within the input text. First, the distribution is Zipfian (Manning & Schütze, 1999) and is overwhelmed by common stop words ("of", "the", "and", "to", "a", etc.). A simple technique to alleviate this problem is to maintain a domain-dependent stop word list and filter stop words out of the distribution before sentence scoring. This is a simple solution that works well in practice but is strongly dependent on having a domain specific list that does not filter too aggressively or vice versa. Methods have been proposed to shift probability mass from the stop words to the more important content words in a domain-independent fashion (Darling & Song, 2011a), and topic modeling based techniques have been proposed that learn content distributions that are separate from background word distributions (stop-words) and document specific distributions in the multi-document summarization context where one is interested in the important content across a document set (Daumé & Marcu, 2006; Haghighi & Vanderwende, 2009). Topic modeling-based techniques seem to perform well for small research-style datasets that concentrate on news summarization, but these techniques have problems scaling when the input grows to thousands or even hundreds of thousands of documents because inference (learning the posterior distributions upon which the summarization algorithm depends) can be very slow. Starting with a simple SumBasic-like approach (Nenkova, et al., 2006) and adding logic as time and resources permit is a sensible and sane approach.

Employing the basic techniques described above results in a quick-to-implement domain- and genre-independent summarization system. The achievable quality is another question entirely, however. As discussed earlier, sentence selection in this context works well when the input consists of a common topic, and it works even better when the writing is succinct and focused. This is clearly not the case in attempting to summarize disparate customer or citizen comments that may be completely off-topic, discussing a different product, referring to a different aspect of a product, etc. The above-described methods are useful, but in this context they are useful as the final step in a pipeline of data processing components that each help to mark-up, add structure, and organize the input.

Making use of existing components and tying their output together through the UNIX-inspired pipes and filters, or pipeline processing systems, has a strong history in achieving complex results in computer science and the UNIX environment (Ritchie, 1980). Likely due to its success, this approach is also very common in opinion summarization work. Blair-Goldensohn, et al. (2008) employ a pipeline of components that (1) extracts phrases from the input; (2) classifies their sentiment; (3) extracts aspects; and (4) selects representative sentences. Hu & Liu (2004) summarize opinions by (1) identifying frequent features; (2) extracting opinion words; (3) classifying opinion; and (4) generating a summary. At a more specific level, an input first has to be assembled which requires the user to pin down what universe she is interested in having a view into. This could include all comments made during a specific time period on a specific Internet forum, or it could be subject-specific such as the results of an information retrieval query over a collection of comments that include references to a particular author. Once the input has been narrowed down, a first component is often used as a filter both to weed out comments that do not contain opinion or that consists of spam, and because the more obvious uninteresting text that is filtered out early, the less processing the later modules in the pipeline will have to perform. Blair-Goldensohn, et al., (2008) use a sentiment classifier early on to filter out comments that do not show a strong sentimental valence, but other early filtering modules might attempt to filter out spam or other off-topic noise. A simple example pipeline-based opinion summarization framework flowchart is shown in Figure 3.

There are two broad classes of types of components that are made use of in opinion summarization. One considers supervised classification where a machine-learning based system learns to generalize on unseen texts by being trained on labeled examples, and the other class consists of view- or model-specific components that are carefully designed to perform a distinct function often in an unsupervised manner. In the processing pipeline context, nearly all of the solutions described in the literature make use of a comment / sentence polarity classification module that fits into the latter class of types (Blair-Goldensohn,

et al., 2008; Balahur, et al., 2009). The most common approach for this task is using an opinion lexicon such as WordNet Affect (Strapparava & Valitutti, 2004) or SentiWordNet (Esuli & Sebastiani, 2006) which assigns a sentiment value to all words appearing in the lexicon. The lexicons themselves are either built by hand or learned statistically from a large set of labeled documents. Opinion lexicons assign negative scores to words associated with negative opinions ("horrible", "bad", "disgusting"), and positive scores to words associated with positive opinions ("excellent", "good", "delicious"). It is immediately apparent that these lexicons are highly domain dependent and we will touch upon this again in the following section. Several of these lexicons have been put together and are available freely on the Internet and the performance of methods that make use of these lexicons is generally good. Balahur, et al. (2009) achieve increased performance by averaging over several different available lexicons. Other approaches that are generally more applicable to longer texts such as movie reviews include supervised machine learning methods making use of common binary classifiers where simple unigram binary features have shown to result in strong performance (Pang, et al., 2002).

Figure 3. An example pipeline-based opinion summarization framework made up of a spam filtering component, an aspect clustering component, and a sentence selection component. Another common addition would be a sentiment classifier.

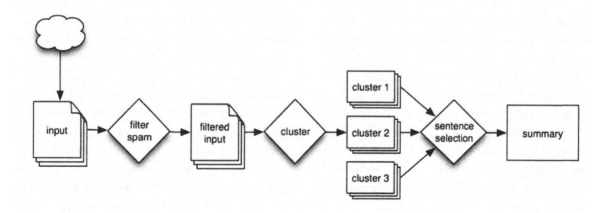

Employing supervised machine learning techniques, the first class type mentioned above, can help to simplify our tasks as less work and thought are often required to go into the design of a specific model. In a generative (unsupervised) model, for example, strong assumptions must be made and carefully thought-out structure must be induced to be sure that the kinds of patterns that we are interested in might be unearthed. For comment selection, for example, we may be interested in having a step in the processing pipeline that filters out comments that do not contain opinion. As discussed previously, modeling opinion is a task fraught with difficulty. Instead, the problem can be simplified and training data can be labeled by considering a simpler task: label comments as either evaluative or non-evaluative (Zhai, et al., 2011). Then, when the classifier is learned, it may automatically uncover latent connections that would have been impossible or extremely difficult to derive manually through rules or by imposing constraints on a generative model.

Combining simple binary classifiers arranged into a pipeline fits with our simple view of iteratively building up a real-world user opinion text summarization system because it only requires examples of what the developer wants to stay and what should be filtered out. In our experience this approach has worked well both in its ease of implementation and in results when compared to more complex approaches such as multi-class classification. Similar results have been observed in other areas that involve marking up input at two or more distinct levels (Lamb, et al., 2013). Finally, this class of approach has also been used to adapt a generic summarization technique to the problem of query-focused summarization where the summary to be constructed should address the user's need outlined in a query. Wang, et al. (2011), for example, employ a binary classifier to first filter out sentences that do not pertain to the user query, and then run a generic summarization method. This technique fits exactly into the framework that we are advocating here.

The overarching problem associated with making heavy use of supervised classification modules, as mentioned in numerous machine learning papers throughout the literature, is the need for large amounts of training data. This is often the rationale for developing complex unsupervised techniques that perform part-of-speech tagging, for example, even at the expense of much poorer performance than the supervised alternatives. The reason that these poorly-performing alternatives are highly popular in research is that for complex labeling tasks such as labeling parts of speech, generating training data is extremely expensive as it requires professional linguists and great deals of time (and money). However, in general, the types of classification tasks that we are interested in for components in an opinion summarization system are not very complex. Rather than having to select from upwards of 40 very specific classes of language syntax use, we normally only want to know if, for example, a text consists of spam or not. When the labeling task is easy, half the problem has been solved. The next problem consists of finding labelers.

Amazon Mechanical Turk (AMT) and other crowdsourcing platforms have become both a hot topic in computer science and sociological research, and an important tool for machine learning researchers (Paollaci, 2010). AMT allows users to submit tasks that are then proposed to workers who can read the description of the task and then choose to attempt the task in return for some payment. The system has become an extremely efficient and highly used way to quickly obtain labels for supervised classification experiments in machine learning, and it is an excellent resource for building a text summarization system that is made up of binary classification components that require training data. The quality of the labels tends to vary with the price that is offered for a successfully completed task, and users will often include tests to ensure that workers are not simply randomly selecting inconsistent answers. Further, users can specify that their tasks are only available to workers who have proven track records or that meet other minimum requirements. Besides AMT, and depending on the labeling task, there are many other methods for building up training data to help build a robust summarization system that is strongly based on supervised classification methods to help filter and structure the input before the final phase of content extraction.

Finally, while traditional news summarization results in a plaintext file consisting of the extracted sentences, there is much room for improvement in the final step of the summarization pipeline: summary output generation. Hu & Liu (2004) advocate a simple feature-based summary that is a good starting point for a large swath of opinion summarization systems. It consists of a hierarchically structured summary that lists the product or service under consideration at the top level, the aspects being considered at the next sub-level, and the positive and negative ranking for that aspect at the final sub-level. Within the final sub-level there are sets of individual review sentences that provide examples of the given sub-category. This outlines a simple way to present structured linked information that gives a succinct overview of the domain at issue. Another simplified view of this type of hierarchically organized opinion summarization is shown in (Blair-Goldensohn, et al., 2008). Generally, a good strategy to follow is to include meta-information that can easily be numerically presented and that is tied to examples. An example might be a positive vs. negative pie chart giving an overview of citizen sentiment with respect to an aspect of a recently proposed law.

This section has outlined a framework for employing simple, often statistical, techniques to iteratively build up a summarization system that is efficient, of high quality, scalable, and can easily improve as the needs and budget of the user or developer grow. We advocate initially implementing a basic sentence selection system grounded in scoring sentences or comments based on term frequency as in SumBasic (Nenkova, et al., 2006; Darling, 2010). If too many undesirable comments

or sentences are being selected, a simple binary classifier can be introduced as a first step in the user opinion summarization pipeline. This classifier should label texts as desirable or not before passing the desirable texts onto the sentence selection module. The classifier – numerous high quality and free software implementations of binary classification through SVMs or logistic regression are available – can first be trained with a small set of hand-labeled examples. If this does not result in high enough accuracy, more training data can be created by posting a task to Amazon Mechanical Turk. Further, the threshold for accepting a text can be either decreased or increased depending on the results that are being obtained. If too many texts are being filtered out, for example, then the threshold can be decreased and more trust can be put in the final sentence selection step in the pipeline. In the next section we will highlight the importance of incorporating domain knowledge into the summarization development process and explain some of the ways that domain knowledge has been used in text summarization research.

Domain Knowledge

As alluded to in the previous section, domain knowledge is vastly important in implementing a practical summarization system. Simply understanding some very basic patterns in the common writing style employed in a domain can lead to small but powerful changes in the quality of a summary. This section will discuss the approaches that can be taken to understand what kind of domain knowledge should be taken into account, and how to maximize the profit that can be unearthed with taking the proper knowledge into consideration. We will primarily consider opinion summarization in the product/service review industry (Liu & Zhang, 2012) and political opinion feedback, but will also address summarization-related domain knowledge in legal (Yousfi-Monod, et al., 2010) and medical (Sarkar, 2009) summarization.

In an opinion summarization system, one of the most important aspects to highlight is the opinion valence with respect to an aspect. In political opinion feedback, for example, decision makers will be principally concerned with whether an enacted policy decision was met with frustration or bliss. As sentiment classification is often performed with the help of sentiment lexicons, we begin here. Blair-Goldensohn, et al. (2008) showed that performance in sentiment classification is highly dependent on having a quality domain-dependent sentiment lexicon. In experiments performed by the author, SentiWordNet and other movie review-specific sentiment lexicons result in performance that is worse than random on a political opinion feedback dataset. This sort of behavior is to be expected, however, because the words that we use in different contexts often have different meanings. With respect to our book publisher case study, a particularly apt example would be the different treatment in this domain versus an automotive review domain for the word "unpredictable". For book reviews, *unpredictable* is often a very good thing; for an automobile, it is clearly the opposite.

The next domain-dependent consideration to explore is the building of word distributions for clustering and sentence selection. The key question is, for a given domain, what do we care about? For an automobile manufacturer, the users may want to strictly focus on problems that are being discussed by its consumers, and there is often an associated jargon to consider. For automobiles we might want to specifically focus on words that describe problems specific to the automobile context: "wind", "noise", "rumbling", or "blind spot". For books, a lot of the roughly domain independent words will remain important such as "enjoyable" or "excellent" but there are others that we might consider and that we could learn using some statistical techniques (Blitzer, et al., 2007). Words learned specifically for a "books" domain might include "reader" and "engaging". In addition to statistical techniques, there are other more direct methods to learn domain-important

words. Chen, et al. (2008) conducted live interviews with experts in the petroleum industry to identify keywords for performing text summarization specific to the oil and gas drilling domain. This information is used to boost words' weights that are considered to often occur in important sentences. Other examples include concentrating on common terminology for medical summarization (Nenkova & McKeown, 2011).

Separate from these domain-independent techniques that are used to learn domain-specific features, a thorough understanding of the domain and the types of inputs that one expects to encounter can be imperative in constructing a text summarization system. This includes imposing assumptions on how the input is structured and using that to be able to perform a more nuanced processing of the content. A common example of being able to make strong assumptions of the structure of the input is in the legal domain. Yousfi-Monod, et al. (2010) summarize legal documents by learning a Naive Bayes classifier with domain-specific features. The features are chosen by a precise understanding of the textual structure that all legal decisions share, and the parameters are learned from a set of decision-summary pairs. Note that even within the legal domain there are differences by field that can be considered to achieve a higher performing system. Yousfi-Monod, et al. limited their experiments to the Immigration Law and Tax domains (separately) where specific content words were used as some of the features. Kumar and Raghuveer (2012) perform legal decision summarization by considering that each judgment can be segmented into seven distinct rhetorical classes that include: identifying the case, establishing the facts, arguments, history, analysis, ratio of the decision, and final decision. They are then more easily able to select sentences from each of the distinct categories and create a summary that provides a good overview of the case in question.

In addition to domain-specific vocabulary and being able to make assumptions with respect to the structure of the input, there are other creative ways to take advantage of domain dependent summarization system development. Some examples include making use of domain-specific meta-information such as click-through data for web page summarization, and considering the social nature of asynchronous communication that is observed in online discussion forums (Zhou & Hovy, 2006). Whatever methods are considered in designing a text summarization system for user opinions, in nearly every case thinking carefully about the specific constraints and idiosyncrasies in a domain and taking advantage of these through imposing structural assumptions and tailoring the method as best as possible is of utmost importance.

When beginning in a particular domain, the first step should always be to manually explore some exemplary data. Performing some simple statistical tests will give a good idea of what kinds of domain-specific stop-words exist, and these can then be compared to a domain-independent list (widely available on the Internet) to see which kinds of domain-specific words may need to be added. If very distinct themes arise in different opinions, it may be very important to try to cluster texts as an early step in the summarization pipeline. As with any data-centered task, achieving a thorough understanding of at least a subset of exemplary data for the domain is an imperative first step in deciding where to allocate resources in the summarization project. In the next section we discuss means to determine whether the developed solution is performing at an acceptable level.

Testing and Evaluation

An all-important step in developing any type of software system for academic or practical use is evaluation. While strong and sober evaluation is required for proving and justifying the claims of a novel technique in academia, it is equally as important in developing real-world systems to be sure that the product will provide the intended results for the customer. As in pure summarization research, evaluation in practice is difficult for a myriad of reasons. As Nenkova and Passoneau note, "all research in summarization evaluation has indicated that no single good model exists" (Nenkova & Passonneau, 2004). The ROUGE evaluation metric – the most widely used in the summarization literature – is premised on the assumption that even humans cannot agree on what is important and therefore what should be included in a summary (Lin, 2004). Rendering real-world evaluation even more difficult is that, as we have defined the problem, the inputs are huge and therefore no gold standard exists, and it would be impossible to even create one because keeping thousands or millions of texts in mind and then creating a summary represents a prohibitive task (making the problem all the more interesting for automatic techniques). Despite this seemingly arduous problem, however, there is nothing that suggests that evaluation to a gold standard in large-input (i.e. opinion or comment) summarization is necessarily at all useful (Blair-Goldensohn, et al., 2008). This section will discuss two useful alternative approaches to testing and evaluation that center upon the end-task that the system was designed to support, and that involve breaking the problem down as described in the "simple methods" section and testing each module independently when such a task is achievable. In product or service opinion summarization, for example, this might be the efficiency with which a user can make a purchasing decision thanks to the output of one summarization system over another. We will also briefly make reference to some work in the literature that aims to evaluate summarization systems where no gold standards exist.

In the standard supervised classification framework of machine learning, the developer has access to labeled training data which is commonly randomly separated into three distinct sets: development, training, and testing. The development data is used during the design and development phase where the model is defined and implemented. Training data is then used to learn the parameters of the model which will in turn be used to predict the labels for the held-out testing data. Gauging performance of the algorithm is as simple as reporting precision and recall statistics. This approach exists in summarization (Kupiec, et al., 1995; Celikyilmaz & Hakkani-Tur, 2010), but is not fully applicable here because there is generally no ground truth on which we can compute precision or recall. This leads to difficulties with development because it is difficult to determine whether the system is working properly or – even if the implementation matches the envisioned model – the model leads to good performance. Nevertheless, this apparent problem forces us to reconsider the purpose of evaluation. In academia, evaluation has often been narrowed down to achieving high (or low) numbers on a specific dataset, and the connection to the real world problem has whittled (Wagstaff, 2012). Instead, we want to consider the results that are achieved directly with respect to the task that our method aims to improve. In opinion summarization, this could range from a highly subjective rating of whether the user is happy with the system, to how quickly a task can be accomplished when the user has access to one tool versus a different tool. A wide-ranging experiment in our case study could look at whether the use of an opinion summarization system within a publishing company could lead to increased profits.

Running a study that concentrates on how different summaries actually help people perform their tasks has been suggested in the literature (Blair-Goldensohn, et al., 2008). To design such a study, it is imperative that the task must be formally defined. While a formal description is important, some of the elements may include subjective judgments. For example, a literary agent may have a propensity to understand the subjective "buzz" (positive or negative) that a new novel has been garnering. The task could be

arriving at the point where the agent feels that she has enough information to pass an opinion on the generated buzz. The study could then determine whether the opinion summarization system is working at improving the agent's efficiency; in other words, does the presence of the system allow the agent to make a judgment more quickly and therefore be able to take an action that could increase a book release's momentum or cut the publisher's losses?

In addition to expensive and time-consuming "live studies", there are other avenues for system evaluation especially in the context of the pipeline of classifiers approach advocated in this Chapter. By measuring the performance of the components that make up our system individually, we can be confident that local improvements will cascade to global improvements throughout the system. The clearest example of this involves concentrating on particular components in our system and testing them individually when there are discrete or ground truth-based answers that we have access to. If a spam filter or a sentiment classifier is implemented by way of a supervised classifier, then we can test the performance of these discrete components on held out test data. If we can improve the precision of our spam filter by some non-negligible amount, for example, then we can be confident that our final summary will likely be improved because the later components did not have to consider the same amount of non-relevant text.

Earlier we noted that while obtaining labeled training data is generally time consuming and expensive, the types of labels that we require in opinion summarization development are generally such that obtaining them can be "outsourced" to services like Amazon's Mechanical Turk and other crowdsourcing platforms. While being an excellent source for obtaining labeled training data for building supervised classification components useful for opinion summarization systems, crowdsourcing can also be extremely useful for testing a proposed system. This can be done by either asking workers to rate the accuracy of the system's components individually, or by having them give ratings on usability or perceived efficiency when having access to the system's full or partial output.

Finally, there has been some research into assessing automatic text summarization performance when no reference summary exists. Louis & Nenkova (2012), for example, consider methods that score a summary by how similar it is to the centroid of a set of other machine-produced summaries. This approach is premised on the idea that the average of numerous disparate techniques should generally come out to the important content present in an input. Nevertheless, though this type of work is interesting, it is difficult to apply to large scale opinion summarization because each system will be highly specialized and comparing it to other types of systems will likely result in a meaningless comparison. Further, as expressed earlier, similarity to some envisioned gold standard (even where it is a latent invention in this case) does not adequately reflect the purpose of our task. Instead, evaluation should concentrate principally on improving the user's efficiency and in improving the given system through quantitative measurable tests that give a view to the accuracy that is being achieved in the components that make up the system.

Following this discussion, we therefore advocate the following initial approach to testing an opinion summarization pipeline. First, each of the components should be tested objectively by examining precision and recall statistics on held out test data. This ensures that the system is working as envisioned technically. Then, a large scale study can be undertaken on the effectiveness of the system at solving the given task, whether that task is increasing efficiency in a company or feeling that citizen opinions are more readily reaching the decision makers in a city government. Though this latter approach is clearly more subjective, it is an important step

in ensuring that the use of the system is worth the effort and expense.

CONCLUSION AND FUTURE RESEARCH DIRECTIONS

This Chapter has aimed to present a view of some of the existing techniques that are used in real world text summarization of large-scale user opinion data. Throughout the Chapter we have argued that the current best thing that we can do with summarization in a real-world scenario involves summarizing opinions gathered through the Web 2.0 framework. We advocated the use of simple, generally modular techniques, to be able to quickly build a functioning, maintainable, and extensible system. In particular, pointers were given in the literature to examples of pipeline-based techniques, how the components used in their systems are generally implemented, and what techniques represent sane decisions to begin with when first building a summarization system. We also enforced the importance of domain dependence and a strong evaluation and testing plan. These three broad areas form the basis of a high quality real world large scale user opinion summarization system.

Although automatic text summarization has been studied since the 1950's (Luhn, 1958) and therefore represents one of the oldest application areas in NLP, there is a tremendous array of research directions that exist for future study. Across all domains, camps, and sub-views of text summarization, the *holy grail* represents a full move from *extractive* summarization to *abstractive* summarization. While baby steps have been taken (Genest & Lapalme, 2012), we are still far from this type of true human-level summarization, and some authors believe that we will not arrive there until we have access to deep language understanding (Darling, 2010). Despite the gulf that separates our current levels from the envisioned capabilities of the future, there are many research areas that promise to bridge the gulf and they fall across the areas of natural language generation (Reiter & Dale, 2000), text-to-text translation, shallow paraphrasing, and others. For now, incremental improvements will be observed as minor iterations are made on the components that make up summarization pipelines.

REFERENCES

Balahur, A., Lloret, E., Boldrini, E., Montoyo, A., Palomar, M., & Martínez-Barco, P. (2009, September). Summarizing threads in blogs using opinion polarity. In *Proceedings of the Workshop on Events in Emerging Text Types* (pp. 23-31). Association for Computational Linguistics.

Barzilay, R., & Elhadad, M. (1997, August). Using lexical chains for text summarization. In *Proceedings of the ACL Workshop on Intelligent Scalable Text Summarization* (Vol. 17, pp. 10-17). ACL.

Blair-Goldensohn, S., Hannan, K., McDonald, R., Neylon, T., Reis, G. A., & Reynar, J. (2008). Building a sentiment summarizer for local service reviews. In *Proceedings of WWW Workshop on NLP in the Information Explosion Era*. IEEE.

Blitzer, J., Dredze, M., & Pereira, F. (2007). Biographies, Bollywood, boom-boxes and blenders: Domain adaptation for sentiment classification. In *Proceedings of Annual Meeting-Association for Computational Linguistics* (Vol. 45, p. 440). ACL.

Carbonell, J., & Goldstein, J. (1998). The use of MMR, diversity-based reranking for reordering documents and producing summaries. In *Proceedings of the 21st Annual International ACM SIGIR Conference on Research and Development in Information Retrieval* (pp. 335-336). ACM.

Celikyilmaz, A., & Hakkani-Tur, D. (2010). A hybrid hierarchical model for multi-document summarization. In *Proceedings of the 48th Annual Meeting of the Association for Computational Linguistics* (pp. 815-824). Association for Computational Linguistics.

Chen, Y. Y., Foong, O. M., Uong, S. P., & Kurniawan, I. (2008). Text summarization for oil and gas drilling topic. *Proceeding of World Academy of Science and Technology, 32*, 37–40.

Chieze, E., Farzindar, A., & Lapalme, G. (2010). An automatic system for summarization and information extraction of legal information. In *Semantic Processing of Legal Texts* (pp. 216–234). Springer. doi:10.1007/978-3-642-12837-0_12

Dang, H. T. (2006). Overview of DUC 2006. In *Proceedings of Document Understanding Conference, DUC 2006*. NIST.

Darling, W. M. (2010). Multi-document summarization from first principles. In *Proceedings of the Third Text Analysis Conference, TAC-2010*. NIST.

Darling, W. M., & Song, F. (2011a). Probabilistic document modeling for syntax removal in text summarization. In *Proceedings of the 49th Annual Meeting of the Association for Computational Linguistics: Human Language Technologies* (pp. 642-647). ACL.

Darling, W. M., & Song, F. (2011b). Pathsum: A summarization framework based on hierarchical topics. In *Proceedings of Canadian AI Workshop on Automatic Text Summarization 2011*. AI.

Daumé, H., III, & Marcu, D. (2006). Bayesian query-focused summarization. In *Proceedings of the 21st International Conference on Computational Linguistics and the 44th Annual Meeting of the Association for Computational Linguistics* (pp. 305-312). Association for Computational Linguistics.

Edmundson, H. P. (1969). New methods in automatic extracting. *Journal of the ACM, 16*(2), 264–285. doi:10.1145/321510.321519

Erkan, G., & Radev, D. R. (2004). LexRank: Graph-based lexical centrality as salience in text summarization. *Journal of Artificial Intelligence Research, 22*, 457–479.

Esuli, A., & Sebastiani, F. (2006). Sentiwordnet: A publicly available lexical resource for opinion mining. []. LREC.]. *Proceedings of LREC, 6,* 417–422.

Genest, P. E., & Lapalme, G. (2012, July). Fully abstractive approach to guided summarization. In *Proceedings of the 50th Annual Meeting of the Association for Computational Linguistics: Short Papers* (vol. 2, pp. 354-358). Association for Computational Linguistics.

Gong, Y., & Liu, X. (2001). Generic text summarization using relevance measure and latent semantic analysis. In *Proceedings of the 24th Annual International ACM SIGIR Conference on Research and Development in Information Retrieval* (pp. 19-25). ACM.

Haghighi, A., & Vanderwende, L. (2009). Exploring content models for multi-document summarization. In *Proceedings of Human Language Technologies: The 2009 Annual Conference of the North American Chapter of the Association for Computational Linguistics* (pp. 362-370). Association for Computational Linguistics.

Halevy, A., Norvig, P., & Pereira, F. (2009). The unreasonable effectiveness of data. *IEEE Intelligent Systems, 24*(2), 8–12. doi:10.1109/MIS.2009.36

Hovy, E., & Lin, C. Y. (1998). Automated text summarization and the SUMMARIST system. In *Proceedings of a Workshop.* Association for Computational Linguistics.

Hu, M., & Liu, B. (2004). Mining and summarizing customer reviews. In *Proceedings of the Tenth ACM SIGKDD International Conference on Knowledge Discovery and Data Mining* (pp. 168-177). ACM.

Kim, S. M., & Hovy, E. (2005). Automatic detection of opinion bearing words and sentences. In *Proceedings of the International Joint Conference on Natural Language Processing* (IJCNLP) (pp. 61-66). IJCNLP.

Kumar, R., & Raghuveer, K. (2012). Legal document summarization using latent dirichlet allocation. *International Journal of Computer Science and Telecommunications, 3,* 114–117.

Kupiec, J., Pedersen, J., & Chen, F. (1995). A trainable document summarizer. In *Proceedings of the 18th Annual International ACM SIGIR Conference on Research and Development in Information Retrieval* (pp. 68-73). ACM.

Lamb, A., Paul, M. J., & Dredze, M. (2013). Separating fact from fear: Tracking flu infections on Twitter. In *Proceedings of HLT-NAACL* (Vol. 2013). NAACL.

Lerman, K., Blair-Goldensohn, S., & McDonald, R. (2009). Sentiment summarization: Evaluating and learning user preferences. In *Proceedings of the 12th Conference of the European Chapter of the Association for Computational Linguistics* (pp. 514-522). Association for Computational Linguistics.

Lin, C. Y. (1999, November). Training a selection function for extraction. In *Proceedings of the Eighth International Conference on Information and Knowledge Management* (pp. 55-62). ACM.

Lin, C. Y. (2004). Rouge: A package for automatic evaluation of summaries. In *Proceedings of the ACL-04 Workshop* (pp. 74-81). ACL.

Lin, C. Y., & Hovy, E. (1997). Identifying topics by position. In *Proceedings of the Fifth Conference on Applied Natural Language Processing* (pp. 283-290). Association for Computational Linguistics.

Lin, C. Y., & Hovy, E. (2000). The automated acquisition of topic signatures for text summarization. In *Proceedings of the 18th Conference on Computational Linguistics* (vol. 1, pp. 495-501). Association for Computational Linguistics.

Litvak, M., Last, M., & Friedman, M. (2010). A new approach to improving multilingual summarization using a genetic algorithm. In *Proceedings of the 48th Annual Meeting of the Association for Computational Linguistics* (pp. 927-936). Association for Computational Linguistics.

Liu, B. (2012). Sentiment analysis and opinion mining. *Synthesis Lectures on Human Language Technologies*, 5(1), 1–167. doi:10.2200/S00416ED1V01Y201204HLT016

Liu, B., Hu, M., & Cheng, J. (2005). Opinion observer: analyzing and comparing opinions on the web. In *Proceedings of the 14th International Conference on World Wide Web* (pp. 342-351). ACM.

Liu, B., & Zhang, L. (2012). A survey of opinion mining and sentiment analysis. In *Proceedings of Mining Text Data* (pp. 415–463). Springer. doi:10.1007/978-1-4614-3223-4_13

Louis, A., & Nenkova, A. (2012). Automatically assessing machine summary content without a gold standard. *Computational Linguistics*, 1–34.

Lu, Y., Zhai, C., & Sundaresan, N. (2009). Rated aspect summarization of short comments. In *Proceedings of the 18th International Conference on World Wide Web* (pp. 131-140). ACM.

Luhn, H. P. (1958). The automatic creation of literature abstracts. *IBM Journal of Research and Development*, 2(2), 159–165. doi:10.1147/rd.22.0159

Manning, C. D., & Schütze, H. (1999). *Foundations of statistical natural language processing*. Cambridge, MA: MIT Press.

McKeown, K. R., Klavans, J. L., Hatzivassiloglou, V., Barzilay, R., & Eskin, E. (1999). Towards multidocument summarization by reformulation: Progress and prospects. In *Proceedings of the National Conference on Artificial Intelligence* (pp. 453-460). John Wiley & Sons Ltd.

Nenkova, A. (2005, July). Automatic text summarization of newswire: Lessons learned from the document understanding conference. In *Proceedings of the National Conference on Artificial Intelligence* (Vol. 20, p. 1436). Menlo Park, CA: AAAI Press.

Nenkova, A., & McKeown, K. (2011). *Automatic summarization*. Delft, The Netherlands: Now Publishers Inc.

Nenkova, A., & Passonneau, R. (2004). Evaluating content selection in summarization: The pyramid method. In *Proceedings of HLT-NAACL*. NAACL.

Nenkova, A., Vanderwende, L., & McKeown, K. (2006). A compositional context sensitive multidocument summarizer: exploring the factors that influence summarization. In *Proceedings of the 29th Annual International ACM SIGIR Conference on Research and Development in Information Retrieval* (pp. 573-580). ACM.

Okurowski, M. E., Wilson, H., Urbina, J., Taylor, T., Clark, R. C., & Krapcho, F. (2000). Text summarizer in use: Lessons learned from real world deployment and evaluation. In *Proceedings of the 2000 NAACL-ANLP Workshop on Automatic Summarization* (pp. 49-58). Association for Computational Linguistics.

Owczarzak, K., & Dang, H. T. (2011). Overview of the TAC 2011 summarization track: Guided task and AESOP task. In *Proceedings of the Text Analysis Conference* (TAC 2011). Gaithersburg, MD: TAC.

Pang, B., Lee, L., & Vaithyanathan, S. (2002). Thumbs up? Sentiment classification using machine learning techniques. In *Proceedings of the ACL-02 Conference on Empirical Methods in Natural Language Processing* (vol. 10, pp. 79-86). Association for Computational Linguistics.

Paolacci, G., Chandler, J., & Ipeirotis, P. (2010). Running experiments on amazon mechanical turk. *Judgment and Decision Making*, 5(5), 411–419.

Reiter, E., & Dale, R. (2000). *Building natural language generation systems*. Cambridge, UK: Cambridge University Press. doi:10.1017/CBO9780511519857

Ritchie, D. M. (1980). The evolution of the UNIX time-sharing system. In *Language Design and Programming Methodology* (pp. 25–35). Springer. doi:10.1007/3-540-09745-7_2

Sarkar, K. (2009). Using domain knowledge for text summarization in medical domain. *International Journal of Recent Trends in Engineering*, *1*(1).

Singhal, A. (2001). Modern information retrieval: A brief overview. *A Quarterly Bulletin of the Computer Society of the IEEE Technical Committee on Data Engineering*, *24*(4), 35–43.

Strapparava, C., & Valitutti, A. (2004). WordNet-Affect: An affective extension of WordNet. []. LREC.]. *Proceedings of LREC*, *4*, 1083–1086.

Wagstaff, K. (2012). Machine learning that matters. *arXiv preprint arXiv:1206.4656*.

Wang, D., Zhu, S., Li, T., Chi, Y., & Gong, Y. (2011). Integrating document clustering and multidocument summarization. *ACM Transactions on Knowledge Discovery from Data*, *5*(3), 14. doi:10.1145/1993077.1993078

Yousfi-Monod, M., Farzindar, A., & Lapalme, G. (2010). Supervised machine learning for summarizing legal documents. In *Proceedings of Advances in Artificial Intelligence* (pp. 51–62). Springer. doi:10.1007/978-3-642-13059-5_8

Zhai, Z., Liu, B., Zhang, L., Xu, H., & Jia, P. (2011). Identifying evaluative sentences in online discussions. In *Proceedings of National Conf. on Artificial Intelligence (AAAI-2011)*. AAAI.

Zhou, L., & Hovy, E. (2006). On the summarization of dynamically introduced information: Online discussions and blogs. In *Proceedings of AAAI Symposium on Computational Approaches to Analysing Weblogs (AAAI-CAAW)* (pp. 237-242). AAAI.

ADDITIONAL READING

Bird, S., Klein, E., & Loper, E. (2009). *Natural Language Processing with Python*. Sebastopol, CA: O'Reilly Media.

Blei, D., Ng, A., & Jordan, M. (2003). Latent Dirichlet Allocation. *Journal of Machine Learning Research*, *3*, 993–1022.

Crespi, I. (1997). *The public opinion process: How the people speak*. Mahwah, NJ: Lawrence Erlbaum Associates.

Endres-Niggemeyer, B. (1998). *Summarizing Information*. New York, NY: Springer-Verlag. doi:10.1007/978-3-642-72025-3

Fattah, M. A., & Ren, F. (2008). Automatic text summarization. In *Proceedings of World Academy of Science* (Vol. 27, pp. 192–195). Engineering and Technology.

Gupta, V., & Lehal, G. S. (2010). A survey of text summarization extractive techniques. *Journal of Emerging Technologies in Web Intelligence*, *2*(3), 258–268. doi:10.4304/jetwi.2.3.258-268

Hovy, E., & Marcu, D. (2005). Automated text summarization. The Oxford handbook of computational linguistics, 583-598. Oxford: Oxford University Press.

Hu, M., & Liu, B. (2004, August). Mining and summarizing customer reviews. In *Proceedings of the tenth ACM SIGKDD international conference on Knowledge discovery and data mining* (pp. 168-177). ACM.

Indurkhya, N., & Damerau, F. J. (Eds.). (2010). *Handbook of natural language processing* (Vol. 2). Boca Raton, FL: CRC Press.

James, A. (1994). *Natural Language Understanding*. Boston, MA: Addison-Wesley.

Jurafsky, D., & Martin, J. H. (2000). *Speech and Language Processing: An Introduction to Natural Language Processing, Computational Linguistics and Speech Recognition*. Upper Saddle River, NJ: Prentice Hall.

Liu, B. (2012). Sentiment analysis and opinion mining. *Synthesis Lectures on Human Language Technologies, 5*(1), 1–167. doi:10.2200/S00416ED1V01Y201204HLT016

Mani, I. (2001). *Automatic Summarization*. Philadelphia, PA: John Benjamins Publishing Company.

Mani, I., & Maybury, M. T. (1999). *Advances in automatic text summarization*. Cambridge, MA: MIT Press.

Manning, C. D., & Schuetze, H. (1999). *Foundations of statistical natural language processing*. Cambridge, MA: MIT Press.

Marcu, D. (2000). *The Theory and Practice of Discourse Parsing and Summarization*. Cambridge, MA: MIT Press.

Mitkov, R. (Ed.). (2005). *The Oxford Handbook of Computational Linguistics*. New York, NY: Oxford University Press. doi:10.1093/oxfordhb/9780199276349.001.0001

Nenkova, A., & McKeown, K. (2011). *Automatic summarization*. Delft: Now Publishers Inc.

Reiter, E., & Dale, R. (2000). *Building Natural Language Generation Systems*. Cambridge: Cambridge University Press. doi:10.1017/CBO9780511519857

Sparck Jones, K., & Endres-Niggemeyer, B. (1995). Automatic summarizing. *Information Processing & Management, 31*(5), 625–630. doi:10.1016/0306-4573(95)92254-F

KEY TERMS AND DEFINITIONS

Abstractive Summarization: Performing summarization by paraphrasing or re-writing the content from the input in a more succinct version.

Extractive Summarization: Performing summarization by selecting existing sentences from the input and using them to construct the output summary.

NLP: Natural Language Processing; the field of research that covers computers understanding and manipulating human language. Text summarization is an area that is sometimes seen as part of NLP and other times seen as borrowing techniques from NLP.

Redundancy: The needless repeating of semantically identical information. It is to be avoided in automatic text summarization to keep room for as much novel information as possible.

Reference Summary: A summary written by a human that is used for evaluating the automatic output of summarization systems.

ROUGE: Recall-Oriented Understudy for Gisting Evaluation; the standard in reference-based automatic evaluation for text summarization.

Stop-Words: Words that do not contain any semantic information and are therefore commonly ignored when calculating word use statistics for text summarization. In English, these words include "the", "and", "of", "a", etc.

SumBasic: A simple embodiment of sentence scoring and selection based on term frequency.

Supervised Learning: Machine learning techniques that make use of data with labels or annotations. Commonly used in opinion summarization system modules that aim to filter out certain types of texts.

Text Analysis Conference: The premiere practical text summarization conference that is the source of most of the summarization data used in the literature.

Chapter 8
Novel Text Summarization Techniques for Contextual Advertising

Giuliano Armano
University of Cagliari, Italy

Alessandro Giuliani
University of Cagliari, Italy

ABSTRACT

Recently, there has been a renewed interest on automatic text summarization techniques. The Internet has caused a continuous growth of information overload, focusing the attention on retrieval and filtering needs. Since digitally stored information is more and more available, users need suitable tools able to select, filter, and extract only relevant information. This chapter concentrates on studying and developing techniques for summarizing Webpages. In particular, the focus is the field of contextual advertising, the task of automatically suggesting ads within the content of a generic Webpage. Several novel text summarization techniques are proposed, comparing them with state of the art techniques and assessing whether the proposed techniques can be successfully applied to contextual advertising. Comparative experimental results are also reported and discussed. Results highlight the improvements of the proposals with respect to well-known text summarization techniques.

INTRODUCTION

The creation of a shortened but meaningful version of a text by a computer program, called Text Summarization (TS), is an old challenge in text mining. Given a text, its summary (i.e., a non-redundant extract from the original text) is returned.

This chapter is focused on studying and developing techniques for summarizing webpages. In particular, the interest is concentrated on the field of Contextual Advertising (CA), a form of online advertising. CA is the task of automatically suggesting ads within the content of a generic webpage. A commercial intermediary, the ad network, is usually in charge of optimizing the selection of ads with the twofold goal of increasing revenue (shared between publisher and ad network)

DOI: 10.4018/978-1-4666-5019-0.ch008

and improving user experience. Ads are selected and served by automated systems based on the content displayed to the user (Anagnostopoulos et al., 2007), (Broder et al., 2007), (Deepayan et al., 2008), (Lacerda, et al., 2006)(Ribeiro-Neto et al, 2005).

The motivation of the proposed research activity is that nowadays, ad networks need to deal in real time with a large amount of data, involving billions of pages and ads. Hence, efficiency and computational costs are crucial factors in the choice of methods and algorithms. A common methodology for Web advertising in real time is focused on the contributions of the different fragments of a webpage. The methodology relies on the adoption of a text summarization task for summarizing the webpage. Extraction-based techniques are usually adopted with the goal of fulfilling the given real time constraint. This methodology allows to identify short but informative excerpts of the webpage by selecting meaningful blocks of text. Several novel TS techniques that take into account further fragments, such as the title of the webpage, are proposed. Experiments confirm the effectiveness of the proposed techniques with respect to the state-of-the-art techniques. A further proposal is motivated by the evolution of the Web. In fact, classical techniques are often not easily applicable to dynamic webpages that typically rely on Microsoft Silverlight, Adobe Flash, Adobe Shock-wave, or contain applets written in Java. Conventional parsing methods are often not applicable to a webpage created on-the-fly. Therefore, snippets –i.e., page excerpts provided together with user query results by search engines– should be adopted to perform text summarization on webpages. Each study is conducted along two directions: comparing the proposed approach with classic text summarization technique and assessing whether the proposals can be successfully applied to CA. After a brief survey of relevant related work on text summarization and Contextual Advertising, the proposed techniques are compared with classic methods. Then, a description about several

Contextual Advertising systems, implemented according to the proposed techniques, is provided. Experimental results, obtained by running the systems on relevant data, are also reported and discussed. A discussion on further issues and relevant solutions ends the chapter.

BACKGROUND

This section is aimed at giving a summary about TS and CA, recalling the main contributions in these fields. Then, the section provides the reasons why TS should be performed by a CA system. Finally, a generic architecture for CA is illustrated, describing also the baseline system to be used as starting point for experiments.

Text Summarization

Text summarization is an old challenge in text mining. During the 60's, a large amount of scientific papers and books have been digitally stored and made searchable. Due to the limitation of storage capacity, documents were stored, indexed, and made searchable only through their summaries. For this reason, the automatic creation of text summaries became a primary task and several techniques were defined and developed.

More recently, there has been a renewed interest on automatic text summarization techniques. The internet has caused a continuous growth of information overload. The problem now is no longer due only to limited storage capacity, but also to retrieval and filtering needs. Since digitally stored information is more and more available, users need suitable tools able to select, filter, and extract only relevant information.

Therefore, text summarization is currently adopted in several fields of information retrieval and filtering (Baeza-Yates & Ribeiro-Neto, 1999), such as, information extraction (Rau et al., 1989), text mining (Witten et al., 1999), document classification (Shen et al., 2004), recommender systems

(Ricci et al., 2010), and contextual advertising (Anagnostopoulos et al., 2007).

The research on automatic summarization is characterized by three important aspects: (i) summaries may be produced from a single document or multiple documents; (ii) summaries should preserve important information; and (iii) summaries should be short.

The development of automatic text summarization methods yielded two main approaches: (i) those that extract information from the source documents (extraction-based approaches) and (ii) those that abstract from the source documents (abstraction-based approaches) (Kolcz et al., 2001). The former impose the constraint that a summary uses only components extracted from the source document. These approaches are mainly concerned with what the summary content should be, usually relying solely on extraction of sentences. The latter relax the constraints on how the summary is created. These approaches put strong emphasis on the form, aiming to produce a grammatical summary, which usually requires advanced language generation techniques. Although potentially more powerful, abstraction-based approaches have been far less popular than extraction-based approaches, mainly because it is easier to generate the latter, and because even simple summaries are quite effective in carrying over relevant information about a document (Brandow et al., 1995).

Most early works on single-document summarization have been proposed by Luhn (1958). They are based on word frequencies. Simple summarization-like techniques have been applied for long time to enrich the set of features used in text categorization. Baxendale (1958) adopted sentence positions as useful features to identify meaningful fragments of documents, whereas Edmundson (1969) considered cue words and titles for deriving the summarized text.

A further common strategy consists of giving extra weight to words appearing in the title of a story (Mladenic & Grobelnik, 1998) or treating the

title-words as separate features, even if the same words were present elsewhere in the text body (Dumais et al., 1998). It has been also noticed that many documents contain useful formatting information, loosely defined as context, that can be utilized when selecting the salient words, phrases or sentences. For example, Web search engines select terms differently according to their HTML markup (Belew, 2000). Summaries, rather than full documents, have been successfully applied to document clustering (Ganti et al., 1999). Ker and Chen (2000) evaluated the performance of a categorization system using title-based summaries as document descriptors. In their experiments with a probabilistic TF-IDF based classifier, they showed that title-based document descriptors positively affect the performance of categorization.

Several approaches have been recently proposed by relying on Machine Learning techniques for single and multi-document summarization, such as Bayesian statistics (Blei, 2006)(Mcargar 2004)(Kraaij, 2001) or neural networks (Wang et al., 2006)(Kaikhah, 2004)(Yong et al., 2005). The next section reports a discussion about the motivations of adopting simple techniques in CA.

Contextual Advertising

Online Advertising is an emerging research field, at the intersection of Information Retrieval, Machine Learning, Optimization, and Microeconomics. Its main goal is to choose the right ads to present to a user engaged in a given task, such as sponsored search advertising or CA.

Sponsored search advertising (or paid search advertising) puts ads on the page returned from a Web search engine following a query. CA (or content match) puts ads within the content of a generic, third party, webpage. A commercial intermediary, namely ad-network, is usually in charge of optimizing the selection of ads with the twofold goal of increasing revenue (shared between publisher and ad-network) and improving user experience. In other words, CA is a form of targeted advertising for ads appearing on Web sites or other media, such as content displayed in mobile browsers. The ads themselves are selected and served by automated systems based on the content displayed to the user.

CA is the economic engine behind a large number of non-transactional sites on the Web. A main factor for the success in CA is the relevance to the surrounding scenario. Each solution for CA evolved from search advertising, where a search query matches with a bid phrase of the ad. A natural extension of search advertising is extracting phrases from the target page and matching them with the bid phrases of ads. Yih et al. (2006) propose a system for phrase extraction, which uses a variety of features to determine the importance of page phrases for advertising purposes. To this end, the authors proposed a supervised approach that relies on a training set built using a corpus of pages in which relevant phrases have been annotated by hand.

Ribeiro-Neto et al. (2005) examine a number of strategies to match pages and ads based on extracted keywords. They represent both pages and ads in a vector space and propose several strategies to improve the matching process. In particular, the authors explore the use of different sections of ads as a basis for the vector, mapping both page and ads in the same space. Since there is a discrepancy between the vocabulary used in the pages and in the ads (the so called "impedance mismatch"), the authors improved the matching precision by expanding the page vocabulary with terms from similar pages.

In a subsequent work, Lacerda et al. (2006) propose a method to learn the impact of individual features by using genetic programming. The results show that genetic programming helps to find improved matching functions.

Broder et al. (2007) classify both pages and ads according to a given taxonomy, and match ads to the page falling in the same node of the taxonomy. Each node of the taxonomy is built as a set of bid phrases or queries corresponding to a certain topic. Results show a better accuracy than that of classic systems (i.e., systems based on syntactic match only). Let us also note that, to improve performance, this system may be used in conjunction with more general approaches.

Another approach that combines syntax and semantics has been proposed in (Armano et al. 2011). The corresponding system, called ConCA (Concepts on Contextual Advertising), relies on ConceptNet, a semantic network able to supply commonsense knowledge (Liu & Singh 2004).

Since bid phrases are basically search queries, another relevant approach is to view CA as a problem of query expansion and rewriting. Murdock et al. (2007) consider a statistical machine translation model to overcome the problem of the impedance mismatch between page and ads. To this end, they propose and develop a system able to re-rank the ad candidates based on a noisy-channel model. In a subsequent work, the authors used a machine learning approach, based on the model described in (Broder et al., 2007), to define an innovative set of features able to extract the semantic correlations between the page and ad vocabularies (Ciaramita et al., 2008a).

Many of the techniques used in CA to place ads in webpages may be used to place ads in response to a user's query, as in Sponsored Search. Sponsored Search can be thought of as a document retrieval problem, where ads are documents to be retrieved in response to a query. Ads could be partly represented by their keywords. Carrasco et al. (2003) approach the problem of keyword suggestion by clustering bi-partite advertiser-keyword graphs. Joachims (2002) propose to use click-data for learning ranking functions resulting from a search engine as an indicator of relevance. Ciaramita et al. (2008b) studied an approach to learn and evaluate sponsored search systems based solely on click-data, focusing on the relevance of textual content.

Text Summarization in Contextual Advertising

Nowadays, ad-networks need to deal in real time with a large amount of data, involving billions of pages and ads. Therefore several constraints must be taken into account for building CA systems. In particular, efficiency and computational costs are crucial factors in the choice of methods and algorithms.

In the most common scenario, the ad-network returns the ads that are most suitable for the page content. The elaboration is usually performed via JavaScript modules embedded in the webpage code: when the user's browser requests to load a page, the modules should analyze the webpage content and select the right ads while the page is loading on the browser. Consequently, the ad-network engine has only a couple of hundreds of milliseconds to provide the ads.

In most cases, this low latency requirement does not allow for pages to be fetched and analyzed online. Although the pages could be fetched and analyzed offline, this approach works well only for static content pages that are displayed repeatedly. But nowadays the Web is highly dynamic: most of the news sites, forums, blogs, and social networks personal pages are constantly changing. Furthermore, some pages cannot be accessed in advance because they belong to the "invisible Web", that is, they do not exist, except as a result of a user query. Moreover, some pages could not be accessible for all users, since they require cookies or authorizations present on the user's computer but not on the ad server's platform. All these examples show the crucial need of suggesting ads while the page is being served to the user, with the limitation of the amount of time allotted for the content analysis.

Anagnostopoulos et al. (2007) present a methodology for Web advertising in real time, focusing on the contributions of the different fragments of a webpage. This methodology allows identifying short but informative excerpts of the webpage by using several text summarization techniques, in conjunction with the model developed in Broder at al. (2007).

The Baseline Architecture

The CA problem can be formulated as follows: let P be the set of webpages and let A be the set of ads that can be displayed. Let f be a utility function that measures the matching between an ad and a webpage, i.e. $f : P \times A \to R$, where R is a totally ordered set (e.g., non-negative integers or real numbers within a certain range). For each $p \in P$, we want to select an $a' \in A$ that maximizes the page utility function. More formally:

$$\forall p \in P, \quad a'_p = \arg\max_{a \in A} f(p, a)$$

A typical view of CA is sketched in Figure 1, which illustrates a generic architecture that can give rise to specific systems, depending on the choices made on each involved module. Notably, most of the state-of-the-art solutions are compliant with this view. The architecture encompasses three modules, each responsible for a specific task.

- **Text Summarizer:** Its goal is to generate a short representation of any given webpage with a negligible loss of information. First, the input HTML page is transformed into an easy-to-process document in plain-text format, while maintaining important information. The page is parsed to identify and remove noisy elements, such as tags, comments and other non-textual items. Then, stop-words are removed from each textual excerpt. The document is then typically tokenized and each term stemmed. The stemmer algorithm mostly used in practice is the well-known Porter's algorithm (Porter, 1980).

Figure 1. A generic architecture for CA

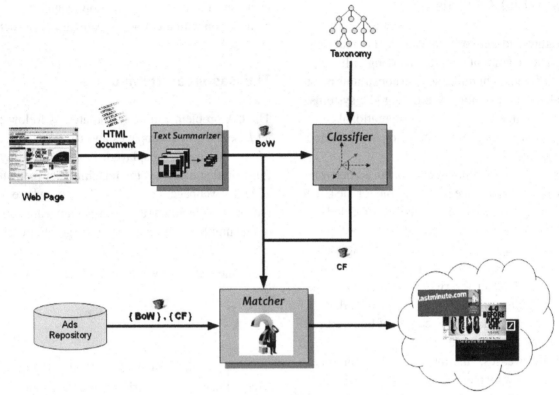

Finally, extraction-based techniques are typically applied to the blocks that form a webpage (Kolcz et al., 2001), e.g., appropriate paragraphs and titles of the page. The text summarizer outputs a vector representation of the original HTML document as bag of words (BoW), each word being weighted by TFIDF (Salton & McGill, 1984). Let us recall that, for each term tk, the TFIDF determines the weight wjk of tk in the document dj.

- **Classifier:** Text summarization is a purely syntactic analysis and the corresponding webpage classification is usually inaccurate. To alleviate possible harmful effects of summarization, both page excerpts and ads are classified according to a given set of categories (Anagnostopoulos et al., 2007). The corresponding classification-based features (CF) are then used in conjunction with the original BoW.

A typical solution consists of adopting a centroid-based classification technique (Han & Karypis, 2000), which represents each class with its centroid calculated starting from the training set. A page is classified measuring the distance between its vector and the centroid vector of each class by adopting the cosine similarity.

- **Matcher:** It is devoted to suggest ads (a) to a webpage (p) according to a similarity score based on both BoW and CF (Anagnostopoulos et al., 2007). In formula (α is a global parameter that allows to control the emphasis of the syntactic component with respect to the semantic one):

$$score(p,a) = \alpha \cdot sim_{BoW}(p,a) + (1-\alpha) \cdot sim_{CF}(p,a)$$

where, $sim_{BoW}(p,a)$ and $sim_{CF}(p,a)$ are cosine similarity scores between p and a using BoW and CF, respectively.

TEXT SUMMARIZATION APPROACHES

In this section, after giving a brief recall of some classic baseline techniques, some novel methods are shown, with comparative experiments in order to evaluate the effectiveness of the proposals. The proposals are based on two main ideas; the former relies on the choice of text fragments and is similar to the baseline approaches, the latter relies on the adoption of the snippet as summary of a webpage.

Baseline Techniques

As baseline, the techniques proposed by Kolcz et al (2001) are considered. In this work seven straightforward (but effective) extraction-based text summarization techniques have been proposed and compared. In all cases, a word occurring at least three times in the body of a document is considered a keyword, while a word occurring in the title of a document is a title-word.

For the sake of completeness, let us recall the techniques; each technique is characterized by the fragments taken into account as summary. Summaries are made, respectively, by:

- Title (T), the title of a document;
- First Paragraph (FP), the first paragraph of a document;
- First Two Paragraphs (F2P), the first two paragraphs of a document;
- First and Last Paragraphs (FLP), the first and the last paragraphs of a document;
- Paragraph with most keywords (MK), the paragraph that has the highest number of keywords;

- Paragraph with most title-words (MT), the paragraph that has the highest number of title-words;
- Best Sentence (BS), sentences in the document that contain at least 3 title-words and at least 4 keywords.

The effectiveness of these techniques could be attributed to the fact that a document (e.g., a scientific paper) is usually written to capture the user's attention with the headlines and initial text (e.g., the abstract or the introduction). The last part of a document could also contain relevant content (e.g., the conclusions). As the input of a contextual advertiser is an HTML document, CA systems typically rely on extraction-based approaches, which are applied to the relevant blocks of a webpage (e.g., the title of the webpage, its first paragraph, and the paragraph which has the highest title-word count).

Development of Novel Extractive Techniques

The methods proposed by Kolcz et al. were introduced and evaluated for conventional documents (e.g., books, news, scientific papers). Since, in CA, the input is an HTML code the classic methods could be less effective. A webpage is usually more concise and noisy than a textual document, and it is not often written in "standard English". In fact, on the one hand a webpage is shorter than a paper, and could contain different items that lie outside from the body content (such as, meta-data or anchor text); on the other hand, the frequency of slang, typos, and non-conventional textual elements (e.g., emoticons or abbreviations) is higher than in textual documents, particularly in blogs, social networks, personal pages, and other user generated pages.

To improve the performance of the algorithms proposed by Kolcz et al., additional features are used in conjunction with the classic features. The selected feature has been the title of the webpage (usually wrapped by the "title" tag). In contrast to the techniques proposed by Kolcz et al., the title is not the headline of a textual section (contained for instance in the "h1" tags). The novel proposals can be summarized as follows:

- Title and First Paragraph (TFP), the title of a document and its first paragraph;
- Title and First Two Paragraphs (TF2P), the title of a document and its first two paragraphs;
- Title, First and Last Paragraphs (TFLP), the title of a document and its first and last paragraphs;
- Most Title-words and Keywords (MTK), the paragraph with the highest number of title-words and that with the highest number of keywords.

A further technique is defined. It is called NKeywords (NK), and it selects the N most frequent keywords[1].

Experimental Results

Experiments are performed with the goal to compare the proposed techniques with the baseline techniques. To this end, a suitable system (depicted in Figure 2) is devised, in which *Text Summarizer* is the module aimed at performing text summarization and the *Classifier* is a centroid-based classifier adapted to classify each page, in order to calculate precision, recall, and F-measure of the proposed text summarization techniques. The proposed text summarization techniques are evaluated by a Rocchio classifier (Rocchio, 1971), with only positive examples and no relevance feedback, previously trained with about 100 webpages per class. A summary is classified measuring the distance between its vector and the centroid vector of each class by adopting the cosine similarity. Thus, summaries are classified by considering the highest score(s) obtained by such computation.

Experiments are performed on the BankSearch Dataset (Sinka & Corne, 2002), which is built using the Open Directory Project and the Yahoo! Categories2. The dataset consists of about 11,000 webpages manually classified in 11 different classes. Figure 3 shows the overall hierarchy. The 11 selected classes are the leaves of the taxonomy, together with the class Sport, which contains Web documents from all sites that were classified as Sport, except for the sites that were classified as Soccer or Motor Sport. The authors show that this structure provides a good test not only for generic classification/clustering methods, but also for hierarchical techniques.

In order to evaluate the effectiveness of the classifier, a preliminary experiment, in which

Figure 2. The system adopted to perform comparative experiments on text summarization

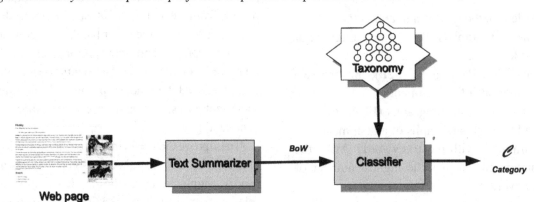

Figure 3. Class hierarchy of the BankSearch Dataset

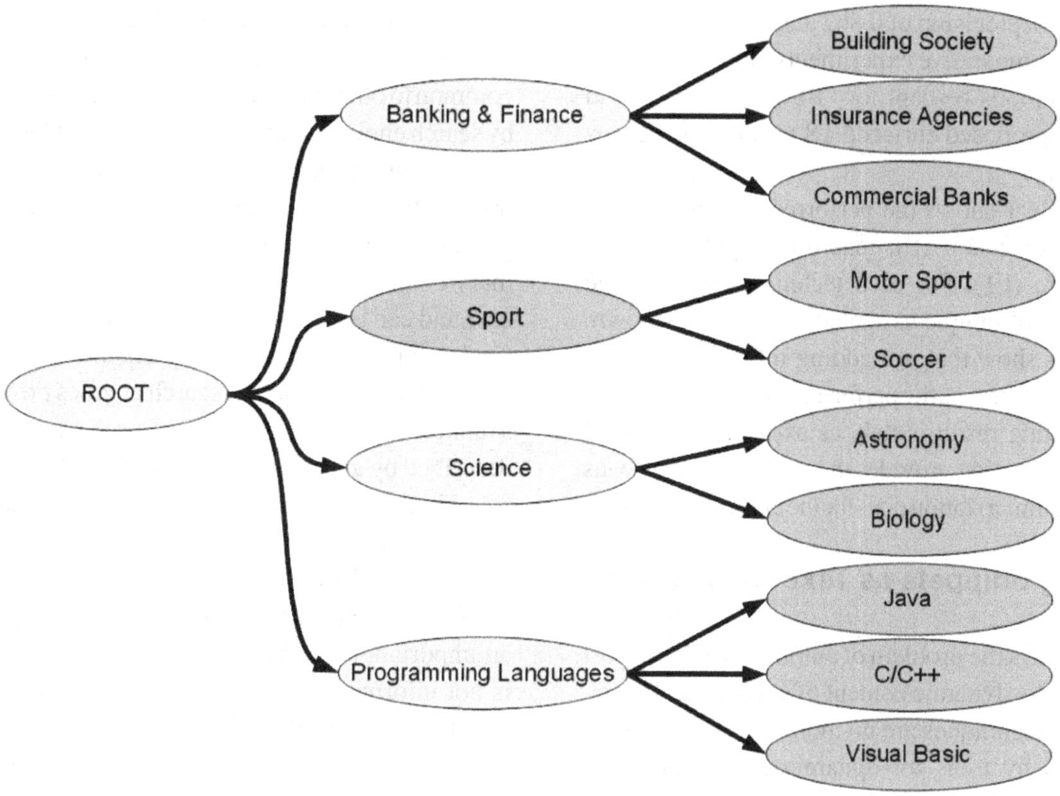

Table 1. Comparative results of TS techniques

	P	R	F1	T
T	**0.798**	0.692	0.729	3
FP	0.606	0.581	0.593	13
F2P	0.699	0.673	0.686	24
FLP	0.745	**0.719**	**0.732**	24
MK	0.702	0.587	0.639	25
MT	0.717	0.568	0.634	15
TFP	0.802	0.772	0.787	16
TF2P	0.822	0.789	0.805	27
TFLP	**0.832**	**0.801**	**0.816**	26
MTK	0.766	0.699	0.731	34

pages are classified without relying on text summarization, is also performed. The classifier showed a precision of 0.862 and a recall of 0.858. Then, comparative experiments among the baseline methods (except for "Best Sentence"[3]) and for the proposed enriched TS techniques are performed.

Table 1 shows the performances in terms of macro-precision (P), macro-recall (R), and F-measure (F1). For each technique, the average number of unique extracted terms (T) is shown. Results show that just adding information about the title improves the performances of TS. Another interesting result is that, as expected, the TFLP summarization provides the best performance, as FLP summarization does for the classic techniques.

Using Snippets as Text Summaries

Nowadays the problem of automated TS is in part due to the dynamic content of a webpage. In fact, classic techniques are no more available for Web created by tools for dynamic generation, such as Microsoft Silverlight[4], Adobe Flash[5], Adobe Shockwave[6], and for pages that contain applets written in Java. Hence, a novel summarization method relies on the adoption of snippets (i.e., the page excerpts provided by search engines following a user's query). Notably, at least in principle, snippets provide a relevant content of the suggested links in few lines and features. The adoption of snippets as summaries has been investigated in (Armano et al., 2012).

A general definition of snippet is "a small piece of something". In programming, it refers to a small region of re-usable source code, machine code, or text. Snippets are often used to clarify the meaning of an otherwise cluttered function, or to minimize the use of repeated code that is common to other functions. Snippets are also used by search engines to provide an excerpt of the corresponding webpage according to the keywords used in the query. A snippet can be considered as a topic-driven summarization, since the summary content depends on the preferences of the user and can be accessed via a query, making the final summary focused on a particular topic. In replying to a user's query, search engines provide a ranked list of related webpages, each page being described by a title, a set of snippets, and its URL (see Figure 4). The title is usually directly taken from the title tag of the page, whereas the URL is the http address of the page.

For a search engine the choice of a snippet, is an important task. If a snippet shown to the user is not informative, the user may click on pages that do not contain the information s/he is looking for, or s/he may not click on helpful pages. Moreover, poorly chosen snippets can lead to a bad search experience.

Snippets are usually directly taken from the description meta tag, if available. If the description meta tag is not provided, the search engine may use the description for the site provided by the Open Directory Project (aka, DMoz)[7], or a summary extracted from the main content of the page.

Snippet extraction depends on the search engine used. Google[8] not always uses the meta description of the page. In fact, if the content provided by the Web developer in the description meta tag

Figure 4. An example of results given by Yahoo! search engine for the query "Information retrieval"

Introduction to **Information Retrieval** - The Stanford NLP ...   Title

Introduction to **Information Retrieval**. This is the companion website for the following book. Christopher D. Manning, Prabhakar Raghavan and Hinrich Schütze ...   Snippets

nlp.stanford.edu/IR-book/information-retrieval-book.html - Cached   URL is not helpful, or of less than reasonable quality, then Google replaces it with its own description of the site. By doing so, Google snippets will be different depending on the users' search query. Yahoo![9] provides a patent application used to decide which snippet to show to users. The gist of the patent application is based on three main aspects[10]: (i) a query-independent relevance for each line of text, i.e., a degree to how a line of text summarizes the document; (ii) a query-dependent relevance of each of the lines of text, i.e., a relevance of the line of text to the query; and (iii) the intent behind a query. To our best knowledge, Bing[11] developers do not give information on how snippets are extracted.

Experimental Results

To evaluate the method the centroid classifier, described in the previous section, has been adopted.

Experiments have been performed on the Bank-Search dataset. Moreover, a further, self-made, dataset has been used. The dataset is extracted by the DMoz directory, and it is the sub-tree rooted by the category "Recreation". It consists of about 5000 webpages classified in 18 categories (see Figure 5). As for the Banksearch dataset, the selected pages are distinct for each category.

The baseline for comparative experiments is the text summarization technique called TFLP

(Title, First and Last Paragraph summarization), described in the previous section. As already pointed out, that technique has shown the best results compared with the state-of-the-art techniques proposed by Kolcz et al. As for snippets, Yahoo! Is queried and the returned snippets are used. Experiments consider the snippets themselves (S) and in conjunction with the title of the corresponding webpage (ST). To be able to process the same number of pages independently by the adopted text summarization technique and to provide a fair comparison, dynamic pages from both datasets are disregarded.

Table 2 reports the corresponding experimental results, in terms of precision (P), recall (R), and F-measure (F1). The Table gives also the average number of extracted terms (T).

The results show that all techniques obtained better results in BankSearch. Moreover, they point out that, in both datasets, results obtained by relying on snippets together with the title (ST) are comparable with those obtained by adopting TFLP. In particular, TFLP performs slightly better in BankSearch, whereas ST performs slightly better in Recreation. This proves that snippets can be used as text summarization techniques, especially when classical techniques cannot be applied, as in the case of dynamic webpages.

Figure 5. Taxonomy of recreation dataset

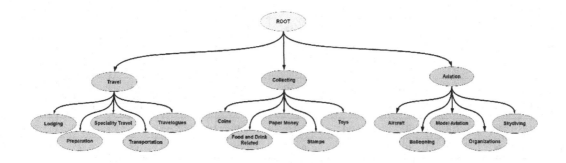

Table 2. Results of text summarization techniques comparison

	BankSearch			Recreation		
	TFLP	**S**	**ST**	**TFLP**	**S**	**ST**
P	0.849	0.734	0.806	0.575	0.544	0.595
R	0.845	0.730	0.804	0.556	0.506	0.554
F1	0.847	0.732	0.805	0.565	0.524	0.574
T	26	12	14	26	11	13

TEXT SUMMARIZATION IN CONTEXTUAL ADVERTISING

Since the main interest is the study of the impact of the syntactic phase on CA, a CA system for each technique is implemented, and the performances are evaluated by means of comparative experiments.

The Impact of the Enriched Techniques

The impact of the summarization techniques is evaluated on the implementation of the system described in the background section, comparing results while varying the adopted TS technique. Let us note that, even if modern advertising networks should work in real time, for the sake of completeness also performances without exploiting Text Summarization have been evaluated (the first row in Table 3).

Experiments are performed on the BankSearch dataset. As for advertisements, a repository of ads has been manually built. Each ad is represented by the webpage code, processed in the same way as for the input page (target page). Five relevant ads are selected for each category, with a total of 55 ads.

CA systems choose the relevant ads contained in the repository according to the scores obtained by the Matcher. The ads with the highest scores are displayed on the target page.

Five different experiments have been performed for each system, in which from 1 to 5 ads are selected for the target page, respectively. Table 3 reports, for each TS technique, the preci-

Table 3. Comparative results on CA

	P@1	α_b	**P@2**	α_b	**P@3**	α_b	**P@4**	α_b	**P@5**	α_b
no TS	0.785	0.0	0.779	0.0	0.775	0.0	0.769	0.0	0.753	0.2
T	0.680	0.1	0.675	0.1	0.652	0.1	0.639	0.1	0.595	0.3
FP	0.488	0.2	0.476	0.3	0.448	0.3	0.421	0.2	0.391	0.1
F2P	0.613	0.2	0.609	0.2	0.588	0.1	0.558	0.2	0.514	0.3
FLP	0.674	0.0	0.653	0.0	0.617	0.2	0.582	0.2	0.546	0.1
MK	0.631	0.2	0.620	0.1	0.581	0.1	0.541	0.2	0.500	0.3
MT	0.640	0.4	0.617	0.3	0.610	0.2	0.586	0.1	0.547	0.3
TFP	0.744	0.0	0.707	0.3	0.691	0.1	0.669	0.0	0.637	0.1
TF2P	0.740	0.0	0.723	0.1	0.721	0.1	**0.712**	0.1	**0.678**	0.0
TFLP	**0.768**	0.2	**0.750**	0.2	**0.729**	0.3	0.701	0.3	0.663	0.0
MTK	0.711	0.2	0.698	0.1	0.685	0.2	0.663	0.2	0.608	0.2

sion at k (k = [1, ..., 5]) in correspondence of the best value of α (α_b). Note that small variations of precision hold for α ranging from 0.2 to 0.4. For each text summarization technique the associated summarizer is implemented in the baseline system.

As expected, the best results are obtained without adopting any Text Summarization technique. Among the selected techniques, TFLP allows to obtain the best performances in terms of P@1, P@2, and P@3, whereas TF2P in terms of P@4 and P@5.

To further highlight the impact of TS, Table 4 reports the results obtained by using TFLP while varying α for the p@1. The best precision, for each value of k, is highlighted in bold. A value of 0.0 means that only semantic analysis is considered, whereas a value of 1.0 considers only the syntactic analysis. A comparative study of the role of the α parameter is reported in Figure 6, in which the behavior of P@1 by varying α is reported, for each classic and novel techniques. Note that this figure better highlights that TFLP is the best technique.

The Impact of Snippets

Being interested in studying the impact of snippets, a suitable system is devised for experiments (see Figure 7). The system takes a webpage as input. First, the BoW builder issues queries to Yahoo!, asking for the URL of each webpage of the dataset, and uses the returned snippets. Then, stop-words are removed and a stemming task is performed.

This module outputs a vector representation of the original text as BoW, each word being represented by its TFIDF. Starting from the BoW provided by the BoW builder, the Classifier classifies the page according to the given taxonomy based on a centroid-based approach. This module outputs a vector representation in terms of Classification Features (CF), each feature corresponding to the score given by the classifier for each category. Finally, the Matcher ranks the categories according to the scores given by the classifier (i.e., the CF of the target page) and, for each category, randomly extracts from the ads repository a corresponding ad.

Table 4. Results with TFLP by varying α

α	p@1	p@2	p@3	p@4	p@5
0.0	0.765	0.746	0.719	0.696	**0.663**
0.1	0.767	0.749	0.724	0.698	**0.663**
0.2	**0.768**	**0.750**	**0.729**	0.699	0.662
0.3	0.766	0.749	**0.729**	**0.701**	0.661
0.4	0.756	0.747	**0.729**	0.698	0.658
0.5	0.744	0.735	0.721	0.693	0.651
0.6	0.722	0.717	0.703	0.681	0.640
0.7	0.685	0.687	0.680	0.658	0.625
0.8	0.632	0.637	0.635	0.614	0.586
0.9	0.557	0.552	0.548	0.534	0.512
1.0	0.408	0.421	0.372	0.388	0.640

Figure 6. The behavior of p@1 by varying α

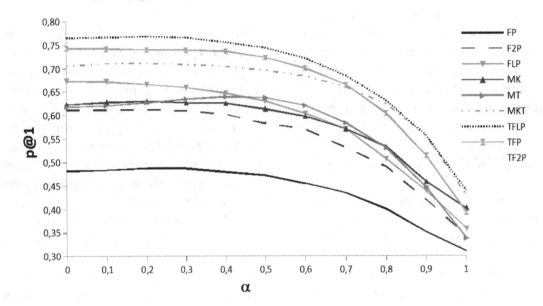

Figure 7. The implemented system

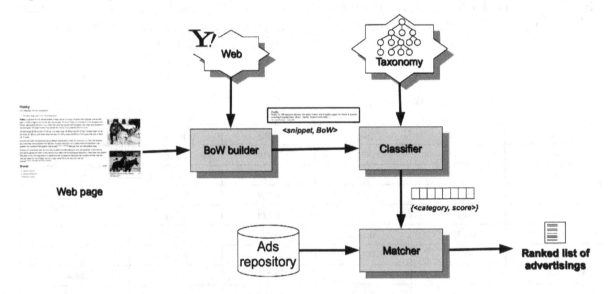

The proposed system, except for the adopted Text Summarization technique, is compliant with the baseline system, in which only CF are considered in the matching phase.

System Performances

To assess the effectiveness of the proposed approach, experiments have been performed on the Recreation dataset. As for the ads we used the ad repository described in the Experimental Results

Table 5. Precision at k of the proposed CA system by adopting: TFLP (CA_{TFLP}), the sole snippets (CA_S); and the snippets together with the page title (CA_{ST})

k	CA_{TFLP}	CA_S	CA_{ST}
1	**0.868**	0.837	0.866
2	0.835	0.801	**0.836**
3	0.770	0.746	**0.775**
4	0.722	0.701	**0.729**
5	0.674	0.657	**0.681**

section. In that repository, each ad is represented by the webpage of a product or service company.

Performances have been calculated in terms of precision at k with $k \in [1, 5]$, i.e., the precision in suggesting k ads.

The evaluation regards the performances obtained by using as text summarization technique: TFLP (the resulting system being CA_{TFLP}); the sole snippets (the resulting system being CA_S); and the snippets together with the page title, (the resulting system being CA_{ST}). Let us recall that, since the focus of this Chapter is on text summarization, comparative experiments among the implemented CA system and selected state-of-the-art systems are out of the scope of this work. Nevertheless, let us stress the fact that CA_{TFLP} coincides with the system proposed in the previous section, in which α parameter is set to 0 (i.e., only CF are considered in the matching phase).

Table 5 shows that, for all the compared systems, the results are quite good, especially in suggesting 1 or 2 ads. It also clearly shows that, except for k = 1, CA_{ST} is the system that performs better. The results highlight the effectiveness of the adoption of snippets as text summarization technique in the for CA.

FUTURE RESEARCH DIRECTIONS

Regarding to CA, the main issue is to analyze the webpage content on-the-fly. Real time analysis should use a reduced amount of resources. This aspect leads to the development of extraction-based techniques, rather than abstraction-based methods. As for future directions, focusing on further semantic techniques is an important direction. The main idea is to improve syntactic techniques by exploiting semantic information (such as, synonyms and hypernyms) extracted from a lexical database or a semantic net.

CONCLUSION

This chapter describes study, development, and experimentation of text summarization techniques. In particular, some straightforward extraction-based techniques have been proposed, such techniques being based on taking into account the information of the title of a webpage. Experimental results confirm the hypothesis that adding such information to well-known techniques leads to improved performance. Then, has been proposed the adoption of snippets as summaries of a webpage. The comparative study showed that the proposed snippet text summarization technique has similar performance, in terms of precision, recall, and F-1 with respect to the proposed extraction technique. The impact of each summarization technique has been studied and evaluated in a CA system. Experimental results confirmed the intuition that the adoption of enriched extractive techniques improves the performance of classic methods, in particular by taking into account the information of webpage title. Furthermore, the impact of snippets has also been studied in the field of CA. The adoption of snippets as text summarization technique in CA showed that performance, calculated in terms of precision@k, are quite good, especially in suggesting 1 or 2 ads and that the system that uses both snippets and title is the one with the best performances.

REFERENCES

Anagnostopoulos, A., Broder, A. Z., Gabrilovich, E., Josifovski, V., & Riedel, L. (2007). Just-in-time contextual advertising. In *Proceedings of the 16th ACM Conference on Information and Knowledge Management* (pp. 331–340). ACM.

Armano, G., Giuliani, A., & Vargiu, E. (2011). Semantic enrichment of contextual advertising by using concepts. In *Proceedings of International Conference on Knowledge Discovery and Information Retrieval*. IEEE.

Armano, G., Giuliani, A., & Vargiu, E. (2012). Using snippets in text summarization: A comparative study and an application. *In Proceedings of CEUR Workshop Proceedings*. CEUR.

Baeza-Yates, R. A., & Ribeiro-Neto, B. (1999). *Modern information retrieval*. Boston, MA: Addison-Wesley Longman Publishing Co., Inc.

Baxendale, P. (1958). Machine-made index for technical literature–An experiment. *IBM Journal of Research and Development, 2*(4), 354–361. doi:10.1147/rd.24.0354

Belew, R. K. (Ed.). (2000). *Finding out about: A cognitive perspective on search engine technology and the WWW*. Cambridge, UK: Cambridge University Press.

Blei, D., & Lafferty, J. D. (2006). Dynamic topic models. In *Proceedings of the 23rd International Conference on Machine Learning*, (pp. 113–120). ACM.

Brandow, R., Mitze, K., & Rau, L. F. (1995). Automatic condensation of electronic publications by sentence selection. *Information Processing & Management, 31*, 675–685. doi:10.1016/0306-4573(95)00052-I

Broder, A., Fontoura, M., Josifovski, V., & Riedel, L. (2007) A semantic approach to contextual advertising. In *Proceedings of the 30th Annual International ACM SIGIR Conference on Research and Development in Information Retrieval* (pp. 559–566). ACM.

Carrasco, J., Fain, D., Lang, K., & Zhukov, L. (2003). Clustering of bipartite advertiser-keyword graph. In *Proceedings of the Workshop on Clustering Large Datasets*. IEEE.

Ciaramita, M., Murdock, V., & Plachouras, V. (2008a). Semantic associations for contextual advertising. *Journal of Electronic Commerce Research Special Issue on Online Advertising and Sponsored Search, 9*(1), 1–15.

Ciaramita, M., Murdock, V., & Plachouras, V. (2008b). Online Learning from click data for sponsored search. In *Proceeding of the 17th International Conference on World Wide Web*. IEEE.

Deepayan, C., Deepak, A., & Vanja, J. (2008). Contextual advertising by combining relevance with click feedback. In *Proceeding of the 17th International Conference on World Wide Web* (pp. 417–426). ACM.

Dumais, S., Platt, J., Heckerman, D., & Sahami, M. (1998). Inductive learning algorithms and representations for text categorization. In *Proceedings of the 7th International Conference on Information and Knowledge Management*, CIKM '98 (pp. 148–155). ACM.

Edmundson, H. P. (1969). New methods in automatic extracting. *Journal of the ACM, 16*(2), 264–285. doi:10.1145/321510.321519

Ganti, V., Gehrke, J., & Ramakrishnan, R. (1999). CACTUS: Clustering categorical data using summaries. In *Proceedings of the 5th ACM SIGKDD International Conference on Knowledge Discovery and Data Mining,* KDD '99, (pp. 73–83). ACM.

Han, E. H., & Karypis, G. (2000). Centroid-based document classification: Analysis and experimental results. In *Proceedings of the 4th European Conference on Principles of Data Mining and Knowledge Discovery,* PKDD'00 (pp. 424–431). Springer-Verlag.

Joachims, T. (2002). Optimizing search engines using clickthrough data. In *Proceedings of the ACM Conference on Knowledge Discovery and Data Mining (KDD).* ACM.

Kaikhah, K. (2004). Automatic text summarization with neural networks. In *Proceedings of the 2nd IEEE International Conference on Intelligent Systems* (pp. 40-44). IEEE.

Ker, J., & Chen, J. (2000). A text categorization based on summarization technique. In *Proceedings of the ACL-2000 Workshop on Recent Advances in Natural Language Processing and Information Retrieval,* (vol. 11, pp. 79–83). Association for Computational Linguistics.

Kolcz, A., Prabakarmurthi, V., & Kalita, J. (2001). Summarization as feature selection for text categorization. In *Proceedings of the 10th International Conference on Information and Knowledge Management* (pp. 365–370). ACM.

Kraaij, W., Spitters, M., & Heijden, M. (2001). Combining a mixture language model and naïve Bayes for multi-document summarization. In *Proceedings of the DUC2001 Workshop (SIGIR2001),* (pp. 95-103). New Orleans, LA: ACM.

Lacerda, A., Cristo, M., Goncalves, M. A., Fan, W., Ziviani, N., & Ribeiro-Neto, B. (2006). Learning to advertise. In *Proceedings of the 29th Annual International ACM SIGIR Conference on Research and Development in Information Retrieval* (pp. 549–556). ACM.

Liu, H., & Singh, P. (2004). ConceptNet: A practical commonsense reasoning tool-kit. *BT Technology Journal, 22,* 211–226. doi:10.1023/B:BTTJ.0000047600.45421.6d

Luhn, P. H. (1958). The automatic creation of literature abstracts. *IBM Journal of Research and Development, 2*(2), 159–165. doi:10.1147/rd.22.0159

McCargar, V. (2004). Statistical approaches to automatic text summarization. *Journal of Information Science, 30*(4), 365–380.

Mladenic, D., & Grobelnik, M. (1998). Feature selection for classification based on text hierarchy. In *Proceedings of Text and the Web, Conference on Automated Learning and Discovery CONALD-98.* CONALD.

Murdock, V., Ciaramita, M., & Plachouras, V. (2007). A noisy-channel approach to contextual advertising. In *Proceedings of the Workshop on Data Mining and Audience Intelligence for Advertising (ADKDD).* ADKDD.

Porter, M. (1980). An algorithm for suffix stripping. *Program, 14*(3), 130–137. doi:10.1108/eb046814

Rau, L. F., Jacobs, P. S., & Zernik, U. (1989). Information extraction and text summarization using linguistic knowledge acquisition. *Information Processing & Management, 25,* 419–428. doi:10.1016/0306-4573(89)90069-1

Ribeiro-Neto, B., Cristo, M., Golgher, P. B., & Silva de Moura, E. (2005). Impedance coupling in content-targeted advertising. In *Proceedings of the 28th Annual International ACM SIGIR Conference on Research and Development in Information Retrieval* (pp. 496–503). ACM.

Ricci, F., Rokach, L., Shapira, B., & Kantor, P. B. (Eds.). (2010). *Recommender systems handbook*. Berlin: Springer.

Rocchio, J. (1971). Relevance feedback in information retrieval. In *The SMART retrieval system: Experiments in automatic document processing* (pp. 313–323). Upper Saddle River, NJ: Prentice Hall.

Salton, G., & McGill, M. (1984). *Introduction to modern information retrieval*. New York: McGraw- Hill Book Company.

Shen, D., Chen, Z., Yang, Q., Zeng, H. J., Zhang, B., Lu, Y., & Ma, W. Y. (2004). Webpage classification through summarization. In *Proceedings of the 27th Annual International ACM SIGIR Conference on Research and Development in Information Retrieval*, SIGIR '04 (pp. 242–249). ACM.

Sinka, M., & Corne, D. (2002). A large benchmark dataset for web document clustering. In Soft Computing Systems: Design, Management and Applications, (pp. 881–890). Press.

Wang, J. B., Hong, P., & Hu, J. S. (2006). Automatic keyphrases extraction from document using neural network. In *Proceeding of the 4th International Conference on Advances in Machine Learning and Cybernetics (ICMLC'05)* (pp. 633-641). ICMLC.

Witten, I. H., Bray, Z., Mahoui, M., & Teahan, B. (1999). A new frontier for lossless compression. In *Proceedings of the Conference on Data Compression,* DCC '99. IEEE.

Yih, W. T., Goodman, J., & Carvalho, V. R. (2006). Finding advertising keywords on webpages. In *Proceedings of the 15th International Conference on World Wide Web* (pp. 213– 222). ACM.

Yong, S. P., & Ahmad, I. Z. Abidin, & Chen, Y.Y. (2005). A neural based text summarization system. In *Proceedings of the 6th International Conference of Data Mining* (pp. 45-50). ACM.

ADDITIONAL READING

Barzilay, R., & Elhadad, M. (1997). Using Lexical Chains for Text Summarization. In *Proceedings of the ACL Workshop on Intelligent Scalable Text Summarization*, 10-17. Madrid, Spain.

Chakrabarti, D., Agarwal, D., & Josifovski, V. (2008). Contextual advertising by combining relevance with click feedback. In *proceeding of the 17th International Conference on World Wide Web 2008*, 417-426. Beijing, China.

Erkan, G., & Radev, D. R. (2004). LexRank: graph-based lexical centrality as salience in text summarization. [AI Access Foundation, USA.]. *Journal of Artificial Intelligence Research, 22*(1), 457–479.

Fan, T.-K., & Chang, C.-H. (2009). Sentiment-Oriented Contextual Advertising. In *ECIR '09 Proceedings of the 31th European Conference on IR Research on Advances in Information Retrieval*, 202 - 215. Springer-Verlag Berlin, Heidelberg.

Gong, Y., & Liu, X. (2001). Generic text summarization using relevance measure and latent semantic analysis. In *24th Annual International ACM SIGIR Conference on Research and Development in Information Retrieval*, 19-25. New Orleans, LA, United States

Hearst, M. A. (1997). TextTiling: Segmenting Text into Multi-paragraph Subtopic Passages. *Computational Linguistics, 23*(1), 33–64.

Hu, M., & Liu, B. (2004). Mining and summarizing customer reviews. In *KDD-2004 - Proceedings of the Tenth ACM SIGKDD International Conference on Knowledge Discovery and Data Mining*, 168-177. Seattle, WA, United States.

Icon Group International, Inc. Staff (eds.) (2009). *The 2009 Report on Online Contextual Advertising: World Market Segmentation by City.* http://books.google.it/books?id=viJZPgAACAAJ

Knight, K., & Marcu, D. (2002). Summarization beyond sentence extraction: A probabilistic approach to sentence compression. *Artificial Intelligence, 139*(1), 91–107. doi:10.1016/S0004-3702(02)00222-9

Kupiec, J., Pedersen, J., & Chen, F. (1995). Trainable document summarizer. In *Proceedings of the 18th Annual International ACM SIGIR Conference on Research and Development in Information Retrieval*, 68-73. Seattle, WA, USA.

Li, W., Wang, X., Zhang, R., Cui, Y., Mao, J., & Jin, R. (2010). Exploitation and exploration in a performance based contextual advertising system. In *KDD '10 Proceedings of the 16th ACM SIGKDD international conference on Knowledge discovery and data mining*, 27-36. ACM New York, NY, USA.

Lin, C., & Hovy, E. (2003). Automatic evaluation of summaries using N-gram co-occurrence statistics. In *NAACL '03: Proceedings of the 2003 Conference of the North American Chapter of the Association for Computational Linguistics on Human Language Technology*, 71–78. Association for Computational Linguistics, Morristown, NJ, USA.

Mani, I. (1999). *Advances in Automatic Text Summarization. MIT Press Cambridge* (M. T. Maybury, Ed.). MA, USA.

Pak, A. N., & Chung, C.-W. (2010). A Wikipedia Matching Approach to Contextual Advertising. [Kluwer Academic Publishers Hingham, MA, USA.]. *World Wide Web (Bussum), 13*(3), 251–274. doi:10.1007/s11280-010-0084-2

Salton, G., Singhal, A., Mitra, M., & Buckley, C. (1997). Automatic text structuring and summarization. *Information Processing & Management, 33*(2), 193–207. doi:10.1016/S0306-4573(96)00062-3

Turney, P. D. (2000). Learning algorithms for keyphrase extraction. *Information Retrieval, 2*(4), 303–336. doi:10.1023/A:1009976227802

Yazdanifard, R., & Mostaf Hossein, S. (2013). Theoretical model for contextual advertising on social networks. *WIT Transactions on Engineering Sciences, 80*, 679–686.

Yeh, J.-Y., Ke, H.-R., Yang, W.-P., & Meng, I.-H. (2005). Text summarization using a trainable summarizer and latent semantic analysis. *Information Processing & Management, 41*(1), 75–95. doi:10.1016/j.ipm.2004.04.003

Zhang, W., Wang, D., Xue, G.-R., & Zha, H. (2012). *Advertising Keywords Recommendation for Short-Text Web Pages Using Wikipedia. ACM Transactions on Intelligent Systems and Technology (TIST) 3(2). Article No. 36.* NY, USA: ACM New York.

KEY TERMS AND DEFINITIONS

Classification: The task of determining and assigning class labels to data. In other words, given an input, classification consists of identifying the class(es) to which the input belongs.

Contextual Advertising (CA): A form of targeted advertising for advertisements appearing on websites or other media, such as content displayed in mobile browsers. Advertisements are selected and served by automated systems based on the content displayed to the user.

Feature Selection: The technique used for selecting a subset of relevant features for describing input data, with the goal of building robust learning models.

Information Retrieval: The task of representing, storing, organizing, and accessing information items.

Text Summarization: A technique aimed at producing summaries from textual documents. A summary is a text produced from one or more texts that conveys important information from the original text(s) with the mandatory constraint that the summary length must not be longer than half of the original text(s), but usually significantly less than that.

ENDNOTES

[1] N is a global parameter that can be set starting from some relevant characteristics of the input

(e.g., from the average document length).

[2] http://www.dmoz.org and http://www.yahoo.com, respectively

[3] This method was defined to extract summaries from textual documents, such as articles, scientific papers and books. In fact, we are interested in summarizing HTML documents, which are often too short to find meaningful sentences composed by at least 3 title-words and 4 keywords in the same sentence.

[4] http://www.microsoft.com/silverlight/

[5] http://www.adobe.com/products/flash-player.html

[6] http://get.adobe.com/it/shockwave/

[7] http://dmoz.org

[8] http://www.google.com

[9] http://www.yahoo.com

[10] http://www.seobythesea.com/2009/12/how-a-search-engine-may-choose-search-snippets/

[11] http://www.bing.com

Chapter 9
NewSum:
"N-Gram Graph"-Based
Summarization in the Real World

George Giannakopoulos
NCSR "Demokritos", Greece & SciFY Not-for-Profit Company, Greece

George Kiomourtzis
SciFY Not-for-Profit Company, Greece & NCSR "Demokritos", Greece

Vangelis Karkaletsis
NCSR "Demokritos", Greece

ABSTRACT

This chapter describes a real, multi-document, multilingual news summarization application, named NewSum, the research problems behind it, as well as the novel methods proposed and tested to solve these problems. The system uses the representation of n-gram graphs in a novel manner to perform sentence selection and redundancy removal for the summaries and faces problems related to topic and subtopic detection (via clustering) and multi-lingual applicability, which are caused by the nature of the real-world news summarization sources.

INTRODUCTION

Automatic summarization has been under research since the late 50's (Luhn, 1958) and has tackled a variety of interesting real-world problems. The problems faced range from news summarization (Barzilay & McKeown, 2005; Huang, Wan, & Xiao, 2013; Kabadjov, Atkinson, Steinberger, Steinberger, & Goot, 2010; D. Radev, Otterbacher, Winkel, & Blair-Goldensohn, 2005; Wu & Liu, 2003) to scientific summarization (Baralis & Fiori, 2010; Teufel & Moens, 2002; Yeloglu, Milios, & Zincir-Heywood, 2011) and meeting summarization (Erol, Lee, Hull, Center, & Menlo Park, 2003; Niekrasz, Purver, Dowding, & Peters, 2005).

The significant increase in the rate of content creation due to the Internet and its social media aspect, moved automatic summarization research to a multi-document requirement, taking into account the redundancy of information

DOI: 10.4018/978-1-4666-5019-0.ch009

across sources (Afantenos, Doura, Kapellou, & Karkaletsis, 2004; Barzilay & McKeown, 2005; J. M Conroy, Schlesinger, & Stewart, 2005; Erkan & Radev, 2004; Farzindar & Lapalme, 2003). Recently, the fact that the content generated by people around the world is clearly multilingual, has urged research to revisiting summarization under a multilingual prism (Evans, Klavans, & McKeown, 2004; Giannakopoulos et al., 2011; Saggion, 2006; Turchi, Steinberger, Kabadjov, & Steinberger, 2010; Wan, Jia, Huang, & Xiao, 2011).

However, this volume of summarization research does not appear to have reached a wider audience, possibly based on the evaluated performance of automatic systems, which consistently perform worse than humans (John M Conroy & Dang, 2008; Hoa Trang Dang & Owczarzak, 2009; Giannakopoulos et al., 2011).

In this chapter, we show how a novel, multilingual multi-document news summarization method, without the need for training, can be used as an everyday tool. We show how we designed and implemented an automatic summarization solution, named NewSum, which summarizes news from a variety of sources, using language-agnostic methods. We describe the requirements studied during the design and implementation of NewSum, how these requirements were met and how people evaluated the outcome of the effort.

Our main contributions in this chapter are, thus, as follows:

- We briefly study the requirements of a real-world summarization application, named NewSum. We describe task-aware specifications based on user and application context limitations (e.g. device, communication), source limitations and legal limitations.
- We describe a generic, language-agnostic method for extractive summarization, taking into account redundancy constraints. The method needs no training and mini-

mizes the effort of crossing language boundaries, since it functions at the character level.
- We describe an open architecture for responsive summarization on a mobile setting.
- We provide an evaluation of the system based on non-expert evaluations, to represent market applicability of the system.

In the following section we provide some background on automatic summarization to sketch the related summarization research.

BACKGROUND

In this section, we briefly discuss summarization methods and systems that have been available as either research efforts, but also as real applications. We refer to the projects that aim at summarization and sketch the current state-of-the-art of the summarization sub-domains of salience detection and redundancy removal.

Summarization has been defined as a reductive transformation of a given set of texts, usually described as a three-step process: selection of salient portions of text, aggregation of the information for various selected portions, (optionally) abstraction of this information and, finally, presentation of the final summary text (S. Jones, 1999; I. M. Mani & Bloedorn, 1999). The summarization research community addresses major problems that arise during the summarization process.

- How can one group texts into topics, given a big set of texts of varying topics?
- How can one detect and select salient information to be included in the summary (ideally without training)?
- How can one avoid redundant or repeated information in the output summary, especially when multiple documents are used as input to the summarization process?

- Can one develop methods that will function independently from the language of documents? To what degree can this independence be achieved?

Up to date, many summarization systems have been developed, presented and evaluated, especially within such endeavors as the Document Understanding Conferences (DUC) and Text Analysis Conferences (TAC)[1].

The summarization community has moved from single-text (single-document) to multi-text (multi-document) input and has also reached such domains as opinion summarization and "trend" summarization, as in the case of NTCIR[2].

Different evaluations performed in recent years have proved that the multi-summarization task is highly complex and demanding, and that automatic summarizers have a long way to go to perform equally well to humans (Dang & Owczarzak, 2008; Dang, 2005, 2006).

A study on how well a system can perform summarization (Genest, Lapalme, Yousfi-Monod, & Montréal, 2009) compared two basic methods of summarization: the extractive and the abstractive. In extractive summarization the summarizer forms a summary by selecting sentences from the original texts. In the abstractive approach, which is how humans tend to summarize, the summarizer creates a (mental) abstraction of the information and then composes a new text based on this abstraction. The study showed that extractive summarization has an upper limit of performance. This upper limit in the study was the performance of humans (considered the best summarizers), who applied extractive summarization through simple sentence selection and reordering. Abstractive summarization seems to be able to perform better than the extractive process.

In the domain of news summarization, there exist efforts that provided publicly available, proof-of-concept systems. Such systems are the NewsInEssence system (D. Radev et al., 2005), the Columbia NewsBlaster (Evans et al., 2004) and

the multilingual NewsGist (Kabadjov et al., 2010). A number of commercial efforts for products and services related to summarization are currently available. We briefly overview these efforts in the following paragraphs.

Related Summarization Systems and Software

Summly (summly.com) is a single-document summarizer, applied on web pages and has just recently been embedded into the Yahoo! mobile application. Wavii (wavii.com) is an application offering a social media view of news integration, by generating a stream of summarized news. It is multi-document, but applied on a single language (English). It was recently bought by Google and is currently unavailable. Another effort is that of iResearch Reporter (iresearch-reporter.com), which is an English-only summarization solution, provided via a web interface. It is search-based, meaning that it summarizes the results of searches in a structured report. Similarly, JistWeb and JistDesktop (jastatechnologies.com) are a set of web and desktop based tools that summarize search results into a single document. Ultimate Research Assistant (urast.com) is a search-based, multi-document, multilingual summarizer. It incorporates no redundancy removal and provides both web-based access and also via a programmatic Application Programming Interface (API).

TLDR Reader (tldrstuff.com) is a mobile application that provides single document summaries on articles and pages. It only works on English texts. TLDR can be also used via an (API). ReadBorg (readborg.com), based on the TextTeaser summarizer, provides single document summaries of news in English. The summarization service is provided as a website and also via a web service API.

Other efforts and products related to NewSum include EMMNewsExplorer (emm.newsexplorer. eu) which is a web-based news aggregator applied on many languages, which however provides no summary – similarly to a variety lots of aggregators like Google News (news.google.com), Fark (fark.com) and others.

What none of the above solutions provide is a multilingual, multi-document, news clustering and summarizing infrastructure and front-end software, offering an effective glimpse of news, made to suit mobile user needs.

In the next paragraphs we overview research works on the summarization subtasks of salience (or importance) detection and redundancy removal, to support the novelty of our n-gram graph based proposed methods.

Sentence and Information Salience

To determine salience of information, researchers have used *positional and structural* properties of the judged sentences with respect to the source texts. These properties can be the sentence position (e.g., number of sentence from the beginning of the text, or from the beginning of the current paragraph) in a document, or the fact that a sentence is part of the title or of the abstract of a document (Edmundson, 1969; D. R. Radev, Jing, Stys, & Tam, 2004). Also, the *relation* of sentences with respect to a user-specific query or to a specified topic (J. M Conroy et al., 2005; Park, Lee, Ahn, Hong, & Chun, 2006; Varadarajan & Hristidis, 2006) are features providing evidence towards importance of information. Cohesion (proper name anaphora, reiteration, synonymy, and hypernymy) and coherence - based on Rhetorical Structure Theory (Mann & Thompson, 1987) - relations between sentences were used in (I. Mani, Bloedorn, & Gates, 1998) to define salience. The idea was that of a graph, where each sentence is a vertex. Vertices in this graph are connected by edges when there is a cohesion or coherence relation between them (e.g. common anaphora). The salience of a sentence, given this graph, is computed as the result of an operation dependent on the graph representation (e.g. spreading activation starting from important nodes). Before

studying the graph-based methods any further, we first overview other common approaches to salience detection in summarization.

Oftentimes, following the *bag-of-words* assumption, a sentence is represented as a word-feature vector, as in (Torralbo, Alfonseca, Guirao, & Moreno-Sandoval, 2005). In such cases, the sequence of the represented words is ignored. The vector dimensions represent word frequency or the Term Frequency - Inverse Document Frequency (TF-IDF) value of a given word in the source texts. In other cases, further analysis is performed, aiming to reduce dimensionality and produce vectors in a *latent topic space* (Flores, Gillard, Ferret, & Chandelar, 2008; Steinberger & Jezek, 2004). Vector representations can be exploited for measuring the semantic similarity between information chunks, by using measures such as the cosine distance or Euclidean distance between vectors.

When the feature vectors for the chunks have been created, clustering of vectors can be performed for identifying clusters corresponding to specific topics. A cluster can then be represented by a single vector, for example the centroid of the corresponding cluster's vectors (Radev, Jing, & Budzikowska, 2000). Chunks closest to these representative vectors are considered to be the most salient. We must point out that for the aforementioned vector-based approaches one needs to perform preprocessing to avoid pitfalls due to stop-words and inflection of words that create feature spaces of very high dimension.

However, the utility of the preprocessing step, which usually involves stemming and stop-word removal, is an issue of dispute (Ledeneva, 2008; Leite, Rino, Pardo, & Nunes, 2007).

More recent approaches use *machine learning techniques* and sets of different features to determine whether a source text chunk (sentence) should be considered salient and included in the output summary. In that case the feature vector calculated for every sentence may include information like sentence length, sentence absolute position in the text, sentence position within its corresponding paragraph, number of verbs and so forth - e.g. see Teufel & Moens (2002).

It has been shown that for specific tasks, such as the news summarization task of DUC, simple *positional features* for the determination of summary sentences can be very promising for summarization systems (Dang, 2005). However, in other domains or genres these features are not adequate. The example of short stories falls into this type of case, where a completely different approach is needed to perform the summarization (Kazantseva & Szpakowicz, 2010): the specific summary type described may be expected to describe the setting without giving away the details or surprises of the plot. In (Jatowt & Ishizuka, 2006), we find an approach where time-aware summaries take into account the frequency of terms over time in different versions of web pages to determine salience.

The notion of Bayesian expected risk (or loss) is applied in the summarization domain by Kumar, Pingali, & Varma (2009), where the selection of sentences is viewed as a decision process. In this process the selection of each sentence is considered a risky decision and the system has to select the sentences that minimize the risk.

The CLASSY system (J. M Conroy, Schlesinger, & O'Leary, 2007; J. M. Conroy, Schlesinger, & O'Leary, 2009) extracts frequently occurring ("signature") terms from source texts, as well as terms from the user query. Using these terms, the system estimates an "oracle score" for sentences, which relates the terms contained within the candidate sentences to an estimated "ideal" distribution based on term appearance in the query, the signature terms and the topic document cluster. Different optimization methods (e.g. Integer Linear Programming) can then be used to determine the best set of sentences for a given length of summary, given sentence weights based on their "oracle score".

Focusing on the graph-related literature on multi-document summarization, we visit a number of works that build on graph structures to build summaries. In (Varadarajan & Hristidis, 2006) the authors create a graph, where the nodes represent text chunks and edges indicate relation between the chunks. In that work, the maximum spanning tree of the document graph that contains all the keywords is considered an optimal summary. More recently, the G-FLOW method (Christensen, Mausam, & Etzioni, 2013) builds on estimated discourse relations to build Approximate Discourse Graphs (ADGs). The summarizing process then uses the graph to select one from various candidate extractive summaries, maximizing coherence. The candidate summaries are also graded via a regression model of salience (based on ROUGE scores of training corpora) and a redundancy detector (based on information extraction). The result is a summarizer that searches through possible ordered lists of sentences - by applying a stochastic hill-climbing algorithm - to find a summary that contains maximally salient, non-redundant sentences that form a maximally coherent text.

In multi-document summarization, different iterative ranking algorithms like PageRank (Brin & Page, 1998) and HITS (Kleinberg, 1999) over graph representations of texts have been used to determine the salient terms over a set of source texts (Mihalcea, 2005). Salience has also been determined based on the fact that documents can be represented as "small world" topology graphs (Matsuo, Ohsawa, & Ishizuka, 2001). In these graphs important terms appear highly linked to other terms. Finding the salient terms, one can determine the containing sentences' salience and create the final summary.

In another approach (Hendrickx & Bosma, 2008), content units (sentences) are assigned a normalized value (0 to 1) based on a set of graphs representing different aspects of the content unit. These aspects include: query-relevance;

cosine similarity of sentences within the same document (termed *relatedness*); cross-document relatedness, which is considered an aspect of redundancy; redundancy with respect to prior texts; and coreference based on the number of coreferences between different content units. All the above aspects and their corresponding graphs are combined into one model that assigns the final value of salience using an iterative process. The process spreads importance over nodes based on the "probabilistic centrality" method that takes into account the direction of edges to either augment or penalize the salience of nodes, based on their neighbors' salience.

In a related study of graph methods for multi-document summarization (Ribaldo, Akabane, Rino, & Pardo, 2012), we see that cross-document structure (via the Cross-document Structure Theory) can be embedded into a sentence-by-sentence similarity graph to enrich available information. Then, node traits such as node grade, clustering coefficient are used to select the most salient sentences across all source texts.

In a recent work by Cai and Li (2012), the authors use a mutual reinforcement principle to determine salient sentences in a query-driven summarization task. The idea is that "a sentence should be ranked higher if it is contained in the theme cluster which is more relevant to the given query while a theme cluster should be ranked higher if it contains many sentences which are more relevant to the given query". To apply this intuition on importance propagation, the authors form a two-layered graph. One layer of the graph contains vertices mapped to topic clusters; the other layer contains vertices mapped to sentences. Edges are drawn between vertices weighted by the cosine similarity of the corresponding vector space representations of the vertex items. Two reinforcement-based methods - Reinforcement After Relevance Propagation (RARP) and Reinforcement During Relevance Propagation (RDRP) – are proposed to determine the importance of sentences in the graph.

In the MUSE multi-document summarizer system (Litvak & Last, 2012) a set of features related to graphs are used as input features to a genetic algorithm. The algorithm, exploiting a training document set, creates a weighting scheme that allows ranking sentences based on the graph (and several other types of) features. The graph is MUSE shows positional proximity between words (Litvak, Last, & Friedman, 2010): nodes are words and edges are drawn between words that are found to be consequtive in the original text.

Within this work, we tackle the problems of salience detection in extractive multi-document summarization using a unified, language independent and generic framework based on n-gram graphs.

The contributed methods offer a basic, language-neutral, easily adaptable set of tools. The basic idea behind this framework is that neighborhood and relative position of characters, words and sentences in documents offer more information than that of the `bag-of-words' approach. Furthermore, the methods go deeper than the word level of analysis into the sub-word (character n-gram) level, which offers further flexibility and independence from language and acts as a uniform representation for sentences, documents and document sets.

As opposed to related works, we do not use centrality traits of the n-gram graph nodes or other graph properties to determine salience. We do not use training or search to rank our sentences. We do not apply propagation of some kind to determine importance. Salience in our system is determined via a set of similarity operators that are applied between topic- and sentence-representative n-gram graphs. The representative graphs are generated via a custom graph merging operator applied on sets of sentence n-gram graphs.

The work presented in this book heavily builds upon conclusions and lessons from a previous technical report (Giannakopoulos, Vouros, & Karkaletsis, 2010). However, the summarization method described herein has significantly different analysis and steps e.g., for subtopic detection, as well as a different overall approach on segmentation (no sub-sentential chunking), essentially constituting a completely novel method of summarization.

Redundancy Detection

A problem that is somewhat complementary to salience selection is that of *redundancy detection*. Redundancy indicates the unwanted repetition of information in a summary. Research on redundancy has given birth to the Marginal Relevance measure (Carbonell & Goldstein, 1998) and the Maximal Marginal Relevance (MMR) selection criterion. The basic idea behind MMR is that "good" summary sentences (or documents) are sentences (or documents) that are relevant to a topic without repeating information already in the summary. The MMR measure is a generic linear combination of any two principal functions that can measure relevance and redundancy.

Another approach to the redundancy problem is that of the Cross-Sentence Informational Subsumption (CSIS) (Radev et al., 2000), where one judges whether the information offered by a sentence is contained in another sentence already in the summary. The "informationally subsumed" sentence can then be omitted from the summary. The main difference between the two approaches is the fact that CSIS is a binary decision on information subsumption, whereas the MMR criterion offers a graded indication of utility and non-redundancy.

Other approaches, overviewed in (Allan, Wade, & Bolivar, 2003), use statistical characteristics of the judged sentences with respect to sentences already included in the summary to avoid repetition. Such methods are the New-Word and Cosine Distance methods (Larkey, Allan, Connell, Bolivar, & Wade, 2003) that use variations of the bag-of-words based vector model to detect similarity between all pairs of candidate and summary sentences. Other,

language model-based methods create a language model of the summary sentences, either as a whole or independently, and compare the language model of the candidate sentence to the summary sentences model (Zhang, Callan, & Minka, 2002). The candidate sentence model with the minimum KL-divergence from the summary sentences' language model is supposed to be the most redundant.

The CLASSY system (Conroy et al., 2009) represents documents in a term vector space and enforces non-redundancy through the following process: Given a pre-existing set of sentences A corresponding to a sentence-term matrix M_A, and a currently judged set of sentences B corresponding to a matrix M_B, B is judged using the term sub-space that is orthogonal to the eigenvalues of the space defined by A; this means that only terms that are not already considered important in A will be taken into account as valuable content.

The G-FLOW method (Christensen, Mausam, & Etzioni, 2013) uses a triple representation to represent sentences and to determine redundancy across sentences.

In this work, we have used and a statistical, graph-based model of sentences by exploiting character n-grams. The strategy, similarly to CSIS, compares all the candidate sentences and determines the redundant ones. We use no deep analysis and we function in a language-independent manner, by using the sub-word (character-based) representation of n-gram graphs. The redundant sentences are removed from the list of candidate sentences before generating the summary.

In the following sections, we provide the study and details related to our proposed method: we overview the requirements of a real world news summarization system; we discuss the research problems behind some of the requirements and how a novel method of summarization and an open architecture were devised to provide a solution. We then provide an evaluation of our approach based on user studies and we conclude the chapter.

NEWSUM: NEWS SUMMARIZATION IN THE REAL WORLD

Real-World Requirements

We saw that, in the summarization domain, a variety of problems arise when attempting to provide human-level summaries. NewSum was our effort to provide a task-specific - or "full-purpose" as Sparck-Jones put it (K. S. Jones, 2007) - implementation of a summarization system with one specific goal: allow humans to get a maximum coverage picture of everyday news in a limited time, avoiding redundancy. The implied process for the generation of summaries in such a system, as was indicated in the introduction, is as follows. First, we gather articles from various news sources, which we then group. The grouping is based on the real events they refer to. We determine the most important aspects of an event. Then we try to detect and extract the most representative sentences covering these aspects to form a summary, while avoiding redundancy of information.

We identified several user requirements plausible related to a news summarization application. First, the summary should be provided with minimal delay (ideally in real-time). Second, all the implementation details should be hidden behind a friendly and effective interface. Third, the system should be multilingual to maximize the impact of the application.

We decided that another important aspect of our system would be a feature allowing the user to provide feedback on the summaries. This would support error detection and analysis, as well as an estimation of how users (who are usually non-experts in linguistics) perceive the performance of the system.

One thing we should stress here is that we decided to follow a strategy which would be penalized in most summarization research tracks (e.g., TAC, DUC): our summaries would not be cohesive, fluent summaries; they would be a set of points. The promise of the system, essentially based on a corresponding specification, is to provide the main points of an event and the user is made aware of this promise. We selected this approach because we assumed that a user expecting a cohesive, fluent, short text summary will be disappointed if he sees an extractive summary (i.e., a collection of extracted sentences). We remind the reader that the assumption is completely in line with the task-specific requirements we have set: extractive summaries may well be suited for a daily news update.

Another aspect of the user requirements is related to the provenance of information. When an application consumes and broadcasts content, the application publisher should be aware of the legal problems that may arise: an application cannot claim ownership of the content it uses from external sources. Especially in our case, where the system draws from copyrighted material we wanted to:

- Make "fair use" of the provided material.
- Point to our source, to allow the user to check the full text and verify the validity of the summary.
- Provide a list of all the sources used for an event, even if the sentences used in the summary are only from a subset. This implies that there are cases where different sources have significant overlap of information, and the text from one subsumes the text from the other. This is very common in the world of news.
- Allow the user to select a subset of sources for the summaries (based on his preferences).

Given the above discussion, more requirements were added to the original set. Summaries were to be provided as sets of sentences/points. In each such point we should refer to the original source, while also keeping links to all the sources that were used to describe the event. Finally, we should allow the user to select a subset of the available sources to suit one's need.

We said that the aim of NewSum was not clearly a research aim, but the processing we needed to perform demanded the support of a variety of research domains to build a usable system. In the following section we show how different research domains map to the individual steps of the processing NewSum performs.

From N-Gram Graphs to Markov Clustering

We have claimed that the steps for analyzing content into summaries are four: gather articles from various news sources; group articles into news events; determine the most important aspects of an event; determine the most representative sentences covering these aspects; avoid redundancy of information in the summary. The only step that does not require a research effort is the gathering step (which we will describe in the next section). The other steps are mapped to corresponding research domains as follows: the grouping of articles and the detection of important aspects is mapped to text clustering; the selection of important sentences is mapped to salience detection in the summarization domain; the avoidance of repetition of information is mapped to redundancy removal.

We note that NewSum is multilingual, i.e. language-agnostic, which sets an important requirement on the applicable research methods. Previous research (Giannakopoulos & Karkaletsis, 2009; Giannakopoulos & Palpanas, 2009; Giannakopoulos et al., 2010) has shown that the n-gram graph text representation is a powerful tool that allows representing texts and combining them, comparing them regardless of underlying language. N-gram

graphs have, notably, given birth to state-of-the-art summary evaluation methods (Giannakopoulos & Karkaletsis, 2013; Giannakopoulos et al., 2008). In the following paragraphs we review the basics of n-gram graphs and see how they were combined with Markov Clustering (MCL) (Dongen, 2000) to achieve text clustering. We also describe how they were an indispensable part of the summarization pipeline, providing - together with the n-gram graph framework algorithms and operators - a generic tool for summarization subtasks.

N-Gram Graphs: The Basics

An n-gram graph is a graph representing how n-grams are found to be neighbors, within a distance of each other, in a given text. An n-gram is a, possibly ordered, set of words or characters, containing n elements. The n-gram graph is a graph $G =< V, E, L, W >$, where V is the set of vertices, E is the set of edges, L is a function assigning a label to each vertex and to each edge and W is a function assigning a weight to every edge. The graph has n-grams labeling its vertices $v \in V$. The edges $e \in E$ connecting the n-grams indicate proximity of the corresponding vertex n-grams. Our chosen labeling function L assigns to each edge $e =< v_1, v_2 >$ the concatenation of the labels of its corresponding vertices' labels in a predefined order: e.g., $L(e) = L(v_1) + SEP + L(v_2)$, where SEP is a special separator character and the operator + is, in this context, the operator of string concatenation. For directed graphs the order is essentially the order of the edge direction. In undirected graphs the order can be the lexicographic order of the vertices' labels.

It is important to note that in n-gram graphs each vertex is unique. To ensure that no duplicate vertices exist, we also require that the labeling function is a one-to-one function. The weight of the edges can indicate a variety of traits: distance between the two neighboring n-grams in the original text, or the number of co-occurrences within a given window (we note that the meaning of distance and window size changes by whether we use character or word n-grams). In our implementation we apply as weight of an edge, the frequency of co-occurrence of the n-grams of its constituent vertices in the original text.

We repeat that the edges E are assigned weights of $c_{i,j}$ where $c_{i,j}$ is the number of times a given pair S_i, S_j of n-grams happen to be neighbors in a string within some distance D_{win} of each other. The distance d of two n-grams S_i, which starts at position i, and S_j, which starts at position j, is $d = |i - j|$. The selection of a distance value allows different levels of fuzziness in our representation. We note that more in depth analysis of different types of n-gram graphs can be found in the corresponding original paper on n-gram graphs (Giannakopoulos et al., 2008).

Here, we will briefly illustrate the process of mapping a string to a *character n-gram graph*, which is a language-agnostic version of n-gram graphs.

Given a string, e.g. "abcdef", 2 steps are needed to form an n-gram graph (cf. Figure 1):

- First we extract all (overlapping) unique n-grams, e.g. 2-grams and form one node per

n-gram. In our example this would be: "ab", "bc", "cd", "de", "ef".

- Second, we connect with edges all the n-grams that are found to be neighbors. Two n-grams are considered neighbors, when they are found to be within D characters of each other in the original string. In the example of the figure, "ab" is a neighbor of "bc" for D=3, but "ab" is not a neighbor of "ef".

Once we have drawn the edges, we assign weights to them. The weight of an edge indicates the number of times the two node n-grams were found to be neighbors in the original string (thus, the weight is a positive integer number). In our string all n-grams are found to be neighbors only once. Due to the fact that in this work we look for neighbors in both directions (left and right) the resulting graph has two edges per pair of neighboring n-grams and is essentially equivalent to an undirected graph.

Given this process, we can represent everything from a single sentence to a whole text as an n-gram graph. We note that no preprocessing (stemming,

Figure 1. From string to n-gram graph

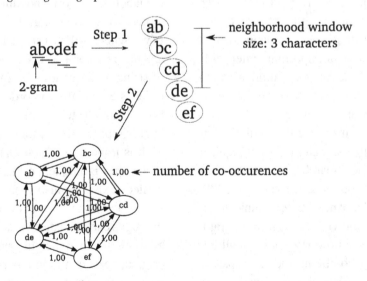

lemmatization, punctuation removal or stop-word removal) is performed on the string.

A second way to use the n-gram graphs is to use *token (e.g., word) n-grams*. In this case some preprocessing is implied, even if only to split the text into tokens. The mapping process is the same, with the difference that distances are measured in tokens instead of characters.

Given a set of n-gram graphs, we can perform several operators (Giannakopoulos, 2009). The *conjunction operator* is a binary operator which keeps the common part (edge set) between two graphs A and B. For a common edge (i.e, an edge that appears in A and in B, regardless of its weight) with weights w_A and w_B in the corresponding graphs, the weight in the resulting graph is the average of w_A and w_B. The *update operator* allows merging a set of graphs into a representative (or class) graph. The merged graph contains all the edges of the source graphs, and common edges in the source graphs result in a single edge with averaged weight in the resulting graph (Giannakopoulos & Karkaletsis, 2011).

On the other hand, several similarity functions have been used to compare n-gram graphs (Giannakopoulos et al., 2008). In this work, we use the *Size Similarity* (SS), *Value Similarity* (VS) and the *Normalized Value Similarity* (NVS) functions.

The SS function is simply the ratio of the edge counts of two graphs. Thus, given two graphs G_1 and G_2, with corresponding edge counts of $|G_1|$ and $|G_2|$, then

$$SS(G_1, G_2) = min(|G_1|, |G_2|) / max(|G_1|, |G_2|)$$

We note that to form the ratio we always use the minimum count as the nominator and the maximum count as the denominator. The SS function is trivial, in that it pays no attention to the contents of the graphs, but only to their relative size (edge count).

The VS function compares two graphs based on their common edges and also takes into account their edge weights and relative graph sizes. In VS

(G_1, G_2), each edge e that is common between G_1, G_2 and has a weight of w_1, w_2 in the corresponding graphs, contributes a value of $VR(e) = min(w_1, w_2) / max(w_1, w_2)$ to the similarity. If SR is the sum of all the VR values for all the common edges between G_1, G_2, then

$$VS = SR / max(|G_1|, |G_2|)$$

The NVS function is calculated as

$$NVS = VS / SS$$

NVS ignores the relative graph sizes, but takes into account common edges and edge weights. We note that all three similarity functions reported here return values between 0.0 (no similarity) and 1.0 (maximum similarity).

In the case where each string is represented with two different n-gram graphs, e.g. a 2-gram graph and a 3-gram graph, one can calculate the *Overall Similarity* (OS) between two strings S_1 and S_2, taking into account both levels of analysis. We first calculate the similarities between the graphs with equal n values (2-gram graph of S_1 and 2-gram graph of S_2, then, 3-gram graph of S_1 and 3-gram graph of S_2), which gives e.g. V_2 and V_3. Then, we calculate OS as the weighted average of the similarities:

$$OS = (2xV_2 + 3xV_3)/(2+3)$$

Once again, the similarity values output from OS are between 0.0 and 1.0, assigning higher importance to higher n-grams (the weighting factor).

In the following paragraphs we describe how the above representation and operators – termed the *n-gram graph framework* - can be applied to face the different research problems NewSum needs to face.

Event Detection as Text Clustering

In NewSum we have used two sets of hand-picked sources: one for Greek and one for English news. Each source provided news via an RSS feed, which encodes article information in a semi-structured manner. Each feed was assigned a category label by its publisher. Given this set of sources providing news feeds, we needed to group news items per news category into events. We need to perform this grouping, because a summary makes more sense per event than over irrelevant documents.

The topic clustering needs to be a very responsive process, thus we used a mechanism similar to blocking for entity resolution - e.g. see (Elmagarmid, Ipeirotis, & Verykios, 2006). The idea is that we use a very quick, similarity-based process to perform the clustering into events, however in our case we have a bias to cluster precision than recall. In other words, we do not mind that much if the cluster misses a single text, but we do mind if the cluster contains an irrelevant text. This is related to the fact that an irrelevant text in a news cluster causes problems in all the following steps, while the missing text may simply be found in a separate cluster (possibly alone) and thus no significant loss is conceded.

The document clustering has several steps, as follows. First, we pre-process the text (including the title) to keep only *Capitalized* words and numbers that appear. This step attempts to perform a very simplistic and high-speed named entity recognizer equivalent, with the addition of a number recognizer. This heuristic implies that the named entities and the numbers are the main identifying information a news item. The output of the process is a series of tokens which are either capitalized words or numbers.

For example, given the title "U.S. tells North Korea new missile launch would be huge mistake", the resulting series would be <"U.S.", "North", "Korea">.

We then use word n-gram graphs to represent the series (n takes values in {1,2} and D=3). This representation implies that the way entities and numbers are found to co-occur in the above series is important and not simply the series themselves. This approach also helps with noise from the previous step, since the co-occurrence of entities is important and, thus, noise may be isolated (it does not repeatedly co-occur with other entities).

Based on the word n-gram graphs, we compare all possible pairs of texts. We use a heuristic rule to connect two texts as referring to the same event: the NVS should be above 0.20 while the SS should be above 0.10. This heuristic (converging to these values through trial and error experiments), is based on the assumptions that we need the texts to be overlapping over a certain degree (NVS threshold), but we also need them to be comparable in size (SS threshold). The success over previously unseen instances given the above values was a cluster precision of over 95% with a cluster recall of about 65%. We note that cluster precision indicates the percentage of texts that were correctly positioned within a cluster (based on the cluster topic). Cluster recall indicates the percentage of the texts that belong to a topic which indeed were assigned to the cluster topic. What this achieved is that we were very strict in our selection of the texts for a given topic: no irrelevant texts should enter. If they did, then the summary would make no sense. The second part of the heuristic related to the size similarity (SS) was inserted to avoid problems of very short texts that appeared to have significant overlaps with almost any other text (due to commonly used words). The result of this step was that texts talking about the same event are connected to each other via a "talk about the same event" relation.

The final step is based on the assumption of transitivity of the relation "talk about the same event". Thus, if A and B "talk about the same event" and B and C "talk about the same event", then A and C "talk about the same event". This assumption completes the clustering process, by forming groups of texts, where all texts within a group talk about a single event.

Given the clusters of texts, we now need to detect topics and subtopics that form the essence of each event. In the next paragraphs we focus on this detection process.

Subtopic Detection and Representation

In NewSum we consider that an event has several aspects, or subtopics. This approach builds on existing related efforts, exploiting (sub-)topic detection for summarization like (Angheluta, De Busser, & Moens, 2002).

In our approach, we start by segmenting the text into sentences. In order to remain maximally language independent we use a statistical sentence splitter (SentenceDetectorME class of the Apache OpenNLP java package[3]) to perform the splitting. Our splitter is trained per language and creates a maximum entropy classifier which can determine split-points in a given sentence. We have trained the splitter on both English and Greek texts to support both languages.

We continue by comparing all pairs of sentences, based on their character n-gram representation. We use character 3-grams and a neighborhood distance of 3 to represent the sentences. These values have been shown to perform well in a variety of settings (Giannakopoulos & Karkaletsis, 2011; Giannakopoulos et al., 2008). The output of this step is a similarity matrix between sentences, based on the NVS between the n-gram graphs of the sentence pairs.

We then apply Markov Clustering - MCL (Dongen, 2000) - on the similarity matrix. The result of this process is a set of hard clusters (i.e., no sentence can belong to two clusters at the same time) which we consider as representing different subtopics of an event. Essentially, what we claim is that sentences that are similar to each other in terms of their character n-gram graphs, may talk about the same subtopic. This claim is in agree-

ment with the distributional similarity hypothesis: texts that have a similar distribution of n-grams are likely to speak about the same topic. Since the n-gram graphs represent the co-occurrence statistics of the n-grams in a text and the similarity functions measure the similarity these statistics, our claim is indeed in agreement.

MCL is an unsupervised way to determine automatically – and efficiently – a good number of subtopics, based on the similarities among sentences. This provides an advantage over methods like k-means, which would need an explicit number of topics (k) to work. Furthermore, MCL is very quick to converge, which offers an advantage to several well-known statistical methods for clustering, such as LDA (Blei, Ng, & Jordan, 2003).

Given the subtopics, described as sets of sentences that cover the same subtopics, we now need to extract the essence of each subtopic. In the n-gram graph framework, we consider that the essence of a set of graphs is the maximum common sub-graph of all the set. Thus, to extract the essence of a subtopic, we use the conjunction operator over all pairs of n-gram graphs within a subtopic sentence cluster. In other words, if a subtopic T_i consists of sentences $\{S_1, S_2, ..., S_n\}$ represented by the corresponding character n-gram graphs $\{G_1, G_2, ..., G_n\}$, and x is the conjunction operator, then the essence E_i of T_i is:

$$E_i = G_1 \times G_2 \times ... \times G_n$$

For a whole event, the subtopic detection and essence extraction process results in a set of n-gram graphs, each of which represents the essence of a subtopic. In order to provide the essence of the whole event, we simply need to combine these essences into one representative graph. To this end we use the update operator over all the essences of the subtopics. The resulting merged graph E_O is the overall representative graph of the event.

Measuring Salience and Avoiding Redundancy

We presume that a sentence is salient if it is similar to the essence of an event. Going back to the n-gram graph framework, the value similarity (VS) is the type of similarity that takes into account whether a given n-gram graph is maximally similar to another, also using the relative size. In other words, VS is the best choice when we want to take into account the overlap between two graphs (vs. the maximum *possible* overlap based on the graph sizes, which is reflected by NVS).

In order to provide a salience based ordering of sentences, we compare (the graph of) each sentence from the source documents of an event cluster to (the graph of) the essence of the event. Ordering the sentences based on their similarity to the essence, we have a salience-based list of candidates for our final summary.

Naively, we could start creating the summary by simply running through the candidate sentences in descending order of similarity to the essence. However, several sentences might talk about the same thing, especially since we are in a multi-document setting. To avoid this problem and tackle redundancy, we perform an a priori filtering of redundant sentences based on the candidate list.

The algorithm starts with the most salient sentence S_1. It compares it to all the following candidate sentences S_i, i>1, by terms of NVS on their character n-gram graphs. If the similarity is above a given threshold (heuristically chosen value in our current setting: 0.3), it means that the later candidate repeats the information of the first candidate and is removed from the candidate list. We iteratively repeat the filtering process for each sentence S_j, j>1, until we reach the end of the candidate list and have removed all redundant sentences.

The result of this process is a set of sentences, which maximally cover the essence of a topic, without repeating information. This set of sentences is, for NewSum, the optimal subset of sentences from the original documents that can form an extractive summary.

To exploit the results of this process, we created the NewSum application, which provides the infrastructure, the interface and the feedback mechanisms that allow using and evaluating our summarization system in a real-life setting. We elaborate on the NewSum application details in the next paragraphs.

NewSum: The Architecture and the Application

The NewSum application integrates all the conducted research into one, free, open-source application, while taking into account real-world requirements. In the NewSum application the main entities are the news article, the news source, the news category, the news feed, the news summary and the news event (or topic). A *news article* is a time and date annotated piece of news, providing a title and the article body. The annotation is implied in the RSS feed (cf. *news feed* below) that provides the article. The *news source* is essentially a news site providing a variety of articles via RSS feeds. The *news category* is a label describing the broad domain of a news article or a news source. Examples of such categories are: world news, local news, politics, science, etc. In most cases a news source is pre-assigned a category by its editor. NewSum uses this information to create its own news categories. The *news feed* is a specific type of web resource (RSS feed), identified by a URL, which provides articles for a specific news category in a semi-structured manner. The *news summary* is a list of sentences (bullets) related to an event. Each sentence is annotated with its originating news feed. If different source texts contain the same sentence, then either of the sources may appear as the origin of the sentence. The *news event (or news topic)* is an abstraction of a real world event. It is described by a set of news articles referring to the event, a title (derived from the most recent news article) and a date. The date of the news event is the date of the latest news article contained in the news event. News aggregators often perform clustering of news articles to form news topic article sets.

Having described the main entities in the New-Sum application, we overview the architecture of the NewSum system built by the analysis server, the web service and the clients.

The *NewSum analysis server* is the processing backbone of the NewSum architecture. At the server we gather and analyze all the articles from a set of predefined news sources, ending up with the processed summaries. The server periodically queries the news sources for new articles. It performs all the analysis required to order the sentences based on salience but it does not remove redundancy at this point. This last step is kept for the moment when a client requests a summary, because clients can choose their news sources and, thus, redundancy can only be determined after a client requests a summary for a given event for a given subset of the data sources.

In order for client software to use the NewSum analysis server output, we provide a web service endpoint (via the Open Source Edition of the Glassfish Server[4]) which simply serves the analyzed, summarized information: t*he NewSum web service*. The endpoint provides the Application Programming Interface (API) for interoperating with the server, getting the detected news topics and the summaries. The web service provides all the required methods to:

- Read the news categories the server covers.
- Get the possible sources that a user can select.
- Read the events (or topics) available at the server, using specific sources.
- Get the summary of a given event, using specific sources.

The NewSum web service makes sure that all the details of the analysis are hidden from client applications and that information is provided at a per-request basis. This latter strategy is meant to minimize network load and latency and allows more flexibility to the client and lower overhead to the server. Furthermore, the fact that the web service is independent of the analysis server allows better workload management and minimizes the impact of one subsystem to the other. Finally, it fulfills the requirements related to speed and responsiveness, since all the data that are sent are a priori available (provided as the output of the execution cycles of the analysis server).

To provide a friendly user interface, independent from the underlying infrastructure, we have created different *NewSum clients* corresponding to different settings. The main client is the Android client, which can be used on portable and mobile devices. In collaboration with the NewSum community, we are also implementing web-based versions of NewSum, as well as a variety of widgets aimed at desktop and virtual desktop settings (e.g., Windows widgets, KDE widget, iGoogle widget). The clients are built upon client libraries that facilitate developers in their application building effort and boost the reusability of the system.

In Figure 2 we provide two snapshots of the NewSum Android application. In the first part we show the basic interface, including the preferences dialog that shows the actions available for selecting sources and categories. In the second part we show how NewSum renders summaries as lists of sentences, also providing the referring link back to the source document on the Web. The reader should also note the five-star rating bar that provides a simple-to-use evaluation interface for the summary viewed.

NewSum[5] will be available as an open source project, building upon the well-established JInsect framework of n-gram graphs (Giannakopoulos, 2010), which is also an open source, free project. It is an effort completed by SciFY[6], with the research support of the SKEL Lab of NCSR "Demokritos". The Android application, as well as some web-based preview versions, are available via the SciFY site.

Figure 2. NewSum snapshots: (a) The main screen with the options menu (b) The summary screen

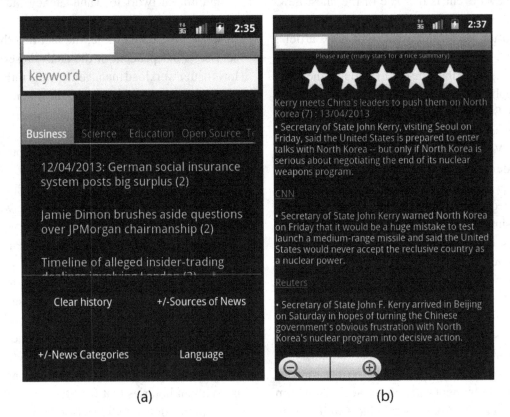

(a)   (b)

Concerning the performance and computational requirements of the summarization method over real data, we note the following: for a total of 110 sources (news feeds) over 18 categories the running time of the whole summarization pipeline (gather, cluster, extract summary) at a server with 8 CPU cores (Intel Xeon at 2.2 GHz) and 12GB of system memory is less than 2 minutes. The implementation is fully parallelizable, scaling with more CPUs.

Both the application and the research behind NewSum make more sense if enough people find its results usable. To determine whether such summarization software makes sense, we conducted evaluations on two main aspects: one on the application usability and one on the summary quality, using the feedback mechanics of the software itself. We elaborate on these evaluations in the next paragraphs.

Evaluation of Summaries

NewSum had two main questions that needed an answer:

- What do people think about the summaries provided?
- Does the use of NewSum (or a similar application) facilitate reading news, by providing global information from various sources?

We conducted three independent studies to answer these questions. Two studies (one preliminary and one more advanced) were meant to answer the summary quality question. The third was meant to answer the question of whether NewSum serves its purpose.

The first user study related to summary quality was conducted during an "open beta" phase of the application. The "open beta" took place between January 2013 and March 2013. During this phase 18 volunteer beta testers were asked to use the program and provide feedback on the summaries they read. The grades were assigned using a 5-star scale: the 1-star rating was mapped to a value of "unacceptable", while the 5-star rating was mapped to a value of "excellent". The feedback we gathered contained 119 different summary ratings. The distribution of grades over all the summaries, from all the users is illustrated in Figure 3. No information was kept related to who sent the rating and thus user bias cannot be determined in this preliminary dataset. The per language performance - 88 instances for Greek and 31 for English - is similar to the overall distribution of grades, with the Greek average rating having a value of 3.89 (and standard deviation of 1) and the English average a value of 3.55 (with a standard deviation of 1). A Kolmogorov-Smirnoff test (preferred over t-test due to the abnormality of the distributions) showed that we cannot reject that the two distributions (Greek and English grades) are derived from the same distribution. In other words, the two distributions appear very similar. In

the rating, grade 1 was meant to indicate "useless or nonsensical summary", grade 3 was mapped to "Acceptable" and grade 5 to "Excellent". What is very interesting is that the percentage of summaries with a grade of 3 or higher is almost 87% of the total summaries. This showed that, even though there is space for improvement, most of the times the summary is at least usable (or much better). Moreover, 2 out of 3 summaries were graded with 4 or 5 ("very good" or "excellent" grades).

In the second study, which started within the CICLing 2013 conference, a newer version of the NewSum application, as well as a website were used to conduct a second experiment. This time an anonymized, persistent user ID was assigned to each participating user. We meant to measure the individual bias of users towards higher or lower grades. Figure 4 illustrates the distribution of grades over all languages and users.

An ANOVA test indicated that the user is indeed a statistically significant factor related to the summary grades assigned (F-value: 4.162, p-value: $<10^{-6}$). The language was similarly highly statistically significant, and this was also shown by the average performances: for Greek

Figure 3. Preliminary "Open Beta" summary grades (119 ratings: 31 for English, 88 for Greek)

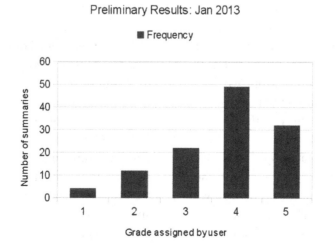

Figure 4. User-aware evaluation summary grades (720 ratings: 267 for English, 453 for Greek)

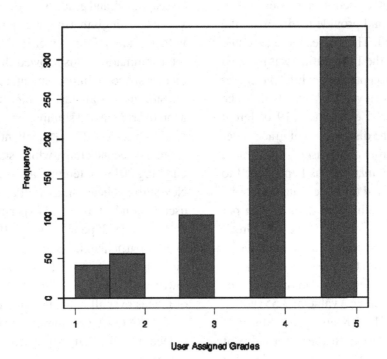

the average was 4.14 (with a standard deviation of 1.07), while for English the average was 3.73 (with a standard deviation of 1.34). This showed that fine-tuning may make sense on individual languages. In both languages the average performance was good, with more than 90% of the summaries having an acceptable (or better) grade for Greek and more than 80% for English. We stress that Greek and English news do not appear simultaneously in the interface (a program option changes the language used in the application). Of course, we could not test where the users originated from and thus part of the bias may relate to the fluency of the users related to one of the languages.

As a result of the deliberately open experiment setting, users varied heavily as related to their contribution: 58 users contributed ratings, with an average contribution of about 12 ratings each, but the median was between 6 and 7 comments,

while a single user provided almost 120 ratings. We tried to remove the user with the 120 ratings, in case he dominated the ratings, but there was slight change in the mean evaluation numbers (-0.01 in the Greek case and -0.15 in the English case).

We also checked via ANOVA whether the source of the data (mobile application or web site) was important for the grading and we found out that it was not statistically significant for the evaluation. Thus, the interface did *not* cause a bias related to the perceived quality of a summary.

Overall, our evaluation showed that the *users think highly of the summaries NewSum creates in both Greek and English*. We should however note that applying the same evaluation at large scale with more information per user, would significantly help detect and remove biases from specific user backgrounds and groups. We are also planning to allow richer feedback in the next versions, to be able to perform better error analysis and also allow our system to learn from user feedback via machine learning.

To answer the question of whether a summarization application facilitates news reading, we performed a small scale user experience experiment, limited to 18 Greek and 7 English beta testers. These testers, who were recruited via an open call, were provided a questionnaire that measured different aspects of user experience. The question we will discuss here was expressed as "The use of NewSum allowed me to get informed of the latest news more globally and thoroughly than before". The answer allowed a 5-scale response from "I totally disagree" to "I totally agree". 11 out of 18 (61%) Greek users and 4 out of 7 (58%) English users have an answer of 4 or 5 to this question. Only 1 user per language thought that NewSum did not really help (2, in the 5-scaled response). The mean grade for Greek was 4 with a standard error of 0.24; for English the mean was 3.86 with a standard error of 0.46. Thus, these preliminary results indicate that users tend to believe that NewSum can improve their news reading, fulfilling its purpose.

FUTURE RESEARCH DIRECTIONS

What is obvious from our research so far is that summarization can be a useful tool. It appears that optimizing existing algorithms to different needs is the way to engineer generic research tools into usable applications, with a societal and commercial impact. Projects like the NOMAD project[7], harvesting information from a variety of sources and aiming to provide actionable updates to decision makers, are examples of the value summarization can bring into this exploding user content generation era.

Summarization is essential due to the increase of content. The applicability of summarization will lie in its ability to gather possible millions of sources (texts or other types of data) and combine them into coherent summaries. Such an approach

implies research efforts towards a variety of domains as follows.

- Large scale summarization: How can we analyze millions (or more) texts and sources to provide summarized information in a timely/responsive manner?
- Language-independent summarization: How can we provide summarization infrastructures over languages that have not been tackled so far, but have millions of speakers and writers (e.g., Chinese, Hindi)?
- Sentiment and argument summarization: Summarizing news has been the focus of numerous research efforts. However, there are many more types of information that would benefit from summarization. Summarizing sentiment and arguments can be of critical importance in domains like policy modeling and business intelligence, since it can provide actionable feedback for decision support. But how can we achieve the summarization in such complex domains, and indeed provide summaries that make sense and can be used as social evidence?
- Summarization as a scientific tool: How can we summarize research in an effective way, to support such domains as bio-informatics, where the production of papers and studies is difficult for researchers to cope with?
- Holistic summarization: How can we combine different types of content (unstructured, semi-structured, fully-structured) into fused summaries of information? Such summaries could provide invaluable feedback for decision support, without the need to skim through completely different types of data to get updated on facts and numbers.

Several ongoing efforts have been fueling the research in these domains and much more is to be seen in the foreseeable future. What we would like to add to this set of research efforts is:

- An effort that would focus on the generalization ability of existing summarization systems and results to new domains and languages.
- An effort that would allow to measure the extrinsic value of summarization systems from the stakeholders: the users.

NewSum is, for, us a milestone towards these two dimensions of summarization system research.

CONCLUSION

In this chapter we presented a multilingual, multi-document summarization method, implemented within a real-world setting. We discussed user and system requirements related to a news summarization application. We showed how existing research, mostly based on n-gram graphs, can support and implement a summarization system that covers different languages – namely Greek and English. We overviewed an effective system, called NewSum, which provides a full infrastructure and user endpoints for the exploitation of summarization on texts provided by real news providers. We finally described how user studies indicate that summarization is a feasible and useful way to facilitate users in everyday news search. We also described two studies indicating the performance of the presented system, from the viewpoint of (non-linguist) users, i.e. the market setting.

We learnt many lessons throughout our effort. First, summarization is useful and can help people, starting today. Second, there exist ways to be language-agnostic in one's methods of summarization. The n-gram graph framework is an effective method to begin with, offering an efficient way to analyze, represent and act upon texts for summarization purposes. Third, we learnt that open, per task evaluations can help judge the usefulness of

an approach on a real setting. Integrating response mechanisms in applications and using user feedback may be a good way to perform such an evaluation. Fourth, our open source effort showed that openness allows combining and improving systems, reusing expertise and promoting common experience on a subject. NewSum was built on open source principles, using open source software and will be provided as an open source application itself. Finally, open architectures allow combining different components of summarization under a unified interface. This leads to an implied proposal: why not use summarization applications as a means to evaluate underlying summarization methods?

In future work we plan to apply the proposed methods on existing copora of multi-document, multi-lingual summarization (e.g. from the MultiLing workshops) to test the cross-language applicability. We also plan to incorporate weights for different sources to support different levels of confidence for different sources. Finally, in the implementation of the project, we mean to test this summarization method versus other state-of-the-art methods, within an open evaluation setting.

Summarization is an indispensible tool for the information overload era. Researchers should also heed popular needs related to summarization and provide the tools and infrastructures to quantify these needs and accordingly evaluate existing systems. This is the main way to large-scale adoption of summarization and to the full exploration of its potential.

ACKNOWLEDGMENT

The research leading to these results has received funding from the OntoSum project (www.ontosum.org). The method is being exploited for argument summarization within the NOMAD FP7 EU project (www.nomad-project.eu), which has partially funded related extensions of the NewSum summarization technology.

REFERENCES

Afantenos, S. D., Doura, I., Kapellou, E., & Karkaletsis, V. (2004). Exploiting cross-document relations for multi-document evolving summarization. *Lecture Notes in Artificial Intelligence, 3025*, 410–419.

Allan, J., Wade, C., & Bolivar, A. (2003). Retrieval and novelty detection at the sentence level. In *Proceedings of the 26th Annual International ACM SIGIR Conference on Research and Development in Information Retrieval* (pp. 314–321). ACM.

Angheluta, R., De Busser, R., & Moens, M.-F. (2002). The use of topic segmentation for automatic summarization. In *Proceedings of the ACL-2002 Workshop on Automatic Summarization*. Retrieved from https://www.law.kuleuven.be/icri/publications/51DUC2002.pdf

Baralis, E., & Fiori, A. (2010). Summarizing biological literature with BioSumm. In *Proceedings of the 19th ACM International Conference on Information and Knowledge Management* (pp. 1961–1962). Retrieved from http://dl.acm.org/citation.cfm?id=1871785

Barzilay, R., & McKeown, K. R. (2005). Sentence fusion for multidocument news summarization. *Computational Linguistics, 31*(3), 297–327. doi:10.1162/089120105774321091

Blei, D. M., Ng, A. Y., & Jordan, M. I. (2003). Latent dirichlet allocation. *Journal of Machine Learning Research, 3*, 993–1022.

Brin, S., & Page, L. (1998). The anatomy of a large-scale hypertextual web search engine. *Computer Networks and ISDN Systems, 30*(1-7), 107–117.

Cai, X., & Li, W. (2012). Mutually reinforced manifold-ranking based relevance propagation model for query-focused multi-document summarization. *IEEE Transactions on Audio, Speech, and Language Processing, 20*(5), 1597–1607. doi:10.1109/TASL.2012.2186291

Carbonell, J., & Goldstein, J. (1998). Use of MMR, diversity-based reranking for reordering documents and producing summaries. In *Proceedings of the 21st Annual International ACM SIGIR Conference on Research and Development in Information Retrieval* (pp. 335–336). ACM Press.

Christensen, J., Mausam, S. S., & Etzioni, O. (2013). Towards coherent multi-document summarization. In *Proceedings of NAACL-HLT* (pp. 1163–1173). Retrieved from http://www.aclweb.org/anthology/N/N13/N13-1136.pdf

Conroy, J. M., & Dang, H. T. (2008). Mind the gap: Dangers of divorcing evaluations of summary content from linguistic quality. In *Proceedings of the 22nd International Conference on Computational Linguistics (Coling 2008)* (pp. 145–152). Manchester, UK: Coling 2008 Organizing Committee. Retrieved from http://www.aclweb.org/anthology/C08-1019

Conroy, J. M., Schlesinger, J. D., & O'Leary, D. P. (2007). CLASSY 2007 at DUC 2007. In *Proceedings of Document Understanding Conference (DUC) Workshop 2006*. DUC.

Conroy, J. M., Schlesinger, J. D., & O'Leary, D. P. (2009). CLASSY 2009: Summarization and metrics. In *Proceedings of the Text Analysis Conference (TAC) 2009*. TAC.

Conroy, J. M., Schlesinger, J. D., & Stewart, J. G. (2005). CLASSY query-based multi-document summarization. In *Proceedings of the Document Understanding Conf. Wksp. 2005 (DUC 2005) at the Human Language Technology Conf./Conf. on Empirical Methods in Natural Language Processing (HLT/EMNLP 2005)*. DUC.

Dang, H. T. (2005). Overview of DUC 2005. In *Proceedings of the Document Understanding Conf. Wksp. 2005 (DUC 2005) at the Human Language Technology Conf./Conf. on Empirical Methods in Natural Language Processing (HLT/EMNLP 2005)*. HLT.

Dang, H. T. (2006). Overview of DUC 2006. In *Proceedings of HLT-NAACL 2006*. NAACL.

Dang, H. T., & Owczarzak, K. (2008). Overview of the TAC 2008 update summarization task. In *Proceedings of TAC 2008 Workshop - Notebook Papers and Results* (pp. 10–23). Retrieved from http://www.nist.gov/tac

Dang, H. T., & Owczarzak, K. (2009, November 16). *Overview of the TAC 2009 summarization track*. Paper presented at the TAC 2009. Retrieved from http://www.nist.gov/tac/publications/2009/presentations/TAC2009_Summ_overview.pdf

Dongen, S. (2000). Performance criteria for graph clustering and Markov cluster experiments. Amsterdam, The Netherlands: CWI (Centre for Mathematics and Computer Science).

Edmundson, H. P. (1969). New methods in automatic extracting. *Journal of the ACM, 16*(2), 264–285. doi:10.1145/321510.321519

Elmagarmid, A., Ipeirotis, P. G., & Verykios, V. (2006). Duplicate record detection: A survey. *SSRN eLibrary*. Retrieved from http://papers.ssrn.com/sol3/papers.cfm?abstract_id=1281334

Erkan, G., & Radev, D. R. (2004). Lexpagerank: Prestige in multi-document text summarization. In *Proceedings of EMNLP* (pp. 365–371). EMNLP.

Erol, B., Lee, D. S., Hull, J., Center, R. C., & Menlo Park, C. A. (2003). Multimodal summarization of meeting recordings. In *Proceedings of Multimedia and Expo, 2003*. ICME.

Evans, D. K., Klavans, J. L., & McKeown, K. R. (2004). Columbia newsblaster: Multilingual news summarization on the web. In *Demonstration Papers at HLT-NAACL 2004* (pp. 1–4). Academic Press. doi:10.3115/1614025.1614026

Farzindar, A., & Lapalme, G. (2003). Using background information for multi-document summarization and summaries in response to a question. In *Proceedings of DUC03: NAACL 2003 Workshop in Automatic Text Summarization*. NAACL.

Flores, J. G., Gillard, L., Ferret, O., & de Chandelar, G. (2008). Bag of senses versus bag of words: Comparing semantic and lexical approaches on sentence extraction. In *Proceedings of TAC 2008 Workshop - Notebook Papers and Results* (pp. 158–167). Retrieved from http://www.nist.gov/tac

Genest, P. E., Lapalme, G., Yousfi-Monod, M., & Montréal, Q. (2009). HEXTAC: The creation of a manual extractive run. In *Proceedings of TAC2009 Notebook*. TAC.

Giannakopoulos, G. (2009). *Automatic summarization from multiple documents*. University of the Aegean. Retrieved from http://www.iit.demokritos.gr/~ggianna/thesis.pdf

Giannakopoulos, G. (2010). *JInsect: The n-gram graph framework implementation*. Retrieved from http://sourceforge.net/projects/jinsect/

Giannakopoulos, G., El-Haj, M., Favre, B., Litvak, M., Steinberger, J., & Varma, V. (2011). TAC2011 multiling pilot overview. In *Proceedings of TAC 2011 Workshop*. TAC.

Giannakopoulos, G., & Karkaletsis, V. (2009). N-gram graphs: Representing documents and document sets in summary system evaluation. In *Proceedings of Text Analysis Conference TAC2009*. TAC.

Giannakopoulos, G., & Karkaletsis, V. (2011). AutoSummENG and MeMoG in evaluating guided summaries. In *Proceedings of TAC 2011 Workshop*. TAC.

Giannakopoulos, G., & Karkaletsis, V. (2013). *Together we stand NPowER-ed*. Paper presented at the CICLing 2013. Karlovasi, Greece.

Giannakopoulos, G., Karkaletsis, V., Vouros, G., & Stamatopoulos, P. (2008). Summarization system evaluation revisited: N-gram graphs. *ACM Trans. Speech Lang. Process., 5*(3), 1–39. doi:10.1145/1410358.1410359

Giannakopoulos, G., & Palpanas, T. (2009). Adaptivity in entity subscription services. In *Proceedings of ADAPTIVE2009*. ADAPTIVE.

Giannakopoulos, G., Vouros, G., & Karkaletsis, V. (2010). *MUDOS-NG: Multi-document summaries using n-gram graphs* (Tech Report). Retrieved from http://arxiv.org/abs/1012.2042

Hendrickx, I., & Bosma, W. (2008). Using coreference links and sentence compression in graph-based summarization. In *Proceedings of TAC 2008 Workshop - Notebook Papers and Results* (pp. 429–435). Retrieved from http://www.nist.gov/tac

Huang, X., Wan, X., & Xiao, J. (2013). Comparative news summarization using concept-based optimization. *Knowledge and Information Systems*, 1–26.

Jatowt, A., & Ishizuka, M. (2006). Temporal multi-page summarization. *Web Intelligence and Agent Systems*, 4(2), 163–180.

Jones, K. S. (2007). Automatic summarising: The state of the art. *Information Processing & Management*, 43(6), 1449–1481. doi:10.1016/j.ipm.2007.03.009

Jones, S. (1999). Automatic summarizing: Factors and directions. In *Proceedings of Advances in Automatic Text Summarization* (pp. 1–12). Academic Press.

Kabadjov, M., Atkinson, M., Steinberger, J., Steinberger, R., & van der Goot, E. (2010). NewsGist: A multilingual statistical news summarizer. In J. L. Balcázar, F. Bonchi, A. Gionis, & M. Sebag (Eds.), *Machine learning and knowledge discovery in databases* (pp. 591–594). Springer. Retrieved from http://link.springer.com/chapter/10.1007/978-3-642-15939-8_40

Kazantseva, A., & Szpakowicz, S. (2010). Summarizing short stories. *Computational Linguistics*, 36(1), 71–109. doi:10.1162/coli.2010.36.1.36102

Kleinberg, J. M. (1999). Authoritative sources in a hyperlinked environment. *Journal of the ACM*, 46(5), 604–632. doi:10.1145/324133.324140

Kumar, C., Pingali, P., & Varma, V. (2009). Estimating risk of picking a sentence for document summarization. In *Proceedings of the 10th International Conference on Computational Linguistics and Intelligent Text Processing* (pp. 571–581). IEEE.

Larkey, L. S., Allan, J., Connell, M. E., Bolivar, A., & Wade, C. (2003). UMass at TREC 2002: Cross language and novelty tracks. [National Institute of Standards & Technology.]. *Proceedings of TREC*, 2002, 721–732.

Ledeneva, Y. (2008). Effect of preprocessing on extractive summarization with maximal frequent sequences. [MICAI.]. *Proceedings of MICAI*, 2008, 123–132.

Leite, D. S., Rino, L. H. M., Pardo, T. A. S., & Nunes, M. das G. V. (2007). Extractive automatic summarization: Does more linguistic knowledge make a difference? In *Proceedings of the Second Workshop on TextGraphs: Graph-Based Algorithms for Natural Language Processing* (pp. 17–24). Rochester, NY: Association for Computational Linguistics. Retrieved from http://www.aclweb.org/anthology/W/W07/W07-0203

Litvak, M., & Last, M. (2012). Cross-lingual training of summarization systems using annotated corpora in a foreign language. *Information Retrieval*, 1–28.

Litvak, M., Last, M., & Friedman, M. (2010). A new approach to improving multilingual summarization using a genetic algorithm. In *Proceedings of the 48th Annual Meeting of the Association for Computational Linguistics* (pp. 927–936). Retrieved from http://dl.acm.org/citation.cfm?id=1858776

Luhn, H. P. (1958). Automatic creation of literature abstracts. *IBM Journal of Research and Development*, 2(2), 159–165. doi:10.1147/rd.22.0159

Mani, I., Bloedorn, E., & Gates, B. (1998). Using cohesion and coherence models for text summarization. In *Proceedings of Intelligent Text Summarization Symposium* (pp. 69–76). Academic Press.

Mani, I. M., & Bloedorn, E. M. (1999). Summarizing similarities and differences among related documents. *Information Retrieval*, *1*(1), 35–67. doi:10.1023/A:1009930203452

Mann, W. C., & Thompson, S. A. (1987). *Rhetorical structure theory: A theory of text organization*. Los Angeles, CA: University of Southern California, Information Sciences Institute.

Matsuo, Y., Ohsawa, Y., & Ishizuka, M. (2001). A document as a small world. In Proceedings the 5th World Multi-Conference on Systemics, Cybenetics and Infomatics (Vol. 8, pp. 410–414). IEEE.

Mihalcea, R. (2005). Multi-document summarization with iterative graph-based algorithms. In *Proceedings of the First International Conference on Intelligent Analysis Methods and Tools (IA 2005)*. McLean.

Niekrasz, J., Purver, M., Dowding, J., & Peters, S. (2005). Ontology-based discourse understanding for a persistent meeting assistant. In *Proceedings of the AAAI Spring Symposium Persistent Assistants: Living and Working with AI*. AAAI.

Park, S., Lee, J. H., Ahn, C. M., Hong, J. S., & Chun, S. J. (2006). Query based summarization using non-negative matrix factorization. In *Proceeding of KES*, (pp. 84–89). KES.

Radev, D., Otterbacher, J., Winkel, A., & Blair-Goldensohn, S. (2005). NewsInEssence: Summarizing online news topics. *Communications of the ACM*, *48*(10), 95–98. doi:10.1145/1089107.1089111

Radev, D. R., Jing, H., & Budzikowska, M. (2000). Centroid-based summarization of multiple documents: Sentence extraction, utility-based evaluation, and user studies. *ANLP/NAACL Workshop on Summarization*.

Radev, D. R., Jing, H., Stys, M., & Tam, D. (2004). Centroid-based summarization of multiple documents. *Information Processing & Management*, *40*(6), 919–938. doi:10.1016/j.ipm.2003.10.006

Ribaldo, R., Akabane, A. T., Rino, L. H. M., & Pardo, T. A. S. (2012). Graph-based methods for multi-document summarization: Exploring relationship maps, complex networks and discourse information. In *Computational Processing of the Portuguese Language* (pp. 260–271). Springer. Retrieved from http://link.springer.com/chapter/10.1007/978-3-642-28885-2_30

Saggion, H. (2006). Multilingual multidocument summarization tools and evaluation. In *Proceedings, LREC 2006*. LREC.

Steinberger, J., & Jezek, K. (2004). Using latent semantic analysis in text summarization and summary evaluation. [ISIM.]. *Proceedings of ISIM*, *04*, 93–100.

Teufel, S., & Moens, M. (2002). Summarizing scientific articles: Experiments with relevance and rhetorical status. *Computational Linguistics*, *28*(4), 409–445. doi:10.1162/089120102762671936

Torralbo, R., Alfonseca, E., Guirao, J. M., & Moreno-Sandoval, A. (2005). Description of the UAM system at DUC-2005. In *Proceedings of the Document Understanding Conf. Wksp. 2005 (DUC 2005) at the Human Language Technology Conf./Conf. on Empirical Methods in Natural Language Processing (HLT/EMNLP 2005)*. HLT.

Turchi, M., Steinberger, J., Kabadjov, M., & Steinberger, R. (2010). Using parallel corpora for multilingual (multi-document) summarisation evaluation. *Multilingual and Multimodal Information Access Evaluation*, 52–63.

Varadarajan, R., & Hristidis, V. (2006). A system for query-specific document summarization. In *Proceedings of the 15th ACM International Conference on Information and Knowledge Management*, (pp. 622–631). ACM.

Wan, X., Jia, H., Huang, S., & Xiao, J. (2011). Summarizing the differences in multilingual news. In *Proceedings of the 34th International ACM SIGIR Conference on Research and Development in Information* (pp. 735–744). ACM.

Wu, C. W., & Liu, C. L. (2003). Ontology-based text summarization for business news articles. In *Proceedings of the ISCA 18th International Conference on Computers and their Applications*, (pp. 389–392). ISCA.

Yeloglu, O., Milios, E., & Zincir-Heywood, N. (2011). Multi-document summarization of scientific corpora. In *Proceedings of the 2011 ACM Symposium on Applied Computing* (pp. 252–258).

Zhang, Y., Callan, J., & Minka, T. (2002). Novelty and redundancy detection in adaptive filtering. In *Proceedings of the 25th Annual International ACM SIGIR Conference on Research and Development in Information Retrieval* (pp. 81–88). ACM.

ADDITIONAL READING

Abuobieda, A., Salim, N., Kumar, Y. J., & Osman, A. H. (2013). An improved evolutionary algorithm for extractive text summarization. In *Intelligent Information and Database Systems* (pp. 78–89). Springer. Retrieved from http://link.springer.com/chapter/10.1007/978-3-642-36543-0_9

Amigó, E., Gonzalo, J., & Verdejo, F. (2012). The heterogeneity principle in evaluation measures for automatic summarization. In *Proceedings of Workshop on Evaluation Metrics and System Comparison for Automatic Summarization* (pp. 36–43). Stroudsburg, PA, USA: Association for Computational Linguistics. Retrieved from http://dl.acm.org/citation.cfm?id=2391258.2391263

Angheluta, R., De Busser, R., & Moens, M.-F. (2002). The use of topic segmentation for automatic summarization. In *Proceedings of the ACL-2002 Workshop on Automatic Summarization*. Retrieved from https://www.law.kuleuven.be/icri/publications/51DUC2002.pdf

Das, D., & Martins, A. F.. (2007). A survey on automatic text summarization. *Literature Survey for the Language and Statistics II course at CMU*.

Fattah, M. A., & Ren, F. (2009). GA, MR, FFNN, PNN and GMM based models for automatic text summarization. *Computer Speech & Language*, 23(1), 126–144. doi:10.1016/j.csl.2008.04.002

Filippova, K., Surdeanu, M., Ciaramita, M., & Zaragoza, H. (2009). Company-oriented extractive summarization of financial news. In *Proceedings of the 12th Conference of the European Chapter of the Association for Computational Linguistics* (pp. 246–254).

Huang, X., Wan, X., & Xiao, J. (2013). Comparative news summarization using concept-based optimization. *Knowledge and Information Systems*, 1–26.

Jones, K. S., & others. (1999). Automatic summarizing: factors and directions. *Advances in automatic text summarization*, 1–12.

Kumar, N., Srinathan, K., & Varma, V. (2012). Using graph based mapping of co-occurring words and closeness centrality score for summarization evaluation. *Computational Linguistics and Intelligent Text Processing*, 353–365.

Lerman, K., & McDonald, R. (2009). Contrastive summarization: an experiment with consumer reviews. In *Proceedings of Human Language Technologies: The 2009 Annual Conference of the North American Chapter of the Association for Computational Linguistics, Companion Volume: Short Papers* (pp. 113–116).

Owczarzak, K., Conroy, J. M., Dang, H. T., & Nenkova, A. (2012). An Assessment of the Accuracy of Automatic Evaluation in Summarization. *NAACL-HLT*, *2012*, 1.

Pitler, E., Louis, A., & Nenkova, A. (2010). Automatic evaluation of linguistic quality in multi-document summarization. In *Proceedings of the 48th Annual Meeting of the Association for Computational Linguistics* (pp. 544–554). Retrieved from http://dl.acm.org/citation.cfm?id=1858737

Radev, D. R., Hovy, E., & McKeown, K. (2002). Introduction to the special issue on summarization. *Computational Linguistics*, *28*(4), 399–408. doi:10.1162/089120102762671927

Saggion, H., Torres-Moreno, J. M., Cunha, I., & SanJuan, E. (2010). Multilingual summarization evaluation without human models. In *Proceedings of the 23rd International Conference on Computational Linguistics: Posters* (pp. 1059–1067). Retrieved from http://dl.acm.org/citation.cfm?id=1944688

Wang, D., Zhu, S., Li, T., & Gong, Y. (2013). Comparative Document Summarization via Discriminative Sentence Selection. [TKDD]. *ACM Transactions on Knowledge Discovery from Data*, *7*(1), 2. doi:10.1145/2435209.2435211

Zhang, J., Cheng, X., & Xu, H. (2008). GSP-Summary: a graph-based sub-topic partition algorithm for summarization. In *Information Retrieval Technology* (pp. 321–334). Springer. Retrieved from http://link.springer.com/chapter/10.1007/978-3-540-68636-1_31

KEY TERMS AND DEFINITIONS

Mobile Application: A software application which runs on a mobile platform (e.g., Android).

Multi-Document Summarization: The process of applying summarization to a set of documents to create one representative summary for the whole set.

Multilingual Summarization: The process of applying a summarization algorithm on texts of different languages (possibly not simultaneously).

N-Gram Graph: A text representation representing how n-grams co-occur within a given text.

N-Gram Graph Framework: The set of algorithms applicable on the n-gram graph representation, together with the representation itself, usable as an analysis method and toolkit.

Summary: A reductive transformation of a text, keeping as much information as possible.

Summary Evaluation: The process of evaluating a summary.

ENDNOTES

[1] See http://duc.nist.gov/ and http://www.nist.gov/tac/ for more information on DUC and TAC.

[2] See http://research.nii.ac.jp/ntcir/ for more information on NTCIR.

[3] See http://opennlp.apache.org/ for more information on the Apache OpenNLP library.

[4] See http://glassfish.java.net/ for more information on the Glassfish server.

[5] See http://www.scify.gr/site/en/our-projects for more information on the NewSum project.

[6] See http://www.scify.org for more information on SciFY.

[7] See http://www.nomad-project.eu for more information on the NOMAD project.

Chapter 10
New Formats and Interfaces for Multi-Document News Summarization and its Evaluation

Bettina Berendt
KU Leuven, Belgium

Mark Last
Ben-Gurion University of the Negev, Israel

Ilija Subašić
KU Leuven, Belgium

Mathias Verbeke
KU Leuven, Belgium

ABSTRACT

News production, delivery, and consumption are increasing in ubiquity and speed, spreading over more software and hardware platforms, in particular mobile devices. This has led to an increasing interest in automated methods for multi-document summarization. The authors start this chapter with discussing several new alternatives for automated news summarization, with a particular focus on temporal text mining, graph-based methods, and graphical interfaces. Then they present automated and user-centric frameworks for cross-evaluating summarization methods that output different summary formats and describe the challenges associated with each evaluation framework. Based on the results of the user studies, the authors argue that it is crucial for effective summarization to integrate the user into sense-making through usable, entertaining, and ultimately useful interactive summarization-plus-document-search interfaces. In particular, graph-based methods and interfaces may be a better preparation for people to concentrate on what is essential in a collection of texts, and thus may be a key to enhancing the summary evaluation process by replacing the "one gold standard fits all" approach with carefully designed user studies built upon a variety of summary representation formats.

DOI: 10.4018/978-1-4666-5019-0.ch010

1. INTRODUCTION

Automatic text summarization is a computer-aided process of distilling the most important information from one or several textual sources on a common topic. Based on the number of input sources, summarization methods are categorised into single-document and multi-document approaches. The output of most summarization methods is a natural-language text in itself.

One distinguishes between summarization by extraction and by abstraction (Hahn & Mani, 2000). Extractive methods select elements from the original text(s) and recompile them to form a summary. Abstractive methods build an internal semantic representation and then use natural-language generation techniques to create a summary. Due to the remaining limitations of natural-language generation methods, extractive summarization remains the dominant approach today.

In this chapter, we focus on extractive summarization of text streams, particularly news streams. In this domain, *multi-document* summarization is especially relevant because of the multitude of sources. Popular applications of these ideas are news aggregators such as Google News[1] or Yahoo News[2]. However, these do not aim at producing a coherently-seeming natural-language text, but a search-engine-type collation of information. This echoes the findings of Barzilay, McKeown, and Elhadad (1999) that pure extraction may be inappropriate in multi-document summarization especially of news texts, because it may produce summaries which are overly verbose or biased towards some sources. In contrast to the static methods of multi-document summarization, STORIES (Subašić & Berendt, 2010a) is designed for both summarization and search in a time-indexed collection of documents. STORIES uses *story graphs* to represent summaries.

The classical summary evaluation methods suffer from severe limitations, especially when applied to Temporal Text Mining techniques, which may produce summaries in both textual and graph formats. Hence, we present an automated and a user-centric framework for the cross-evaluation of news summaries. An initial user study of the proposed frameworks provides encouraging results. We use these results to outline directions for future work.

The contribution of this chapter is threefold: *First*, we give an overview of key concepts and formats of text summarization in general and news summarization in particular (Section 2). *Second*, we present a critical re-assessment of evaluation methodology. In Section 3, we discuss the issue of evaluation of summarization methods, highlighting in particular the difficulties of cross-evaluating text-based as well as the emerging multitude of non-text-based summaries. We also take a closer look at a form of human input that is crucial for all automated evaluations: the "ground truth" summaries and their construction.

We argue that current practice severely limits our ability to evaluate automatic methods and that this calls for interactive, graphical approaches. *Third*, in Sections 4 and 5 we propose a new approach to evaluating summarization methods. We describe the automated and the user-centric frameworks for cross-evaluating methods that output different summary formats, and we describe the challenges associated with each evaluation framework. In Section 6, we draw conclusions from these findings and outline key elements of future multi-document summarization methods.

2. KEY CONCEPTS AND FORMATS IN TEXT SUMMARIZATION

Extractive summarization aims at the selection of a subset of the most relevant fragments from a source text into the summary. The fragments can be paragraphs (Salton, Singhal, Mitra, & Buckley, 1997), sentences (Luhn, 1958), keyphrases (Turney, 2000; Litvak, Aizenman, Gobits, Last, & Kandel, 2011) or keywords (Litvak & Last, 2008).

Extractive summarization usually consists of *ranking*, where each fragment of a summarized text gets a relevance score, and *extraction*, where the top-ranked fragments are gathered into a summary, according to their appearance in the original text.

While in *generic summarization,* the only input for a system is a document (or documents) to summarize, in *query-based summarization* a query expressing the user's interest has to be provided. In a query-based summary, the fragment rankings must take into account the content of a given query, making the extract adaptable to the user's information needs.

Various text representation models have been utilised across different summarization approaches. In addition to the traditional "bag-of-words" model, graphs are becoming increasingly popular, due to their ability to enrich the document representation with syntactic and semantic relations. Erkan and Radev (2004) and Mihalcea (2005) introduced LexRank and TextRank, respectively – algorithms for unsupervised extractive summarization that rely on the application of iterative graph-based ranking algorithms, such as PageRank (Brin & Page, 1998) and HITS (Kleinberg, 1999). Their methods represent a document as a graph of sentences interconnected by similarity relations. MUSE (Litvak & Last, 2013) uses two graph-based models, which are based on sentence and word segmentation, respectively. MUSE also uses features calculated from the document structure and its vector-space representation.

In addition to these questions of format, two features of the underlying corpora have received increased attention in recent years: multilinguality and temporality (for example, see the multilingual multi-document summarization task and the multilingual summary evaluation tracks at MultiLing 2013[3]). We will present key features of multilingual summarization with reference to the MUSE approach, then give an overview of approaches in temporal summarization with a focus on representation formats, and illustrate this with the STORIES approach.

2.1 The MUSE Approach for Multilingual Static Summarization

The MUSE (MUltilingual Sentence Extractor) approach (Litvak & Last, 2013) uses a linear combination of 31 language-independent features from various categories for ranking each sentence in a document. Language-independent features do not require any morphological or syntactic analysis of the summarized text, and they may include the sentence position in a document, the number of characters and words in a sentence, the similarity of the sentence to the document title, and other statistical metrics. In contrast, language-specific features of a sentence may include the presence of cue words or the number of certain parts-of-speech. For example, "to sum up" in English may be an indicator that the following is a summarizing sentence, and a high number of nouns in a sentence may indicate a high amount of topical information in this sentence. MUSE finds the best set of feature weights by a genetic algorithm trained on a collection of human-generated document summaries. Obviously, the quality of the resulting sentence ranking model directly depends on the number and the quality of the training summaries.

Formally, the MUSE model for sentence scoring can be expressed by the following formula:

$$Score = \sum w_i \times r_i,$$

where r_i is the value of ith sentence feature and w_i is its weight in the linear combination.

The MUSE approach builds upon two main modules: the *training module* activated offline, and the *summarization module* operating online.

The *training module* receives as input a corpus of documents, each accompanied by one or several gold-standard summaries: abstracts or extracts compiled by human assessors. The set of documents may be either monolingual or multilingual, and their summaries have to be in the same language as the original text. As a second parameter, the module obtains a user-specified set of sentence features computed by the system. Then, the training module applies a genetic algorithm to sentence-feature matrices of pre-computed sentence scores for each input feature, with the purpose of finding the best linear combination of features that maximises the value of ROUGE (Lin & Hovy, 2003, see Section 3.1 below) as a fitness function. The output of the training module is a vector of weights for user-specified sentence ranking features.

The *summarization module* performs an on-line summarization of input text(s). Each sentence of an input text document obtains a relevance score according to the trained model, and the top-ranked sentences are extracted to form the summary in their original order. To avoid duplicate content, a new sentence is added if and only if it is not similar to the previously selected sentences. The length of the resulting summaries is limited by a user-specified value (maximum number of words or sentences in the text extract or a maximum extract-to-text ratio). The summarization module is expected to use the model trained on the same language as that of the input texts. If such a model is not available (no annotated corpus in the text language), the user can choose from the following: (1) a model trained on some other language/corpus, or (2) a model trained on a parallel corpus generated by a machine translation tool. Both approaches were shown by Litvak and Last (2013) to provide a reasonable performance while saving significant annotation efforts.

2.2 Summarizing Temporally-Indexed Texts

The above methods are not directly applicable to the news summarization domain, as they ignore the potentially dynamic nature of the summarized texts. Moreover, they all produce output summaries in strictly textual, non-interactive format, which may not represent well the temporal characteristics of a news stream. Temporality is, on the one hand, a feature of the documents in a news corpus. On the other hand, it may govern what is expected of a summary. In particular, readers often want to know what happened in a particular time period, such that the expected summaries are query-based, with the query being a time period. Further restrictions may be added, as we discuss with respect to the STORIES method below. We begin with an overview of prominent approaches to news summarizations in the literature.

First Story Detection (FSD; Allan, Lavrenko, & Jin, 2000) is a Topic Detection and Tracking (TDT; Allan, 2002) task incorporating the temporal dimension of a corpus. Sometimes this task is also referred to as the Online New Event Detection (ONED) task. In this task, a system has to decide whether a newly arrived document discusses "a new event" or not. In TDT, events are defined as "something that happens at a particular time and place" (Allan, Lavrenko, & Jin, 2000). During and after the seven years in which the TDT framework was active, a number of approaches to solving the FSD task have been developed. Allan, Lavrenko, and Jin (2000) generated queries and used cosine similarity to compare them with already seen documents. Luo, Tang and Yu (2007) tackled these problems and explored document source quality, efficient indexing, and user interfaces for FSD. An interesting extension of the FSD task was described by Nallapati, Feng, Peng, and Allan (2004): going beyond detecting events towards discovering relations between events. A more recent application of FSD to social-network status update data was described by Petrović, Osborne, and Lavrenko (2010).

The DUC (Document Understanding Conference) Update Summarization task[4][5] outputs a set of 100-word summaries for a number of time periods so that the summaries contain information from previous periods. A LexRank-inspired approach to update summarization was proposed by Chen and Chen (2008). Other methods specifically designed for update summarization used information-distance-based summaries (Long,

Huang, Zhu, & Li, 2009), integer linear programming (Gillick & Favre, 2009), or latent semantic analysis (Steinberger & Ježek, 2009).

In the TREC Novelty Detection Task, participants are given a set of documents on a topic, and their task is to extract sentences that are relevant to the topic and to select sentences that are "new". In this context, "new" is defined as containing information that has not appeared previously in a topic's set of documents. Experiences with running the TREC Novelty Detection Task were summarized by Soboroff and Harman (2005). In 2012, TREC started the Temporal Summarization task.[6]

In contrast to the previous tasks that focus on the detection of a new element or breakpoint in a stream of documents, *story tracking* is the activity of following one story over time and summarizing it. This task has been popularized by Temporal Text Mining. *Temporal Text Mining (TTM)* methods output bursty (novel) patterns that point to the changes in the story they track, and the subjects arising from these changes. *Subjects* constitute the high-level story; they can be events (e.g. a specific ski slalom in the Winter Olympics) or topics (e.g. doping).[7] The patterns consist of *story elements*, syntactical units extracted from the underlying documents. For example, an element could be a term, and the pattern could be this term plus some score assigned to it. We also define a *story representation* as a set of bursty story elements used to represent a subject. Story elements have different levels of expressiveness. TTM methods operate on sub-sentence story elements, and we distinguish the following *elements*: tokens, n-grams, and n-gram groups. Further filters are possible, producing elements such as terms with frequencies or other weights above a threshold, or n-grams denoting named entities.

A *token* is a series of characters not containing any of a set of predefined delimiters. *N-grams* are content-bearing tokens. Basic n-grams are unigrams (1-grams), where every token is a unigram. More advanced n-grams are sequences of *n* contiguous (or non-contiguous) tokens extracted from the text. Non-consecutive, or skip-m n-grams, contain *n* tokens appearing in a window of *m* tokens. *N-gram groups* are collections of n-grams pointing to the same subject. These groups can be n-gram cluster centre values, latent variables' probability distributions over n-grams, or some other way of grouping by similarity.

In general, elements are associated with some weight. We focus on the *burst scores* assigned by the respective TTM method. This score may be a probability of an element appearing in a bursty subject, the relative importance in a bursty subject cluster centre, or a weight in a latent component. Regardless of their mathematical specifics, these burst scores provide an ordering on the elements that can be used for ranking the elements in query generation.

Based on the differences in their story representations, we distinguish between three types of TTM tracking methods: (a) keyword representation, (b) group representation, and (c) combo representation methods. Type (a) methods use a list of bursty n-grams ranked by their burst scores (Kleinberg, 2002; Fung, Yu, Yu, & Lu, 2005; Gruhl, Guha, Kumar, Novak, & Tomkins, 2005; He, Chang, Lim, & Zhang, 2007; Smith, 2002). Type (b) methods assemble bursty n-grams into groups which point to subjects (Fung et al., 2005; Wang & McCallum, 2006; Mei & Zhai, 2005; Schult & Spiliopoulou, 2006; Janssens, Glänzel, & Moor, 2007). Type (c) methods use a combination of the previous two approaches (Subašić & Berendt, 2010a; Allan, Gupta, & Khandelwal, 2001).

2.3 The STORIES Approach for Temporal Summarization

STORIES (Subašić & Berendt, 2010a) comprises summarization and search. Both steps are time-indexed and therefore user-directed in the STORIES tool (Subašić & Berendt, 2010b). For pre-processing, a corpus of text-only documents is transformed into a sequence-of-terms representation. Basic term statistics are calculated to identify candidates for story basics: the top-ranked words based on term frequency, TF.IDF weights, regular terms plus named entities, and all terms.

For the summarization of a time-indexed subset of the whole corpus, c_t for period t, the frequency of the co-occurrence of all pairs of content-bearing terms b_j in documents is calculated as the number of occurrences of both terms in a window of w terms, divided by the number of all documents in c_t. We call this measure *local relevance* with LR_t $(b_1, b_2) = freq_t (b_1, b_2)$. LR normalised by its counterpart in the whole corpus C yields *time relevance* as the measure of burstiness: $TR_t (b_1, b_2) = (freq_t (b_1, b_2) / freq_C (b_1, b_2))$. Thresholds are applied to avoid singular associations in small sub-corpora and to concentrate on those associations that are most characteristic of the period and most distinctive relative to others. This gives rise to the *story graphs $G_t = <V_t, E_t>$*. The edges E_t are the story elements: all pairs (b_1, b_2) with absolute frequencies and TR above the respective thresholds. The nodes are the terms involved in at least one association in this symmetric graph: $V_t = \{ b_j \mid \exists b_k : (b_j, b_k) \in E_t \}$. From each document, we extract sentences containing "facts", short statements with semantic role labelling, as returned by Open Calais[8]. The full set of these sentences for each time period is indexed using Lucene[9]. We then use story graphs to filter the most important facts: for each of the graph's edges, we query the index, using node names of the edge as query terms, and select the top sentences as defined by Lucene. We treat the resulting set of short textual statements as a summary of the story.

Search can be constrained by the nodes of a subgraph of the story graph. Retrieval is then restricted to documents relevant to these subgraphs. The selection of documents of the starting corpus C corresponds to a top-level query; this query is expanded by all nodes of the subgraph as additional query terms, subject to the time restriction.

Thus, like MUSE, STORIES focusses on graph representations. In contrast to MUSE graphs, which represent a single text document, STORIES graphs represent a multi-document story. Another difference is that in the MUSE graph representation, the window size w is usually equal to one (the co-occurring terms have to be adjacent to each other). Both approaches extend the bag-of-words idea by taking co-occurrence as well as sequence into account. Other summarization approaches extend this by forming a graph based on additional syntactic and/or semantic information. For example, based on semantic role labelling and the merging of synonyms, triples can be formed and event templates filled (Trampus & Mladenic, 2009).

3. CHALLENGES IN EVALUATING AUTOMATED TEXT-BASED SUMMARIES

In this section, we first give a brief overview of classical cross-evaluation methods and sketch their limitations. We then present a cognitive hypothesis that allows us to make different formats of summaries comparable.

3.1 Classical Evaluation Methods of Textual Summaries

Summary quality can be evaluated in an *intrinsic* or *extrinsic* manner, depending on whether the goal is to assess the summary itself (i.e. according to its information content) or its effectiveness for reaching the goals of a third-party application (e.g. information retrieval). In intrinsic evaluation, the summary informativeness is determined by comparing its content to a gold standard summary. In the case of the extrinsic evaluation, the third-party system performance is evaluated. For example in the text categorisation domain, a document summary can serve as a noise filter, and the question that should be asked is whether categorization performance can be increased by using the summary rather than the entire document.

Another aspect for summary evaluation approaches is the automation issue. Evaluation can be human-assisted or automated. In human-assisted evaluation approaches, human participation is an integral part of the evaluation process. For example, in Pyramid evaluation (Nenkova, Passonneau, & McKeown, 2007), pieces of information that are conceptually equal across model summaries (Summary Content Units) are manually identified. In the DUC'04 conference[10], summaries were evaluated with respect to linguistic quality aspects (grammaticality, non-redundancy, referential clarity, focus, structure, and coherence). Each quality aspect has a related question to be answered by human assessors according to a five-point scale. In automated evaluation approaches, a summary quality is determined exclusively by computers. For example, ROUGE (Recall-Oriented Understudy for Gisting Evaluation) (Lin & Hovy, 2003) automatically compares a computer-generated summary to gold standard summaries (generated by human annotators) in terms of overlapping units such as n-grams, word sequences, and word pairs. It has been shown that a quality ranking of summaries by the ROUGE measures is highly correlated with a quality ranking of these summaries by humans (Lin & Hovy, 2003), meaning that ROUGE scores can select the "best" summaries.

3.2. The Problem of the "Ground Truth" Summaries

Automated evaluation methods use text similarity measures (such as different variations of ROUGE) to compare system summaries to human (peer) summaries provided by native language speakers (assessors). Usually, the assessors are required to spend a certain amount of time on reading each article from a conventional computer screen and then choose the most important (key) sentences containing a pre-defined number of words. One popular collection of summarized documents in English is the corpus from the single-document summarization task at the Document Understand-

ing Conference 2002[11]. This benchmark dataset contains 533 news articles, each accompanied by two to three human-generated *abstracts* of approximately 100 words each. Though DUC 2002 still serves as a widely recognised benchmark for single-document summarization, the best ROUGE-1 score (Lin & Hovy, 2003) achieved on it by a supervised system is only 50.11% (Mihalcea, 2005). Since supervised summarization systems learn from the human summaries, this result indicates the low degree of actual inter-assessor agreement, implying that the human assessors participating in the experiment had a poor understanding of their summarization task and interpreted it in a variety of ways. Another important implication of the above result, confirmed by the published performance of state-of-the-art summarization methods (e.g. TextRank, see Mihalcea, 2005, and MUSE, see Litvak & Last, 2013), is that no automated summarization system can be expected to exceed the 50 percent recall on this corpus.

For the Arabic language, a corpus compiled from 90 news articles was generated by Litvak and Last (2013). Each article was summarized by three native Arabic speakers, who selected the most important sentences into an *extractive* summary of approximately 100 words each. All assessors were provided with the *Tool Assisting Human Assessors (TAHA)* software tool, which allowed the assessors to easily select the sentences to be included in the document extract. On this relatively small corpus, the agreement between assessors measured by the ROUGE-1 score reached 75 percent on average.

For the Hebrew language, Litvak and Last (2013) built a corpus of 120 news articles having 250 to 830 words each from the websites of the *Haaretz* newspaper[12], *The Marker* newspaper[13], and manually translated articles from *WikiNews*[14]. The articles were summarized by human assessors using the TAHA software. In total, 126 undergraduate students participated in the experiment. Each participant was randomly assigned ten different documents and instructed to choose the most important sentences in each document subject to the following constraints: (a) spend at least five minutes on each document, (b) ignore dialogs and quotations, (c) read the whole document before beginning sentence extraction, (d) ignore redundant, repetitive, and overly detailed information, and (e) remain within the minimal and maximal summary length limits (95 and 100 words, respectively).

Summaries were assessed for quality by comparing each student's extract to those of all the other students using the ROUGE evaluation toolkit and the ROUGE-1 metric. The summaries of the assessors who received an average ROUGE score below 0.5, i.e. who agreed with the rest of the assessors in fewer than 50% of cases, were removed from the corpus. Also, the time spent by an assessor on each document was checked (with respect to the requirements). The final corpus of summarized Hebrew texts was compiled from the summaries of about 60% of the assessors, with an average of five *extracts* per single document. The average ROUGE score of the selected assessors was 54 percent only, only slightly higher than the quality of the DUC 2002 corpus.

The above-mentioned results in three different languages pose a severe limit on the maximum achievable accuracy of automated summarization systems. Consequently, user satisfaction with the output of these systems is expected to be low as well. As long as these subjective evaluation methods remain in use, a significant breakthrough in the single-document and multi-document summarization technology is highly unlikely. Graph-based interfaces may be a key to enhancing the consistency of "gold standard" summaries and improving the usability of text summarization systems.

3.3 Summary Representation Formats and Cognitive (Re)Representation Formats

As described in Section 2, there is an increasing multitude of formats in summarization. This raises the question which ones are "better" than others, i.e. how to cross-evaluate them. While we have described the increasing move away from sentential summaries (natural-language texts), particularly in the news summarization domain, in this section we want to argue why for cross-evaluation, we believe we need to go back to sentences. In particular, we propose a hypothesis about the cognitive representation of such summaries. The latter served as a starting point for our evaluation framework, presented next. Advocating, on the one hand, non-sentential, graph-based summaries and arguing, on the other hand, for text as a common format for cross-evaluation, may seem like a paradox. We will come back to this and propose steps towards a resolution in Section 4.

News texts are typically (factual) *narrative texts*: temporal sequences of events, described in terms of answers to the "W" questions: Who? When? Where? What? The focus of the text is typically on a series of actions. So a good summary of one news text or several news texts is likely to focus on the most relevant actions/events, i.e. itself be a narrative. The "W"s at first sight appear to suggest a tabular format, but a closer look at the multitude of different real-life events (i.e. in particular the "what") suggests that the richness of natural language is more appropriate. We therefore hypothesise that human news consumers, the ultimate target group of summaries, are likely to "translate" news summaries of whatever form into sentences in their head anyway, and that this translation will determine their actual mental model. In order to compare automatic summarization techniques based on this assumption, we therefore need to transform non-textual summary elements or patterns into sentences. The most direct way of doing this is to *use the patterns as selectors of sentences* – thus we *extend* the patterns into a form of extractive summarization.[15] To assess the quality of this (re-)construction of presumed novel "facts" in the story, we then build on existing techniques for cross-evaluating sentential summaries to compare specific TTM methods with one another.

While we believe that ultimately, a news-summary user's "translation" into sentences will determine this user's mental model of the story, it is quite possible that different formats offered by automatic summarizers support this construction in different ways. *The automated cross-evaluation cannot demonstrate the superiority of a pattern type.* Therefore, we complement the automated cross-evaluation framework by a user-centric cross-evaluation of methods. Thus, we now let human end-users perform the reconstruction-by-selection that we modelled in the first stage. Here, the algorithms can no longer be evaluated in isolation but as part of an interactive user interface, and the evaluation criteria need to be extended by usability criteria.

4. HOW CAN DIFFERENT FORMATS BE COMPARED? A FRAMEWORK FOR CROSS-EVALUATING TTM METHODS

In this section, we will describe the procedures for automatic and for user-assisted evaluations of news summaries in a graph-based format. The general schema for automated evaluation, together with results from a case study, have first been presented in (Subašić & Berendt, 2010c, 2013). The general schema for user-centric evaluations is presented in Section 4.2. Results from an instance of the general schema for user-centric evaluation are presented in Section 5.

4.1 Cross-Evaluating TTM Methods: Automated Approaches

The evaluation procedure is composed of the following steps: (a) generation of interesting patterns,

(b) generation of a "ground truth", (c) pattern-to-query transformation, (d) sentence retrieval using generated queries, and (e) comparison of retrieved sentences and editor-selected "fact" sentences. For step (a), we apply the respective TTM methods, which regard bursty patterns as interesting, see Section 3, or frequency as a baseline form of interestingness in patterns, see Section 5.1. Steps (b)-(e) are explained in the present section.

A note on temporal indexing that concerns all of the following subsections: we use techniques for generating a summary of events in a given period t within a story. Thus, the patterns are generated to be bursty within t, the documents are grouped into sets belonging to t, and the resulting retrieved sentences and editor-selected sentences likewise belong to t. In principle, any temporal structure could be applied; for simplicity, in our evaluation study we partitioned the whole story time into periods of equal length.

4.1.1 Crowdsourcing the Ground Truth?!

To compile ground-truth descriptions for corpora, we turned to the Web itself. The Web not only provides us with a wealth of documents, but also with summaries of events and their progression. Such "timeline" documents are particularly interesting when they have already undergone a process of testing for and creating a form of consensus – i.e. a form of inter-rater agreement. Documents authored in Wiki fashion and in particular Wikipedia articles, which are often written and re-written by hundreds of people, are good examples. While there is often extensive disagreement in Wikipedia (Viégas, Wattenberg, & Dave, 2004), it is generally acknowledged that text portions that remain in a Wikipedia article represent consensus (Kriplean, Beschastnikh, McDonald, & Golder, 2007; Adler, de Alfaro, Pye, & Raman, 2008) – with the big advantage that this is not a consensus between two or three raters, but between a much larger number of people. We therefore chose, wherever possible, this form of "crowdsourcing the ground truth" to create our set of ground-truth sentences. To maintain the time-indexed nature of temporal text mining, only sentences that contained a date specification (identified via a set of regular expressions) were selected from these documents. This approach works very well for many stories of common interest, see (Subašić & Berendt, 2010a, 2013).

Of course, this approach is not without problems. First, a story has to have raised enough interest to have inspired authors to write and publish a timeline document. Second, these documents are subject to the same quality challenges as other Wikipedia entries. Third, their authors have not written "their" parts independently, such that it is not straightforward to measure inter-rater agreement with the usual metrics. Fourth, it is difficult to account for authors' self-selection bias (although problems of self-selection can also not be ruled out when using the standard methods of assessor recruitment). Finally, the information sources of the Wikipedia authors may be different from the article corpus used by a TTM method.

We observed two cases in which the Wikipedia-based approach fails or in which other timeline documents are superior. The first case is a story in which developments happen at a certain time, but get discovered (and reported) only much later. The resulting reporting, in the timeline, of the dates on which events happened cannot serve as a summary of the reporting documents that appeared at this time. An example of this case was the Enron story (Wikipedia contributors, 2013). We decided not to cover such stories. The second case are special-interest stories for which more detailed sources exist. We found this to be the case for celebrity reporting and chose the timeline provided by a fan site as the ground truth.

In sum, we believe that this method of defining a ground truth cannot replace others, but that it can be a useful complement. Future work should investigate to what extent this method can help avoid the problems mentioned above in Section 3.2.

4.1.2 From Patterns to Sentences: Query Generation and Sentence Retrieval

Due to differences in the expressiveness levels of story representations, comparing the patterns directly with editor-selected sentences would be biased towards the patterns with sentence-like structure. Therefore, to make direct comparisons possible, we developed a process for identifying the sentences that story elements resemble best. This task is akin to that of sentence retrieval: given a query, rank sentences based on some measure of their similarity to that query. Our approach is therefore to transform the patterns into queries and then use sentence retrieval. Direct comparisons are then possible on the retrieved sentences. The process is shown, along with an example for the combo method STORIES, in Figure 1. For keyword-based methods, word conjunctions are formed; for group-based methods, conjunctions are formed from words within a group. We used the Query-likelihood retrieval method (QL) with Jelinek-Mercer topic smoothing for sentence retrieval, as suggested by the use of this method as a baseline by Murdock and Croft (2005).

The inputs for this model are an index of pseudo-documents and a set of queries used for retrieval. We use the set of all sentences from the complete document set as the index. Queries are obtained from story representations of evaluated TTM tracking methods.

We form two types of queries. *Generic query generation* uses the top-ranking bursty elements from each story-representation method. *Specific*

Figure 1. The evaluation pipeline (top) and an example (bottom). The example turns a STORIES pattern (the subgraph highlighted in red constitutes the query) into a set of retrieved sentences.

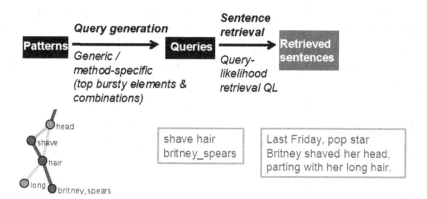

query generation combines the basic story elements into more complex queries to account for the semantics of different story representations. An example are subgraphs-as-queries for the STORIES method, as shown in the example in Figure 1.

For a given TTM method, we use each generic query to retrieve the top-ranked sentences using QL, as well as each specific query. This creates two sets of retrieved sentences per method.

4.1.3 Quality Measures: Comparing Retrieved "Facts" with Editor-Selected "Ground-Truth" Sentences

The quality of such a summary can be assessed by the degree to which the retrieved sentences (the presumed novel "facts") resemble the "ground-truth" sentences. The challenge is to measure an aggregate reconstruction quality over the possible/plausible fact constructions. We compare retrieved sentences with ground-truth sentences in an IR-style evaluation employing measures for scoring each TTM method.

The "recall-oriented" aggregate measure *maxMR* measures how well a ground-truth sentence is recalled. It uses an atomic measure *sim* of sentence-to-sentence fit (ROUGE2 or ROUGE. SU4, although others are also possible), and then uses the whole corpus to normalise this, accounting for differences in the number of retrieval candidates over periods. For each ground-truth sentence, the best-fitting sentence is found in the sentences retrieved by the query. The best *possible* fit is the maximum over all sentences indexed with the same time period. Formally:

$$maxMR_t = avg_{s \in G_t} (max_{r \in R_t} sim(r, s) / max_{r \in A_t} sim(r, s)),$$

where *G* are the ground-truth sentences, *A* all sentences from the documents, and $R \subseteq A$ the sentences retrieved by the bursty patterns of the method under consideration, each for period *t*.

The "precision-oriented" aggregate measure *maxMP* scales *maxMR* to reward methods that retrieve fewer sentences:

$$maxMP_t = maxMR_t \times min(|G_t|, |R_t|) / |R_t|.$$

Each method's overall scores are formed by aggregating their *maxMR*$_t$ and *maxMP*$_t$ over all periods *t*. (The aggregation method can for example be an average if time is partitioned into equal-sized periods.)

With the help of the Friedman/Tukey multiple comparison test (Kendall, 1976), we can then determine, for a group of methods, which ones differ from one another in a statistically significant way and which ones do not, thus identifying a *group* of top performers. We evaluated the methods named above and varied a number of parameters including how many of the top-ranking patterns were used for sentence retrieval. For example, methods that belong to the top performers even when only their top 5 patterns are used, can be considered to be high-precision in more senses than one: a small number of their top patterns retrieves a small number of sentences, and these do well at recalling relevant ground-truth sentences.

4.1.4 Case Study: An Automated Evaluation of Several TTM Methods

In (Subašić & Berendt, 2010c, 2013), we presented a case study of the above evaluation framework that evaluated three methods over five corpora: (Kleinberg, 2002) as a representative of keyword representations, (Mei & Zhai, 2005) as a representative of group representations, and STORIES (Subašić & Berendt, 2010a) as a representative of combo representations (see Section 2.2 for a definition of the three types of representation). The study varied a number of parameters for pattern generation and sentence retrieval. The results suggest that the STORIES method is the most robust of all tested methods. The research also shows that using bursty patterns' internal structure for connecting them with ground truth sentences improves the results.

4.1.5 Limitations

Any given TTM method constructs a certain pattern type *and* extracts certain information from a corpus. Through the proposed mapping to a *common* format, namely sentences, we were able to make different TTM methods comparable. This automated comparison thus focused on the extracted information and – by construction – abstracted from the differences in pattern type.

The automated comparison cannot demonstrate the superiority of a pattern type also for a second

reason: For any given extracted information (here operationalised as a given set of retrieved sentences R^*) and any given pattern type, one can define a TTM algorithm that generates patterns of this type that will retrieve R^*.[16]

Thus, such comparisons cannot answer an important question that a system designer would ask: Are certain pattern types better for humans? Do they present better affordances for the (re)construction of events, do they give people faster insights into a story, do they lead to a more enjoyable user experience? The usefulness of the automated comparison method described above also strongly depends on the quality of the "ground-truth" sentences selected by the editors or the annotators. As shown in Section 3.2 above, this can be the weakest link in the evaluation pipeline.

In the next section, we will therefore propose a complementary cross-evaluation methodology. We will argue that in user-centric evaluations, we can fix the algorithm and thus the information presented and vary the pattern type.

4.2 Cross-Evaluating TTM Methods and Interfaces: User-Centric Approaches

Various approaches to (news-)story tracking led to the development of different research areas like update summarization and temporal text mining. In this section and the following one, we focus on the users and investigate document-search interfaces for story tracking. We propose a set of tasks and measures to evaluate document-search interfaces for story tracking. To the best of our knowledge, this is the first cross-evaluation study of document-search interfaces in the context of story tracking, and the first systematic account of its relation to automated cross-evaluation.

Many tasks related to information retrieval have been approached with interaction in mind (Ruthven, 2008), and several of these tasks have been assessed using standardised evaluation frameworks (Dumais & Belkin, 2005). However, all of these disregard the temporal dimension of corpora and thus are not fully appropriate for interactive story tracking evaluation. We transform the story tracking task into a fact finding and summary creation task. On one side this is similar to the fact finding tasks of the HARD track (Allan, 2004), but we provide a broader description of the topics and include search over several time periods.

In the following, we describe the specific choices made in our evaluation of different aspects of our TTM method STORIES (see Section 2.3), but frame this specific user experiment in terms of a general scheme for cross-evaluating TTM methods.

4.2.1 From Patterns to Sentences: The User Task

We framed the story tracking task as an interactive IR task of fact finding and summary creation. Patterns were given to users as summaries and document-search interfaces. We asked them to identify sentences from the documents that "best describe the time period they belong to". We refer to the resulting interactive interfaces as *summarization interfaces*. To simulate story tracking, the task should be solved in a number of consecutive time periods.

4.2.2 Quality Measures: Summary Quality and Other Indicators of Usability and Usefulness

We defined five sets of measures to capture the various aspects of interfaces for story tracking. The first two are observation-based, the remaining ones are based on self-reports and assess subjective evaluations of various aspects of usability and usefulness of the summarization interfaces in relation to the task.

- **Summary Quality Measures:** We quantify the summary quality using the measures for automatic story tracking evaluation de-

scribed above. For each user and period, *maxMR* is calculated.[17]

- **User Activity Measures:** Activity measures show the level of user engagement in story tracking. We wish to investigate whether different summarization interfaces provide an incentive for corpus exploration. We defined four activity measures: query length (number of words), number of issued queries, number of accessed documents, and exploration time.

- **Other Usability and Usefulness Measures:** Questionnaires were used to assess users' subjective impressions of usability and usefulness. Questions centring on the summarization interface asked how well the summarization interface supports the following activities: quick scan of the documents, exploration of the different aspects of the document set, and discovery of relevant documents. Other questions refer to the task and users' own performance within the summarization interface: how tedious and overwhelming the task was, and how they perceived their success in solving the task. We also requested a ranking of the summarization interfaces based on four criteria: easy to learn, easy to use, suitable to solving the task, and personal preference.

5. USER-CENTRIC EVALUATION OF STORY TRACKING METHODS: A CASE STUDY

In this section, we describe a detailed example of the user-centric cross-evaluation described in general terms in the previous section.

5.1 Pattern Types, Tested Aspects, and their Operationalisation as Summarization Interfaces

To compare different TTM methods, one needs to offer them in interfaces that resemble one another as much as possible. We presented users with four different summarization interfaces (SIs). One was the STORIES interface, in which users interact with the story graph by selecting edges that they find relevant. These edges are then transformed into a query by concatenating the names of nodes they connect. The system returns a set of relevant documents for this query. The main components of STORIES are temporal patterns that we use as *suggestions* and visual graph-based *search*. (Recall from Figure 1 that a search query is submitted by marking a subgraph.) To test these components, we created two further SIs: GRAPH, a graph-based visual search interface based on non-temporal patterns, and SUGGEST, a text-based search using temporal patterns presented as a list. We added a standard keyword-based interface (S.BOX) as a baseline SI. Figure 2 shows the SIs we tested. GRAPH and STORIES look the same, and S.BOX and SUGGEST differ only in the presence of a bigram list (marked by a red rectangle in the figure).

- **Generating Suggestions and Graphs:** We generated two types of suggestions, temporal and non-temporal. First, we extracted the content-bearing terms, defined as the 150 top-TF.IDF terms. The suggestions were generated for a time period t as described in Section 2.3. For the temporal suggestions used in STORIES and SUGGEST, the *TR* measure was used for the edge weights, and for the non-temporal in GRAPHS, the *LR* measure was used. Finally, we sorted the edges by weight and kept the top 30.

5.2 Method

- **Participants:** We recruited 24 participants (9 female) using a student forum. As an incentive for participation, we offered a 20 Euros voucher for a retail store. Participants had a wide range of study directions, and most (16) were PhD or Master students.

- **Materials:** The corpora we collected each consist of two parts: the document set and the ground-truth set. The document set is divided into stories which are the subcorpora discussing the same news subjects. The subject is regarded as a higher-level news story. In total, we compiled four stories covering: Britney Spears, the Greek debt crisis, the BP oil spill, and the Chilean miners' accident. A ground-truth set was created for each story, using the technique described in Section 4.1.1. Participants explored the document sets using the four SIs described in Section 5.1.

- **Design:** Each user tested all SIs and was assigned a unique ordering of them. We counterbalanced the order by generating all possible orderings of the four interfaces. There was no reason to expect an effect of the order of the stories; therefore, this was kept constant. This produced a total of 24 orderings. Using a single SI, a participant always explored the same news story.

- **Procedure:** The participants were asked to read the task instruction and solve the task of identifying sentences from the documents that "best describe the time period they belong to". To simulate story tracking, the task was solved in three consecutive time periods.

Before using each SI, participants were provided with a tutorial followed by a test run. For each period, participants were presented with the interface and the initial document list sorted by date and relevance. A time limit of seven minutes

Figure 2. Screenshots of the interfaces: (a) graph-based interfaces STORIES and GRAPH; (b) text-based interfaces SUGGEST and S.BOX. SUGGEST and S.BOX are identical except for the highlighted area (marked with a red rectangle), which is visible only in SUGGEST.

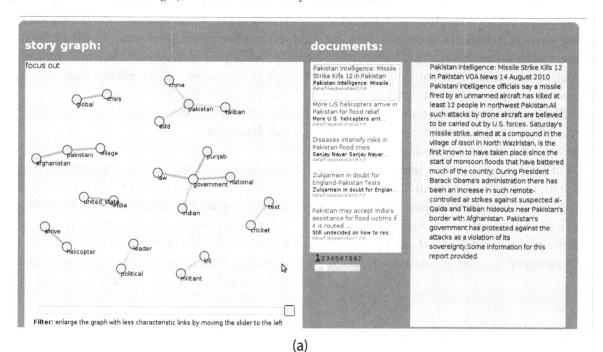

(a)

(b)

per period was set, following a pilot study in which participants completed the task without the time limit. After seven minutes, participants could finish reading the document they were inspecting at that moment and select sentences from it, but neither search for nor read further documents.

Before solving the tasks, participants filled in a demographics pre-study questionnaire, and after each SI they filled in a post-system questionnaire, in which they rated the interface-specific "other usability and usefulness measures" described in Section 4.2.2 on a five-point Likert scale. At the end of the study (after the fourth SI), participants were given an exit questionnaire in which they were asked to compare all the SIs they had used. Together with this exit questionnaire, participants were presented with the screenshots of the SIs

in the same order as they had been used during the study.

Participants were tested in individual sessions lasting about two hours each. After the second SI test was completed, there was a 15 minute break. The participants worked with a Mac minicomputer using a 17" monitor, with the Web-based software and documents residing on a server.

5.3 Results

The value for all summary quality measures (Figure 3a) was always highest for the graph-based interfaces (GRAPH and STORIES). We tested the differences using the Kruskal-Wallace test (due to the non-normal distribution used instead of ANOVA) with Tukey's HSD correction for multiple comparisons. No statistically significant dif-

Figure 3. Study results for the observed measures, summary quality (a: top) and user activity (b: bottom left); and comparative measures (c: bottom right). S2: bigram overlap, S4: skip-4 bigram overlap, all: averaged over all periods, last: last period only.

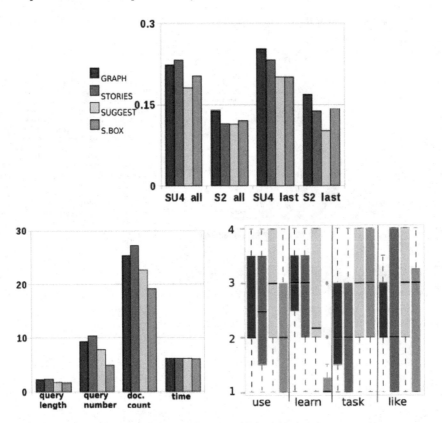

ferences in summary quality were found between interfaces. The analysis of user activity measures (Figure 3b) showed that on average, participants used more and longer queries with GRAPH and STORIES. The longest queries (avg. 2.33) were issued with STORIES and the shortest (1.7) with S.BOX. The differences were statistically significant *(p < .05)* between all interfaces except between GRAPH and STORIES. With the average of 10.4 queries per period, STORIES engaged participants to issue the highest number of queries. The fewest queries were issued using S.BOX (4.84). The differences between S.BOX and all other interfaces were statistically significant. As expected, issuing more queries resulted in more document accesses. With STORIES, participants on average read around 27 documents. The only statistically significant difference was between STORIES and S.BOX. We found no differences between interfaces in exploration time.

The self-reported measures were analysed assuming equal distances between the scores on the Likert scale; averages are shown in Table 1. On average, users found that the graph-based interfaces provided for an *easier access* to the relevant documents and *exploration* of aspects in a story. Participants rated the task as slightly more *tedious* to complete with graph-based interfaces. However, the differences between interfaces were not significant for any measure.

The results of interface comparison (Figure 3c) show that participants ranked S.BOX as the *easiest for using and learning*. On the other two criteria, users ranked GRAPH and STORIES as the *most fitting to the task* of the study, and they expressed *personal preference* towards them. All four criteria were tested using the Friedman test with Tukey's HSD. With regard to the criterion *easy to learn*, only the differences between S.BOX and all others were significant *(p < .05)*. For the criterion *easy to use*, the only significant difference of ranking was that between S.BOX and GRAPH. For both the criteria *fitting to the task* and *personal preference*, there was a significant difference between the ranks of GRAPH and STORIES and the ranks of SUGGEST and S. BOX.

5.4 Discussion

For all interfaces, we found no statistically significant differences in summary quality measures. The observed low performance of participants is most likely the cause of the lack of differentiation between the interfaces. We speculate that the reason for a low performance is the complexity of the task. Creating a summary may be a job more suited to professional journalists than to regular web users. Nevertheless, we discovered several valuable insights into interfaces for story tracking. First, we observed that with time, summary quality improves. In the last periods, summary quality was higher than in the first two by around 20% for GRAPH and STORIES. In addition, we found that GRAPH and STORIES engaged participants in deeper exploration of the document set: they issued more queries and longer queries, and they accessed more documents compared to other inter-

Table 1. Average values of self-reported measures

	GRAPH	STORIES	SUGGEST	S.BOX
Quick scan	3.76	3.32	3.11	3.39
Aspect exploration	3.62	3.32	3.06	3.13
Relevant documents	3.81	3.55	3.22	3.35
Overwhelming	2.95	2.91	2.56	2.17
Tedious	2.67	2.86	2.83	2.65
Successful	3.81	3.50	3.50	3.70

faces. All interfaces except S.BOX include query suggestions, and queries can be issued without typing. This provides an easier way of querying, and the study shows that users will use facilitated querying (clicking rather than typing) if provided.

For the self-reported measures, we found no statistically significant differences, but the analysis of the direct comparison of the interfaces shows that users expressed higher preference for using graph-based interfaces and ranked these two interfaces as the most fitting to the task of the study. The biggest differences were found between SUGGEST and STORIES/GRAPH. This suggests that out of graph representation and suggestion generation components, the first one is a more important one. This may indicate that temporal patterns are not more useful than non-temporal ones for graphs, or alternatively that the difference is due to the low performance on the tasks. As this study does not follow the full factorial design, this finding should be interpreted keeping this in mind. For most criteria, the standard search-box interface is outperformed by graph interfaces.

In sum, although text-based interfaces are still the most widely used interfaces for search today, we were able to show that graph-based interfaces can provide for a different, and for some users better, search experience without diminishing the task performance.

We recognise a number of limitations of this study. It is not clear whether the task we defined is a "good" simulation of story tracking. We asked participants to rate, on a five-point scale, how similar the defined task is to the way they follow news, and the average rating was just over three (neutral). Another issue concerns current habits: although users had not seen the interfaces prior to the study, text-based interfaces resemble most commonly used search interfaces. Thus, some bias towards these interfaces was expected, as shown by user perception on learning and operating difficulty. Also, the study should be replicated with more users.

6. CONCLUSION AND FUTURE RESEARCH DIRECTIONS

In this chapter, we have investigated the summarization of multiple news documents and the challenges this poses for evaluation. In particular, we have taken a close look at the role of the sentential format. We have described several new alternatives to presenting summaries as natural-language texts, looking in particular at graph-based formats. In this concluding section, we will summarize the main points and extend the discussion in order to outline directions for future work.

First, we have argued that to compare different approaches to summarization with one another, we need to map them to a common format. We have argued that the mental models that users construct of news texts are likely to be sentential and that therefore a *mapping of summaries to a sentential format is advantageous for the purposes of comparison*. However, such comparisons themselves rely on the existence and availability of a ground truth, which is also sentential – although studies have shown this to be a non-robust procedure of representing a common understanding of multiple texts. This shows that *a sentential format is also problematic for the purposes of comparison*.

Can the non-sentential formats that we have discussed offer a way out of this dilemma? The results of our user study suggest that it is essential for effective summarization to integrate the user into sense-making through usable, entertaining and ultimately useful interactive summarization-plus-document-search interfaces. Today's news aggregators are just the beginning in this. In particular, we believe that interactive graphical summaries, such as STORIES, illustrate the potentials of future multi-document summarization. Other graph-based text representations, such as those used by MUSE, can also be adapted for the interactive summarization purposes.

This may be leveraged in two ways that focus on users in their roles as assessors and as end users, respectively. First, graph-based methods and interfaces may be a better *preparation* for people to concentrate on what is essential in a collection of texts, and thus may be a key to enhancing the consistency of "gold standard" summaries for evaluating various summarization tasks. Such high-quality summarization corpora should also enhance the performance of supervised summarization methods that heavily depend on the quality of their training data. Second, it is also conceivable that the quest for "the best" summarization is bound to fail because *there is no summary that is best for everyone*, that instead, the best summary is one which stimulates the end user to engage in interactive and individual sense-making. This perspective augments machine intelligence (through automatic summarization, query-dependence and user-adaptivity) by a focus on usability. Such a paradigm shift towards user-customised summaries should also change the way we evaluate text summarization techniques and replace the "one gold standard fits all" approach with carefully designed user studies built upon a variety of summary representation formats.

While graph-based interfaces can provide such usability, an outlook on future summarization should also consider the broader context of new devices and use cases. The increasing importance of mobile devices especially for the consumption of news presents an interesting test case. On the one hand, the limitations of screen resolution both in display and in the granularity of interactivity appear to favour text as a more "robust" representation format. A recent example is the success of the summarization app Summly, which was recently bought by Yahoo! (Winch, 2013). Summly uses a proprietary single-document extractive summarization algorithm, which compresses the content of news articles into 2-3 key sentences that fit onto an iPhone screen. The users can link to the original article if they like the summary. Another example is the summarization app based on MUSE[18].

The current popularity of short texts probably also results from habits of information consumption and production shaped by Twitter. On the other hand, devices are developing fast and becoming increasingly available in a variety of screen sizes. Also, visual information presentation is hugely popular on mobile devices, and it may often be easier to apprehend at a glance than textual information ("a picture says more than a thousand words"), especially when information is consumed on the move. We believe that this presents a good starting point for graph-based summarization formats to exploit and shape visual literacy for complementary and/or improved ways of presenting information on mobile devices.

These developments may also be accompanied by advances in summarization of other types of content, for which not even people's mental models of summaries may be sentential. As an example, take sports reports. These are also narratives (and news), but for many purposes the information need may be much more schematic: who played against whom in what, and which score was the result? For such purposes, a tabular summary of key variables' values may be optimal (such that the summary can easily be used to compare teams' performance, create statistics, etc.), see Narrative science[19] and (Levy, 2012). Appropriate formats may change even more when content in other modes of discourse is summarized. For example, for product reviews as a form of *argumentative/evaluative text*, the desired summarization may be an aggregate such as the relative number of positive vs. negative opinions on a product feature, calling for extractive-abstractive hybrids (Carenini & Cheung, 2008). For search results (which may be considered a form of *descriptive text*), the current user interfaces of Web search engines suggest that a list format, or a combination of list and aspect-oriented results, is desired. *Expository texts* such as scientific essays may require yet other contents and formats of summarization. The extension of the analysis presented in this paper to different types of summarization is an exciting area of future research. Such further analysis should assist in choosing the best summarization interfaces and formats for different content types and user devices.

REFERENCES

Adler, B. T., de Alfaro, L., Pye, I., & Raman, V. (2008). Measuring author contributions to the Wikipedia. In Proceedings of WikiSym'08 (pp. 15:1-15:10). New York: ACM.

Allan, J. (Ed.). (2002). *Topic detection and tracking: Event-based information organization.* Norwell, MA: Kluwer Academic Publishers. doi:10.1007/978-1-4615-0933-2

Allan, J. (2004). HARD track overview in TREC 2004 – High accuracy retrieval from documents. In E. M. Voorhees & L. P. Buckland (Eds.), TREC. Gaithersburg, MD: National Institute of Standards and Technology (NIST).

Allan, J., Gupta, R., & Khandelwal, V. (2001). Temporal summaries of news topics. In W. B. Croft, D. J. Harper, D. H. Kraft, & J. Zobel (Eds.), *Proceedings of SIGIR* (pp. 10-18). New York: ACM.

Allan, J., Lavrenko, V., & Jin, H. (2000). First story detection in TDT is hard. In *Proceedings of the 9th CIKM* (pp. 374-381). New York: ACM.

Barzilay, R., McKeown, K., & Elhadad, M. (1999). Information fusion in the context of multi-document summarization. In R. Dale & K. W. Church (Eds.), *Proceedings of ACL* (pp. 550-557). Stroudsburg, PA: Association for Computational Linguistics.

Brin, S., & Page, L. (1998). The anatomy of a large-scale hypertextual web search engine. *Computer Networks and ISDN Systems, 30*, 107–117. doi:10.1016/S0169-7552(98)00110-X

Carenini, G., & Cheung, J. C. K. (2008). Extractive vs. NLG-based abstractive summarization of evaluative text: The effect of corpus controversiality. In M. White, C. Nakatsu, & D. McDonald (Eds.), *Proceedings of INLG*. Stroudsburg, PA: Association for Computational Linguistics.

Chen, C. C., & Chen, M. C. (2008). TSCAN: A novel method for topic summarization and content anatomy. In *Proceedings of the 31st SIGIR* (pp. 579-586). New York: ACM.

Dumais, S. T., & Belkin, N. J. (2005). The TREC interactive tracks: Putting the user into search. [Gaithersburg, MD: National Institute of Standards and Technology] [NIST]. *Proceedings of TREC, 05*, 22–31.

Enron Scandal. (2013, May 28). *Wikipedia*. Retrieved 13, 2013, from http://en.wikipedia.org/w/index.php?title=Enron_scandal&oldid=545449463

Erkan, G., & Radev, D. R. (2004). LexRank: Graph-based lexical centrality as salience in text summarization. *Journal of Artificial Intelligence Research, 22*, 457–479.

Fung, G. P. C., Yu, J. X., Yu, P. S., & Lu, H. (2005). Parameter free bursty events detection in text streams. In *Proceedings of VLDB* (pp. 181-192). New York: ACM.

Gillick, D., & Favre, B. (2009). A scalable global model for summarization. In *Proceedings of the Workshop on Integer Linear Programming for Natural Language Processing* (pp. 10-18). Stroudsburg, PA: Association for Computational Linguistics.

Gruhl, D., Guha, R. V., Kumar, R., Novak, J., & Tomkins, A. (2005). The predictive power of online chatter. In *Proceedings of SIGKDD* (pp. 78-87). New York: ACM.

Hahn, U., & Mani, I. (2000). The challenges of automatic summarization. *IEEE Computer*, *33*(11), 29–36. doi:10.1109/2.881692

He, Q., Chang, K., Lim, E.-P., & Zhang, J. (2007). Bursty feature representation for clustering text *streams*. In *Proceedings of SDM*. Minneapolis, MN: SIAM. Retrieved July 13, 2013 from http://www.siam.org/proceedings/datamining/2007/dm07_050he.pdf

Janssens, F. A. L., Glänzel, W., & De Moor, B. (2007). Dynamic hybrid clustering of bioinformatics by incorporating text mining and citation analysis. In *Proceedings of SIGKDD* (pp. 360-369). New York: ACM.

Kendall, M. (1976). *Rank correlation methods*. Oxford, UK: Oxford University Press.

Kleinberg, J. (1999). Authoritative sources in a hyperlinked environment. *Journal of the ACM*, *46*(5), 604–632. doi:10.1145/324133.324140

Kleinberg, J. (2002). Bursty and hierarchical structure in streams. In *Proceedings of SIGKDD* (pp. 91-101). New York: ACM.

Kriplean, T., Beschastnikh, I., McDonald, D. W., & Golder, S. A. (2007). Community, consensus, coercion, control: CS*W or how policy mediates mass participation. In *Proceedings of the 2007 ACM Conference on Supporting Group Work (GROUP '07)* (pp. 167-176). New York: ACM.

Levy, S. (2012). Can an algorithm write a better news story than a human reporter? *Wired*. Retrieved July, 13, 2013 from http://www.wired.com/gadgetlab/2012/04/can-an-algorithm-write-a-better-news-story-than-a-human-reporter/

Lin, C.-Y., & Hovy, E. (2003). Automatic evaluation of summaries using N-gram co-occurrence statistics. In *Proceedings of the 2003 Conference of the North American Chapter of the Association for Computational Linguistics on Human Language Technology (NAACL'03)* (pp. 71-78). Morristown, NJ: Association for Computational Linguistics.

Litvak, M., Aizenman, H., Gobits, I., Last, M., & Kandel, A. (2011). DegExt: A language-independent graph-based keyphrase extractor. In *Proceedings of the 7th Atlantic Web Intelligence Conference* (AWIC 2011) (pp. 121-130). Berlin: Springer.

Litvak, M., & Last, M. (2008). Graph-based keyword extraction for single-document summarization. In *Proceedings of the Workshop on Multi-Source Multilingual Information Extraction and Summarization* (pp. 17-24). Stroudsburg, PA: Association for Computational Linguistics.

Litvak, M., & Last, M. (2013). Cross-lingual training of summarization systems using annotated corpora in a foreign language. *Information Retrieval*, *5*(16), 629-656. doi:10.1007/s10791-012-9210-3 PMID:24078787

Long, C., Huang, M., Zhu, X., & Li, M. (2009). Multi-document summarization by information distance. [Silver Spring, MD: IEEE Computer Science Press.]. *Proceedings of ICDM*, *2009*, 866–871.

Luhn, H. P. (1958). The automatic creation of literature abstracts. *IBM Journal of Research and Development*, *2*, 159–165. doi:10.1147/rd.22.0159

Luo, G., Tang, C., & Yu, P. S. (2007). Resource-adaptive real-time new event detection. [New York: ACM.]. *Proceedings of SIGMOD*, *2007*, 497–508.

Mei, Q., & Zhai, C. (2005). Discovering evolutionary theme patterns from text: An exploration of temporal text mining. In *Proceedings of SIGKDD* (pp. 198-207). New York: ACM.

Mihalcea, R. (2005). Language independent extractive summarization. In *Proceedings of AAAI* (pp. 1688-1689). AAAI Press.

Murdock, V., & Croft, W. B. (2005). A translation model for sentence retrieval. In *Proceedings of HLT/EMNLP*. Stroudsburg, PA: Association for Computational Linguistics.

Nallapati, R., Feng, A., Peng, F., & Allan, J. (2004). Event threading within news topics. [New York: ACM.]. *Proceedings of CIKM, 2004*, 446–453. doi:10.1145/1031171.1031258

Nenkova, A., Passonneau, R., & McKeown, K. (2007). The pyramid method: Incorporating human content selection variation in summarization evaluation. *ACM Transactions on Speech and Language Processing, 4*(2).

Petrović, S., Osborne, M., & Lavrenko, V. (2010). Streaming first story detection with application to Twitter. In *Proceedings of HLT '10: Human Language Technologies: The 2010 Annual Conf. of the North American Chapter of the Association for Computational Linguistics* (pp. 181-189). Morristown, NJ: Association for Computational Linguistics.

Ruthven, I. (2008). Interactive information retrieval. *Annual Review of Information Science & Technology, 42*(1), 43–91. doi:10.1002/aris.2008.1440420109

Salton, G., Singhal, A., Mitra, M., & Buckley, C. (1997). Automatic text structuring and summarization. *Information Processing & Management, 33*(2), 193–207. doi:10.1016/S0306-4573(96)00062-3

Schult, R., & Spiliopoulou, M. (2006). Discovering emerging topics in unlabelled text collections. In *Proceedings of ADBIS* (pp. 353-366). Berlin: Springer.

Smith, D. A. (2002). Detecting and browsing events in unstructured text. In *Proceedings of SIGIR* (pp. 73-80). New York: ACM.

Soboroff, I., & Harman, D. (2005). Novelty detection: the TREC experience. In *Proceedings of the Conference on Human Language Technology and Empirical Methods in Natural Language Processing* (pp. 105-112). Morristown, NJ: Association for Computational Linguistics.

Steinberger, J., & Ježek, K. (2009). Update summarization based on novel topic distribution. In *Proceedings of the 9th ACM Symposium on Document Engineering* (pp. 205-213). New York: ACM.

Subašić, I., & Berendt, B. (2010a). Discovery of interactive graphs for under-standing and searching time-indexed corpora. *Knowledge and Information Systems, 23*(3), 293–319. doi:10.1007/s10115-009-0227-x

Subašić, I., & Berendt, B. (2010b). Experience stories: A visual news search and summarization system. In *Proceedings of ECML/PKDD* (vol. 3, pp. 619-623). Berlin: Springer.

Subašić, I., & Berendt, B. (2010c). From bursty patterns to bursty facts: The e ectiveness of temporal text mining for news. []. Amsterdam, The Netherlands: IOS Press.]. *Proceedings of ECAI, 215*, 517–522.

Subašić, I., & Berendt, B. (2013). Story graphs: Tracking document set evolution using dynamic graphs. *Intelligent Data Analysis, 17*(1), 125–147.

Trampus, M., & Mladenic, D. (2009). Constructing event templates from written news. In *Proceedings of Web Intelligence/IAT Workshops* (pp. 507–510). Silver Spring, MD: IEEE Computer Science Press.

Turney, P. D. (2000). Learning algorithms for keyphrase extraction. *Information Retrieval, 2*(4), 303–336. doi:10.1023/A:1009976227802

Viégas, F. B., Wattenberg, M., & Dave, K. (2004). Studying cooperation and conflict between authors with history flow visualizations. In *Proceedings of CHI* (pp. 575-582). New York: ACM.

Wang, X., & McCallum, A. (2006). Topics over time: A non-Markov continuous-time model of topical trends. In *Proceedings of SIGKDD* (pp. 424-433). New York: ACM.

Winch, J. (2013). British teen sells Summly app. for millions. *The Telegraph.* Retrieved March, 25, 2013 from http://www.telegraph.co.uk/finance/newsbysector/mediatechnologyandtelecoms/9952658/ British-teen-sells-Summly-app-for-millions.html

ADDITIONAL READING

Balasubramanian, N., Allan, J., & Croft, W. B. (2007). A comparison of sentence retrieval techniques. In *Proc. 30th SIGIR* (pp. 813-814). New York: ACM.

Barzilay, R., Elhadad, N., & McKeown, K. (2002). Inferring strategies for sentence ordering in multidocument news summarization. *Journal of Artificial Intelligence Research, 17,* 35–55.

Bollegala, D., Okazaki, N., & Ishizuka, M. (2006). A bottom-up approach to sentence ordering for multi-document summarization. In *Proceedings of the 21st International Conference on Computational Linguistics and the 44th annual meeting of the Association for Computational Linguistics (ACL-44).* Association for Computational Linguistics (pp. 385-392). Stroudsburg, PA, USA.

Bysani, P. (2010). Detecting novelty in the context of progressive summarization. In *Proceedings of the NAACL HLT 2010 Student Research Workshop (HLT-SRWS '10). Association for Computational Linguistics* (pp. 13-18). Stroudsburg, PA, USA.

Filippova, K. (2010). Multi-sentence compression: finding shortest paths in word graphs. In *Proceedings of the 23rd International Conference on Computational Linguistics (COLING '10). Association for Computational Linguistics* (pp. 322-330). Stroudsburg, PA, USA

Giannakopoulos, G., & Karkaletsis, V. (2010). Summarization System Evaluation Variations Based on N-Gram Graphs. *TAC 2010 Proceedings Papers.*

Li, T., & Shen, C. (2010). Multi-document summarization via the minimum dominating set. In *Proceedings of the 23rd International Conference on Computational Linguistics (COLING '10)* (pp. 984-992). Association for Computational Linguistics, Stroudsburg, PA, USA.

Lin, H., & Bilmes, J. (2010). Multi-document Summarization via Budgeted Maximization of Submodular Functions. In *Proceedings of the 2010 Annual Conference of the North American Chapter of the Association for Computational Linguistics (HLT '10)* (pp. 912-920). Stroudsburg, PA, USA: Association for Computational Linguistics.

McKeown, K., Passonneau, R. J., Elson, D. K., Nenkova, A., & Hirschberg, J. (2005). Do summaries help? In *Proceedings of the 28th annual international ACM SIGIR conference on Research and development in information retrieval (SIGIR '05)* (pp. 210-217). New York, NY, USA.

Murdock, V. (2006). Aspects of sentence retrieval. Doctoral dissertation, University of Massachusetts Amherst, Amherst, Massachusetts. Retrieved July 13, 2013, from http://maroo.cs.umass.edu/pdf/IR-542.pdf

Nenkova, A., & McKeown, K. (2012). A survey of text summarization techniques. In C. C. Aggarwal, & C. Zhai (Eds.), *Mining Text Data* (pp. 43–76). New York: Springer. doi:10.1007/978-1-4614-3223-4_3

Saggion, H. (2006). Multilingual Multidocument Summarization Tools and Evaluation. *International Conference on Language Resources and Evaluation (LREC).*

Schlesinger, J. M. (November 14-15, 2011). CLASSY 2011 at TAC: Guided and Multi-lingual Summaries and Evaluation Metrics. *Proceedings of the Fourth Text Analysis Conference (TAC 2011)*. Gaithersburg, Maryland, USA: National Institute of Standards and Technology.

Wan, X. (2010). Towards a unified approach to simultaneous single-document and multi-document summarizations. In *Proceedings of the 23rd International Conference on Computational Linguistics (COLING '10)* (pp. 1137-1145). Stroudsburg, PA, USA: Association for Computational Linguistics.

Wan, X., Li, H., & Xiao, J. (2010). Cross-language document summarization based on machine translation quality prediction. In *Proceedings of the 48th Annual Meeting of the Association for Computational Linguistics (ACL '10)* (pp. 917-926). Stroudsburg, PA, USA.

Wan, X., & Yang, J. (2008). Multi-document summarization using cluster-based link analysis. In *Proceedings of the 31st annual international ACM SIGIR conference on Research and development in information retrieval (SIGIR '08)* (pp. 299-306). ACM.

Wang, D., & Li, T. (2010). Many are better than one: improving multi-document summarization via weighted consensus. In *Proceeding of the 33rd international ACM SIGIR conference on Research and development in information retrieval (SIGIR '10)* (pp. 809-810). New York, NY, USA.

Wang, D., Zhu, S., Li, T., & Gong, Y. (2009). Multi-document summarization using sentence-based topic models. In *Proceedings of the ACL-IJCNLP 2009 Conference Short Papers (ACL Short '09)* (pp. 297-300). Association for Computational Linguistics, Stroudsburg, PA, USA.

Wei, F., Li, W., Lu, Q., & He, Y. (2010). A document-sensitive graph model for multi-document summarization. *Knowledge and Information Systems, 22*(2), 245–259. doi:10.1007/s10115-009-0194-2

Xiaodan, X. (2010). Study on Sub Topic Clustering of Multi-documents Based on Semi-supervised Learning. 2nd International Workshop on Database Technology and Applications. Wuhan, China: IEEE Computer Society.

Xiong, Y., Liu, H., & Li, L. (2010). Multi-Document summarization based on improved features and clustering. *International Conference on Natural Language Processing and Knowledge Engineering (NLP-KE)* (pp. 1-5).

Zhang, J., Cheng, X., Xu, H., Wang, X., & Zeng, Y. (2008). Summarizing Dynamic Information with Signature Terms Based Content Filtering. Retrieved 09 06, 2011, from *TAC 2008 Proceedings Papers*. Retrieved November 21, 2012 from http://www.nist.gov/tac/publications/2008/papers.html

Zhao, L., & Wu, L. (2009). Using query expansion in graph-based approach for query-focused multi-document summarization. *Information Processing & Management, 45*(1), 35–41. doi:10.1016/j.ipm.2008.07.001

Zhou, L., & Lin, C. (2006). ParaEval: using paraphrases to evaluate summaries automatically. In *Proceedings of the main conference on Human Language Technology Conference of the North American Chapter of the Association of Computational Linguistics (HLT-NAACL '06)* (pp. 447-454). Stroudsburg, PA, USA: Association for Computational Linguistics.

KEY TERMS AND DEFINITIONS

Burst: Sudden surge of importance of some element, where the importance of an element can be measured with frequency, probability, etc.

Bursty Pattern: A text pattern from a story going through a burst.

Extractive Summarization: Selection of a subset of the most relevant fragments from a source text into the summary. The fragments can be paragraphs, sentences, keyphrases or keywords.

Generic Summarization: Processes only a document (or a set of documents) to be summarized.

Language-Independent Sentence Features: Statistical features that do not require any morphological or syntactic analysis of the summarized text.

Language-Specific Sentence Features: Features that require dictionaries and Natural Language Processing (NLP) tools.

MUSE (MUltilingual Sentence Extractor): An extractive generic single-document summarization approach, which uses a linear combination of language-independent features for ranking each sentence in a text document.

Query-Based Summarization: Processes a document (or a set of documents) to be summarized as well as a query expressing the user's interest.

ROUGE (Recall-Oriented Understudy for Gisting Evaluation): An automated method for comparing a computer-generated summary to gold standard summaries (generated by human annotators) in terms of overlapping units such as n-grams, word sequences, and word pairs.

Story: A set of time-stamped documents related to the same subject (e.g. all news reports about a specific natural disaster such as earthquake in Japan 2002).

Temporal Text Mining: A family of temporal text mining methods that outputs bursty text patterns (bursty patterns).

ENDNOTES

1   http://news.google.com
2   http://news.yahoo.com
3   http://multiling.iit.demokritos.gr/pages/view/662/multiling-2013/
4   In 2008, DUC became a Summarization track in the Text Analysis Conference (TAC).
5   http://www-nlpir.nist.gov/projects/duc/duc2007/tasks.html#pilot
6   http://www.trec-ts.org/home

7   Thus, in TDT evaluation, events correspond to story subjects. In that sense, FSD differs from story tracking in that it aims to detect documents discussing a new story subject. However, it is easy to imagine that all documents of an incoming stream belong to the same story. It this case the "new events" would correspond to developments, making FSD more similar to our notion of the story tracking task.
8   http://www.opencalais.com/
9   http://lucene.apache.org
10   http://duc.nist.gov/duc2004/protocol.html
11   http://duc.nist.gov
12   http://www.haaretz.co.il
13   http://www.themarker.com
14   http://en.wikinews.org/wiki
15   We do not attempt an abstractive technique in which novel sentences are generated. Abstraction would require an added sentence-building component – which would then affect the overall performance. Also, the influence of the pattern-generation component resp. abstraction component might be hard to disentangle.
16   This general statement is a conjecture, which we believe to be true due to the many degrees of freedom of how TTM algorithms may be defined. We invite attempts to prove or disprove this conjecture.
17   *maxMP* could also be used, but only adds new information when results are aggregated over periods and/or stories. In our experiment described in Section 5, we focused on the fine-grained results that only aggregate across users and therefore did not use *maxMP*.
18   https://itunes.apple.com/sl/app/muse-summary-test/id643238319?mt=8
19   http://narrativescience.com/

Section 3
Multilingual Summarization

Chapter 11
Multilingual Summarization Approaches

Kamal Sarkar
Jadavpur University, India

ABSTRACT

As the amount of on-line information in the languages other than English (such as Chinese, Japanese, German, French, Hindi, etc.) increases, systems that can automatically summarize multilingual documents are becoming increasingly desirable for managing information overload problem on the Web. This chapter presents an overview of automatic text summarization with special emphasis on multilingual text summarization. The various state-of-the-art multilingual summarization approaches have been grouped based on their characteristics and presented in this chapter.

INTRODUCTION

Summarization is a kind of human ability. Since the time immemorial, some form of summarization has been used to store knowledge, transmit knowledge and memorize the key facts about anything.

Today, in the age of electronic media, it is hard to imagine everyday life without some form of summarization. News headlines are summaries, written in a terse stylized language, of material in a news articles. Abstracts of the scientific articles are a traditional form of author-written summaries. Other form of summaries include reviews of books or movies, Minutes of a meeting, a stock market bulletin, an abridgement of a book, a resume, an obituary, initial search hits returned by the search engines and so on.

The human experts for an area can write good summaries for the articles related to that area. This indicates that the human summarizers require background knowledge while writing the summaries. The summaries are very much subjective

DOI: 10.4018/978-1-4666-5019-0.ch011

in nature. The human summarizers may differ in their viewpoints for summarizing the same article. So, the human produced summaries suffer from the bias of the authors. But, there is no question of bias when summaries are produced by the machines. Ideally, the machine-generated summaries should contain the best and important information.

Due to the lack of proper mathematical model of human cognition, it is difficult to explain how human learns to summarize. Since the human cognition is not computable or the present paradigms of computation are inadequate for computing the human cognition, it is hardly possible for the machines to generate summaries as the human does. However, given a compression ratio, a machine can distinguish between the more relevant textual units and the less relevant textual units and select or reformulate the more relevant textual units for the generation of the summaries. Thus, the machine can produce sub-optimal results without depending on the exact mathematical formulation of the cognition process that humans apply to summary generation.

The World Wide Web (WWW) has introduced us with a new paradigm of knowledge sharing, transmission and consumption. The number of web pages available on the Internet almost doubles every year. Though English is dominating language on the web, the number of documents written in the languages other than English (such as Chinese, Japanese, German, French, Hindi etc.) is also increasing daily at unprecedented rate. With this rapid growth of the World Wide Web, information overload is becoming a problem for an increasingly large number of people. The traditional search engines such as Yahoo, Google etc. have revolutionized searching capabilities along with the intelligent visualization of search results to facilitate browsing on the Web. A keyword-based search using the engines results in links to web pages along with snippet of its contents where these keywords have occurred. This snippet actually helps the reader decide whether the retrieved link is worth reading in detail or not. So, in some sense these snippets serve as indicative summaries. It is also very difficult for the users to go through all the hits that the traditional search engines return and find the relevant information from the collection. This has created a growing need for the development of a new way of managing a vast hoard of information. Automatic summarization can be an indispensable solution to reduce the information overload problem on the web. Not only for the online application, but also for the offline applications such as searching information on a large corpus of offline documents, the text summarization tools can be useful.

Definition of Summary

It is very difficult to define what a summary is. The following are the definitions of "summary" found in various sources.

- **(Oxford Dictionary Online 2009):** "A brief statement of the main points of something."
- **(Cambridge Dictionaries Online 2009):** "A short clear description that gives the main facts or ideas about something."
- **(Radev et.al. 2002):** "A text that is produced from one or more texts, that conveys important information in the original text(s), and that is no longer than half of the original text(s) and usually significantly less than that. Text here is used rather loosely and can refer to speech, multimedia documents, hypertext, etc."

Definition of Automatic Summarization

The following are the definitions of "automatic text summarization" found in various sources.

- **(Mani and Maybury 1999):** "To take an information source, extract content from it, and present the most important content to the user in a condensed form and in a manner sensitive to the user's or application's needs."

- **(Mani 2001):** "A process to produce a condensed representation of the content of its input for human consumption."
- **(Sparck Jones 1999):** "A reductive transformation of source text to summary text through content condensation by selection and/or generalization on what is important in the source."

Types of Summaries

Extract vs. Abstract

Based on the relationship between the input and the summary produced by the summarizer, a distinction can be made between *extracts* and *abstracts*. An *extract* is a summary consisting of a number of salient text units selected from the input. An *abstract* is a summary, which represents the subject matter of the article with the text units, which are generated by reformulating the salient units selected from the input. An abstract may contain some text units, which are not present in the input text.

Single Document vs. Multi-Document

Text Summarization is broadly categorized as *single document summarization* (the input is only one document) and *Multi-document summarization* (the input is a cluster of related documents) based on the input source.

Another type of summarization is called multi-document multilingual summarization where the input consists of multiple related documents and documents are written in multiple languages and the summary is produced in a chosen language. A single document summary or a multi-document summary can either be an extract or an abstract.

Indicative vs. Informative vs. Critical Summary

Based on the purpose of summary generation, a summary can be categorized as indicative, informative or critical summary. An indicative summary provides an indication about the document content for using it as the entry point (or a reference function) that help the user to decide whether the document worth in-depth reading. Informative summary covers all salient information in the document at some level of detail, i.e., it will contain information about all the different aspects such as article's purpose, scope, approach, results and conclusions etc. It is expected that informative summary can be used as the document surrogate and sometimes, users may read the summary in place of the document to satisfy the information needs. But, depending on the user's information needs, how much a summary is informative can be represented by a scale on which the document itself is placed at the rightmost point (maximally informative) and a system produced summary is placed somewhere on the scale. For example, an abstract of a medical research article is more informative than its headline.

A critical summary covers the subject matter of the source and also expresses the abstractor's views on and evaluation of the quality of the work reported by the authors in the article. For example, reviews are critical summaries, which involve inclusion of opinions, feedback, weakness, strong points, recommendations etc.. It may also include something beyond what is found in the source.

Generic vs. Query Focused

Based on the type of user a summary is intended for, it can be categorized as generic summary or query-focused summary. Generic summaries are aimed at a broad readership community. Generic summary should serve the purpose of using it as document surrogate. User focused (query focused) summaries are tailored to the requirements of a particular user or group of users. Query focused summary as returned in response to a query given by the user should contain specific material important and relevant with respect to the user's query.

Multilingual Summarization

Multilingual summarization is defined by Mani (2001) as "processing several languages, with summary in the same language as input."

In broader sense, the definition of *Multilingual text summarization* can be extended to the following:

If L is a set of natural languages, multilingual text summarization can be defined as a process that can accept a single document stated in one language $\ell \in L$ or can accept a cluster of related documents typed in one language /multiple different languages selected from L to produce a summary in the language same as the input or the language chosen from *L* by the user.

Cross-language document summarization is a type of multilingual summarization where a summary is produced in a language (e.g. Chinese) different from the language (e.g. English) of the source documents.

Multilingual text summarization is relatively harder because it should be capable of processing multiple languages and there are idiosyncrasies across the languages. Many approaches to multilingual text summarization have already been developed. Major approaches to multilingual text summarization are presented in the next section.

MAJOR MULTILINGUAL SUMMARIZATION APPROACHES

Multilingual summarization approaches can be broadly categorized as *language independent multilingual summarization* approaches and *language dependent multilingual summarization* approaches.

Language Independent Approaches

Text summarization techniques which do not use much of semantic or language specific information can be easily extended to computing multilingual text summarization. These kinds of text summarization approaches which have language independence properties can be used for summarizing documents written in multiple languages. Only systems that perform equally well on different languages without language-specific knowledge (including linguistic analysis) can be considered language-independent summarizers. Language independent approaches can be divided into two types: language independent single document text summarization approaches and language independent multi-document text summarization approaches.

Language Independent Single Document Multilingual Text Summarization Approaches

In this section, the various text summarization methods that use language independent features for generating summary from a text are discussed.

Position Based Methods (Baxendale, 1958)

The positional information of a sentence in a document is used to compute the score for the sentence. The position based method that gives more importance to the sentences appears earlier in the document is also called *lead method* (Mani, 2001). According to this method, the score of the sentence i is computed using the following formula:

$$\text{SCORE}(S_i) = \frac{1}{i} \tag{1}$$

Some other methods that use positional information assign scores to the sentences based on their closeness to the borders. According to this method, the sentences which appear in the beginning or the last paragraphs are assigned more weights. The following formula is used to compute the score for a sentence at position i in a document.

$$\text{SCORE}(S_i) = \max\left(\frac{1}{i}, \frac{1}{n - i + 1}\right) \quad (2)$$

where n is the total number of sentences in a document.

Edmundsonian Methods and its Variants

Edmundson (1969) conducted experiments with a corpus (collection) of 200 scientific articles on chemistry. The methods he used are: (1) cue method that uses cue words for assigning weight to a sentence, (2) title method that assigns score to a sentence based on the sum of weights of title words present in a sentence, (3) key method that assigns score to a sentence based on sum of the weights of keywords contained in a sentence and (4) position method that assigns score to a sentence based on its position in the document. The first three methods consider word level features and the fourth method considers a sentence level feature. Word level features are selected after excluding a list of stop words called stop-list. *Stop-list* includes words which are insignificant and less informative such as articles, preposition etc. Edmundson developed a hybrid method that linearly combines the four basic methods namely cue, title, key and position.

The cue method considers *Cue words* as the feature. Cue words are the words that affect the summary worthiness of the sentences. A dictionary of cue words which exclude stop words are compiled from a corpus. After a study on a hetero-

geneous corpus of 100 documents and manually created extracts of those documents, cue words are compiled based on three important statistical parameters: frequency (number of occurrences of a word in a corpus), dispersion (number of documents in which the word occurred) and the selection ratio (ratio of the number of occurrences in the sentences in the extracts to the number of occurrences in all sentences in the corpus). The cue words are divided into two categories: bonus words (Example: "significant") and stigma words (Example: "hardly", "impossible"). According to Edmundson, bonus words include "comparatives", "superlatives", "adverbs of conclusion", "value terms", etc. and stigma words include "anaphoric expressions, belittling expressions, "insignificant detail expressions and hedging expressions" etc.. The final *Cue* weight for each sentence is the sum of the *Cue* weights of its constituent words

The key method considers keywords as the feature. Keywords are extracted based on a frequency based term filtering technique. All words in a document are sorted in decreasing order of their frequencies and the non-cue words whose frequencies are above a cut off are selected as the keywords. Here word frequency is taken as the word-weight and the weights of the keywords contained in a sentence are added to obtain the score for a sentence.

Location method considers location of a sentence as a feature. The location feature has been used in the Edmundsonian approach in two ways: (1) a list of short headings like "conclusion", "introduction" is manually created and sentences occurring under those headings are assigned positive weights (2) sentences occurring in the first paragraph and last paragraph of the document are assigned positive weights.

The Title method creates, for each document, a title glossary consisting of all non-Null words of the title, subtitle, and headings for that document. Positive weights are assigned to the words that occur in the title glossary. The final title weight for each sentence is the sum of the title weights of its constituent words.

The overall method for the linear combination of the four features to score sentences is the following:

$$W = a1 * C + a2 * K + a3 * T + a4 * L \qquad (3)$$

where C=Cue word, K=Key word, T =Title and L=location and a_1, a_2, a_3 and a_4 are the parameters which can be regarded as feature weights for four features respectively. These four feature weights are manually adjusted by comparing documents and the manually created extracts. Edmundson's evaluations on test data reveal that key words are poorer than the other three features and the combination of cue-title-location was the best. As the individual feature, location is the best and key word feature alone is the worst.

A variant of Edmundsonian approach presented in (Sarkar, 2012a & 2012b) uses two important features for sentence ranking: thematic term and position. These features are basically variants of the features used in Key method and position method proposed by Edmundson (1969):

Thematic terms in a document are the terms having TF*IDF weights greater than a predefined threshold. Term frequency (TF) is combined with inverse document frequency (IDF) for assigning weights to a keyword. TF stands for term frequency which is computed as the number of times a term (keyword) occurs in a document and IDF stands for inverse document frequency (IDF) which is computed using the formula log(N/df) where N is the number of documents in a corpus and df is the number of documents in which a term occurs at least once. df is computed over the a large corpus. The sentence score is computed as the sum of TF*IDF weights of the keywords contained in a sentence. In this work, the positional score of a sentence is computed in such a way that the first sentence of a document gets the highest score and the last sentence gets the lowest score and the sentence length feature is considered to penalize the sentences which are too short and too long.

LUHN Method (Luhn, 1958)

The significance factor of a sentence in the Luhn method is derived from an analysis of its words and based on a combination of two measurements: the frequency of word occurrence, and the relative position of keywords (significant words selected based on some criteria) within the sentence. Thus the sentence score depends on the number of keywords within the sentence and the linear distance between them due to the intervention of non-significant words. Luhn suggests that the optimal limit of intervening non-significant words between the bracketing keywords should be set to 4 or 5 non-significant words. According to the Luhn method, the score of the ith portion of a sentence bracketed by keywords is computed as follows:

$$SCORE_i = \frac{S_i^2}{N_i} \qquad (4)$$

where: S_i is the number of keywords in the ith portion and N_i is the total number of words in the ith portion.

After computing scores for the different portions of the sentence S, the overall score for the sentence is computed as follows:

$$SCORE(S) = \max_{i \in C} \{SCORE_i\} \qquad (5)$$

where C is the portions of the sentence S bracketed by keywords. $Score_i$ is the score of the ith portion of a sentence.

TF*ISF Based Method

This work presented in (Neto et al., 2000) proposes a new extractive text-summarization algorithm based on the importance of the topics contained in a document. In this approach, the document is partitioned by using the TextTiling algorithm, which identifies topics (coherent segments of text) based on the TF-IDF (TF: term frequency, IDF: inverse document frequency) metric. Then for each topic, the relative relevance in the document is computed using the measure TF-ISF (Term Frequency - Inverse *Sentence* Frequency), which is basically the adaptation of the well-known TF-IDF (Term Frequency – Inverse *Document* Frequency) measure. Finally, the summary is generated by selecting from each topic a number of sentences proportional to the importance of that topic. TF*ISF represents a product of term frequency and inverse sentence frequency. The score for a textual unit is calculated as an average TFISF for all the words in the textual unit:

$$\text{SCORE(S)} = \sum_{t \in S} \text{f(t)} \times \text{isf(t)} \tag{6}$$

where $f(t)$ stands for frequency of the term t and

$$\text{isf (t)} = 1 - \frac{\log(\text{n(t)})}{\log(\text{n})} \tag{7}$$

where n is the number of sentences in the document and $n(t)$ is the number of sentences containing t.

SVD based Method (Steinberger and Jezek, 2004)

SVD *(Singular Value Decomposition)* can be used as a method for transforming correlated variables into a set of uncorrelated ones that better expose the various relationships among the original data items. At the same time SVD is a method for identifying and ordering the dimensions along which data points exhibit the most variation. SVD derives the latent semantic structure of the document represented by the matrix A which is

term-sentence matrix where a column i represents weighted term-frequency vector corresponding to the sentence i in the document. According to Gong and Liu (2001), one should create a $m \times n$ term-sentence matrix $A = [A_1, A_2, \ldots, A_n]$, where each column A_i represents the weighted term-frequency vector of the ith sentence in the document, and apply SVD to the matrix A: $A = U\Sigma V^T$. SVD maps m-dimensional space spawned by weighted term frequency vectors to the r- dimensional singular vector space. This operation reflects the breakdown of the original document into r linearly independent base vectors or concepts. The summarization method proposed by Gong and Liu (2001) chooses the most informative sentence for each topic, i.e., the kth sentence chosen is the one with the largest index value in the kth right singular vector in matrix V^T.

The improved summarization method introduced by Steinberger and Jezek (2004) selects the sentences whose vector-representation in the matrix $\Sigma^2 \cdot V^T$ has the greatest 'length'. Intuitively, the idea is to choose the sentences with the greatest combined weight across all important topics. More formally, sentence score is calculated as a length of the sentence vector in $\Sigma^2 \cdot V^T$ after computing SVD.

Graph-Based Method

A graph based method represents a document as a graph where each node represents a sentence and an edge between two nodes is weighted by the similarity relationship between two sentences representing the nodes. ML_TR is a multilingual version of TextRank (Mihalcea, 2005) without morphological analysis. Each document is represented as a graph of nodes. The overlap of two sentences is determined simply as the number of common tokens between the two sentences, normalized by the length of these sentences. The score of a sentence is equal to the PageRank (Brin and Page, 1998) score of the corresponding node in the representation graph:

$$WS(V_i) =$$

$$(1\text{-}d) + d * \sum_{v_j \in In(v_i)} \frac{w_{ji}}{\sum_{v_k \in out(v_j)} w_{jk}} ws(v_j) \qquad (8)$$

where $In(V_i)$ is the set of vertices that point to V_i (predecessors), $Out(V_j)$ is the set of vertices that vertex V_j points to (successors), d is the damping factor, which integrates into the model the probability of jumping from a given vertex to another random vertex in the graph (setting the value of d to 0.85 implies that the probability of jumping to a completely new node is set to 0.15), and w_{ji} is the weight assigned to the edge connecting the two vertices: V_j and V_i are equal to the similarity value between the corresponding sentences. The appropriate value of d for an application is determined through experimentation.

Other Methods

A Multilingual summarization system called MUSE (Litvak et al., 2010) uses a language independent approach for extractive summarization based on the linear optimization of several sentence ranking measures using a genetic algorithm. The MUSE is multilingual single-document extractive summarization system where summarization is considered as an optimization or a search problem. According to this approach, a set of features are linearly combined to score sentences in a document and the genetic algorithm is applied for finding the best weight configuration used for feature combination. The weight model learned for one language is applied to another language to determine efficacy of the model across the different languages.

A language independent approach to multilingual text summarization is also presented in (Patel, 2007). This approach uses structural and statistical factors (rather than semantic factors) to make the system language independent. This approach has been tested on English and three Indian languages namely Hindi, Gujarati and Urdu.

Language Independent Multi-Document Multilingual Text Summarization Approaches

There are a number of multi-document text summarization techniques (Erkan et al., 2004; Radev et al., 2004.; Hatzivassiloglou et al., 2001; Wan et al., 2006; Sarkar, 2009) for English that can be easily extended to summarize a cluster of documents typed in either English or in a language other than English such as Japanese, Dutch etc. Though the existing multi-document summarization techniques with language independence properties can be easily extended to multilingual summarization, there are only a limited number of such techniques which have been properly tested on multilingual datasets. For many cases, the language independent single document text summarization features such as TF, TF*IDF, position, title/headline, centroid have been extended to use in language independent multi-document multilingual summarization tasks.

MEAD (Radev et al., 2004) is a multi-document multilingual extractive summarization platform which uses a text summarization approach having four stages: preprocessing and clustering, feature extraction, feature combination and sentence reranking. The features which are used for developing this system are:

- **Centroid:** A pseudo document containing a set of words (centroid vector) whose weights are greater than a predefined threshold. Cosine overlap with the centroid vector of the cluster is considered as the feature value.
- **Similarity-With-First:** Cosine overlap with the first sentence (or title if exists) in the document is considered as the feature value.
- **Length:** The value of this feature is 1 if the length of a sentence is greater than a predefined value, 0 otherwise.

- **RealLength:** Length of a sentence in words
- **Position:** Position of the sentence in the document
- **QueryOverlap:** Cosine overlap with the query sentence
- **KeywordMatch:** Full match from a list of keywords
- **CosineCentrality:** Eigenvector centrality of the sentence on the lexical connectivity matrix with a defined threshold

NewGist is a multilingual statistical news summarizer (Kabadjov, 2010) that uses a language independent approach to multi-document text summarization. This approach uses Singular Value Decomposition (SVD) for prominent sentence selection. Since SVD has the advantage of being language independent, the approach presented in (Kabadjov, 2010) is applied for a variety of languages.

Language Dependent Multilingual Summarization Approaches

Multilingual text summarization approaches that utilize language specific knowledge such as morphological information, semantic information retrieved from the Wordnet, Language specific resources such as parallel corpora, thesaurus etc. can be considered to be language dependent approaches. Language specific knowledge is necessary for machine translation of documents from one language to another language. Multilingual summarization approaches that translate all documents to a specific language can be named as translation based approaches and these can also be regarded as language dependent approaches since translation based approaches mostly depend on automatic translation of documents, which uses language specific knowledge.

Language Dependent Single Document Multilingual Summarization Approaches

When the summarization system can accept single document stated in one language chosen from a set of languages and produce a summary in the language same as the input or the language chosen by the user, the summarization process can be called as *Single Document Multilingual Summarization*. Like monolingual text summarization, single document multilingual summarization produces a summary that can be of the various types such as *extract, abstract, indicative, informative, critical, generic and query focused* etc. as discussed earlier in this chapter.

The single document multilingual summarization approach presented in (Hovy and Lin, 1999) is used to develop the SUMMARIST system which extracts sentences from documents in a variety of languages, and translates the resulting summary to a language chosen by a user. It operates on texts in English, Spanish, French, German, Indonesian languages. Its older versions can also process Arabic and Japanese documents. This system has been coupled with the Information Retrieval system called MuST (Lin, 1999) which uses query translation to allow a user to search for documents in a variety of languages, summarize the documents using SUMMARIST, and translate the summary.

The Keizai system (Ogden et al., 1999) accepts an English query, uses query translation to search for Japanese and Korean documents and extracts passages containing query terms for generating query-specific summaries in the language same as that of the input documents. It also translates the original summaries to English using the machine translation facilities for Japanese and Korean.

Language Dependent Multi-Document Multilingual Summarization Approaches

A multi-document summarization system that can process a group of languages is called multi-document multilingual summarization system. The input to a language dependent multi-document multilingual summarization approach is a cluster of related documents coming from the different language sites.

Sarkar and Bandyopadhyay (2005) presented the architecture of multilingual summarization system for Indian languages. The architecture of the system proposed in (Sarkar and Bandyopadhyay, 2005) is shown in Figure 1.

The system shown in Figure 1 has three major components: several monolingual news clusterers, a multilingual news clusterer, and a news summarizer. The monolingual news clusterer receives a news stream from multiple online newspapers in its respective language, and directs them into several output news streams by using events. The multilingual news clusterer then matches and merges the news streams of the same event but in different languages in a cluster. The task for the multilingual clusterer is to align the news clusters in the same topic set, but in different languages. It is similar to document alignment in comparable corpus. The news summarizer summarizes the news stories for each event by creating the clusters of sentences (MU: meaningful units) and select-

Figure 1. Architecture of the multilingual summarization system

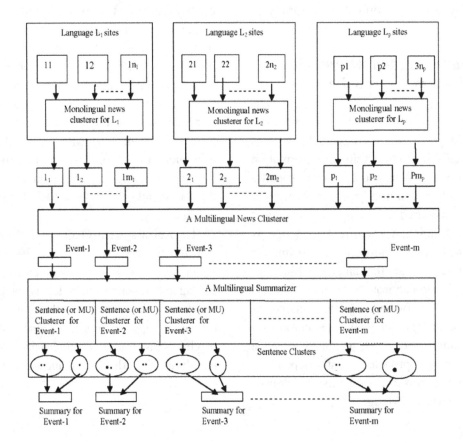

ing the representatives from each cluster to form the summary. The possible tasks for each component depend on the languages used.

Chen and Lin (2000) also describe a system whose architecture is almost similar to that of the system proposed in (Sarkar and Bandyopadhyay, 2005).

Evans and Klavans (2004) have developed a multilingual version of Columbia Newsblaster as a testbed for multilingual multi-document summarization. The system collects, clusters, and summarizes news documents from sources all over the world daily. It crawls news sites in many different countries, written in different languages, extracts the news text from the HTML pages, uses a variety of methods to translate the documents for clustering and summarization, and produces an English summary for each cluster.

Evans and McKeown (2005) presents an approach that identifies similarities and differences across documents written in different languages for summarizing topically clustered documents from two sources, English and machine translated Arabic texts. This approach to multilingual multi-document summarization clusters all input document sentences, and identifies sentence clusters that contain information exclusive to the Arabic documents, information exclusive to the English documents, and similar information between the two.

Wan el al. (2010) presents a cross-lingual multidocument summarization approach which is tested on the manually translated version of DUC 2001 dataset. In this approach, each English document set is summarized to produce a Chinese summary. This approach has several important steps: (1) prediction of the translation quality of each English sentence in the document set using the SVM regression method, (2) selection of the English summary sentences based on translation quality and informativeness, and (3) translation of the generated English summary to form the Chinese summary.

Wan (2011) proposes a cross-lingual multidocument summarization approach that uses the bilingual information from both the source and translated documents. Two summarization methods (SimFusion and CoRank) have been proposed to leverage the bilingual information in the graph-based ranking framework for cross-language summary extraction.

SOME EXISTING MULTILINGUAL SUMMARIZERS

Open Text Summarizer (OTS): This is a multilingual summarizer which is able to generate summaries in more than 25 languages, such as English, German, Spanish, Russian or Hebrew. This approach used in this system identifies keywords by means of word occurrence, and assigns a score to a sentence based on the keywords it contains. Some language-specific resources, such as stemmers and stop word lists are employed. It has been shown that this system obtains better performance than other multilingual text summarization systems (Yatsko and Vishnyakov, 2007).

MS Word 2007 Summarizer (MS Word): This summarizer is available with Microsoft Word 2007 and it also generates summaries in several languages. Since it is a commercial system, its implementation details are not revealed.

Essential Summarizer (Essential): This text summarization system is a commercial version of the one presented in (Lehmam, 2010). It relies on linguistic techniques to perform semantic analysis of written text, taking into account discursive elements of the text. It can produce summaries in twenty languages.

MULTILINGUAL SUMMARIZATION TASK AT DUC AND TAC

For summary evaluation, the Document Understanding Conference (DUC) (Over et al., 2007) was the main evaluation forum from 2000 until 2007. Over the course of its first six years DUC has examined automatic single and multi-document summarization of newspaper/wire articles, with both generic tasks and various focused tasks. Nowadays, the Text Analysis Conference (TAC)[1] provides a forum for assessment of different information access technologies including text summarization.

Out of the past DUCs and TACs, only a few has included multilingual text summarization tasks in the list of official tasks. DUC 2004 had two tasks, the task 3 and task 4 for cross-lingual single-document and multidocument summarization respectively. In DUC 2004, task 3 was to generate very short cross-lingual single-document summaries and task 4 was to generate short cross-lingual multi-document summaries. The data used for these tasks is obtained in three different ways: (1) automatic English translations of Arabic documents document (2) manual English translation of Arabic documents and (3) English translation produced by the MT (machine translation) system.

Recently, TAC 2011 Summarization Track had a task on multilingual text summarization (the task name was MultiLing task) that aimed to evaluate the application of (partially or fully) language-independent summarization algorithms on a variety of languages. Each system participating in the task had been called to provide summaries for a range of different languages, based on corresponding corpora. Participating systems applied their methods on at least two languages. Evaluation favored systems that applied their methods in more languages. The MultiLing task was to generate a single, fluent, representative summary from a set of documents describing an event sequence. The language of the document set was within a given range of languages. All documents in a set shared the same language. The output summaries were generated in the language of the source documents. The set of languages that were considered are: Arabic, Czech, English, French, Hebrew and Hindi. The evaluation of the

summaries was performed using automatic (AutoSummENG, ROUGE) and manual processes (Overall responsiveness score). The participating systems were 8, some of which providing summaries across all languages.

SUMMARY EVALUATION

Summary can be evaluated either intrinsically or extrinsically. Since intrinsic evaluation is more challenging and it has gained great attention in the last years, we only focus on this type of evaluation.

The summary evaluation methods can be broadly categorized as human evaluation methods and automatic (machine-based) evaluation methods. A human evaluation is done by comparing system-generated summaries with reference/model summaries by human judges. According to some predefined guidelines, the judges assign a score in a predefined scale to each summary under evaluation. Quantitative scores are given to the summaries based on the different qualitative features such as information content, fluency etc.

Informativeness of s summary has been commonly accessed employing *recall, precision and F-measure*. In this method, an automatic summary (peer summary) is compared to a human written one and the common sentences between them are counted. Nenkova (2006) defines recall based on which portion of sentences selected by human is also selected by the summarization system, whereas precision is defined as fraction of these sentences identified by the summarization system are correct. F-measure is defined as a combination of precision and recall. The main drawback of this measure is that it may evaluate two equally valid summaries differently. It may happen when the sentences in a peer summary poorly match with those in the model summary.

Relative utility was then proposed by Radev and Tam (2003) to overcome this drawback. In this method, multiple judges are allowed to assign scores to the sentences in a document based on how they are suitable for a summary. The score for a sentence ranges between 0 and 10. The higher a sentence is ranked, the more suitable for the summary is. Finally, a summary is evaluated using these weights to score sentences in a summary.

The Pyramid method (Nenkova et al., 2007) identifies information with same meaning across the model summaries called *summarization content units (SCUs)* that are used for comparison of information in summaries. SCUs emerge from annotation of a corpus of summaries and are not bigger than a clause. SCUs that appear in more manual summaries will get greater weights, so a pyramid will be formed after SCU annotation of manual summaries. At the top of the pyramid there are SCUs that appear in majority of the summaries and thus they have the greatest weight. The lower in the pyramid the SCU appears, the lower its weight is because it is contained in fewer summaries. The SCUs in peer summary are then compared against an existing pyramid to evaluate how much information agrees between the peer summary and model summary.

The above mentioned two valuation methods namely relative utility, pyramid method require some human annotations to identify important information content. The main problems with human evaluation are: (1) the evaluation process is tedious (2) it suffers from the lack of consistency. Two human judges may not agree on each other's judgments.

Automatic Summary Evaluation Metric

Automatic evaluation (machine based) is consistent with a judgment. The automatic evaluations may lack the linguistic skills and emotional perspective that a human has. Hence although automatic evaluation is not perfect compared to the human evaluation, it is popular primarily because the evaluation process is quick even if summaries to be evaluated are large in number. Since automatic evaluation is performed by a machine, it follows

a fixed logic and always produces the same result on a given summary. Since automatic evaluation processes are free from human bias, it provides a consistent way of comparing the various summarization systems.

ROUGE (Recall-Oriented Understudy for Gisting Evaluation)

It is an automatic summary evaluation tool. ROUGE has been developed based on the ideas used for developing BLEU (Bilingual Language Evaluation Understudy).

BLEU (Papineni et al., 2002) is an *n*-gram-based evaluation metric for machine translation. The BLEU considers precision metric which computes the percentage of *n*-grams in a system generated summary that match *n*-grams in the reference summaries. In BLEU, brevity penalty is applied if the candidate summary is shorter than the references. BLEU provides a precision measure because it measures how much of the content that appears in a candidate translation should properly appear in an ideal translation. As such it rewards systems that rarely say the wrong thing, but doesn't penalize systems that fail to say the right things. For this reason, BLEU has not been widely used for evaluation of summarization. To overcome the limitations of BLEU with respect to summary evaluation, University of Southern California's Information Sciences Institute (ISI) developed the recall-based metric called Recall Oriented Understudy of Gisting Evaluation (ROUGE) (Lin, 2004). ROUGE calculates the word *n*-gram overlap of a summary submitted for evaluation (peer) with a set of human-generated summaries (models). The *n*-gram overlap of a peer with the models is the number of *n*-grams in the peer that also occur in the models.

ROUGE was used in DUC 2004 for automatic evaluation of the summaries. It was the older version of the ROUGE package which was based on n-gram overlap between the system-produced and reference summaries. The older version of

ROUGE, such as ROUGE 1.4.2, reports separate scores for 1, 2, 3, and 4-gram matching between the model summaries and the generated summary. This version of ROUGE evaluates summaries using a recall-based measure that requires the length of system generated summary and reference summary to be the same. The score ROUGE-N is computed using the following formula:

$$ROUGE-N = \frac{\sum_{S\in(\text{Reference Summaries})} \sum_{gram_n \in S} \text{Count}_{\text{match}}(gram_n)}{\sum_{S\in(\text{Reference Summaries})} \sum_{gram_n \in S} \text{Count}(gram_n)} \quad (9)$$

where ROUGE-N is an n-gram recall between a candidate summary and a set of reference summaries, n stands for the length of the n-gram, $gram_n$ and $Count_{match}(gram_n)$ is the maximum number of n-grams co-occurring in a candidate summary and a set of reference summaries (Lin and Hovy, 2003). The older versions of ROUGE, such as ROUGE 1.4.2, used in the DUC 2004 evaluations produces only the recall score which is not always useful in distinguishing between a good summary and a bad summary because one can easily generate texts that score highly using the ROUGE-measurements but are not really good summaries. More recent versions of ROUGE such as ROUGE 1.5.5, which calculates both precision and recall values, is a good way to detect whether the system generated summaries are good or bad and it seems to be much harder to achieve high precision and recall than just a high recall. Some important ROUGE scores are discussed below.

- Rouge-N: it counts contiguous n-grams, where n ranges from 1 to 4.
- Rouge-L: it computes longest common subsequence. Given two sequences X and Y, a longest common subsequence of X and Y is a common subsequence with maximum length.

- Rouge-W: it is like Rouge-L but uses a weighting factor for longest number of consecutive matching words. ROUGE-W favors strings with consecutive matches.
- Rouge-S: it uses skip bigrams: pairs of words in sentence order, ignoring gaps. It allows arbitrary gaps in matches as LCS (Longest Common Subsequence) but count all in sequence pairs; while LCS only counts the longest subsequences. For example, the sentence, "police killed the gunman" has the following skip bigrams: ("police killed", "police the", "police gunman", "killed the", "killed gunman", "the gunman"). One can limit the maximum skip distance, between two in-order words that is allowed to form a skip-bigram. If the maximum skip distance is set to 4 then only word pairs of at most 4 words apart can form skip-bigrams.
- Rouge-SU: it includes unigrams in the skip bigrams.

ROUGE-1, ROUGE-2 and ROUGE-SU metrics have been widely used in the NLP community for automatic summary evaluation.

Though ROUGE is a novel automatic summary evaluation tool used for summary evaluation at many past DUC conferences organized by NIST (National Institute of Standards and Technology), it is not flawless. In (Sjobergh, 2007) it was shown that a very poor summary can easily get higher ROUGE scores.

AutosummENG *(Giannakopoulos et al., 2008)*

It is another automatic *n*-gram based summary evaluation method which is recently developed has been proven to have higher correlation with human judgments than ROUGE. This method differs from ROUGE in three main aspects: (1) the type of statistical information extracted (*n*-gram characters), (2) the representation used for the extracted information (graph), and (3) the method used for calculating similarities between the summaries. Here the comparison between the summaries is carried out by comparing their *n*-gram character graph representations. The degree of similarity between the graphs corresponding to the peer summary and the model summary is considered as score for summary evaluation.

Multilingual Summary Evaluation

Since a machine generated summary is evaluated by comparing it to a set of reference summaries, the summary evaluation methods which are used for evaluating summaries produced by monolingual summarizer can also be used for multilingual summary evaluation.

Since the methodologies (except basic element (BE)-based evaluation component (Hovy el al., 2006) of ROUGE package) used in implementing ROUGE and AutosummENG are language independent, these two have been used as the official tools for multilingual summary evaluation tasks at TAC 2011 (Giannakopoulos et al, 2011).

CONCLUSION AND FUTURE DIRECTIONS

Multilingual text summarization is expected to be able to summarize multiple documents coming from multiple sources where the languages for the sources are different. In fact, multilingual text summarization, in real sense, requires merging multi-source information in several languages and this makes multilingual summarization task more challenging.

Though many language independent text summarization techniques have been tested for multiple languages, there are a few number of multilingual summarization systems that can summarize a cluster of documents written in the different languages. The main difficulties for developing this kind of multilingual summarization systems

are unavailability of multilingual resources and relatively slow progress in the machine translation system development for so many languages across the countries throughout the world.

Though multilingual multidocument text summarization in resource poor languages for which the machine translation systems are not matured till date is not an easy task, it can be attempted by linking the sentences in different languages across the documents and grouping them to produce the themes and selecting representative sentences from each theme to create a summary in the language specified by the user. In this method, instead of using document level translation at the initial stage of the summarization process, the translation of the representative sentences can done at the later stage of the summarization process to reduce the translation overhead and translational error. For linking the sentences in different languages across the documents, resolution of word level translational ambiguities, developments of modules for named entity recognition, transliteration and matching the named entities across the documents written in different languages are required. Machine learning algorithms can be used to learn from a corpus of sentence pairs and develop a model that can determine whether a given pair of sentences written in different languages is topically linked or not.

REFERENCES

Baxendale, P. (1958). Man-made index for technical literature - An experiment. *IBM Journal of Research and Development*, 2(4), 354–361. doi:10.1147/rd.24.0354

Brandow, R., Mitze, K., & Rau, L. F. (1995). Automatic condensation of electronic publications by sentence selection. *Information Processing & Management*, 31(5), 675–685. doi:10.1016/0306-4573(95)00052-I

Brin, S., & Page, L. (1998). The anatomy of a large-scale hypertextual web search engine. *Computer Networks and ISDN Systems, 30*(1-7), 107–117.

Chen, H. H., & Lin, C. J. (2000). A multilingual news summarizer. In *Proceedings of the 18th International Conference on Computational Linguistics* (pp. 159–165). IEEE.

Edmundson, H. P. (1969). New methods in automatic extracting. *Journal of the Association for Computing Machinery, 16*(2), 264–285. doi:10.1145/321510.321519

Erkan, G., & Radev, D. R. (2004). LexRank: Graph-based lexical centrality as salience in text summarization. *Journal of Artificial Intelligence Research, 22,* 457–479.

Evans, D., & McKeown, K. (2005). Identifying similarities and differences across English and Arabic news. In *Proceedings of International Conference on Intelligence Analysis* (pp. 23–30). IEEE.

Evans, D. K., & Klavans, J. L. (2004). Columbia newsblaster: Multilingual news summarization on the web. In *Demonstration Papers at HLT-NAACL 2004*. Boston, MA: NAACL. doi:10.3115/1614025.1614026

Giannakopoulos, G., El-Haj, M., Favre, B., Litvak, M., Steinberger, J., & Varma, V. (2011). Multiling pilot overview. In *Proceedings of TAC 2011*. TAC.

Giannakopoulos, G., Karkaletsis, V., Vouros, G., & Stamatopoulos, P. (2008). Summarization system evaluation revisited: N-gram graphs. *ACM Transactions on Speech and Language Processing, 5*(3), 5. doi:10.1145/1410358.1410359

Gong, Y., & Liu, X. (2001). Generic text summarization using relevance measure and latent semantic analysis. In *Proceedings of the 24th ACM SIGIR Conference on Research and Development in Information Retrieval* (pp. 19–25). ACM.

Hatzivassiloglou, V., Klavans, J. L., Holcombe, M. L., Barzilay, R., Kan, M.-Y., & McKeown, K. R. (2001). SimFinder: A flexible clustering tool for summarization. In *Proceedings of NAACL, Workshop on Automatic Summarization*. Pittsburgh, PA: NAACL.

Hovy, E., & Lin, C. Y. (1999). Automated text summarization in SUMMARIST. In I. Mani, & M. Maybury (Eds.), *Advances in automatic text summarization* (pp. 81–94). Cambridge, MA: MIT Press.

Hovy, E., Lin, C. Y., Zhou, L., & Fukumoto, J. (2006). Automated summarization evaluation with basic elements. In *Proceedings of the Fifth Conference on Language Resources and Evaluation* (LREC 2006) (pp. 604-611). LREC.

Kabadjov, M., Atkinson, M., Steinberger, J., Steinberger, R., & Goot, E. V. D. (2010). News-Gist: A multilingual statistical news summarizer. In *Proceedings of the European Conference on Machine Learning and Knowledge Discovery in Databases: Part III* (pp. 591–594). IEEE.

Lehmam, A. (2010). Essential summarizer: Innovative automatic text summarization software in twenty languages. In Adaptivity, Personalization and Fusion of Heterogeneous Information (pp. 216–217). Academic Press.

Lin, C.-Y. (1999). Training a selection function for extraction. In *Proceedings of the Eighteenth International Conference on Information and Knowledge Management* (CIKM'99) (pp. 1-8). CIKM.

Lin, C. Y. (2004). Rouge: A package for automatic evaluation of summaries. In *Proceedings of the ACL-04 Workshop* (pp. 74-81). ACL.

Lin, C.-Y., & Hovy, E. (1997). Identifying topics by position. In *Proceedings of the 5th Applied Natural Language Processing Conference* (pp. 283–290). New Brunswick, NJ: Association for Computational Linguistics.

Lin, C.-Y., & Hovy, E. (2003). Automatic evaluation of summaries using n-gram concurrence. In *Proceedings of 2003 Language Technology Conference* (HLT-NAACL 2003). Edmonton, Canada: NAACL.

Litvak, M., Last, M., & Friedman, M. (2010). A new approach to improving multilingual summarization using a genetic algorithm. In *Proceedings of the 48th Annual Meeting of the Association for Computational Linguistics* (pp. 927–936). ACL.

Luhn, H. P. (1958). The automatic creation of literature abstracts. *IBM Journal of Research and Development, 2*(2), 159–165. doi:10.1147/rd.22.0159

Mani, I. (2001). Automatc summarization, book, volume 3 of natural language processing. Amsterdam: John Benjamins Publishing Company.

Mani, I., & Maybury, M. (Eds.). (1999). *Advances in automatic text summarization*. Cambridge, MA: MIT Press.

Mihalcea, R. (2005). Language independent extractive summarization. In *Proceedings of the 20th National Conference on Artificial Intelligence* (pp. 1688–1689). AAAI.

Nenkova, A. (2006). *Summarization evaluation for text and speech: Issues and approaches.* INTERSPEECH.

Nenkova, A., Passonneau, R., & McKeown, K. (2007). The pyramid method: Incorporating human content selection variation in summarization evaluation. *ACM Transactions on Speech and Language Processing, 4*(2), 4. doi:10.1145/1233912.1233913

Neto, J. L., Santos, A. D., Kaestner, C. A. A., & Freitas, A. A. (2000). *Generating text summaries through the relative importance of topics* (pp. 300–309). Lecture Notes in Computer Science Berlin: Springer. doi:10.1007/3-540-44399-1_31

Ogden, W., Cowie, J., Davis, M., Ludovik, E., Molina-Salgado, H., & Shin, H. (1999). Getting information from documents you cannot read: An interactive cross-language text retrieval and summarization system. In *Proceedings of SIGIR/DL Workshop on Multilingual Information Discovery and Access (MIDAS)*. ACM.

Over, P., Dang, H., & Harman, D. (2007). DUC in context. *Information Processing & Management, 43*(6), 1506–1520. doi:10.1016/j.ipm.2007.01.019

Papineni, K., Roukos, S., Ward, T., & Zhu, W. J. (2002). BLEU: A method for automatic evaluation of machine translation. In *Proceedings of the 40th Annual Meeting on Association for Computational Linguistics* (pp. 311-318). ACL.

Patel, A., Siddiqui, T., & Tiwary, U. S. (2007). A language independent approach to multilingual text summarization. In Proceedings of Large Scale Semantic Access to Content (Text, Image, Video, and Sound), RIAO 2007 (pp. 123–132). RIAO.

Radev, D., Allison, T., Blair-Goldensohn, S., Blitzer, J., Celebi, A., & Drabek, E. … Zhang, Z. (2004). MEAD - A platform for multidocument multilingual text summarization. In *Proceedings of the 4ᵗʰ International Conference on Language Resources and Evaluation*. IEEE.

Radev, D., Hovy, E., & McKeown, K. (2002). Introduction to the special issue on text summarization. *Computational Linguistics, 28*(4). doi:10.1162/089120102762671927

Radev, D. R., Jing, H., Sty, M., & Tam, D. (2004). Centroid-based summarization of multiple documents. *Journal of Information Processing and Management, 40*(6), 919–938. doi:10.1016/j.ipm.2003.10.006

Radev, D. R., & Tam, D. (2003). Summarization evaluation using relative utility. In *Proceedings of the Twelfth International Conference on Information and Knowledge Management* (pp. 508-511). IEEE.

Sarkar, K. (2009). Sentence clustering-based summarization of multiple text documents. *TECHNIA – International Journal of Computing Science and Communication Technologies, 2*(1).

Sarkar, K. (2012a). Bengali text summarization by sentence extraction. In *Proceedings of International Conference on Business and Information Management* (pp. 233-245). IEEE.

Sarkar, K. (2012b). An approach to summarizing Bengali news documents. In *Proceedings of the International Conference on Advances in Computing, Communications and Informatics*. ACM.

Sarkar, K., & Bandyopadhyay, S. (2005). A multilingual text summarization system for Indian languages. In *Proceedings of Simple 2005*. IIT Kharagpur.

Sjöbergh, J. (2007). Older versions of the ROUGEeval summarization evaluation system were easier to fool. *Information Processing & Management, 43*(6), 1500–1505. doi:10.1016/j.ipm.2007.01.014

Sparck-Jones, K. (1999). Automatic summarizing: Factors and directions. In I. Mani, & M. Maybury (Eds.), *Advances in automatic text summarization*. Cambridge, MA: MIT Press.

Steinberger, J., & Jezek, K. (2004). Text summarization and singular value decomposition. *Lecture Notes in Computer Science*, 245–254. doi:10.1007/978-3-540-30198-1_25

Wan, X. (2011). Using bilingual information for cross-language document summarization. In *Proceedings of ACL*. ACL.

Wan, X., Li, H., & Xiao, J. (2010). Cross-language document summarization based on machine translation quality prediction. In *Proceedings of ACL 2010*. ACL.

Wan, X., & Yang, J. (2006). Improved affinity graph based multi-document summarization. In *Proceedings of HLT-NAACL, Companion Volume: Short Papers* (pp. 181–184). NAACL.

Yatsko, V., & Vishnyakov, T. (2007). A method for evaluating modern systems of automatic text summarization. *Automatic Documentation and Mathematical Linguistics, 41*, 93–103. doi:10.3103/S0005105507030041

ADDITIONAL READING

Carbonell, J., & Goldstein, J. (1998t). The use of MMR, diversity-based reranking for reordering documents and producing summaries. In Proceedings of the 21st annual international ACM SIGIR conference on Research and development in information retrieval (pp. 335-336). ACM.

Celikyilmaz, A., & Hakkani-Tur, D. (2010). A hybrid hierarchical model for multi-document summarization. In Proceedings of the 48th Annual Meeting of the Association for Computational Linguistics (pp. 815-824). Association for Computational Linguistics.

Das, D., & Martins, A. F. (2007). A survey on automatic text summarization. Literature Survey for the Language and Statistics II course at CMU.

Evans, D. K., McKeown, K., & Klavans, J. L. (2005). Similarity-based multilingual multi-document summarization.

Fung, P., & Ngai, G. (2006). One story, one flow: Hidden Markov Story Models for multilingual multidocument summarization. [TSLP]. *ACM Transactions on Speech and Language Processing, 3*(2), 1–16. doi:10.1145/1149290.1151099

Gupta, S., Nenkova, A., & Jurafsky, D. (2007, June). Measuring importance and query relevance in topic-focused multi-document summarization. In Proceedings of the 45th Annual Meeting of the ACL on Interactive Poster and Demonstration Sessions (pp. 193-196). Association for Computational Linguistics.

Hachey, B., Murray, G., & Reitter, D. (2006). Dimensionality reduction aids term co-occurrence based multi-document summarization. In Proceedings of the Workshop on Task-Focused Summarization and Question Answering (pp. 1-7). Association for Computational Linguistics.

Hakkani-Tur, D., & Tur, G. (2007). Statistical sentence extraction for information distillation. In Acoustics, Speech and Signal Processing, 2007. ICASSP 2007. IEEE International Conference on (Vol. 4, pp. IV-1). IEEE.

Hassel, M., & Mazdak, N. (2004). FarsiSum: a Persian text summarizer. In Proceedings of the Workshop on Computational Approaches to Arabic Script-based Languages (pp. 82-84). Association for Computational Linguistics.

Hovy, E. (2003). The Oxford Handbook of Computational Linguistics Oxford University Press, Oxford, 2003, chapter 32.

Ježek, K., & Steinberger, J. (2008). Automatic Text Summarization (The state of the art 2007 and new challenges). *Proc. of Znalosti, 2008*, 1–12.

Ko, Y., & Seo, J. (2008). An effective sentence-extraction technique using contextual information and statistical approaches for text summarization. *Pattern Recognition Letters*, *29*(9), 1366–1371. doi:10.1016/j.patrec.2008.02.008

Kupiec, J., Pedersen, J., & Chen, F. (1995). A trainable document summarizer. In Proceedings of the 18th annual international ACM SIGIR conference on Research and development in information retrieval (pp. 68-73). ACM.

Lin, C. Y., & Hovy, E. (1997). Identifying topics by position. In Proceedings of the fifth conference on Applied natural language processing (pp. 283-290). Association for Computational Linguistics.

Nenkova, A. (2005). Automatic text summarization of newswire: Lessons learned from the document understanding conference. In AAAI (Vol. 5, pp. 1436-1441

Nenkova, A., & McKeown, K. (2012). A survey of text summarization techniques. In Mining Text Data (pp. 43-76). Springer US.

Qazvinian, V., Radev, D. R., Mohammad, S. M., Dorr, B. J., Zajic, D. M., Whidby, M., & Moon, T. (2013). Generating Extractive Summaries of Scientific Paradigms. [JAIR]. *Journal of Artificial Intelligence Research*, *46*, 165–201.

Radev, D. R., & McKeown, K. R. (1998). Generating natural language summaries from multiple on-line sources. *Computational Linguistics*, *24*(3), 470–500.

Saggion, H., & Lapalme, G. (2002). Generating indicative-informative summaries with sumUM. *Computational Linguistics*, *28*(4), 497–526. doi:10.1162/089120102762671963

Sarkar, K., Nasipuri, M., & Ghose, S. (2011). Using Machine Learning for Medical Document Summarization. *International Journal of Database Theory and Application*, *4*, 31–49.

Sekine, S., & Nobata, C. (2003). A survey for multi-document summarization. In *Proceedings of the HLT-NAACL 03 on Text summarization workshop* (pp. 65–72). Volume 5.

Spärck Jones, K. (2007). Automatic summarising: The state of the art. *Information Processing & Management*, *43*(6), 1449–1481. doi:10.1016/j.ipm.2007.03.009

KEY TERMS AND DEFINITIONS

Abstract: A summary, which represents the subject matter of the article with the text units, which are generated by reformulating the salient units selected from the input. An abstract may contain some text units, which are not present in the input text.

Automatic Text Summarization: A process to produce a condensed representation of the content of its input for human consumption.

Cross-Language Document Summarization: It is a type of multilingual summarization where a summary is produced in a language (e.g. Chinese) different from the language (e.g. English) of the source documents.

Extract: A summary consisting of a number of salient text units selected from the input.

Multidocument Summarization: a summarization process that creates a summary from multiple documents describing the similar topics or events.

Multilingual Document Clustering: A process to partition the documents written in different languages into groups by matching and merging the documents describing the similar events in a group.

Multilingual Summarization: A process which can handle several languages and produce a summary in the language of the input or the language specified by the user.

Single Document Summarization: A summarization process that creates a summary from one document only.

ENDNOTES

[1]   http://www.nist.gov/tac

Chapter 12
Aspects of Multilingual News Summarisation

Josef Steinberger
University of West Bohemia, Czech Republic

Hristo Tanev
Joint Research Centre, Italy

Ralf Steinberger
Joint Research Centre, Italy

Vanni Zavarella
Joint Research Centre, Italy

Marco Turchi
Fondazione Bruno Kessler, Italy

ABSTRACT

In this chapter, the authors discuss several pertinent aspects of an automatic system that generates summaries in multiple languages for sets of topic-related news articles (multilingual multi-document summarisation), gathered by news aggregation systems. The discussion follows a framework based on Latent Semantic Analysis (LSA) because LSA was shown to be a high-performing method across many different languages. Starting from a sentence-extractive approach, the authors show how domain-specific aspects can be used and how a compression and paraphrasing method can be plugged in. They also discuss the challenging problem of summarisation evaluation in different languages. In particular, the authors describe two approaches: the first uses a parallel corpus and the second statistical machine translation.

INTRODUCTION

News gathering and analysis systems, such as *Google News* or the *Europe Media Monitor*[1], gather tens or hundreds of thousands of articles per day. Efforts to summarise such highly redundant news data are motivated by the need to automatically inform news end users of the main contents of up to hundreds of news articles talking on a particular

event, e.g. by sending a breaking news text message or an email. Due to the high multilinguality of the raw news data, any summariser must be multilingual.

In this chapter, we first present an overview of summarisation approaches and a discussion of their possible application to other languages. We study deeply one particular approach based on Latent Semantic Analysis (LSA) (Steinberger et al., 2012) because LSA was shown to be a high-performing method across many different

DOI: 10.4018/978-1-4666-5019-0.ch012

languages in the multilingual task of the Text Analysis Conference(TAC[2]) in 2011. We start from the basic LSA approach (Steinberger and Jezek, 2009).

We then discuss the more challenging task of *aspect-based* summarisation, as defined at TAC'2010[3]. In the aspect scenario, the goal is to produce a summary from articles about a specific event which falls into a predefined domain (e.g. terrorist attacks), for which we have defined aspects that should be mentioned in the summary (e.g. what, when, where happened; who were the victims, perpetrators, etc.). This scenario forces systems to make use of information extraction and to look at the content selection from a more semantic point of view. We will show how an event extraction system can be used to detect pieces of required information and then to extract the related content (Steinberger et al., 2011).

The majority of approaches to automatically summarising documents are limited to selecting the most important sentences. We will therefore dedicate some effort to discussing sentence compression/paraphrasing approaches aiming at more human-like summaries, which typically consist of shorter sentences than automatic summaries. As the ultimate goal is to apply the approach to multiple languages, we will discuss how far we can get with a statistical sentence compression/paraphrasing method (Steinberger et al., 2010).

TAC/DUC evaluation campaigns were the most important events to perform large-scale experiments and discuss evaluation methodology in the last years. We follow the TAC roadmap and discuss the multilingual issue. Evaluation of automatically produced summaries in different languages is a challenging problem for the summarisation community because human efforts are multiplied to create model summaries for each language. At TAC'11, six research groups spent a considerable effort on creating evaluation resources in seven languages (Giannakopoulos et al., 2012). Thus compared to the monolingual evaluation, which requires writing model summaries and evaluating

outputs of each system by hand, in the multilingual setting we need to obtain translations of all documents into the target language, write model summaries and evaluate the peer summaries for all the languages. We will discuss findings of the TAC's multilingual task which was the first shared task to evaluate summaries in more than two languages. We will then propose two possibilities how to lower the huge annotation costs:

First, we will consider using a parallel corpus for the multilingual evaluation task. Because of the unavailability of parallel corpora suitable for news summarisation we will follow an effort to create such a corpus (Turchi et al., 2010). The approach is based on the manual selection of the most important sentences in a cluster of documents from a sentence-aligned parallel corpus, and by projecting the sentence selection in one language to various target languages. Although model summaries were not created, and texts were taken from a slightly different genre (news commentaries), the evaluation results are directly comparable across languages.

Second, we will discuss using Machine Translation (MT) to achieve multilingual summarisation evaluation. In the last fifteen years, research on MT has made great strides allowing human beings to understand documents written in various languages. Nowadays, on-line services such as Google Translate and Bing Translator can translate text into more than 50 languages, showing that MT is not a pipe-dream. We thus investigate how machine translation can be plugged in to evaluate summaries in other languages. We will try to see whether machine-translated models can perform close to manually created evaluation models (Steinberger and Turchi, 2012).

The remainder of the chapter is organized as follows: It contains two main sections, each discussing several aspects: In the first section, we describe several approaches aimed at building coherent summaries by selecting the most informative sentences from a set of documents. We also describe the specific case of aspect-based summarisation, importance of temporal analysis and that of compression and paraphrasing techniques. The second section is dedicated to issues concerning the evaluation of multilingual summaries. With that regard, we will investigate how parallel data and how statistical machine translation can be used. After the core two sections, we follow performance of the LSA-based summariser, as a representative of multilingual approaches, at the TAC 2008-2011 evaluations in the results section.

BACKGROUND

Automatic news summarisation deals with the problem of producing a succinct informative gist for a set of news articles about the same topic. The aim of the task could be that the target language of the summary be the same as the input articles (standard single-/multi-document summarisation) (Nenkova and Louis, 2008) or that the languages of summary/input articles be different (cross-language document summarisation) (Wan et al., 2010). Moreover, the task of handling several languages, with summary and input articlesbeing in the same language, has been termed as multilingual summarisation (Litvak et al., 2010).

Summarisation has been an active area of research for several decades (Luhn, 1958; Edmundson, 1969), but in particular over the past seventeen years. The area initially focused on single-document summarisation (Mani and Maybury, 1999), a fact reflected by the first US NIST-organized *Document Understanding Conference* (DUC) evaluation exercises (Over et al., 2007). Then, over the past decade the emphasis shifted to multi-document summarisation exemplified by latter DUCs followed by the *Text Analysis Conference* (TAC). However, it has been only recently that interest in multilingual summarisation has risen (Kabadjov et al., 2013; Litvak et al., 2010).

MULTILINGUAL SUMMARISATION

Extractive Summarisation

Work on Text Summarisation has been quite varied and abundant. A basic processing model for Text Summarisation, proposed by Sparck-Jones (1999) comprises three main stages: source text interpretation (I) to construct a source representation (e.g., lexical chains, semantic graphs, discourse models), source representation transformation(T) to form a summary representation (e.g., Singular Value Decomposition, SVD), and summary text generation (G). More practically-motivated approaches that use shallow linguistic analysis and only partially cover this processing model, as well as more ambitious ones attempting all three stages using deep semantic analysis have been proposed in the literature.

There are approaches based on shallow linguistic analysis such as word frequencies (Luhn, 1958), cue phrases (e.g., "in conclusion", "in summary") and location (e.g., title, section headings) (Edmundson, 1969); there are machine learning approaches that combine a number of surface features (Kupiec et al., 1995) and/or more elaborate features exploiting discourse structure (Teufel and Moens, 1999) to train classifiers using specialized corpora formed by pairs of documents and their hand-written summaries; there are also more sophisticated approaches, but still working at the surface level, exploiting cohesive relations like co-reference (Boguraev and Kennedy, 1999) and lexical cohesion (Barzilay and Elhadad, 1999) to identify salience or purely lexical approaches trying to identify 'implicit topics' by conflating words using methods inspired by Latent Semantic Analysis (LSA) (Gong and Liu, 2002); using yet deeper linguistic analysis, there are approaches purely based on discourse structure (e.g., RST) (Marcu, 1999) and others combining discourse structure with surface features (Hovy and Lin, 1999) or lexical with higher level semantic information such as anaphora (Steinberger et al., 2007); and finally there are knowledge-rich approaches, where the source undergoes a substantial semantic analysis during the process of filling in a predefined template (McKcown and Radev, 1995) or the source data is available in a more structured way (i.e., events have been identified already) (Maybury, 1999).

Summarisation Based on LSA

Approaches based on term co-occurrence (e.g. LSA) represent a good base for building a language-independent (or multilingual) summariser. The LSA approach (Steinberger and Ježek, 2009) first builds a term-by-sentence matrix from the source, then applies Singular Value Decomposition (SVD) and finally uses the resulting matrices to identify and extract the most salient sentences. SVD finds the latent (orthogonal) dimensions, which in simple terms correspond to the different topics discussed in the source.

More formally, it constructs the terms by sentences association matrix A. Each element of A indicates the weighted frequency of a given term in a given sentence. Having m distinguished terms and n sentences in the documents under consideration the size of A is m x n. Element a_{ij} of A represents the weighted frequency of term i in sentence j and is defined as:

$$a_{i,j} = L_{i,j} \cdot G_i,$$

where $L_{i,j}$ is the local weight of term i in sentence j and G_i is the global weight of term i in the document set. The weighting scheme found to work best (Steinberger et al., 2007) uses a binary local weight and an entropy-based global weight:

$$L_{i,j} = 1 \text{ if term } i \text{ appears at least once in sentence } j; \text{ otherwise } L_{i,j} = 0,$$

$$G_i = 1 - \sum_{j=0}^{j<n} \frac{p_{i,j} \log p_{i,j}}{\log n}, p_{i,j} = \frac{t_{i,j}}{g_i},$$

where $t_{i,j}$ is the frequency of term i in sentence j, g_i is the total number of times that term i occurs in the whole set of documents and n is the number of sentences in the set.

After that step Singular Value Decomposition (SVD) is applied to the above matrix. The SVD of an m x n matrix is defined as:

$$A = U \cdot S \cdot V^T,$$

where U (m x n) is a column-orthonormal matrix, whose columns are called left singular vectors. The matrix contains representations of terms expressed in the newly created (latent) dimensions. S (n x n) is a diagonal matrix, whose diagonal elements are non-negative singular values sorted in descending order. V^T (n x n) is a row-orthonormal matrix which contains representations of sentences expressed in the latent dimensions. The dimensionality of the matrices is reduced to r most important dimensions and thus, we receive matrices U' (m x r), S' (r x r) a V'^T (r x n). The value of r can be set according to the summarisation ratio ($r = summarisation\_ratio \cdot n$). For example, having 200 sentences to be summarised to 5%, r will be set up to 10. Another possibility is to learn the optimal r from the training data (Steinberger and Ježek, 2009).

From the mathematical point of view SVD maps the m-dimensional space specified by matrix A to the r-dimensional singular space. From an NLP perspective, what SVD does is to derive the latent semantic structure of the document set represented by matrix A: i.e. a breakdown of the original documents into r linearly-independent base vectors which express the main 'topics' of the document set. SVD can capture interrelationships among terms, so that terms and sentences can be clustered on a 'semantic' basis rather than on the basis of words only. Furthermore, as demonstrated in [4], if a word combination pattern is salient and recurring in a document set, this pattern will be captured and represented by one of the singular vectors. The magnitude of the corresponding singular value indicates the importance degree of this pattern within the document set. Any sentences containing this word combination pattern will be projected along this singular vector, and the sentence that best represents this pattern will have the largest index value with this vector. Assuming that each particular word combination pattern describes a certain topic in the document (LSA topic), each singular vector can be viewed as representing such a topic (Ding, 2005),the magnitude of its singular value representing the degree of importance of this topic.

Matrix V^T contains representation of sentences in the LSA topics and S contains importance of those topics. Thus their product, matrix $F = S \bullet V^T$, represent the sentence latent space weighted by topic importance. Sentence selection starts with measuring the length (Euclidean norm) of sentence vectors in matrix F. The length of the vector can be viewed as a measure for importance of that sentence within the top LSA topics. It was called *co-occurrence sentence score* in (Steinberger et al., 2011). The sentence with the largest score is selected as the first to go to the summary (its corresponding vector in F is denoted as f_{best}). After placing it in the summary, the topic/sentence distribution in matrix F is changed by subtracting the information contained in that sentence:

$$F^{(it+1)} = F^{(it)} - \frac{f_{best} \cdot f_{best}^T}{f_{best}^2} \cdot F^{(it)} \qquad (1)$$

The vector lengths of similar sentences are decreased, thus preventing within-summary redundancy. After the subtraction of information in the selected sentence, the process continues with the sentence which has the largest co-occurrence sentence score computed on the updated matrix F. The process is iteratively repeated until the required summary length is reached.

Aspect-Driven Summarisation

TAC'10 encouraged a deeper semantic analysis of the source documents by its new Guided summarisation task. Summarisers were given a list of aspects for each article category, and the summary should include those aspects if possible. The task naturally led to the integration with information extraction tools.

Steinberger et al. (2011) proposed an approach which works in multiple languages. It used an event extraction system that is focused on similar issues as the categories defined for TAC'10. For capturing other aspects they automatically learned terms semantically related to a manually created set of seed terms. The aim was to select frequently mentioned information, whilst at the same time making sure that this information also captures the required aspects. Thus, a combination of the co-occurrence-based information from LSA and the aspect information coming from the event extraction system was proposed.

The event extraction system (NEXUS), which was used in the experiments, analyses news articles reporting on violent events, natural or man-made disasters (see Tanev et al. (2008) for a detailed system description). The system identifies the type of the event (e.g., flooding, explosion, assassination, kidnapping, air attack, etc.), number and description of the victims, as well as descriptions of the perpetrators and the means used by them. For example for the text *"Three people were shot dead and five were injured in a shootout"*, NEXUS will return an event structure with three slots filled: The *event type slot* will be set to *shooting*; the *dead victims slot* will be set to *three people*; and the *injured slot* will be set to *five*. Event extraction is deployed as a part of the EMM family of applications, described in (R.Steinberger et al., 2009). NEXUS relies on a mixture of manually created linguistic rules, linear patterns, acquired through machine learning procedures, plus domain knowledge, represented as domain-specific heuristics and taxonomies. In the summarisation experiments the event extraction system was run on each news article from the corpus and the extracted slots were mapped to the summarisation aspects.

It was found out that some of the aspects, relevant to the summarisation task, correspond to the information extracted by NEXUS. In particular, the aspects *what happened, perpetrators* and *who affected* have corresponding slots in the event structures of NEXUS.

In our summarisation experiments we ran the event extraction system on each news article from the corpus and we mapped extracted slots to summarisation aspects. This was done in the following way: The event type (e.g., terrorist attack) was mapped to the aspect *what happened*; the slot *perpetrator* was mapped to the aspect *perpetrators*; and the values for the aspect *who affected* were obtained as a union of the event slots: *dead victims, injured, arrested, displaced, kidnapped, released hostages* and *people left without homes*. At the end, from a fragment like: *"three people died and many were injured"*, the system will extract two values for the aspect *who affected*, namely *"three people"* and *"many"*.

For the other aspects lexica were generated using *Ontopopulis*, a system for the automatic learning of semantic classes, based on distributional semantics (see Tanev et al. (2006) for algorithm overview and evaluation). As an input, it accepts a list of words, which belong to a certain semantic class, e.g. *"disasters"*, and then it learns additional words, which belong to the same class, e.g. *"earthquake"*, *"flooding"*, etc. Clearly, the system output needs to be manually cleaned, in order to build an accurate lexicon. Since the terms are ordered by reliability (more reliable terms are at the top), the users can review the list top-down deciding where to stop on the basis of their availability or the quality of the list around the point reached within the list. The unrevised items are discarded. Another possibility is to skip the manual reviewing process and take all the terms up to a certain threshold. This approach, however, cannot guarantee very high accuracy.

Four lexica were learned using Ontopopulis, followed by manual cleaning. Each lexicon was relevant to a specific summary aspect. The four aspects covered by our lexica are: *"damages"*, *"countermeasures"*, *"resource"*, and *"charges"*. Here we give a short sample from each of the learned lexica:

1. **Damages:** Damaged, destroyed, badly damaged, extensively damaged, gutted, torched, severely damaged, burnt, burned;
2. **Countermeasures:** Operation, rescue operation, rescue, evacuation, treatment, assistance, relief, military operation, police operation, security operation, aid;
3. **Resource:** Water, food, species, drinking water, electricity, gas, forests, fuel, natural gas;
4. **Charges:** Rape, kidnapping, aggravated, murder, attempted murder, robbery, aggravated assault, theft, armed robbery.

The words and multi-word units from these four lexicons were used to trigger the corresponding summary aspects.

The identified aspects were used to boost the co-occurrence-based scores of the sentences that contained them. For each document set an aspect-by-sentence matrix which contained Boolean values to store an aspect's presence/absence in sentences was built. The length of the sentence vector in the aspect matrix worked as a booster for the co-occurrence score. After selecting a sentence, the influence of the aspects mentioned there was lowered. For details see Steinberger et al. (2011).

Temporal Analysis

Temporal analysis is important in various summarisation subtasks. It can help to identify date and time of the event in the case of event-focused topics (the *when* aspect in the case of the guided summarisation task). It can provide important features for summary sentence ordering in the case of story-focused summaries. Steinberger et al. (2012) integrated into the processing chain a temporal analysis module which deals with the detection and normalisation of so called temporal expressions (timex), whose extent and classification are defined in partial compliance with the TIMEX2 standard (Ferro et al., 2005).

Temporal expressions are categorized into a small set of temporal types (Date, Duration, Period and Set), and include constructions such as numerical and non-numerical dates, underspecified dates ("in March 2002"), absolute, relative or deictic expressions (e.g. "in March 2002", "in March", "last month", respectively), fuzzy time references ("in a few months") and their compositions ("a year before last Monday").

Timex processing consists of a Recognition and a Normalization stage. In the Recognition phase, they are detected and segmented in text through local finite-state parsing performed by a cascade of hand-coded, partially language-dependent rules. Rules build a more abstract, intermediate typed feature structure-like representation of the temporal expressions, which is then exploited by a language-independent Normalization module. This latter performs, first, "anchor selection", that is it determines and maintains a reference time for relative timex resolution, by starting using the article creation date and updating it along the resolution process according to a simple heuristic: find the closest preceding resolved timex, within the same sentence, with a compatible level of granularity (e.g. a relative timex such as "in the afternoon" can be resolved by a day granularity timex like "the day after" but not by "in 2010"). Then, it uses the reference time to resolve relative timexes, computes exact calendar values of the time expressions and finally normalizes them according to the machine-readable TIMEX2 standard (Zavarella and Tanev, in press) Finally, the

most frequent normalized timex of type Date in the article set was simply taken as the time of the target event. The whole method is highly limited in recall by exclusively focusing on explicit temporal expressions and ignoring other temporal relation markers. Also, anaphoric event references in text are not detected, so that a sentence containing, for example, the phrase "*after the attack on Bagdad*", will not trigger any additional piece of temporal information, with respect to a previously detected terrorist attack event.

Compression and Paraphrasing Techniques

Empirical evidence shows that human summaries contain on average more and shorter sentences than system summaries (6 sentences vs. 4 sentences in TAC'09 data – Turchi et al., 2010). By compressing and/or rephrasing, the saved space in the summary could be filled in by the next most salient sentences, and thus the summary can cover more content from the source texts. Turchi et al. (2010) and Steinberger et al. (2012) tried to investigate language-independent possibilities to achieve this goal. The initial experimental results showed that the approach is feasible, since it produced summaries, which when evaluated against the TAC'09 data yield ROUGE scores comparable to the average of the participating systems. However, it achieved lower scores compared to the sentence-extractive summariser.

The approach starts by identifying the most salient terms in each selected sentence. For each term it computes the term salience score from the LSA. Matrix U contains representation of terms in the LSA topics and S contains importance of those topics. Thus their product, matrix $T = U \cdot S$, represents the term latent space weighted by topic importance. Notice the analogy with the LSA-based sentence selection approach. For each term i, the salience score is given by $\|t_i\|$. In addition, language model probabilities up to 4-grams were computed. The salience score should reflect the local importance of the term within the document set (mainly nouns) and language model probabilities should add the globally important terms (e.g. verbs). After normalising scores of each feature and combining them, each term ended up with a score reflecting its importance in the sentence. The final term sequence consisted of the top 70% terms. To make the sequence more readable, the sentences were reconstructed by the noisy-channel model primarily used by SMT systems, adding the most probable content (mainly stopwords) to connect the sentence fragments. The interpretation of the noisy channel in this application consists of looking at a stemmed string without stopwords and imagining that it was originally a long string and that someone removed or stemmed some text from it. In the proposed framework, reconstruction consists of identifying the original long string (for details see Turchi et al. (2010)). The term selection gives compression capabilities and the reconstruction adds paraphrasing capabilities.

SUMMARY EVALUATION IN MULTIPLE LANGUAGES

Evaluation of automatically produced summaries in different languages is a challenging problem for the summarisation community, because human efforts are multiplied to create model summaries for each language. Unavailability of parallel corpora suitable for news summarisation adds even another annotation load because documents need to be translated to other languages. At the last TAC'11 campaign, six research groups created evaluation resources in seven languages (Giannakopoulos et al., 2012). Compared to the monolingual evaluation, which requires writing model summaries and evaluating outputs of each system by hand, in the multilingual setting we need to obtain translations of all documents into the target language, write model summaries and evaluate the peer summaries for all the languages.

The Multilingual task of TAC'11 (Giannakopoulos et al., 2012) aimed at evaluating the application of (partially or fully) language-independent summarisation algorithms on a variety of languages. The task was to generate a representative summary (250 words) of a set of 10 related news articles. It included 7 languages (English, Czech, French, Hebrew, Hindi, Greek and Arabic). Annotation of each language sub-corpus was performed by a different group. English articles were manually translated to the target languages, 3 model summaries were written for each topic. Eight groups (systems) participated in the task; however, not all systems produced summaries for all languages. Human annotators scored each summary, both models and peers, on a 5-to-1 scale. The score corresponded to the overall responsiveness of the main TAC task – equal weight of content and readability.

Although the manually assigned grades showed a clear gap between human and automatic summaries, there were 5 systems for English and 1 system for French which were not significantly worse than at least one model. ROUGE (Lin, 2004) is widely used for English evaluations because of its simplicity and its high correlation with manually assigned content quality scores on overall system rankings, although per-case correlation is lower. As it compares n-grams in a system and reference summaries, it is possible to use it for evaluating summaries in other languages. However, it performs worse in the case of specific languages (e.g. languages with free word order) and more effort should be allocated to find a more appropriate set of evaluation methods. Although using n-grams with n greater than 1 gives limited possibility to reflect readability in the scores when compared to reference summaries, ROUGE is considered mainly as a content evaluation metric.

Using Parallel Data

A method, and related resources, which allows saving precious annotation time and that makes the evaluation results across languages directly comparable was introduced by Turchi et al. (2010). This approach relies on parallel data and it is based on the manual selection of the most important sentences in a cluster of documents from a sentence-aligned parallel corpus, and by projecting the sentence selection to various target languages.

In extractive summarisation, a single or multi-document summary is produced by selecting the most relevant sentences. It can then be evaluated by comparing these sentences with a gold standard of manually selected sentences. If sentence alignment information is available for a parallel text collection, the gold standard of one language can be projected to all the other languages. The more languages there are in the parallel corpus, the more time can be saved with this method. Sentences are not always aligned one-to-one because a translator may decide, for stylistic or other reasons, to split a sentence into two or to combine two sentences into one. Translations and original texts are never perfect, so that it is also possible that the translator accidentally omits or adds some information, or even a whole sentence. For these reasons, aligners such as Vanilla[4], which implements the Gale and Church (2012) algorithm, can be used.

Using Statistical Machine Translation

Steinberger and Turchi (2012) addressed the same problem of reducing annotation time and generating models, but from a different perspective. Instead of using parallel data and annotation projection or full documents, they investigated the use of machine translation at a different level of summary evaluation. While the approach of Turchi et al. (2010) is focused on sentence selection evaluation, the strategy of Steinberger and Turchi (2012) can also evaluate generative summaries, because it works at the summary level.

When we want to evaluate a summary on language A and we have evaluation resources in language B we can translate the summary to language A. Another approach, investigated by Steinberger and Turchi (2012), is to produce models in one pivot language (e.g., English) and translate them automatically to all other languages. In the results section we discuss the results of using both machine-translated model and system summaries.

RESULTS

In this section, we will show how the language-independent LSA-based summariser performs on different datasets. The next part shows how the summariser can compete with systems adapted for English at the TAC evaluation campaigns. A manual multilingual evaluation will then show how the summariser behaves when it is run on various languages. And finally, the two approaches, which lower the annotation costs, will be evaluated: using parallel and translated data.

LSA-Based Summariser vs. State-of-the-Art on English (TAC2008-2011)

In this section we report the results of the multilingual LSA-based summariser in all four TAC evaluation exercises. In 2008 and 2009, the basic summarisation task required systems to produce a short (100 words) summary of a set of English newswire articles (initial summaries). The update task aimed at producing a summary of a set of chronologically newer articles under the assumption that the user has already read a given set of earlier articles (used for the creation of an initial summary). In 2010 and 2011, the automatic summaries were supposed to include predefined category-related aspects resulting in the Guided summarisation task. The summaries submitted by participating systems were evaluated against human-created summaries based on various evaluation measures. Overall responsiveness evaluated the degree to which a summary is responding to the information need contained in the topic statement, considering the summary's content as well as its linguistic

Table 1. Overall responsiveness score of the multilingual LSA-based summariser and its variants throughout the TAC 2008 – 2011 evaluations (English initial summaries). It shows the best TAC system's score. LSA=system based on latent semantic analysis, +entities=addition of entities into the LSA matrix in 2009 was discussed in Kabadjov et al.(2013),+aspects = sentence selection also based on the aspect information, +compression = compression/paraphrasing method included. Score (rank/total number of participating systems).The scale is from 5=very good to 1=very poor.

	Best System	LSA	+ Entities	+ Aspects	+ Temporal Analysis	+ Compression
TAC 2008	2.792	2.667 (10/58)				
TAC 2009	3.080		2.978 (2/52)			
TAC 2010	3.170		2.890 (19/43)	2.980 (10/43)		
TAC 2011	3.159				2.977 (12/50)	2.341 (43/50)

quality. In Table 1, we report and compare overall responsiveness scores of different variants of the multilingual LSA-based summariser.

In 2008, the summaries of the LSA-based summariser were ranked 10th from a total of 58 participating systems. They were not statistically significantly worse than those of the best TAC system indicating that even a simple language-independent summariser can perform close to the best systems for English. In 2009, the system with more semantic representation, which included entities (see Kabadjov et al. (2013)),was ranked 2nd overall although the approach was multilingual. The TAC 2010 and TAC 2011 LSA-based summariser, which extracted and used aspects for the guided summarisation task, was ranked still at the state-of-the-art level (10thout of 43 and 12thout of 50). The sentence-generative summaries submitted to TAC 2011 suffered from worse readability, which also affected content-based scores. This showed that they still cannot compete with sentence-extractive summaries.

Mutlilingual Manual Evaluation (TAC Mutliling 2011)

TAC 2011 included a pilot multilingual evaluation task. The aim was to generate again a representative summary of a set of 10 documents describing an event sequence – a set of atomic event descrip-

tions, sequenced in time, that share main actors. An important difference compared to the main TAC summarisation task was that the limit of summary length was set to 250words.Human annotators scored each summary on the5-to-1 scale, similarly to the overall responsiveness of the main TAC task, with equal weight of content and readability.

The LSA-based system received the highest score in the case of 5 languages – Czech, English, French, Hebrewand Greek (see Table 2). For Arabic it was lower than baseline (the start of the centroid article) and for Hindi three other systems performed better. Looking at the average across languages, the summariser received a score of 3.37 indicating positive above-average (> 3) quality of the produced summaries. The basic lexical version of the summariser was used for the experiments. The only resource dependent on the language was a list of stopwords. It did not use the entity detection, event extraction and temporal analysis tools because they had not been developed for all the languages of the task yet. However, all these extensions were designed to work highly multilingually. So far, NER has been introduced for 20 languages, event extraction for 8 languages and temporal analysis for 4 languages. Thus these extensions could improve the summariser's performance at the cost of limiting the set of target languages.

Table 2. Overall responsiveness score of the TAC 2011 Mutliling task for all languages. The best system's score and the one of the LSA-based are reported. Score (rank/total number of participating systems). The scale is from 5=very good to 1=very poor.

	Best System	LSA
Arabic	3.77	3.43(4/9)
Czech	3.40	3.40(1/7)
English	3.57	3.57(1/10)
French	3.23	3.23(1/9)
Hebrew	3.87	3.87(1/7)
Hindi	2.73	2.47(4/9)
Greek	3.63	3.63(1/7)

Evaluation on Parallel Data

This section will discuss the evaluation on a parallel corpus done by Turchi et al. (2010). The binary model considered a sentence important if it was selected by at least two annotators (there were 4 annotations in total). The score of a system summary can then be computed as: the number of sentences in the intersection between the system summary and the sentences selected by at least two annotators divided by the number of sentences in the system summary. Table 3 shows the results of this evaluation approach.

We can see that the LSA summarizer selected on average over 5 sentences from 10 (56%) that at least two annotators marked as important. We can also observe that it is significantly better than baselines for all languages. It was also interesting to see that such a language-independent summariser selects on average only 35% of the same sentences for a language pair. Agreement peaks do exist, like the Czech-Russian pair (41%), which may be due to the fact that they are both Slavic languages and thus have similar properties. This indicates that there is a real need for multilingual summarisation evaluation, even if the sum-

Table 3. Summary evaluation on the parallel corpus from Turchi et al. (2010) using binary model - summary length is 10 sentences. It compares the LSA approach with 2 baselines: random sentence selection (Random) and selecting the first sentences from each article(Lead). The values are ratios of the number of sentences in the intersection between the system summary and the sentences selected by at least two annotators divided by the number of sentences in the system summary (10).

	Random	Lead	LSA
Arabic	22%	25%	60%
Czech	21%	25%	70%
English	21%	25%	60%
French	21%	25%	45%
German	22%	20%	55%
Russian	24%	25%	50%
Spanish	21%	30%	50%

mariser in principle uses only statistical, language-independent features.

Evaluation on Translated Data

The study in Steinberger and Turchi (2012)addressed the same problem. It investigated whether we can annotate in one language and instead of using sentence selection and its projection to other languages in a parallel corpus they proposed to use Machine translation. This approach is not constrained on sentence selection as the one using parallel corpus and thus the experiments were run on the TAC Multiling 2011 corpus.

There are two basic possibilities how we can evaluate a summary in language B given that we have model summaries in language A. Table 4 compares translating a system summary from language B to A and translating models from A to B. Thanks to the nature of the multilingual corpus, we can use translation of models from more languages. We analyse the ROUGE-SU4 score (Lin, 2004), which is more suitable than ROUGE-2 for languages with free word order. The figures show correlations of system rankings (both model and system summaries included) provided by ROUGE to system rankings generated using grades manually assigned to each summary.

Three languages were analysed: English, French and Czech. The translation approach discussed in (Turchi et al., 2012) was used to build four models covering the following language pairs: En-Fr, En-Cz, Fr-En and Cz-En. Performance was evaluated using the Bleu score (Papineni et al., 2002): En-Fr 0.23, En-Cz 0.14, Fr-En 0.26 and Cz-En 0.22.

The results indicate (correlations were not always enough statistically significant, see the p-value) that the use of translated models or summaries did not alter much the overall system ranking. A drop in ROUGE score was evident, and it strongly depended on the translation performance.

Table 4. Evaluation of using machine-translated data from Steinberger et al. (2012).Each row corresponds to one evaluation settings: using original/translated models (2ndcolumn), evaluating original/translated system summaries (3rd column), Bleu score capturing quality of the machine translator, an average of ROUGE-SU4 system scores and the correlations of the system ranking provided by ROUGE to the system ranking based on manually-assigned grades.

Evaluation Language	Model Summaries	System Summaries	Translation Quality (BLEU)	Avg. System ROUGE-SU4	R.-SU4&Grades Correlation
EN	EN models	EN summaries		.183	.723(p<.02)
	EN models	FR summaries translated to EN	0.26	.184	.581(p<.05)
	EN models	CZ summaries translated to EN	0.22	.217	.777 (p<.02)
	FR models translated to EN	EN summaries	0.26	.170	.785 (p<.01)
	CZ models translated to EN	EN summaries	0.22	.162	.692 (p<.02)
	FR&CZ models translated to EN	EN summaries	0.26&0.22	.153	.759 (p<.01)
FR	FR models	FR summaries		.207	.700(p<.02)
	FR models	EN summaries translated to FR	0.23	.190	.839 (p<.01)
	EN models translated to FR	FR summaries	0.23	.186	.559 (p<.1)
CZ	CZ models	CZ summaries		.211	.636(p<.1)
	CZ models	EN summaries translated to CZ	0.14	.160	.620(p<.05)
	EN models translated to CZ	CZ summaries	0.14	.172	.651 (p<.1)

FUTURE RESEARCH DIRECTIONS

We have seen that our automatic summariser does not select the same sentences in the different language versions of a parallel corpus. As this behaviour is relevant for the language independence assumption of our system, we feel that we need to analyse the reasons for this different sentence selection.

Regarding the selection of the most important sentences by the human annotators, we would like to deepen our insights regarding the human choice of summary-worthy sentences. Besides the fact that the most relevant aspects should be covered in a summary, it may be necessary to look at the human selection behaviour in enumerations, such as pros and cons regarding a certain argument or subject.

In our work up to now, we have identified a whole range of issues that would improve the summary result. We aim at improving each of them.

Regarding aspect-driven summarisation, we are interested in automatically identifying for any news cluster what the most relevant and important expected information aspects are and to focus the summary on those. Identifying these aspects could be achieved through a rough classification of the news and its vocabulary into major event classes. Identifying the *When, Where* and *Why* aspects is challenging, especially for multiple languages.

Regarding compression and paraphrasing, we are considering using more features and working harder on making the summaries more readable.

A thorough human analysis of the current results of our basic sentence selection summaries shows that using some simple heuristics will increase the readability a lot and it will at the same time reduce the summary length, leaving more space for further information aspects and details. Steps we currently work on are to use a word n-gram overlap measure to reduce the redundancy and repetition in sentences and phrases, such as the full titles of entities mentioned. Another promising step is to delete or avoid location and source information frequently found in first sentences of news articles as these are misleading and also disturbing when found in the middle of a summary.

Regarding summary evaluation, we plan to participate in the *Multiling* workshop at ACL'2013, by adding more languages and extending the evaluation corpus. Running the Machine Translation evaluation experiments on such an extended corpus will help us find more evidence. We would also be interested in researching evaluation methods that are more meaningful than ROUGE and that would work with different languages.

The study of Wan et al. (2011) investigated the task of finding and summarising the major differences between the news articles about the same event in two languages. Also our ultimate goal is to produce a real cross-lingual summariser that is able to identify new information aspects across languages in order to benefit from information complementarity across languages. Incorporating a sentiment analysis component would enable to analyse also different opinions about the same event expressed in different languages.

CONCLUSION

Automatic multi-document summarisation is an important task which has the potential to reduce information overload and to enable users finding more information in less time. The task is rather challenging and complex. Many research avenues can be explored to build summarisers and to improve them. For highly multilingual summarisation software, the methods must be kept relatively simple (e.g. by mostly using statistics, machine learning and annotation projection) as any extended human effort is prohibitive for most system developers. The performance ranking at the multilingual summary evaluation task at TAC2011 of the LSA and entity-based system showed that – with enough effort and resources – one can do better, but having achieved the top performance in most of the non-English languages also showed that this simple method produces results that can be considered a rather high-level baseline that is not that easy to pass. Working on paraphrasing and on sentence compression allows interesting and promising extensions to the base sentence selection approach. The two strands of studies carried out on evaluating automatic summaries in various languages while keeping the human annotation effort low – using annotation projection in parallel corpora and making use of machine translation – help close the annotation effort gap so that such solutions are quintessential for anybody working on summarisation covering several languages.

REFERENCES

Barzilay, R., & Elhadad, M. (1999). Using lexical chains for text summarization. In *Advances in Automatic Text Summarization*. Cambridge, MA: MIT Press.

Boguraev, B., & Kennedy, C. (1999). Salience-based content characterisation of text documents. In *Advances in Automatic Text Summarization*. Cambridge, MA: MIT Press.

Ding, C. (2005). A probabilistic model for latent semantic indexing. *Journal of the American Society for Information Science and Technology*, *56*(6). doi:10.1002/asi.20148

Edmundson, H. (1969). New methods in automatic extracting. *Journal of the Association for Computing Machinery*, *16*(2), 264–285. doi:10.1145/321510.321519

Ferro, L., Gerber, L., Mani, I., Sundheim, B., & Wilson, G. (2005). *TIDES 2005 standard for the annotation of temporal expressions (Technical Report)*. The MITRE Corporation.

Giannakopoulos, G., El-Haj, M., Favre, B., Litvak, M., Steinberger, J., & Varma, V. (2012). TAC 2011 multiling pilot overview. In *Proceedings of the Text Analysis Conference 2011*. NIST.

Gong, Y., & Liu, X. (2002). Generic text summarization using relevance measure and latent semantic analysis. In *Proceedings of ACM SIGIR*. ACM.

Hovy, E., & Lin, C. (1999). Automated text summarization in summarist. In *Advances in Automatic Text Summarization*. Cambridge, MA: MIT Press.

Jones, K. S. (1999). Automatic summarising: Factors and directions. In *Advances in Automatic Text Summarization*. Cambridge, MA: MIT Press.

Kabadjov, M., Steinberger, J., Pouliquen, B., Steinberger, R., & Poesio, M. (2009). Multilingual statistical news summarisation: Preliminary experiments with English. In *Proceedings of the Workshop on Intelligent Analysis and Processing of Web News Content at the IEEE/WIC/ACM International Conferences on Web Intelligence and Intelligent Agent Technology (WIIAT)*. IEEE/ACM.

Kabadjov, M., Steinberger, J., & Steinberger, R. (2013). Multilingual statistical news summarization. In T. Poibeau, H. Saggion, J. Piskorski, & R. Yangarber (Eds.), *Multi-source, multilingual information extraction and summarization* (pp. 229–252). Berlin: Springer. doi:10.1007/978-3-642-28569-1_11

Kupiec, J., Pedersen, J., & Chen, F. (1995). A trainable document summarizer. In *Proceedings of the 18th Annual International ACM SIGIR Conference on Research and Development in Information Retrieval* (pp. 68–73). ACM.

Lin, C. Y. (2004). ROUGE: A package for automatic evaluation of summaries. In *Proceedings of the Workshop on Text Summarization Branches Out*. ACL.

Litvak, M., Last, M., & Friedman, M. (2010). A new approach to improving multilingual summarization using a genetic algorithm. In *Proceedings of the 48th Annual Meeting of the Association for Computational Linguistics* (pp. 927–936). ACL.

Luhn, H. (1958). The automatic creation of literature abstracts. *IBM Journal of Research and Development, 2*(2), 159–165. doi:10.1147/rd.22.0159

Mani, I., & Maybury, M. (1999). *Advances in automatic text summarization*. Cambridge, MA: MIT Press.

Marcu, D. (1999). From discourse structures to text summaries. In *Advances in automatic text summarization*. Cambridge, MA: MIT Press.

Maybury, M. (1999). Generating summaries from event data. In *Advances in automatic text summarization*. Cambridge, MA: MIT Press.

McKeown, K., & Radev, D. (1995). Generating summaries of multiple news articles. In *Proceedings of the 18th Annual International ACM SIGIR Conference on Research and Development in Information Retrieval* (pp. 74–82). ACM.

Nenkova, A., & Louis, A. (2008). Can you summarize this? Identifying correlates of input difficulty for generic multi-document summarization. In *Proceedings of the 46th Annual Meeting of the Association for Computational Linguistics* (pp. 825–833). ACL.

Over, P., Dang, H., & Harman, D. (2007). DUC in context. *Information Processing & Management, 43*(6), 1506–1520. doi:10.1016/j.ipm.2007.01.019

Pouliquen, B., Kimler, M., Steinberger, R., Ignat, C., Oellinger, T., Blackler, K., et al. (2006). Geocoding multilingual texts: Recognition, disambiguation and visualisation. In *Proceedings of the 5th International Conference on Language Resources and Evaluation* (LREC 2006) (pp. 53–58). ELRA.

Pouliquen, B., & Steinberger, R. (2009). Automatic construction of multilingual name dictionaries. In C. Goutte, N. Cancedda, M. Dymetman, & G. Foster (Eds.), *Learning machine translation*. Cambridge, MA: MIT Press.

Steinberger, J., & Ježek, K. (2009). Update summarization based on novel topic distribution. In *Proceedings of the 9th ACM DocEng Conference*. ACM.

Steinberger, J., Kabadjov, M., Pouliquen, B., Steinberger, R., & Poesio, M. (2010b). WB-JRC-UT's participation in TAC 2009: Update summarization and AESOP tasks. In *Proceedings of the Text Analysis Conference 2009*. NIST.

Steinberger, J., Kabadjov, M., Steinberger, R., Tanev, H., Turchi, M., & Zavarella, V. (2012). Towards language-independent news summarization. In *Proceedings of the Text Analysis Conference 2011*. NIST.

Steinberger, J., Poesio, M., Kabadjov, M., & Ježek, K. (2007). Two uses of anaphora resolution in summarization. *Information Processing & Management, 43*(6), 1663–1680. doi:10.1016/j.ipm.2007.01.010

Steinberger, J., Tanev, H., Kabadjov, M., & Steinberger, R. (2011). Aspect-driven news summarization. *International Journal of Computational Linguistics and Applications, 2*(1-2).

Steinberger, J., & Turchi, M. (2012). Machine translation for multilingual summary content evaluation. In *Proceedings of the NAACL Workshop on Evaluation Metrics and System Comparison for Automatic Summarization* (pp. 19-27). ACL.

Steinberger, J., Turchi, M., Kabadjov, M., Cristianini, N., & Steinberger, R. (2010). Wrapping up a summary: From representation to generation. In *Proceedings of the 48th Annual Meeting of the Association for Computational Linguistics* (pp. 382-386). ACL.

Steinberger, R., Pouliquen, B., & van der Goot, E. (2009). An introduction to the europe media monitor family of applications. In *Proceedings of Information Access in a Multilingual World of the SIGIR*. ACM.

Tanev, H., & Magnini, B. (2006). Weakly supervised approaches for ontology population. In *Proceedings of the 11th Conference of the European Chapter of the Association for Computational Linguistics* (EACL). ACL.

Tanev, H., Piskorski, J., & Atkinson, M. (2008). Real-time news event extraction for global crisis monitoring. In *Proceedings of 13th International Conference on Applications of Natural Language to Information Systems* (NLDB 2008). NLDB.

Teufel, S., & Moens, M. (1999). Sentence extraction as a classification task. In *Advances in automatic text summarization*. Cambridge, MA: MIT Press.

Turchi, M., Atkinson, M., Wilcox, A., Crawley, B., Bucci, S., Steinberger, R., & van der Goot, E. (2012). ONTS: Optima news translation system. In *Proceedings of EACL 2012* (pp. 25-32). ACL.

Turchi, M., Steinberger, J., Kabadjov, M., & Steinberger, R. (2010). Using parallel corpora for multilingual (multi-document) summarisation evaluation. In *Multilingual and Multimodal Information Access Evaluation (LNCS)* (Vol. 6360, pp. 52–63). Berlin: Springer. doi:10.1007/978-3-642-15998-5_7

Wan, X., Jia, H., Huang, S., & Xiao, J. (2011). Summarizing the differences in multilingual news. In *Proceedings of the 34th International ACM SIGIR Conference on Research and Development in Information Retrieval* (pp. 735–744). ACM.

Wan, X., Li, H., & Xiao, J. (2010). Cross-language document summarization based on machine translation quality prediction. In *Proceedings of the 48th Annual Meeting of the Association for Computational Linguistics* (pp. 917–926). ACL.

Zavarella, V., & Tanev, H. (2013). FSS-TimEx for TempEval-3: Extracting temporal information from text. In *Proceedings of Second Joint Conference on Lexical and Computational Semantics (*SEM)*, (pp.58-63). ACL.

ADDITIONAL READING

Barzilay, R., & Elhadad, M. (1999). Using lexical chains for text summarization. In *Advances in Automatic Text Summarization*. MIT Press.

Boguraev, B., & Kennedy, C. (1999). Salience-based content characterisation of text documents. In *Advances in Automatic Text Summarization*. MIT Press.

Boudin, F., Huet, S., & Torres-Moreno, J. M. (2010). A graph-based approach to cross-language multi-document summarization. In *Research journal on Computer science and computer engineering with applications* (Polibits), 43 (pp. 113–118).

Clarke, J., & Lapata, M. (2008). Global inference for sentence compression: An integer linear programming approach. In *Journal of Artificial Intelligence Research*, 31 (pp. 273–318).

Erkan, G., & Radev, D. (2004). LexRank: Graph-based centrality as salience in text summarization. In *Journal of Artificial Intelligence Research* (JAIR).

Giannakopoulos, G., El-Haj, M., Favre, B., Litvak, M., Steinberger, J., & Varma, V. (2012). TAC 2011 Multiling pilot overview. In *Proceedings of the Text Analysis Conference* 2011, NIST.

Gong, Y. & Liu, X. (2002). Generic text summarization using relevance measure and latent semantic analysis. In *Proceedings of ACM SIGIR'02*. ACM.

Hovy, E. (2005). Automated text summarization. In Ruslan Mitkov (ed.), *The Oxford Handbook of Computational Linguistics* (pp. 583–598). Oxford University Press.

Jones, K. S. (1999). Automatic summarising: Factors and directions. In *Advances in Automatic Text Summarization*. MIT Press.

Kabadjov, M., Steinberger, J., & Steinberger, R. (2013). Multilingual Statistical News Summarization. In Thierry Poibeau, Horacio Saggion, Jakub Piskorski & Roman Yangarber (Eds.), *Multisource, Multilingual Information Extraction and Summarization* (pp. 229-252). Springer.

Knight, K., & Marcu, D. (2002). Summarization beyond sentence extraction: A probabilistic approach to sentence compression. *Artificial Intelligence, 139*(1) (pp. 91–107).

Kupiec, J., Pedersen, J. & Chen, F. (1995). A trainable document summarizer. In *Proceedings of the 18th Annual International ACM SIGIR Conference on Research and Development in Information Retrieval* (pp. 68–73). ACM.

Lin, C.Y. (2004). ROUGE: a package for automatic evaluation of summaries. In *Proceedings of the Workshop on Text Summarization Branches Out*. ACL.

Litvak, M., Last, M., & Friedman, M. (2010). A new approach to improving multilingual summarization using a genetic algorithm. In *Proceedings of the 48th Annual Meeting of the Association for Computational Linguistics* (pp. 927–936). ACL.

Marcu, D. (1999). From discourse structures to text summaries. In *Advances in Automatic Text Summarization*. MIT Press.

McKeown, K., & Radev, D. (1995). Generating summaries of multiple news articles. In *Proceedings of the 18th Annual International ACM SIGIR Conference on Research and Development in Information Retrieval* (pp. 74–82). ACM.

Nenkova, A., Passonneau, R., & McKeown, K. (2007). The pyramid method: incorporating human content selection variation in summarization evaluation. *ACM Transactions on Speech and Language Processing, 4*(2).

Over, P., Dang, H., & Harman, D. (2007). DUC in context. *Information Processing and Management, 43*(6), 1506–1520.

Owczarzak, K., Conroy, J., Trang Dang, H., & Nenkova, A. (2012). An Assessment of the Accuracy of Automatic Evaluation in Summarization. In *Proceedings of the NAACL Workshop on Evaluation Metrics and System Comparison for Automatic Summarization*. ACL.

Steinberger, J. & Turchi, M. (2012). Machine Translation for Multilingual Summary Content Evaluation. In *Proceedings of the NAACL Workshop on Evaluation Metrics and System Comparison for Automatic Summarization* (pp. 19-27), ACL.

Steinberger, J., Kabadjov, M., Steinberger, R., Tanev, H., Turchi, M., & Zavarella, V. (2012). Towards language-independent news summarization. In *Proceedings of the Text Analysis Conference 2011*, NIST.

Steinberger, J., Poesio, M., Kabadjov, M., & Ježek, K. (2007). Two uses of anaphora resolution in summarization. *Information Processing and Management, 43*(6), 1663–1680.

Steinberger, J., Turchi, M., Kabadjov, M., Cristianini, N., & Steinberger R. (2010). Wrapping up a Summary: from Representation to Generation. In *Proceedings of the 48th Annual Meeting of the Association for Computational Linguistics* (pp. 382-386), ACL.

Turchi, M., Steinberger, J., Kabadjov, M. &Steinberger, R. (2010). Using Parallel Corpora for Multilingual (Multi-Document) Summarisation Evaluation. In *Multilingual and Multimodal Information Access Evaluation*, (LNCS 6360, pp. 52-63), Springer.

Wan, X., Jia, H., Huang, S., Xiao, J. (2011). Summarizing the differences in multilingual news. In *Proceedings of the 34th international ACM SIGIR conference on research and development in information retrieval* (pp. 735–744).ACM.

Wan, X., Li, H.& Xiao, J. (2010). Cross-language document summarization based on machine translation quality prediction. In *Proceedings of the 48th Annual Meeting of the Association for Computational Linguistics* (pp. 917–926).ACL.

KEY TERMS AND DEFINITIONS

Aspect-Driven Summarisation: It is a summarisation task, in which a summariser is given a list of aspects for each article category, and the summary should include those aspects if possible.

Cross-Lingual Summarisation: It is a summarisation task, in which the languages of the summary and input articles are different.

Latent Semantic Analysis: It is a fully automatic mathematical/statistical technique which is able to extract and represent the meaning of terms on the basis of their contextual usage.

Multilingual Summarisation Evaluation: It is a task of evaluating quality of automatically produced summaries in a set of languages.

Multilingual Summarisation: It is a summarisation task, in which the languages of the summary and input articles are the same, however, the summariser can process articles in a set of languages.

Parallel Corpus: It is a collection of texts placed alongside its translations. Texts and corresponding translations are usually aligned at sentence level.

Text Analysis Conferences: It is a series of evaluation workshops organized by NIST (US National Institute for Standards and Technology) to encourage research in Natural Language Processing and related applications, by providing a large test collection, common evaluation procedures, and a forum for organizations to share their results.

ENDNOTES

[1] http://emm.newsbrief.eu/overview.html.

[2] The National Institute of Standards and Technology (NIST) initiated the Document Understanding Conference (DUC) series to evaluate automatic text summarisation. Its goal is to further progress in summarisation and enable researchers to participate in large-scale experiments. Since 2008 DUC has moved to TAC (Text Analysis Conference) that follows the summarisation evaluation roadmap with new or upgraded tracks.

[3] http://www.nist.gov/tac/2010/Summarization/Guided-Summ.2010.guidelines.html.

[4] http://nl.ijs.si/telri/Vanilla/.

Chapter 13
Language Independent Summarization Approaches

Firas Hmida
LINA Nantes-University, France

ABSTRACT

In this chapter, the authors introduce monolingual and multilingual summarization and present the problem of dependence of language and linguistic knowledge of the process. Then they describe the most influential works and techniques in the field of automatic multilingual and language-independent summarization. This section is presented as a solution to solve the problem already explained. The authors present several language independent approaches and used techniques. In the next section, they study the behavior of these methods by discussing their limitations and perspectives.

INTRODUCTION

Automatic summarization is a difficult problem of Natural Language Processing (NLP). It is highly language dependent. Indeed, the increasing volume and variety of electronic information, whether on the Internet or networks companies, makes it difficult to access the required information without recourse to language tools. This makes it very complicated to generate summaries because it requires language skills and knowledge of the world that remain virtually impossible to incorporate in a computer system.

Since multilingual summarization stems from the monolingual summarization, the former have to face many language-dependent challenges in order to be able to deal with different languages. To avoid this problem a lot of works in this area have turned towards language independent summarization.

In the first section we describe the task of summarization and present the problem of dependence of language and linguistic knowledge of the process. Then we describe the most influential work and techniques in the field of automatic multilingual summarization. This section will be presented as a solution to solve the problem already explained in the introduc-

DOI: 10.4018/978-1-4666-5019-0.ch013

tion. We present several language independent approaches and used techniques. In the next section we study the behavior of these methods by discussing their limitations and perspectives. As usual, we will end this chapter with a conclusion referring to the automatic evaluation of multilingual summaries.

BACKGROUND

An automatic summarization synthesizes a compressed representation of an information source while maintaining the important information of the original content. It is a very complicated task. However, generally, people still produce summaries so efficiently. Works in this field aimed to imitate the cognitive process of generating a summary. Since a long time, researches have focused on scientific documents and also on press reports. This work deals only with text summarization. We can distinguish two types of summaries: the first one is the single-document summary, when the source document is unique, whereas, in the second one, the multi-document summary, analyzed information may come from several documents. The summary can also have different purposes: It can be generic if it treats all the topics in a document with the same degree of importance, but if it deals with only one specific part of the information required, it is called an oriented summary.

One can think of an approach to summarization as being an extract or an abstract method, with rather different implications. The method using the extraction consists on selecting textual units (words, sentences, etc...) which are supposed to contain important information from the document and then assemble those units to produce an "extract". In other words, an extract is a part taken from a source document in order to provide an overview of its content (Boudin,

2008). An "abstract" is to understand the contents of a source document and reformulate them. It is a gloss describing those contents with an implicit way, which means that they don't have to feature with the same language used in the original document. (Lin and Hovy, 2003) said that nearly 65% of the sentences in manually created summaries are extracted from the source document without any modification.

The multilingual summarization stems from the monolingual automatic summarization: They both have the same functionalities, but the multilingual summarization comes up with a new dimension: globally, it is defined as a process that involves more than one language in the automatically text summarization process.

Multilingual/language-independent summarizer needs to show a good and an equal ability to deal with different languages without any special adjustment such as modifying the algorithm and/or requiring some additional data in each language. The majority of multilingual summarization of documents/queries, written in a foreign language, use automatic (and/or manual) translation as a pre-processing or/and a post-processing step (Chenn & Lin, 2000) and (Ogden, & al.1999). In such cases, the summarization accuracy may be considerably affected by the quality of translation. The automatic translation is known as a very complicated and challenging process, and existing tools usually suffer from the lack of the results' accuracy, therefore, summarization systems are facing a noisy output. In order to deal with multilingual contents, only few works do not employ translation or any other complementary tool. Another simple technique has been included by the authors of (Salton & al. 1997), (Radev & al.2004); it consists in using a graph representation of the text and a similarity measure between the text units that can be easily applied to several languages.

TOWARDS LANGUAGE-INDEPENDENT SUMMARIZATION

The following list is a summary of some features that we need to take into consideration when dealing with a multilingual summarization system. Particularly, these are challenges we must reveal when working with multiple language.

- **Tokenization:** Because languages encode word boundaries differently, tokenization is a first obstacle to overcome when building a summarization for different languages. Languages such as English identify token boundaries via whitespace and punctuation but other languages such as Chinese require a more complex segment to extract tokens from a stream of text that does not contain any whitespaces. A token is a word in languages such as English but may be something else in another language. Other languages (e.g. Arabic) that process a rich morphology may require an even more fine-grained tokenization up to the morph level.
- **Anaphoric Expression:** The identification of anaphora (i.e, pronouns, discourse markers and definite noun phrases) can help to make a more structured summary. Some techniques exist for monolingual summarization, but concerning multilingual summarization, some challenges appear: names are written differently and that discourse markers, have different semantics in different languages.
- **Discourse Structure:** The identification of a document structure can help to improve the coherence of a summary. However, different languages don't express the same structure of a text with the same way.
- **Machine Translation:** The state-of-the-art machine translation technology has not reached yet the perfect level to guarantee high-quality translation. While designing a

multilingual summarization system, developers must answer an important question: When should we use a machine translation in the system? If the text is generated as the start components developed for the source language, it can be reused (e.g, tokenizer). If translation is done after identifying the summary-worthy sentences, language-independent systems have to be used to preprocess the text accordingly.

Solutions and Recommendations

In this section we are dealing with sentence extraction applied to document summarization and describing the text representation models used in the state of the art. These methods can be applied for multilingual summarization because they are more or less language-independent. Most of language-independent sentence scoring methods introduced in the literature can be classified as frequency, position, and length or title-based. Frequency and title are calculated thanks to a vector representation of a text, whereas position and length-based methods calculate scores using the whole structure of the document. The description of each approach includes a reference to the original work where this method was proposed for extractive summarization.

Classic Approach

Researches on automatic summarization can probably be traced back in the late 1950s with Luhn's work on summarization. Luhn was the first to describe a statistical method, simple and specific to scientific documents, to calculate the frequency of terms (words) in a sentence. The majority of jobs today are based on this method. Among the most commonly used techniques of Luhn, the stemming. Luhn also introduced a manually created "anti-dictionary" (Stop-List) that contains stop-words. This list can be used to select common terms from the parsed and the Stop

List. The Luhn's algorithm also eliminates the less frequent terms to preserve the most common terms which are not tools. After this preprocessing the words preserved in the scanned document are called significant (i.e important). Thus, it assigns a score to each sentence as meaningful terms; it contains and extracts the top ranked ones to produce a summary.

Subsequently, (Edmundson, 1969) was the first to use the structure of the text. Indeed, he has extended the work of Luhn by introducing an important evidence such as the position of sentences, the presence of words from the document's structure (eg, titles, etc. ..) and the presence of keywords (meaning, impossible, in conclusion, etc. ..). According to the study of Edmundson, the combination of criteria – position, title word, and word index – is more efficient than the distribution of frequent words. It also shows that the position of the sentence in the document is the most important parameter. Note that the position of the sentence in the text depends on the type of document. In the case of scientific articles, the last sentences (from the conclusion) are often the most important ones, while for the news papers' articles the sentences at the beginning are usually preferred (Brandow & al., 1995).

Approaches by Learning

The approaches by learning tried to learn methods to automatically generate summaries. Thus, these researches seemed to be interesting. A famous example of learning techniques in automatic summarization is the weight measurement (ie frequency) of words. Measurement tf.idf (Term Frequency, Inverse Document Frequency) is used to highlight the most significant words in a document.

(Kupiec et al. 1995) describe a method arising from (Edmundson, 1969). They used data consisting on pairs of document-summary. Their learning process is guided by a Bayesian classifier that decides according to the probability of the sentence, if it is selected or not. They used two new parameters: the length of the sentence and the presence of capitalized words. (Aone et al. 1999) have extended this work using more valuable parameters as the presence of signature-words.

(Lin, 1999) chose to model the problem of extracting sentences thanks to decision trees and also evaluated several baselines (references) with different parameters. The evaluation was done by comparing the sentences extracted by the system with those extracted manually. The decision tree classifier seemed to be generally more efficient. At the end of his work, Lin concluded that some of the parameters were independent from each other.

(Radev et al. 2004) were interested in multi-document summaries. They relied on the algorithm Maximal Marginal Relevance (MMR) proposed in (Goldestein, 1998). The principle of this algorithm is based on the idea of maximizing the relevance of sentences used faced to an application, while minimizing the redundancy of information added to the summary. (Radev et al., 2004) used the concept of centroid in their approach as a query. Each source is represented by a vector (called centroid) in the data base which consists in all words appearing in the document. The components of this vector are normalized frequencies tf.idf. Thus, each document is represented by centroid:

$$\left(D\right) = \left(w1, w2, w3, ..., w_{|D|}\right)$$

with an index word in the document. (Radev et al. 2004) use three criteria to extract a sentence: its centrality, its position and redundancy compared to the first sentence of the document. The measure of the centrality of a sentence is the total weight of all the terms. The value associated with the position is calculated by:

$$\frac{|D| - j + 1}{|D|}$$

with *j* is the rank of the sentence in the text and not in all documents.

Redundancy is the scalar product between the vector of the weights of words in the sentence and the first sentence of the document. Subsequently, the three parameters are normalized in the interval] 0,1 [:

$$Redundancy\left(phrasei, phrase\right) = \frac{\left\langle phrasei \cdot phrase1 \right\rangle}{\left\| phrasei \right\| \cdot \left\| phrase1 \right\|}$$

One technique to minimize redundancy among the sentences of a summary, uses the similarity measure between sentences such as dividing the number of common words between two sentences by the total number of words:

$$Redundancy_{summary} = \frac{\left| commonwords \right|}{\sum \left| sentence \right|}$$

The score associated with each sentence is obtained after subtracting the measure of similarity with the sentence with the highest score, from the total of the three criteria.

$$Score\left(sentencei\right) = \left(Centrality + position + redundancy\right) - Redundancy_{summary}$$

Other studies have chosen to use the Hidden Markov Models and neural networks. But these approaches have shown some limits. However, many systems involved in Text Analysis Conference (TAC), are used in most learning.

Graph-Based Approaches

Ranking algorithms based on the graphs are widely used in researches on the Internet. Applied to the automatic summaries, they have recently been more popular. These algorithms analyze the positions of Web pages in the network without knowing their contents. Indeed, each web page is represented by a vertex. Edges represent links to Web pages. The most influent nodes are those which maintain the most important links with others. This type of method highlights the centrality (importance) of a page by taking advantage of the whole content of the Web.

Projected on automatic summarization, this method means that the text is represented by a graph whose vertices represent sentences. These vertices are joined by edges weighted by the value of similarity between sentences. Among the approaches which are based on this method we can find (Erkan and Radev, 2004; Mihalcea, 2004; Moreno and Boudin, 2009). The selected sentences are the most prestigious in the graph or the most central ones.

(Mihalcea, 2004) proposed a method based on graphs in which he assessed the similarity between the vertices by the sum of terms in common between the two sentences, divided by the sum of the log of each sentence length. Thus, the relevance of a sentence is pulled through its influence in the graph. (Mihalcea, 2004) has used the PageRank technique to accord a score to each vertex. The final score of each sentence corresponds to the pair containing the sum of the scores of all phrases that are directly related to the needed sentence, and the similarity among sentences. The best classified phrases according to the final score are extracted to produce the summary.

(Boudin & Moreno, 2009) have extended the approach (Mihalcea, 2005) using a similarity measure which allows the approximation of sentences morphologically close. Indeed, they proposed to combine the similarity measure between two sentences (already existing in (Mihalcea, 2004; Erkan & Radev, 2004)), with a measurement of the longest common substring (LCS), which increases the similarity between vertices in a graph. They changed the formula LCS by LCS* in 2010. The sentence with the highest score is preferred. In order to minimize redundancy intra-summarized (Boudin, Moreno, 2009-2010) fixed a similarity threshold intraphrases applied upstream.

Global Approaches

(McDonald, 2007) was the first to propose a global approach to solve the summarization problem as an instance of the problem of quadratic *Knapsack Problem problem* (in winch sentences match to items of the knapsack). McDonald unfortunately does not include the redundancy of information in the summary generally, but rather measure the overlap between each pair of sentences. This approach is innovative but it does not solve the problem of redundancy.

(Gillick & al., 2008-2009) provide an innovative approach by defining the problem of automatic summarization as a maximum coverage problem. This approach solves this problem with integer linear program (ILP). The purpose of (Gillick & al., 2008-2009) was to maximize bi-grams lemme (truncated words of their termination) called concepts. The choice of this method is inspired by the evaluation method ROUGE-2. (Gillick et al., 2008-2009) applied a preprocessing to scan documents to ignore the terms that appear in stop world list, but not concepts that contain at least one relevant words. A concept is called relevant only if it appears in more than 3/10 documents. More sentence cover concepts, more it is important. Formally, the constraints are: the maximum size of the summary (100 words), the concepts and phrases have binary values to indicate whether a phrase or concept appears in the summary, sentence is selected if and only if all its concepts are, and that if a concept is selected when there is at least one selected sentence. This property tends to avoid redundancy and increases the coverage concept.

FUTURE RESEARCH DIRECTIONS

Having studied the behavior of many approaches for automatic summary, we observed that most of them use the model of bag-of-words to represent the text sentences. Intuitively, we suggest the following question: "Can we apply these approaches to languages of which we know neither the limits of phrases or word boundaries?" Summary generation systems presuppose the segmentation of text into sentences. For most languages using the Latin alphabet, for example French or English, a cutting by spaces and punctuation symbols is a good approximation for segmentation into tokens. Humans recognize sentences as a result of words that lie between punctuations such as the so-called major point, exclamation point or question mark. But in the case of the writing systems used for example to write Chinese, Japanese, or Vietnamese, typography is not used to indicate borders between the same linguistic units: in Vietnamese, which uses a variant of the Latin alphabet, space separates sub-lexical units.

In Chinese or Japanese only signs punctuation indicate boundaries between lexical units; characters which also represent sub-word units are directly juxtaposed. The step of lexical segmentation is a difficult problem for these languages called non- segmented languages, and gives rise to an abundant literature (Zhao & Liu, 2010), including the Francophone community (Seng & al., 2009; Wu, 2010). This work may also be useful for segmented languages, due to non-correspondence between separators and boundaries of lexical units, which are difficult to define and identify whatever language is (Zhikov & al., 2010).

These methods are difficult to assess because they do not follow a given standard. In return, they have a greater potential to adapt to the dynamics of language (domain change, geographical variants, diachronic, treatment neologisms), and can be used for segmentation with little or no language.

These approaches can be adapted to many languages or designed to language-independent system and will not need further adaptation for processing new languages. We have identified several language-dependent factors in existing summarization systems:

- **Sentence Segmentation:** Most extractive summarizers rely on sentence boundaries, which can be detected using punctuation and abbreviation lists.
- **Tokenization:** Rules to split a sequence of words are language independent, and can be non trivial, as for instance in Chinese.
- **Relevance Assessment:** Relies mostly on comparing word frequency histograms, and involves language-dependent stopword lists.
- **Morphological, Syntactic and Semantic Analysis, Information Extraction:** High-level processing often requires dictionaries and corpora to train the analyzers.
- **Training Data:** Any supervised summarizer needs training data from the same language as used in the documents to be summarized.

(Hmida & Favre, 2011) focused on the notion of word, the notion of sentence and stop-word lists. They modified a system based on the Maximal Marginal Relevance (MMR) algorithm (Carbonell and Goldstein, 1998) in order to remove or reduce those factors. In particular, sentence segmentation is replaced by a crude heuristic: use the last character of the input documents as splitting point; the need for word tokenization is replaced by using character n-grams to represent the content of sentences (Damashek, 1995) ; stop-word lists are not needed because we only include character sequences of length n, with n long-enough to cover multiple words relevance is assessed at the n-gram level instead of the word level using the unmodified cosine/tf.idf framework.

- **Sentence Segmentation:** The problem of automatic detection of sentence arises because of the ambiguity of certain punctuation marks. The characters that represent punctuation marks are language dependent, and therefore, we propose to use a crude heuristic: consider the last character of text to be summarized as the punctuation mark that indicates the limit between sentences.
- **Tokenization:** In order to reduce the dependence to language, we ignore the notion of word and we use n-grams of characters as tokens to represent sentences. In the following we call term n-grams of all characters in a text.
- **Importance of Words:** The discriminative power of terms in the context of a similarity measure between sentences depends on their relative importance to all documents. We used the metric proposed in tfidf (Salton and Buckley, 1988) to determine the importance of a term in a set of documents without use of external resources. In particular, we use the following tf:idf weighting scheme.

EVALUATION

Problematic

Evaluate a summary is a problem in itself that the proposed solutions have responded only partially.

Several methods for evaluating automatic summaries have emerged. Usually, each proposed system is accompanied by an assessment procedure, but in most cases, because of the difficulties of implementing rigorous assessment, works are done with little significant corpus.

However, evaluations carried on some systems as well as the collaborative work with professional summarizers (Endres-Niggemeyr & al., 1995) or in comparison with the summaries produced by professionals (Saggion & Lapalme, 1998) revealed difficulty in carrying out standard summaries: there is no specific criteria for determining what is a good summary. Indeed what is considered relevant to a reader is not necessarily relevant for another.

Generally, people are extremely efficient summarizers. Based on this assumption, the evaluation followed - and that seems the most effective method is to compare the summaries of a system to those of humans.

These difficulties have led many researchers to take a different lane in which systems are better suited to the specific needs of users:

The origin of this observation is the fact that there are no clear criteria determining what is a good summary. Summaries are also very different depending on their intended users. Thus, we do not produce the same summary of an innovative scientific article if you must send it to the general directorate, the patent department for legal consultation, laboratory development, services general press... Summaries depend also on types of texts. It is not just the same way to summarize a narrative text, a scientific article dealing with theoretical or experimental science, legal articles, etc.. Therefore, there is no ideal summary that is independent of user requests and the types of texts. These different findings led research teams to expand the field of their research aiming either single non-target automatic summaries, but systems tailored to the specific needs of a task identification or information retrieval. We call these systems automatic information filtering systems. (Minel, 2003)

The same problem has been analyzed in the Document Understanding Conference (DUC) (section DUC) conferences: the discussion about the evaluation DUC 2002 turned on the problem of finding an agreement on what constitutes a good summary (Harman, 2002). Thus, in the

task of DUC 2003 multi-document summary is similar to DUC in 2002 but was asked to human summarizers to determine how they wrote the summary.

Evaluation systems that take peer summaries and reference as input and per comparison to produce evaluation results are called automated evaluations. To validate the effectiveness of an automatic evaluation, it must correlated to human assessments.

We present the evaluation of automatic summarization under the gaze of the campaign Document Understanding Conference (DUC) organized by NIST[1].

Recall-Oriented Understudy for Gisty Evaluation (ROUGE)

These measures are proposed by (Lin, 2004) for automated evaluation of summaries. They are based on the calculation of similarity between candidate summaries (produced by systems) and references (i.e gold) summaries (produced by humans). They involve the n-grams of common words between these two summaries. So ROUGE is a recall-oriented metric:

$$ROUGE = \frac{number of common words}{nubmer of reference words}$$

- **ROUGE-(N):** Calculates the co-occurrences of N-grams of words within a summary candidate and a set of reference summaries.
- **ROUGE-SU(M):** Adaptation of ROUGE-2 using bigrams with holes (skip units (SU)) with maximum size M and counting unigrams.

This kind of measurement is constantly improving and tends to integrate design elements (entity-relationship). It comes closer to a space of representation of information and get away from the area of linguistic instantiation. Automatic measurement is essential for improving systems because it takes much less time and does not require human operator.

Pyramid

The pyramid method is a manual method for summarization evaluation. It was developed by Nenkova et al. (2007) in an attempt to address the fact that different humans choose different content when writing summaries. The pyramid method uses multiple human summaries to create a gold-standard and expoits the frequency of information in the human summaries in order to assign importance to different facts.

Indeed, Pyramid is a list of Summary Content Units[2] (SCUs) from summaries of reference. These units are weighted and ranked according to their frequency in the reference, in the form of a pyramid, where does the name. The top-ranked units are then the most important. Subsequently, a score is attributed to abstracts: the sum of the weights of the units they contain, divided by the sum of the weights of the units in the reference summaries. This type of evaluation, no automated, has the disadvantage of being extremely time consuming expertise. Indeed, learning how to build a pyramid of SCUs, as well as construct are time-consuming.

Document Understanding Conference (DUC)

Document Understanding Conference[3] (DUC) is an evaluation campaign organized by National Institute of Standards and Technology since 2001. It aims to promote progress in the field of automatic text summarization but also to provide an international experimental space for researchers in this area and allow to evaluate their systems by a group of independent persons. DUC campaigns successively proposed produc-

tion tasks generic summaries single and multi documents (2001-2003), short summaries of single and multi-documents (2003-2004), summaries multi-oriented documents (2003-2007) and summaries put oriented to multi-day documents (2007-2008).

In the context of these campaigns, the evaluation of systems is carried out on the bottom and on the form of summaries produced. DUC became since 2008 Text Analysis Conference (TAC).

Text Analysis Conference (TAC)

The task of TAC-2011, for example, aims to assess the implementation of algorithms summary, partially or completely independent of the language on several languages. Each system participating in the mission is expected to provide summaries for a range of seven different languages, based on on corresponding corpus. Participantssont systems required to apply their methods over at least two languages. The evaluation is supportive of systems that apply their methods in other languages, The languages used are: Arabic, Czech, English, French, Greek, Hebrew and Hindi.

All documents in a dataset share the same language. Summaries must be generated in the same language as their source material and should contain between 240 and 250 words.

Evaluation in DUC and TAC

ROUGE is heavily used during the DUC campaigns notably ROUGE-2 and ROUGE-SU(4) are imposed for automatic assessment .

However, summaries evaluation can not be limited to automatic evaluation. In order to assess the participants summaries within the framework of DUC and TAC, a group of independent persons carry out intrinsically the assessment on the bottom and on the form of summaries. A quality score is awarded by the judges based on the following criteria to judge the linguistic form:

- **Grammaticality:** The presence of ungrammatical errors.
- **Non-Redundancy: The** appearance of unnecessary repetitions in the summary.
- **Clarity References:** Reference errors pronouns and nominal groups.
- **Preview Focus:** Belonging information to the desired context.
- **Structure and Coherence:** The structure and coherence of informations.

For each of these criteria a score between 1 and 5 is given: 1 being very poor and 5 is very good (if a human summary). This manual evaluation is paramount and justifies the success of DUC and TAC campaigns. (Boudin, 2007) says that this is the only way to judge the form of a summary.

CONCLUSION

All approaches described above attempt to maximize a score assigned to abstracts, manually or automatically based on reference summaries. The quality measures the most commonly used are n-grams comparisons between reference summaries and automatic summaries, and ROUGE metrics. These methods based on word frequency and other criteria surface exploit some of the information contained in the documents. The fact that many sentences are strongly related in content, reflecting their importance is not exploited. In addition, such systems reflects the centrality of phrases, but does not reflect nor leverages diversity (that sentences express different information).

Otherwise we can no longer be limited by analyzing summaries with statistical models which can identify the importance of the selected text segments morphologically, syntactically and pragmatically analyzed. Therefore, it must extend the analysis to the overall summary. That means that the summary, which was considered as an object to be seen and analyzed in a wider dimension than the textual units that compose it. Extractive methods

have the advantage of extracting sentences with good grammaticality. But instead, they "suffer" at the coherence and cannot include references (ie pronouns, etc.).. That is why recent research in the field, are directed to methods abstractive. A reduction in the dependence of language for syntactic or semantic parsers will have a major impact on the Automatic Language Processing.

REFERENCES

Aone, C., Okurowski, M. E., Gorlinsky, J., & Larsen, B. (1999). A trainable summarizer with knowledge acquired from robust NLP techniques. In *Advances in automated text summarization.* Cambridge, MA: MIT Press.

Boudin, F. (2008). *Exploration d'approches statistiques pour le résumé automatique de texte.* (PhD Thesis).

Boudin, F., Bechet, F., El-Beze, M., Favre, B., Gillard, L., & Torres-Moreno, J. M. (2007). The lia summarization system at duc-2007. In *Proceedings of DUC 2007 Document Understanding Conference.* DUC.

Boudin, F., & Torres-Moreno, J.-M. (2009). A maximization-minimization approach for update text summarization. In *Current issues in linguistic theory: Recent advances in natural language processing.* John Benjamins Publishers.

Carbonell, J., & Goldstein, J. (1998). The use of MMR, diversity-based reranking for reordering documents and producing summaries. In *Proceedings of the 21st Annual International ACM SIGIR Conference on Research and Development in Information Retrieval.* ACM.

Chen, H. H., & Lin, C. J. (2000). A multilingual news summarizer. *In Proceedings of the 18th International Conference on Computational Linguistics,* (pp. 159-165). ACL.

Damashek, M. (1995). Gauging similarity with n-grams: Language-independent categorization of text. *Science, 267*(5199), 843. doi:10.1126/science.267.5199.843 PMID:17813910

Edmundson, H. P. (1969). New methods in automatic extracting. *Journal of the ACM, 16*(2), 264–285. doi:10.1145/321510.321519

Endres-Niggemeyer, B., Maier, E., & Sigel, A. (1995). How to implement a naturalistic model of abstracting: Four core working steps of an expert abstractor. *Information Processing & Management*, 631–674. doi:10.1016/0306-4573(95)00028-F

Erkan, G., & Radev, D. R. (2004). Lexrank: Graph-based centrality as salience in text summarization. *Journal of Artificial Intelligence Research, 22*(1), 457–479.

Gillick, D., Favre, B., & Tür, D. H. (2008). The ICSI summarization system at TAC 2008. In *Proceedings of the First Text Analysis Conference.* Academic Press.

Hmida, F., & Favre, B. (2011). LIF at TAC multiling: Towards a truly language independent summarizer. In *Proceedings of Text Analysis Conference.* TAC.

Kupiec, J., Pedersen, J., & Chen, F. (1995). A trainable document summarizer. In *Proceedings of the 18th Annual International ACM SIGIR Conference on Research and Development in Information Retrieval*, (pp.68-73). ACM.

Lin, C. Y. (2004). Rouge: A package for automatic evaluation of summaries. In *Proceedings of the Workshop Text Summarization Branches Out*, (pp. 74-81). Academic Press.

Lin, C. Y., & Hovy, E. H. (2003). Automatic evaluation of summaries using n-gram co-occurrence statistics. In *Proceedings of Language Technology Conference.* Academic Press.

Lin, N. (1999). Social networks and status attainment. *Annual Review of Sociology*, 467–487. doi:10.1146/annurev.soc.25.1.467

Luhn, H. P. (1958). The automatic creation of literature abstracts. *IBM Journal of Research and Development, 2*(2), 159–165. doi:10.1147/rd.22.0159

McDonald, R. (2007). A study of global inference algorithms in multi-document summarization. In *Advances in information retrieval.* Berlin: Springer. doi:10.1007/978-3-540-71496-5_51

Mihalcea, R. (2004). Graph-based ranking algorithms for sentence extraction, applied to text summarization. In *Proceedings of the ACL 2004 on Interactive Poster and Demonstration Sessions.* ACL.

Mihalcea, R. (2005). Language independent extractive summarization. In *Proceedings of the 20th National Conference on Artificial Intelligence*, (pp. 1688-1689). AAAI.

Minel, J. L. (2002). *Filtrage sémantique: Du résumé à la fouille de textes.* Hermès Science Publications. Retrieved from http://hal.archives-ouvertes.fr/hal-00022142/en/

Nenkova, A., Passonneau, R., & McKeown, K. (2007). The pyramid method: Incorporating human content selection variation in summarization evaluation. *ACM Transactions on Speech and Language Processing, 4*(2).

Ogden, W., Cowie, J., Davis, M., Ludovik, E., Molina-Salgado, H., & Shin, H. (1999). Getting information from documents you cannot read: An interactive cross-language text retrieval and summarization system. In *Proceedings of Joint ACM DL/SIGIR Workshop on Multilingual Information Discovery and Access.* ACM.

Radev, D. R., Jing, H., Stys, M., & Tam, D. (2004). Centroid-based summarization of multiple documents. *Information Processing & Management*, *40*(6), 919–938. doi:10.1016/j.ipm.2003.10.006

Saggion, H., & Lapalme, G. (1998). Where does information come from? Corpus analysis for automatic abstracting. *Rencontre Internationale sur l'extraction le Filtrage et le Résumé Automatique*, 72-83.

Salton, G., & Buckley, C. (1988). Term-weighting approaches in automatic text retrieval. *Information Processing & Management*, *24*(5), 513–523. doi:10.1016/0306-4573(88)90021-0

Salton, G., Singhal, A., Mitra, M., & Buckley, C. (1997). Automatic text structuring and summarization. *Information Processing & Management*, *33*(2), 193–207. doi:10.1016/S0306-4573(96)00062-3

Zhao, H., & Liu, Q. (2010). The CIPS-SIGHAN CLP 2010 Chinese word segmentation bakeoff. In *Proceedings of the First CPS-SIGHAN Joint Conference on Chinese Language Processing*, (pp. 199--209). CPS.

Zhikov, V., & Takamora, H. (2010). An efficient algorithm for unsupervised word segmentation with branching entropy and MDL. In *Proceedings of the 2010 Conference on Empirical Methods in Natural Language Processing*, (pp. 832–842). NLP.

ADDITIONAL READING

Bird, S., Klein, E., & Loper, E. (2009). *Natural Language Processing with Python*. O'Reilly.

Cunningham, H. (2002). GATE, a general architecture for text engineering. *Computers and the Humanities*, *36*(2), 223–254. doi:10.1023/A:1014348124664

Evans, D., & McKeown, K. (2005). Identifying similarities and differences across English and Arabic news. In: *Proceedings of International Conference on Intelligence Analysis*, pp. 23-30.

Ji, H., Favre, B., Lin, W., Gillick, D., Hakkani-Tur, D., & Grishman, R. (2013). *Open-domain Multi-Document Summarization via Information Extraction: Challenges and Prospects* (pp. 177–201). Multi-source, Multilingual Information Extraction and Summarization. doi:10.1007/978-3-642-28569-1_9

Krenn, B., & Samuelsson, C. (1997). *The Linguist's Guide to Statistics – Don't Panic*.

Manning, C. D., & Schütze, H. (1999). *Foundations of Statistical Natural Language Processing*. MIT Press.

Saggion, H. (2008). A robust and adaptable summarization tool. *Traitement Automatique des Langues*, *49*(2), 103–125.

Saggion, H., Torres-Moreno, J., Cunha, I., & SanJuan, E. (2010). Multilingual Summarization Evaluation without Human Models. In *Proceedings of the 23rd International Conference on Computational Linguistics: Posters*, pp. 1059-1067

Siddharthan, A., & Mckeown, K. (2005). Improving Multilingual Summarization: Using Redundancy in the Input to Correct MT errors. In *Proceedings of the conference on Human Language Technology and Empirical Methods in Natural Language Processing*, pp. 33--40.

Wan, S., & Paris, C. (2008). In-browser summarisation: generating elaborative summaries biased towards the reading context. In *Proceedings of the 46th Annual Meeting of the Association for Computational Linguistics on Human Language Technologies: Short Papers*, pp. 129-132.

KEY TERMS AND DEFINITIONS

Document Understanding Conference (DUC): An evaluation campaign organized by National Institute of Standards and Technology since 2001. DUC became since 2008 (TAC).

Information Extraction (IE): A field of Artificial Intelligence concerned with the extraction of structured information from structured and/or unstructured data.

Multilinguism: A field of linguistic (and NLP) concerned with data containing more than one language.

Natural Language Processing (NLP): A field of computer science concerned with linguistic and Artificial Intelligence in order to translate the human language processing to machine language.

Recall-Oriented Understudy for Gisty Evaluation (ROUGE): Proposed for automated evaluation of summaries and based on the similarity between summaries and references.

Text Alanalysis Conference (TAC): An evaluation workshops providing a large test collection and evaluations to encourage researche in NLP.

Text Summarization: A compressed representation of an information source while maintaining the important information of the original content.

ENDNOTES

[1]   Web Site: http://doc.nist.gov
[2]   A description of content units and their use in annotation ca be found in http://www1. cs.columbia.edu/~ani/DUC2005/AnnotationGuide.htm
[3]   Web Site: http://duc.nist.gov/

Compilation of References

Adler, B. T., de Alfaro, L., Pye, I., & Raman, V. (2008). Measuring author contributions to the Wikipedia. In Proceedings of WikiSym'08 (pp. 15:1-15:10). New York: ACM.

Afantenos, S. D., Doura, I., Kapellou, E., & Karkaletsis, V. (2004). Exploiting cross-document relations for multi-document evolving summarization. *Lecture Notes in Artificial Intelligence, 3025,* 410–419.

Afantenos, S., Karkaletsis, V., & Stamatopoulos, P. (2005). Summarization from medical documents: A survey. *Artificial Intelligence in Medicine, 33*(2), 157–177. doi:10.1016/j.artmed.2004.07.017 PMID:15811783

Aggarwal, C. C. (2011). An introduction to social network data analytics. In *Social network data analytics.* New York: Springer. doi:10.1007/978-1-4419-8462-3_1

Ahmad, K., Vrusias, B., & Oliveira, P. C. (2003). Summary evaluation and text categorization. In *Proceedings of the 26th Annual International ACM SIGIR Conference on Research and Development in Informaion Retrieval* (pp. 443-444). ACM.

Aker, A., Cohn, T., & Gaizauskas, R. (2010). Multidocument summarization using A* search and discriminative training. In *Proceedings of the 2010 Conference on Empirical Methods in Natural Language Processing, EMNLP '10.* (pp. 482–491). EMNLP.

Alfonseca, E., & Rodriguez, P. (2003). Generating extracts with genetic algorithms. In *Proceedings of the 2003 European Conference on Information Retrieval (ECIR'2003).* (pp. 511–519). ECIR.

Allan, J. (2004). HARD track overview in TREC 2004 – High accuracy retrieval from documents. In E. M. Voorhees & L. P. Buckland (Eds.), TREC. Gaithersburg, MD: National Institute of Standards and Technology (NIST).

Allan, J., Gupta, R., & Khandelwal, V. (2001). Temporal summaries of news topics. In W. B. Croft, D. J. Harper, D. H. Kraft, & J. Zobel (Eds.), *Proceedings of SIGIR* (pp. 10-18). New York: ACM.

Allan, J., Lavrenko, V., & Jin, H. (2000). First story detection in TDT is hard. In *Proceedings of the 9th CIKM* (pp. 374-381). New York: ACM.

Allan, J., Papka, R., & Lavrenko, V. (1998). On-line new event detection and tracking. In *Proceedings of the 21st Annual International ACM SIGIR Conference on Research and Development in Information Retrieval, SIGIR '98.* ACM.

Allan, J., Wade, C., & Bolivar, A. (2003). Retrieval and novelty detection at the sentence level. In *Proceedings of the 26th Annual International ACM SIGIR Conference on Research and Development in Information Retrieval* (pp. 314–321). ACM.

Allan, J. (2002). *Topic detection and tracking: Event-based information organization.* Norwell, MA: Kluwer Academic Publishers. doi:10.1007/978-1-4615-0933-2

Amini, M. R., & Usunier, N. (2007). *A contextual query expansion approach by term clustering for robust text summarization.* Paper presented at Document Understanding Conference 2007. Rochester, NY.

Anagnostopoulos, A., Broder, A. Z., Gabrilovich, E., Josifovski, V., & Riedel, L. (2007). Just-in-time contextual advertising. In *Proceedings of the 16ᵗʰ ACM Conference on Information and Knowledge Management* (pp. 331–340). ACM.

Ancona, M., Scagliola, N., & Traverso, A. (2005). *Application of 3G cellular phones to cultural heritage: The agamemnon project*. Paper presented at the International Workshop on Recording, Modeling and Visualization of Cultural Heritage. New York, NY.

André, P., Bernstein, M. S., & Luther, K. (2012). Who gives a tweet? Evaluating microblog content value. In *Proceedings of the ACM 2012 Conference on Computer Supported Cooperative Work*. IEEE.

Angheluta, R., De Busser, R., & Moens, M.-F. (2002). The use of topic segmentation for automatic summarization. In *Proceedings of the ACL-2002 Workshop on Automatic Summarization*. Retrieved from https://www.law.kuleuven.be/icri/publications/51DUC2002.pdf

Antikytera Mechanism. (n.d.). *Wikipedia*. Retrieved from http://en.wikipedia.org/wiki/Antikythera_mechanism

Aone, C., Okurowski, M. E., Gorlinsky, J., & Larsen, B. (1999). A trainable summarizer with knowledge acquired from robust NLP techniques. In *Advances in automated text summarization*. Cambridge, MA: MIT Press.

Armano, G., Giuliani, A., & Vargiu, E. (2011). Semantic enrichment of contextual advertising by using concepts. In *Proceedings of International Conference on Knowledge Discovery and Information Retrieval*. IEEE.

Armano, G., Giuliani, A., & Vargiu, E. (2012). Using snippets in text summarization: A comparative study and an application. *In Proceedings of CEUR Workshop Proceedings*. CEUR.

Arora, R., & Ravindran, B. (2008). Latent dirichlet allocation and singular value decomposition-based multi-document summarization. In *Proceedings of the Eighth IEEE International Conference on Data Mining (ICDM 2008)*. IEEE Press.

Baeza-Yates, R. A., & Ribeiro-Neto, B. (2011). *Modern information retrieval the concepts and technology behind search* (2nd ed.). Harlow, UK: Pearson Education Ltd.

Baeza-Yates, R., & Ribeiro-Neto, B. (1999). *Modern information retrieval*. New York: ACM Press.

Baker, C. F., & Fellbaum, C. (2009). WordNet and FrameNet as complementary resources for annotation. In *Proceedings of the Third Linguistic Annotation Workshop*, ACL-IJCNLP, (pp. 125–129). ACL.

Baker, L. D., & McCallum, A. K. (1998). Distributional clustering of words for text classification. In *Proceedings of the 21ˢᵗ Annual International ACM SIGIR Conference on Research and Development in Information Retrieval* (pp. 96-103). New York: ACM Press.

Balahur, A., Lloret, E., Boldrini, E., Montoyo, A., Palomar, M., & Martínez-Barco, P. (2009, September). Summarizing threads in blogs using opinion polarity. In *Proceedings of the Workshop on Events in Emerging Text Types* (pp. 23-31). Association for Computational Linguistics.

Baralis, E., & Fiori, A. (2010). Summarizing biological literature with BioSumm. In *Proceedings of the 19th ACM International Conference on Information and Knowledge Management* (pp. 1961–1962). Retrieved from http://dl.acm.org/citation.cfm?id=1871785

Barzilay, R., & Elhadad, M. (1997). Using lexical chains for text summarization. In *Proceedings of the ACL/EACL'97 Workshop on Intelligent Scalable Text Summarization* (pp. 10–17). ACL.

Barzilay, R., McKeown, K., & Elhadad, M. (1999). Information fusion in the context of multi-document summarization. In R. Dale & K. W. Church (Eds.), *Proceedings of ACL* (pp. 550-557). Stroudsburg, PA: Association for Computational Linguistics.

Barzilay, R., & McKeown, K. R. (2005). Sentence fusion for multidocument news summarization. *Computational Linguistics*, *31*(3), 297–327. doi:10.1162/089120105774321091

Baxendale, P. (1958). Machine-made index for technical literature–An experiment. *IBM Journal of Research and Development*, *2*(4), 354–361. doi:10.1147/rd.24.0354

Becker, H., Chen, F., Iter, D., Naaman, M., & Gravano, L. (2011). Automatic identification and presentation of Twitter content for planned events. In *Proceedings of International AAAI Conference on Weblogs and Social Media*. AAAI.

Becker, H., Iter, D., Naaman, M., & Gravano, L. (2012). Identifying content for planned events across social media sites. In *Proceedings of the Fifth ACM International Conference on Web Search and Data Mining*, WSDM '12. ACM.

Becker, H., Naaman, M., & Gravano, L. (2010). Learning similarity metrics for event identification in social media. In *Proceedings of WSDM*, (pp. 291–300). WSDM.

Becker, H., Naaman, M., & Gravano, L. (2011). Beyond trending topics: Real-world event identification on Twitter. In *Proceedings of ICWSM*. ICWSM.

Becker, H., Naaman, M., & Gravano, L. (2011). Selecting quality Twitter content for events. In *Proceedings of International AAAI Conference on Weblogs and Social Media*. AAAI.

Belew, R. K. (Ed.). (2000). *Finding out about: A cognitive perspective on search engine technology and the WWW*. Cambridge, UK: Cambridge University Press.

Bell, T. C., Cleary, J. G., & Witten, H. (1990). *Text compression*. Englewood Cliffs, NJ: Prentice Hall.

Benson, E., Haghighi, A., & Barzilay, R. (2011). Event discovery in social media feeds. In *Proceedings of the 49th Annual Meeting of the Association for Computational Linguistics: Human Language Technologies*. ACL.

Berkelaar, M. (1999). *lp-solve free software*. Retrieved from http://lpsolve.sourceforge.net/5.5/

Berryman, M. J., Allison, A., & Abbott, D. (2002). Signal processing and statistical methods in analysis of text and DNA. In *Proceedings of SPIE: Biomedical Applications of Micro and Nanoengineering*. SPIE.

Beverungen, G., & Kalita, J. (2011). Evaluating methods for summarizing twitter posts. In *Proceedings of WSDM'11*. Hong Kong, China: WSDM.

Blair-Goldensohn, S., Hannan, K., McDonald, R., Neylon, T., Reis, G. A., & Reynar, J. (2008). Building a sentiment summarizer for local service reviews. In *Proceedings of WWW Workshop on NLP in the Information Explosion Era*. IEEE.

Blei, D., & Lafferty, J. D. (2006). Dynamic topic models. In *Proceedings of the 23rd International Conference on Machine Learning*, (pp. 113-120). ACM.

Blei, D. M. (2012). Probabilistic topic models. *Communications of the ACM*, *55*(4), 77–84. doi:10.1145/2133806.2133826

Blei, D. M., Griffiths, T. L., Jordan, M. I., & Tenenbaum, J. B. (2004). Hierarchical topic models and the nested Chinese restaurant process. In *Neural Information Processing Systems*. Cambridge, MA: The MIT Press.

Blei, D., M., Andrew, Y. N., & Jordan, I. M. (2003). Latent dirichlet allocation. *Journal of Machine Learning Research*, *3*, 993–1022.

Bliki Engine. (n.d.). Retrieved from http://code.google.com/p/gwtwiki/

Blitzer, J., Dredze, M., & Pereira, F. (2007). Biographies, Bollywood, boom-boxes and blenders: Domain adaptation for sentiment classification. In *Proceedings of Annual Meeting-Association for Computational Linguistics* (Vol. 45, p. 440). ACL.

Bogdanovych, A. (2007). *Virtual institutions*. (PhD Thesis). University of Technology of Sydney, Sydney, Australia.

Boguraev, B., & Kennedy, C. (1999). Salience-based content characterisation of text documents. In *Advances in Automatic Text Summarization*. Cambridge, MA: MIT Press.

Boudin, F. (2008). *Exploration d'approches statistiques pour le résumé automatique de texte*. (PhD Thesis).

Boudin, F., Bechet, F., El-Beze, M., Favre, B., Gillard, L., & Torres-Moreno, J. M. (2007). The lia summarization system at duc-2007. In *Proceedings of DUC 2007 Document Understanding Conference*. DUC.

Boudin, F., & Torres-Moreno, J.-M. (2009). A maximization-minimization approach for update text summarization. In *Current issues in linguistic theory: Recent advances in natural language processing*. John Benjamins Publishers.

Boyd, D. M., & Ellison, B. N. (2007). Social network sites: Definition, history, and scholarship. *Journal of Computer-Mediated Communication*, *13*(1), 210–230. doi:10.1111/j.1083-6101.2007.00393.x

Brandow, R., Mitze, K., & Rau, L. (1995). Automatic condensation of electronic publications by sentence selection. *Information Processing & Management, 31*(5), 675–685. doi:10.1016/0306-4573(95)00052-I

Brin, S., & Page, L. (1998). The anatomy of a large-scale hypertextual web search engine. *Computer Networks and ISDN Systems, 30,* 107–117. doi:10.1016/S0169-7552(98)00110-X

Broder, A., Fontoura, M., Josifovski, V., & Riedel, L. (2007) A semantic approach to contextual advertising. In *Proceedings of the 30th Annual International ACM SIGIR Conference on Research and Development in Information Retrieval* (pp. 559–566). ACM.

Cai, X., & Li, W. (2012). Mutually reinforced manifold-ranking based relevance propagation model for query-focused multi-document summarization. *IEEE Transactions on Audio, Speech, and Language Processing, 20*(5), 1597–1607. doi:10.1109/TASL.2012.2186291

Carbonell, J., & Goldstein, J. (1998). The use of MMR, diversity-based reranking for reordering documents and producing summaries. In *Proceedings of the 21st Annual International ACM SIGIR Conference on Research and Development in Information Retrieval* (pp. 335-336). ACM.

Carenini, G., & Cheung, J. C. K. (2008). Extractive vs. NLG-based abstractive summarization of evaluative text: The effect of corpus controversiality. In M. White, C. Nakatsu, & D. McDonald (Eds.), *Proceedings of INLG*. Stroudsburg, PA: Association for Computational Linguistics.

Carletta, J. (1996). Assessing agreement on classification tasks: The Kappa statistic. *Computational Linguistics, 22*(2), 249–254.

Carrasco, J., Fain, D., Lang, K., & Zhukov, L. (2003). Clustering of bipartite advertiser-keyword graph. In *Proceedings of the Workshop on Clustering Large Datasets*. IEEE.

Celeux, G., & Govaert, G. (1992). A classification EM algorithm for clustering two stochastic versions. *Journal of CSDA, 14*(3), 315–332.

Celikyilmaz, A., & Hakkani-Tur, D. (2010). A hybrid hierarchical model for multi-document summarization. In *Proceedings of the 48th Annual Meeting of the Association for Computational Linguistics* (pp. 815-824). Association for Computational Linguistics.

Chakrabarti, D., & Punera, K. (2011). Event summarization using tweets. In *Proceedings of the Fifth International AAAI Conference on Weblogs and Social Media* (pp. 66-73). AAAI.

Chen, C. C., & Chen, M. C. (2008). TSCAN: A novel method for topic summarization and content anatomy. In *Proceedings of the 31st SIGIR* (pp. 579-586). New York: ACM.

Chen, H. H., & Lin, C. J. (2000). A multilingual news summarizer. In *Proceedings of the 18th International Conference on Computational Linguistics* (pp. 159–165). IEEE.

Chen, S. F., & Goodman, J. (1998). *An empirical study of smoothing techniques for language modeling (Technical Report)*. Cambridge, MA: Harvard University.

Chen, Y. Y., Foong, O. M., Uong, S. P., & Kurniawan, I. (2008). Text summarization for oil and gas drilling topic. *Proceeding of World Academy of Science and Technology, 32,* 37–40.

Chieze, E., Farzindar, A., & Lapalme, G. (2010). An automatic system for summarization and information extraction of legal information. In *Semantic Processing of Legal Texts* (pp. 216–234). Springer. doi:10.1007/978-3-642-12837-0_12

Chong Tat Chua, F., & Asur, S. (2013). Automatic summarization of events from social media. In *Proceedings of the Seventh International AAAI Conference on Weblogs and Social Media* (ICWSM). AAAI.

Christensen, J., Mausam, S. S., & Etzioni, O. (2013). Towards coherent multi-document summarization. In *Proceedings of NAACL-HLT* (pp. 1163–1173). Retrieved from http://www.aclweb.org/anthology/N/N13/N13-1136.pdf

Chua, F. C. T., & Asur. (2013). Automatic summarization of events from social media. In *Proceedings of the Seventh International AAAI Conference on Weblogs and Social Media* (ICWSM 2013). AAAI.

Ciaramita, M., Murdock, V., & Plachouras, V. (2008). Online Learning from click data for sponsored search. In *Proceeding of the 17th International Conference on World Wide Web*. IEEE.

Ciaramita, M., Murdock, V., & Plachouras, V. (2008). Semantic associations for contextual advertising. *Journal of Electronic Commerce Research Special Issue on Online Advertising and Sponsored Search, 9*(1), 1–15.

Clough, P. D. (2003). *Measuring text reuse*. (PhD Thesis). University of Sheffield, Sheffield, UK.

Conroy, J. M., & Dang, H. T. (2008). Mind the gap: Dangers of divorcing evaluations of summary content from linguistic quality. In *Proceedings of the 22nd International Conference on Computational Linguistics (Coling 2008)* (pp. 145–152). Manchester, UK: Coling 2008 Organizing Committee. Retrieved from http://www.aclweb.org/anthology/C08-1019

Conroy, J. M., & O'Leary, D. P. (2001). Text summarization via hidden markov models. In *Proceedings of the 24th Annual International ACM SIGIR Conference on Research and Development in Information Retrieval* (pp. 406-407). ACM.

Conroy, J. M., Schlesinger, J. D., & O'Leary, D. P. (2007). CLASSY 2007 at DUC 2007. In *Proceedings of Document Understanding Conference (DUC) Workshop 2006*. DUC.

Conroy, J. M., Schlesinger, J. D., & O'Leary, D. P. (2009). CLASSY 2009: Summarization and metrics. In *Proceedings of the Text Analysis Conference (TAC) 2009*. TAC.

Conroy, J. M., Schlesinger, J. D., & Stewart, J. G. (2005). CLASSY query-based multi-document summarization. In *Proceedings of the Document Understanding Conf. Wksp. 2005 (DUC 2005) at the Human Language Technology Conf./Conf. on Empirical Methods in Natural Language Processing (HLT/EMNLP 2005)*. DUC.

Conroy, J. M., Schlesinger, J. D., O'Leary, D. P., & Goldstein, J. (2006). *Back to basics: CLASSY 2006*. Paper presented at Document Understanding Conference 2006. Rochester, NY.

Conroy, J. M., Schlesinger, J. D., Rankel, P. A., & O'Leary, D. P. (2010). *Guiding CLASSY toward more responsive summaries*. Paper presented at Text Analysis Conference 2010. Gaithersburg, MD.

Cordeiro, M. (2012). Twitter event detection: Combining wavelet analysis and topic inference summarization. In *Proceedings of Doctoral Symposium on Informatics Engineering*. DSIE.

Cormen, T. H., Leiserson, C. E., & Rivest, R. L. (2011). *Introduction to algorithms*. Cambridge, MA: The MIT Press.

Cover, T. M., & Thomas, J. A. (1991). *Elements of information theory*. New York: Wiley-Blackwell. doi:10.1002/0471200611

Crochemore, M., & Rytter, W. (2003). *Jewels of stringology: Text algorithms* (2nd ed.). Singapore: World Scientific Publishing.

Cunningham, H., Maynard, D., Bontcheva, K., & Tablan, V. (2002). GATE: A framework and graphical development environment for robust NLP tools. In *Proceedings of the 40th Anniversary Meeting of the Association for Computational Linguistics (ACL'02)*. Philadelphia, PA: ACL.

Damashek, M. (1995). Gauging similarity with n-grams: Language-independent categorization of text. *Science, 267*(5199), 843. doi:10.1126/science.267.5199.843 PMID:17813910

Dang, H. (2005). Overview of DUC 2005. In *Proceedings of the Document Understanding Conferences (DUC)*. Vancouver, Canada: NIST.

Dang, H. T. (2006). Overview of DUC 2006. In *Proceedings of Document Understanding Conference*, DUC 2006. NIST.

Dang, H. T., & Owczarzak, K. (2008). Overview of the TAC 2008 update summarization task. In *Proceedings of TAC 2008 Workshop - Notebook Papers and Results* (pp. 10–23). Retrieved from http://www.nist.gov/tac

Dang, H. T., & Owczarzak, K. (2009, November 16). *Overview of the TAC 2009 summarization track*. Paper presented at the TAC 2009. Retrieved from http://www.nist.gov/tac/publications/2009/presentations/TAC2009_Summ_overview.pdf

Darling, W. M. (2010). Multi-document summarization from first principles. In *Proceedings of the Third Text Analysis Conference*, TAC-2010. NIST.

Darling, W. M., & Song, F. (2011). Probabilistic document modeling for syntax removal in text summarization. In *Proceedings of the 49th Annual Meeting of the Association for Computational Linguistics: Human Language Technologies* (pp. 642-647). ACL.

Darling, W. M., & Song, F. (2011). Pathsum: A summarization framework based on hierarchical topics. In *Proceedings of Canadian AI Workshop on Automatic Text Summarization 2011*. AI.

Das, D., & Martins, A. F. T. (2007). *A survey on automatic text summarization*. Retrieved from http://www.cs.cmu.edu/~nasmith/LS2/das-martins.07.pdf

Das, D., & Martins, A. (2007). *A survey on automatic text summarization. Literature Survey for the Language and Statistics II Course at CMU*. Pittsburgh, PA: CMU.

Daumé, H., III, & Marcu, D. (2006). Bayesian query-focused summarization. In *Proceedings of the 21st International Conference on Computational Linguistics and the 44th Annual Meeting of the Association for Computational Linguistics* (pp. 305-312). Association for Computational Linguistics.

De Silva, L., & Jayaratne, L. (2009). *Semi-automatic extraction and modeling of ontologies using wikipedia XML corpus,* Applications of Digital Information and Web Technologies.

Deepayan, C., Deepak, A., & Vanja, J. (2008). Contextual advertising by combining relevance with click feedback. In *Proceeding of the 17th International Conference on World Wide Web* (pp. 417–426). ACM.

DeJong, G. F. (1982). An overview of the frump system. In W. Lehnert, & M. Ringle (Eds.), *Strategies for natural language processing* (pp. 149–176). Academic Press.

Delort, J., & Alfonseca, E. (2012). DualSum: A topic-model based approach for update summarization. In *Proceeding of EACL 2012*. Avignon, France: EACL.

Didion, J. (2012). *The java wordnet library (JWNL)*. Retrieved from http://sourceforge.net/projects/jwordnet/

Digital Buzz. (2012). *Infographic: Social media statistics for 2012*. Retrieved from http://www.digitalbuzzblog.com/social-media-statistics-stats-2012-infographic/

Ding, C. (2005). A probabilistic model for latent semantic indexing. *Journal of the American Society for Information Science and Technology, 56*(6). doi:10.1002/asi.20148

Doddington, G. (2002). Automatic evaluation of machine translation quality using n-gram co-occurrence statistics. In *Proceedings of the Second International Conference on Human Language Technology Research* (pp. 138-145). San Francisco, CA: Morgan Kaufmann.

Donaway, R. L., Drummey, K. W., & Mather, L. A. (2000). A comparison of rankings produced by summarization evaluation measures. In *Proceedings of NAACL-ANLP 2000 Workshop on Text Summarization* (pp. 69-78). Association for Computational Linguistics.

Dongen, S. (2000). Performance criteria for graph clustering and Markov cluster experiments. Amsterdam, The Netherlands: CWI (Centre for Mathematics and Computer Science).

DUC. (2002). *Document understanding conference*. Retrieved from http://duc.nist.gov/pubs.html#2002.

DUC. (2004). *The document understanding conference*. Retrieved from http://duc.nist.gov

Dumais, S., Platt, J., Heckerman, D., & Sahami, M. (1998). Inductive learning algorithms and representations for text categorization. In *Proceedings of the 7th International Conference on Information and Knowledge Management,* CIKM '98 (pp. 148–155). ACM.

Dumais, S. T., & Belkin, N. J. (2005). The TREC interactive tracks: Putting the user into search.[Gaithersburg, MD: National Institute of Standards and Technology] [NIST]. *Proceedings of TREC, 05*, 22–31.

Earl, L. (1970). Experiments in automatic extracting and indexing. *Information Storage and Retrieval, 6*(4), 313–330. doi:10.1016/0020-0271(70)90025-2

Edmunds, M.G., & Freeth, T. (2011). Using computation to decode the first known computer. *IEEE Computer*, 32-39.

Edmundson, H. P. (1969). New methods in automatic abstracting. *Journal of the Association for Computing Machinery, 16*(2), 264–285. doi:10.1145/321510.321519

Eisenstein, J. (2013). Phonological factors in social media writing. In *Proceedings of the NAACL/HLT 2013 Workshop on Language Analysis in Social Media* (LASM 2013). Atlanta, GA: LASM.

Elmagarmid, A., Ipeirotis, P. G., & Verykios, V. (2006). Duplicate record detection: A survey. *SSRN eLibrary*. Retrieved from http://papers.ssrn.com/sol3/papers.cfm?abstract_id=1281334

Endres-Niggemeyer, B., Maier, E., & Sigel, A. (1995). How to implement a naturalistic model of abstracting: Four core working steps of an expert abstractor. *Information Processing & Management*, 631–674. doi:10.1016/0306-4573(95)00028-F

Enron Scandal. (2013, May 28). *Wikipedia*. Retrieved 13, 2013, from http://en.wikipedia.org/w/index.php?title=Enron_scandal&oldid=545449463

Erkan, G., & Radev, D. R. (2004). Lexpagerank: Prestige in multi-document text summarization. In *Proceedings of EMNLP* (pp. 365–371). EMNLP.

Erkan, G., & Radev, D. (2004). LexRank: Graph-based lexical centrality as salience in text summarization. *Journal of Artificial Intelligence Research*, 457–479.

Erol, B., Lee, D. S., Hull, J., Center, R. C., & Menlo Park, C. A. (2003). Multimodal summarization of meeting recordings. In *Proceedings of Multimedia and Expo, 2003*. ICME.

Esuli, A., & Sebastiani, F. (2006). Sentiwordnet: A publicly available lexical resource for opinion mining.[). LREC.]. *Proceedings of LREC*, 6, 417–422.

Evans, D., & McKeown, K. (2005). Identifying similarities and differences across English and Arabic news. In *Proceedings of International Conference on Intelligence Analysis* (pp. 23–30). IEEE.

Evans, D. K., Klavans, J. L., & McKeown, K. R. (2004). Columbia newsblaster: Multilingual news summarization on the web. In *Demonstration Papers at HLT-NAACL 2004* (pp. 1–4). Academic Press. doi:10.3115/1614025.1614026

Farzindar, A. (2012). Industrial perspectives on social networks. In *Proceedings of EACL 2012 - Workshop on Semantic Analysis in Social Media*. EACL.

Farzindar, A., & Inkpen, D. (Eds.). (2012). *Proceedings of the workshop on semantic analysis in social media (SASM)*. Avignon, France: Association for Computational Linguistics.

Farzindar, A., & Khreich, W. (2013). A Survey of Techniques for Event Detection in Twitter, accepted in special Issue of the Computational Intelligence, an International Journal, on Semantic analysis in social networks.

Farzindar, A., & Lapalme, G. (2003). Using background information for multi-document summarization and summaries in response to a question. In *Proceedings of DUC03: NAACL 2003 Workshop in Automatic Text Summarization*. NAACL.

Farzindar, A., & Lapalme, G. (2004). LetSum, an automatic legal text summarizing system, legal knowledge and information systems. In *Proceedings of Jurix 2004: the Sevententh Annual Conference*. Berlin: IOS Press.

Farzindar, A., Danescu-Niiculescu-Mizil, C., Gamon, M., Inkpen, D., & Nagarajan, M. (Eds.). (2013). *Proceedings of the NAACL/HLT workshop on language analysis in social media* (LASM 2013). Atlanta, GA: NAACL.

Ferro, L., Gerber, L., Mani, I., Sundheim, B., & Wilson, G. (2005). *TIDES 2005 standard for the annotation of temporal expressions (Technical Report)*. The MITRE Corporation.

Filatova, E. (2004). Event-based extractive summarization. In *Proceedings of ACL Workshop on Summarization* (pp. 104–111). ACL.

Firmin, T., & Chrzanowski, M. J. (1999). An evaluation of automatic text summarization systems. In I. Mani, & M. T. Maybury (Eds.), *Advances in automatic text summarization* (pp. 325–336). Cambridge, MA: MIT Press.

Flores, J. G., Gillard, L., Ferret, O., & de Chandelar, G. (2008). Bag of senses versus bag of words: Comparing semantic and lexical approaches on sentence extraction. In *Proceedings of TAC 2008 Workshop - Notebook Papers and Results* (pp. 158–167). Retrieved from http://www.nist.gov/tac

Fox, D., Hightower, J., Liao, L., Schulz, D., & Borriello, G. (2003). Bayesian filtering for location estimation. *IEEE Pervasive Computing / IEEE Computer Society [and] IEEE Communications Society*, 2, 24–33. doi:10.1109/MPRV.2003.1228524

Frawley, W. (1992). *Linguistic semantics*. New York: Routledge.

Friedman, J. H. (2001). Greedy function approximation: A gradient boosting machine. *Annals of Statistics*, 29, 1189–1232. doi:10.1214/aos/1013203451

Fujisaka, T., Lee, R., & Sumiya, K. (2010). Discovery of user behavior patterns from geo-tagged micro-blogs. In *Proceedings of the 4th International Conference on Uniquitous Information Management and Communication*, ICUIMC '10. ACM.

Fung, G. P. C., Yu, J. X., Yu, P. S., & Lu, H. (2005). Parameter free bursty events detection in text streams. In *Proceedings of VLDB* (pp. 181-192). New York: ACM.

Ganti, V., Gehrke, J., & Ramakrishnan, R. (1999). CACTUS: Clustering categorical data using summaries. In *Proceedings of the 5th ACM SIGKDD International Conference on Knowledge Discovery and Data Mining, KDD '99*, (pp. 73–83). ACM.

Genest, P. E., & Lapalme, G. (2012, July). Fully abstractive approach to guided summarization. In *Proceedings of the 50th Annual Meeting of the Association for Computational Linguistics: Short Papers* (vol. 2, pp. 354-358). Association for Computational Linguistics.

Genest, P. E., Lapalme, G., Yousfi-Monod, M., & Montréal, Q. (2009). HEXTAC: The creation of a manual extractive run. In *Proceedings of TAC2009 Notebook*. TAC.

Giannakopoulos, G. (2009). *Automatic summarization from multiple documents*. University of the Aegean. Retrieved from http://www.iit.demokritos.gr/~ggianna/thesis.pdf

Giannakopoulos, G. (2010). *JInsect: The n-gram graph framework implementation*. Retrieved from http://sourceforge.net/projects/jinsect/

Giannakopoulos, G., & Karkaletsis, V. (2009). N-gram graphs: Representing documents and document sets in summary system evaluation. In *Proceedings of Text Analysis Conference TAC2009*. TAC.

Giannakopoulos, G., & Karkaletsis, V. (2011). AutoSummENG and MeMoG in evaluating guided summaries. In *Proceedings of TAC 2011 Workshop*. TAC.

Giannakopoulos, G., & Karkaletsis, V. (2013). *Together we stand NPowER-ed*. Paper presented at the CICLing 2013. Karlovasi, Greece.

Giannakopoulos, G., & Palpanas, T. (2009). Adaptivity in entity subscription services. In *Proceedings of ADAPTIVE2009*. ADAPTIVE.

Giannakopoulos, G., El-Haj, M., Favre, B., Litvak, M., Steinberger, J., & Varma, V. (2011). TAC 2011 multiling pilot overview. In *Proceedings of Text Analysis Conference (TAC-2011)*. National Institute of Standards and Technology.

Giannakopoulos, G., Karkaletsis, V., & Vouros, G. (2006). *Automatic multi-document summarization and prior knowledge: Past, present and vision* (Technical Report DEMO-2006-2). Demokritos, Greece: NCSR.

Giannakopoulos, G., Vouros, G., & Karkaletsis, V. (2010). *MUDOS-NG: Multi-document summaries using n-gram graphs* (Tech Report). Retrieved from http://arxiv.org/abs/1012.2042

Giannakopoulos, G., Karkaletsis, V., Vouros, G., & Stamatopoulos, P. (2008). Summarization system evaluation revisited: N-gram graphs. *ACM Trans. Speech Lang. Process.*, 5(3), 1–39. doi:10.1145/1410358.1410359

Gillick, D., & Favre, B. (2009). A scalable global model for summarization. In *Proceedings of the NAACL HLT Workshop on Integer Linear Programming for Natural Language Processing* (pp. 10–18). NAACL.

Gillick, D., Favre, B., & Tür, D. H. (2008). The ICSI summarization system at TAC 2008. In *Proceedings of the First Text Analysis Conference*. Academic Press.

Gionis, A., Indyk, P., & Motwani, R. (1999). Similarity search in high dimensions via hashing. In *Proceedings of the 25th International Conference on Very Large Data Bases*, VLDB '99. Morgan Kaufmann Publishers Inc.

Goldstein, J., Kantrowitz, M., Mittal, V., & Carbonell, J. (1999). Summarizing text documents: Sentence selection and evaluation metrics. In *Proceedings of the 22nd Annual International ACM SIGIR Conference on Research and Development in Information Retrieval* (pp. 121-128). ACM.

Gong, S., Qu, Y., & Tian, S. (2010). Summarization using wikipedia. In *Proceedings of the Text Analysis Conference*. TAC.

Gong, Y., & Liu, X. (2001). Generic text summarization using relevance measure and latent semantic analysis. In *Proceedings of the 24th ACM SIGIR Conference on Research and Development in Information Retrieval* (pp. 19–25). ACM.

Good, I. J. (1953). The population frequencies of species and the estimation of population parameters. *Biometrika, 40*(3/4), 237–264. doi:10.2307/2333344

Greek Gods. (n.d.). *Wikipedia*. Retrieved from http://en.wikipedia.org/wiki/Category:Greek_gods

Gruhl, D., Guha, R. V., Kumar, R., Novak, J., & Tomkins, A. (2005). The predictive power of online chatter. In *Proceedings of SIGKDD* (pp. 78-87). New York: ACM.

Gu, H., Xie, X., Lv, Q., Ruan, Y., & Shang, L. (2011). ETree: Effective and efficient event modeling for real-time online social media networks. In Proceedings of Web Intelligence and Intelligent Agent Technology (WI-IAT), 2011 IEEE/WIC/ACM, (Vol. 1, pp. 300–307). IEEE.

Haghighi, A., & Vanderwende, L. (2009). Exploring content models for multi-document summarization. In *Proceedings of Human Language Technologies: The 2009 Annual Conference of the North American Chapter of the Association for Computational Linguistics* (pp. 362-370). Association for Computational Linguistics.

Hahn, U., & Mani, I. (2000). The challenges of automatic summarization. *IEEE Computer, 33*(11), 29–36. doi:10.1109/2.881692

Halevy, A., Norvig, P., & Pereira, F. (2009). The unreasonable effectiveness of data. *IEEE Intelligent Systems, 24*(2), 8–12. doi:10.1109/MIS.2009.36

Han, E. H., & Karypis, G. (2000). Centroid-based document classification: Analysis and experimental results. In *Proceedings of the 4th European Conference on Principles of Data Mining and Knowledge Discovery,* PKDD'00 (pp. 424–431). Springer-Verlag.

Hand, T. F. (1997). A proposal for task-based evaluation of text summarisation systems. In *Proceedings of the ACL/EACL'97 Workshop on Intelligent Scalable Text Summarization* (pp. 31-38). ACL.

Harabagiu, S., & Lacatusu, F. (2010). Using topic themes for multi-document summarization. *ACM Transactions on Information Systems, 28*(3), 13:1-13:47.

Harman, D., & Over, P. (2004). The effects of human variation in duc summary evaluation. In *Proceedings of Text Summarization Branches out Workshop at ACL 2004*. ACL.

Hassanpour, S., O'Connor, M. J., & Das, A. K. (2011). A framework for the automatic extraction of rules from online text. *LNCS, 6826*, 266–280.

Hassel, M., & Sjobergh, J. (2006). Towards holistic summarization: Selecting summaries, not sentences. In *Proceedings of LREC - International Conference on Language Resources and Evaluation*. LREC.

Hastie, T., Tibshirani, R., & Friedman, J. (2009). *The elements of statistical learning: Data mining, inference, and prediction* (2nd ed.). Berlin: Springer. doi:10.1007/978-0-387-84858-7

Hatzivassiloglou, V., Klavans, J. L., Holcombe, M. L., Barzilay, R., Kan, M.-Y., & McKeown, K. R. (2001). SimFinder: A flexible clustering tool for summarization. In *Proceedings of NAACL, Workshop on Automatic Summarization*. Pittsburgh, PA: NAACL.

He, Q., Chang, K., Lim, E.-P., & Zhang, J. (2007). Bursty feature representation for clustering text *streams*. In *Proceedings of SDM*. Minneapolis, MN: SIAM. Retrieved July 13, 2013 from http://www.siam.org/proceedings/datamining/2007/dm07_050he.pdf

He, Z., Chen, C., Bu, J., Wang, C., Zhang, L., Cai, D., & He, X. (2012). *Document summarization based on data reconstruction.* Paper presented at the Twenty-Sixth AAAI Conference on Artificial Intelligence. New York, NY.

Help Formatting. (n.d.). *MediaWiki*. Retrieved April 10, 2013, from http://www.mediawiki.org/wiki/Help:Formatting

Hendrickx, I., & Bosma, W. (2008). Using correference links and sentence compression in graph-based summarization. In *Proceedings of TAC 2008 Workshop - Notebook Papers and Results* (pp. 429–435). Retrieved from http://www.nist.gov/tac

Herrera, J. P., & Pury, P. A. (2008). Statistical keyword detection in literary corpora. *The European Physical Journal C, 63*(1), 135–146.

Hmida, F., & Favre, B. (2011). LIF at TAC multiling: Towards a truly language independent summarizer. In *Proceedings of Text Analysis Conference*. TAC.

Hogenboom, F., Frasincar, F., Kaymak, U., & Jong, F. (2011). An overview of event extraction from text. In *Proceedings of Workshop on Detection, Representation, and Exploitation of Events in the Semantic Web* (DeRiVE 2011). CEUR.

House, D. (1997). *Interactive text summarization for fast answers*. Retrieved from http://www.mitre.org/pubs/edge/july_97/tirst. htm

Hovy, E., & Lin, C. Y. (1998). Automated text summarization and the SUMMARIST system. In *Proceedings of a Workshop*. Association for Computational Linguistics.

Hovy, E., Lin, C. Y., Zhou, L., & Fukumoto, J. (2006). Automated summarization evaluation with basic elements. In *Proceedings of the Fifth Conference on Language Resources and Evaluation* (LREC 2006) (pp. 604-611). LREC.

Hovy, E., Lin, C.-Y., & Zhou, L. (2005). Evaluating DUC 2005 using basic elements. In *Proceedings of the Document Understanding Conferences (DUC)*. Vancouver, Canada: NIST.

Hovy, E., Lin, C.-Y., Zhou, L., & Fukumoto, J. (2006). Automated summarization evaluation with basic elements. In *Proceedings of the Fifth Conference on Language Resources and Evaluation (LREC)* (pp. 899-902). Genoa, Italy: LREC.

Hovy, E., & Lin, C. Y. (1999). Automated text summarization in SUMMARIST. In I. Mani, & M. Maybury (Eds.), *Advances in automatic text summarization* (pp. 81–94). Cambridge, MA: MIT Press.

Hu, M., & Liu, B. (2004). Mining and summarizing customer reviews. In *Proceedings of the Tenth ACM SIGKDD International Conference on Knowledge Discovery and Data Mining* (pp. 168-177). ACM.

Hu, M., Sun, A., & Lim, E. (2007). Comments-oriented blog summarization by sentence extraction. In *Proceedings of 16th CIKM*, (pp. 901—904). CIKM.

Huang, X., Wan, X., & Xiao, J. (2013). Comparative news summarization using concept-based optimization. *Knowledge and Information Systems*, 1–26.

Janssens, F. A. L., Glänzel, W., & De Moor, B. (2007). Dynamic hybrid clustering of bioinformatics by incorporating text mining and citation analysis. In *Proceedings of SIGKDD* (pp. 360-369). New York: ACM.

Jatowt, A., & Ishizuka, M. (2006). Temporal multi-page summarization. *Web Intelligence and Agent Systems, 4*(2), 163–180.

Java, A., Song, X., Finin, T., & Tseng, B. (2007). Why we Twitter: Understanding microblogging usage and communities. In *Proceedings of the 9th WebKDD and 1st SNA-KDD 2007 Workshop on Web Mining and Social Network Analysis*, WebKDD/SNA-KDD '07. ACM.

Jing, H., McKeown, K., Barzilay, R., & Elhadad, M. (1998). Summarization evaluation methods: Experiments and analysis. In *Working Notes of the Workshop on Intelligent Text Summarization* (pp. 60-68). Academic Press.

Joachims, T. (2002). Optimizing search engines using clickthrough data. In *Proceedings of the ACM Conference on Knowledge Discovery and Data Mining (KDD)*. ACM.

Johnson, F. C., Paice, C. D., Black, W. J., & Neal, A. P. (1993). The application of linguistic processing to automatic abstract generation. *Journal of document and text management, 1*(3), 215-241.

Jones, S., Lundy, S., & Paynter, G. W. (2002). Interactive document summarization using automatically extracted keyphrases. In *Proceedings of the 35th Hawaii Int. Conf. on System Science*. IEEE.

Jones, K. S. (1999). Automatic summarising: Factors and directions. In *Advances in Automatic Text Summarization*. Cambridge, MA: MIT Press.

Jones, K. S. (2007). Automatic summarising: The state of the art. *Information Processing & Management, 43*(6), 1449–1481. doi:10.1016/j.ipm.2007.03.009

Jones, S. (1999). Automatic summarizing: Factors and directions. In *Proceedings of Advances in Automatic Text Summarization* (pp. 1–12). Academic Press.

Jurafsky, D., & Martin, H. J. (2009). *Speech and language processing an introduction to natural language processing, computational linguistics, and speech recognition* (2nd ed.). Upper Saddle River, NJ: Prentice Hall.

Kabadjov, M., Atkinson, M., Steinberger, J., Steinberger, R., & Goot, E. V. D. (2010). NewsGist: A multilingual statistical news summarizer. In *Proceedings of the European Conference on Machine Learning and Knowledge Discovery in Databases: Part III* (pp. 591–594). IEEE.

Kabadjov, M., Steinberger, J., Pouliquen, B., Steinberger, R., & Poesio, M. (2009). Multilingual statistical news summarisation: Preliminary experiments with English. In *Proceedings of the Workshop on Intelligent Analysis and Processing of Web News Content at the IEEE/WIC/ACM International Conferences on Web Intelligence and Intelligent Agent Technology (WIIAT)*. IEEE/ACM.

Kabadjov, M., Steinberger, J., & Steinberger, R. (2013). Multilingual statistical news summarization. In T. Poibeau, H. Saggion, J. Piskorski, & R. Yangarber (Eds.), *Multi-source, multilingual information extraction and summarization* (pp. 229–252). Berlin: Springer. doi:10.1007/978-3-642-28569-1_11

Kaikhah, K. (2004). Automatic text summarization with neural networks. In *Proceedings of the 2nd IEEE International Conference on Intelligent Systems* (pp. 40-44). IEEE.

Kallel, F. J., Jaoua, M., Hadrich, L. B., & Hamadou, A. B. (2004). Summarization at LARIS laboratory. In *Proceedings of the Document Understanding Conference*. Academic Press.

Kalman, D. (2006). A singularly valuable decomposition: The SVD of a matrix. *The College Mathematics Journal, 27*(1), 2–23. doi:10.2307/2687269

Karmarkar, N. (1984). New polynomial-time algorithm for linear programming. *Combinatorica, 4*, 373–395. doi:10.1007/BF02579150

Katz, S. (1987). Estimation of probabilities from sparse data for the language model component of a speech recognizer. *IEEE Transactions on Acoustics, Speech, and Signal Processing, 35*(3), 400–401. doi:10.1109/TASSP.1987.1165125

Kazantseva, A., & Szpakowicz, S. (2010). Summarizing short stories. *Computational Linguistics, 36*(1), 71–109. doi:10.1162/coli.2010.36.1.36102

Kendall, M. (1976). *Rank correlation methods*. Oxford, UK: Oxford University Press.

Ker, J., & Chen, J. (2000). A text categorization based on summarization technique. In *Proceedings of the ACL-2000 Workshop on Recent Advances in Natural Language Processing and Information Retrieval,* (vol. 11, pp. 79–83). Association for Computational Linguistics.

Khachiyan, L. G. (1996). Rounding of polytopes in the real number model of computation. *Mathematics of Operations Research, 21*, 307–320. doi:10.1287/moor.21.2.307

Khachiyan, L. G., & Todd, M. J. (1993). On the complexity of approximating the maximal inscribed ellipsoid for a polytope. *Mathematical Programming, 61*, 137–159. doi:10.1007/BF01582144

Khuller, S., Moss, A., & Naor, J. S. (1999). The budgeted maximum coverage problem. *Information Processing Letters, 70*(1), 39–45. doi:10.1016/S0020-0190(99)00031-9

Kim, S. M., & Hovy, E. (2005). Automatic detection of opinion bearing words and sentences. In *Proceedings of the International Joint Conference on Natural Language Processing (IJCNLP)* (pp. 61-66). IJCNLP.

Klein, D., & Manning, C. D. (2003). Accurate unlexicalized parsing. In *Proceedings of the 41st Meeting of the Association for Computational Linguistics,* (pp. 423-430). ACL.

Kleinberg, J. (1998). Authoritative sources in a hyperlinked environment. In *Proceedings of the Ninth Annual ACM-SIAM Symposium on Discrete Algorithms (SODA '98)*. ACM.

Kleinberg, J. (2002). Bursty and hierarchical structure in streams. In *Proceedings of SIGKDD* (pp. 91-101). New York: ACM.

Kleinberg, J. M. (1999). Authoritative sources in a hyperlinked environment. *Journal of the ACM, 46*(5), 604–632. doi:10.1145/324133.324140

Kolcz, A., Prabakarmurthi, V., & Kalita, J. (2001). Summarization as feature selection for text categorization. In *Proceedings of the 10ʰ International Conference on Information and Knowledge Management* (pp. 365–370). ACM.

Kraaij, W., Spitters, M., & Heijden, M. (2001). Combining a mixture language model and naïve Bayes for multi-document summarization. In *Proceedings of the DUC2001 Workshop (SIGIR2001)*, (pp. 95-103). New Orleans, LA: ACM.

Kriplean, T., Beschastnikh, I., McDonald, D. W., & Golder, S. A. (2007). Community, consensus, coercion, control: CS*W or how policy mediates mass participation. In *Proceedings of the 2007 ACM Conference on Supporting Group Work (GROUP '07)* (pp. 167-176). New York: ACM.

Krippendorff, K. (1980). *Content analysis: An introduction to its methodology*. Beverly Hills, CA: Sage Publications.

Krishnamurthy, B., Gill, P., & Arlitt, M. (2008). A few chirps about Twitter. In *Proceedings of the First Workshop on Online Social Networks*, WOSN '08. ACM.

Kumar, C., Pingali, P., & Varma, V. (2009). Estimating risk of picking a sentence for document summarization. In *Proceedings of the 10th International Conference on Computational Linguistics and Intelligent Text Processing* (pp. 571–581). IEEE.

Kumar, R., & Raghuveer, K. (2012). Legal document summarization using latent dirichlet allocation. *International Journal of Computer Science and Telecommunications, 3*, 114–117.

Kupiec, J., Pedersen, J., & Chen, F. (1995). A trainable document summarizer. In *Proceedings of the 18ʰ Annual International ACM SIGIR Conference on Research and Development in Information Retrieval*, (pp. 68-73). ACM.

Lacerda, A., Cristo, M., Goncalves, M. A., Fan, W., Ziviani, N., & Ribeiro-Neto, B. (2006). Learning to advertise. In *Proceedings of the 29ʰ Annual International ACM SIGIR Conference on Research and Development in Information Retrieval* (pp. 549–556). ACM.

Lamb, A., Paul, M. J., & Dredze, M. (2013). Separating fact from fear: Tracking flu infections on Twitter. In *Proceedings of HLT-NAACL* (Vol. 2013). NAACL.

Larkey, L. S., Allan, J., Connell, M. E., Bolivar, A., & Wade, C. (2003). UMass at TREC 2002: Cross language and novelty tracks.[National Institute of Standards & Technology.]. *Proceedings of TREC, 2002*, 721–732.

Lavrenko, V., & Croft, W. B. (2001). Relevance based language models. In *Proceedings of the 24th Annual International ACM SIGIR Conference on Research and Development in Information Retrieval*, SIGIR '01. ACM.

Ledeneva, Y. (2008). Effect of preprocessing on extractive summarization with maximal frequent sequences. [MICAI.]. *Proceedings of MICAI, 2008*, 123–132.

Lee, R., & Sumiya, K. (2010). Measuring geographical regularities of crowd behaviors for Twitter-based geo-social event detection. In *Proceedings of the 2nd ACM SIGSPATIAL International Workshop on Location Based Social Networks*, LBSN '10. ACM.

Lehmam, A. (2010). Essential summarizer: Innovative automatic text summarization software in twenty languages. In Adaptivity, Personalization and Fusion of Heterogeneous Information (pp. 216–217). Academic Press.

Leite, D. S., Rino, L. H. M., Pardo, T. A. S., & Nunes, M. das G. V. (2007). Extractive automatic summarization: Does more linguistic knowledge make a difference? In *Proceedings of the Second Workshop on TextGraphs: Graph-Based Algorithms for Natural Language Processing* (pp. 17–24). Rochester, NY: Association for Computational Linguistics. Retrieved from http://www.aclweb.org/anthology/W/W07/W07-0203

Lerman, K., Blair-Goldensohn, S., & McDonald, R. (2009). Sentiment summarization: Evaluating and learning user preferences. In *Proceedings of the 12th Conference of the European Chapter of the Association for Computational Linguistics* (pp. 514-522). Association for Computational Linguistics.

Levy, S. (2012). Can an algorithm write a better news story than a human reporter? *Wired*. Retrieved July, 13, 2013 from http://www.wired.com/gadgetlab/2012/04/can-an-algorithm-write-a-better-news-story-than-a-human-reporter/

Li, J., & Li, S. Wang. X., Tian, Y., & Chang, B. (2012). Key laboratory of computational linguistics. Peking University.

Lin, C. (2004). ROUGE: A package for automatic evaluation of summaries. In *Proceedings of the 42nd Annual Meeting of the Association for Computational Linguistics*. ACL.

Lin, C. Y. (1999, November). Training a selection function for extraction. In *Proceedings of the Eighth International Conference on Information and Knowledge Management* (pp. 55-62). ACM.

Lin, C. Y., & Hovy, E. (1997). Identifying topics by position. In *Proceedings of the Fifth Conference on Applied Natural Language Processing* (pp. 283-290). Association for Computational Linguistics.

Lin, C. Y., & Hovy, E. (2000). The automated acquisition of topic signatures for text summarization. In *Proceedings of the 18th Conference on Computational Linguistics* (vol. 1, pp. 495-501). Association for Computational Linguistics.

Lin, C. Y., & Hovy, E. H. (2003). Automatic evaluation of summaries using n-gram co-occurrence statistics. In *Proceedings of Language Technology Conference*. Academic Press.

Lin, C.-Y. (1999). Training a selection function for extraction. In *Proceedings of the Eighteenth International Conference on Information and Knowledge Management* (CIKM'99) (pp. 1-8). CIKM.

Lin, C.-Y. (2001). *Summary evaluation environment*. Retrieved from http://www.isi.edu/~cyl/SEE

Lin, C.-Y., & Hovy, E. (2002). Manual and automatic evaluation of summaries. In *Proceedings of the ACL 2002 Workshop on Automatic Summarization*, (vol. 4, pp. 45-51). Association for Computation Linguistics.

Lin, C.-Y., & Hovy, E. (2003). Automatic evaluation of summaries using n-gram concurrence. In *Proceedings of 2003 Language Technology Conference* (HLT-NAACL 2003). Edmonton, Canada: NAACL.

Lin, C.-Y., & Och, F. J. (2004). Automatic evaluation of machine translation quality using longest common subsequence and skip-bigram statistics. In *Proceedings of the 42nd Annual Meeting on Association for Computational Linguistics* (pp. 605-612). Association for Computational Linguistics.

Lin, C.-Y., & Och, F. J. (2004). ORANGE: A method for evaluating automatic evaluation th metrics for machine translation. In *Proceedings of the 20th International Conference on Computational Linguistics* (pp. 501-507). Association for Computational Linguistics.

Lin, D., & Pantel, P. (2002). Concept discovery from text. In *Proceedings of the 19th International Conference on Computational Linguistics (COLING-02)* (pp. 1-7). Taipei, Taiwan: Association for Computational Linguistics.

Lin, H., & Bilmes, J. (2010). Multi-document summarization via budgeted maximization of submodular functions. In *Proceedings of the 2010 Annual Conference of the North American Chapter of the Association for Computational Linguistics (HLT '10)* (pp. 912-920). Stroudsburg, PA: Association for Computational Linguistics.

Lin, N. (1999). Social networks and status attainment. *Annual Review of Sociology*, 467–487. doi:10.1146/annurev.soc.25.1.467

Lin, Y., Sundaram, H., & Kelliher, A. (2009). *Summarization of large scale social network activity: Acoustics, speech, and signal processing*. Academic Press.

Litvak, M., & Last, M. (2008). Graph-based keyword extraction for single-document summarization. In *Proceedings of the Workshop on Multi-Source Multilingual Information Extraction and Summarization* (pp. 17-24). Stroudsburg, PA: Association for Computational Linguistics.

Litvak, M., & Vanetik, N. (2012). Polytope model for extractive summarization. In *Proceedings of International Conference on Knowledge Discovery and Information Retrieval* (pp. 281-286). Academic Press.

Litvak, M., Aizenman, H., Gobits, I., Last, M., & Kandel, A. (2011). DegExt: A language-independent graph-based keyphrase extractor. In *Proceedings of the 7th Atlantic Web Intelligence Conference* (AWIC 2011) (pp. 121-130). Berlin: Springer.

Litvak, M., Last, M., & Friedman, M. (2010). A new approach to improving multilingual summarization using a genetic algorithm. In *Proceedings of the 48th Annual Meeting of the Association for Computational Linguistics* (pp. 927–936). ACL.

Litvak, M., & Last, M. (2013, September). Cross-lingual training of summarization systems using annotated corpora in a foreign language. *Information Retrieval*, 5(16), 629-656.

Liu, B., Hu, M., & Cheng, J. (2005). Opinion observer: analyzing and comparing opinions on the web. In *Proceedings of the 14th International Conference on World Wide Web* (pp. 342-351). ACM.

Liu, K.-L., Li, W.-J., & Guo, M. (2012). Emoticon smoothed language models for Twitter sentiment analysis. In *Proceedings of the Twenty-Sixth AAAI Conference on Artificial Intelligence*. AAAI.

Liu, B. (2012). Sentiment analysis and opinion mining. *Synthesis Lectures on Human Language Technologies*, 5(1), 1–167. doi:10.2200/S00416ED1V01Y201204HLT016

Liu, B., & Zhang, L. (2012). A survey of opinion mining and sentiment analysis. In *Proceedings of Mining Text Data* (pp. 415–463). Springer. doi:10.1007/978-1-4614-3223-4_13

Liu, D., Wang, Y., Liu, C., & Wang, Z. (2006). Multiple documents summarization based on genetic algorithm. *Fuzzy Systems and Knowledge Discovery*, 4223, 355–364. doi:10.1007/11881599_40

Liu, H., & Singh, P. (2004). ConceptNet: A practical commonsense reasoning tool-kit. *BT Technology Journal*, 22, 211–226. doi:10.1023/B:BTTJ.0000047600.45421.6d

Li, W. (1992). Random texts exhibit Zipf's-law-like word frequency distribution. *IEEE Transactions on Information Theory*, 1842–1845. doi:10.1109/18.165464

Long, C., Huang, M., Zhu, X., & Li, M. (2009). Multi-document summarization by information distance.[Silver Spring, MD: IEEE Computer Science Press.]. *Proceedings of ICDM*, 2009, 866–871.

Long, R., Wang, H., Chen, Y., Jin, O., & Yu, Y. (2011). Towards effective event detection, tracking and summarization on microblog data. In *Web-Age Information Management (LNCS)* (Vol. 6897, pp. 652–663). Berlin: Springer. doi:10.1007/978-3-642-23535-1_55

Louis, A., & Nenkova, A. (2012). Automatically assessing machine summary content without a gold standard. *Computational Linguistics*, 1–34.

Lu, Y., Zhai, C., & Sundaresan, N. (2009). Rated aspect summarization of short comments. In *Proceedings of the 18th International Conference on World Wide Web* (pp. 131-140). ACM.

Luhn, H. P. (1958). The automatic creation of literature abstracts. *IBM Journal of Research and Development*, 2(2), 159–165. doi:10.1147/rd.22.0159

Luo, G., Tang, C., & Yu, P. S. (2007). Resource-adaptive real-time new event detection.[New York: ACM.]. *Proceedings of SIGMOD*, 2007, 497–508.

Makhorin, A. O. (2000). *GNU linear programming kit*. Retrieved from http://www.gnu.org/software/glpk/

Makino, T., Takamura, H., & Okumura, M. (2011). Balanced coverage of aspects for text summarization. *In Proceedings of Text Analysis Conference*. TAC.

Mani, I. (2001). Automatc summarization, book, volume 3 of natural language processing. Amsterdam: John Benjamins Publishing Company.

Mani, I., Bloedorn, E., & Gates, B. (1998). Using cohesion and coherence models for text summarization. In *Proceedings of Intelligent Text Summarization Symposium* (pp. 69–76). Academic Press.

Mani, I. (2000). *Automatic summarization*. Amsterdam: John Benjamins Publishing Company.

Mani, I. M., & Bloedorn, E. M. (1999). Summarizing similarities and differences among related documents. *Information Retrieval*, 1(1), 35–67. doi:10.1023/A:1009930203452

Mani, I., Firmin, T., House, D., Chrzanowski, M., Klein, G., & Hirschman, L. et al. (1998). *The TIPSTER SUMMAC text summarisation evaluation: Final report*. The MITRE Corporation.

Mani, I., & Maybury, M. (1999). *Advances in automatic text summarization*. Cambridge, MA: MIT Press.

Manning, C. D., & Schutze, H. (1999). *Foundations of statistical natural language processing*. Cambridge, MA: MIT Press.

Mann, W. C., & Thompson, S. A. (1987). *Rhetorical structure theory: A theory of text organization*. Los Angeles, CA: University of Southern California, Information Sciences Institute.

Marcu, D. (2000). *DUC summarization roadmap*. Paper presented at NIST Ad-Hoc Review Committee for Planning Long-Term Research and Evaluation in Question Answering and Summarization. Retrieved from http://www-nlpir.nist.gov/projects/duc/roadmap.html

Marcu, D. (1999). From discourse structures to text summaries. In *Advances in automatic text summarization*. Cambridge, MA: MIT Press.

Markov, A. (1913). An example of statistical investigation in the text of 'Eugene Onyegin' illustrating coupling of 'tests' in chains. In *Proceedings of the Academy of Sciences of St. Petersburg* (pp. 153-162). Academy of Sciences of St. Petersburg.

Marquez, L., Carreras, X., Litkowski, K. C., & Stevenson, S. (2008). Semantic role labeling: An introduction to the special issue. *Computational Linguistics, 34*(2), 145–159.

Massoudi, K., Tsagkias, M., Rijke, M., & Weerkamp, W. (2011). Incorporating query expansion and quality indicators in searching microblog posts. In *Proceedings of the 33rd European Conference on Advances in Information Retrieval*, ECIR'11. Springer-Verlag.

Mathioudakis, M., & Koudas, N. (2010). TwitterMonitor: Trend detection over the Twitter stream. In *Proceedings of SIGMOD Conference*. Indianapolis, IN: ACM.

Matsuo, Y., Ohsawa, Y., & Ishizuka, M. (2001). A document as a small world. In Proceedings the 5th World Multi-Conference on Systemics, Cybenetics and Infomatics (Vol. 8, pp. 410–414). IEEE.

Maybury, M. (1999). Generating summaries from event data. In *Advances in automatic text summarization*. Cambridge, MA: MIT Press.

McCargar, V. (2004). Statistical approaches to automatic text summarization. *Journal of Information Science, 30*(4), 365–380.

McDonald, D. M., & Chen, H. (2006). Summary in context: Searching versus browsing. *ACM Transactions on Information Systems, 24*(1), 111–141. doi:10.1145/1125857.1125861

McDonald, R. (2007). A study of global inference algorithms in multi-document summarization. In *Advances in information retrieval*. Berlin: Springer. doi:10.1007/978-3-540-71496-5_51

McKeown, K. R., Klavans, J. L., Hatzivassiloglou, V., Barzilay, R., & Eskin, E. (1999). Towards multidocument summarization by reformulation: Progress and prospects. In *Proceedings of the National Conference on Artificial Intelligence* (pp. 453-460). John Wiley & Sons Ltd.

McKeown, K., & Radev, D. (1995). Generating summaries of multiple news articles. In *Proceedings of the 18th Annual International ACM SIGIR Conference on Research and Development in Information Retrieval* (pp. 74–82). ACM.

McKeown, K., Passonneau, R. J., Elson, D. K., Nenkova, A., & Hirschberg, J. (2005). Do summaries help? In *Proceedings of the 28th Annual International ACM SIGIR Conference on Research and Development in Information Retrieval (SIGIR '05)* (pp. 210-217). New York, NY: ACM.

Mei, Q., & Zhai, C. (2005). Discovering evolutionary theme patterns from text: An exploration of temporal text mining. In *Proceedings of SIGKDD* (pp. 198-207). New York: ACM.

Melamed, I. D. (1995). Automatic evaluation and uniform filter cascades for inducing n-best translation lexicons. In *Proceedings of the 3rd Workshop on Very Large Corpora (WVLC3)* (pp. 184-198). WVLC.

Melville, P., Sindhwani, V., & Lawrence, R. (2009). Social media analytics: Channeling the power of the blogosphere for marketing insight. In *Proceedings of the Workshop on Information in Networks* (WIN-2009). New York: WIN.

Metzler, D., Cai, C., & Hovy, E. H. (2012). Structured event retrieval over microblog archives. In *Proceedings of HLT-NAACL*, (pp. 646–655). NAACL.

Metzler, D., Dumais, S., & Meek, C. (2007). Similarity measures for short segments of text. In *Proceedings of the 29th European Conference on IR Research*, ECIR'07. Springer-Verlag.

Mihalcea, R. (2004). Graph-based ranking algorithms for sentence extraction, applied to text summarization. In *Proceedings of the ACL 2004 on Interactive Poster and Demonstration Sessions*. ACL.

Mihalcea, R. (2005). Language independent extractive summarization. In *Proceedings of the 20th National Conference on Artificial Intelligence*, (pp. 1688-1689). AAAI.

Mihalcea, R. (2005). Multi-document summarization with iterative graph-based algorithms. In *Proceedings of the First International Conference on Intelligent Analysis Methods and Tools (IA 2005)*. McLean.

Mihalcea, R., & Tarau, P. (2005). A language independent algorithm for single and multiple document summarization. In *Proceedings of IJCNLP*, (vol. 5). IJCNLP.

Mihalcea, R., & Tarau, P. (2004). Textrank: Bringing order into texts.[EMNLP.]. *Proceedings of EMNLP, 2004*, 404–411.

Miike, S., Itoh, E., Ono, K., & Sumita, K. (1994). A full-text retrieval system with a dynamic abstract generation function. In *Proceedings of the 17th Annual International ACM SIGIR Conference on Research and Development in Information Retrieval* (pp. 152-161). ACM.

Miller, G. (1995). WordNet: A lexical database for English. *Communications of the ACM, 38*(11), 39–41. doi:10.1145/219717.219748

Minel, J. L. (2002). *Filtrage sémantique: Du résumé à la fouille de textes*. Hermès Science Publications. Retrieved from http://hal.archives-ouvertes.fr/hal-00022142/en/

Minel, J., Nugier, S., & Piat, G. (1997). How to appreciate the quality of automatic text summarisation? Examples of FAN And MLUCE protocols and their results on SERAPHIN. In I. Mani & M. Maybury (Ed.), *Proceedings of ACL/EACL Workshop on Intelligent Scalable Text Summarization* (pp. 25-30). ACL.

Mithun, S. (2012). *Exploiting rhetorical relations in blog summarization*. (PhD thesis). Department of Computer Science and Software Engineering, Concordia University, Montreal, Canada.

Mladenic, D., & Grobelnik, M. (1998). Feature selection for classification based on text hierarchy. In *Proceedings of Text and the Web, Conference on Automated Learning and Discovery CONALD-98*. CONALD.

MultiLing. (2013). Retrieved from http://multiling.iit.demokritos.gr/pages/view/662/multiling-2013

Murdock, V., & Croft, W. B. (2005). A translation model for sentence retrieval. In *Proceedings of HLT/EMNLP*. Stroudsburg, PA: Association for Computational Linguistics.

Murdock, V., Ciaramita, M., & Plachouras, V. (2007). A noisy-channel approach to contextual advertising. In *Proceedings of the Workshop on Data Mining and Audience Intelligence for Advertising (ADKDD)*. ADKDD.

Murphy, K. P. (2012). *Machine learning: A probabilistic perspective*. Cambridge, MA: MIT Press.

Naaman, M., Becker, H., & Gravano, L. (2011). Hip and trendy: Characterizing emerging trends on Twitter. *Journal of the American Society for Information Science and Technology, 62*(5), 902–918. doi:10.1002/asi.21489

Nallapati, R., Feng, A., Peng, F., & Allan, J. (2004). Event threading within news topics.[New York: ACM.]. *Proceedings of CIKM, 2004*, 446–453. doi:10.1145/1031171.1031258

National Institute of Standards and Technology (NIST). (2011). *Document understanding conferences*. Retrieved July 21, 2013 from http://duc.nist.gov

National Institute of Standards and Technology (NIST). (2013). *Text analysis conference (TAC)*. Retrieved July 21, 2013 from http://www.nist.gov/tac

Nenkova, A. (2005). Automatic text summarization of newswire: Lessons learned from the document understanding conference. In *Proceedings of the 20th National Conference on Artificial Intelligence* (pp. 1436-1441). AAAI.

Nenkova, A., & Louis, A. (2008). Can you summarize this? Identifying correlates of input difficulty for generic multi-document summarization. In *Proceedings of the 46th Annual Meeting of the Association for Computational Linguistics* (pp. 825–833). ACL.

Nenkova, A., & Passonneau, R. (2004). Evaluating content selection in summarization: The pyramid method. In *Proceedings of HLT-NAACL*. NAACL.

Nenkova, A., Passonneau, R., & McKeown, K. (2007). The pyramid method: Incorporating human content selection variation in summarization evaluation. *ACM Transactions on Speech and Language Processing, 4*(2).

Nenkova, A., Vanderwende, L., & McKeown, K. (2006). A compositional context sensitive multi-document summarizer: exploring the factors that influence summarization. In *Proceedings of the 29th Annual International ACM SIGIR Conference on Research and Development in Information Retrieval* (pp. 573-580). ACM.

Nenkova, A. (2006). *Summarization evaluation for text and speech: Issues and approaches*. INTERSPEECH.

Nenkova, A., & McKeown, K. (2011). Automatic summarization. *Foundations and Trends in Information Retrieval, 5*(2-3), 103–233. doi:10.1561/1500000015

Nenkova, A., & McKeown, K. (2012). A survey of text summarization techniques. In *Mining Text Data* (pp. 43–76). Berlin: Springer. doi:10.1007/978-1-4614-3223-4_3

Nenkova, A., Passonneau, R., & McKeown, K. (2007). *The pyramid method: Incorporating human content selection variation in summarization evaluation*. ACM Transactions on Speech and Language Processing. doi:10.1145/1233912.1233913

Neto, J. L., Santos, A. D., Kaestner, C. A. A., & Freitas, A. A. (2000). *Generating text summaries through the relative importance of topics* (pp. 300–309). Lecture Notes in Computer ScienceBerlin: Springer. doi:10.1007/3-540-44399-1_31

New Media Trend Watch. (2013). *Social networking and UGC*. Retrieved from http://www.newmediatrendwatch.com/world-overview/137-social-networking-and-ugc

Niekrasz, J., Purver, M., Dowding, J., & Peters, S. (2005). Ontology-based discourse understanding for a persistent meeting assistant. In *Proceedings of the AAAI Spring Symposium Persistent Assistants: Living and Working with AI*. AAAI.

Nishikawa, H., Hasegawa, T., & Kikui, G. (2010). Opinion summarization with integer linear programming formulation for sentence extraction and ordering. In Proceedings of Coling 2010: Poster Volume (pp. 910–918). Coling.

NIST. (2003). *The 2003 NIST machine translation evaluation plan (MT-03)*. Retrieved from http://www.itl.nist.gov/iad/mig/tests/2003/doc/mt03_evalplan.v2.pdf

Ogden, W., Cowie, J., Davis, M., Ludovik, E., Molina-Salgado, H., & Shin, H. (1999). Getting information from documents you cannot read: An interactive cross-language text retrieval and summarization system. In *Proceedings of Joint ACM DL/SIGIR Workshop on Multilingual Information Discovery and Access*. ACM.

Okurowski, M. E., Wilson, H., Urbina, J., Taylor, T., Clark, R. C., & Krapcho, F. (2000). Text summarizer in use: Lessons learned from real world deployment and evaluation. In *Proceedings of the 2000 NAACL-ANLP Workshop on Automatic Summarization* (pp. 49-58). Association for Computational Linguistics.

Open University. (2001). *Networks 3 - Assignment and transportation* (2nd ed.). Open University Worldwide.

Ortuño, M., Carpena, P., Bernaola-Galván, P., Muñoz, E., & Somoza, A. M. (2002). Keyword detection in natural languages and DNA. *Europhysics Letters, 57*, 759–764. doi:10.1209/epl/i2002-00528-3

Ouyang, Y., Li, W., Li, S., & Lu, Q. (2011). Applying regression models to query-focused multi-document summarization. *Information Processing & Management, 47*, 227–237. doi:10.1016/j.ipm.2010.03.005

Over, P., Dang, H., & Harman, D. (2007). DUC in context. *Information Processing & Management, 43*(6), 1506–1520. doi:10.1016/j.ipm.2007.01.019

Owczarzak, K., & Dang, H. T. (2011). Overview of the TAC 2011 summarization track: Guided task and AESOP task. In *Proceedings of the Text Analysis Conference* (TAC 2011). Gaithersburg, MD: TAC.

Page, L., Brin, S., Motwani, R., & Winograd, T. (1999). *The pagerank citation ranking: Bringing order to the web*. Stanford Digital Libraries.

Paice, C. D., & Jones, P. A. (1993). The identification of important concepts in highly structured technical papers. In *Proceedings of the 16th Annual International ACM SIGIR Conference of Research and Development in Information Retrieval* (pp. 69-78). ACM.

Pang, B., Lee, L., & Vaithyanathan, S. (2002). Thumbs up? Sentiment classification using machine learning techniques. In *Proceedings of the ACL-02 Conference on Empirical Methods in Natural Language Processing* (vol. 10, pp. 79-86). Association for Computational Linguistics.

Paolacci, G., Chandler, J., & Ipeirotis, P. (2010). Running experiments on amazon mechanical turk. *Judgment and Decision Making, 5*(5), 411–419.

Papineni, K., Roukos, S., Ward, T., & Zhu, W. J. (2002). BLEU: A method for automatic evaluation of machine translation. In *Proceedings of the 40th Annual Meeting on Association for Computational Linguistics* (pp. 311-318). ACL.

Paranjpe, D. (2009). Learning document aboutness from implicit user feedback and document structure. In *Proceedings of the 18th ACM Conference on Information and Knowledge Management*, CIKM '09. ACM.

Park, S., Lee, J. H., Ahn, C. M., Hong, J. S., & Chun, S. J. (2006). Query based summarization using non-negative matrix factorization. In *Proceeding of KES*, (pp. 84–89). KES.

Pastra, K., & Saggion, H. (2003). Colouring summaries BLEU. In *Proceedings of the EACL 2003 Workshop on Evaluation Initiatives in Natural Language Processing: Are Evaluation Methods, Metrics and Resources Reusable?* (pp. 35-42). Association for Computational Linguistics.

Patel, A., Siddiqui, T., & Tiwary, U. S. (2007). A language independent approach to multilingual text summarization. In Proceedings of Large Scale Semantic Access to Content (Text, Image, Video, and Sound), RIAO 2007 (pp. 123–132). RIAO.

Patel, C., Supekar, K., & Lee, Y. (2003). OntoGenie: Extracting ontology instances from WWW. In *Proceedings of Human Language Technology for the Semantic Web and Web Services*. ISWC.

Petrović, S., Osborne, M., & Lavrenko, V. (2010). Streaming first story detection with application to Twitter. In *Proceedings of HLT '10: Human Language Technologies: The 2010 Annual Conf. of the North American Chapter of the Association for Computational Linguistics* (pp. 181-189). Morristown, NJ: Association for Computational Linguistics.

Phuvipadawat, S., & Murata, T. (2010). Breaking news detection and tracking in Twitter. In *Proceedings of IEEE/WIC/ACM International Conference on Web Intelligence and Intelligent Agent Technology* (WI- IAT). IEEE.

Pingali, P., Rahul, K., & Vasudeva, V. (2007). *IIIT Hyderabad at DUC 2007.* Paper presented at Document Understanding Conference 2007. Rochester, NY.

Popescu, A.-M., & Pennacchiotti, M. (2010). Detecting controversial events from Twitter. In *Proceedings of the 19th ACM International Conference on Information and Knowledge Management*, CIKM '10. ACM.

Popescu, A.-M., Pennacchiotti, M., & Paranjpe, D. (2011). Extracting events and event descriptions from Twitter. In *Proceedings of the 20th International Conference Companion on World Wide Web*. ACM.

Porter, M. (1980). An algorithm for suffix stripping. *Program, 14*(3), 130–137. doi:10.1108/eb046814

Pouliquen, B., Kimler, M., Steinberger, R., Ignat, C., Oellinger, T., Blackler, K., et al. (2006). Geocoding multilingual texts: Recognition, disambiguation and visualisation. In *Proceedings of the 5th International Conference on Language Resources and Evaluation* (LREC 2006) (pp. 53–58). ELRA.

Pouliquen, B., & Steinberger, R. (2009). Automatic construction of multilingual name dictionaries. In C. Goutte, N. Cancedda, M. Dymetman, & G. Foster (Eds.), *Learning machine translation*. Cambridge, MA: MIT Press.

Radev, D. R., & Tam, D. (2003). Summarization evaluation using relative utility. In *Proceedings of the Twelfth International Conference on Information and Knowledge Management* (pp. 508-511). IEEE.

Radev, D. R., Jing, H., & Budzikowska, M. (2000). Centroid-based summarization of multiple documents: Sentence extraction, utility based evaluation, and user studies. In *Proceedings of NAACL-ANLP 2000 Workshop on Text Summarisation* (pp. 21-29). NAACL.

Radev, D., Allison, T., Blair-Goldensohn, S., Blitzer, J., Celebi, A., & Drabek, E. … Zhang, Z. (2004). MEAD - A platform for multidocument multilingual text summarization. In *Proceedings of the 4ᵗʰ International Conference on Language Resources and Evaluation*. IEEE.

Radev, D., Blair-Goldensohn, S., & Zhang, Z. (2001). Experiments in single and multidocument summarization using MEAD. In *Proceedings of First Document Understanding Conference*. Academic Press.

Radev, D., Teufel, S., Saggion, H., Lam, W., Blitzer, J., Qi, H., et al. (2003). Evaluation challenges in large-scale document summarization. In *Proceedings of the 41st Annual Meeting of the Association for Computational Linguistics* (pp. 375-382). Association for Computational Linguistics.

Radev, D. R., Jing, H., Stys, M., & Tam, D. (2004). Centroid-based summarization of multiple documents. *Information Processing & Management, 40*(6), 919–938. doi:10.1016/j.ipm.2003.10.006

Radev, D., Hovy, E., & McKeown, K. (2002). Introduction to the special issue on text summarization. *Computational Linguistics, 28*(4). doi:10.1162/089120102762671927

Radev, D., Otterbacher, J., Winkel, A., & Blair-Goldensohn, S. (2005). NewsInEssence: Summarizing online news topics. *Communications of the ACM, 48*(10), 95–98. doi:10.1145/1089107.1089111

Rau, L. F., Jacobs, P. S., & Zernik, U. (1989). Information extraction and text summarization using linguistic knowledge acquisition. *Information Processing & Management, 25*, 419–428. doi:10.1016/0306-4573(89)90069-1

Reeve, L. H., & Hyoil, H. (2007). A term frequency distribution approach for the duc-2007 update task. In *Proceedings of the Document Understanding Conference*. DUC.

Reiter, E., & Dale, R. (2000). *Building natural language generation systems*. Cambridge, UK: Cambridge University Press. doi:10.1017/CBO9780511519857

Ribaldo, R., Akabane, A. T., Rino, L. H. M., & Pardo, T. A. S. (2012). Graph-based methods for multi-document summarization: Exploring relationship maps, complex networks and discourse information. In *Computational Processing of the Portuguese Language* (pp. 260–271). Springer. Retrieved from http://link.springer.com/chapter/10.1007/978-3-642-28885-2_30

Ribeiro-Neto, B., Cristo, M., Golgher, P. B., & Silva de Moura, E. (2005). Impedance coupling in content-targeted advertising. In *Proceedings of the 28ᵗʰ Annual International ACM SIGIR Conference on Research and Development in Information Retrieval* (pp. 496–503). ACM.

Ricci, F., Rokach, L., Shapira, B., & Kantor, P. B. (Eds.). (2010). *Recommender systems handbook*. Berlin: Springer.

Ritchie, D. M. (1980). The evolution of the UNIX time-sharing system. In *Language Design and Programming Methodology* (pp. 25–35). Springer. doi:10.1007/3-540-09745-7_2

Rocchio, J. (1971). Relevance feedback in information retrieval. In *The SMART retrieval system: Experiments in automatic document processing* (pp. 313–323). Upper Saddle River, NJ: Prentice Hall.

Ruthven, I. (2008). Interactive information retrieval. *Annual Review of Information Science & Technology, 42*(1), 43–91. doi:10.1002/aris.2008.1440420109

Rutman, L. (1984). *Evaluation research methods: A basic guide*. Beverly Hills, CA: Sage Publications.

Saggion, H. (2006). Multilingual multidocument summarization tools and evaluation. In *Proceedings, LREC 2006*. LREC.

Saggion, H., & Lapalme, G. (1998). Where does information come from? Corpus analysis for automatic abstracting. *Rencontre Internationale sur l'extraction le Filtrage et le Résumé Automatique, 72-83.*

Saggion, H., Bontcheva, K., & Cunningham, H. (2003). Robust generic and query-based summarisation. *In Proceedings of the Tenth Conference on European Chapter of the Association for Computational Linguistics* (pp. 235–238). EACL.

Saggion, H., Radev, D., Teufel, S., & Lam, W. (2002). Meta-evaluation of summaries in a cross-lingual environment using content-based metrics. In *Proceedings of the 19th International Conference on Computational Linguistics* (pp. 1-7). ACL.

Saggion, H., Radev, D., Teufel, S., Lam, W., & Strassel, S. M. (2002). Developing Infrastructure for the evaluation of single and multi-document summarization systems in a cross-lingual environment. In *Proceedings of the Third International Conference on Language Resources And Evaluation (LREC 2002)* (pp. 747-754). LREC.

Sakaki, T., Okazaki, M., & Matsuo, Y. (2010). Earthquake shakes Twitter users: Real-time event detection by social sensors. In *Proceedings of the 19th international conference on World Wide Web*, WWW '10. ACM.

Salton, G., & Buckley, C. (1988). Term-weighting approaches in automatic text retrieval. *Information Processing & Management*, *24*(5), 513–523. doi:10.1016/0306-4573(88)90021-0

Salton, G., & McGill, M. J. (1983). *Introduction to modern information retrieval*. New York: McGraw Hill.

Salton, G., Singhal, A., Mitra, M., & Buckley, C. (1997). Automatic text structuring and summarization. *Information Processing & Management*, *33*(2), 193–207. doi:10.1016/S0306-4573(96)00062-3

Salton, G., Wong, A., & Yang, C. S. (1975). Vector space model for automatic indexing. *Communications of the ACM*, *18*(11), 613–620. doi:10.1145/361219.361220

Sankaranarayanan, J., Samet, H., Teitler, B. E., Lieberman, M. D., & Sperling, J. (2009). TwitterStand: News in tweets. In *Proceedings of the 17th ACM SIGSPATIAL International Conference on Advances in Geographic Information Systems*, GIS '09. ACM.

Sarah, M., & Taylor, S. M. (2004). Information extraction tools: Deciphering human language. *IT Professional*, *6*(6), 28–34. doi:10.1109/MITP.2004.82

Sarkar, K. (2009). Sentence clustering-based summarization of multiple text documents. *TECHNIA – International Journal of Computing Science and Communication Technologies*, *2*(1).

Sarkar, K. (2012). Bengali text summarization by sentence extraction. In *Proceedings of International Conference on Business and Information Management* (pp. 233-245). IEEE.

Sarkar, K. (2012). An approach to summarizing Bengali news documents. In *Proceedings of the International Conference on Advances in Computing, Communications and Informatics*. ACM.

Sarkar, K. (2009). Using domain knowledge for text summarization in medical domain. *International Journal of Recent Trends in Engineering*, *1*(1).

Sarkar, K., & Bandyopadhyay, S. (2005). A multilingual text summarization system for Indian languages. In *Proceedings of Simple 2005*. IIT Kharagpur.

Savoy, J. (2013). *IR multilingual resources at UniNE*. Retrieved from http://members.unine.ch/jacques.savoy/clef/

Schenker, A., Bunke, H., Last, M., & Kandel, A. (2005). *Graph-theoretic techniques for web content mining*. Singapore: World Scientific.

Schlesinger, J. M., & Conroy, J. D. (2011). CLASSY 2011 at TAC: Guided and multi-lingual summaries and evaluation metrics. In *Proceedings of the Fourth Text Analysis Conference (TAC 2011)*. Gaithersburg, MD: National Institute of Standards and Technology.

Schult, R., & Spiliopoulou, M. (2006). Discovering emerging topics in unlabelled text collections. In *Proceedings of ADBIS* (pp. 353-366). Berlin: Springer.

Schutz, A., & Buitelaar, P. (2005). *RelExt: A tool for relation extraction from text in ontology extension*. Academic Press. doi:10.1007/11574620_43

Sharifi, B., Hutton, M., & Kalita, J. (2010). Experiments in microblog summarization. In *Proceedings of NAACL-HLT 2010*. Los Angeles, CA: NAACL.

Shen, C., & Li, T. (2010). Multi-document summarization via the minimum dominating set. In *Proceedings of the 23rd International Conference on Computational Linguistics (COLING '10)* (pp. 984-992). Association for Computational Linguistics.

Shen, D., Chen, Z., Yang, Q., Zeng, H. J., Zhang, B., Lu, Y., & Ma, W. Y. (2004). Webpage classification through summarization. In *Proceedings of the 27th Annual International ACM SIGIR Conference on Research and Development in Information Retrieval,* SIGIR '04 (pp. 242–249). ACM.

Shen, D., Sun, J. T., Li, H., Yang, Q., & Chen, Z. (2007). Document summarization using conditional random fields. In *Proceedings of the 20th International Joint Conference on Artificial Intelligence,* (vol. 7, pp. 2862-2867). IEEE.

Sheskin, D. J. (2000). *Handbook of parametric and nonparametric statistical procedures* (2nd ed.). Academic Press.

Shi, L., & Mihalcea, R. (2004). *Open text semantic parsing using FrameNet and WordNet.* Paper presented at HLT-NAACL 2004. New York, NY.

Siegel, S., & Castellan, N. J. Jr. (1988). *Nonparametric statistics for the behavioral sciences.* New York: McGraw-Hill.

Singhal, A. (2001). Modern information retrieval: A brief overview. *A Quarterly Bulletin of the Computer Society of the IEEE Technical Committee on Data Engineering, 24*(4), 35–43.

Sinka, M., & Corne, D. (2002). A large benchmark dataset for web document clustering. In Soft Computing Systems: Design, Management and Applications, (pp. 881–890). Press.

Sjöbergh, J. (2007). Older versions of the ROUGEeval summarization evaluation system were easier to fool. *Information Processing & Management, 43*(6), 1500–1505. doi:10.1016/j.ipm.2007.01.014

Smith, D. A. (2002). Detecting and browsing events in unstructured text. In *Proceedings of SIGIR* (pp. 73-80). New York: ACM.

Soboroff, I., & Harman, D. (2005). Novelty detection: the TREC experience. In *Proceedings of the Conference on Human Language Technology and Empirical Methods in Natural Language Processing* (pp. 105-112). Morristown, NJ: Association for Computational Linguistics.

Sparck Jones, K. (1999). Automatic summarising: Factors and directions. In I. Mani, & M. Maybury (Eds.), *Advances in automatic text summarisation* (pp. 1–12). Cambridge, MA: MIT Press.

Spark-Jones, K., & Galliers, R. J. (1995). Evaluating natural language processing systems: An analysis and review. *Lecture Notes in Artificial Intelligence, 1083.*

Steinberger, J., & Ježek, K. (2009). Update summarization based on novel topic distribution. In *Proceedings of the 9th ACM DocEng Conference.* ACM.

Steinberger, J., & Kabadjov, M. (2011). JRC's participation at TAC 2011: Guided and multilingual summarization tasks. In *Proceedings of the Fourth Text Analysis Conference (TAC 2011).* Gaithersburg, MD: National Institute of Standards and Technology.

Steinberger, J., & Turchi, M. (2012). Machine translation for multilingual summary content evaluation. In *Proceedings of the NAACL Workshop on Evaluation Metrics and System Comparison for Automatic Summarization* (pp. 19-27). ACL.

Steinberger, J., Kabadjov, M., Pouliquen, B., Steinberger, R., & Poesio, M. (2010b). WB-JRC-UT's participation in TAC 2009: Update summarization and AESOP tasks. In *Proceedings of the Text Analysis Conference 2009.* NIST.

Steinberger, J., Kabadjov, M., Steinberger, R., Tanev, H., Turchi, M., & Zavarella, V. (2012). Towards language-independent news summarization. In *Proceedings of the Text Analysis Conference 2011.* NIST.

Steinberger, J., Turchi, M., Kabadjov, M., Cristianini, N., & Steinberger, R. (2010). Wrapping up a summary: From representation to generation. In *Proceedings of the 48th Annual Meeting of the Association for Computational Linguistics* (pp. 382-386). ACL.

Steinberger, J., & Jezek, K. (2004). Text summarization and singular value decomposition. *Lecture Notes in Computer Science,* 245–254. doi:10.1007/978-3-540-30198-1_25

Steinberger, J., & Jezek, K. (2004). Using latent semantic analysis in text summarization and summary evaluation. [ISIM.]. *Proceedings of ISIM, 04,* 93–100.

Steinberger, J., Poesio, M., Kabadjov, M., & Ježek, K. (2007). Two uses of anaphora resolution in summarization. *Information Processing & Management, 43*(6), 1663–1680. doi:10.1016/j.ipm.2007.01.010

Steinberger, J., Tanev, H., Kabadjov, M., & Steinberger, R. (2011). Aspect-driven news summarization. *International Journal of Computational Linguistics and Applications, 2*(1-2).

Steinberger, R., Pouliquen, B., & van der Goot, E. (2009). An introduction to the europe media monitor family of applications. In *Proceedings of Information Access in a Multilingual World of the SIGIR*. ACM.

Strapparava, C., & Valitutti, A. (2004). WordNet-Affect: An affective extension of WordNet.[). LREC.]. *Proceedings of LREC, 4*, 1083–1086.

Subašić, I., & Berendt, B. (2010). Experience stories: A visual news search and summarization system. In *Proceedings of ECML/PKDD* (vol. 3, pp. 619-623). Berlin: Springer.

Subašić, I., & Berendt, B. (2010). Discovery of interactive graphs for under-standing and searching time-indexed corpora. *Knowledge and Information Systems, 23*(3), 293–319. doi:10.1007/s10115-009-0227-x

Subašić, I., & Berendt, B. (2010). From bursty patterns to bursty facts: The e ectiveness of temporal text mining for news.[). Amsterdam, The Netherlands: IOS Press.]. *Proceedings of ECAI, 215*, 517–522.

Subašić, I., & Berendt, B. (2013). Story graphs: Tracking document set evolution using dynamic graphs. *Intelligent Data Analysis, 17*(1), 125–147.

TAC. (2011). *The text analysis conference*. Retrieved 2011 30-October from http://www.nist.gov/tac/

Takamura, H., & Okumura, M. (2009). Text summarization model based on maximum coverage problem and its variant. In *Proceedings of the 12th Conference of the European Chapter of the Association for Computational Linguistics* (pp. 781–789). EACL.

Tanev, H., & Magnini, B. (2006). Weakly supervised approaches for ontology population. In *Proceedings of the 11th Conference of the European Chapter of the Association for Computational Linguistics* (EACL). ACL.

Tanev, H., Piskorski, J., & Atkinson, M. (2008). Real-time news event extraction for global crisis monitoring. In *Proceedings of 13th International Conference on Applications of Natural Language to Information Systems* (NLDB 2008). NLDB.

Teufel, S., & Moens, M. (1999). Sentence extraction as a classification task. In *Advances in automatic text summarization*. Cambridge, MA: MIT Press.

Teufel, S., & Moens, M. (2002). Summarizing scientific articles: Experiments with relevance and rhetorical status. *Computational Linguistics, 28*(4), 409–445. doi:10.1162/089120102762671936

Tf-idf. (n.d.). *Wikipedia*. Retrieved April 10, 2013, from http://en.wikipedia.org/wiki/Tf-idf

Torralbo, R., Alfonseca, E., Guirao, J. M., & Moreno-Sandoval, A. (2005). Description of the UAM system at DUC-2005. In *Proceedings of the Document Understanding Conf. Wksp. 2005 (DUC 2005) at the Human Language Technology Conf./Conf. on Empirical Methods in Natural Language Processing (HLT/EMNLP 2005)*. HLT.

Toutanova, K., & Manning, C. D. (2000). Enriching the knowledge sources used in a maximum entropy part-of-speech tagger. In *Proceedings of the Joint SIGDAT Conference on Empirical Methods in Natural Language Processing and Very Large Corpora* (EMNLP/VLC-2000), (pp. 63-70). ACM.

Toutanova, K., Brockett, C., Gamon, M., Jagarlamudi, J., Suzuki, H., & Vanderwende, L. (2007). *The PYTHY summarization system: Microsoft research at DUC 2007*. Paper presented at Document Understanding Conference 2007. Rochester, NY.

Trampus, M., & Mladenic, D. (2009). Constructing event templates from written news. In *Proceedings of Web Intelligence/IAT Workshops* (pp. 507–510). Silver Spring, MD: IEEE Computer Science Press.

Tratz, S., & Hovy, E. (2008). Summarization evaluation using transformed basic elements. In *Proceedings of the Text Analysis Conference (TAC-08)*. Gaithersburg, MD: NIST.

Tucker, R. (1999). *Automatic summarising and the CLASP system*. (PhD thesis). University of Cambridge Computer Laboratory, Cambridge, UK.

Turchi, M., Atkinson, M., Wilcox, A., Crawley, B., Bucci, S., Steinberger, R., & van der Goot, E. (2012). ONTS: Optima news translation system. In *Proceedings of EACL 2012* (pp. 25-32). ACL.

Turchi, M., Steinberger, J., Kabadjov, M., & Steinberger, R. (2010). Using parallel corpora for multilingual (multi-document) summarisation evaluation. In *Multilingual and Multimodal Information Access Evaluation (LNCS)* (Vol. 6360, pp. 52–63). Berlin: Springer. doi:10.1007/978-3-642-15998-5_7

Turian, J. P., Shen, L., & Melamed, I. D. (2003). Evaluation of machine translation and its evaluation.[New Orleans, LA: MT.]. *Proceedings of MT Summit, IX*, 386–393.

Turney, P. D. (2000). Learning algorithms for keyphrase extraction. *Information Retrieval, 2*(4), 303–336. doi:10.1023/A:1009976227802

Tversky, A. (1977). Features of similarity. *Psychological Review, 84*(4), 327–352. doi:10.1037/0033-295X.84.4.327

van Rijsbergen, C. (1979). *Information retrieval* (2nd ed.). London: Butterworths.

Varadarajan, R., & Hristidis, V. (2006). A system for query-specific document summarization. In *Proceedings of the 15th ACM International Conference on Information and Knowledge Management*, (pp. 622–631). ACM.

Verma, R., Ping, C., & Wei, L. (2007). A semantic free-text summarization system using ontology knowledge. In *Proceedings of Document Understanding Conference*. DUC.

Viégas, F. B., Wattenberg, M., & Dave, K. (2004). Studying cooperation and conflict between authors with history flow visualizations. In *Proceedings of CHI* (pp. 575-582). New York: ACM.

Voorhees, E. M., & Tice, D. M. (2000). Overview of the TREC-9 question answering track. In *Proceedings of the Ninth Text REtrieval Conference (TREC-9)*. TREC.

Voorhees, E. M. (2000). Variations in relevance judgments and the measurement of retrieval effectiveness. *Information Processing & Management, 36*(5), 697–716. doi:10.1016/S0306-4573(00)00010-8

Wagstaff, K. (2012). Machine learning that matters. *arXiv preprint arXiv:1206.4656.*

Wan, X. (2011). Using bilingual information for cross-language document summarization. In *Proceedings of ACL*. ACL.

Wan, X., & Yang, J. (2006). Improved affinity graph based multi-document summarization. In *Proceedings of HLT-NAACL, Companion Volume: Short Papers* (pp. 181–184). NAACL.

Wan, X., & Yang, J. (2008). Multi-document summarization using cluster-based link analysis. In *Proceedings of the 31st Annual International ACM SIGIR Conference on Research and Development in Information Retrieval (SIGIR '08)*. ACM.

Wan, X., Jia, H., Huang, S., & Xiao, J. (2011). Summarizing the differences in multilingual news. In *Proceedings of the 34th International ACM SIGIR Conference on Research and Development in Information* (pp. 735–744). ACM.

Wan, X., Li, H., & Xiao, J. (2010). Cross-language document summarization based on machine translation quality prediction. In *Proceedings of ACL 2010*. ACL.

Wang, D., Li, T., Zhu, S., & Ding, C. (2008). Multi-document summarization via sentence-level semantic analysis and symmetric matrix factorization. In *Proceedings of the 31st Annual International ACM SIGIR Conference on Research and Development in Information Retrieval*, (pp. 307-314). ACM.

Wang, G., Yu, Y., & Haiping, Z. (2007). *PORE:* Positive-only relation extraction from wikipedia text. In *Proceedings of the 6th International Semantic Web and 2nd Asian Conference on Asian Semantic Web Conference*, (pp. 580-594). Springer.

Wang, J. B., Hong, P., & Hu, J. S. (2006). Automatic keyphrases extraction from document using neural network. In *Proceeding of the 4th International Conference on Advances in Machine Learning and Cybernetics (ICMLC'05)* (pp. 633-641). ICMLC.

Wang, X., & McCallum, A. (2006). Topics over time: A non-Markov continuous-time model of topical trends. In *Proceedings of SIGKDD* (pp. 424-433). New York: ACM.

Wang, D., Zhu, S., Li, T., Chi, Y., & Gong, Y. (2011). Integrating document clustering and multidocument summarization. *ACM Transactions on Knowledge Discovery from Data, 5*(3), 14. doi:10.1145/1993077.1993078

Wan, X. (2008). Using only cross-document relationships for both generic and topic-focused multi-document summarizations. *Information Retrieval, 11*(1), 25–49. doi:10.1007/s10791-007-9037-5

Weber, R. P. (1990). *Basic content analysis* (2nd ed.). Thousand Oaks, CA: Sage Publications.

Weerkamp, W., & Rijke, M. (2008). Credibility improves topical blog post retrieval. In *Proceedings of ACL*, (pp. 923–931). ACL.

Weng, J., & Lee, B. S. (2011). Event detection in Twitter. In *Proceedings of ICWSM*. ICWSM.

Winch, J. (2013). British teen sells Summly app. for millions. *The Telegraph*. Retrieved March, 25, 2013 from http://www.telegraph.co.uk/finance/newsbysector/mediatechnologyandtelecoms/9952658/ British-teen-sells-Summly-app-for-millions.html

Witten, I. H., Bray, Z., Mahoui, M., & Teahan, B. (1999). A new frontier for lossless compression. In *Proceedings of the Conference on Data Compression, DCC '99*. IEEE.

Witten, H., & Bell, T. C. (1991). The zero-frequency problem: Estimating the probabilities of novel events in adaptive text compression. *IEEE Transactions on Information Theory, 37*(4), 1085–1094. doi:10.1109/18.87000

Woodsend, K., & Lapata, M. (2010). Automatic generation of story highlights. *In Proceedings of the 48th Annual Meeting of the Association for Computational Linguistics* (pp. 565–574). ACL.

Wu, C. W., & Liu, C. L. (2003). Ontology-based text summarization for business news articles. In *Proceedings of the ISCA 18th International Conference on Computers and their Applications*, (pp. 389–392). ISCA.

Xu, W., Grishman, R., Meyers, A., & Ritter, A. (2013). A preliminary study of tweet summarization using information extraction. In *Proceedings of the NAACL/HLT 2013 Workshop on Language Analysis in Social Media* (LASM 2013). Atlanta, GA: NAACL.

Yang, Y., Pierce, T., & Carbonell, J. (1998). A study of retrospective and on-line event detection. In *Proceedings of the 21st Annual International ACM SIGIR Conference on Research and Development in Information Retrieval*, SIGIR '98. ACM.

Yang, Y., Zhang, J., Carbonell, J., & Jin, C. (2002). Topic-conditioned novelty detection. In *Proceedings of the Eighth ACM SIGKDD International Conference on Knowledge Discovery and Data Mining*. ACM.

Yatsko, V., & Vishnyakov, T. (2007). A method for evaluating modern systems of automatic text summarization. *Automatic Documentation and Mathematical Linguistics, 41*, 93–103. doi:10.3103/S0005105507030041

Yeloglu, O., Milios, E., & Zincir-Heywood, N. (2011). Multi-document summarization of scientific corpora. In *Proceedings of the 2011 ACM Symposium on Applied Computing* (pp. 252–258).

Yih, W. T., Goodman, J., & Carvalho, V. R. (2006). Finding advertising keywords on webpages. In *Proceedings of the 15th International Conference on World Wide Web* (pp. 213– 222). ACM.

Yong, S. P., & Ahmad, I. Z. Abidin, & Chen, Y.Y. (2005). A neural based text summarization system. In *Proceedings of the 6th International Conference of Data Mining* (pp. 45-50). ACM.

Yousfi-Monod, M., Farzindar, A., & Lapalme, G. (2010). Supervised machine learning for summarizing legal documents. In *Proceedings of Advances in Artificial Intelligence* (pp. 51–62). Springer. doi:10.1007/978-3-642-13059-5_8

Zavarella, V., & Tanev, H. (2013). FSS-TimEx for TempEval-3: Extracting temporal information from text. In *Proceedings of Second Joint Conference on Lexical and Computational Semantics (*SEM)*, (pp.58-63). ACL.

Zhai, Z., Liu, B., Zhang, L., Xu, H., & Jia, P. (2011). Identifying evaluative sentences in online discussions. In *Proceedings of National Conf. on Artificial Intelligence (AAAI-2011)*. AAAI.

Zhang, Y., Callan, J., & Minka, T. (2002). Novelty and redundancy detection in adaptive filtering. In *Proceedings of the 25th Annual International ACM SIGIR Conference on Research and Development in Information Retrieval* (pp. 81–88). ACM.

Zhao, D., & Rosson, B. R. (2009). How and why people Twitter: The role that micro-blogging plays in informal communication at work. In *Proceedings of the ACM 2009 International Conference on Supporting Group Work*. ACM.

Zhao, H., & Liu, Q. (2010). The CIPS-SIGHAN CLP 2010 Chinese word segmentation bakeoff. In *Proceedings of the First CPS-SIGHAN Joint Conference on Chinese Language Processing*, (pp. 199--209). CPS.

Zhikov, V., & Takamora, H. (2010). An efficient algorithm for unsupervised word segmentation with branching entropy and MDL. In *Proceedings of the 2010 Conference on Empirical Methods in Natural Language Processing*, (pp. 832–842). NLP.

Zhou, L., & Hovy, E. (2006). On the summarization of dynamically introduced information: Online discussions and blogs. In *Proceedings of AAAI Symposium on Computational Approaches to Analysing Weblogs (AAAI-CAAW)* (pp. 237-242). AAAI.

Zhou, L., Lin, C.-Y., Munteanu, D. S., & Hovy, E. (2006). ParaEval: Using paraphrases to evaluate summaries automatically. In *Proceedings of the Main Conference on Human Language Technology Conference of the North American Chapter of the Association of Computational Linguistics (HLT-NAACL '06)* (pp. 447-454). Stroudsburg, PA: Association for Computational Linguistics.

Zhou, L., Ticrea, M., & Hovy, E. (2005). Multi-document biography summarization. In *Proceedings of Conference on Empirical Methods in Natural Language Processing (EMNLP)*. EMNLP.

Zipf, G. K. (1949). *Human behavior and the principle of least effort*. Reading, MA: Addison-Wesley.

About the Contributors

Alessandro Fiori received the European Ph.D. degree from Politecnico di Torino, Italy. He is project manager at the Institute for Cancer Research and Treatment (IRCC) of Candiolo, Italy, since January 2012. His research interests are in the field of data mining, in particular bioinformatics and text mining. His activity is focused on the development of information systems and analysis frameworks oriented to the management and integration of biological and molecular data. His research activities are also devoted to text summarization and social network analysis.

* * *

Massimo Ancona received the Laurea degree in Mathematics from the University of Genova in 1965. From 1971, he was with the research staff of The "Laboratorio di Analisi Numerica" of the Italian Research Council (CNR) of Pavia, and in 1976, he was with the research staff of The "Istituto per la Matematica Applicata" of the CNR of Genova. Since 1985, he has been an Associate Professor of the Departement of Mathematics and since 1992 of DISI (Dipartimento di Informatica e Scienza dell'Informazione) of the University of Genova. Since 2002, he was full professor of DIBRIS (Dipartimento di Informatica, Bioingegneria, Robotica, e Ingegneria dei Sisitemi) of the University of Genova. He has been the local responsible of the following research projects in Computers and Archaeology: CNR project "Beni Culturali" Unita` DISI di Genova; European project IST--2-1A-20805 "PAST"; European project IST 508013 "Agamemnon" (http://services.txt.it/agamemnon).

Giuliano Armano obtained his Ph.D. degree in Electronic Engineering from the University of Genoa, Italy, in 1990. He is associate professor of computer engineering at the Dept. of Electrical and Electronic Engineering (DIEE), University of Cagliari, leading also the IASC (Intelligent Agents and Soft-Computing) group. At the Faculty of Engineering, he is currently teaching the following courses: (1) Fundamentals of Databases and of Bioinformatics, (2) Fundamentals of Computer Science 1, and (3) Object-Oriented Programming and Scripting in Python. His educational background ranges over expert systems and machine learning, whereas his current research activity is focused on machine learning and pattern recognition techniques, mainly experimented in the field of bioinformatics, information retrieval, and text categorization. Author or co-author of several international journals, Prof. Armano has organized various international events (conferences, workshops, and special issues) in the fields of software agents and bioinformatics.

Bettina Berendt is a professor in the Declarative Languages and Artificial Intelligence (DTAI) group at the Department of Computer Science of KU Leuven, Belgium. She studied Business Studies, Economics, and Artificial Intelligence/Informatics at Freie Universität Berlin, Germany, and the Universities of Cambridge and Edinburgh, UK. She holds a PhD in Computer Science/Cognitive Science from the University of Hamburg, Germany, and a Habilitation in Information Systems at Humboldt University Berlin, Germany. In her research, teaching, and project activities, she aims at defining and developing human-centric data mining. Concrete research interests include Web and text mining, privacy, and feedback and awareness tools for information literacy. Further details can be found at http://people.cs.kuleuven.be/~bettina.berendt/.

William Darling is a Research Engineer in the Machine Learning for Services (MLS) Group at Xerox Research Centre Europe. His research interests include statistical machine learning and natural language processing which encompasses probabilistic topic models, automatic text summarization, sentiment analysis, part-of-speech tagging, and others. He is also interested in the intersection of computer science and the social sciences, especially with respect to the application of AI to law. William received his Ph.D. in Computer Science from the University of Guelph in 2012 where the title of his thesis was "Generalized Probabilistic Topic and Syntax Models for Natural Language Processing." He also has LL.B. (common law) and B.C.L. (civil law) degrees from McGill University (2007) and an H.B.Sc. in Physics and Computer Science from Trent University (2004).

Paulo Cesar Fernandes de Oliveira received his BSc degree in Computer Science from the Federal University of Santa Catarina State, Brazil. The Ph.D. degree in Computer Science, he received from the University of Surrey, UK. He is now an Associate Professor at Anhanguera University – Joinville, Brazil. In addition, he is an IEEE and ACM member. His research interests are in language engineering (e.g. natural language processing), automatic text summarization, language and computer interface, information retrieval, knowledge management, AI applications in industrial engineering, and data mining/Web mining.

Atefeh Farzindar is the founder of NLP Technologies Inc., a Canadian company established in 2005, and specializing in natural language processing and automatic summarization of structured texts such as legal decisions, machine translation, and social media monitoring. Mrs. Farzindar obtained a joint Ph.D. degree in Computer Science from Université de Montréal and her Doctorate in Languages, Computer, and Cognition from Paris-Sorbonne University. She gathered academic and industrial experience in various positions in industry and academia. She is adjunct professor at the Department of Computer Science, Université de Montréal, General co-chair of AI/GI/CRV 2013 and 2014 Conference (Artificial Intelligence, Graphics Interface, and Computer and Robot Vision), Industry Chair of the Canadian Artificial Intelligence Association (CAIAC), Vice President of the Canadian Language Technologies Research Centre (LTRC), Member of the Canadian Advisory Committee for International Organization for Standardization (ISO), and Chair of technology sector of Language Industry Association Canada (AILIA) since 2009. She organized several conferences in Artificial Intelligence in collaboration with Canadian Artificial Intelligence Association (CAIAC) and workshops with the Association for Computational Linguistics (ACL) in Social Media. She co-edited two special issues on social media analysis for the *International Journal of Computational Intelligence* (CI) and *Journal TAL* (La Revue Internationale Traitement Automatique des Langues), an international journal on natural language processing.

George Giannakopoulos works as a Research Fellow in NCSR "Demokritos," Greece, and is co-founder of the Not-for-Profit Company, SciFY, which brings Artificial Intelligence applications and systems to the public as open systems (open source, open hardware) for free. He has been awarded a Best Paper award in 2009 (Adaptive 2009 Conference). His research interests include natural language understanding, automatic summarization, machine learning, knowledge representation, as well as adaptive systems. He has participated as a researcher in a number of EU and government funded projects (OntoSum, OKKAM, SYNC3, NOMAD). He is the organizer of the MultiLing community on Multilingual Multi-Document Summarisation and the corresponding workshops (co-located with TAC 2011 and ACL 2013). He has been a PC member for various conferences and workshops (e.g., ACL, NAACL, EM-NLP, LSHTC). Has has also acted as a reviewer for well-known journals (*Applied Artificial Intelligence, International Journal on Artificial Intelligence Tools, International Journal on Advances in Intelligent Systems, COIN*).

Alessandro Giuliani received his Ph.D. in Electronic and Computer Engineering at the University of Cagliari, in 2012. He is currently a Post-doc at the Dept. of Electrical and Electronic Engineering (DIEE), University of Cagliari, in the IASC (Intelligent Agents and Soft-Computing) group, led by Prof. G. Armano. In 2011, he worked as intern at Yahoo! Labs in Barcelona (Spain). Alessandro Giuliani is a co-organizer of the annual International Workshop on Information Filtering and Retrieval (DART). His main research focus ranges over information retrieval, information filtering, text categorization, and Web mining. In particular, he is investigating several algorithms, techniques, and applications on contextual advertising.

Hyoil Han is an Associate Professor in the Division of Computer Science at Marshall University. She obtained her BS and MS degrees from Korea University and Korea Advanced Institute of Science and Technology, respectively. She worked for Samsung Electronics and Korea Telecom before obtaining a PhD in Computer Science and Engineering from the University of Texas at Arlington in 2002. Dr. Han's research areas lie in the merging of techniques from the fields of databases and artificial intelligence and applying the new, combined techniques to Biomedical Informatics and the Semantic Web with an emphasis on text/data mining and text summarization. Dr. Han is a member of the ACM and has published over 40 papers in the refereed literature related to her research.

Firas Hmida is currently a PhD student in Laboratoir d'Informatique Nantes-Atlantique at the University of Nantes. His research interests include automated text summarization, multilingualism, sentiment analysis, information extraction, and text understanding with a focus on statistical approaches. He received his Master degree from the University of Marseille, France, in 2011 on fundamental computing, and he participated with Benoit Favre in TAC2011 with a language independent summarizer. Firas was a research engineer at Semantic Group Company (SucceedTogether) between 2011 and 2012 where he contributed methods for sentiment analysis. Then, he held the same position at LIF laboratory of Marseille, working with the speech group. Since 2013, he is a PhD student working on Context Rich Knowledge and Translation.

Vangelis Karkaletsis is Research Director at NCSR "Demokritos," and head of the SKEL Lab of the Institute of Informatics and Telecommunications. His research interests lie in Language and Knowledge Engineering, as applied to content analysis, natural language interfaces, ontology engineering, and personalization. He has acted as coordinator and technical manager in several research projects (MedIEQ, QUATRO Plus, OntoSum, INDIGO, NOMAD) and work package manager in others (BOEMIE project). He was the local Chair of EACL-09. He is co-founder of the spin-off company 'i-sieve' technologies, which focuses on sentiment analysis applications. He has authored more than 140 scientific texts (book chapters, journal articles, conference proceedings), including 2 patents. He has been a reviewer for a variety of high-impact journals, including JNLE, *IEEE Intelligent Systems*, KAIS, and others. He has also co-edited several special issues, including "Information Extraction and Summarization from Medical Documents" issue of the *Journal of Artificial Intelligence in Medicine*.

George Kiomourtzis works as a Research Assistant in NCSR "Demokritos," Greece, and is Lead Developer and Project Manager of the NewSum project in SciFY Not-for-Profit Company. He has had more than 7 years of experience in technical studies related to energy installations, including significant experience in CAD/CAM design. He has also worked as a Python and Java developer, recently focusing on Artificial Intelligence and Natural Language Processing applications. These include such systems as the NewSum summarization software (infrastructure, APIs, and end-user interfaces) and the PServer personalization platform. He participates in the NOMAD EU project as Research Assistant, working on the linguistic analysis pipeline Work Package and on system integration.

Mark Last is an Associate Professor at the Department of Information Systems Engineering, Ben-Gurion University of the Negev, Israel, and the Head of the Data Mining and Software Quality Engineering Group. Prof. Last obtained his Ph.D. degree from Tel Aviv University, Israel, in 2000. He has published over 170 papers and 10 books on data mining, text mining, and software engineering. Prof. Last is a Senior Member of the IEEE Computer Society and a Professional Member of the Association for Computing Machinery (ACM). He currently serves as an Associate Editor of *IEEE Transactions on Cybernetics and Pattern Analysis and Applications*. Prof. Last has co-chaired seven international conferences and workshops on data mining, software engineering, and Web intelligence. His current research interests are focused on data mining, cross-lingual text mining, and security informatics. Further details can be found at http://www.bgu.ac.il/~mlast/.

Marina Litvak has obtained a Ph.D. in Information Systems Engineering from Ben-Gurion University of the Negev in 2010. She is currently a faculty member at Department of Software Engineering of Shamoon College of Engineering in Beer Sheva, Israel. Her research interests include information retrieval, text mining, automated summarization, social networks analysis, and recommender systems.

Angela Locoro earned one degree in modern literature and one in computer science from the University of Genova, where she also attended the PhD Course in Electronic and Computer Engineering, Robotics, and Telecommunications. She is presently working as a postdoctoral fellow at the Computer Science Department of the same University within the group of Artificial Intelligence. Her research interests include Knowledge Representation, Semantic Web technologies, and Natural Language Processing (with a major focus on Word Sense Disambiguation). In particular her main publications focus on ontology matching, ontology learning from texts, concepts disambiguation, and automatic classification of documents based on standard metadata infrastructures for digital libraries.

Uri Mirchev is a software engineer with a background in information systems and text mining. He holds an MSc degree in Information Systems Engineering from Ben-Gurion University of the Negev, Israel. He is currently working as an installation software developer for an Internet company. His professional interests include text summarization and data mining.

Kamal Sarkar received his B.E degree in Computer Science and Engineering from the Faculty of Engineering, Jadavpur University, in 1996. He received the M.E degree and Ph.D. (Engg) in Computer Science and Engineering from the same University in 1999 and 2011, respectively. In 2001, he joined as a lecturer in the Department of Computer Science and Engineering, Jadavpur University, Kolkata, where he is currently an associate professor. His research interest includes text summarization, natural language processing, machine learning, Web mining, knowledge discovery from text data.

Sean Sovine studied mathematics and computer science at Marshall University in Huntington, WV. His research interests in the field of computer science are in the areas of machine learning and cyber security. He has done research in the area of multi-document summarization, and has had work published at the 26th International Conference of the Florida Artificial Intelligence Research Society.

Josef Steinberger works at the University of West Bohemia, Czech Republic, as an assistant professor. His research interests are in the area of text summarization, sentiment analysis, co-reference resolution, and information extraction, with special interest in multilingual solutions. After receiving a Ph.D. degree in computer science from the University of West Bohemia, he worked at the Joint Research Centre, European Commission, as a researcher in multilingual text mining.

Ralf Steinberger is a computational linguist (Ph.D. from University of Manchester, UK) with background in theoretical linguistics, specialising in multilingual text mining and methods to provide cross-lingual information access. Since 1998, he has been working at the European Commission's Joint Research Centre, where he leads the Language Technology activities. Before, he worked at the Sharp Laboratories of Europe in Oxford (UK), the Kyushu Institute of Technology in Iizuka (Japan), and the Institute for Applied Information Sciences in Saarbrücken (Germany).

Ilija Subasic is a data scientist with a background in information systems and a strong interest in Web mining. He holds an MPhil degree in Informatics from the University of Novi Sad, Serbia, on folksonomy generation, and a PhD degree in Computer Science from KU Leuven, Belgium, on temporal text analysis for online news analysis. His specific interests include temporal summarization of content, visual Web search, personal data organization, and online news search. Lately, he has been working as a consultant on projects regarding the aggregation of crowd-sourced data and personal data organization. More information on his research can be found at http://scholar.google.co.uk/citations?user=_7D39PYAAAAJ&hl.

Hristo Tanev works in the Joint Research Centre, European Commission, as a researcher in multilingual text mining. His research interests are in the area of event extraction, information fusion, unsupervised lexical acquisition, pattern learning, and sentiment analysis. He has a Ph.D. degree in Computer Science from the University of Plovdiv, Bulgaria.

Marco Turchi is a researcher at the Fondazione Bruno Kessler in the Human Language Technology group. His current research is centered on SMT techniques applied to news domain, in particular, on the use of translated documents in different NLP tasks such as document summarization, event extraction, and sentiment analysis. Before moving to the FBK, he worked at the European Commission's Joint Research Centre and the University of Bristol.

Natalia Vanetik has obtained a Ph.D. in Computer Science from Ben-Gurion University of the Negev in 2009. She is currently a faculty member at Department of Software Engineering of Shamoon Academic College of Engineering in Beer Sheva, Israel. Her research interests include data mining, combinatorial optimization, text mining and text analysis, and biological data mining.

Mathias Verbeke is a Ph.D. student in Machine Learning in the Declarative Languages and Artificial Intelligence group of the Department of Computer Science at KU Leuven, Belgium. He holds an MSc in Informatics from KU Leuven, his thesis focusing on integrating data mining techniques in literature-search engines. His research interests include machine learning, computational linguistics, and Web and news mining. More information can be found at http://people.cs.kuleuven.be/~mathias.verbeke/.

Vanni Zavarella works in the Joint Research Centre, European Commission, as a researcher in multilingual text mining. His research interests are in the area of Information Extraction, with a focus on temporal and spatial event information and sentiment analysis. He has a Master degree in Computational Linguistics from University of Nancy, France.

Index